ANTHROPOLOGY

ANTHRO-POLOGY

AN INTRODUCTION
TO PRIMITIVE CULTURE

By

Alexander Goldenweiser

PROFESSOR OF THOUGHT AND CULTURE
University of Oregon, Portland Extension

VISITING PROFESSOR OF SOCIOLOGY
Reed College

F. S. CROFTS & CO., NEW YORK, 1937

To Ethel

FOREWORD

Initially this book was planned as a revision of *Early Civilization*. What followed was not unlike the philosopher's story of the shoe. At first the shoe was new. Then the heel wore out and was replaced. A little later the sole gave out and a new one was substituted. Finally, the uppers refused to serve and new uppers were provided. Now, is the shoe the old shoe or is it a new one? Do not ask the philosopher: before you finish with him, you might have to go barefoot. Ask the wearer; he will tell you it is the old shoe. He knows because he wore it all along. It may pinch a little now since the new uppers were sewed in, but it is the same good old shoe all right. Ask the Old Woman who lived in a Shoe. She will know. Surely her shoe has needed many repairs, considering its generous juvenile population. But it is to her the same shoe in which she has made her home for these many years. So also with *Early Civilization* and *Anthropology, an Introduction to Primitive Culture*. To me it is the same book. The latter grew out of the former without breach of continuity. As the years flitted by and with them promises to the publisher, changes and ever new changes were introduced. A radical revision was undertaken in 1929–30, at Washington, D. C. At that time I was fortunate in securing the faithful assistance of Mrs. Dora Fox, to whom I want to express my belated recognition. Finally, in January 1936, the decision was taken to go through with it. Meanwhile my idea of the book had changed so thoroughly as to make it a 'revision' merely *pro forma*. Five months later, when on the last day of June we boarded our train for the East, the *Anthropology* was finished.

The reader is invited to look upon the book as a new one. In his eyes the work need not bear any allegiance to *Early Civilization*, nor—if perchance he has read the earlier book—will he find many similarities between the two. The entire plan of the work is different. The four chapters of Part I are devoted to a discussion of man, physical and psychic, in his relation to the animals and to culture, a topic disposed of in *Early Civilization* in a small section of one chapter. The descriptive chapters of the latter have vanished. After considerable hesitation, I decided to abandon this procedure, which, under the protective guise of concreteness, inevitably comprised but a very superficial sketch of primitive cultures. In place of this the reader will find in the twenty-two chapters of Part II, the major portion of this book, a large number of concrete and fairly detailed sketches of the different aspects of primitive culture —industry, art, religion, social organization—as exhibited in many different tribes. Here also some of the relevant theoretical problems are discussed, though relatively briefly. In this section much of the factual material already assembled in *Early Civilization* has been incorporated: facts are facts and do not wear with use. The different aspects of primitive culture are brought to a focus in Chapter XXV, 'Primitive Life and Thought,' which is based on the last chapter of *Early Civilization* but also contains many new features gleaned from further study and reflection. Chapters XXV and XXVI, 'Theories of Early Mentality,' of the old book have been scrapped. Of the five chapters of the new Part III, devoted to the processes of culture, one is almost entirely new, and three are entirely so. Here I examine the relations of culture to physical environment, discuss the phenomena of cultural diffusion and assimilation, and present a sketch of the theories of evolution and progress.

In addition the book contains two chapters of a kind not usually found in anthropological texts, namely Chapter IV, 'How Anthropologists Work,' and Chapter XXVI, 'The White Man's Burden.' In Chapter IV the reader is inducted into the methods used by field anthropologists in collecting their material. In Chapter XXVI the attempt is made to tell the disheartening story of the contacts of White civilization with the cultures of living primitives. There is much in this story for us to be ashamed of, and for this reason, if for no other, it should be told. A section of this chapter is devoted to a brief account of the Indian administration of Commissioner John Collier. Although I do not share his optimistic faith in the possibility of saving the cultures of our Indians from dissolution and disappearance, no one can appreciate more than I do his noble effort to lighten the plight of Indian tribes in this last hour of their existence as the bearers of an autonomous culture.

Every book comprises two basic elements: that which is written, and the writing itself. The first element is the content of the book. Here an author's obligation is to those who have collected the materials and invented the theories. The choice is his, the labour theirs. The second element, the writing of the book, includes the form, that is, the manner of writing, and the writing as a process—an act of will. In form this book differs from *Early Civilization*, which was my maiden effort in the art of presentation and possessed all the earmarks of such a performance. It differs also from my theoretical articles, especially the earlier ones, which bore evidence of a heavy and pedantic German upbringing (in

Russia!) and of a taste that might be described as Hegelian. I used to think that a sentence was the grander the less it was comprehensible. This affliction needed a radical remedy. The cure came *via* lecturing, especially public lecturing in adult groups, as at the New School for Social Research in New York, or at the University of Oregon Extension in Portland. As one acquires the habit of speaking in the presence of dozens of eager eyes, the call for simplicity and clarity becomes categorical. One learns to take his cue from the faces and demeanour of the audience. The frank puzzlement on the countenance of a listener, the tortured efforts of another, the unashamed snore from still another, are signs of trouble that simply cannot be disregarded. And so one learns the art of directness, of simple diction, of lucid exposition. When he subsequently turns from speaking to writing, the habit persists. It is as if he were taking his audience with him into the very sanctum of the study. If the text of the *Anthropology* should indicate that I have learned my lesson, I owe this to my audiences, to whom I want at this place to express my obligation.

There are, however, some persons to whom a more individual and intimate acknowledgement is due. Of these Miss Claire Gallagher, my graduate assistant at Reed College, comes first. Without her faithful and thankless labour of taking down dictation and preparing first copy, the writing, as act, could not have been accomplished. The magnitude of her task, moreover, was enhanced by the fact that the whole thing was done under the constant pressure of academic duties. A debt only less great is due to Miss Brunhilde Kaufer, one of my Reed graduates, who by some miracle managed to survive the sustained flood of material, and succeeded in turning out the final copy on schedule and in a form acceptable to the publisher.

There are obligations and obligations. Some are intangible. Under this head I want to mention the names of two friends, my 'adopted sisters' and the sweetest women alive, Frances L. Barnes and Grace De Graff. They did not take dictation nor did they prepare copy; in my classes they sat only casually. But they wanted the book. They felt that I should write it. When all seemed to indicate that the thing could not be done, they never faltered in their faith. In whatever way I may have failed in carrying out this task, at least I have not disappointed them: the book is written.

Still another person has contributed her share to make the act of writing possible: my wife, Ethel. Her contribution is the dearer because she is so little aware of it. A man busy upon a book is a formidable animal, best appreciated at a distance. He does not speak, he does not hear, he remembers nothing except irrelevancies, namely, things bearing upon the book. To share one's habitation with such a creature is an achievement little short of the heroic. My wife stood up nobly under the strain. For days and weeks on end she practised without grumbling the bitter art of self-effacement. In the words of the Melanesians, she 'grew' me, while the book was growing under my hands. To her also I owe the preparation of the list of tribes for the final Map, the list of personal names, and the list of illustrations.

I should not close this lengthy yet all too brief list of acknowledgements without mentioning, humbly and gratefully, the name of my publisher, F. S. Crofts. He has shown almost superhuman patience in waiting for years for a book which, in all probability, was never to come. Whether now when it is about to see the light, he is to be rewarded for his stoicism, lies on the knees of the gods.

ALEXANDER GOLDENWEISER

January 29, 1937
Portland, Oregon

CONTENTS

CONTENTS

Part III

THE WAYS OF CULTURE

LIST OF ILLUSTRATIONS

LIST OF PLATES

PART I

ANIMAL, MAN, AND CULTURE

Chapter I

ANIMAL AND MAN

Man and Nature

To the scientist, man is part of the order of nature. In certain respects he is like the rest of the physical world. Man has size, weight, shape, and colour. He occupies space and his movements are controlled by the same laws and limiting conditions that apply to any physical object. If he falls from a cliff he will fall like a stone, and the law of falling bodies will describe his behaviour accurately and without residue.

Man is also like all chemical things. In innumerable ways his body is a chemical laboratory. The fundamental law of life, namely, to absorb foreign substances into one's body, there to transmute them into one's own substance, and thereby to live and grow, is in essence a chemical process. The processes of vision, breathing, digestion, as well as those humanly even more significant but as yet little known or understood processes of glandular action, imply chemical transmutations. Man, then, is a chemical laboratory.

Man is like all living things in these respects, and also in certain further respects. The ultimate unit of his body is a cell, which combines with the traits of physical and chemical things certain additional features of sensitivity and response which distinguish living substances from other substances. Man, then, is like a plant: as an organism, he first of all vegetates. In order to live, he must absorb food, as does the plant. He multiplies by reproduction, as does a plant, even though the method is different. His life as an individual has a beginning, an unfoldment and an end, as have the lives of all plants.

Man has yet more characteristics in common with animals. All animals, even those least differentiated from plants, have a capacity that plants lack almost completely, namely, that of a relative freedom of movement. By and large, plants are tied to the 'ground.' Before they can absorb nourishment, it must come within their reach. Plants have roots which greatly enlarge the range within which food is available. Beyond this they cannot go. Animals, above the very simplest, go after

3

their food; they travel to reach it, as man does.[1] In several additional senses man is like all vertebrate animals. The skeletal framework of his body is built about a spinal column. It is symmetrically and bilaterally distributed on its sides. The symmetry of the human body, like that of all vertebrates, is bilateral—not spherical, as is that of many known invertebrate animals. Right and left are in symmetry, but not front and back or top and bottom. In common with many invertebrates, but especially with all vertebrates, man has a nervous system, the major parts of which are: the brain, situated at the front or top of the spinal cord, the central apparatus of nervous co-ordination and control; and the spinal cord itself, the principal centre of muscular response and control. Beyond this, as in all vertebrates and most animals generally, the nervous system expands in an ever more refined network through all parts of the body, thus insuring sensitivity even in its remotest corners, as well as expeditious communication with the nervous centres.

Another order of vertebrates comes still nearer to man, namely the mammals, with whom man shares the additional trait of bringing live offspring into the world, fed for a time by the mother's milk. Among the mammals the different orders resemble man in different ways. Humans share the hunting "instinct" with the animals of prey, gregariousness with the grass-eaters.

From a purely physical standpoint, the next higher order of resemblance is found with the monkeys. Like man, they have arms and hands. In this respect some monkeys are, in fact, more human than humans, in that they possess four arms and hands, with the tail as a near fifth. In physiognomy and the expression of emotions the higher monkeys are almost preposterously human. At the top rung of the ladder, finally, we find the Anthropoid Apes, the gibbon, orang-utan, gorilla, and chimpanzee. These are the man-like creatures *par excellence* in the animal world. In skeletal framework, muscular, physiological and neural organization the Anthropoids are like man in numerous particular and detailed features. They are, moreover, more nearly adjusted to the erect gait than any other animal, short of man himself. As Huxley once said, there is more difference between the Anthropoids and the other animals, including the monkeys, than between the Anthropoids and man (see Plate I).

Now it will be seen what was meant by saying that man is part of

---

[1] This differentiation between plants and animals applies more precisely to the higher orders, especially the terrestrial ones. Between the lower orders of aquatic animals and some aquatic plants the distinction cannot always be drawn with precision.

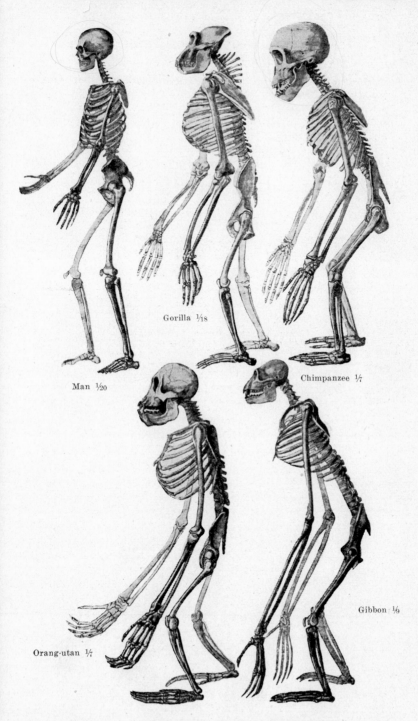

Man 1/20   Gorilla 1/18   Chimpanzee 1/7

Orang-utan 1/7   Gibbon 1/9

PLATE I. MAN AND THE ANTHROPOIDS

The Chimpanzee and Orang skeletons belong to young specimens in which the resemblance to man is more striking. (Ernst Haeckel, *Der Kampf um den Entwickelungs-Gedanken.*)

the order of nature. In so and so many respects he is like all physical things, like all chemical substances, like living creatures, like plants, like animals, like vertebrates, like mammals, like monkeys, and like the Anthropoids. In so and so many respects he is of one kind with all these things and creatures.

I might venture the guess that many a reader, while running over these pages, will think: he is talking about evolution! Now this is not, strictly speaking, true. I have not said a word about evolution. All I have done is to present factual evidence of man's similarities to the different orders of natural things. Everyone knows that classification—the next step after description in all scientific procedure—is based on the noting of similarities and differences and followed by grouping similar things together, and different things apart. On the basis of the facts here presented any unprejudiced person would group man with the rest of nature, and more particularly with the animals, and still more particularly with the higher animals, especially the Anthropoid Apes. This is what is meant by saying: To the scientist, man is part of the order of nature.

We may, however, go one step further. Taught by experience, we ascribe similarity or resemblance in living things to genetic relationship. Because all men are alike, more like each other than they are like anything else, we classify them as belonging to genus *Homo,* a group of common biological ancestry. When we are confronted with two White men, we do not hesitate to class them with the White race. When, in addition, they have blond hair, blue eyes, tall stature, long heads, we are almost certain that they are Nordics. Once more, then, a reduction to common ancestry. If, finally, they display resemblances in form of face, finer shades of eye colour, size and shape of mouth, form of nose, curvature of the ear, they are declared to be brothers. And the more minute these resemblances, the greater our astonishment should they prove not to be closely related. Here empirical judgment runs parallel with the verdict of science. When we become acquainted with the manifold resemblances, in structure and function, between man and the vertebrates, mammals, monkeys, apes, we should not waver in ascribing these also to genetic relationship, community of descent. And, the more detailed the resemblances, the closer must be the common ancestor. This is not evolution. It is a statement of facts, described and classified, plus an indication of the direction in which an interpretation must lie.[2]

[2] In Chapter XXX we shall return to this subject, to deal, in a brief résumé, with the theory or theories of evolution.

There will be those, of course, who prefer to deal with the history of the earth, inanimate and animate, in terms of creation. With them we have no quarrel; there is no disputing about faith. This much, however, can be added by way of clarifying the issue: Suppose the Divine Being is held responsible for the creation of man and of all the species of animals. Then there are two alternatives. Either the Creator gave the animal series the form which to a scientist means genetic unity, because this was the only way in which the series could be created. If so, divine authority is added to that of the scientist and to the common-sense hunch of the plain man, in support of the naturalistic view. Or the Creator deliberately cast his handiwork into a mould which would befog and mislead the minds of thinking men—but I doubt whether the advocates of creationism would care to ascribe to the Divine Intelligence a scheme so diabolical.

Beyond the Animal

Man then is very much of one kind with the higher animals, the Anthropoid Apes above all. He has, we saw, so much in common with them that in any unprejudiced view he must without hesitation be classed with these creatures. In saying this, one should, of course, not imply that any or all of these highest mammals are to be regarded as the direct ancestors of mankind. This is patently not the case. The gibbon, for example, with his enormously elongated arms, is in this feature less like man than some of the monkeys in his own ancestral tree. In other words, the Anthropoid Apes, each one in its own way, represent specializations in development which are not on the direct route to man. Close relatives of ours these Anthropoids certainly are, but along a collateral, not a direct line of descent.

So far we have dealt, however briefly, with man's similarities with other animals. The time has now come to stress the differences. Rooted in a common animal tree of descent and relationship, man has, in his own and unique way, become a species like unto itself: just man. In the process of becoming human, man's prehuman ancestor had to undergo a number of striking and, as the future proved, significant changes. He learned to stand erect [3] without difficulty, to walk and breathe in

---

[3] This, be it noted, is an art that will be learned. Speaking strictly physically, man's posture on the soles of his feet is one of unstable equilibrium, both as to standing and as to walking. Construct a doll of human size, stand it up without support, and it will fall at the first opportunity. The baby learns to stand and walk gradually, if not as gradually as is at times supposed. I knew a little girl once who, when she was learning to walk, was supported by being held up by the

his own peculiar way. The human hand developed, unique in its capacity and versatility. Radical changes took place in the sensory relationship to nature: the sense of smell receded, that of sight came to the fore. The arms, though relatively shorter than among the Anthropoids, became longer and stronger than they were among the lower monkeys, the spider monkey excepted,—in relation, be it understood, to the length of the body. The foot, which makes bipodal standing, walking and running possible, became flattened out and lost its prehensile proclivities. Thus the foot specialized, whereas the hand became more versatile. The eyes moved to the front and learned to co-operate in vision. The animal snout receded and a real nose made its appearance. The skull, no longer carried in front of the body but perched on top of it, became larger and was supported by readjusted muscles. The human animal, finally, became more moderate in procreation than most of its prehuman forebears. Let us consider, one by one, some of these items in man's advance beyond the animal.

We know, of course, that many animals below the apes can on occasion stand erect. None of them, however, are comfortable when doing so. The bear, who wobbles along on all fours when in peace and undisturbed, assumes an erect position when ready to meet and hug an adversary. He does not, however, like to do so, and when the job is done he returns to his more normal position. A horse can rear, and with a little training can persist in this erect position for some time. This, however, is for the horse a position of unstable equilibrium, as many a rider has discovered to his grief when carelessly pulling on the reins of a rearing horse, thus making it fall backwards. And so on with many others.

Perhaps the real development in the direction of the upright posture began with the gibbon. Though eminently an arboreal creature, the gibbon may be called an 'erect climber,' and when on the ground, it is an 'erect biped.' In animals which walk on all fours, the spine and the long axis of the body cavity run approximately parallel to the ground. The internal organs are packed in these cavities in such a way as to be supported by the cage formed by the ribs, by the wall of the abdomen, and by the front portion of the pelvis which in these animals is greatly elongated, forward and backward. In an animal adapted for an upright posture, on the other hand, the contents of the abdomen must be so fixed and suspended that they will not slip downward in

top of her dress. After she had mastered the art, she continued for some time to hold herself by the scruff of the neck while walking, having evidently been conditioned to accept this gesture as part of the walking process.

that position. In the upright primates, including the gibbon, chimpanzee, orang-utan and gorilla, as well as man, the bowels and the other viscera are closely bound to the back wall of the abdominal cavity or suspended from the head end. That this adjustment, even in the human, is not quite perfect may be gathered from the fact that some members of the species suffer from an intestinal dislocation called a 'rupture,' which must be remedied by artificial means to patch up what nature has imperfectly constructed. In conjunction with this goes the reduction of the tail which has already proceeded far among the Anthropoids. In man it is normally absent—externally, that is. Here again abnormalities will occur—and a human infant is sometimes born with a diminutive tail.

The new posture creates a condition to which the process of breathing must be adjusted. In the pronograde animals, or quadrupeds, inspiration is brought about merely by the muscles which are attached to the immovable shoulder girdle which pulls the flexible rib-case forward and downward, but when the body axis is changed and the spine comes to stand perpendicularly to the ground, a new method of respiration develops which may be called 'internal': the thorax is enlarged for the drawing in of the air by the lowering of the floor of the diaphragm in the thoracic cavity. With this also goes a gradual change in the shape of the vertebral column, which ultimately assumes a somewhat S-like form.

And then the hand! The utilization of the fore limb as a supporting organ in walking upon the ground obviously must and did result in the stiffening and fixation of its mobile elements. The fore limbs of quadrupeds, whether with claw-equipped paws or hoofs, are good enough for the purposes they must serve, but they are not hands. For discriminate grasping and versatile manipulation they are useless. If any of these animals, for example the cats, did develop great skill in tree climbing, they achieved this by means of specialized claws with which to dig into the bark of a tree. The development of the prehensile fore limb in tree climbing is thus a necessary preamble to the human hand.

It is significant in this connection that the hind limbs of an animal, owing to their very position, are better adapted for supporting the weight of the body than for grasping and exploring. The fore limbs, on the other hand, which are nearer to the central part of the nervous system, that is, the brain, as well as to the organs of sight and smell, are exploited for purposes of investigation, defence, and attack. Among the tree-climbing preprimate monkeys, the hind limbs adjusted themselves to the arboreal life by developing prehensile facilities, almost or even quite equalling those of the fore limbs, thus initiating a stage in animal evolution known as 'four-handed.' It must, however, be remembered that among the tree-climbing monkeys, as well as the gibbon, the hand is primarily adjusted to climbing, grasping of branches, and the supporting of a considerable weight suspended from it. Thus the hand in these creatures is narrow and long, and so are the digits. The thumb, having no particular use in this set of functions, is abbreviated and relatively supernumerary; in certain instances, in fact, it disappears altogether. Only later, following along the line marked out by the chimpanzee and gorilla, the human hand, now devoted mainly to exploration and manipulation, becomes more moderate in length, increases in width, and becomes equipped with a thoroughly adequate thumb which moves freely in a direction towards the other digits and effectively co-operates with them.

In these new situations the sense organs were also readjusted. The land-grubbing quadrupeds are nose-minded. The nose, with its highly developed sensory equipment, is in them the forepost of the organism. It guides them, informs them, and warns them. Up in the trees the usefulness of the organ of smell is greatly reduced. In place of this, what becomes necessary is a multiplicity of rapid and accurate muscular co-ordinations which must have their sensory and external, as well as their internal and neural, representations. Not only is the nose in its earlier forms an exploratory organ, by smelling, but also a tactile one: it actually bumps into things. Such accessory organs as feelers and whiskers are symptomatic of this function. The value of all this is enhanced by a projecting muzzle or snout. If the food is to be seized with the teeth, the jaws should project considerably beyond the visual plane, else the eyes would cease to function properly by being submerged in the food. It is, moreover, important for the animal to be able to look about while it is eating. In the life in the tree all this is no longer so necessary, and so we find that the monkeys and Anthropoids undergo marked diminution in the forward projection of the snout, even though it should not be forgotten, as a check on these somewhat speculative statements, that the gorilla and orang, each in its own way, have protruding snouts.

In the arboreal monkeys as well as the Anthropoids, markedly the gibbon, the arms underwent a lengthening comparable to the lengthening of man's legs. In the case of the gibbon, as already stated, this process was extreme, its arms becoming enormous in proportion both to the hind limbs and to the size of the body. The ape-like prehuman ancestor, on descending to the ground, had no longer any use for this excessive length of arm, and so man's arms are relatively short when compared to his extremely long legs; they are, however, long enough and strong enough for the purposes for which henceforth they are to be devoted, namely reaching, grasping, exploring, manipulating, and lifting. When it was no longer necessary to lift one's own weight by the arms, they could be devoted to lifting other weights, while one's feet were firmly planted on the ground. Thus a shortening of the forearm set in.

Next to the arm and hand, the leg and foot. The erect position and the associated function of adequately supporting the weight of the body and balancing it upon the foot expressed themselves in the lengthening of the leg, the strengthening of the leg muscles and the supporting bones. From this standpoint man's legs are further ahead in comparison with those of the Anthropoids than the latter's arms are in comparison with those of man. The major adjustment, however, was that undergone by the foot, which from a grasping organ became a supporting one. Many terrestrial quadrupeds are digitigrade: they walk upon their toes. The primates, on the other hand, are plantigrade: they walk on the soles of their feet. When the foot was transformed into a supporting organ, the great toe was brought into line with the other toes; also it increased in length, thus becoming the principal base for the support of the body, as has been experienced by those who have for one reason or another lost the use of that organ or the organ itself. Even the presence of an enveloping and reinforcing shoe does not quite suffice to make up for the loss of a big toe. The toe altogether lost its original twist and was turned out so that the nail was now directed upward and the plantar surface rested upon the ground. Thus equipped, the foot no longer needed the active co-operation of the lesser toes, which became reduced in size and almost degenerate in their passive immobility.[4]

In this connection Hooton remarks that the foot developed into a specialist, exclusively and effectively devoted to the purpose of walking, running, and in other ways supporting the body, whereas the hand, in comparison, became a versatile organ, doing a great many things exceedingly well.[5]

[4] It must, of course, be remembered that this relatively recent recession in the strength, mobility, and independence of the toes can within limits be rescinded under duress, as has been demonstrated more than once by people born without arms, and less satisfactorily by those who have lost them in later years. By the exercise of infinite patience and much practice, they learn to make very adequate use of their toes, even to the extent of wielding a violin bow.

[5] E. A. Hooton, *Up from the Ape*, p. 134. This entire sketch of the emergence of man from his prehuman ancestors is no more than a paraphrase of Hooton's exceedingly able presentation of the topic.

Associated with the reduction of the snout is the displacement of the eyes from the lateral to the frontal plane, a change which seems to have made possible stereoscopic vision.[6] To this might be added the further fact that the reduction of the interorbital space, possibly associated with the diminution of the olfactory sense, also enhanced the possibility of stereoscopic vision.

With all of these dislocations and shifts in the development of the sensory equipment goes a change in the shape of the snout. In a quadruped the skull is suspended from the end of the spine by two knobs or condiles on the occipital or back surface of the cranium. The head of the animal is not balanced on the end of the spine but is supported by powerful muscles and ligaments which are attached to the long spines of the vertebrae and elsewhere. The mammalian snout projects along the line of the vertebral column. When an animal like a dog squats upon its haunches or sits upon its hind legs, it lowers its muzzle so that the head rotates forward and downward through almost a quarter of a circle, and the long axis of the snout and skull is now perpendicular to the axis of the spine. The nodding of the head is accomplished by the skull moving forward upon its occipital condiles. In the erect-sitting arboreal animals this change in the position of the head tends to become permanent, 'the condillar knobs and the occipital foramen between them migrate from their original position on the back of the skull to a new site at the base of the skull, so that the head may now be said to "rest" upon the spinal column instead of being suspended from it.'[7] At this stage, however, the head does not balance upon the spine, on account of the forward projection of the muzzle and the lack of development of the occipital parts of the brain, to offset the protrusion of the snout. As the snout recedes, a process associated with the freeing of the fore limbs and the habit of hand feeding, a simultaneous backward growth of the occipital lobes of the brain takes place; this provides cortical representation for the sense of vision, now on the ascendant. These associated changes are already observable in the Tarsius monkey and they become even more noticeable in the Anthropoids and in man.

Another feature which man probably owes to his arboreal ancestry is a reduction in the number of the young. One might conjecture that the very activity of an arboreal life would be prohibitive of pregnancy involving more than one or two offspring. If this be not so, there is the

---

[6] Hooton here warns against the assumption that such a frontal position of the eyes was a direct or mechanical effect of the shortening of the muzzle.

[7] E. A. Hooton, *op. cit.*, pp. 97–98. (By permission of The Macmillan Company, publishers.)

additional factor of caring for several young simultaneously in a tree, certainly a difficult task, at least for a larger animal. 'The lowest Primates,' writes Hooton, 'such as Lemurs, often produce two young at a birth; the lowliest of the New World monkeys, the Marmosets, usually have three young at once; but in the rest of the monkeys and the higher forms, one monkey at a time is the rule. The number of pairs of breasts on the mother's body are reduced in accordance with the diminishing number of offspring produced at a single pregnancy.' [8]

Over and above all these changes, and by far exceeding them in significance, is the growth of the brain with the accompanying changes in the shape of the skull. Our insight into the nature of the factors responsible for this fateful growth and of the mechanisms by which it was achieved is so fragmentary and imperfect that it will perhaps be best to pass over in silence the scientific speculations bearing on this point. Suffice it to say that a fairly steady growth is observable when the New World monkeys are compared with those of the Old World. The brain of the gibbon is intermediate between those of the Old World monkeys and those of the other Anthropoids. The orang-utan has a more voluminous brain, with more convolutions and fissured surface than has the gibbon; the brain of the chimpanzee is still larger, and that of the gorilla is largest of all and most closely comparable in pattern to that of man. Even the gorilla's brain, however, is no more than 1/150 to 1/200 of his body weight, whereas the human brain approximates 1/50 of the body weight.[9]

[8] *Ibid.*, p. 76. It is interesting to note that the gestation period of the chimpanzee is the same as that of man: nine months. The period is eight months in the orang and gorilla and probably seven in the gibbon.

[9] Hooton, *op. cit.*, Part 2, 'The Primate Life Cycle,' pp. 46–206.

Chapter II

RACE

What Is Race?

The Variability of a Group. Race to the anthropologist is a purely physical concept. To define race is to characterize a group of men from the standpoint of their common hereditary physical traits. Race, therefore, as a student of mine once put it, is inherited breed. Or more fully, a race is a subdivision of mankind having certain inborn physical traits in common. Now a layman in reading such a definition might conclude that races or physical types are characterized, say, by certain sizes, weights, head-forms, skin colour, or what not, in such a way that all the individuals of the race or type are identical in the possession of these traits. The scientist knows and the observant layman suspects that such is, in fact, not the case. Similarity or identity in a physical trait is found in a group of men only under conditions of artificial selection. The Prussian king, Frederick the Great, we are told, had an inordinate liking for tall men. Being a king, he ordered for himself a guard of grenadiers all of whom were six-footers. Even here, of course, there was some variation, but for all practical purposes, six-footers they were. This, however, was not a natural group; it was an artificial one, deliberately selected. Natural groups always vary. When we say that Scotchmen are tall, Swiss or Italians relatively short, what is meant is not that all Scotchmen are six-footers nor that every Scotchman is taller than any Swiss. Clearly, this is not so. The short Scotchman, Harry Lauder for example, is certainly shorter than many a Swiss; and if you compare a random group of Scotchmen with a random group of Swiss, you will find a very large number of individuals in the two groups to be of the same size. The same applies to all other traits.

Further, if a group of people in a natural population are classified according to a physical trait, such as size, weight, or shape of head, the situation works out in the following way. Suppose we take size. Then we shall find a considerable number of persons who will be of a size somewhere between the tallest and the smallest member of the group; a smaller number of people will be either shorter or taller than

13

those in the first group; and so on, until we come to the extremes, where a very small number of people will be found to be either much taller or much shorter than a vast majority of the group. A distribution of this sort, also referred to as the dispersion of a group, can be readily represented by a curve in which the sizes will be indicated on the base-line, whereas the curve itself will represent the end-points of the verticals corresponding to the number of cases of each size.

It is important to note in this connection that the number of cases connected with each size is as significant as the variability itself. Disregard this factor and the whole thing becomes absurd and will lead to meaningless results. Take, for example, a class of students. Somewhere in the second row sits a girl with a pug nose. Now you might conceive the idea that the nose of this girl represents the type of nose of the class. Should anyone point out to you that the girl to her left has a different nose, say a straight Greek one, whereas the boy to her right has a different one again, say a convex nose with a drooping tip, popularly known as a Jewish or 'Semitic' nose, you might answer that these noses are deviations from the type. Proceeding, then, on this basis you could successfully arrange the class, as to noses, from the standpoint of their differences from the nose of that particular initial girl. This result, however, will mean precisely nothing, excepting only this: that any unselected group of individuals varies as to nose. On the other hand, if you count up the pug noses and the straight noses and the convex noses and the other kinds of noses in the class, always mindful of the number of persons possessing a particular kind of nose, and represent this distribution in a curve such as mentioned before, the result will actually reveal the variability of the group, as to nose. If the class, moreover, is a large one and as a group accidental or non-selected, in so far as nose is concerned, then it can pass for a fair sample of the population of the district, and what you will have is a measure of the nasal type of the local population.

Laymen, impatient of complicated calculations or procedures, might object to this on the ground that taking an average of the noses would be just as good and much simpler. Now an average, with reference to any particular measurable thing, is, of course, the sum-total of the individual measurements, divided by the number of cases. The average has a meaning. A group of an average size of 6 feet is a taller group, by and large, than one with an average size of 5 feet 5 inches. Still, the average alone gives one a very imperfect idea of the actual character of the group, as to this particular trait. This can be illustrated by the simplest of examples. Take three men, one 6 feet tall, another

5 feet 10 inches, and still another 5 feet 8 inches. The average size of the group of three will be 5 feet 10 inches. Then take another group of three men: the tallest is 6 feet 2 inches, the next 5 feet 10 inches, and the smallest 5 feet 6 inches. The average size is 5 feet 10 inches. Finally, take a third group: all three men are 5 feet 10 inches. The average of the group is once more 5 feet 10 inches. It will be seen, then, that the average is the same in all three cases, even though the groups are very different indeed. This is what is meant by saying that an average gives us no idea of the dispersion or variability of a group. We may have a highly uniform group, with the smallest and the tallest being very much like the average, and a highly variable one where the smallest is much smaller and the tallest much taller than the average. Yet both groups may have the same average. Variability then is significant. It follows from this that to do justice to the principle of variability, some measure should be found which would give an idea of the variability of a group about its average. Such a measure has, in fact, been found by mathematicians, and it is designated by a somewhat mystifying symbol, the Greek letter σ (sigma). We need not here analyze the nature of that figure any further. Suffice it to say that it is a measure of the variability of the group. If the group is relatively uniform with reference to a certain trait, so that its extremes vary but little from the average, the σ will be small. If, on the other hand, the dispersion of the group with reference to the trait is great, so that the extremes are very different from the average, the σ will be large. In calculating the σ, both the range of variability and the number of cases for each measurement are taken into account.

The final point which emerges from these considerations is this: the characterization of a group with reference to a certain trait is one thing; the placing of an individual into a certain group, another. Suppose you are interested in a group from the standpoint of shape of head.[1] You find it long-headed. Now in any long-headed population, or a sample of it, there will be numbers of individuals with relatively round heads. Suppose then you take another population, a round-headed one or a sample of it. Here you will discover numbers of individuals with

[1] The shape of head is computed from the length and the width of the head. The length is measured from the glabella, the bony point between the eyes, to a point at the back of the head farthest removed from the glabella, as the crow flies. The width of the head is measured from a point a little back of and above one ear to a similar point near the other ear. The shape of the head indicated by the so-called 'cephalic index' is the percentile relation of width to length of head: $w \times 100 \div l$. A cephalic index of 100 would mean that width equalled length: a perfectly round head. The nearer to 100 the index, the wider or broader the head; the further from 100 the index, the longer the head.

relatively long heads. You will find, in the end, that some of these relatively long-headed individuals in your round-headed group will be identical in head-shape with some of the relatively round-headed individuals in the long-headed group. In other words, the two series will overlap. Or, to put it still differently, there will be a considerable number of individuals who might be allocated to either one of the two series. It follows from this that if you pick up a man at random and measure his head, then—unless indeed he is an extreme long-head or an extreme round-head—your knowledge of this measurement will not suffice to determine to what kind of population he belongs: he might either represent a relatively long-headed variant in a round-headed population or a relatively round-headed variant in a long-headed one. The lesson we should learn from these considerations, but usually do not, is this: when one compares, say, two groups of people with reference to any trait, it is important to know how much overlapping there is between the dispersions of that trait in the two groups or in adequate samples of the two groups. If the overlapping is large, a separation of the groups as distinct, with reference to this trait, will evidently be artificial and is likely to lead to error or confusion. Only when the overlapping is slight, or when there is no overlapping, can the groups be regarded as thoroughly different with reference to a particular trait. Finally, when we speak of types, races, or sub-races, we refer or should refer to the characteristics of groups rather than to those of individuals.

The Stability of Physical Types. Our second preliminary problem is that of the stability of physical traits. We need no knowledge of scientific theory or method to state that human groups differ in their physical characteristics. The question is: in how far are these physical group characteristics stable? Now the three factors that can conceivably affect the physical character of a group are these: intermarriage, within or without the law; selection; physical environment. Without going into this matter further, for the moment, we all know that interbreeding of a group of one type with a group of a different type will affect the character of both groups. When Whites breed with Negroes, Chinamen with Whites or Negroes, Indians with Whites, long-heads with round-heads, tall groups with short groups, things happen which change the physical traits of these groups.

Another possible cause for a change in physical type is selection. Without stopping to consider this factor either, we might state that it is at least possible that individuals possessing a certain trait or lacking one will die out in a population because of their inability to endure certain conditions. It has been assumed, for example, that some of the inhabitants of the Arctic regions, such as the Eskimo, have undergone a selective process with reference to their capacity to endure extremely low temperatures. As a result, the present Eskimo population is better able to carry on in its forbidding environment than were its ancestors. We need not pass here on the correctness of the hypothesis in this particular instance (*cf.* p. 75, n. 3). I cite it merely as an illustration of what is meant by a change in the type of a group under the influence of selection.

Another possible cause for change in a group is the influence of physical environment. If the physical environment of a group changes, or if the group moves into a new and different physical environment, will it persist in its physical characteristics or will it change? Let us consider this last point.

By an act of Congress of February 20, 1907, a Commission was created, consisting of three senators, three members of the House of Representatives, and three persons appointed by the President of the United States, to make an investigation of immigration in the United States. The labours of the Commission were to extend to many different fields appertaining to different phases of the life, welfare, occupations, criminality, assimilability, etc., of the immigrants in this country. One of these investigations referred to the changes in bodily form of the descendants of European immigrants in the United States; this was under the supervision of Professor Franz Boas of Columbia University. In the words of the director, an attempt was made to solve the following questions: (1) Is there a change in the type of development of the immigrant and his descendant due to his transfer from his home surroundings to the congested parts of New York? (2) Is there a change in the type of the adult immigrant arriving on the shores of our continent?

In view of the complexity of the problem and the limitation of time and money, Boas first undertook a preliminary investigation of two types of immigrants in New York City, namely the East European Jew and the South Italian. The result of this preliminary inquiry was the discovery that the descendants of both kinds of immigrants did change in America. In connection with one measurement, namely the shape of the head, the result was this: The cephalic index is about 78 among the Sicilians born in Sicily. They are, therefore, decidedly long-headed. The cephalic index among American-born descendants of Sicilians rises to 80: they become more broad-headed. The cephalic index of East European Jews born in Europe is about 84, which is a round or broad head. Among the Jews of East European ancestry born in America, it sinks to 81: they become more long-headed. It will be seen that, in this instance, the cephalic indices of the two groups became less different among the individuals born in America than they were among the immigrants themselves: the difference between the indices of Sicilians and Eastern Jews in Europe is 6 units, whereas the difference between the indices of their descendants in America is only 1 unit.[2]

Boas then proceeded with a more ambitious investigation of the immigrants and their descendants. In order to conduct his inquiry within the limits of the time and money available, he restricted the investigation to immigrants in New York City. He further restricted the range of the groups investigated to five racial sub-types, the Scotch, Bohemians, East European Jews, and two types of Italians. The measurements taken comprised height, standing and sitting; weight; cephalic index; facial index;[3] colour of the eyes; and colour of the hair. The individuals investigated were the immigrants themselves born in Europe, their children born in Europe, and their children born in the United States. The latter were subdivided into 10 groups, those born 1 year after the arrival of the mother, 2 years, 3 years, and up to 10 years after the arrival of the mother in this country.[4]

The results of this inquiry were as definite as they were surprising and significant. It was found that (1) the descendants of these immigrants differed in physical type from their parents and their brothers and sisters born in Europe; (2) the change in physical type was specific for each one of the five sub-racial groups; and (3) this change in each type was cumulative, that is, it increased from year to year. For ex-

[2] This preliminary result was promptly seized upon by the press as a confirmation of the 'melting pot' idea. At last, it was claimed, scientific evidence was forthcoming of the operation of this heretofore somewhat mystic entity, the American scene. The peoples who came to our shores would become as one and rapidly so. This popular version of Boas's initial report was, needless to say, quite beside the mark. Boas himself never regarded this reduction of the difference in the cephalic indices of the Italians and Jews as more than a peculiar coincidence, due to the fact that the long-headed individuals happened to change in the direction of broadheadedness, whereas the broad-headed ones changed in the direction of longheadedness, thus moving towards the ultimate limit of a common figure. What struck Boas and stimulated him to continue the investigation was not this feature of the result, but the fact that there *was* a change and that the direction of the change differed for the two types in question.

[3] In the facial index the breadth of the face is expressed as a percentage of its length.

[4] These measurements were taken by Boas's assistants, including the present writer, who worked in groups of two, one investigator taking the measurements, the other recording the figures. Some of the measurements were secured in schools, but a larger number were obtained by house-to-house canvassing and at such gatherings as the yearly athletic contests of the Scotch clans.

ample, if the cephalic index tended towards greater long-headedness, the children born 1 year after the arrival of the mother were a little more long-headed than the European parents or the European-born children; those born 2 years after the arrival of the mother exhibited this trait to a greater extent; and so on up to those children born 10 years after the arrival of the mother, who were the most long-headed of all.

Such were the results. How could they be interpreted? Fortunately, the conditions of this particular investigation were such that two of the possible causes for change in type would be eliminated at the outset. Change through intermarriage was excluded because the parents of the European and American children were the same. The possibility of selection was also precluded because the time involved was so short. The residual possible cause was, therefore, to be seen in the effect of the American physical environment on the European-born types. Just precisely what is meant by environment here is another question. It might cover climate, location, eating habits—the last factor combining both physical environment and certain cultural elements—or perhaps some other as yet unidentified factor of the physical environment. As there was neither time nor money to pursue this research any further, no more specific conclusion could be formulated than that the change was due to immigration into a different environment. As so often in science, the answer also set a problem.

These results, which may be justly characterized as revolutionary, have an obvious bearing on the general problem of the stability of racial types, and this again should reflect on our view of the history of man in its physical aspect. If change of environment affects physical type, the various races and sub-races of mankind must have been subject to this influence again and again during their frequent wanderings over the earth. On a small or large scale, in Asia and Africa, Europe and America, as well as between the different continents, movements of peoples of all types and descriptions are known to have occurred from the most primitive times, and there must have been other movements of which no evidence has been preserved. If the results of this investigation can be generalized—and if true, they must have general validity —then all such movements must have been accompanied by change in physical type. Thus the picture of race in history shifts from one of stability to one of recurrent changes.

The Races of Man

Physical Characteristics of the Races. From the standpoint of the cultural anthropologist, the presence of race is an encumbrance. In his concrete studies he practically always disregards it. He can do so with impunity, for it is obvious even to the casual observer that the cultural differentiation of mankind has proceeded much further than the racial one, and that within each race all sorts of cultures are to be found, not only qualitatively different ones, but also different in degree of advancement. Much as the cultural anthropologist would like to disregard race altogether, he may not do so, quite. In the first place, if he is a field worker gathering fresh material at its source, he frequently finds himself in a position where he must study man physical as well as man cultural. Even more important is the fact that whatever race may or may not mean inherently, it does mean a great deal psychologically and socially. It is, as has been said, a state of mind. It may, in fact, be asserted without exaggeration that the layman is more acutely sensitive to the problems of race in its physical and psychological aspects than he is to the details of primitive culture.

To deal with *Homo sapiens* from the standpoint of race means to classify. This, as everyone knows, is easier said than done. Classifications of races have been undertaken from the most ancient times on, certainly since the days of Herodotus, and races are still being classified and reclassified. As a sample, this is what Boas writes in a little article, 'The History of the American Race': 'Man had arisen from his animal ancestors. His upright posture, his large brain, the beginnings of articulate and organized language and the use of tools mark the contrast between him and animals. Already differentiation of human types had set in. From an unknown ancestral type that may have been related to the Australoid type, two fundamentally distinct forms had developed— the Negroid type and the Mongoloid type. The former spread all around the Indian Ocean; the latter found its habitat in northern and central Asia, and also reached Europe and the New World. The uniformity of these types ceased with their wide spread over the continents, and the isolation of small communities. Bushmen, Negroes, and Papuans mark some divergent developments of the one type; American Indians, East Asiatics, and Malays, some of the other. The development of varieties in each group showed similarities in all regions where the type occurred. The races located on both sides of the Pacific Ocean exhibited the tendency to low pigmentation of skin, eyes and hair, to a strong development of the nose, and to a reduction of the size of the face.

Thus types like the Europeans, the Ainu of Japan and some Indian tribes of the Pacific coast, exhibit certain striking similarities in form. This tendency to parallel modification of the type indicates early relationship.' [5]

This statement is helpful, in so far as it indicates the two contrasting physical groups which make up mankind: one, East Asiatic or Mongoloid to which the American Indian and the White are related; the other, African or Negro to which are related the Australian, partially the Melanesian, as well as the Negritos of the Philippines, Indo-China, and the Andaman Islands, the last three being pigmoid races. As a statement and as a fact this grouping is helpful, but we cannot go very far with it unless more detailed characterization of at least the major types of man physical has also been made. And it is precisely this that is so difficult. If there were some one physical trait on the basis of which a sufficient number of racial types could be differentiated, the situation would be only half bad. This, however, is not the case.

If you take skin colour, a rather elusive trait except at extremes, it is easy enough to differentiate the Negro or Negroid from the Mongoloid, but further than this it is difficult to go with any degree of assurance. The White at his whitest can be easily enough distinguished from the Mongolian at his yellowest, but there are so many White people with relatively dark complexions of a Mongoloid tint, that a distinction of the White race from the Mongolian, on the basis of this trait, can at best bring out only the extreme variants. Similarly, the Negro as a group is darker than the Australian as a group, but the overlapping is so marked that most Negroes could not be distinguished from most Australians by skin colour alone. Needless to say, the subracial groups are even less easily distinguishable on the ground of complexion. Some students have emphasized the whiteness of the White, as a racial trait, so strongly that they found it desirable to differentiate groups like the Hindu and Arab and some others, as a Brown race, thus separating it from the White. Now, whatever use there may be in this grouping from other standpoints, in point of complexion neither the Hindu nor the Arab can be satisfactorily distinguished from at least the Mediterranean branch of the White race, including such peoples as Italians, Greeks, and Spaniards. And so on with the rest.

Or take hair. In one sense the texture and form of the hair might be regarded as a good racial trait, in so far as one race, the Negro, has frizzly or kinky hair, relatively thin and light in weight, whereas another, the Mongolian, has straight hair which is thick and very heavy.

[5] *Annals of the New York Academy of Sciences*, vol. XXI, 1912, pp. 177–178.

But here once more the major usefulness of the differentiation comes to an end. The American Indian, who in other respects can be differentiated from the Mongolian, is indistinguishable from him in the character of his hair: it is black and straight and thick and heavy and it grows long, if one lets it. The Negro and the Australian differ, in so far as the hair of the Australian is usually wavy. But in this very waviness of hair the Australians are like many Whites, and they are like the White race in general in the hairiness of their faces and bodies.

In view of the impossibility of classifying the races on the basis of any one trait, anthropologists and comparative anatomists are in the habit of using a complex of traits as a basis of racial classification. Of the individual traits comprised in such a complex only a very few prove to be exclusively characteristic of any one race or of all of its members, but the complex as a whole serves the ends of classification well enough.

It will suffice for our purposes if we classify on the basis of such a complex the following five representative racial types: the Negro, Australian, Mongolian, American Indian, and White. Briefly, the grouping of typical traits in these five races is as follows.

First the Negro: His complexion is dark, sometimes almost black. The hair is frizzly, often kinky, relatively sparse even on the head and definitely so on the face and body. The nose is thick and fleshy with moderately low back. The nostrils are large with a characteristic lateral spread along the surface of the face, whereas the septum of the nose extends slantingly from the tip of the nose to a point on the face some distance below the tip; this gives the Negro nose a moderately pug appearance and results in the partial visibility of the nostrils in front view (see Plate II). The lips of the Negro are large and fleshy, with an unusually large surface of externally visible mucous membrane. Thus they look as if they were partially turned inside out. A certain number of Negroes tend to be prognathic, meaning by this that their jaws protrude: the upper and lower jaws meet at an obtuse angle.

Second, the Australian: The complexion here also is dark, but not as dark as that of a Negro. The hair is usually wavy, ample on the head and exceedingly so on the face and body generally. The nose varies from a Negroid variety to one with a considerably more prominent back. Perhaps the most marked racial peculiarity of the Australian is the unusual development of the supra-orbital ridges, the bones which form the upper part of the skeletal frame of the eye and are situated right under the eyebrows. In addition to this, there seems to be a tendency for limbs to grow relatively long in relation to the length of the body; this applies especially to the legs.

PLATE II.   A ZULU WARRIOR IN FIGHTING TRIM

PAWNEE WIND RIVER SHOSHONI

CROW

PLATE III. PLAINS INDIAN TYPES

(Clark Wissler, *American Indians of the Plains.*)

Third, the Mongolian: The complexion is a sort of lightish brown, not very pure. The hair is black, straight, thick, and heavy. The hairiness of the face and body is slight. The cheek bones are prominent. The nose is flatter than that of the Negro but not so thick. The root of the nose, between the eyes, is thick and fatty, frequently without any elevation. This trait can often be observed on our own infants. The eye is almond-shaped, with thick eyelids, and is slanted from the nose upward, so that the corners of the eye near the nose are lower than the opposite corners.

Fourth, the American Indian: In complexion there is here considerable variability from a relatively dark brown, darker than the Mongolian variety, to a relatively light palish brown. The hair is characteristically of the precise Mongolian type, black, straight, thick, and heavy, with slight hairiness of face and body. The nose is variable. The so-called classical Indian nose, with a very high bridge and convex, is very pronounced and distinctive when it occurs, but it does not occur very often. In many regions of both American continents it is very rare or unknown. The cheek bones are high, not only the upper but frequently also the lower ones, which makes for a broad face; and as the face is also long, at least in many cases, the result is a large face, rather typical of the Indian, though of course not universal (Plate III). The Indian face has also been described as pentagonal (see Figs. 67 and 68, p. 191).

Fifth and last, the White: This race is most difficult to characterize for the reason of its extreme variability, a significant feature in the light of what was said a little while ago. In complexion, hair-form and hair-texture, eyes, nose, lips, shape of head and face, as well as size, there is here more variation, as between man and man, than in any other race. The complexion, nominally white, varies from the paleness of the northern Europeans, the so-called Nordics, to the relatively dark skin of the Mediterraneans—as dark, let me repeat, as that of many Arabs and Hindus. The hair varies in colour from black through all shades of brown, from very dark brown to auburn, light brown, or blond, to the flaxen or very pale yellowish white of some Swedes and Dutchmen. The blond and some of the brown varieties of hair are occasionally tinged with red, which occurs in the form of the so-called Titian hair, a darkish golden red type, regarded by many as very attractive, to the pronounced red hair, 'like fire,' regarded by most people as very unattractive. In form the hair varies from straight, through all degrees of waviness, to almost kinky hair. Similarly, the eye varies from the very dark brown, almost black eye of the southern Europeans through all shades of dark and light brown, brownish grey, brownish green, and a large number of shades of blue, from dark blue to a very pale watery blue. Grey eyes, in different shades, though rare, are not unknown. The different varieties of blue eyes belong on the whole to the northern peoples of the White race, but are also known in more southern regions. Again, the nose may be narrow or broad, with slight or very pronounced nostrils, with a low, moderate, or high bridge. It may be straight, convex in a variety of kinds, and concave. When the latter kind of nose is combined with a slanting septum, revealing the nostrils in front view, we have the pug nose. It may be noted at once that what is typical here are not so much the physical features themselves as their variability, to which may be added the general tendency towards low pigmentation, as revealed in complexion, colour of hair, and colour of eyes. This classification does not, of course, exhaust all the varieties of mankind, but let me only add that neither the Melanesian nor the Polynesian falls precisely into any of these groupings. However, the base of the Melanesian type is certainly Negroid, whereas that of the Polynesian is almost certainly White; but there are also Mongolian and probably Negroid components in the Polynesian, and perhaps non-Negroid ones in the Melanesian.

Having thus settled the problem of racial classification, at least roughly, I shall add a few explanatory remarks with reference to a number of particular traits mentioned above.

The colour of human hair is prevailingly dark or black. It is such among all the races except the White, and is also, of course, commonly such in the White race. The lighter varieties of hair are frequent only in middle and northern Europe or among peoples whose ancestors lived there, but they also occur, although not frequently, even among the extreme eastern Mediterraneans. Reddish hair has also been reported among Polynesians, which is significant on account of their early affiliation with White ancestors.

Straight hair is circular in cross section, which makes for greater rigidity and straightness. Curly hair is oval in cross section: the more flattened the oval, the greater the curliness.[6] The hair of the Mongolian,

---

[6] Hooton here adds an interesting detail. He writes: 'It is very doubtful if hair form is modifiable by environment. "Naturally curly" hair becomes more curly in damp weather, but artificially curved hair straightens out when exposed to moisture. "Permanent waving" of the hair is accomplished by twisting the hair and applying to it intense heat, while keeping the hair moist. Straightening of the hair is effected by ironing it out under moist heat. Apparently hair that is "permanently waved" is little affected by subsequent damp weather, but the wave is gradually lost as the hair grows out and is cut. Straightened hair becomes curved, however, as soon as the atmosphere gets humid. These considerations make it probable that there is some relationship between heat and moisture and curvature of the hair.'

in addition to being straight, is also heavy; according to Hooton, it is almost twice as heavy as a like volume of Negro hair, while that of the Whites is intermediate in weight. Among the Whites, the hair of the Nordics is the lightest in weight, that of the Alpines comes next, and the Mediterraneans have the heaviest hair.

Complexion depends on the amount of granular pigment segregated in the deeper layers of the epidermis. This pigment, called melanin or 'black substance,' consists of very dark brown or black granules, closely packed together within the cells if the granules are numerous, but sparsely set if the amount of melanin is small. In accordance with the thickness of the pigment the skin appears yellowish, brown, or black.[7]

The nose, which plays, as we saw, an important part as a racial feature, can vary both in shape and in size, the former being more important as a racial trait. Hooton gives excellent characterizations of the Negro and Mongolian noses which may be quoted in full: 'The Negro nose *par excellence* has a slightly depressed root which is low and broad; the concave or straight bridge is of great breadth, and of low or medium height; the tip is thick and bulbous and turned upward; the wings are very thick and flaring, the nostrils round or with their long axes directed transversely and frontally visible. The septum is thick and inclined upward, although viewed from the side it is convex. The whole nose is short and very broad at the tip and wings.'[8] Compared with this the Mongolian nose differs in that 'its root is much lower and not as broad, and is almost never depressed at nasion. . . . Often the Mongoloid nose shows practically no elevation of the root. The bridge is also much lower than that of the Negro and much narrower. The tip is not swollen and the wings are much thinner and less flaring. The nostrils are round or broadly oval and directed forward, the tip and septum elevated. The septum is thinner than that of the Negro and does not usually show a convexity. In profile the Mongoloid nose is strongly concave, whereas some Negro noses are slightly convex and many straight.'[9]

Among the many and varied noses of the White race the one that has

(E. A. Hooton, *Up from the Ape*, p. 437. By permission of The Macmillan Company, publishers.)

[7] The blue birth-marks often seen on the skin of the sacral region in Mongoloids, and similar blue birth-marks found in various parts of the bodies of Europeans, are usually caused by large pigmented cells in the lower part of the true skin (dermis). The blue tinge is imparted by the brown pigment granules showing through the imperfectly transparent, superficial layers of the skin. (*Ibid.*, p. 442.)

[8] *Ibid.*, p. 429.

[9] *Ibid.*, p. 430.

aroused the greatest attention and comment is perhaps the so-called Semitic or Jewish nose which anthropologists prefer to call Armenoid. In describing this type of nose Hooton almost waxes dramatic, and so we may let him have his say once more: 'This nose is remarkable for its great length, great height, convexity, and depression of its thick tip. It is not a narrow nose, especially at its lower end, which shows heavy wings curving back so as to expose a large part of the inner wall of the nostrils. Very often this kind of nose has no depression either at nasion or below it, but continues the forehead slope without a dip, ending in a thick, rounded, and depressed tip with a concave and downward sloping septum. The eminence or hump in the bridge may be very marked or hardly perceptible, but the tip is almost invariably thickened and depressed and the wings coarse and recurved. This nose was found among the ancient Sumerians, Babylonians, Assyrians, Hittites, and Persians, and it is an inescapable feature of many Syrians, Armenians, Jews, Greeks, Turks, and other Levantine peoples of today. A modified form of this nose with a considerable refinement of the tip and wings occurs in the tall, brachycephalic Balkan group sometimes called the "Dinaric race." ' [10] This is the type of nose referred to before which also occurs among the Negroids of Oceania, the Melanesians and Papuans, and occasionally in Australia, combining, in these instances, most of the characters of the Armenoid nose in exaggerated form.[11]

An additional word is due to the eye of the Mongolian before we close this topic. As already stated, in many cases but not universally, this eye is slanting from the nose upwards. What is notable here is that this peculiarity of the Mongolian eye is not due to any characteristics of the skull. Even in the slantest-eyed Mongolian, the skeletal position of the eye sockets is perfectly horizontal. The peculiarity, then, is due to the fatty and dermal tissues. Hooton distinguishes two varieties of the Mongolian eye. In the first, the fold of skin covers up the free edge of the upper eyelid from corner to corner, overhanging the inner corner and concealing the lachrymal duct. This type of fold is the complete

[10] *Ibid.*, pp. 431–432.

[11] As between the large-nostrilled nose of the Negro and the nose of the northern inhabitants with its greatly reduced nasal aperture, Hooton refers to an interesting theory which is mentioned here for what it may be worth. The broad-nosed races who live in hot climates, it is thought, can breathe in great quantities of warm air without undue cooling of the respiratory organs. Among the northern peoples, on the other hand, with their narrow noses lined with thin mucous membrane, the air is warmed as it is breathed in, and is thus prevented from lowering the body temperature. It is interesting in this connexion that the Eskimo has one of the narrowest nasal apertures.

Mongoloid fold—it does not represent the better known, because more peculiar form. In the second variety of fold the overhanging skin begins on the inner or medial part of the upper eyelid, covering the upper edge of the inner part and extending downward to conceal the lachrymal duct. It is in this case that the position of the eye acquires the slanting appearance, thus giving rise to the typical 'Mongolian eye.' [12]

Race Mixture. Much more important, practically and even theoretically, than to realize the differences between racial traits is to be aware of the fact that everywhere on earth racial distinctions have been subjected and continue to be subjected to obliteration, recombination, or perhaps reconstitution, through the physical mixture of individuals representing these different types. I have already indicated that the very fact of an extraordinary variability in the White race points to an unusually varied ancestry. It is well known that such variability is characteristic of domesticated when compared with wild animals, the domesticated varieties being produced by the peculiarities of many artificial environments and the deliberate efforts of animal fanciers. It would, for example, be impossible to duplicate in nature 'in the raw' the enormous variability of the domesticated dog from the diminutive Spaniel and lap-dog to the enormous Dane, Newfoundland, and St. Bernard. It is in fact quite remarkable, as has been pointed out long ago by Eduard Hahn, that dog knows dog, however he may look and of whatever size or shape he may be. (*Cf.* p. 112, footnote 7.) The same, of course, is true in man, but on a less marked scale and with the regrettable difference that man seems to be less inclined to recognize his kind even though the contrast may not be so great.

It does not require any extraordinary depth, acumen, or scholarship to realize how thoroughgoing and omnipresent has been the process of racial mixture. Man is a great traveller. Under pressure of climatic or human

[12] Before closing the description of the races let me draw attention here to a very important point made by Hooton, namely that the vast majority of the so-called racial traits are expressed in features which are, so far as one can see, of no survival value. In the nose, for example, the shape may possibly be of significance, as suggested above, but its size, however interesting aesthetically or otherwise, is an utterly indifferent matter in the struggle for existence. The same is true of shape of eye, head-form, the character of the jaw, the colour, texture or form of the hair, and so on through a large number of traits. In other words, from the standpoint of human biology in relation to its geography, these differences may be regarded as playful variations. They are what they are, but might also have been quite different, without in either case being of any serious biological significance. Hypothetically at least, this state of affairs may be taken as symptomatic of what might be true in the psychological sphere also. If there are any differences here which in any sense can be regarded as racial, perhaps these also fall into the field of playful variants: nothing that really counts, merely something that differs.

factors, in quest of richer harvests or an easier life, or just following that blind urge for adventure which may be regarded as the geographical expression of human imagination, people have always moved about, in smaller or larger groups, for short or for long distances. In the course of these wanderings and dislocations they have been coming in contact with groups of men somewhat differently shaped or coloured, and with them they have mated. The early Malays crossed the outskirts of an enormous continent to find themselves far from their East Asiatic home on the edge of South Africa, where a very different nature and a very different type of man were awaiting them. Before the present pacifism of the Chinese was born, the Mongolian inhabitants of China moved in repeated militant thrusts in a southerly direction, finding there other peoples who, though Mongolian, were of a different sub-variety. The entire development of the Negro tribes of northern Africa has been affected by Mongolian and other West Asiatic invasions, long before the 'civilized' Europeans discovered the home of the Negro as something worthy of exploration, annexation, and exploitation. When the Arabs embraced the Mohammedan creed in the seventh century A.D. and carried the new message along the broad strips of northern Africa, they mixed with the native Negroes, and when early in the eighth century they crossed into Spain, they brought to Europe not only science, philosophy, medicine, and art, but also Negro blood. These Arabs, in the course of several centuries, intermarried with native Europeans. Among the Arabs were many Jews who themselves had been touched by Negro blood and had interbred with the Arabs; so there was a Negro strain in them also. During the residence of the Arabs in Spain, and later after the expulsion of the Jews from Spain, Negro strains were communicated to other Europeans through both these sources. After the discovery of America, 'blood mixture' on a large scale proceeded between the White settlers and the Indians. Later in the seventeenth and eighteenth centuries, during the period of the slave trade, Negroes were imported to America who mixed with the Whites as well as with the Indians. And the offspring of the Whites who had already mixed with Indians, now mixed with the Negroes. Nor was the Indian the only source through which Mongolian blood penetrated into the domain of the White race. The early history of Russia, or the country north of the ancient Pontus or Black Sea which was to become Russia, tells of never ending streams of Mongolian invaders. In the middle of the first millennium B.C., and then again a thousand years later, they came in irresistible waves, until in the thirteenth century, under the mighty Genghis Khan and his successor Batu, the Mongolians subjugated the entire plain of European Russia and then clung to its edges, to mix with the White race, for a period of two and a half centuries, transforming into Mongolian likeness not only the Alpine or Alpinoid Russian population of the south, but even the Jews of that region, who to this day can be readily recognized as the carriers of Mongolian strains. And the mixture continues. In Madagascar the Mongoloid Malay has mixed with the Negro and the Negroid, and here also both have mixed with the White. How in the face of all these facts, which as here presented are but a sample of the real story, the idea of racial purity can continue to persist in the minds of men, is a fact that nothing can explain except the blind stubbornness of dogma backed by prejudice. Pure race was once a fact, but this was long, long ago. Then it became a myth. Of late the myth has been turning into a nightmare, and the time is more than ripe for man to wake up and realize where he stands or who he is.

Race, Language, and Culture. The association of a physical type with a particular language and a special kind of culture is not altogether a fiction. In the case of the Eskimo, for example, we find an instance of a people with somewhat marked physical characteristics, plausibly due to inbreeding, who speak a number of languages which, though differentiated, have numerous characteristics in common, and possess a culture which in the midst of minor differences reveals many basic similarities. The case of the Eskimo, however, is instructive because fairly unique and certainly exceptional. The remote and forbidding environment does not invite intrusion, and is almost prohibitive of permanent or protracted residence for anyone but the Eskimo themselves. Such is not the case in most other regions of the globe. Under normal conditions physical type, language, and culture possess mobilities of their own. Each changes, but not under the same conditions nor at the same rate. Physical type can, of course, only be affected by another physical type when actual mating takes place; mere spatial coexistence does not suffice here. Language, though more stubborn in its passage from one group to another than is generally supposed, will become seriously modified when two or more groups coexist in the same locality for any length of time. This can be illustrated in all so-called marginal areas. The citizens of Alsace and Lorraine, for example, are linguistically as French as they are German; whereas those of Switzerland, itself a marginal area to Germany, France, and Italy, converse glibly in all three languages, mixing them up on occasion. The Finns, a Mongolian tribe with a Uro-Altaic language and possessing in modern days a culture almost completely Scandinavian, have during the eighteenth and nineteenth centuries absorbed the Russian language, but very little of Russian culture. The Mongolian Magyars of Hungary, through prolonged intermarriage with Mid-Europeans, have lost many of their Mongolian features; they have also absorbed the culture of Middle Europe, Germanic in its essential traits. To be sure, the majority of Hungarians also know German, but they have preserved the Hungarian language, which happens to be related to that of the Finns. The American Negro, after his forced transportation from Africa, has remained a Negro physically even though not without marked modifications in type, but his languages and cultures have vanished, except for a few disjointed fragments. Culturally and linguistically the Negro is an American. The peoples on the two sides of the Rhine, those of southern Germany and northern France, though differing in language and culture, represent the same Alpine physical type. And so it goes in innumerable other instances.

In view of all this, it is most important to separate these three domains in our investigations and discussions. A classification of peoples from the standpoint of language need not have any meaning culturally, and certainly has no meaning physically. A classification from the standpoint of physical type is equally without bearing on either culture or language. The point here made, though theoretically obvious and from this standpoint scarcely deserving emphasis, is nevertheless worth making for the reason that we are so prone to endow linguistic groupings with cultural significance and to ascribe cultural complexes, such as those of nations, to the influence of racial or sub-racial qualities. As a preamble to the discussion of the psychology of race it is therefore worth our while to comment briefly upon our habits of thought with reference to so-called national characteristics.

The Russians of the nineteenth century were regarded as intelligent, temperamental, unreliable, great linguists. It was also thought that somehow Asiatic and European traits were combined in their national psychology: scratch a Russian, it was said, and you will find a Tartar. Now, apart from obvious inaccuracies and equally patent exaggerations, the general picture as just given is a fairly true one, in so far as certain groups of nineteenth-century Russia are concerned. What is at fault is the accompanying interpretation: once a Russian always a Russian. These traits were, on the contrary, the expression of an historic past and a cultural *status quo*. Even the notorious linguistic capabilities of Russians can be readily explained away by the simple fact that in the Russian nobility and upper middle class children were brought up under the guidance of foreign tutors, German, French, and English, and thus imbibed these languages early in life. Those who have listened to the French or English conversation of those Russians who had learned these tongues in later years and under less favourable conditions, soon enough disabused themselves of any illusions as to the linguistic ability of the Russian stock. And finally, how many of the old Russian traits still survive in the U.S.S.R., or will be recognizable another generation hence?

The same is true of Germany. The Germans of the end of the eighteenth century and the beginning of the nineteenth were romantic, philosophical, sentimental, chummy (*gemütlich*) and, on the whole, pacific. The change came with the rise of Prussia, the consolidation of Germany after the Franco-Prussian War, and the forced moulding of German character into a nation of dogmatic, pedantic, goose-stepping, and potentially militaristic citizens. The transformation has occurred under our very eyes, as it were. It is the more illuminating and instructive, I might add, perhaps overoptimistically, as what has happened in one direction may happen again, in another.

The French are noted for their logical precision and what is called *ésprit*, a peculiar sparkling sort of intelligence not unrelated to wit. The French, however, did not possess these qualities in the days of Caesar. In his comments on their ancient forebears—and he was a shrewd observer and a trenchant writer—we hear nothing of logical precision or any particular intellectual sparkle. We know, on the other hand, how the remarkable development of philosophy and science and literature in seventeenth- and eighteenth-century France resulted in a new form of culture and mental orientation. This, combined with the elaborate court life in the era from Louis XIV to the beginning of the nineteenth century, gave the 'French mind' those qualities of mental precision and articulatory grace which in more recent days have been justly placed in the centre of French culture.

Similarly, when Napoleon designated the English as 'a nation of shopkeepers' he was combining a highly one-sided selection of a trait with the subjective colouration rooted in his hatred of the English—well-founded, in the light of his personal history. But it would be no more justifiable to identify his characterization with English character than to regard as significant the singling out of the 'man of property' in Galsworthy's *Forsyte Saga*. What I am trying to convey is not that these characterizations are necessarily untrue—some of them may be profoundly true—but that they are worthless if extended beyond a given time and place, and that in any case they have no relation whatsoever to the biological inheritance of the group.

Mental Characteristics of the Races. When it comes to the psychology of race I always think of the apochryphal volume on Iceland in which there was a chapter on snakes. It opened like this: 'There are no snakes in Iceland,' and there it also closed. As I have already repeatedly stated, to the anthropologist race physical is a special and technical pursuit. In his studies of primitive culture he is accustomed to disregard it. The same is true of race psychological. We do not find in anthropological field work any of those captions under which racial psychology is dealt with so glibly in the books of innocent laymen or less innocent race mythologists. We hear nothing of the stolidity of the American Indian, or the reserve of the Mongolian, or the emotional instability of the Negro, any more than we do of the hysterical emotional make-up of the 'savage' or the improvidence of the primitive. What the anthropologist finds is man to whom nothing human is foreign: *all the fundamental traits of the psychic make-up of man anywhere are present everywhere.* The basic differences between the shrewd and intelligent, on the one hand, and the stupid and gullible, on the other, with all the intervening gradations, confront the student of human culture, and in particular the anthropologist, everywhere he goes. Nor is he the only one to draw the distinction; the people observed by him draw it too, and often they draw it for him.

Similarly, man's proclivity to religious emotion and his artistic impulse are found in every tribe. In this case also men, primitive or modern, are strictly comparable. But here further application brings out the fact that not any man can be a shaman, nor can any man or woman draw, paint, carve, or embroider as well as any other. On the contrary, ability is there, it counts, and it is differential. Wherever man is found we know there is society, a social organization, a form of leadership. The edicts of society become dogma, they are enforced by special pressure and protected by penalization, and the official representatives of social authority (or even the self-named despots) are, by and large, everywhere individuals with a certain practical knowledge of people, an ability to control them, a capacity to rise to an occasion, a certain poise in crucial situations, and so on.

Everywhere, again, man invents. He combines and recombines old things and ideas into new ones, and he applies them in such a way that they work in a material and stubborn world. Again and again, we shall see in the course of our investigation how significant in the history of civilization were just the early basic inventions, many of which still survive, notwithstanding the enormous overlay contributed by human originality or shrewdness in later periods. Quite as in the case of racial prejudice within the modern world itself, contradictory qualities are wont to be ascribed to the primitive with the greatest ease. For example, he is characterized, even by some of those who might know better, as an inveterate supernaturalist, addicted to ideas charged with emotion and incapable of putting two and two together because, we are told, two to him is not 'two' but something else, probably mystical and intangible. On the other hand, we also hear that the 'savage' is incurably practical, that he does not do anything but what he must or needs to do, that even his religion is dominated by the needs of the morrow or the day, that fundamentally he is most unimaginative: he cannot see beyond his nose —and this he takes for something else. Characterizations such as this are worse than wrong: they are half-true in the vicious sense of losing the half-truth each contains through a blind spot with reference to the other half. The primitive must live. The protective armour of his culture is not as proof against accident or misfortune as is that of ours. The pressure, therefore, of daily tasks and needs is enormous. In this sense, the primitive is and must be practical: he attends to the business of living. But also, he has imagination. He transcends the day and the morrow and the needs of the body, in the name of ideas, faiths, the enjoyment of fancy or of play. From this standpoint it is unfortunate that the study of primitive languages is so technical and difficult a task. The idea is still prevalent among the laity that just as the primitive is only half a man, so his language is only half a language. How far from the truth this is! The languages of the primitives are elaborate mechanisms, comprising ample vocabularies and complex grammatical structures, in which the unconscious capacity of man for the formation of what one might call organic concepts and categories is as conspicuous as in any grammar or language. Not only can the primitives use their languages but these, in their case, represent culture, life, the entire mental content. The attritions and simplifications which have reduced our own day-by-day talk to a mere skeleton, if a dynamic one, have as yet not set in. It is for this reason that the language of primitives, like that of peasants, over-flows with rich and picturesque content. It holds and gives forth not only the framework of a culture but all of its overtones and shadings. It abounds in proverbs, where these prevail, and popular sayings in which the observations and shrewdness or the prejudices and foibles of the people are expressed. It possesses all the flexibility of a tool constantly put to many and varied uses. It can be said, with probability, that if a primitive visitor could encompass the real nature of our conversational language, the day-by-day words and phrases of our Western civilization, he would be prompted to puzzlement or even contempt. What kind of people are these, he might exclaim, who cannot even talk!

We constantly forget that the achievements of what we call 'our' civilization are peaks attained by a few, for which the vast majority of us are not and could not be responsible, and which this majority cannot understand, frequently being ignorant even of their very existence.

The honest psychologist of race can glean nothing from the comparative study of brains. How much do we know about brains anyway, or their precise relation to mentality in particular and to psychic life in general? Whatever evidence there is certainly indicates that there is room for all human wisdom and all human foolishness within a wide range of brain size, weight, and structure. Beyond this, what we know as to what a brain can do is always *ex post facto*: the only convincing and unanswerable proof is performance. When it has done it, we know it can do it. The obvious inference from this is that we do not know what a given brain or a given set of brains, such as that comprised in the heads of a primitive tribe, could and might do in a different setting.

Consider this: The development of White man's civilization, our Western culture, is not, as one might at first think, a series of events that have recurred again and again, so that one might say: at any place or time when a group of the White race tackled civilization it pulled it up to heights beyond the reach of others. Nothing of the sort! In the course of a few thousands of years the development of this civilization has been so continuous—not from year to year or century to century necessarily, but from thing to thing and from idea to idea—that the entire story is really merely an elaborate statement of one historic phenomenon or 'event,' in the broadest sense. White man in his progress has never been out of reach of other White men before him to tack on to.

This is one thing, and then there is the other: How old really is this civilization of ours? We like to trace it back to the Greeks. This is, of course, subjective and inaccurate, but suppose we take the Greeks. Two of the outstanding achievements of modern civilization, which by its own proclamation belong to its very essence, are science and technology. Now science, as we understand it, was as non-existent among the Greeks as it could well be among a people so enamoured with intellectual endeavour. They knew little about experiment and nothing about measurement, nor were they either able or willing to divest scientific terms and concepts of the baggage of mysticism and aestheticism which barred the way to further achievement. As to technology, they were about on the level of the smallest modern country town, however 'one by two.' The technical, mechanical, or power phase of modern civilization would have surprised Aristotle or Hippocrates as much as it would have surprised Howitt's Australian chieftain or a magic-working shaman of eastern

Siberia. When Marco Polo visited China, in the second half of the thirteenth century, and communed with Kublai Khan—Marco Polo, incidentally, being not the first but the third European visitor to these
lands during that century, the first two having been Franciscan monks—
he found and heard things there which kept him in constant amazement.
It is said that he brought Christianity to the Chinese, which it seems they
were not in a hurry to accept; but he brought back philosophic doctrines,
technical knowledge, and a vision of policy and statecraft which Europe
was only too eager to grasp and make its own. To the Chinese of those
days, if they only had gone out of their way to know our ancestors and
had been as prejudiced then as we are today, these ancestors of ours
would have appeared as little more than pale-faced weaker brothers, as
much behind in civilization as their washed-out countenances stood below the Mongolian standards of beauty.

When one considers our persistent inability to draw inferences from
historic examples, he almost despairs of the ultimate victory of rationality which, in our racial pride, we claim to have already achieved. Thinking back only a little, we find ourselves holding the same supercilious
and contemptuous notions about the Japanese that are still prevalent
among us about the Chinese. What is it that so suddenly brought about a
change of attitude towards these easternmost representatives of the
Asiatic Mongolians? Merely this. When the Japanese threw open their
harbours to American and European commerce, or when Commodore
Perry threw them open for them, they seized upon the advantages of
Western civilization with a zest and effectiveness which must have proved
no less surprising to thoughtful Japanese than it did to us. The result
was that they learned Western commerce; in its wake came industries,
industries engendered science, and the national consciousness of having
become an active participant in this heretofore foreign world of the
Western nations stimulated thought about national grandeur and defence—a very appropriate thought under the conditions. Presently Japan
became a power amongst other powers. Still its status, it must be admitted, remained a lowly one until 1905; then it went up with flying
colours, after the war with Russia, whose badly equipped and worse led
legions had by that time acquired a European reputation of invincibility.
Only then did the cloak of prejudice fall. It is not necessary to ask here
whether China would have to undergo a similar transformation to gain
that objective or receive that reward. The point is that the history of
China certainly represents a much more impressive picture of cultural
achievement than did that of Japan before its opening to Western influence. Still the average American continues to think about the Chinese

as if they were a nation of coolies. Even our outstanding philosopher could not find it in him to say anything better about the Chinese than that under favourable conditions they might successfully learn from us. Fortunately for our self-respect, another outstanding philosopher, from across the seas, insists rather emphatically that there are a number of things that we might learn from the Chinese.

As one becomes immersed in the study of racial psychology, one comes to realize that the significant factor involved is not by any means the psychic differences of the races, but rather the psychic unity of man, a rather discouraging aspect of that psychic unity. What counts and demands attention is not the problematic difference in racial ability but the disability of the genus *Homo*, however *sapiens*, to think intelligently and without prejudice in this field, so heavily charged with emotion, vanity, special pleading, and still lowlier affects.

Chapter III

FROM MIND TO CULTURE

Animal Mind

As it is impossible here to review what is known about the so-called mentality of the different varieties of animals, a few examples will suffice. There lived once a famous horse, *Der kluge Hans* (the intelligent Hans), an unusually bright equine, resident in Berlin, which acquired the reputation of being able to solve simple mathematical problems in addition and multiplication. It would be asked how much is 2 times 4 or 12 and 13, and it would give the correct answer by striking the ground with one of its fore hoofs. Hans promptly became famous and acquired wide publicity, until a young psychologist, Dr. Pfungst, undertook to examine the case more carefully. First suspicion fell on the trainer, who was subsequently found to be perfectly innocent and above board. Having once trained his Hans, he now did nothing to assist him—nothing, that is, he knew of. Whenever Hans was performing, though, the trainer was right there, standing in front of the horse. So Dr. Pfungst invited him to retire; and presently, Hans's mathematical talent retired with him: the horse was no longer able to give the correct answers. Further investigation revealed the fact that Hans was guided by slight and, of course, unconscious automatic movements in the face of the trainer, which gave the horse a clue as to the precise moment at which it should stop striking the ground with its hoof. Now, there are horses and horses; among equines as among humans some are bright, others dumbbells. Evidently Hans was an intelligent horse, but its achievement was after all within the range of horse sense. If, on the other hand, Hans had actually possessed the ability to perform additions and multiplications, there would have been no reason why, with further application, he or some other equally gifted equine could not reach the stage of handling calculus and the like. Apparently there are no such horses. Hans's performance then still lies within the range of reactions guided by sense impressions, in this case minute ones, the discernment and utilization of which require a bright mind, for a horse.

Then we have the fascinating study by Wolfgang Koehler, *The Mentality of Apes*. The author spent large stretches of several years on a

37

banana plantation on Teneriffe (Canary Islands) where he had ample opportunity to study chimpanzees both in the wild and under controlled conditions. What he reports are experiments like this. A chimpanzee placed in a cage was supplied with three boxes, light enough for him to handle and arrange at will. Under the roof of the cage and out of reach of the chimpanzee, even when standing on top of the boxes, except in a certain arrangement, a banana was placed. The latter fact was promptly noted by the Anthropoid. For a long time, however, it made no deliberate or reasoned effort to reach the banana. It kept on playing with the boxes, after the fashion of its kind. Presently it happened that it placed them one on top of the other, which brought it near the banana, but not quite near enough. Upon descending to the foot of the pyramid, the chimpanzee was now visibly disturbed. For a while it sat there looking at the boxes. What it may have thought no one, of course, can tell, but Koehler's hunch about its mental content is expressed in the sentence, 'There is something about those boxes!' In due time, in the course of its manipulations, the chimpanzee did manage to put them together in the right way. Then in an instant it swung itself to the top and grabbed the banana. After repeating this operation a number of times the ape learned to perform it without difficulty or hesitation.

Another instance: This time the banana was placed on the ground outside the cage and the chimpanzee in the cage was supplied with two sticks, neither of which was long enough to enable it to reach the banana by extending the stick between the bars of the cage and pulling it within reach. This chimpanzee had already learned to reach a banana by means of one stick long enough for the purpose. Now, the shorter sticks were made in such a way that they could be fitted together end to end. Again the chimpanzee went through the appearance of longing and despair at seeing the banana it could not reach. Once more, it engaged in a prolonged manipulation of the sticks, without any apparent reference to the banana and without any discernible interest. Presently, however, it happened that the two sticks placed end to end in the right position fitted together, thus forming one long stick. In an instant the chimpanzee stuck the new tool through the bars, pushed the banana towards the cage, grabbed and ate it (in very human fashion). This performance was repeated with ease ever after.

In both of these instances it will be seen that the chimpanzee apparently is incapable of visualizing a fairly complex situation and taking stock of its equipment, in order to figure out in advance the acts necessary to reach the goal. Once the necessary arrangement is brought about by accident, however, it has ample capacity to discern the fitness of the situation, to make the best of it with alacrity, and reproduce it on all future occasions. The chimpanzee's performance, it will be seen, places it on a higher plane of mentality than that of poor clever Hans. As to figuring things out, that is, first imagining then reproducing a situation on the basis of mere 'indicators' in preceding experience, the chimpanzee itself has still far to go.

Perhaps these instances will suffice to indicate that the limitation of the animal mind seems to lie in its incapacity, or more limited capacity, to think in abstract terms or, for short, to *think*. In a broader perspective, again, it is of course obvious that the difference between the mentality here displayed and that of man is merely one of degree.

Human Mind

In point of sheer psychology, mind as such, man is after all no more than a talented animal. The mind of the infant, as it enters the world, is not a fact—it is a potentiality. What this potentiality means we discover in the unfoldment of capacity which soon transcends that of any animal. But at that first fateful moment, ushered in by the baby's first cry, and for some time later, there is as yet no evidence of humanity.

More than this. In spite of all the enormous labour expended on the study of nerve tissue in general and the brain in particular, it would be quite impossible for us to determine by an advance examination, outside or inside, what the youngster was about to unfold into, not only as a particular individual but even as just a human rather than a mere animal. On the other hand, we do know from some few experiences that away from a human setting the potentiality of the baby would be wasted—it would grow up just an animal. The agency which transforms the potential human that has just entered the world into the human of later days, is applied to it very early, and it keeps on being applied for a long time to come. That agency is culture, and the method of its application is education.

We know then that there is culture and that it comes to man in the process of education. But even this is not enough for an exact understanding of what it is that happens here. One of the differences between what occurs in the case of any animal, on the one hand, and in that of man, on the other, is the rate at which they grow up. With variations as between animal and animal, their young mature very fast. It is a matter of mere months. So fast do they mature that were there much for them to learn and had they the ability to do so, they could not, on account of the very shortness of the period separating birth from relative maturity. Then life's problems, with their categorical demands and dangers, must be met if life is to continue. Fortunately for the animal, its life is planned differently. It is equipped by nature with a large assortment of instincts or reaction complexes which make their appearance almost ready for action and develop perfect 'form' after relatively few individual experiences. These instinctive reactions constitute its answers to the problems of life. Being equipped with these answers, or nearly so, by its psychophysical constitution, the animal has very little to learn. What it needs to know for its own purposes it almost knows already.

The factor in human life, on the other hand, which makes acquisition of vast knowledge and the accumulation of experience possible for the young, is the so-called prolongation of infancy in man. Before man becomes a man, he is a baby, a child, an adolescent, for a considerable number of years during which most of his time is absorbed in one or another form of learning. To this he can devote himself with impunity because during these years his life is guarded. The baby or child does not have to pay the consequences of its errors, and is prevented from committing too grievous ones, by the presence of adults. The carefully circumscribed artificial conditions in which it is placed prevent it from putting a premature conclusion to its life through not knowing what it was all about. This factor in human life, once emphasized by the American historian and Spencerian disciple, John Fiske, is next to human psychic quality perhaps the most significant agency in the making of humanity.

Let us then rejoin the baby at its first moment of overt existence, and see what happens. During the first few weeks of its life it learns but little. Nursing is a process common to all mammals, and the baby's adjustment to it is usually rapid and wholly satisfactory. A few weeks later, after the sensory reactions have become properly allocated and defined, the baby begins to explore, not with the nose or ears or even eyes at first, but largely with the hands, often assisted by the mouth. It must be remembered that the baby's initial contact with the world, as something valuable and interesting, comes through touch and taste in the process of nursing. This conditions the direction taken by its earliest explorations of the rest of the world. It explores itself, its own body, for which operation it has unusual facilities. On account of the great flexibility of its limbs, it can readily cover this itinerary which acquaints it with all but a few parts of its body. Even later, when this has been accomplished, its tactual and manipulatory propensities persist. At the age of one and later the baby, though now adequately guided by its eyes as to what to tackle, continues to explore primarily by its hands, still ably assisted by the mouth. Thus it learns to know the world, develops a feel of it. And as I said before, in doing this it is not disturbed or checked in its tracks by the intrusion of demanding and menacing nature. Its efforts are restrained by the crib or the play pen, or the nursery, or the house, and should it be in the open, there is someone there to watch it—or should be.[1]

Now long before this process of a personal and direct acquaintance with the world has gone very far, it is supplemented by another and, humanly speaking, even more typical and significant process. The baby learns not only from its contact with nature but also from its contact with its mother or whatever other individuals are in its vicinity. In addition to checking it when it plays with a knife or is about to jump out of a window, the mother initiates that process (which once begun does not stop for a long time) of acquainting the baby not with the world of things merely but with that of humans. This is culture. It is there when the baby arrives, just as the world of natural things is there. It is not something that comes from the baby; it goes forth towards it. Moreover, the baby must take it and, whatever its nature, it does; meaning by this that any kind of culture, within very broad limits, is acceptable to the baby. This is the basic fact of cultural absorption to which all the later emotions and rationalizations and standardizations become attached. The baby comes into the world without culture. It takes it where it finds it, and what it takes depends on what there is to be taken. At this juncture, let us leave the baby once more.

I said that what the baby takes is what is there to be taken. Now how did it come there in the first place? The culture that exists at any given time and place has come from the past. It is the result of accumulation of things, attitudes, ideas, knowledge, error, prejudice. And the method by which this cultural baggage has been communicated and passed on through the generations is first that of sheer persistence, which refers especially to material things, and second that of verbal communication, which refers to all else, including material things also.

From this angle, the major role of language is that of a culture-carrier, and among primitives where written language does not exist, it is the spoken word that performs this function. Next to the prolonged infancy of man, the culture-bearing function of language is the most important fact in the making of humanity. The primitive knows what he

---

[1] How thoroughly we are adjusted to this feeling of the dependence of a baby on a protective agency can be gathered from that vague sense of uneasiness, a sort of undefined fear for the baby, which seizes an adult when he sees it alone and unprotected by a fence—or a guardian.

knows and thinks what he thinks, in the first place, because he was told so by others. The situation is really not different in modern conditions with reference to that initial baggage that comes to a person in the early years.

Before man begins to learn from anything written or printed, he is already more than half-formed by the things he has heard and absorbed. In this early contact of the adult world with the world of the child two other factors play a part; these come to be of vast significance in society and in the life of the adult. One is the presence of checks and penalties, if only verbal ones. Not being cultured, the baby naturally does most things wrong; that is, it does them differently from the way they are 'being done' in a given society. Here 'the mother' steps in and not only teaches it, or tells it what to do, but also and primarily checks it when it does what should not be done. More often than not, the baby goes where it should not go, for example, into the neighbourhood of the stove or into father's study. It is told and checked and scolded, upon transgression. When it begins to talk, no sooner has it learned to say things at all than it begins to say what it should not say. Once more it is told, checked, and reprimanded. The same is true of the numerous techniques it is gradually made to acquire, such as first letting itself be dressed, then dressing itself, then eating, then washing. We take these things in so matter-of-fact a way, take them for granted as it were, because they are so common and trite and infinitely repetitious. But how really significant they are will be gathered by anyone with a spark of imagination who will try to visualize what a baby might do at a family meal had it never learned either by imitation or by precept how to do what others are doing. Now this process of being told what to do, being checked when one does the wrong thing, and being penalized for doing it, is a prototype of a vast and all-important range of social life. All human institutions, whether the family, or religion, or law, or politics, centre in it.

Another process is this: after the baby has acquired a certain linguistic facility, it begins to concentrate its efforts on the articulation of one little word, 'Why?' Why, indeed? The 'why' of most things and acts and customs is neither apparent nor simple nor, in most instances, known. Still the brat wants to know 'why,' and if the next 'why' is to be sidetracked some answer must be forthcoming to satisfy the baby. In answering these questions 'the mother'—still using her as a symbol for the social world as educator—accepts the *status quo* as certain and impeccable. It is in its light that she answers the baby's queries. Do this because a hunter does it, or a warrior, or a chief, or a medicine-man. Do that because it is what mother does, or father, in fact, 'all our people always did it and you must do it also.' And finally, do this because it is good and if you do it you will be good; do not do that because it is bad and you will be bad if you do it. Now let us state categorically right here that the youthful inquirer is not to be blamed for interposing another 'Why?' after these explanations have been given. All of them, it will be readily conceded, are merely ways of shirking the real answers which, should anyone try to give them, could not be given because one does not know. And so the educator makes out as good a case as he or she can for the *status quo*, by hallowing it with tradition, or by misrepresenting it by means of verbal embellishments, or by rationalizing it through making it seem reasonable, whereas in fact it merely is what it is.

Now this last educational device is particularly characteristic of modern society, much given to rationality, but much more so to rationalization. We are rational in some things but we try to make ourselves out to be rational in all things. The amount of human effort expended in providing rational grounds for fundamentally perfectly indifferent acts, ideas and attitudes, is stupendous, and the educational process is both the primary source and the major field of application of that effort. This is also the basic root of the difference, no matter what the culture, between what people think or say they are and what they actually are, between professions and performance, ideals and actuality. The range of culture designated by the term 'morals,' the sum-total of the standards of behaviour within a given group, is an in-between thing. At one end are the ideals and standards, at the other, the behaviours; in between is the moral code which exerts a constant pull on the behaviours in the direction of the standards.

And now another point. In this inevitably reasoned presentation, the process here analyzed appears as a sort of deliberate give and take, overt and rational. This, however, is very far from being the case. The 'mother' uses her educational technique and the baby submits to it, or does not, very much as a craftsman uses his tool and the material yields or resists. In this process the craftsman is almost as non-deliberate and unthinking as is the tool or the material. The process is largely automatic, at least semi-mechanical, and when pulled into consciousness the overt explanation of it is usually wrong, that is, it does not represent with any degree of accuracy what is actually taking place.

The same in education. The mother educates as she cooks. She says and does what other mothers said and did, her own mother when she was a baby, just as the cook follows established recipes and standardized processes. And the baby responds to the educational mechanism very much as a steak does to the efforts of the cook. It does not know what it is doing, and when it has acquired or learned something, it does not really know what it has learned or how, unless it should be puzzled by what it is doing—and this is not the way of babies, or of adults, for that matter.

When we say that the acquisition of the cultural baggage by the child is an unconscious process, this statement should not be understood as saying that the child is like unto a block of wood on which the educational process makes dents. What is meant is that the whole procedure is so constant, so habitual, and on the whole so uninteresting, that it finds its way into the habits of the child without its becoming aware of what is really occurring. It must be realized that what we receive in education is always mere end-points of things or processes, as they happen to be at a given time and place.

Now all these things and acts are complex, they have their antecedents and histories. But this is not what is communicated to us, at least not on first application. No field of culture illustrates this more strikingly than does that of language. The child absorbs sentences, words, exclamations, meanings. It is not presented with an analysis but with an accomplished fact—the word or sentence. And it picks up the meanings from a feel of the situation, from the effects the words or sentences produce, from the response they evoke, from the pleasures or griefs that accompany them, and then it proceeds to use its 'mother'-tongue and use it well, without, however, knowing it. In other words, the structure of that tongue, the principles upon which it is based, the rules that keep it travelling along certains paths and avoiding others, all remain unknown, profoundly unknown. To bring them into consciousness, to analyze them, requires very deliberate and persistent effort.[2]

What is so conspicuously true of language is also true, if not to the same extent, of other aspects of culture. As we learn to walk without knowing what walking is or how we do it, so we sing and draw and play on an instrument, without any idea of the underlying forms or categories or principles, unless we deliberately turn to these aspects, as a distinct and difficult subject of study and inquiry. The same is true of morals, politics, etiquette, and taste. By the time one reaches the age when self-

---

[2] This is, of course, illustrated by what happens in the case of one's own language, acquired spontaneously in childhood, when compared with foreign languages, taught and learned in later years. We know our language and use it well, or some of us do, but its grammar we know only if we are grammarians. In the case of foreign languages, on the other hand, the diligent ones among us may study and learn the grammars very well, but they will not know the languages or speak them, with any degree of facility or even correctness, unless they have had an opportunity to learn them spontaneously in the process of spoken intercourse, as they learned the mother tongue.

analysis becomes possible, he simply discovers himself as having all these things: certain political views, certain moral convictions, certain standards of social amenity, and even certain kinds of taste. When people say there is no disputing about tastes, this is less than half a truth. Individual tastes in a given community do, of course, differ. But even more conspicuously, they agree; which appears at once when we compare the tastes in houses, vehicles, garments, amenities, of one community with those of another. The general and far-reaching similarity of taste in any community stands out against the background of difference or contrast between it and another. Now all of this is also unconscious and spontaneous in its acquisition. We do not know *how* or *why*, and only slightly *what*. We simply live or act these things, until we stop to turn around and inspect and analyze.

What one acquires deliberately, rationally, thinkingly, one holds on tolerance, as it were, subject to change or revision. About such matters we are ready to differ, to dispute, and to convince one another. A mathematician is not likely to be shocked or insulted when his colleague presents a different analysis of a formula or a different way of arriving at it; neither thinks the worse of the other for the difference. Not so in morals, mores, etiquette, or any of the many things and habits and views we acquire in the way described above: spontaneously, unconsciously. Things annexed in this fashion become part of our very make-up. Just because we do not know them, or what they really are, or how we acquired them, any doubt or criticism or difference impresses us as an impingement upon our very natures, and our protest is accompanied by a more or less violent explosion of emotion. What further intensifies the emotional padding of habits and views thus acquired is the social sanction which supports and hallows them, in any given place and time. Either they are just part of ourselves and we are therefore touchy about them, or they are held as 'convictions,' and as such are unassailable.

It is on this basis that one's allegiance to the minor or major groups to which one belongs gains in strength and becomes surrounded by protective discriminations, criticisms, and resentments against other groups, a process which is almost as spontaneous and automatic as the development of the views and attitudes themselves. In summary it might then be said that culture is historical or cumulative, that it is communicated through education, deliberate and non-deliberate, that its content is encased in patterns (that is, standardized procedures or idea systems), that it is dogmatic as to its content and resentful of differences, that its contribution to the individual is absorbed largely unconsciously, leading to a subsequent development of emotional reinforcements, and that the raising of these into consciousness is less likely to lead to insight and objective analysis than to explanations *ad hoc*, either in the light of the established *status quo*, or of a moral reference more or less subjective, or of an artificial reasonableness or rationality which is read into it; also, finally, that culture in its application and initial absorption is local. The spot and the hour control its impact upon us. People's allegiance to it is itself as spontaneous and non-deliberate as are those negative reactions aroused by differences between one's own culture and that of others.

Chapter IV

HOW ANTHROPOLOGISTS WORK

I think it has become clear by now that the anthropologist deals with the past only inferentially. The presence of archaeological material here and there, or a comparison of several accounts belonging to different periods, enables him to construct a fairly complete picture of a culture in a particular tribe or locality. This picture, however, when at all possible, is lacking in depth: at best it covers but a short span of time, owing to the inevitable limitation of our data. What the anthropologist really deals with, then, is not the past but the present. He studies peoples who, in James Harvey Robinson's phrase, are our primitive contemporaries. That some of the beliefs and customs thus revealed and described may be curiously like those of very early man buried in the remote past and perhaps like those of our own forgotten ancestors, is another story.

Now the study of a culture in general is no easy matter, and that of a primitive culture has difficulties all its own. Special devices and methods have to be employed in order to enable one to record and disentangle cultures so foreign from our own as are those of the primitives. As the English anthropologist, W. H. R. Rivers, used to point out, a wholly untouched primitive tribe does not present the most favourable situation for study. People in general, and primitives in particular, do not think or analyze their culture—they live it. It never occurs to them to synthesize what they live or reduce it to a common denominator, as it were. When the investigator approaches a member of such a tribe, his point of view is not at all apparent to the primitive. If the primitive understands the investigator at all, the fact that this strange fellow is puzzled by the obvious and is asking persistent questions about simple matters known to every child is not calculated to enhance the questioner's reputation for intelligence in the eyes of his informant. The latter, then, is likely to be suspicious of the anthropologist's motives and on his guard generally—a very unfavourable situation for successful field work.

A much more satisfactory set-up is found in those numerous instances where a tribe to be investigated has already experienced the impact of

47

White man's culture and contains among its members at least a few
individuals familiar with White man's ways. Some of those who may be
conversant with the anthropologist's language may then be employed as
interpreters. If the anthropologist is lucky, such an interpreter may also
function as one of his informants. This, however, is not usually the
case. The best informants are likely to be found among the older men
who belong to a period when the culture was relatively untouched,
whereas the best interpreters are most likely to be found among younger
persons who can speak the investigator's language and are somewhat
familiar with his ways, but know less of the group's own past. When the
services of informant and interpreter can be furnished by one and the
same person, the field anthropologist is lucky indeed. This was, for example, the case with the late Chief John Gibson, Seneca Iroquois, who
was an excellent old Indian but also a fairly well educated 'White man'
by training. To such investigators as J. N. B. Hewitt, A. C. Parker, the
present writer, and others, he proved an inexhaustible source of information. Professor Franz Boas was fortunate in his explorations of the
Pacific Coast Indians to have found an equally well informed and 'civilized' native, whose assistance proved invaluable. Paul Radin in his
work among the Winnebago also succeeded in discovering one or two
interpreter-informants of this type, and so did Clark Wissler in his
study of the Pawnee. W. H. R. Rivers, after having spent some months
among the Todas of southern India, was a little vexed to find later that
he could have secured much of the information he had up to that time
collected, from two old men, one belonging to each of the two social
divisions of the tribe.

In the course of a fairly prolonged and varied experience in field investigation, anthropologists have developed certain principles of procedure best fitted to achieve results. It will never do, for example, for
a student, when first contacting a tribe, to set to work immediately, plying the natives with questions and expecting willing answers in return.
He simply will not receive them. The rational approach is rather to
settle down in the camp or village, as inconspicuously as possible, and
spend some time, perhaps a number of weeks, living the life of the natives and participating in their activities. The more successful an anthropologist is in doing this, the better foundation he has laid for his
future work. He acquires the reputation of being a pleasant fellow, not
over-inquisitive, who enjoys taking part in ceremonies, dances, songs,
and palavers. He does not make himself conspicuous by sticking his
nose into affairs that do not concern him, and he is in general an agreeable individual. The ability to 'go native' on the surface is thus a great

boon to the anthropological field student. After a general friendly relationship has thus been established, the work may begin in earnest. During these first preliminary weeks the anthropologist should, of course, keep his eyes open for any person or persons of either sex who may have the reputation of being particularly well informed. If such a person can be discovered, and usually he can, and should he also stand high in the esteem of his fellows, as would a chief, medicine-man, expert craftsman, famous hunter or warrior, the anthropologist feels gratified. Now, at last, he may set to work.

In the initial stages of this process it is advisable to make use of the so-called genealogical method, first extensively used by Rivers but now a common technique among many anthropologists. What is aimed at is to extract from one or more of your informants a genealogy as detailed as possible comprising what is called a family tree. Natives, women even more than men, are usually genealogically minded. In primitive cultures relationships are matters of great importance, and much of the cultural content is lived and remembered in a setting of relatives, more or less close. While such a relationship tree is being worked out, an attempt is made to gather as much initial information as possible about the individuals comprising the genealogy. As all such individuals are related to the informant, he knows them well, their lives and achievements are packed away in his memory, ready for delivery. He is, moreover, likely to be interested in them, and on occasion, to be proud of their deeds or attainments. All of this is of great value to the anthropologist by way of establishing jumping-off places, as it were, from which new starts can later be made. The genealogical method has other features of value. As it presents an objective account, it provides a basis by means of which the data of the informant can be controlled. Suppose, for example, that a woman has given you a group of names of men and women, all her relatives, has indicated the marriages, and enumerated the children in the order of birth. Now, all of this information is part of your genealogical record. Some weeks later, when again at work with this informant, you may casually ask a question or two about these same children, and should it prove that the names and order of births are given as before, you will feel satisfied that the informant is reliable, that his or her memory can be trusted. The informant, in the meantime, is quite unaware of being controlled. Also, a genealogical record presents, in the nature of the case, an excellent sample in which such matters as inheritance of property, or hereditary succession of office—that of a chief, for example, or of a ceremonial leader—are objectively represented. One cannot, of course, be sure that the whole of the matter will be revealed, but as long as one's attention is drawn to such a particular topic, it can then be pursued further by means of comparisons with other genealogies or by additional questioning.

Another method now generally employed is the recording of certain kinds of information in the native tongue. It is obviously impossible for most students to reside in a native tribe long enough for a thorough acquisition of the local language. An exceptionally capable linguist might conceivably accomplish this in a relatively short time, but such are few. On the other hand, certain kinds of material will never be communicated in full detail, with all the niceties and shadings, if the informant is asked to use the language of the investigator. So a compromise device has been hit upon. The informant is permitted to use his own language. He thus begins to feel at home and relaxed in the situation and proceeds to talk at great length, giving an account of a complicated ceremony or telling an elaborate myth. The anthropologist, to be sure, does not understand him, but he uses a phonetic script which enables him to take down, after the fashion of a stenographer, what the informant is saying. At the end of such a session or several sessions, he has in his possession a complete record, freely given by the informant, who has not been interrupted or disturbed during the process of supplying the information. The manuscript, still cryptic to the writer, now becomes the basis for further study with the assistance of the interpreter. First a rough translation is attempted, then the text is utilized, on the one hand, for the purpose of eliciting further information, and, on the other, as a basis for at least a tentative study of the grammatical structure of the language. This has now become possible. By using the forms of speech employed by the informant as leads for further pointed questioning, the student begins to see the outlines of a grammar emerging. As an ultimate result, a more careful analytical translation and, perhaps, an exhaustive grammar may be prepared in due time.

It will be seen that the linguistic method is thus utilized in two contexts: as a tool in studying the native culture, and as an approach to the language itself and its grammatical structure.

Culture is a complicated affair. For purposes of study it is customary to divide the cultural complex into a number of aspects, such as the economic life of a tribe, its technology, social and political structure, religion and magic, mythology and ceremonies, and the pursuits of craft and art. The field-student is to a degree guided by these cultural subdivisions, with the result that in the average anthropological monograph the different cultural aspects are treated separately and under distinct headings. The field-worker, however, should realize the partial artificiality of these divisions. He must ever be cognizant of the fact that a culture to its bearers is their life. To them it represents a more or less unified set of experiences, beliefs, attitudes and practices which the natives themselves never think of separating into aspects corresponding to those currently employed by anthropologists. The different aspects of culture constantly interplay. If you take the family system, for example, it is as such part of the social organization. But a family will be found to function as a ceremonial unit, or as an economic one, and as such it reaches out into another domain of culture. There are also such things as family deities or spirits, specialized creatures standing in an intimate relationship to the life and welfare of a particular family. Here, then, the family interlocks with religion. Special artistic techniques are sometimes found as a family characteristic, hereditary in a family line. Here art plays into the family organization. And so on. A culture is a matter of things and processes, but also of linkages. In the lives of the people themselves it functions as an organic unit, more or less.

As soon as the field-worker takes this fact into consideration he finds his study assuming a dynamic aspect. He becomes interested not only in patterns, systems, forms of organization, but in the functioning of these units or aspects with reference to each other or to the culture at large. The functional aspect of cultural things and processes constitutes the meaning of these things to the people themselves. The field-worker, then, must pay heed to the relatively formal divisions of a culture which may be distinguished for purposes of analysis and detailed study, but he must also be prepared to transcend these divisions, or he is likely to produce, in his account, a merely formal and static picture, lacking the dynamism and vibrance of life itself.

In adopting this method of procedure, the field anthropologist is frequently tempted to read the preconceptions of his own culture into the culture he is studying. William James might have called his predicament 'the anthropologist's dilemma.' This is a dangerous procedure which one learns to avoid only gradually and by experience. The meanings of things and processes are not the same in all cultures, nor are the relations between different aspects of culture. Even though many similarities may subsequently be discovered between culture and culture, the wise course in such matters is to begin by accepting a culture on its own terms, without preconceptions or outside comparisons.

Another problem is this: People at large, and primitives perhaps more than others, accept their culture rather than make it; they live it rather than think it out. The average primitive cannot give a coherent, rational picture of his culture, nor can the average modern. Also, both have at least two sets of ideas about their own culture. On the one hand, they accept it as it is, and may on occasion be able to give an intelligible account of one or another aspect of it. On the other, they also have a more or less ideal picture of the culture or certain aspects of it which to them represents what their culture should be in their estimation. These two pictures of a culture are never identical, but both belong in the story. It follows from this that the account of a culture given by one or two informants should never be accepted uncritically as an accurate statement of the *status quo*. Invariably the ideas entertained by an individual or a group will colour the account. To counteract the aberrations in the cultural picture which come from this source, accounts of a number of informants, taken independently, should be compared, as well as verified by the personal observations of the student as to what actually occurs. For this reason it is also important to receive from informants accounts of conditions or attitudes which they are induced to furnish without knowing that they are doing so. Thus Boas, for example, in his study of the Tsimshian social organization, supplements the data obtained through direct questioning of informants by a reconstruction of the social system and kinship terms as secured from native texts dealing with religion, ceremonialism, and traditional stories. In these accounts the items bearing on social or kinship matters occur incidentally, as parts of an entirely different context. The information on social things that the raconteur is furnishing in such cases can be relied upon to be free from those personal shadings or rationalizations which will inevitably creep into a deliberate and systematic account of the same practices or attitudes. In comparing the accounts of independent informants, moreover, one is led to detect elements of individual variability. This furnishes insight not only into the flexibility of the cultural pattern, but also into the variations in the understanding, abilities, or personal interpretations, as between individual and individual. In the study of religion, for example, especially in tribes with a more or less developed priesthood, it is invariably found that the religious attitudes among the people at large are not identical with the beliefs of the priests, and that within that esoteric group itself there will again be certain individual discrepancies.

In preparing for a field trip the student must, of course, familiarize himself with whatever is already known about the tribe which he is about to visit. He also has a plan of attack, as it were, which he has prepared in advance, and perhaps a special predilection for, or interest in, some particular aspect of the tribal culture. He must, however, be able to handle this preliminary equipment with the greatest plasticity, ever prepared for the unexpected, even though it may cut right across his preconceived ideas or plans. It may be said broadly that every item of practice, belief, or attitude should be recorded as accurately and objectively as possible, whenever it comes to one's attention, no matter how insignificant or irrelevant it might appear. There is no telling where or how it may at some time come to fit into a coherent whole. And should this not prove the case, the loose ends of a culture, apparently or actually unrelated to the rest, have an interest of their own.

Perhaps no one among modern field anthropologists has shown greater ability to absorb a vast array of facts, to interrelate them meaningfully, and to present the results in a cogent and readable form, than Bronislaw Malinowski, author, among other works, of *Argonauts of the Western Pacific, Sex Life of Savages*, and quite recently, *Coral Gardens and Their Magic*. All of these books are based on the author's field studies among the Trobriand Islanders of northwestern Melanesia. Being intensely interested in problems of method, Malinowski has commented upon this subject on several occasions. Let us see what he has to say.

In his last book, a work which, though admirable, is almost top-heavy with methodological excursions, the author makes the following statement: 'The main achievement in field-work consists, not in a passive registering of facts, but in the constructive drafting of what might be called the charters of native institutions. The observer should not function as a mere automaton, a sort of combined camera and phonographic or shorthand recorder of native statements. While making his observations the field-worker must constantly construct: he must place isolated data in relation to one another and study the manner in which they integrate. To put it paradoxically, one could say that "facts" do not exist in sociological any more than in physical reality; that is, they do not dwell in the spacial and temporal continuum open to the untutored eye. The principles of social organization, of legal constitution, of economics and religion have to be constructed by the observer out of a multitude of manifestations of varying significance and relevance. It is these invisible realities, only to be discovered by inductive computation, by selection and construction, which are scientifically important in the study of culture.' [1]

In field-work, as in other matters, self-criticism is one of the conditions of true achievement. The author just quoted once again rises to

[1] B. Malinowski, *Coral Gardens and Their Magic*, p. 317. (Reprinted by permission of George Allen and Unwin, Ltd.)

the occasion. This is what he has to say by way of comment on his own errors: 'I started as all field-workers have to start, with the most superficial method, that of question and answer. I also had naturally to work first through Pidgin-English, since Trobriand cannot be learned except on the spot. Thus I put some such question as, "What man belong him this fellow garden?"—the Pidgin equivalent of, "Who is the owner of this plot?" My inquiries, moreover, were limited to the very few natives who had even a smattering of Pidgin. I was keenly aware of the lack of precision and insight resulting from this approach, and was not surprised that the results were correspondingly contradictory and vague. They varied according to whether the chief was present or not: in the former case he was ostentatiously declared to be the owner of the lands. At other times Bagido'u, whom we know already, would be pointed out. If in the absence of the chief or garden magician the heads of other local sub-clans were present, they would be styled the real owners of the soil. At times my interpreter—I was mainly working through a rascally fellow called Tom, *recte* Gumigawaya—would claim a piece of land as his own and tell me that he was just cultivating that plot. Or again I would walk with him through the gardens and map out the plots in a field and obtain a whole string of names for them. I remember writing out early in my field-work a preliminary account of land tenure which unfortunately I have never published—unfortunately, because it would have been an interesting document of errors in method. There I stated my opinion that in the Trobriands the natives do not really know who owns the land, that the chief has an over-right to the whole territory, vaguely acknowledged when he is not present, but definitely claimed by himself and admitted by the natives who are afraid of him; that the natives have a haphazard way of tilling the soil, there being no definite rules as to who is going to take over a plot. The account contained some elements of truth. What was wrong with it was the perspective in which these elements were placed.' [2]

I had occasion a while ago to comment upon the great value for fieldwork of the so-called genealogical method. But withal, a method is only a method. The test lies in the results. There is such a thing as seeing a mouse brought forth by a mountain. The methodological mechanism may be out of proportion to the results attained: genealogical trees are worth no more than their fruits. Writes Malinowski: 'But before we come to that I want the reader to explore another *impasse* from which I had to retreat, or at least give up as a short-cut to knowledge. I suffered at that

[2] B. Malinowski, *Coral Gardens and Their Magic*, pp. 324–325.

time from a belief in infallible methods in field-work. I still believed that by the "genealogical method" you could obtain a fool-proof knowledge of kinship systems in a couple of days or hours. And it was my ambition to develop the principle of the "genealogical method" into a wider and more ambitious scheme to be entitled the "method of objective documentation." After my Mailu failure—for I was aware that I had failed there to find out all that really matters about land tenure —I had developed a strategy of frontal attack on the subject. Early in my work at Omarakana I mapped out the territory. I plotted out the fields, made rough measurements of the individual plots and, in several cases, made a record of who was cultivating each plot and who owned it. The documents which I thus obtained were very valuable. They are reproduced in this book: the map, the terminology of fields and field boundaries, of plots and plot divisions; also the principles of inheritance, the *pokala* system and the manifold legal claims. This frontal attack, however, resulted in a multiplicity of unconnected and really unfounded claims. My documentation enabled me to draw up the list of legal titles which will be reproduced presently, and I found that this list agreed with that obtained by the question and answer method; and yet, as we shall see, neither of these approaches solves our problem.

'Actually, side by side with these direct attacks, I was all this time accumulating that most valuable knowledge which comes piecemeal from observation of facts.' [3]

In concluding this account of 'how anthropologists work' let me present, in the form of a field-worker's *vade mecum*, the profession of faith, as to field technique, given me by Dr. and Mrs. Melville Jacobs, of the University of Washington, who know more about the Indian tribes of Oregon than any other living persons, and whose sensitive response to the less apparent aspects of native life and attitude serve to give their field studies an altogether exceptional value. This is their profession of faith:

1. Establish a *rapport* with the informant, so he can reveal himself to you frankly. (Then his account will be of theoretical value.)

2. Make him 'fall in love' with you.

3. Discard note-book, pencil, 'turtle-shell glasses.' Be yourself, just an interested friend from the outside.

4. Try to be simple and direct, so as to enchant the informant.

5. 'Sample' the native until you find what he is interested in.

[3] *Ibid.*, p. 327.

6. First talk about indifferent things, so as not to arouse suspicion.

7. Use a number of informants, so they can check each other, helping you to discover the objective 'truth.'

8. Nine to twelve months is a minimum for any sort of productive field study.

9. Native language an essential item (note idioms and 'expressions').

10. Compare the accounts of natives of different ages.

11. Be cognizant of the mentality of the Whites in the neighbourhood.

12. The best information is that given when no pay is expected.

13. Watch the native's opinions about the Whites. (Thus you discover his values.)

14. Return to the same material again and again, from different angles.

15. Make the native function as the leader in your interview with him.

16. Let him tell you about his own childhood.

17. Autobiographical native material is important, but no more so than biographical material.

PART II

PRIMITIVE LIFE AND THOUGHT

Chapter V

MAN AND HIS TOOLS

Animal Adjustments

The animal, as we saw, is not wholly deprived of technique and industry which, in part and in certain instances, survive when a particular individual or generation passes away. These remain as a material setting for posterity to fit into, as is the case with man who is born into a certain economic status and technical equipment. But we also saw that this prehuman material culture is strictly limited. The major part of the economic and technical set-up of the animal constitutes an inherent aspect of his organic frame.

An animal of prey is fitted out by nature with tools or technique, such as the horns or antlers of the buffalo, goat, reindeer and rhinoceros; the powerful tusks and long sharp claws of the cat family—tiger, panther, jaguar, or lion (half cat)—all of whom also possess a special facility for a lightning and accurate leap; the poison fangs of the rattler and its kind, which have the instinctive technique of striking from a coiled position as well as back-striking; the highly sensitive, pliable, and enormously powerful trunk of the elephant, and his equally effective tusks, which he shares with the boar whose impetuous attack is thus rendered well-nigh irresistible except on the part of the most powerful animals; similarly, the incredibly sharp vision of the birds of prey, their powerful beaks and enormous claws.

The same is true of such protective devices as the tough hide of the pachyderms, the odorous sprinkle of the skunk, the sharp quills of the porcupine, the armour-like back of the turtle and the shells of mollusks, as well as the various devices of mimicry or camouflage, such as the stripes of the Bengal tiger or of the zebra, the feigned death of many insects, or the colour of many others which mimics that of their floral background so faithfully as to make them all but invisible. Also, where attractiveness is the objective, in the name of love, the highly elaborate and conspicuous plumage of many birds, the almost ludicrously luxurious fan of the peacock, the sweet, enrapturing voices of the song birds.

In their adjustments to particular types of environment and their

59

functioning in it, animals are equally well fitted out by nature, as illustrated by the hollow and therefore light bones of the birds; the legless, gliding, propulsive locomotion of the snake; the long, narrow, often stream-lined shapes of aquatic mammals and fishes, whose swimming adjustment is further enhanced by beautifully placed and shaped fins and a rudder-like tail; the warm coat-like fur of the Arctic inhabitants, such as the polar bear, beaver, Arctic fox, and certain varieties of seal; the equally adequate protective layer of blubber in others, such as the whales. These adjustments are not always static, provision having often been made for a change of scene, as among squirrels and other furry animals, which change their coats at the approach of winter and then again in spring, or among snakes which periodically shed their skins.

Now all of this is, of course, admirably effective and teleological. However, as these adjustments are once and for all determined by nature and accompanied by appropriate instincts, they constitute a minus as well as a plus. The turtle which carries its armour on or as its back and can instantly hide its legs and head under this protective covering is, thereby, rendered not only clumsy and slow but also helpless when turned on its back, so that when one of its enemies of the cat family succeeds in turning a turtle over, the animal is doomed.[1] What was once an armour now becomes a dish, and the turtle is leisurely consumed by the attacker.[2] Similarly, the gigantic tusks and horns of certain

---

[1] A more precise statement of the situation would be this. Turtles come in two varieties as to limbs: the terrestrial ones have legs, the marine ones, fins. The former are able to right themselves when upside down; of the latter, three subvarieties cannot do this. But *all* turtles have difficulty in performing the operation: they can only do it slowly and after considerable fussing. With the watchful feline standing by, this is as bad as not being able to do it at all. (This information was supplied to me by my friend Isadore Lattman, M.D., who took the trouble to consult an authority.)

[2] Still we know that turtles survive. An interesting insight into nature's devices to supplement inadequate protective structures is gained from an old description by Alexander von Humboldt (*Personal Narrative of Travels to the Equinoctial Regions of America* 1799–1804, vol. II, pp. 189–191). When in the course of his travels in South America he came to the sources of the Orinoco River, he became greatly interested in the major industry of the district centring in turtle eggs. On one occasion he found an agent examining, by means of a long wooden pole, how far the stratum of turtle eggs deposited in this spot extended into the water. It was found that the distance was 120 feet and the average depth was 3 feet. This official placed marks to indicate where each tribe should stop in its labours. When collecting the eggs the Indians remove the earth with their hands, place the eggs in small baskets, carry them to the encampment, and throw them into long troughs of wood filled with water. In these troughs the eggs, broken and stirred with shovels, remain exposed to the sun until the oily part which swims on the surface has time to inspissate. As fast as this collects on the surface of the water, it is taken off and boiled

animals, involving corresponding weight, are not only an asset but also a liability. An enormous enlargement and strengthening of the muscles of the neck is required to support these accoutrements, leading to a decided disproportion in the distribution of weight in such animals, which, anthropomorphizing somewhat, we might describe as an inconvenience. Even the seasonal change of fur or skin does not seem to be a matter of indifference in the organic tone of the animal. Without our presuming too much insight into the animal psyche and speaking behaviouristically, both fur-bearing animals and snakes seem to be in an ugly mood when the process of dermal or superdermal change sets in.

An adjustment, to the extent to which it is specific and unchangeable, precludes the possibility of other adjustments. Thus few animals are fitted for more than the one kind of climate, altitude, food supply, or condition of attack or defence. They do well indeed when finding themselves in situations for which they are fitted, but they are worse than helpless in others. Even such obviously correlated functions as attack and defence are not always equally well served by an animal's equipment. Thus the gazelle and other relatively pacific grass-eating quadrupeds can run like the wind but cannot do much else; so, when they find themselves at bay, the performance is ended, and the lion does the rest. Similarly even the elephant, with his massive bulk, fool-proof hide, enormous strength, and formidable tusks, is helpless when the tiger sinks its claws and teeth into his trunk, which is relatively soft and can be effectively mangled by the ferocious cat.

Now man, in comparison, has been denuded by nature. Like Kipling's

over a quick fire. This animal oil, called *tortoise butter*, is the purpose of all these preparations. The missionaries regard it as almost as good as the best olive oil and it is used for burning in lamps and also for cooking. In his capacity as naturalist eager for information, von Humboldt made certain calculations, too elaborate for reproduction here, in the course of which he came to the conclusion that the annual production of 5000 jars of oil required 330,000 tortoises which must lay 33,000,000 eggs on the three shores where this harvest is gathered. On further reflection he found this enormous figure inadequate to account for the results. The Indians eat a great many of the eggs. Vast numbers are broken during gathering. The number of eggs laid by a turtle frequently falls far below the maximum figure of a hundred odd eggs. Some of the turtles who foregather at this spot do not lay their eggs there, but go off and deposit them in solitude, some weeks later. Many turtles, moreover, are devoured by jaguars (*N.B.*) at the moment when they emerge from the water. Taking into consideration all these factors, the scientist concluded that the number of turtles which annually visit the banks of the Lower Orinoco to deposit their eggs must approximate about 1,000,000. Under such conditions, it will be realized, the jaguars have little chance of putting an end to turtledom. Even though the turtle's armour may be a clumsy and inadequate device, nature has supplemented it with a factor far more powerful and proof against the ferocity of jaguars or man's business proclivities, namely the instinct of procreation, generously exercised.

Mowgli, he is indeed a naked frog. His strength, though considerable, is below that of many an animal, not only the elephant and his tribe, but also the larger members of the cat family or the more massive quadrupeds like horses, buffalo, and the like. His speed on the run, though neither negligible nor useless, is also inferior to that of both kinds of animals just mentioned. On account of his binocular vision, his eye has virtues of its own, but it lacks the adjustment for distance and accuracy possessed by the eye of the eagle or hawk. His skin covering is negligible as a protection against cold, heat, or moisture. His dental equipment, though adequate not only for chewing but, in its more ancient forms, also for biting and tearing, and supported by strong, formerly formidable muscles, is yet inferior to that of the cats or the grass-eating masticators or the wood-gnawing rodents. Thus man is inferior to each of these animals in its special domain of excellence. But also, he is superior to all in his versatility.

And that is the key to man's physical advantage! Just because he is less physically fitted for any particular purpose he is better fitted for many varied purposes. Not being anatomically and instinctively doomed to any special mode of life or any specific kind of physical valour, his physique can bend itself pliably to many different tasks and, with practice, perform many of them well, some well enough, and others superlatively well. In this last respect the human hand with its fingers stands out as man's particular agent of superiority, excellence, versatility, and effectiveness. This organ, together with man's vocal cords and articulating set-up, supported by a brain relieved of much of its instinctive baggage and set free for learning, improvement, and new accomplishments, constitutes the equipment by means of which man, strong in his very limitations and practically unhampered in his range, could make the whole of nature his own and rise above it, to own it, transform it and bend it to his will and purpose.

Nature then left man relatively denuded, but also equipped to overcome this handicap. Not only did it leave him naked, weak, slow, but also less formidable and protected than many of his animal brethren. From one angle, man's emergence from the long range of his more ferocious and dangerous ancestors provides a lesson in disarmament. Animals carry the eternal struggle of tooth and claw, the war of nature against nature, imbedded in their very structures. In comparison, man  is born innocent and helpless, but in his mental and manual equipment he also brings with him into the world a capacity for recreating whatever he has lost in the form of an equipment no longer static and instinctive but removable, interchangeable, infinitely better fitted for all

PLATE IV.   DOBO OR TREE-HOUSE FOR UNMARRIED
WOMEN IN NEW GUINEA

PLATE V.   HULA VILLAGE, NEW GUINEA *

PLATE VI.   A GOARIBARI DUG-OUT CANOE WITH ITS
COMPLEMENT OF WARRIORS *

*Captain Frank Hurley, *Pearls and Savages*. By permission of the publishers,
G. P. Putnam's Sons.

emergencies of time, place and situation. This is the domain of tools and the chapter of man's achievement as the inventor and maker of tools.

Man the Tool Maker

Thus fitted out by nature, man set to work from the very beginning to supplement his psychic and physical potentialities by artificial tools which, appropriately enough, have been called extended sense organs. For the purposes of this chapter, let me add incidentally, I shall use the term 'tool' in a broad sense so as to cover all artificial devices of material culture calculated to enhance man's power, comfort, and security.

Like all animals, man must live somewhere, nor can he stay in the open day and night, exposed to the caprice of the elements and the attacks of his enemies. In very early conditions, man often chose a cave as his retreat. Among primitives, as we know them today, this is rare but not unknown. As a rule we find them erecting one or another sort of habitation. In the crudest form this is nothing but a wind-break, as among the Australians or the Patagonians. Then comes a wide variety of tents, such as the wood and skin ones of northeastern Siberia, the buffalo-hide *tipi* of the Plains Indians, the many varieties of tents of the migratory herders of central and western Asia, including the Arabs of Arabia and of the Sahara beyond. Other primitives, who may also be using another type of habitation, employ the tent under special conditions. For example, the Eskimo, who build tents during the warmer months after their snow houses have melted over their heads, or the Village tribes of the Plains, whose permanent residences are earthen lodges, but who turn to the usual Plains *tipi* when the buffalo hunting season arrives. Still others build huts and houses, as in Africa with its large variety of huts, with circular or rectangular base of mud, earth, or branches and mud combined, and a thatched roof. (Figs. 1–5.) Huge thatched houses over wooden supports are common in South America. Other structures are built mainly of earth, earth and stone, or stone alone, like the earth-lodges of the Mandan and Hidatsa of the Plains, the fortress-like structures of North Africa, the adobe or part-stone houses of the Pueblos, the imposing large stone temples and palaces of the Mexicans and Peruvians. Then there are the bark long-houses of the Iroquois and other kinds of long-houses in northern Melanesia and New Guinea, the spacious wooden structures of the Pacific Coast Indians and Polynesians, houses in trees, houses on boats. (Plates IV and V.)

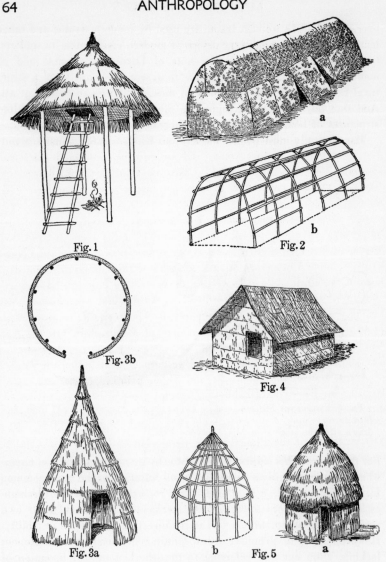

TYPES OF AFRICAN HUTS.
(Drawn by Miss Harriette Akin.)

In this domain of the 'tools of residence,' as in other domains of material culture, the ancient inventions of the primitives have, in the course of cultural development, been added to rather than superseded, all but a few of the earlier forms persisting in later periods or reappearing on special occasions. Tents consisting of goat's hair stuffs over a saddle-like wooden frame are used by modern Arabs, and other tents are used as a temporary device of modern civilization by soldiers, travellers, and vacationists. The huts of European peasants and of many American farmers frequently represent no more than a structural minimum of what a habitation must be if it is to be one at all. And our boys, in their imaginative moments, like to erect nest-like structures of board, as temporary arboreal homes.

Man not only must live somewhere but he also wants to move about.

FIG. 6. EMERGENCY SLEEPING ARRANGEMENT ON THE AMAZON. (W. E. Roth, *An Introductory Study of the Arts, Crafts, and Customs of the Guiana Indians*; drawn after the original by Miss Harriette Akin.)

For this purpose his natural equipment is by no means negligible. Everywhere among primitives pedestrian transportation is the most common form of locomotion on land, and it still remains such even in the highest civilizations, notwithstanding the terrific pull exercised in our own society by the automobile, a pull in the direction of sedentary mobility. However, even in primitive transportation, artificial devices are not lacking. I am not now referring to the wheel, a radical invention of the Old World, associated as a cultural complex with the wagon, the plough, the ox (castrated bull), and historic agriculture. This constitutes part of another story, rich with technological and mythological content, upon which I cannot enter here. True primitives remain on a more modest level. Among the Plains Indians of America a useful device is the travois, a simple triangular arrangement consisting of poles which rest on the back of a dog, man's all but ubiquitous tame companion, and is utilized for the transportation of baggage (Fig. 7). In northern districts, where snow is common, the sleigh or sledge becomes a useful tool of transportation, as for example in America, among the Eskimo and farther south, and in the northern reaches of Asia. The principal, as it were organic, part of a sleigh is, of course, the runners, which, being narrow, provide a gliding surface with a minimum of friction.

The problem of transportation by water has been tackled and solved everywhere, in one way or another. The canoe, of bark or skin, or in the form of a dugout, is found everywhere in America, which is also the region where this particular type of vessel, especially the bark canoe and skin *kayak* (see p. 83), has reached its highest form of development and technical perfection. The wooden canoe and boat are also used (see Plates VI, VII, and VIII), in a variety of forms, in Melanesia and Polynesia; a very crude bark canoe, whole or composite, in Australia. In the Melanesian Archipelago there is also to be found a composite floating contrivance consisting of several unit canoes tied together and used as support for a more or less elaborate house-like superstructure, as well as the interesting outrigger canoe, in which an ordinary canoe, of a narrower pattern than usual, is made seaworthy by a laterally attached light log floating at a little distance from the canoe, or two such logs which flank the vessel, or, on occasion, a smaller second canoe in place of the floating log (see Plate V).[3] The dugout, highly developed in both structural detail and size among the Indians of the North Pacific coast, is found in an equally advanced form in both Melanesia and Polynesia, where it often reaches enormous proportions and is in some instances supplemented by boards built up along the sides in what might more properly be called a boat. In Africa, where navigation is on the whole weakly developed, the dugout of Kamerun is distinguished for its size and elaborate decoration. In California and farther south, in Mexico, Central and South America, the balsa occurs, a float made of bunches of reeds tied together into a floating platform, or a canoe-like structure similarly made of reeds. A wooden float, made out of interconnected logs, is in one form or another widespread among primitive tribes, and modern ones as well, for example, among the loggers of our Northwest.[4]

[3] The outrigger, single or double, is also found in Indonesia and farther west among the littoral and island peoples of South Asia, as far west as India.

[4] It scarcely needs saying that the canoe and the boat have persisted into 'civilization,' as have the tent and the house. Our modern American canoe is akin to the bark canoe of the eastern Indians, and if it is superior, the advantage lies largely in the mechanically secured accuracy of plan and precision of execution.

Nowhere among primitives do we find any mechanical device for the purpose of propelling an aquatic vehicle, with the exception of the ubiquitous oar or paddle, handled by a paddler or oarsman, seated in the vessel or standing up. The sail, though limited in distribution, occurs among primitives, as in the South Seas as well as in an incipient and crude form in Northwest America. Another singular conveyance is the bull-boat, a circular structure made of hide over a support of branches, built neither for comfort nor for speed, which occurs in the American Plains, but also in certain localities of western Asia.

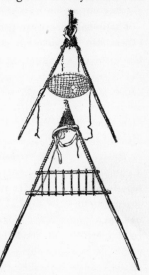

In addition to a place of residence and some device for transportation, terrestrial and aquatic, man also needs to or wants to mitigate his nakedness in one way or another. And so, whether for comfort, protection against weather or enemies, or for embellishment, man has acquired a body-covering or clothes. It may be noted here that clothing among primitives is on the whole relatively simple and light, though not necessarily more comfortable, when compared with that of the civilized. Habitual elaborateness and the considerable weight [5] of clothes are relatively late devices of civilization. The latter-day reduc-

FIG. 7. BLACKFOOT TRAVOIS. (Clark Wissler, *American Indians of the Plains.*)

tion in weight and complexity of attire, conspicuous among Western women, constitutes an altogether recent and urban development, rather limited in its range even today. Many primitives, especially in the warmer regions, go around either altogether naked or graced by a very minimum of sartorial equipment, such as the loin-cloth for men and a corresponding belt-like device for women, as, for example, in Australia, South America, and sections of Africa. When more elaborate attire prevails the stuffs used for wear are in part determined by the materials and the mode of life: in Melanesia and Polynesia, bark-cloth; in Africa, either bark-cloth or cloths woven of fibre in the grasslands, or animal skins in the wooded hunting areas. In America three types of clothing prevail: textile cloth-

[5] This applies to garments, in the narrower sense. When it comes to decorations, as in the case of the metal embellishments of Africa and elsewhere, or of the protective coverings of warriors, as in many different places, primitive attire also reaches very impressive weight.

ing, which occurs in a continuous region starting with Peru in South America and extending northward as far as California and the Southwest; tailored clothing made of hide, in the northern regions of the United States and the whole of Canada, including the Arctic domain of the Eskimo; and robes, which are worn in the northern plains of North America and in the pampas of Argentine.

In comparison with clothing as such, body decorations of a permanent or removable sort are practically ubiquitous. The most common among these are scarification and tattooing, which in a limited form occur

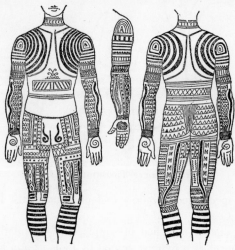

FIG. 8. IGOROT (PHILIPPINES) TATTOOING.

almost everywhere, the latter being developed in exuberant forms in Polynesia, the Philippine Islands (Fig. 8), and elsewhere. The process of being tattooed, incidentally—in the case of a Polynesian chieftain it may take the whole of two years—is a fine illustration of endurance on the part of the subject, persistence and meticulous care on the part of the tattooer, and an exceptionally interesting and intricate form of art in the resulting tattooed body. By way of removable decorations there are anklets; armlets; necklaces of beads, shells, metal, or flowers; varieties of hair decorations; ear pendants, at times weirdly elaborate, as well as lip and nose decorations.

One of the obvious and urgent needs of man, both for the home and on the road, is some kind of vessel or container. In one form or another these are found everywhere, built of wood or bark, bone or stone, or egg shell (of the ostrich). Of special importance are baskets in different varieties of woven technique, clay pots, and boxes. Baskets and pots in a crude form are found, as I said, in many places. Here and there we encounter a highly developed basketry technique, as in certain regions of Brazil, among the Indians of California, the Pueblos, and the Plateau, as well as in the Philippines and the archipelago of southeastern Asia. Similarly with pottery, which occurs in varied and sometimes elaborate forms, highly finished both technically and artistically, as among the Pueblos, the Chiriqui, and the Fiji Islanders. A high development of

FIG. 9. AFRICAN THROWING KNIVES.

boxes with a specialized technique is found among the Indians of the North Pacific Coast.

As already stated, man had to supplement his relatively deficient natural equipment as a fighting animal by tools of attack and defence. Weapons of some sort are used by man everywhere. Of these the most ubiquitous is perhaps the stone knife, the ancestor of the dagger, doing service both as a tool and as a weapon. Next to it comes the club, either altogether of wood, or with a head of bone or stone, or (as in Africa) with a metal edge. In certain sections of North America, as well as in Polynesia, the club has been developed in an enormous variety of forms, reaching at points high technical perfection as well as artistic beauty.[6]

Another very primitive weapon is the spear. Being initially nothing but a long stick with a sharp point, it is evidently a device requiring the least of original inventive effort. In Australia this weapon is universal, being used both in fighting and for hunting such larger animals as the kangaroo. In Melanesia also it is perhaps the most important

[6] The club of the Marquesans is, perhaps, the most artistically cultivated article in the whole expanse of culture, primitive or modern. See Karl von den Steinen, *The Marquesans and Their Art* (in German).

weapon, together with the bow and arrow. In this artistically very sophisticated area the spear and the arrow shaft, as well as the spear-thrower—a device the New Guineans share with the Australians and the Eskimo—have undergone a high technical and artistic elaboration. In the neighbouring Polynesian Islands, the bow and arrow—probably formerly a fighting weapon, now only a toy for practice, sometimes for hunting—has receded before the club, which has become the favourite weapon of war and a hallowed ritual object as well (see Plate IX). In Africa the spear, fitted out with a metal point, is used by most of the tribes inhabiting the vast grasslands of that continent.[7] It is employed both in warfare, together with its usual associate, the shield, and in hunting the wild grass-eaters, the enormous pachyderms and the ferocious and powerful cats—the leopard and the lion. In case of the latter the hunt usually takes the form of a massed assault, the natives riddling the beast with their spears while avoiding its attacks, until it finally succumbs. In India, where the spear is also indigenous, it is used, *inter alia*, in hunting the Bengal tiger. This is a particularly interesting and dangerous form of spear hunting: the hunter is alone; when the tiger is ready to charge, he places himself in position, holding his spear in such a way that the butt-end leans against the ground, while the entire shaft is inclined towards the line of the tiger's charge. When it occurs, and the animal's bulky shape begins to descend, the spearman shifts the point of his weapon to meet the tiger as he approaches the ground. Thus he is pierced—and pinned. In North America, the spear or lance, provided with a stone head, though now practically extinct except among the Californian Hupa and the western Eskimo, must have been widely used in the past, as is attested by archaeological remains among many tribes. This weapon underwent an especially high development among the tribes of the Plains, who must have been acquainted with the stone-headed lance, at least as a hunting implement, even before they entered the plains or became familiar with the horse. A shorter spear, known as a javelin, also occurs in various regions, notably in Australia.

A weapon of extraordinary importance which occurs even among the most primitive tribes, such as the various pygmy groups, is the bow and arrow. It is known in all major culture areas of the primitive world, with the exception of Australia, where a substitute is available in the form of the boomerang, some types of which have ways of their own. The bow, like the knife, club, and spear, survived up to the time of the introduction of firearms and beyond. In recent days it has become a rather

[7] A specialized weapon of Africa, with its iron technique, is the throwing knife, a formidable fighting tool which has a wide distribution (see Fig. 9).

PLATE VII.   LANGALANGA OVERSEAS CANOE, MALA

(Walter Ivens, *Island Builders of the Pacific*. By permission of J. B. Lippincott Co., Publishers.) Such canoes are built of planks, stem and stern being added last.

PLATE VIII.   ANDAMANESE SHOOTING FISH

For larger varieties, like the dugong, they use a harpoon.

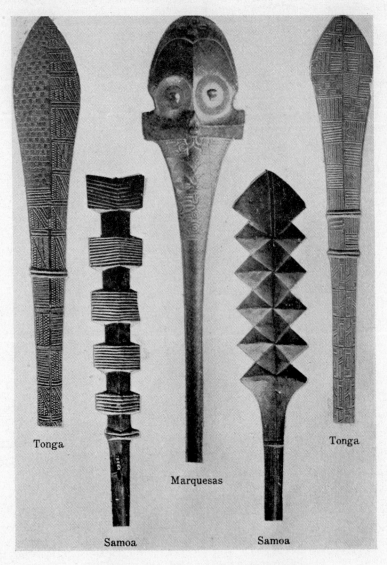

Tonga

Marquesas

Tonga

Samoa

Samoa

PLATE IX.   POLYNESIAN CLUBS

(The butt-ends of the clubs do not appear in the figures.)

popular sporting weapon in the United States and other countries, and is here and there employed in place of a gun by daring Western adventurers on their hunting vacations. Both before and after the introduction of the horse, the Indians of the Plains used the bow and arrow in hunting buffalo. When the animal was at close range, this weapon proved adequate and effective even with so massive a target.

In addition to these weapons of offence man has also learned to use a variety of protective devices to minimize the danger from the weapons of his human opponents. Of these the best known are the shield—which occurs in Australia, Melanesia, Asia, Africa, and America—and a variety of armours in a number of materials and techniques, which are worn on the body, legs, and head. The armour, however, has a more limited distribution.

For fishing, the bow and arrow and the spear are used in different places (see Plate VIII), as well as hooks, nets, and snares. Prompted by the desire to corner his animal prey without direct personal participation, the hunter has practically everywhere introduced a variety of traps and snares, to which I shall return in the section on invention.

We must regard the various devices for making fire as perhaps the peers of all tools, which completely transformed man's life on earth. All are based on the application of one or another kind of friction. Fire in different places is produced by sawing, boring, and striking, an especially interesting and perfected variety of the boring kind being the bow-drill of the Eskimo, the Pacific Northwest Indians, the northeastern Siberians, and other peoples.

All the tools mentioned so far represent man's efforts and successes in using natural materials in dealing with nature in the wild. This is only part of the story of tools. Man, having conquered nature resisting, also learned to subdue and tame her, thus gaining her willing cooperation. This was achieved in the cultivation of plants and the domestication of animals, topics which will be illustrated and commented upon repeatedly in the course of this book. Here only one more word. Man who domesticated animals has also, as we already know, domesticated himself. From this angle, man is one of the animals domesticated by man by means of cultural devices. Nor is this all. Many men and women have also been domesticated in the course of culture history in a special and more sinister sense: they became the slaves of other men. If domestication implies loss of freedom and self-determination and unprotesting submission to the demands of society and the will of the master, then slavery is the most perfect example of domestication, and the most terrible.

Chapter VI

ECONOMIC LIFE AND TECHNICAL ARTS OF THE ESKIMO

Of all the native inhabitants of North America the Eskimo are the most northern. Their habitations and camping grounds extend over the enormous range from South Alaska, where they are in touch with the Tlingit Indians, along the shore and proximate interior as well as the islands of the Arctic coast as far east as Greenland, and south to Newfoundland and the opposing coast, where they come in contact with the northern offshoots of Algonquin-speaking Indians. Of this enormous coast-line the only stretch free from Eskimo habitations is the southern shore of Hudson Bay. Like the American Indians, the Eskimo are of Mongolian derivation, but the isolation of their forbidding habitat has led to prolonged inbreeding, with the result that in their physical appearance the Eskimo can usually be identified as such.[1] (Plate X.)

[1] This is what Hooton has to say about the unusual combination in the Eskimo of a very broad face with a very long head, a so-called disharmonic skull. 'It is commonly supposed that the great development of the chewing muscles in the Eskimo has modified the form of the brain case. The tremendous attachments of the temporal muscles to the side walls of the skull are supposed to have restricted the lateral growth of the brain, compensation taking place by increase in length, thus rendering the Eskimo head excessively dolichocephalic and relatively high or hypsicephalic. The reason for the great masticatory development is supposed to be the tough fish and flesh diet upon which the Eskimo principally subsist. In addition to consuming large quantities of whale, seal, walrus, and other tough meat, the Eskimo are reputed to use their teeth for untying frozen knots and lashings and for various feats of strength. Furthermore, they are reported to soften up leather and prepare it for use in clothing by chewing it. In the evening Eskimo ladies chew up their husbands' frozen boots so that the latter may have nice soft footwear ready for the next morning. All of these facts are correct. The Eskimo have, of all living men, the most powerfully developed chewing apparatus. To the anatomist most Eskimo crania give plain evidence of dental and masticatory hypertrophy.

'But there are grave objections against attributing their excessive dolichocephaly to squeezing of the skull walls by the powerful temporal muscles in chewing tough food. In the first place it is questionable whether the temporal muscles actually exert any great inward pressure upon the skull walls, as their pull is almost straight up and down. The masseters and pterygoids, which also function in chewing, could have no such effect, since they are attached solely to the facial skeleton. Again, the food of the Eskimo is probably not as tough as it is reputed to be.'

Then the author adduces the authority of Stefansson to the effect that 'frozen

Notwithstanding the enormous spread of their habitat, Eskimo culture throughout this range is distinguished by a great uniformity. There are, of course, local variations in detail, but the general type of culture is the same in all its main features. This is true even of the Eskimo language, the local variations of which do not rise beyond dialectic forms, so that an Eskimo from whatever region can understand any other

Fig. 10. The Habitat of the Eskimo. (Reproduced, in simplified form, from E. M. Weyer, *The Eskimos*. By permission of Yale University Press.)

Eskimo or (in cases of extreme distance, as between Greenland and Alaska) he will soon learn to do so. The persistence and conservatism of the culture are no doubt traceable to the Arctic location, which cuts them off from all but casual contacts with other groups, either Indian

fish is about of the consistency of ice cream.' Eskimo women, moreover, who are the ones who 'chew up their husbands' frozen boots,' do not have the very narrow skulls nor the great temporal muscle attachments which are characteristic of the male skull. 'The so-called Eskimo disharmony,' continues Hooton, 'is most pronounced in the Labrador and Greenland Eskimo. The Western Eskimo do not show the peculiar Eskimoid features of the skull in any such marked degree. Indeed they are much less dolichocephalic than the Eastern Eskimo and sometimes approach a brachycephalic head form. Nor am I aware of any differences in diet and masticatory functioning which would account for such variations in skull breadth. It seems to me wholly probable that the Eskimo, like the Cro-Magnon type, have inherited a mixed cranial form—a long, narrow skull from one ancestral strain and a broad face from another. It is much more probable that the strength of the chewing apparatus and its vigorous use in the Eskimo have caused his face and palate to increase in breadth than that they have squeezed out his skull to an excessive dolichocephaly.' (E. A. Hooton, *Up from the Ape*, pp. 404–406. By permission of The Macmillan Company, publishers.)

or White, so that the overwhelming number of contacts of any particular local group are with other Eskimo groups. These latter contacts, let me add, are more frequent than might be suspected, considering the great distances that frequently separate individual camps. The Eskimo are great travellers and frequently go visiting, family and all. Such a visit, involving perhaps two or three hundred miles of travel, often takes the form of a temporary residence, the visiting family remaining with the hosts for a number of months. Under such conditions any tendency towards localism in culture is likely to be checked and widespread uniformity encouraged.

The physical environment of the Eskimo is so forbidding and its peculiarities so extreme that a human group, finding itself in this environment, would perish unless it achieved a very special adjustment to the environmental conditions. This is precisely what has happened in the case of the Eskimo. By means of a large number of special devices they have managed to make the inhospitable Arctic their home, and so well have they solved this difficult problem that occasional visitors from the outside world, such as White traders or ardent anthropologists, have been known to accept the Eskimo mode of life rather than, in their usual fashion, impose theirs upon the Eskimo. The Arctic explorer, Stefansson, for example, as well as the more permanent resident among the Eskimo, Peter Freuchen, may be regarded as samples of partially Eskimoized White men.

For one thing the Eskimo lives in a land of almost perpetual cold, interrupted by relatively short periods of milder weather.[2] Survival here

[2] The prevalence of low temperatures in Eskimoland should not, however, be exaggerated, says Weyer. 'Only a small proportion of the Eskimos live in what can be considered the high Arctic belt, which includes northern Greenland and the Arctic Archipelago with the exception of the southern fringe of Victoria Island and the greater part of Baffin Island. In this belt the average temperature, even of the warmest month of summer, is within ten degrees (F.) above freezing, which is about the same as that during the coldest month of winter in Delaware. Thus, even on the extreme fringe of the inhabited world, the climate in midsummer is comparable with midwinter climate in a densely settled section of the temperate zone. Farther south in the Eskimo region the summer temperatures become increasingly milder; until at Dillingham, Alaska, near the southern limit of the Eskimos in the west, the average temperature of the warmest month (July) is 56°F., which is practically the same as the average temperature of the coldest month at San Diego, California. At Hopedale, Labrador, near the southern limit of the Eskimos in the east, the average temperature of the warmest month (51°F.) is comparable to that of the coldest month at Mobile, Alabama; and at Ivigtut, near the southern tip of Greenland, it is the same as the average of the coldest month at San Francisco. Farther north within the Eskimo province at Point Barrow on the northernmost point of Alaska; at Adelaide Peninsula, on the Arctic coast of Canada; and at Upernivik, in latitude 73°N. on the west coast of Greenland, the average temperature of the warmest month is approximately the same as the average temperature

necessitates protection against the extreme of low temperature, and so we find the Eskimo probably the most warmly clad of primitive groups, with the possible exception of the natives of northeastern Siberia.[3] This attire, very similar for men and women, is made of reindeer hide and comprises trousers, a shirt, an upper garment in the shape of a lengthy jacket, provided with a hood which can be either pulled over the head or pulled back so that it rests on the shoulders and back. In addition there are hide mittens and hide boots made of the same material. This attire is cut to pattern and sewed together by the women. In many instances the several parts of the garment are decorated by geometrically patterned pieces of hide. These decorations, in dark and light colours, provide the borders of Eskimo, as well as Koryak and Chukchee, costumes (Figs. 11–15). The material used for thread is thin string of hide or sinew, and the long needle used for sewing is of bone. These needles, highly prized by the women, are kept, when not in use, in special ivory needle cases, of which there are many varieties and which are usually highly decorated by surface carving (Fig. 16, p. 77).

Not only is it cold in Eskimoland but it is also dark for days, weeks, and months on end. In the more northern regions the sun does not rise at all for several months at a time, and when it rises, it appears above the horizon in the form of a mildly luminous, reddish disk, travels for some distance, always close to the horizon, and then sets. To balance this reign of darkness there are, of course, equally long periods of continuous illumination. Obviously the Eskimo could not exist without some form of artificial lighting, which is provided by sandstone lamps (Fig. 32, p. 93) in which oil or blubber is burned. These lamps, used inside the house, are usually fed by drippings of blubber which fall into the lamp from pieces of rich, fatty meat suspended from wooden supports,

during the coldest month at Victoria, Canada; Portland, Oregon; Nantes, France; and Hankow, China. (E. M. Weyer, *The Eskimos*, p. 20. Reprinted by permission of the Yale University Press.)

[3] 'That Eskimos sometimes suffer from frostbite is mentioned by many Arctic travellers,' writes Weyer. 'Whether their resistance to it is appreciably different from that of other people is open to question. Perhaps those who are not able to endure cold are, as a rule, eliminated fairly early in life. There may be a certain amount of unconscious selection in the killing of some of the children by their parents, a practice general among the Eskimos. No instance appears of testing a child's endurance by exposing it to the cold, but the manner in which infants are exposed to the elements in the natural course of events must have some selective influence. Jenness remarks that he has seen a woman expose an infant to the weather with the thermometer at 30°F. below zero in a thirty-mile-an-hour blizzard while she leisurely changed its garments. Mathiassen writes: "In —20° I have seen a woman bring her nine-months adoptive daughter out of the pouch and sit her on the sledge for a little while with her lower body bare." ' (*Ibid.*, pp. 47–48.)

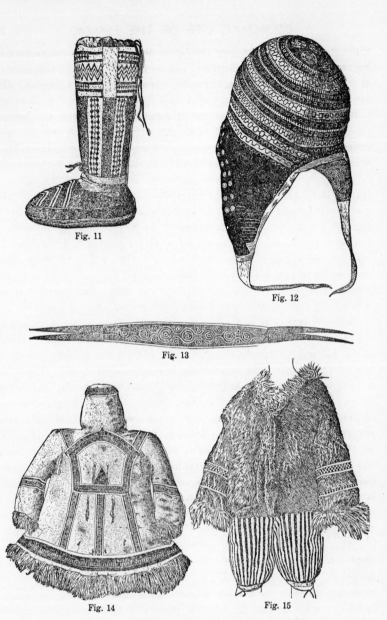

Fig. 11

Fig. 12

Fig. 13

Fig. 14

Fig. 15

FIGS. 11, 12, 13, 14 AND 15. KORYAK CLOTHES. These objects of attire reproduced from W. Jochelson's monograph on the Koryak (*Jesup North Pacific
Expedition*, Vol. VI, Part 2) represent the artistic sartorial technique in skin
and fur at its height. This accomplishment these Siberian natives share with
their neighbours the Chukchee and the American Eskimo.

while it is being cooked over the lamp. In this way the lamps furnish both heat and a moderate degree of light—also, to be sure, an abundance of smoke, an inevitable characteristic of the inside of an Eskimo habitation.

The next problem is that of the habitation itself. Though the Eskimo can stand cold with relative equanimity, even sleeping in the open under conditions prohibitive to others, living without some protective structure or other would be impossible in that climate. The two types

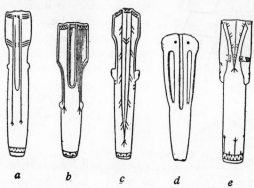

a   b   c   d   e

FIG. 16. ALASKAN NEEDLE CASES. (Franz Boas, *Primitive Art.* By permission of the Institute for Comparative Research in Human Culture, Oslo, Norway.)

of habitation used by the Eskimo are the snow house for the larger part of the year and a skin tent during the short period of relatively mild weather. The material for the snow house is available most of the time and in ample quantity. The structural unit is a fairly large, evenly shaped block of snow, cut in the neighbourhood of the house which is being built, for which purpose a large bone snow knife is used. Usually it is the women who cut and shape these blocks. Ordinarily two or three people co-operate in erecting a house, although under duress, one person, almost always a man but occasionally a woman, may erect a house single-handed. If three persons co-operate, one will be working on the inside and two on the outside of the rising wall, which is built up of superimposed layers of snow blocks. These layers ascend in spiral fashion, so that the surface of each layer is not altogether horizontal. When a new layer is to be laid, the initial block is thus supported not only from the bottom but also from the side, which prevents it from collapsing towards the inside of the house. Unless this device were adopted, the hemispherical form of the house would not be structurally feasible (Fig. 17a). After the larger part of the structure has been finished there remains an opening on the top, which is finally closed by a snow block shaped to fit it. The connecting edges of the separate blocks are smoothed over, on both the inside and the outside of the house. When it is finished, the snow surface is smooth and unbroken. Now the man on the inside of the house is marooned, for there is as yet no entrance.

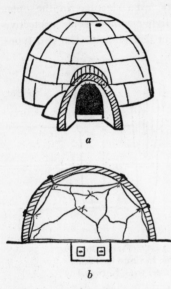

Presently he makes his way out by working a passage through the snow at the ground level, thus forming the opening which is henceforth to serve as the entrance. Usually a covered passage is added, encasing this entrance and extending some distance from the house, with a lateral twist at the end where the real entrance will be. The purpose of this twist is to break the force of the wind. As a further protection from wind and cold, the original entrance of the house, now inside the passage, will frequently be blocked by a piece of ice or frozen snow shaped so as to fit the outline of the entrance; when it is not in use, it may be seen lying in the passageway.

FIG. 17. SNOW HOUSE: *a*, OUTSIDE, *b*, INSIDE. (Franz Boas, *The Central Eskimo*.)

Inside the house itself the whole understructure, except the section that leads to the entrance, consists of a foundation of snow, the two blocks on the sides of the entrance passage being used for the cooking lamps, each attended by a woman, usually the wives of the master of the house; for polygyny is the rule here. In the back of the house another snow platform is erected on which the family bed is made. Discarded wooden implements are placed on it, covered with several layers of heavy skins, and upon these the family lies down for the night, all in a row and naked (for all clothes are discarded upon entering the house).

The only ventilation is provided by a small hole in the roof. With two lamps going and a considerable number of people about, the temperature in the house is high, the air stuffy and filled with smoke— a condition enhanced by the inadequacy of the ventilation through the tiny hole in the roof. Also, the snow, of course, tends to melt from the heat. Stalactite-like little pendants of melting snow gradually form under the dome of the house, and unless proper measures are taken, they

PLATE Xa.   ESKIMO MAN

PLATE Xb.   ESKIMO GIRL

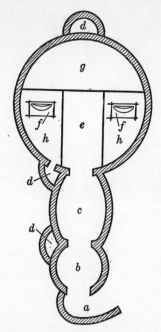

FIG. 18. GROUND PLAN OF ESKIMO SNOW HOUSE OF MORE ELABORATE TYPE.
(Franz Boas, *The Central Eskimo*.)

The section (*a*) in front of the entrance is protected by a semi-circular turn in the wall which prevents the wind and snow from blowing directly into the house. (*b*) is formed by a small dome about six feet in height, while the two doors are about two and one-half feet in height. Equally high is the passage (*c*) formed by an elliptical vault. The door to the main room is about three feet high, while the floor of the latter is about nine inches above the floor of the passage, so that any moisture accumulated on the floor of the main room will flow off into the passage, but the opposite will not occur. The small compartments (*d*) are formed by vaults and may be entered either through small doors from the main room or the passage, or by the removal of one of the snow slabs from the outside. The compartments are used for storing clothing, harness, meat and blubber. Over the entrance to the main room a window is cut through the wall, which is either square or more often arched. This window is covered with the intestines of ground seals, neatly sewed together, the seams extending vertically. In the centre of the window is a hole for looking out, into which a piece of fresh water ice is sometimes inserted.

In the main room, on both sides (*h*) of the door and in the back of the room (*g*) a bank of snow two and one-half feet high is raised, leaving a passage five feet wide and six feet long (*e*). The rear part is the bed (*g*) while on the two sides (*h*) the lamps (*f*) are placed and meat and refuse are heaped.

presently begin to drip. In a crudely or hurriedly built house, this is prevented by one or another of the inmates arising in time and pressing the dripping pendant back into the snowy mass of the roof, where it freezes again—a somewhat annoying and unsatisfactory palliative. In a well-built house, which is the rule, there is no necessity for these extra precautions. In such a house the walls and ceiling are protected on the inside by skins suspended on small ropes which are drawn through the

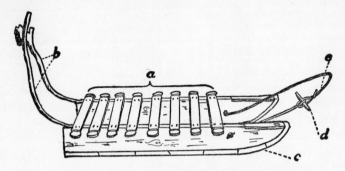

FIG. 19. ESKIMO SLEDGE. (Franz Boas, *The Central Eskimo.*)

Among the tribes where driftwood is plentiful (Hudson and Davis Straits) the best sledges are made with long wooden runners. The sledges have two runners from five to fifteen feet long and twenty inches to two and one-half feet apart. They are connected by cross bars of wood or bone (a) and the back is formed by deer's antlers (b) with the skull attached. This back is used for steering, for attaching the lashing when a load is carried and for hanging the snow knife and the harpoon line upon it. The bottom of the runners is shod with whalebone, ivory or the jaw bones of a whale (c). In long sledges the shoeing is made broadest at the head. When travelling over soft snow, this proves of value, as the snow is pressed down by the broad surfaces of the runners at the head, and the sledge glides over it without sinking in very deeply.

The shoe is either tied or riveted to the runner. In the former case, the lashing passes through sunken drill holes, to prevent friction when moving over the snow. The right and left sides of a whale's jaw are often used for shoes, as they are of the right size, thus providing excellent one-piece shoes. The exposed points of the runners are frequently protected with bone also on the upper side.

The cross bars (a) are lashed to the runners by thongs which pass through two pairs of holes in each bar and corresponding ones in the runners. The bars extend beyond the runners on each side, a sort of neck being formed in the projecting parts by notches on the two sides of the bar (see drawing). When a load is lashed onto the sledge, the thongs are fastened to these necks.

Under the foremost cross bar there is a hole in each runner through which a very stout thong passes, which is prevented by a button from slipping through. One thong ends in a loop (e), to the other a clasp (d) is tied, which, when in use, passes through the loop at the end of the other thong. Upon this line the dogs' traces are strung by means of a small implement with a large and small eyelet: to one the trace is tied, the other is used for stringing the implement upon the stout thong.

walls and held tight by toggles on the outside (see Fig. 17b). When this is done, no further damage ensues; the snow melts from the hot air in the upper section of the room, the water thus formed trickles down the skins along the inner surface of the wall and to the bottom of the house, where it freezes again in the lower temperature. In spring, when the weather becomes warmer, the houses tend to melt. Not infrequently a roof will cave in. For a while the damage may be repaired by a piece of skin to cover the hole. As the warm weather continues, the house becomes uninhabitable.[4] Then the 'summer' tents make their appearance; they are made of skins over a rough assemblage of poles; the skin is pinned to the ground by small blocks of wood and held fast by stones placed on the ground along its periphery. Many houses are more elaborate than those here described, consisting of several semi-spherical snow structures connected by a number of covered snow passages, or of one such structure with a passage and compartments (see diagram, Fig. 18).

Another pressing problem is that of transportation, both on land and on water. This has been admirably solved by means of the sleigh, canoe (*kayak*), and woman's boat (*umyak*). The sleigh is of the same general pattern as most sleighs, and it is pulled by dogs[5] (Fig. 19).

[4] 'What a house to have a second mortgage on!' exclaimed a visitor in my class once; apparently she was better versed in the ways of business than in those of primitives.

[5] At this point a frequently made popular error, to the effect that the Eskimo sleighs are pulled by reindeer, should be corrected. The reindeer, which plays an important part in the economy of the Eskimo, has not been domesticated by them and is therefore not available for transportation purposes. Of course, in more recent days sleighs pulled by reindeer may be readily enough seen in Alaska, and the driver may be an Eskimo. This, however, is a recent phenomenon consequent upon the introduction of domesticated reindeer into Alaska by White men.

As to the dogs, Boas's remarks on their treatment by the Eskimo and on their behaviour are so interesting as to deserve reproduction verbatim. 'The strongest and most spirited dog has the longest trace and is allowed to run a few feet in advance of the rest as a leader; its sex is indifferent, the choice being made chiefly with regard to strength. Next to the leader follow two or three strong dogs with traces of equal length, and the weaker and less manageable the dogs the nearer they run to the sledge. A team is almost unmanageable if the dogs are not accustomed to one another. They must know their leader, who brings them to terms whenever there is a quarrel. In a good team the leader must be the acknowledged chief, else the rest will fall into disorder and refuse to follow him. His authority is almost unlimited. When the dogs are fed, he takes the choice morsels; when two of them quarrel, he bites both and thus brings them to terms [Fig. 20].

'Generally there is a second dog which is inferior only to the leader, but is feared by all the others. Though the authority of the leader is not disputed by his own team, dogs of another team will not submit to him. But when two teams are accustomed to travel in company the dogs in each will have some regard for the leader of the other, though continuous rivalry and quarrels go on between the two leaders. Almost any dog which is harnessed into a strange team will at first be unwilling to draw, and it is only when he is thoroughly accustomed to all his neighbours and has found out his friends and his enemies that he will do his work satisfactorily. Some dogs when put into a strange team will throw themselves down and struggle and howl. They will endure the severest lashing and allow themselves to be dragged along over rough ice without being induced to rise and run along with the others. Particularly if their own team is in sight will they turn back

The sleigh must be strongly built, for driving in the Arctic regions is
not by any means smooth going all the way. There is many a rough
stretch where the tension on the sleigh is considerable. The Eskimo
craftsman, however, builds solidly, though no nails nor anything else
of the sort is used in the framework of the sleigh. Before starting on a
journey, the driver turns his sleigh upside down and wets the bone
surface with water, if it is available, or by spitting on it. The wet strip

and try to get to it. Others, again, are quite willing to work with strange dogs.

'Partly on this account and partly from attachment to their masters, dogs sold
out of one team frequently return to their old homes, and I know of instances in
which they even ran from thirty to sixty miles to reach it. Sometimes they do so
when a sledge is travelling for a few days from one settlement to another, the dogs
not having left home for a long time before. In such cases when the Eskimo go to
harness their team in the morning they find that some of them have run away,

FIG. 20. DOG IN HARNESS. (Franz Boas, *The Central Eskimo.*)

particularly those which were lent from another team for the journey. In order to
prevent this the left fore leg is sometimes tied up by a loop which passes over
the neck. When one is on a journey it is well to do so every night, as some of the
dogs are rather unwilling to be harnessed in the morning, thus causing a great
loss of time before they are caught. In fact such animals are customarily tied up at
night, while the others are allowed to run loose.' (Franz Boas, *The Central Eskimo*,
pp. 533–534.)

of bone presently freezes over, thus providing a perfect gliding surface.

Frequently the Eskimo is forced to travel in a driving storm, a pro-hibitive venture unless some protection is provided for the eyes. This is done in the form of goggles, wooden spectacle-like ovals or disks con-nected across the nose and with narrow slits for the eyes.

The facilities available for navigation are equally adequate and in-genious. The Eskimo *kayak* is a specialized variant of the canoe, differ-ing from the latter only in so far as the entire wooden skeleton is cov-

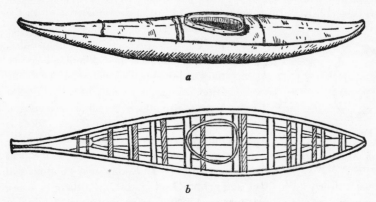

a

b

FIG. 21. KAYAK AND FRAMEWORK. (Boas, *op. cit.*)

ered, top and bottom, with skins sewed together into a solid surface, the only aperture left being located about the centre of the *kayak*. Into this the paddler slips. He is, of course, dressed in the usual thick hide gar-ment and fits into the hole snugly. In this way the *kayak* is transformed into a relatively air-tight vessel, very light and exceedingly seaworthy (Fig. 21). It is propelled by a double-bladed paddle which the Eskimo has learned to use from childhood, thus becoming incredibly expert at it. A skilful paddler has no trouble righting the *kayak* should it capsize. He can, in fact, at will make it do so, describing a complete arc under the water and reappearing on the other side of the *kayak*, whereupon he rights it again and paddles on as if nothing had occurred. The *kayak*, being long, narrow, and light, can be propelled with considerable speed, and is singularly well adapted for navigation in the ice-infested waters of the Arctic Ocean. It is also guaranteed against being 'rubbed in' when an ice-field suddenly closes in upon it, a great menace to any ordinary vessel. On account of its shallow draught and slight weight, the *kayak* is lifted upon the ice, where it sits unhurt, ready for the next journey. A *kayak* is sometimes built for two, but as a rule it is a one-man affair. One of its most important uses is in connexion with the reindeer hunt, the harpoon being the weapon employed. In a pinch several additional persons, a whole family in fact, including wives, offspring, and a dog or two, may be tucked away inside the *kayak*, not a wholesome or comfortable mode of transport but sufficient under duress. Then there is the *umyak*, or woman's boat, so called because it is used for longer journeys when the family travels together, and the rowing is done by the women. It is a less unusual kind of boat, much larger and without an upper skin covering. The body of the boat in this case consists of a wooden frame with skin drawn over it up to the

FIG. 22. THUMB-PROTECTOR USED FOR SHOOTING WITH BOW AND ARROW. (Drawn by Miss Harriette Akin.)

gunwale. The oarsmen, as stated, are women, who use oars instead of paddles.

The food quest in Eskimoland constitutes a pressing and perpetual problem. Often enough, it can only be solved imperfectly; also, there are in it elements of adventure and of danger. The reindeer is hunted in two ways. If a reindeer herd is in the vicinity of the camp—a frequent occurrence—an Eskimo may go alone and shoot a deer with his bow and arrow (see Fig. 22).[6] But there is also a communal reindeer hunt, usually undertaken when a herd of reindeer appears after a long period of scarcity. Then an effort is made to drive the herd, if possible, towards a strip of water, a river or lake, the hunters in their *kayaks* waiting in readiness at the edge. As the animals plunge into the water, a general call to arms is sounded: at once, the hunters, harpoons in hand, paddle furiously after the deer, which are plunging through the water in mortal fear. In the consequent disorder many animals get into each other's way, thus being impeded in their progress. Now it is easy to strike them with a well-aimed harpoon thrown at close

[6] From his observation of the Bear Lake Eskimo, Stefansson states that an effective range of the average Eskimo bow used against the caribou varies between 75 and 90 yards. At 30 or 50 yards the arrow will pass through the thorax or abdomen of an adult caribou and travel several yards beyond. The thrust of the arrow is not powerful enough to break a caribou bone, except perhaps a rib; it will never break a leg, though the point may penetrate a long bone slightly and perhaps stick fast in it. Stefansson adds the interesting detail that 'when an arrow lodges in an animal' every movement of the body causes pain and tends to increase bleeding. For this reason an animal which would have kept moving with a similarly located bullet-wound will lie down if it carries an arrow, and will thus give a chance for a second shot. Far fewer wounded animals escape from the bow-hunters than do from the rifle-using Eskimo. ('Preliminary Anthropological Report of the Stefansson-Anderson Arctic Expedition,' *Anthropological Papers of the American Museum of Natural History*, vol. XIV, 1914, p. 96.)

quarters. On occasions such as this, large numbers of reindeer will be killed at one time. There is jubilation in the village, and an ample food kettle for a long time to come.[7]

The hunting of a seal, the second most important food animal, is a much more difficult procedure. In the winter, when no large gatherings of seals occur, they have to be hunted individually, and the hunter also is usually a single man. Being a mammal and a lung-breather, the seal cannot stay under water indefinitely: every so often it must come up to breathe. To provide for this, the seal makes holes in the ice for breathing purposes, to which he returns periodically. I said 'holes' rather than 'a hole,' because the seal usually has a choice of a few. In the prevailing low temperature such a hole will, of course, quickly freeze

Fig. 23. Seal Trumpet. (Franz Boas, *op. cit.* Drawn by Miss Harriette Akin.)

When stemmed against the ice and applied to the ear, this device makes it easier to hear the seal, as it is approaching the breathing hole.

over, even though the layer of ice will be thin and can be broken through easily enough by the returning seal. During snowfall the breathing-hole, covered over by the snow, is hard to find for an inexperienced hunter. A seasoned hunter, familiar with the habits of seals, will then proceed towards a spot where he knows seal breathing-holes are likely to occur and will locate them in the following way. He goes over the ground carefully, striking the surface from time to time with a cane provided for the purpose; thus he discovers a breathing-hole by a change in the sound. He must proceed very quietly, for the seal is likely to be frightened away by untoward noises. Having discovered the hole, the hunter sits down on a block of ice and is ready to wait. He may wait for a long time, hours or even days. To force himself to be as im-

---

[7] Note here what Weyer says with reference to hunting booty (when he speaks of 'hunting grounds' this should include hunting waters) :

'1. Hunting grounds, or rather the privilege of hunting on them, are a communal right, except in rather rare instances.

'2. The hunter or hunters almost always have the preferential share in the game secured, but part of each catch is generally divided among the community or among those present at the apportioning.

'3. Stored provisions are normally the property of the family or household; but in time of scarcity there is a tendency toward communalism. Hospitality is stressed under all circumstances.' (*The Eskimos*, p. 188.)

mobile as possible, he may tie his legs together loosely with a thong; his harpoon lies near him, at the right, ready to be picked up at short notice. Finally he hears the seal approaching.[8] At once he rises, seizes the harpoon with his right hand, and stands ready in striking position. As soon as the seal's head appears in the hole, he throws the harpoon, striking the seal in the head. The animal, of course, dives back immediately and disappears under the ice. It cannot go very far, though, because the harpoon point, firmly embedded in its body, is attached to a thong held by the hunter in his left hand. A full-grown powerful animal will not bow to the situation without a struggle. It tugs at the thong and not infrequently drags the hunter to the very edge of the hole. In an emergency such as this, the latter may be constrained to call for help, should any be available in the neighbourhood, or he may find himself forced to let go of the thong and thus lose the animal. If all goes well, the wounded seal will return after a while to the same hole, to breathe. When this occurs, the hunter hits it over the head with a club, dispatching it with ease, and then pulls the carcass out onto the surface of the ice. Without losing any time, he will usually skin it with his skinning knife right on the spot, profiting by the occasion to cut off a piece or two of oily blubber to be consumed then and there (Fig. 24).

FIG. 24. PLUGS FOR SEAL WOUNDS. (Drawn by Miss Harriette Akin.)

When inserted into the wound, the plug prevents the loss of the blood so valuable to the Eskimo.

The two weapons used in hunting, as here described, are the bow and arrow and the harpoon. Both are somewhat unusual, in structure as in use. One of the limiting conditions the Eskimo must face in his environment is the rarity of wood. No growing trees being available, he is usually forced to rely on the chance of picking up a piece of driftwood, if he is to use wood at all. This is seldom of the size or quality fit for a bow, and so we find the Eskimo bow made in a variety of ways and materials: a whole wooden bow,[9] or a composite wooden bow (Fig. 25), or a composite bone one

[8] An accessory device used for this purpose is the seal-trumpet (see Fig. 23).

[9] What is done in a particular locality depends, in part, on the available materials. The tribes around Bear Lake, who have been visited by Stefansson, make

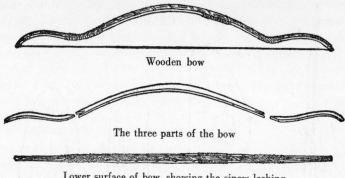

Wooden bow

The three parts of the bow

Lower surface of bow, showing the sinew lashing

FIG. 25. COMPOSITE WOODEN BOW. (Stefansson, *op. cit.*)

(Fig. 26). The arrow used in conjunction with the bow may be made of wood or of bone with a bone or stone point.

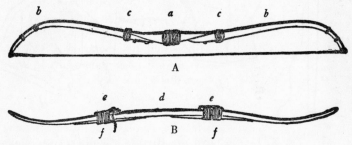

FIG. 26. COMPOSITE BONE BOWS. (Boas, *op. cit.*)

In both cases the bow consists of three pieces of antler. In A there is a stout central piece (*a*) slanted at both ends, to which the other two pieces (*b*) are riveted. The bow is reinforced by sinews, like the wooden variety, and the joints are secured by strong strings (*c*) wound around them. In B the central piece (*d*) is not slanted but cut off straight. The joint on either side is secured by two additional pieces of bone, a short stout one outside (*e*), which prevents the sections from breaking apart, and a long thin one inside (*f*), which provides the needed resiliency.

their bows out of wood, in this case 'exclusively of green spruce trees,' which can be secured. These are chopped down with adzes and roughed out. In midsummer, after the wood has dried for a month or so, it is further shaped with a crooked knife, when it is ready to be made into a bow. The backing used for these bows is usually of the leg sinew of the old bull-caribou, although that of smaller animals and even back sinew is occasionally used. There are three or more different ways of preparing this backing and applying it to the bow. The bow-string is of sinew plaited three-ply into a long slender line. This line is then taken four-, five-, or six-fold and twisted into a round cord one-sixteenth to one-eighth of an inch in diameter. The length of the bow-string, between the tips of the strung bow, is from 4½ to 5½ feet. The larger bow is used by men, whereas the bows used

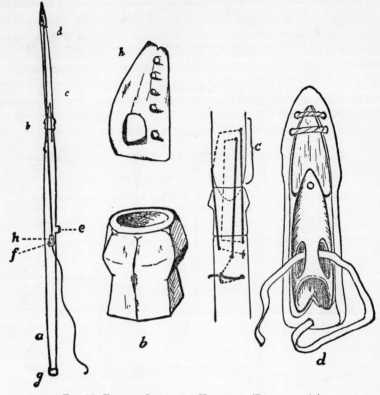

FIG. 27. ESKIMO COMPOSITE HARPOON. (Boas, *op. cit.*)

The harpoon is a most extraordinary contrivance. It is also composite, consisting of four parts (Fig. 27).

The shaft (*a*) consists of a stout pole, from 4 to 5 feet long; to its lower end an ivory knob (*g*) is fastened. At the center of gravity of the shaft a small piece of ivory (*e*) is attached, which supports the hand

by women and boys are smaller in all dimensions, with less sinew backing and a more slender bow-string. The arrows made here are also of wood and may consist of from three to five pieces spliced together. Being themselves ingenious, the Eskimo also accept anything useful that may come from the outside. They have, for example, learned long ago to supplement their original stone and bone arrow-heads with whatever metal became available through contact with the Whites, such as tin, iron, or steel. In addition to the wooden shaft and the metal or stone cutting-blade of the arrow-head, the section of the shaft which is nearest the head is made of caribou antler. This is from 5 to 8 inches in length, slightly flattened or round, and fits by a long spike, like a point or shoulder, into a socket in the front end of the wooden shaft, while a slit in the front end of the antler-piece holds the cutting-blade of the arrow-head.

when the weapon is thrown; at right angles to knob (e) another small ivory knob (f) is inserted in the shaft, which holds the harpoon line. The ivory head (b) is fitted upon the shaft so snugly that no other devices are used to insure its remaining in place. The walrus tusk (c) articulates with (b) by means of a ball-and-socket joint. The point of (c), finally, fits into the lower end of the harpoon point (d), as may be seen in Fig. 27. The walrus tusk is attached by thongs to the shaft, which transforms the latter, the ivory knob, and the tusk into a firm unit. The harpoon line is attached to the point (d) and then another little con-

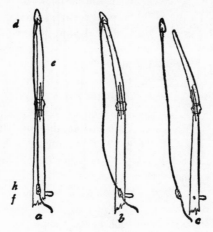

FIG. 28. COMPOSITE HARPOON IN ACTION. (Boas, *op. cit.*)

trivance (h) which is attached to the line is pulled over the ivory knob (f). The line between the point and (h) is just long enough for (h) to reach to (f), and so long as the tusk (c) remains in position, the shaft and point are thus firmly held together. Through two holes in the harpoon-point is drawn and firmly attached another thong which is very long and is held by the hunter in his left hand, whereas the harpoon is thrown with the right. When the harpoon (Fig. 28a) is thrown and the point strikes the animal (seal, walrus, or whale), the tusk moves laterally in the ball-and-socket joint; this diminishes the distance between the point (d) and the knob (f) (as in Fig. 28b), (h) slips off, thus disengaging the line and harpoon point from the shaft (as in Fig. 28c). Thus the precious point, which is often made with great care, is saved to the hunter.

In connection with the bird spear (Fig. 29a) a throwing-board is used, as shown in the drawing (Fig. 29b). The ivory knob (c) at the end of the spear shaft has a small hole, into which the spike (d) at the end of the groove in the throwing-board is inserted when the spear is in position for throwing. When in use, the board is held firmly in the right hand, the first finger passing through hole (e), and the thumb clasping the notch (f), while the points of the other fingers hold to the notches on the opposite side of the board (g). The spear is violently thrust forward by the spike and attains considerable velocity.[10]

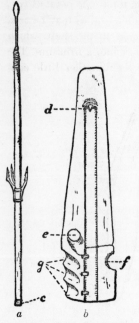

When the harpoon is used on a powerful animal such as a whale, a specially devised seal-skin float is sometimes employed. It consists of a wooden hoop with a seal- or deer-skin stretched over it. Three or four thongs of equal length are fastened to the hoop at equal distances and bound together. At the point of union they are attached to the line. In the drawing (Fig. 30) this contrivance is represented in action in conjunction with five seal-skin floats.

As soon as the animal is struck, it begins to swim away. Then the hoop assumes a position at right angles to the line. Thus a strong resistance comes into play, the speed of the animal is reduced, and its strength is soon exhausted. The buoyancy of the float prevents the animal's escape; moreover, it is unable to dive and is thus forced to remain within sight of the hunter.

Fig. 29. Eskimo Bird Spear and Throwing-Board. (Boas, *op. cit.*)

The most essential accessory of Eskimo technique is, without doubt, the drill used for boring holes in wood and bone (Fig. 31). We saw before that the Eskimo are not acquainted with any kind of nails. Instead, they bore holes in the objects or parts that are to be fitted together; through these holes thongs are drawn and pulled tightly, thus achiev-

---

[10] A similar device, a spear-thrower in this case, occurs also in Australia and Melanesia. On account of the technical requirements of the situation, this device is in principle similar to that of the Eskimo, even though the details of the apparatus are different. There is obviously no probability whatsoever of any historic contact between these two regions. We must therefore regard the Oceanic spear-thrower as having developed independently of the harpoon-thrower of the Eskimo. One peculiarity of the Eskimo thrower which is not duplicated in Oceania or Australia is the grooves described above into which the fingers fit.

ing the purpose at hand. In view of the paucity of wooden material and the unsuitable shapes of bone used, the piecing together of parts of material by means of thongs drawn through holes provides constant occasion for the use of this device. Whenever a wooden spade or spear-thrower breaks, repairs are made in this laborious but adequate fashion. Interestingly enough, the Eskimo with all their ingenuity have no device corresponding to a saw. Thus, when a piece of wood or bone is to be split in two a common method of accomplishing this is by boring a row of contiguous holes and then breaking the piece along the weakened line.[11] It will be evident from this how basic is the device by means of which holes are made. The significance of the drill is enhanced by the fact that the same apparatus is also used for making fire, except that a heavier shaft is then employed.

FIG. 30. COMPOSITE SEAL-SKIN FLOAT WITH HOOP. (Boas, *op. cit.*)

The drill (Fig. 31) has three parts: the shaft (*a*) made of iron (since the introduction of this metal by the Whites); the mouthpiece (*b*), made of wood or bone; and the bow (*c*), made of bone. When the drill is in use the mouthpiece (*b*) is taken between the teeth and held firmly; then the point of the drill is set against the place to be perforated, and the bow is moved to and fro by both hands; as one string winds, the other automatically unwinds. Thus a continuous revolution of the point is secured, and the hole is quickly made. When the drill is used for making fire, hardwood (ground willow) is substituted for the iron shaft (*a*), which is made to revolve against a piece of driftwood (*d*). Presently the driftwood begins to

[11] However, see p. 93. In recent days the Eskimo, ever eager to learn useful techniques, have caught the idea of a saw from the Whites and manufacture crude saws of their own. Such a specimen, very crudely made with an uneven cutting

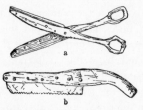

edge, is represented by Stefansson (*b*). Another such borrowed idea are the scissors, a specimen of which, made of bone handles with crudely shaped iron blades, was picked up by Stefansson on Coronation Gulf (*a*).

glow. Against the glowing wood a little moss is next applied, which after some gentle blowing begins to burn.

In his elaborate treatise, *The Graphic Art of the Eskimo*,[12] W. J. Hoffman quotes the following letter which he received in 1894 from Turner, who had prolonged opportunity to study the customs and art of the Eskimo resident in southern Alaska. The letter refers to the methods

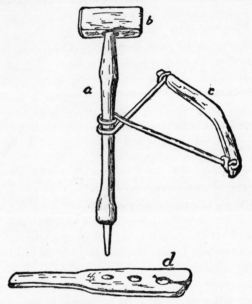

FIG. 31. ESKIMO BOW-DRILL. (Boas, *op. cit.*)

used by the Eskimo in preparing the ivory drill bows, which like many other ivory objects of these people are richly engraved with pictographs. Turner writes as follows: 'The abundance of walrus ivory in the days prior to the advent of Americans . . . permitted the Innuit (Eskimo) to secure the best character of ivory when wanted; hence the selection of a tusk depended entirely upon the want or use to which it was to be applied. Later the best tusks were sold and the inferior qualities retained, as is well shown by the comparison of the older and the more recent implements created from that material.

'The tusk selected was rudely scratched with a fragment of quartz or other siliceous stone along the length of the tusk, until the sharp edge would no longer deepen the groove; the other three sides were scratched

[12] *Report*, U.S. National Museum, 1895, pp. 739–968.

or channelled until the pieces of tusk could be separated. Sometimes this was done by pressure of the hand, or effected by means of a knifeblade-shaped piece of wood, on which was struck a sharp blow, and so skilfully dealt as not to shatter or fracture the piece intended for use. The other side, or slabs, were removed in a similar manner.

'The piece intended for drill bow or other use was now scraped (rubbed) with a fragment of freshly broken basalt, in which the cavities formed additional cutting edges and aided in the collection of

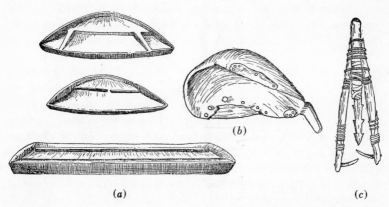

(b)

(a)   (c)

FIG. 32. (a) SANDSTONE LAMPS; (b) BAILING VESSEL WITH PATCHES; (c) AN ELABORATE SPEAR-POINT. The Eskimo way of making the best of the dearth of materials. (Drawn by Miss Harriette Akin after Stefansson, op. cit.)

the bone dust. When this was explained to me, I suggested the use of water, but the native smiled and continued his work. I soon saw he knew better than I how to reduce the size of a strip of walrus ivory. This attrition of the surface was continued until the approximate size was reached. The holes or perforations in the ends were produced by means of stone-drills after a depression had been made by an angular piece of stone, or any stone capable of wearing away the ivory substance. A few grains of sand were put into the shallow cavity and the stone-drill started by means of another drill or by a string or thong similar to the manner of making fire.

'Various sizes of stone drills were made, and by their use the different holes were produced. It is unusual to find two perforations of the same diameter in any object. These stone drills were used in making the long holes in ivory objects of all kinds.

'The final smoothing of the surface of the ivory piece was effected by rubbing it against a fine-grained stone or in the hand where fine sand was held; lastly, two pieces of ivory were rubbed against each other and thus a polished surface produced.

'The etching was done with sharp edges of fragments of flint. Sometimes these stone fragments were skilfully fastened into a piece of wood and used as gravers or even as lancets. In later years files and saws were used to cut the ivory into the required shape, and pieces of steel were used to make the holes. Often a three-cornered file was the instrument used to make the holes.

'The drill bow or other implement or utensil was not produced in a day or even in a month, as these articles were usually created for personal use. I have known of such articles being taken along on a protracted hunting expedition and there worked upon to while away the oftentimes tedious hours of watching game. Again I have known when a native had requested a friend to etch some design, and in their festivals, commemorating their dead, these articles were often presented and highly cherished as gifts. Other articles of ivory often passed as a legacy from a relative to another, and highly valued by the owner.'

Referring finally to the walrus ivory and antler, both of which are employed for engravings, Mr. Turner adds in the same letter: 'You will observe many of the larger objects of ivory and antler have outer or engraved portions of harder substance than the inner or core portion. You will perceive that in bent or curved affairs the outer part is always the denser portion of the material. This or these substances warp or curve because of their unequal density of parts. The native saw that heat would unshape a straight piece of ivory or antler, and, taking advantage of what the sun did, he laid aside the piece where it would become moist, and then placed it before the fire, core next to the fire, and warping was the result.

'In the winter the heat of the sun was not sufficient to produce harm, but when the warm rays began to heat objects, the native was careful to put his ivory or bone implements of the chase in the shade of a house or on the side of his cache, or within a place where heat could not affect it.

'I never saw them dip any such object in hot water or try to bend it by force.'

This account from a student who knew and loved the Eskimo illustrates with great clarity what care was exercised by these people in ascertaining the nature and peculiarities of materials, in adjusting their techniques both to the properties of the substance and to the nature of the object to be fashioned, and the great emotional value that attached

PLATE XIa.
IVORY PIPE-STEM

As an illustration of the engravings made by the Eskimo on such objects as drill-bows, pipe-stems, etc., I include the object on this plate, which represents a pipe-stem. As usual, the designs representing animals, men, and objects, are exceedingly small and very simple in contour, which does not prevent the figures from being admirably expressive of action and even psychic state. On the base-line facing (A), the left-hand figure denotes a habitation with its entrance (a). Seated upon the projecting shelf seat is the drummer, holding the tambourine drum in one hand while with the other he holds a drum-stick (b). The other figures are the dancers, in various attitudes, with hands and fingers extended (c). Upon the roof of the entrance are two men in similar attitudes, while within the entrance is one figure of a man in the attitude of falling forward upon the ground (d). In front of the entrance is a group of figures in threatening attitudes. One of the men seems to be drawing his bow with the intention of shooting the man facing him, who has a hand up as if guarding his face (e). There appears to have been a discussion respecting a seal—lying upon the ground between the men—which led to the disagreement. The next figure is shown in the attitude of spearing a seal in the water (e'), the spear bladder being shown at the upper end of the weapon. The next man is dragging home a seal (f), while the next following is engaged with another seal, stooping down for some reason. The large creature lying upon the base line, next to the right, is a whale (g). One of the hunters has a hatchet and is cutting up the animal, while two assistants are otherwise engaged at either end. Next to the right is another hunter in the act of dragging along his kayak on a sledge (h). The last person has on his sledge a seal which has been captured (i).

If the pipe-stem is turned upside down, further figures will be observed on the new base-line, facing (B), the interpretation of which can be easily made. (For further illustrations of Eskimo engraving see pp. 95, 99, 102, 106, 112.)

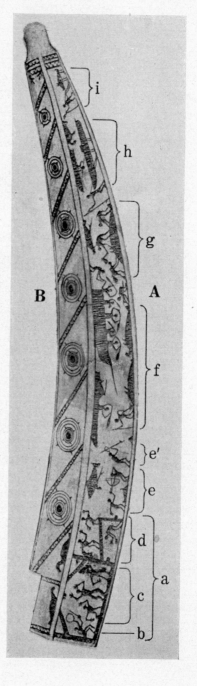

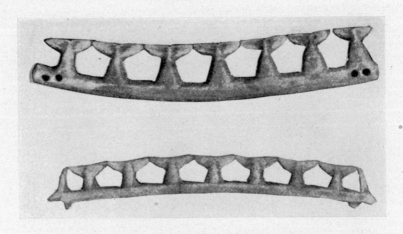

PLATE XIb. ESKIMO CARVINGS OF WHALE TAILS

Illustration of utilization of a slightly stylized realistic feature for decorative effect.

to such objects in the preparation of which untold hours of toil were spent (see Plate XIa).

Settling Disputes Among the Eskimo [13]

Among the Eskimo, as among many other primitive peoples, the custom of blood revenge is one of the ancient means of retaliating for murder. In certain particulars this custom, as we find it among the Eskimo, is rather unique. In commenting on these practices Boas cites a report of Lieutenant A. Gordon from the year 1886 which in substance runs as follows: There once lived in the neighbourhood of Cape Chidleigh, Labrador, a 'good' Eskimo who was christened at the White station Old Wicked, an impassioned man who was continuously threatening to do bodily harm to other natives. When his behaviour at length became unbearable, the Eskimo foregathered and decided that he had to be shot, which was done one afternoon while he was engaged in repairing his snow house. The 'executioner' shot him in the back, killing him instantly. This man then undertook to take care of Old Wicked's wives and children so that they should not become a burden on the group.

This incident, I said, refers to Labrador, whereas the Central Eskimo with whom Boas deals inhabit Baffin Land and the west shore of Hudson Bay. The fact that similar customs prevail in regions so widely separated suggests their antiquity. Another variant of this type of revenge also related by Boas is to the effect that the murderer comes to visit the relatives of the victim and settles down with them, knowing all the time that they are about to kill him in revenge. He is welcomed, and may live on this way quietly for weeks or even months; then he is suddenly challenged to a wrestling match, and if defeated is killed; if victorious, however, he may kill one of the opposite party. Or he may be suddenly attacked while hunting and slain by one of his companions.[14]

Apart from vengeance, there are here other ways of settling grievances, of which the wrestling match mentioned by Boas is one, the other two being a fist fight and a song contest. Each of the three has its own geographical distribution in the vast area inhabited by the Eskimo. The legal nature of all of these fights is seen in the fact that revenge here

[13] Primitive law, as a separate topic, is not treated in this book. Instead, I am inserting here this bit on Eskimo legal procedure. To omit it would have been cruel to the reader.

[14] Franz Boas, *op. cit.*, p. 582.

is not left to the whim of the aggrieved person but is provided an outlet in a specific form. In blood revenge the common custom is for a man to be overtaken suddenly and by stealth, as was the case in the instance reported by Gordon. Here, on the contrary, the man who is about to take revenge meets his opponent eye to eye and subject to the risks involved in a fight, including the possibility of his being bested. The second legal aspect consists in the fact that what is aimed at is not a complete annihilation of the opponent but a mere chastisement or humiliation.

By far the most interesting of the three methods is the song contest. The form it takes in West Greenland is described by Holmes: The contestants stand facing each other. Suddenly one of them starts to sing a satirical song directed against his opponent. While he does so, the other stands by quietly and apparently indifferently. The singer may accompany his song by contemptuous gestures towards his opponent, he may even spit in his face or butt him with his forehead so that he falls over backwards. All this is endured by the other with utmost calm, or at worst, with derisive laughter, so as to show the spectators how indifferent he really is. When the opponent is ready to butt him he shuts his eyes and sticks his head forward in order to meet the blow. In this way they may proceed the whole night long, without otherwise moving from the spot.

The well-known Eskimo explorer, Krantz, makes the following remarks on the subject: When a Greenlander feels himself offended by another he shows no anger nor does he plan revenge, but prepares a satirical song which he recites in the presence of his household, especially the women, accompanying it by dancing until they all know it; then he makes it known in the entire district that he wants to sing against his abuser. The latter appears at a designated spot and while he stands surrounded by the spectators, the accuser sings his song accompanied by dancing and a drum and supported by the exclamations of the crowd, who also repeat every sentence he articulates. The general tenor of his song is, of course, that of a satirical invective against the aggressor. When the singer has finished, the latter steps forward and answers with a similarly composed song, supported by his relatives and friends. This procedure may be repeated again and again. The one who finally has the laugh on his opponent is regarded as having won the contest. The spectators as a group decide the issue. After this the two contestants behave like good old friends.[15]

---

[15] Herbert König, 'Breaches of Law and their Settlement Among the Eskimo,' *Anthropos*, vol. xx, 1925, pp. 276–316 (in German).

The author reproduces a number of these contests which he picked up in Greenland.

Koungak, who is seeking revenge, sings:

> 'Let me follow the women's boat
> as a *kayak* man;
> Let me follow the boat
> with the singers.
> Though I am shy and modest of nature,
> I shall follow as a *kayak* paddler,
> shall follow the singing ones.
> It is not strange that he was joyful,
> he who almost killed his cousin,
> almost killed him with a harpoon.
> It is not surprising that he was pleased,
> that he was joyful.'

Kirdlavik, the accused, dances and sings:

> 'But I only laugh about it.
> I only make fun about it.
> Koungak, it is you who is
> the real murderer.
> The reason why you are so wrathful
> and of such wild disposition
> are your three wives;
> and only three, you think, is not enough.
> Others you should ask to marry them.
> Then all their husbands' catch
> you would receive.
> Koungak, because you do not worry
> about others' opinions,
> always you are hungry.
> Everything you have
> your women had.
> And so you have begun
> to kill the people.'

The second contest is more exciting; the account runs as follows: The old Kilinre beat the drum with the strength of a youth and first sang Marratse's challenge to Eqerko, who had married Marratse's divorced wife. This marriage reawakened the old love and jealousy of Marratse, who challenged his rival to a singing contest. This contest was very

long and lasted, with dance and mimicry, at least an hour. The songs,
in part, go like this.

Marratse sings:

> 'Words I shall split,
> little sharp words, like wood splinters
> from under my ax.
> A song of olden days,
> a breath of the ancestors.
> A song of longing
> for my wife.
> A song that brings
> forgetfulness.
> A cheeky braggart
> has stolen her.
> He has tried
> to belittle her.
> Miserable wretch
> who loves human flesh.
> A cannibal
> from famine days.'

And Eqerko answers, singing:

> 'Cheek which amazes one!
> Laughable fury
> and sham courage.
> A song of derision
> which proclaims my guilt.
> You want to frighten me!
> Me, who defies death
> with indifference.
> Hei! You sing to my wife
> who once was yours.
> Then you were not so worthy
> of love.
> While she was left alone,
> you forgot to exalt her
> in song,
> in challenging, fighting
> song.
> Now she is mine,

nor will she ever be visited
by song-making, false lovers,
abductors of women
in strangers' tents.[16]

Commenting upon the geographical distribution of the different
methods of settling disputes, the author brings out the following in-

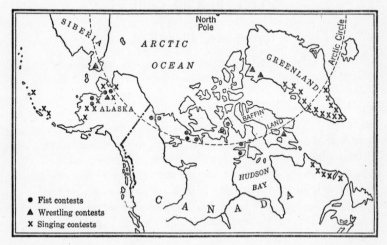

FIG. 33. SETTLING DISPUTES AMONG THE ESKIMO: DISTRIBUTION OF VARIETIES
OF CONTESTS. (After Herbert König, *op. cit.*)

teresting fact. Song contests occur in the marginal districts of the Eskimo
habitat, that is, in Greenland and on the coast of Labrador in the East,
and in Alaska and the Aleutian Islands in the West. The fist contests
are indigenous in the intervening region, around Hudson Bay and the
mouth of the Mackenzie. The wrestling contests again articulate through
Smith's Sound with the fist fights in the East, and through Alaska with
the western area of the singing contests. It appears then that the distribution of the latter is cut into and separated into two areas by the intrusion of the two types of fighting contests.[17] (See Map, Fig. 33.)

[16] *Ibid.*, pp. 314–315. The translation from the German is mine. However true to
the content of the Eskimo original, this double translation can, of course, not aspire to reproduce the form of the native song.
[17] *Ibid.*, p. 295.

Chapter VII

THE FOOD QUEST

Hunters and Plant Gatherers

The preceding sketch of Eskimo technology has made abundantly clear the urgent nature of the primary adjustment to the food supply. The food quest, which is so difficult and arduous among the Eskimo, is only less so among all primitives, especially among those who have not reached the stage of the domestication of animals or the cultivation of plants. Man will eat and he must do so with a degree of regularity. As the food does not come to him, he must go after the food.

In this primary adjustment, woman and man have always co-operated in most primitive societies living in what was sometimes described as 'The Hunting Stage.' Woman has her share of labour as a provider, in so far as it is she rather than the man who goes forth in quest of the products of wild plant nature. In this division of labour, as will be shown in greater detail later on, there are some exceptions, but by and large wild plant gathering falls to the woman, not the man of the primitive group. She digs for yams with a crude stick, as in Australia; she gathers mushrooms and barks and berries or nuts and mosses, according to the opportunities offered by her habitat. The equipment of tools she requires for this work is of the simplest. Not so with man who is the hunter. We saw already how elaborate were the hunting paraphernalia of the Eskimo. While these Arctic people are perhaps somewhat exceptional in this respect, hunting without tools is not possible. It is in this connection that the different hunting tribes of the primitive world have devised such equipment as the spear, the bow and arrow, the Australian boomerang, the almost ubiquitous club, and the well-nigh omnipresent knife. Not satisfied with this, man, as has already been stated, invented a series of further accessory devices for hunting and fishing, such as hooks and nets, snares and traps, in endless variety and profusion. By means of a trap, it becomes possible for the hunter to corner and hold his prey without being personally present at the crucial moment of capture. In one form or another, these various devices are found everywhere, however primitive the particular tribe may be.

The example of the Eskimo has shown that both fishing and hunting may be carried on individually as well as in groups. Both of these features also have a universal distribution. The Australian may follow the kangaroo alone, but he will also participate in communal hunts after smaller fry in which women, old men, and children will lend a hand. The Eskimo, as we saw, also have communal hunts on a large scale in the pursuit of reindeer or walrus. In the Plains of North America the buffalo was hunted individually but also by large groups of tribal dimensions. It is this latter kind of hunt which became an important social institution among these people.

Not only must food be secured, but it must also be prepared for consumption. While the intake of raw food, vegetable or animal, is not unknown either in modern or in primitive society, food of many kinds has been prepared in one way or another to make it palatable for consumption. Also, it has been stored away. This storing and preparation of food called for additional devices, vessels, and habits of procedure. Generally, though not exclusively, this task also falls to the women. Vegetable food, owing to its very nature, is secured more readily, under conditions of less danger, and within a smaller radius from the home. These traits of the plant aspect of the food quest have almost inevitably led to its becoming the monopoly of the housewife, or very nearly so. In these tasks, however, the women were often assisted by the children and the sick and aged as well. Everywhere the sustenance of this part of the household is more regularly and reliably provided by the efforts of the home-bound woman than by those of her roving hunter husband or son. It is, in fact, a familiar spectacle among all primitive hunters that the man returning from a more or less arduous chase may yet reach home empty-handed and himself longing for food. Under such conditions, the vegetable supply of the family has to serve his needs as well as those of the rest of the household.

Especially in connection with the preparation of meat for consumption, most of the many devices employed in cooking in modern days had already been known to the primitives, such as roasting, boiling, steaming, preserving, drying, spicing, and the like. Nor should it be forgotten that the variety of eatables thus made available is often very considerable, even in a primitive community. The recipes, moreover, in accordance with which particular dishes are to be prepared may lack none of the precision, complexity, or elaboration of detail made familiar by modern cookbooks. Professor Franz Boas, who knew his Kwakiutl so intimately, was able to secure from their women several hundred cooking recipes which would have done honour to any similar modern collection.

By and large, of course, the food quest is not a matter of fun, nor can it be taken lightly. It is hard work, continuous, often boring, not infrequently dangerous, but on occasion it may also become highly absorbing, exciting, and dramatic. As an illustration of the more spectacular varieties of hunting and fishing, let me offer a few descriptions, including a whale hunt among the Eskimo, one variety of buffalo hunt among the Plains Indians, and an elaborate fishing expedition of the Maori.

An Eskimo Whale Hunt

This sketch, comprising a picturesque account of an Eskimo whale hunt under modern conditions and in co-operation with White men, is borrowed from *Eskimo*, by Peter Freuchen, who of all White men now living, with the possible exception of Stefansson, has identified himself most thoroughly and sympathetically with the life of these Arctic hunters.

This is Freuchen's tale: 'At last they sighted a whale. The water which the whale spouted each time it came to the surface showed from afar where it was. The blowing indicated that the animal must be a good sized one and easy to approach closely. Here was a splendid chance for a good catch and helmsman and harpooner kept an alert watch on their distant prey. First they must discover the direction the whale was taking. They made all preparations for the animal was making straight for their boat and Mala [the Eskimo hero of Freuchen's story] realized that they would soon make their first catch. The excitement of the hunt gripped them all as they rowed toward the whale. The animal apparently suspected nothing and was speeding calmly through the water.

' "Can any life be happier than that of a whale?" thought Mala. The whale need only dive deep enough to obtain its food; it opens its mouth, pushes out its mighty tongue and keeps on swimming while its gullet rakes in the small fish. As soon as its mouth is filled sufficiently the whale locks in the prey with its tongue and presses out the water, while the food is retained by the baleen which forms a fringe-like sieve extending from the upper jaw. The food of the whale consists of millions of little fish, and the only thing the whale has to do after locking up his prey is to swallow it and that, after all, is the greatest joy of every living being. There cannot be any doubt that whales have every reason to be satisfied with their lot.

'Now the boat was quite close to the whale. The men who had never before caught whales felt their hearts pounding, and were very careful to observe all precautionary measures. As soon as they reached the wake of the whale, they pulled in the oars, laying them very quietly in the bottom of the boat, so that no noise should scare the whale away. The water around them seemed to be boiling with tiny air bubbles ejected by the gigantic creature. The tell-tale bubbles made it possible for them to follow its trail. Whales are very wary; they know from great distances when a boat is crossing their course. Since they usually keep on in a straight line, it is possible either to follow them or, with luck, to approach them from straight ahead when they float on the surface breathing-in air. They cannot see straight ahead, as their eyes are on either side of their heads, and if approached noiselessly from the front, they are a sure prey. However, should they suddenly turn and catch a glimpse of the boat, they lose no time in vanishing from sight.

'The men used small paddles and brought the boat to without a ripple. They could see nothing, but they felt instinctively that the mighty animal was coming to the surface. Presently the colossus became visible; a mighty spout of water rose high in the air. Fetid air had to be exhaled and fresh air inhaled repeatedly before the whale could dive for food again. After all there was nothing in the world for it to fear—not for an animal of such great bulk as this giant! There were no enemies here. The whale floated serenely on the surface and the helmsman did not dare to utter a word of command. Everyone thought of the instructions he had been given before and tried to do his best. The most important thing now was to get ahead, speedily and noiselessly. In case they bungled the job, hell would break loose.

'Then everything happened quickly: The harpooner hurled his spear-like weapon deep into the body of the whale.

'At that moment, the fear of death nearly overcame them. What a tremendous lashing of the tail! How the water boiled all around them! And then, with indescribable speed, the whale made for the sheltering depths. The swiftness with which the line unrolled from the box! It rushed out of the containers, first out of the one, then out of the other. If anybody had stood in the way, the line would have snapped off his legs. If the line should become entangled now, the whale would pull the boat beneath the surface of the sea.

'Mala felt a sinking sensation in his stomach. This, certainly, was different from hunting a miserable little seal which one could hold on to with one hand, provided one's line was strong. How excitement could bring out the sweat! Big beads of perspiration gathered on his forehead.

'Not before the whale had reached the bottom of the sea and the line had stopped uncoiling, did they receive an order, "Back water!" They obeyed and the harpooner took a deep breath. As soon as the line tightened, there was a jerk. It was certain that the barbed hooks of the harpoon had struck, despite the tremendous pull exerted by the whale when it made its wild rush for safety. There was a muffled detonation. An explosive, imbedded in the head of the harpoon, had been discharged by the desperate struggling of the beast. The charge must have torn terrible holes in the mighty body. Now all depended on whether the harpoon had penetrated the body of the animal in a straight line; otherwise the explosive would do no more harm to the whale than injure one side and pass out of the body again.

'To all appearances the shot had been a bull's eye, and the giant was even now resting on the bottom of the sea, limp with terror and excruciating pain. Perhaps its whole belly had been ripped open! And up above, on the surface of the sea, the men tore and pulled on the line, enlarging the wound and increasing the whale's agonies.

' "Row on—and keep rowing," the helmsman shouted. Now they must locate the hiding place of the whale. Besides, a steady pull had to be exerted on the line so that the whale could not turn over and draw the boat under water. If this should happen, one quick motion must sever the line; a hatchet was held in readiness. Then the prey would be lost for ever.

'What terrible tension this waiting meant! The kind of suspense that sets one's nerves a-tingle when some terrific danger looms near might be so racking as to be nigh unbearable but, at the same time, it furnishes good sport for hardy men. It seemed to Mala as if there was no end to their trying wait. The whale must have stored up a great amount of air in its lungs to last so long beneath the waves!

'Suddenly it appeared! The line slackened with incredible speed. The whale rose quickly to the surface, plainly exhausted. The white men consulted their watches. Mala, looking at the sky, judged that the sun had travelled the breadth of two fingers since the whale had been harpooned. The water, spouting through the nostrils of the whale, was reddened with blood, proof that the lungs had been punctured and that the battle would be over soon. All at once, however, the whale rallied; it no longer seemed in the least exhausted. Now they must get close to the animal and hurl into his huge bulk additional harpoons in order to finish it off—a dangerous job that required great care.

'Carefully, they paddled close to the whale and again the beast was harpooned, this time with a smaller barbed spear. The animal hardly moved from the spot. As soon as the harpoon penetrated the body of the whale, the trigger line was pulled and there was an explosion opening new wounds. And then it rushed ahead madly through the water, pulling along the boat at a terrific rate of speed. There was still strength in the King of the Seas. Northward the boat sped. Like wounded rein-

FIG. 34. HAULING IN A WALRUS. (Drawn by Miss Harriette Akin after O. T. Mason, *The Human Beast of Burden.*)

deer in the snow, the whale left behind tracks, easy to discern. How brave this whale was! Now it made straight for the mountainous shore whence the hunters had come. . . .

'Often a whale which is already considered a sure catch causes much trouble; in case the animal should take its course through fields of dangerous ice floes, the line must be severed to avoid disaster. Game and line and everything is lost then. This time, however, the whale gradually weakened, the men once more pulled at the oars and when the edge of the ice was reached, the King of the Seas was dead. It was Mala's boat which had made the first catch of the season. The skipper heaped unstinting praise upon the entire crew. . . .

'The helmsman ordered one of the white sailors to hoist a red flag on a boat-hook, as a signal to the other boats that they had made a catch and needed assistance in cutting up the carcass.' [1]

[1] Peter Freuchen, *Eskimo*, trans. Branden, pp. 56–59. (Reprinted by permission of the Liveright Publishing Corporation.)

Hunting the Buffalo

The scene now shifts to the Plains Indians. During the years 1832–1839 an English traveller and artist, George Catlin, journeyed widely among the Indians of North America. Fortunately for us, he was prevailed upon by friends to record his experiences in a series of letters and notes on the manners, customs, and condition of the North American Indians (this being the title of his two-volume work published in London in 1841). Although he often wrote loosely and always painted badly, his descriptions and drawings record much that in later years could only be gathered by reconstruction and speculation. Coming upon the Indians of the Plains at a time when the buffalo still roamed the grasslands in countless thousands, he was in a position to witness these intrepid hunters in their massed and devastating attacks on the animal in which the culture of the Plains was rooted.[2] I reproduce his description of a buffalo hunt of the kind known as a 'surround.' The tribes participating in this affair, the Minitarees (more commonly known as Hidatsa) and Mandan, constitute together with the Arikara the northern branch of the Siouan-speaking Indians of the eastern Plains, also called the Village tribes on account of the earth-lodge settlements or villages in which they lived when not following the buffalo. During these tribal hunts, on the other hand, they used the typical Plains *tipis* which, when camp was struck, were arranged in the form of the so-called Camp Circle. Follows Catlin's account:

'The Minitarees, as well as the Mandans, had suffered for some months past for want of meat, and had indulged in the most alarming fears that the herds of buffalo were emigrating so far off from them that there was great danger of their actual starvation, when it was suddenly announced through the village one morning at an early hour that a herd of buffaloes was in sight. A hundred or more young men mounted their horses, with weapons in hand, and steered their course to the prairies. . . .

'The plan of attack, which in this country is familiarly called a surround, was explicitly agreed upon, and the hunters, who were all mounted on their "buffalo horses" and armed with bows and arrows or long lances, divided into two columns, taking opposite directions, and drew themselves gradually around the herd at a mile or more dis-

[2] For a more detailed sketch of Plains life, see pp. 171–172.

tance from them, thus forming a circle of horsemen at equal distances apart, who gradually closed in upon them with a moderate pace at a signal given. The unsuspecting herd at length "got the wind" of the approaching enemy and fled in a mass in the greatest confusion. To the point where they were aiming to cross the line the horsemen were seen, at full speed, gathering and forming in a column, brandishing their weapons, and yelling in the most frightful manner, by which they turned the black and rushing mass, which moved off in an opposite direction, where they were again met and foiled in a similar manner, and wheeled back in utter confusion; by which time the horsemen had closed in from all directions, forming a continuous line around them, whilst the poor affrighted animals were eddying about in a crowded and confused mass, hooking and climbing upon each other, when the work of death commenced. I had rode up in the rear and occupied an elevated position at a few rods' distance, from which I could (like the general of a battle-field) survey from my horse's back the nature and the progress of the grand *mêlée*, but (unlike him) without the power of issuing a command or in any way directing its issue.

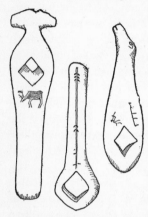

Fig. 35. Eskimo Arrow-Straighteners. (Drawn by Miss Harriette Akin after Stefansson, *op. cit.*)

'In this grand turmoil a cloud of dust was soon raised, which in part obscured the throng where the hunters were galloping their horses around and driving the whizzing arrows or their long lances to the hearts of these noble animals; which in many instances, becoming infuriated with deadly wounds in their sides, erected their shaggy manes over their bloodshot eyes and furiously plunged forward at the sides of their assailants' horses, sometimes goring them to death at a lunge and putting their dismounted riders to flight for their lives. Sometimes their dense crowd was opened, and the blinded horsemen, too intent on their prey amidst the cloud of dust, were hemmed and wedged in amidst the crowding beasts, over whose backs they were obliged to leap for security, leaving their horses to the fate that might await them in the results of this wild and desperate war. Many were the bulls that turned upon their assailants and met them with desperate resistance, and many were the warriors who were dismounted and saved themselves by the superior muscles of their legs; some who were closely pursued by the

bulls wheeled suddenly around, and snatching the part of a buffalo
robe from around their waists, threw it over the horns and eyes of the
infuriated beast, and darting by its side drove the arrow or the lance
to its heart; others suddenly dashed off upon the prairie by the side
of the affrighted animals which had escaped from the throng, and
closely escorting them for a few rods, brought down their heart's blood
in streams and their huge carcasses upon the green and enamelled turf.

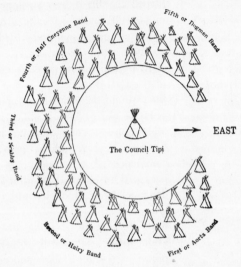

FIG. 36. THE CHEYENNE CAMP CIRCLE. (Wissler, *op. cit.*, after Dorsey.)

'In this way this grand hunt soon resolved itself into a desperate battle, *and in the space of fifteen minutes resulted in the total destruction
of the whole herd,* which in all their strength and fury were doomed,
like every beast and living thing else, to fall before the destroying
hands of mighty man.

'I had sat in trembling silence upon my horse and witnessed this extraordinary scene, which allowed not one of these animals to escape
out of my sight. Many plunged off upon the prairie for a distance, but
were overtaken and killed, and although I could not distinctly estimate
the number that were slain, yet I am sure that some hundreds of these
noble animals fell in this grand *mêlée.* Amongst the poor affrighted
creatures that had occasionally dashed through the ranks of their
enemy and sought safety in flight upon the prairie (and in some instances had undoubtedly gained it), I saw them stand awhile, looking
back, when they turned, and, as if bent on their own destruction, re-
traced their steps, and mingled themselves and their deaths with those

of the dying throng. Others had fled to a distance on the prairies, and for want of company, of friends or of foes, had stood and gazed on till the battle scene was over, seemingly taking pains to stay and hold their lives in readiness for their destroyers until the general destruction was over, when they fell easy victims to their weapons, making the slaughter complete.' [3]

After quoting the above passage of Catlin's, W. T. Hornaday makes the following remark: 'It is to be noticed that *every animal* of this entire herd of several hundred was slain on the spot, and there is no room to doubt that at least half (possibly much more) of the meat thus taken was allowed to become a loss. People who are so utterly senseless as to wantonly destroy their own source of food, as the Indians have done, certainly deserve to starve.' [4]

The statement of our author is charged with sinister irony. Catlin could not have foreseen, but Hornaday knew and described the havoc, complete and irretrievable, wrought among the bisons by the White hunters who by means of their rifles, backed up by a psychology no less savage nor more provident than that of the Indians, all but achieved that extermination of this indigenous American animal which had been begun by the Indians [5] (Fig. 37).

A Maori Fishing Expedition

For an illustration of primitive fishing operations on a large scale let me now turn to the Maori. In his valuable book, *Primitive Economics*

---

[3] George Catlin, *Letters and Notes* etc., pp. 199–201.

[4] 'The Extermination of the American Bison,' *Smithsonian Report*, U. S. National Museum, 1887, p. 482.

[5] Nor was the surround the only devastating method employed in hunting down the buffalo. There was also the 'still hunt,' in which a single hunter, armed with a repeating rifle and shooting from ambush, could lay low dozens of buffalo almost at will. Hornaday mentions a certain 'Capt. Jack Brydges, of Kansas, who was one of the first to begin the final slaughter of the southern herd, who killed, by contract, one thousand one hundred and forty-two buffaloes in six weeks.' Another method was chasing the buffalo on horseback or 'running buffalo.' This was an exciting procedure, full of danger, not alone for the hunted animal, but for the hunter and his mount as well. When practised by the Indians, before the introduction of the repeating rifle, it gave the buffalo an almost fair chance. The lance or bow and arrow could be used effectively only at close range. This implied dangerous proximity to the powerful creatures, as well as numerous opportunities for a fall with its attending hazards. All this changed with the coming of the modern rifle and the Colt's revolver. The latter, in particular, proved vastly superior even to the rifle. Held in one hand, it could be fired with greater precision than a rifle, which required the use of both hands. Shooting with a rifle from the back of a galloping horse is no easy matter. It was his skill at this particular

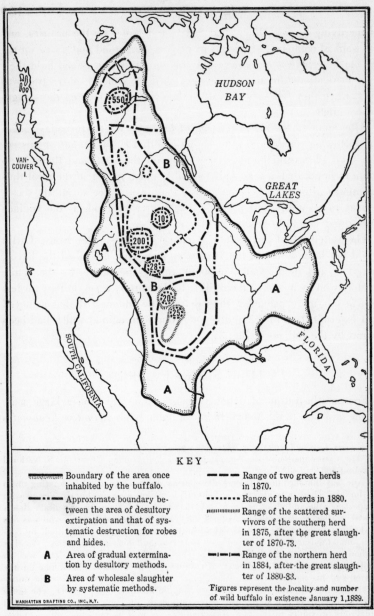

KEY

▬▬▬▬ Boundary of the area once inhabited by the buffalo.	▬ ▬ ▬ Range of two great herds in 1870.
▬··▬··▬ Approximate boundary between the area of desultory extirpation and that of systematic destruction for robes and hides.	········ Range of the herds in 1880.
	▭▭▭▭▭ Range of the scattered survivors of the southern herd in 1875, after the great slaughter of 1870-73.
A Area of gradual extermination by desultory methods.	▬ı▬ı▬ı Range of the northern herd in 1884, after the great slaughter of 1880-83.
B Area of wholesale slaughter by systematic methods.	Figures represent the locality and number of wild buffalo in existence January 1, 1889.

MANHATTAN DRAFTING CO., INC., N.Y.

FIG. 37. THE EXTERMINATION OF THE BUFFALO. (After W. T. Hornaday, *The Extermination of the American Bison.*)

of the New Zealand Maori, Raymond Firth reproduces the following condensed account from a sketch given by Captain Gilbert Mair of a spectacular fishing display made in the year 1886 by Chief Te Pokiha with his great fishing net. The operation of one of these enormous nets was a complicated affair requiring participation of many individuals and competent direction as well. The account runs as follows:

'The net used in this affair was a huge one, measuring by veracious report, 95 chains in length. It was made at Maketu during the winter months of 1885, by several hundred of Ngati-Pikiao of Arawa, on the initiative of their chief, Te Pokiha Raranui. The net was taken in sections to a flat below the village and was there set up with appropriate magic by the learned old men of the tribe. It was of such a size that no single canoe would hold it, and it was therefore taken out on a platform placed over two war canoes lashed together, the whole being propelled by thirty men. The control of the enterprise was in the hands of one Te Whanarere, an expert in fishing, who in order best to supervise the workers, ascended to the top of a high telegraph tower near by, and thence gave out his commands. Shoal after shoal of fish he allowed to pass untouched, while crew and waiting crowd grew impatient, but the old man was wise in the lore of fish and nets. At last he gave the signal to encircle what appeared to be an insignificant brown patch on the water. *"Haukotia mai!"* came his cry: *"Intercept it!"* The paddles dipped furiously, the craft forged along, and the net was paid out by six men. After the shoal was encircled a great portion of the net was still unused, but nevertheless it was found impossible to haul the seine, in spite of the large numbers of people who hauled on the ropes. The catch was too great. The unused part of the net was now doubled round the remainder, and the expert came down from the tower and swam out to attend to the work. Under his direction the men hoisted the belly of the net, and so allowed a large part of the catch to escape. This was done twice, and only then could the seine be hauled in to the beach. It was held there by stakes driven firmly in, and the tide allowed to fall. Meanwhile, owing to the *tapu*, the people were not allowed to partake of food—which certainly tended to focus their interest on the work! The resulting catch numbered many thou-

exploit that earned the late W. F. Cody his world-famous nickname, 'Buffalo Bill.' Still another method was 'impounding' or killing in pens. This device enjoyed great popularity among the Indians, as it involved the co-operation of men, women, and children, appropriately stationed over a great distance, all intent on driving the herd toward the pen. Once the animals had entered the enclosure, they could do no more than chase about, wildly and aimlessly, until they were all killed. The methods of hunting here enumerated are but a sample of a much greater variety employed against the buffalo.

sands of fish, and its apportionment was supervised by Te Pokiha himself.'[6]

Domestication and Cultivation

At certain points in the history of the food quest, of labour, transportation, and warfare, certain inventions supervened, perhaps not too often, which placed man in a position of an even greater dominance over nature than he had heretofore enjoyed. With this dominance came greater comfort, security, power, and an almost unlimited range of further opportunities for development. The two inventions, or more correctly, complexes of inventions I have in mind are, of course, the domestication of animals and the cultivation of plants. The wild animal or bird can be of use to man only after its life has been destroyed. To achieve this, it must be hunted, cornered or caught, and killed. Then it, or parts of it, can be used as food, clothing, or ornament. The animal as a source of power or of other useful qualities does not figure in this connection. The domesticated animal loses its freedom and some of its quality, but not all of it. It may now be employed as a source of energy, as a tool of speed, or as a reservoir of useful properties which under domestication may become greatly enhanced with special reference to the needs of man.

In connection with domestication, we have already had occasion to become acquainted with the dog, man's all but ubiquitous companion, helpmate, and friend. Let me repeat here that the domestication of the dog, however, wherever, and whenever it was achieved, must be regarded as a very ancient event in the history of culture, preceding that of the domestication of any other animal. This is attested by the almost universal distribution of the dog including even the most primitive tribes.[7]

The degree of domestication of this animal is not by any means always the same. In Australia, for example, the *dingo* may be described as only half domesticated. Around the camp he is very much in evidence both

[6] Raymond Firth, *Primitive Economics of the New Zealand Maori*, pp. 214–215. (Reprinted by permission of George Routledge and Sons, Ltd.)

[7] All original dogs have been derived from native wolves or some wolf-like animals, perhaps going back to a common Asiatic ancestor. Under the deliberate and non-deliberate artifices of a cultured existence, the race of dogs has multiplied and become diversified enormously in size, shape, and quality. This notwithstanding, as old Eduard Hahn once pointed out, a dog has remained a dog, a fact of which humans are at least vaguely aware, but which to dogs is a matter of utmost certainty. An enormous St. Bernard or Newfoundland, when confronted with a diminutive Spaniel or lap dog, knows that he is in the presence of one of his kind.

numerically and vocally. Being a dog he barks,[8] with reason or without, and to this extent he is of some use to the native as a messenger of trouble or anything else that may be happening. Again as dog, or we might say as wolf, he will go along on the hunt, but he has not in Australia been trained in any of those niceties of the hunting dog's behaviour which we find among other primitives or in modern days. Also, he is not fed. As a result, he frequently looks and is underfed, and puppies in Australia often die prematurely for this reason.

In America, we find the dog utilized for transportation among the Plains Indians, where he pulls the *travois* (see p. 67, Fig. 7), and among the Eskimo where, as we already know, he is employed for pulling the sled. Previously I have described the peculiar niceties and difficulties of the latter situation among the Eskimo. As a watch dog and hunting companion, the dog is employed, more or less effectively, among a great many tribes.

The dog apart, domestication must be recognized as a cultural feature of the Old World. In the two Americas, the only well developed case of domestication is that of the llama of the Peruvian area.[9] In the Old World, on the other hand, we find the ancient domestication of the horse, cattle, camel, donkey, goat, sheep, pig, chicken, and elephant (half-domesticated in India and Indo-China). The South Sea Islanders have learned (probably independently) to domesticate the pig, and they have readily absorbed the domesticated chicken from the Whites. Native Africa abounds in domesticated animals: sheep, goats, donkeys, cattle, and in the North, horses and camels, the latter two certainly of Asiatic derivation. The breeding, herding, and tending of cattle must be recognized as one of the basic socio-economic institutions of Negro Africa, a subject to which I shall return (p. 153).

Just as the domestication of animals made it possible for man to use them as tools, hence as a source of power, so the cultivation of plants greatly enlarged the role played by the vegetable kingdom in human

[8] It is interesting to note that wolves or wild dogs do not bark: they howl. Barking, in other words, is itself a symbol of domestication. It is a sort of cultured or humanized howl.

[9] The words 'well developed' are important here. For there were numerous approaches to domestication. The Pueblo Indians kept eagles in cages and even reared turkeys. In the California-Oregon region, birds, especially those of striking plumage, were frequently caged, then plucked and liberated. Limited bee culture occurred in a number of tribes. The Indians of the North and Northwest often kept bears, foxes, and other animals as pets. The dog, however, and the llama were the only ones to be systematically bred in capitivity and made to do work for man, and of the two the llama, as stated, was restricted to a relatively narrow district.

economy and industry. Cultivation is basically rooted in the sowing of the seed of whatever plant may be involved, preceded by one or another sort of preparation of the soil for the reception of the seed, from the making of a mere hole in the ground by means of a digging stick to a surface loosening of the soil with a hoe and a systematic turning of the soil, to a considerable depth, by means of a plough.[10] Cultivation makes possible a more ready accumulation of substantial quantities of food at a given place and time. It also enhances the possibilities of food storage for future use. In a still broader perspective, cultivation invites sedentary habits of life.

In certain primitive areas, a kind of agriculture exists which fails to qualify as such, in the full sense of the word. I refer to the so-called 'garden culture' of the Kwakiutl Indians, a form of cultivation highly developed among the Melanesians and Polynesians. The difference from agriculture proper here lies in the fact that the tending of whatever plant may be involved—clover among the Kwakiutl, taro, etc., among the South Sea Islanders—consists largely in weeding out the garden patches and protecting them from intrusion by means of fences of some sort but does not include the sowing of the seed.[11] True agriculture occurs in the two Americas in an enormous and practically continuous area of distribution (see pp. 400, n. 17, 456).[12] It is practised in the grassy plains of Africa,

---

[10] In the sequel, I shall have occasion to point out that the plough does not belong to primitive agriculture in the narrower sense. It does not generally occur in Africa, although it is known in the northeastern area where it can be shown to be of Asiatic origin.

[11] When local techniques are examined with sufficient care, a differentiation of primitive agriculture into hoe culture and digging-stick culture proves only partially adequate. On the basis of his intensive study of agricultural methods in Central America, on the one hand, and in the Melanesian-Polynesian area, on the other, K. Sapper distinguishes the planting-stick culture of the former from the digging-stick culture of the South Sea Islanders. The digging stick is a more substantial tool than the planting stick, being approximately twice as wide in cross-section. No real loosening of the soil is effected by the planting stick; instead, it is merely used to make a hole in the ground, which, after deposition of the plant, is lightly covered with loose earth. Much more is accomplished with the digging stick. In preparation for a single taro shoot, the ground is loosened with the digging stick to a depth of ten inches and over a surface some eight inches in diameter. Then the shoot is deposited and the soil somewhat pressed down about it. (K. Sapper, 'Some Notes on Primitive Agriculture,' Globus, Vol. XCVII, 1910, p. 346; in German.)

[12] The vast majority of plants put under cultivation by the American Indians were indigenous in the New World in pre-Columbian days, and foreign to the Old World. According to Spinden, the only two exceptions to this were the common gourd, Lagenaria vulgaris, and the closely related family of species known as cotton, gossypium. Both of these were common to the Old and the New World in 1500. These plants can be readily distributed by wind and water and must have come to the New World from the Old in one of these ways. In Mexico and Peru,

in India, Indonesia, the Malay Archipelago, and certain parts of the Philippine Islands. More often than not, primitive agriculture is woman's work, a rule to which there are some exceptions. In Africa, agriculture and herding co-exist in many tribes, whereas the persons who engage in these pursuits constitute distinct social classes, the herders or breeders usually appearing as the higher class, the agricultural peasants, as the lower one.[13]

As a sample of agricultural activity among the North American Indians, let me now say a few words about the Iroquois-speaking tribes of the Great Lakes region in northwestern New York and southeastern Canada. These tribes were already located in the above region at the discovery of America, although in ultimate derivation they may perhaps have migrated from farther South. We are in possession of many at times detailed descriptions of Iroquoian life dating as far back as the sixteenth century and comprised in the so-called Jesuit Relations. Towards the middle of that century, five of these tribes formed a confederacy usually referred to as the League of the Iroquois.[14] In the beginning of the eighteenth century, one of the Iroquois-speaking tribes, the Tuscarora, who had previously resided in North Carolina, migrated north and was incorporated with the other tribes of the League to which it was related both linguistically and culturally.

The Iroquois, though always practising hunting with skill and enthusiasm, were in the main agriculturists. They cultivated on a large scale the

where agriculture was highly developed, the principal cultivated plants were maize, bean, and squash, as well as the sweet potato, *Ipomœa batatas* (Aztec *camotl*), chile (Aztec), *Capsicum annuum*, and the tomato, *Lycopersicum esculentum* (Aztec *tomatl*), the last two only in Mexico. Cacao, *theobroma cacao* (from Aztec *cacauatl*) was known in Mexico, Central and South America, and the West Indies. When ground, this fruit seed was made into a drink known as *chocolatl*. Among the several plants cultivated by the Peruvians the most common were the potato (see p. 400, footnote 17) and the peanut. In the valleys of the Amazon, Orinoco, and Plata, maize, beans, and squashes were cultivated, maize here ceding first place to manioc or cassava, of which two species were in use, one with a poisonous juice (see p. 123, footnote 4), the other harmless. Tobacco, of several species, was widely cultivated in both continents. In North America maize was the staple crop, usually associated with beans and squashes. In a complete enumeration a number of semicultivated trees, of economic value, would have to be added to this list. Spinden estimates that the annual value, for the United States alone, of the plants brought under cultivation by the Indians amounts to some three billion dollars. (H. J. Spinden, 'The Origin and Distribution of Agriculture in America,' *Nineteenth International Congress of Americanists*, pp. 271–276.)

[13] It is certain that the combination of agriculture and herding characteristic of so many African tribes has been the result of the mixture of pastoral and agricultural tribesmen, although in many particular instances the historical information is lacking by which this reconstruction could be substantiated.

[14] For other data on the League, see p. 334.

bean, squash, and especially the green corn or maize.[15] The Jesuits tell us of the vastness of their fields and the ample granaries found by them among these people. As the region occupied by the Iroquois was a wooded one, the first stage in agriculture consisted in the clearing of the forests, a task of considerable proportions and difficulty in view of the poor technical equipment of the natives who could only dispose of the stone ax. This necessitated the adoption of a special procedure. A ring of bark encircling the tree was cut off with the ax, then the tree was permitted to stand, die, and dry for about a year, whereupon it was chopped down, the residual trunk being softened somewhat on the surface by a fire started about the base of the tree, the upper portion of which was prevented from catching fire by water being thrown at it. The latter function was performed by women, although the other operations connected with the removal of trees were done by the men. After the field was cleared, the agricultural activities were taken over by the women exclusively. They worked in the field, organized in a so-called 'working bee,' usually under the leadership of a woman supervisor. While thus engaged, the women frequently tugged along their babies, securely strapped to wooden carrying boards, which were as a rule hung up on branches of trees at the outskirts of the field, where the cradles could be seen swinging in the breeze while the women were labouring in the field.

These agricultural activities stood in the very centre of the social and ceremonial life of these tribes and deeply affected their mythological ideas. The presiding deities of the Iroquois were the Three Sisters ('Our Mothers'), the Bean, the Squash, and the Corn. About these female deities and the plants which they represented centred the seasonal ceremonies in the form of the Bean Festival, the Squash Festival, and the Corn Festival, the last and most important of the three taking place about the month of September when the corn stood ripe in the fields ready for harvesting. Similar festivals were held at the time when the berries, such as strawberries and raspberries, ripened in the woods and were picked and brought into the village. In the course of these ceremonies which were somewhat uniform in their general structure, prayers were addressed to the gods, in particular the Three Sisters referred to above, to whom praise was given for past favours, and supplications were addressed for their continuance in the future. Many features of the social life of the

[15] Some fifteen or sixteen varieties of corn were distinguished by the Iroquois, and they used perhaps as many as forty recipes for the preparation of corn. The dishes made of beans and squashes were similarly diversified. (For details see F. W. Waugh, 'Iroquois Foods and Food Preparation,' *Memoir 86, No. 12, Anthropological Series*, Geological Survey, Canada.)

Iroquois with which we shall become familiar later on suggest that the great influence enjoyed by women in Iroquoian society is largely to be traced to their importance in tribal economy in their capacity as agricultural workers.

How the different forms of the food quest are to be conceived in relation to their history and succession in the development of human economy is a separate problem to which I shall return in a later chapter (see p. 512).

Chapter VIII

INVENTION

The Nature of Invention

In the first chapter of this book, when dealing with man in his relation to animals, I had occasion to point out that mentality as such, in the sense of a capacity for logical or abstract thought, does not exhaust the range of difference between man and his animal predecessors. It is true, of course, that man can think; but he can also imagine, which is a special and distinct kind of psychic process. Whereas thought, as logic or abstraction, need not lead to anything new, imagination, though leaning upon the actual or existing, in fact or in thought, adds something to that which pre-existed: it opens the doors into the realm of the new, the heretofore non-existing. The quality of the human mind which enables it thus to expand the realm of thought and ultimately of things is usually designated as creativeness. It would perhaps be going beyond actually known facts to state that animals are wholly devoid of this faculty. Seeing that creativeness is of all things the most inherently psychic and therefore 'inward,' there is little hope that we shall ever know whether creativeness has had its beginning with man or was foreshadowed in the psycho-physical organization of animals. Man, at any rate, is a creative animal. He goes beyond the facts, beyond the existing and the known, to add something new which neither existed before nor was thought of. There is, however, creativeness and creativeness. The poet, religionist, artist, are creative; furthermore, the products of their imaginings are not restrained by any necessity to correspond to matter-of-fact reality or to chime with it—these alluring phantoms have their own feet to stand on. If they can cause a thrill or aesthetic satisfaction or stimulate the imagination of others, well and good.

Not so with that special kind of originality designated as the inventive faculty, of which the mechanical aspect is the most typical. An inventor also goes beyond the facts: he transcends the heretofore existing by imagining and inducting something that has not existed before. But also, the product of his inventiveness must operate within the realm of the established and matter-of-fact. In other words, it must work. If it

118

does not concretely and objectively work, it is a failure as an invention. Then indeed we may designate it as sheer phantasy or romance, but no longer as an invention. It is this combination of creative originality, as spiritual and ideal as any, with the requirements of matter-of-factness and operative worth, which constitutes the earmark of inventing and inventions. Among the various tools and devices of primitive man, some discussed in the preceding, others still to be mentioned, there is abundant evidence of the operation of the inventive faculty. As we saw again and again, man is the tool-maker, but he is not born with his tools as are animals with their organic determinants. The tools are not given him: he must conjure them up and, in doing so, he must be guided not by phantasy alone but by the conditions, requirements, and limitations of the given situation. A prayer or magical incantation works as long as its user believes in it. In other words, its operation or effectiveness is a matter of conviction or faith. Not so a mechanical tool: no tool works or can work by faith. Unless it is a fit tool, it will not work. And when we say that it is fit, what is meant is that it works and that it does so in the setting of the operative characteristics of those materials and the matter-of-fact requirements of those processes which constitute the proper and appointed field of the tool. In this spirit man conceived and created his tools, and when he saw that they worked he knew that they were indeed tools, or at least he accepted them as such.

This, then, is the field of invention. At first there was no artificial fire in the world. The only fire man knew was that produced by the forces of nature without his participation, such as a fire brought about by a stroke of lightning, or the burning forest or prairie of whatever origin. When man wanted or, more accurately, needed fire, he did not have it. I say 'needed' rather than 'wanted,' for the chances are that he did not know that he wanted it until he first had it. How then, it may be asked, did he ever come to invent those devices which made the making of fire possible?

The answer is, unpremeditated discovery. An analysis of the different methods of making fire, by sawing, drilling, or striking, reveals the fact that one or another kind of friction is involved in each case. Now friction, whether deliberately induced for a purpose or not, will on occasion produce smoke, a spark, and hence fire. The observation of such natural origination of fire must have been made by man frequently enough. This was not an invention but a discovery. A discovery, let it be noted, is not a mere observation. To see something is not a discovery; however, if what you see is noted as something worth seeing, it may qualify as a discovery. The discovery, again, is not yet an invention. To have seen fire

naturally produced is not equivalent to being able to produce it artificially. It is only when the discovery is harnessed and made to do man's
bidding that it becomes an invention. And it is here that the objective
characteristics and limitations of the matter-of-fact world must be taken
into consideration. Unless this is done, the discovery will prove in vain
and the invention abortive. Let me add to this that primitive man, though
well if not accurately informed about many matters, is eminently
concrete-minded in his knowledge. Of science he has the unorganized
beginnings, but of scientific theory, not even that. Being innocent of any
insight into what we call principles or laws, as in mechanics, the use
he made of his noted observations was purely empirical.

The cruder methods of making fire by sawing or drilling are further
improved by an additional invention in the pump drill of the Iroquois
and other tribes, or the bow drill of the Eskimo and the Pacific Coast
Indians. Thus an unbroken continuity of revolutions is assured and speed
increased. Wherever we look at the field of material culture, it bristles
with inventions. Take, for example, a canoe. The fact that it is narrow
and long is not casual but significant: it stands for lightness, speed, and
manageability. There is no reason to think that this shape occurred to
man when he made his first canoe, or whatever that thing was. There is
no *a priori* reason why man should have attempted to navigate the waters
in an article shaped thus rather than otherwise. In other words, this
particular shape, a combination of narrowness with relative length, which
has long since become the well-nigh universal attribute of all artificial
floating things, must have been discovered as desirable, because adequate
to the requirements, not through any pre-existing knowledge or theory,
but by sheer observation, accidental and uninduced. The oar or paddle,
in all its particulars as well as in its articulation with the boat, represents an invention; so does the fishing hook which, as we saw, has an
enormous distribution in the primitive world. The purpose of a hook is
to hook on to things, and this it does admirably. It is one thing, however,
to have a fish on the hook and another to pull it out of the water with
it, especially when the fish is unwilling. Thus many a fish must have been
lost before a barbed hook was invented, the same being true of the barbed
arrow or spear head. When thus perfected the point is the entering wedge
for the weapon; the barb, on the other hand, impedes its exit. This being
what the occasion required, the barb, as an invention, proved adequate.[1]

[1] I might add that the formulation here presented in which invention is coupled
with discovery, need not be taken as a theoretical dogma, implying the universality
or inevitability of the application of this principle. Granted familiarity with the
relevant processes and man's capacity for imagining new combinations, it is after
all conceivable that here and there inventions were made by a mind unfertilized

The composite harpoon of the Eskimo wears the unmistakable earmarks of an invention or of a series of inventions. Though spear-like articles may be picked up in nature, it knows no composite spears or harpoons. Now this is precisely what a harpoon is: a composite spear. In this case—the history of the article being, as usual, unknown—the origin of the device seems fairly plausible. The utilization of a spear for fishing is of course widespread, and we are safe in assuming that the ancient Eskimo used this weapon for hunting aquatic mammals. These creatures are powerful and not to be downed by one spear wound, nor may victory be expected until the hunter has had a chance to throw at least a second spear. And so the idea arose of preserving contact with the spear, and hence the animal, by attaching it to the hunter by means of a thong held in the left hand while the spear was thrown with the right. When this scheme was put into operation, it would no doubt often happen that the spear, subjected to the double pull of the animal and the thong, would break when the animal attempted to escape, with the result, once more, of the hunter's losing his catch. It is in this situation that some ingenious Eskimo may have thought of making a spear or harpoon operate as a unit by fashioning it in two or more parts in the first place, and then connecting the parts in such a way that they could separate under pressure, without breakage. When this had been carried out the invention was accomplished, for now the tension to which the harpoon was subjected led it to separate along the points of articulation, as determined by its structure.[2] The most important part, namely, the point, now imbedded in the animal,

FIG. 38. GREAT ANDAMAN HARPOON, with major part of shaft omitted. (After A. R. Radcliffe-Brown, *The Andaman Islanders*.)

by appropriate discoveries. Whether and when this happened among primitives it is, of course, impossible to determine, in view of our scant knowledge of the history of primitive inventions. We do, however, know from modern evidence that the process of mental experimentation is not unknown among inventors, rare though it naturally is. Whatever the psychology, let me add, the final test of any invention is its behaviour in a concrete material situation. Only after this test has been successfully passed is the invention recognized as such.

[2] A. R. Radcliffe-Brown describes a composite harpoon among the Andamanese (*The Andaman Islanders*, pp. 441–442). Here it consists of two parts, shaft and point, the latter detachable and—as among the Eskimo—provided with a thong held by the hunter. It is used for hunting turtles and dugongs, aquatic mammals ranging about eight feet in length. Like situation, like invention (see Fig. 38).

preserved its contact with the hunter by means of the thong attached to it and held tight by the hunter. A gigantic creature, like the whale, would in such a case pull the hunter and his boat along with him, a lively process but not necessarily a fatal one to the hunter. In due time the latter could repeat his attack, and not infrequently, victory was his in the end. In the case of a smaller animal, like the seal, the thong is sufficient to prevent it from escaping very far, and when it returns to the original breathing hole for air, the hunter has little trouble in dispatching it. Now this, of course, is not history but an historical hypothesis, but barring details, it does not seem to be a rash one.[3] (See pp. 87–88 and Fig. 27).

Another invention is the feathered attachment to the shafts of arrows, which in some instances runs parallel to the sides of the shaft, in others is spiral with reference to the shaft, which makes it even more effective in so far as a screw-like motion is thereby communicated to the arrow. As a consequence, such an arrow bores its way through the air, as it were, and then similarly through the flesh, making a formidable wound. The German psychologist, Wilhelm Wundt, was inclined to ascribe this invention to magical analogy, the arrow, first identified with a bird, being constructed so as vaguely to resemble one. The greater success of such arrows may then have led to the perfecting of the device. This roundabout way of arriving at the result, *via* magic, though conceivable, is to my mind unnecessary in this instance. A feather might easily chance into this position, say as a decorative attachment to the counterweight placed here to balance the point. This would provide the necessary condition for the pregnant discovery.

A good illustration of the relation between invention and discovery is provided by the release used in traps among many different tribes, the operative item consisting in a sapling bent out of its natural position and attached to a part of the release mechanism (Fig. 39). The pull of the bent sapling provides the necessary tension to keep the device in equi-

---

[3] Obviously enough, the ball-and-socket device connecting the point with the middle part of the composite shaft is a later development or invention, plausibly reducible to the discovery that two objects placed in such a position and subjected to friction, as the position of one with reference to the other varies, will tend to develop a ball-and-socket-like surface of contact. Once such an observation was made, a deliberate shaping of the two pieces into a ball-and-socket form was an easy next step in technique. The fact that two objects in this position will tend to develop such an articulating surface is proved by the presence of the ball-and-socket feature in bones, human and animal. Example: the hip joint. No directing mind can be assumed here, nor can it be held that two bones thus juxtaposed possessed the ball-and-socket feature from the beginning: it was formed mechanically through the continual pressure at the point of contact of the two bones placed in such a dynamic situation. Another possibility is that some Eskimo observed this very fact on a human or animal skeleton, and applied the discovery to the harpoon.

librium until the crucial moment of the release arrives. How, it will be asked, might the idea of a tree acting in this fashion occur to anyone? The answer in this case is at hand. In walking through the jungle many a savage must have had the experience of being struck in the face by a branch dislocated by a man walking ahead of him. Here then was an observation which brought home the fact that a branch or young tree, when bent out of position, presents power. Subsequently, when the hunter needed a source of power to replace himself in conjunction with a

FIG. 39. TRAP OF KALAHARI BUSHMEN. (Drawn by Miss Harriette Akin.)

trap, he thought of the tree and made use of it, fitting its energy into the operative situation.

All the inventions here mentioned and numerous other ones of the same general kind refer to the most primitive conditions; still others, associated with the cultures of more advanced tribes, became responsible for the art of smelting metals and the different devices employed in the domestication of animals and the cultivation of plants.[4]

---

[4] The staple food-plant of South America is cassava or manioc, which, for best results, requires a somewhat dry, sandy soil. It was not cultivated along the moist Andean coast but was in general use in the eastern section of the continent, either alone or in combination with maize. In its natural state cassava contains a poisonous juice unfitting it for consumption. For this reason a special method of preparation had to be adopted. First the cassava is grated, the resulting mess being gathered in a container, called 'cassava canoe.' Then the 'cassava squeezer' or matapi comes into use. The device is made of plaited itiviti strands (Fig. 39a, 1). 'It is next hung up by the collar [Fig. 39a, 2] on to a suitable projecting beam [a], while a strong pole [b], passed through the ankle ring, is tucked under a fork made by tying a strong stick [c] at an acute angle to a house post [d]. The pole acts as a lever, the fork as the fulcrum. By the woman throwing her whole weight, usually sitting, on

It may be observed here incidentally that the operative conditions, or the uses to which an article is to be put, often provide limiting conditions which in a sense predetermine the technical solution, thus leading to comparable results whenever such a solution is reached. Take, for ex-

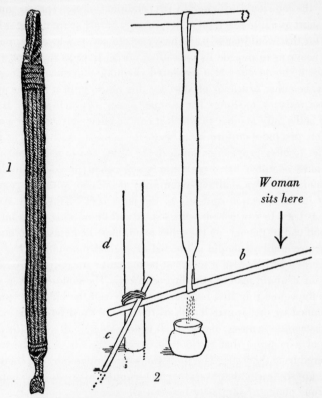

FIG. 39a. MATAPI, OR CASSAVA SQUEEZER. (Walter E. Roth, 'An Introductory study of the Arts, Crafts and Customs of the Guiana Indians,' *38th Report*, Bureau of American Ethnology, pp. 277–299.)

ample, an oar. Abstractly speaking an oar can be long or short, light or heavy, circular in cross-section or flat, wide or narrow, of even width throughout its length or otherwise; also it can be made of more than one material. Now, in accordance with local conditions or chance, most of these shapes and materials may have been used for oars at one time or

the free end of the pole, the matapi is extended, its diameter consequently diminished, the contents squeezed, and the poisonous juice, which is expressed through the interstices of the plait, allowed to run down and drip into a vessel placed beneath to collect it.' (Roth, *op. cit.* under Fig. 39a.)

another and a variety are still being used in a pinch, including even the human arms when a rower or paddler permits his tool to slip into the water and, perhaps, be carried off by the current, leaving him stranded in his boat. But if you want a *good* oar—and this is what at length you do want—the end result is limited by the conditions of use. The oar must not be so short as not to reach the water, or only barely so, nor must it be too long, for that would make it too heavy or clumsy as a lever; it must not be so heavy as to impede its operation, nor so light as to cut off the resistance it should offer in a measured rhythmic movement. It must not, finally, be either brittle or pliable, for this would unfit it for use against a dense resisting medium. The manner again in which an oar is used, which is the only manner in which it can be effectively used in a sitting position, precludes uniformity of shape throughout its length. The blade, in order to offer proper resistance to the water and thus induce propulsion, must be either flat or preferably somewhat curved longitudinally and laterally, like a shallow spoon open at the end, with the concavity facing in the direction opposite to the movement of the boat. Anyone who has tried to row a boat with a stick will know what is meant here. The butt end of the oar, on the other hand, must be adjusted to manipulation: preferably it should not be flat or angular but more or less circular in cross-section. Also it must not be too bulky for a firm grip nor too slight, or it would tend to slip during rowing. The middle section of the oar is the connecting link between the blade and the butt; its length is determined by the proper length of the oar; it must be strong enough to withstand the stresses, and so on. It is desirable, finally, that the oar be made of a material that could float, so that the oar could be readily recovered from the water. The limitations here imposed by the conditions of use are so drastic that every oar is—emphatically—an oar, implying numerous points of similarity between all oars.[5]

The same point applies to numerous other objects, such as canoes, knives, pots, releases in traps, hooks, knots, and so on and on. In all these instances the technical conditions of use are bound to result in similarities, more or less precise, in the objects designed to solve the technical problem. If the situation allowed of only one solution, the object solving it would always be identical. This, of course, is a limiting case. The fewer the possibilities, at any rate, the more likely are similar solutions. As a general result of this principle it is to be expected that many objects or devices, independently invented in different parts of the

[5] See my 'Limiting Possibilities in the Development of Culture' (*History, Psychology, and Culture,* pp. 44–46).

world and in different tribes, will in certain particulars be more or less similar. It is well to remember this point when we come to the discussion of cultural similarities in their relation to diffusion (see p. 470).

It is customary to restrict the term 'invention' to objects or devices. While no objection need be offered to this terminological limitation, it should be understood that from a psychological as well as a mechanical standpoint, the concept 'invention,' with precisely the same connotation, is not less applicable to processes than to things, processes executed by means of tools or by the hands alone. The boat-maker, basket-weaver, wood-carver, carpenter, smith, acrobat, dancer, typist, all employ certain sets of motions to achieve certain desired technical results with speed and accuracy. These motions are themselves subject to certain technical limitations inherent in the operative situation, but they will be found to differ, more or less, as between person and person, with results, perhaps, equally good, or bad, or with varying results. It is well known that a tennis player who has not learned, in the very beginning of his career, the proper grips and positions required by what is called 'form,' is likely to find his game fatally handicapped. Similarly, when a typist acquires the habit of striking the keyboard with one or two fingers, he is well on the way to becoming a poor typist. Now, all these technical achievements can be taught and are being taught by those possessing the technique to others who are learning it. At the same time, we know from experience that the student, though frequently adopting certain peculiarities of the master's technique, also develops certain individual adjustments. Such adjustments or grips or shifts become crystallized as 'motor habits' (Boas) and presently come to operate automatically; so much so that the operator is usually incapable of analyzing what precisely it is he is doing or giving an account of his operations. Probing into the matter further, we discover that such motor habits were dynamic inventions before they became habits. They have about them the earmarks of an invention, in so far as a new element is introduced—in this case a 'position' or motion, not a thing—and fitted into a mechanical, therefore, operative and matter-of-fact, situation so that it works and accomplishes the desired result. The case, I repeat, is strictly parallel to that encountered in the invention of objects or devices, with the only difference that the something invented is not an object but a process. It is interesting to note, in this connexion, that these 'dynamic inventions,' having originated from numerous shifts and counter-shifts in the midst of a moving mechanical complex, seldom rise into consciousness except occasionally at the point where they make their first appearance. Even by a deliberate act of will one does not readily succeed in lifting a motor habit, routinized dynamic invention, into the light of awareness. For this reason the teaching of techniques consists to a large extent in the presentation of examples to be followed, rather than in verbal directions of what one is to do. Anyone who would rely on verbal instruction in teaching a novice how to skate, play billiards, thread a needle, or handle a saw, is almost bound to fail. His example, on the contrary, may well enhance the rapidity of the learning process. 'Let me *show* you how' expresses the pedagogy of these situations.

Primitive and Modern Inventions

It is customary in our mechanical age to think of ourselves, our time, and Western civilization in the light of invention. We feel that we are the inventors *par excellence* and regard mechanical inventions as the very corner-stone of modern culture. To a degree all this is very true. On the other hand and in the context of this book, it will be useful to consider not only the differences but the similarities between modern and primitive invention. The similarities here are considerable. First comes inventiveness itself as a psychological trait, that variety of creativeness which receives its particular stamp from its practical-mindedness. In this respect, as we saw, man differs very markedly from the animal, but as between man and man, all seem to have it without distinction of race but with a marked variability in individual endowment. We do not know, it is true, the precise limits of this variability. Here, as in all similar instances, the difficulty of drawing a sharp line between first and second nature seems insuperable, but that there is such individual variability in mechanical gifts can scarcely be doubted. Some people are born with mechanical fingers while those of others are 'dead'; some can almost be said to see with their finger-tips, whereas others cannot use them even when they see with their eyes. Within these extreme limits there are other variations which, as I said, we cannot with any degree of assurance allocate as inborn or acquired, but it seems certain that such differences between individuals are not restricted to modern man but characterized mankind from the beginning. This statement applies equally to what may more accurately be described as a talent for manipulation, and to that more specifically psychic quality of inventiveness of which we spoke before. At the same time it is important to realize that the inventor, as a professional, is not present among primitives. We know of no primitive individuals who devote themselves wholly or even largely to invention as such. This is both a cause and a consequence of the fact that inventions among primitives are few and far between. Apart from the presence of individual differences in inventive capacity, the principal similarity be-

tween primitive and modern invention lies in the relationship of both to
discovery. The principal difference, on the other hand, as between primitive and modern, lies in the intellectual equipment of the inventor and in
the conditions under which he does his work. Most of the time, at any rate,
the modern inventor is, like his primitive brother, a capable utilizer of
discoveries.

Consider, for example, the role of discovery in the invention of the
incandescent lamp. When Edison entered this field electric lighting based
on the consumption of carbon or other material in an open-air lamp
had already been attempted with partial success. Edison began his
exploration by rapidly reaching the conclusion that an arc-light was
unfit for indoor illumination. What he therefore set out to solve was the
problem of an incandescent electric lamp. At this point the Edison Electric Light Company undertook to finance Edison's labours at his Menlo
Park laboratory. Followed days and nights of unrelenting toil. Not
before forty thousand dollars had been spent on the experiments, did a
lamp, put on the circuit, light up and maintain its light for almost two
days. A new principle of lighting was thus established. But the brittle
filament employed did not come up to commercial requirements. What
was needed was a durable burner. So a search was begun for a material
which could be reduced to a perfectly homogeneous carbon. Here
Edison turns discoverer. He carbonizes everything he can lay his hands
on, tissue paper, soft paper, card boards, threads, fish line, vulcanized
fibre, celluloid, coco-nut hair and shell, varieties of wood, punk, cork,
flax, grasses, weeds. In all, some six thousand substances were carbon-
ized and tested before Edison chanced upon a bamboo binding rim of
a palm-leaf fan, which, finally, proved to possess the properties required in the specifications. A man was then sent to Japan for a supply
of bamboo, and before long the major problem was solved.

Edison, it will be seen, knew what he wanted the 'thing' to do, knew it
more precisely, perhaps, than a primitive would know it in a similar
situation; but he did not know how it would do it or what that thing
would prove to be; and so he launched upon a voyage of discovery, the
end of which proved successful but might have proved a failure, in the
course of which he had to test nature in its myriad forms and wait and
watch for the discovery to come. Knowing what he wanted, he was of
course impatient though persistent, but—quite like his primitive brother
—he was unable to take the next step without a discovery which, as
always, was on the knees of the gods who, in this case, proved kindly
disposed to Edison.

The respect in which Edison's labours differed from those of the

primitive inventor, on the other hand, is this: In the case of Edison, as
of many other modern inventors, a background of technical knowledge
and of human organization were there to expedite and promote his
inventive efforts.[6]

Another recent example of a highly organized attempt at invention is
presented by the history of the once famous Liberty Motor. In this case the
order of events was: first, the realization of a need; then, an organization
of technicians; finally, the requisite invention. What occurred, in brief,
was the following: Some time after America entered the War President
Wilson came to realize that a radical improvement in aeroplane motors
had become a necessity. In consequence he charged his Secretary of the
Treasury, Mr. McAdoo, with the accomplishment of this task. The latter,
who had had previous experience in engineering enterprises, retained two
consulting engineers, the brothers X and Y, and placed them in a position where they could exercise a free hand in the selection of assistants,
the acquisition of laboratory facilities, and the expenditure of practically
unlimited funds. X and Y then proceeded to summon three experts, A, B,
and C, each one of whom was occupying a consulting position with one
of the great automobile concerns: A was a specialist on carbureters,
B on gases, and C on machine-designing. These experts were made familiar with the problem and the requirements that were to be met. The
weight of the motor was not to exceed $1\frac{1}{2}$ to $1\frac{3}{4}$ pounds per horse-power.
This specification was to be adhered to even were the motor to be fed with
very low-grade gasoline, an important provision in view of war conditions. The parts of the motor were to be standardized and made interchangeable so that the motor could be disassembled and reassembled
even under most adverse conditions, and broken or deranged parts could
be promptly replaced. The standardization of the parts of the motor was
required as an essential condition for economical mass production.

Supplied with these specifications, A, B, and C went into consultation
in a room of a Washington hotel and remained there, their meals being
served to them, until the designs for the motor were complete in all
particulars. In view of the many mechanical details involved in this
task, a staff of trained designers were placed at their disposal.

When this much was accomplished, the engineers X and Y 'farmed out'
different parts of the motor to a number of machine-manufacturing concerns, being guided in their choice by the special facilities of these concerns. When the separate parts of the motor were thus produced, they
were brought to Washington and there assembled. The motor was next
subjected to the most exacting experimental tests, more than fulfilling

[6] This sketch is based on Deyer and Martin's book, *Edison, His Life and Inventions*.

all expectations. As usual in such cases, however, certain constituent parts of the motor were found to be slightly altered in shape through the stresses and strains to which they were subjected in the tests, a well-nigh inevitable occurrence no matter how precise or detailed the theoretical specifications. In this final shape, then, the parts of the motor were utilized as models for the building of tools to be employed in the manufacture of the motor. After this was done orders were once more 'farmed out' to concerns located far and wide over the entire country.[7]

In comparing these two modern instances with what we know to be true of primitives, both the similarities and the differences in the two situations come to light. We have professional inventors, the primitives lack them. Among us the inventor is an expert who devotes himself to the task of inventing after the fashion of any specialist; among the primitives inventions are made by ordinary people, though no doubt in many instances the ordinary people are endowed by nature with an inventive bent. Our inventions, therefore, can be anticipated, deliberately planned, and controlled to a nicety; among the primitives none of these things can be done. The modern inventor is a highly trained individual. He is equipped with a body of theoretical knowledge which guides him in his work and saves him from becoming lost in blind alleys.[8] He is also an experienced technician, at home among many varieties of materials and master of many of the often highly specialized skills needed in the handling of tools and the control of mechanical processes. He has been trained in the short-cuts of modern machine production. He can read a blue-print into a machine and visualize a machine from a blue-print. In addition to all this, inventors and technicians have themselves undergone a process of highly diversified specialization, each specialist being

[7] This sketch of the Liberty Motor, when first made in my *Early Civilization*, was accompanied by the following foot-note which I want to reproduce here: 'This history of the "Liberty Motor" is given on the authority of my friend, Ralph A. Gleason, an inventor and engineer, to whom I owe whatever insight I possess into the nature of the mental processes, often so mysterious to the layman, which result in inventions.'

[8] As an additional illustration let me cite the following interesting project. Some three or four years ago the National Physical Laboratory at Teddington, England, announced the plan of constructing a wind-tunnel to test the 'drift' on projectiles, such as shells and bullets. For this purpose use was to be made of the large amount of compressed air accumulated in similar experiments with aeroplanes. This air was to be released through a small tunnel at speeds as high as 700 miles per hour. The projectile or bullet, then, would remain stationary, all the motion being supplied by the air stream. One of these objects was to be suspended in the tunnel, while automatic electric recording instruments were to tell the effect of wind forces. Whether this project was carried into effect I am unable to say. But no matter.

particularly familiar with certain kinds of processes, tools, and problems: mechanical, chemical, structural, and so on.

Of this many-sided training, knowledge, and skill, the primitive inventor, by the grace of God, knows nothing. There is no theoretical knowledge for him to acquire. He is subject to all the vicissitudes of false leads; he is, moreover, a busy man doing all sorts of things as a member of his tribe, for—to remind the reader once more—he is not a professional inventor devoting all his time and thought to the technical task at hand. The modern inventor, before embarking upon a particular invention, familiarizes himself in great detail with everything that has been done before him along similar lines, and the particular direction in which his invention, or improvement on a preceding invention, is to lie, is also clear to his mind. The primitive inventor is not a student of the history of techniques or of tools. Being, as we assumed, of a mechanical turn of mind, he may have paid more attention to the technical devices of his tribe than did some of his mates, but no more than that. Also, he knows but vaguely what it is that he wants to accomplish: the relative definiteness with which the modern inventor can think of something which is as yet not there is itself the product of a highly trained intelligence with a mechanical or technical slant. Then again, the primitive invents in the open, as it were, surrounded by nature in the raw with nothing to go by but the average run of experience, the incidental hints of discovery, and the sparse background of the technical *status quo* of his tribe and culture.

To the modern inventor also nature is an indispensable companion. However, his work is done in a laboratory. Now a laboratory, from one angle, is nature harnessed. The experiments he makes with it under these conditions are condensed in space and in time. Like Edison with his innumerable samples, he merely has to stretch out his hand (or have his assistant do so), and the required substance is produced. The role of accident is thus minimized. Time and space, as I said, are reduced here by the presence in the laboratory of all those elements of nature the inventor is likely to need in his work. He is not forced to rely, as must his primitive brother, on the accident of encountering these elements in the course of his uncontrolled experience. As a result, he is capable of producing in a day or a week or a year what under primitive conditions might take a century or an era, or not occur at all.

The enormous enhancement of inventive possibilities by the availability of a laboratory equipment is carried even further by the presence of human organization and co-operation centered around inventions, as exhibited in the case of the incandescent lamp and in that of the Liberty Motor. This feature also is lacking in the primitive setting: as there are no professional inventors or technological experts, so also there is no co-operation in invention. Each one has to rely on his own wits and the accidents or good fortune of his private experience.

It would seem then that the contrast is overwhelming. This, however, is not the case. Primitive or modern, not everyone can invent. As stated before, there is no reason to doubt that individual variability in mechanical ability or ingenuity is a universal fact, quite independent of time or place or cultural phase. This special ability, as we saw, comprises two factors: originality or imagination, which is a gift for thinking along new lines; and practicality of a special sort, which is a talent for giving the original idea a form calculated to function, when materialized, in an objective and matter-of-fact world. The inventor, to be sure, concocts many devices and can do many things which nature unaided is incapable of accomplishing; nevertheless, in constructing his device with a view to operation, the inventor uses natural materials and must consider their qualities and limitations as well as the operative conditions in which they will function as parts of his device. If he neglects this double orientation, his invention, though still original, will not operate. It might then qualify as a tricky thing, a would-be invention, but not in the proper sense as an invention. Now this combination of the ideal with the real, of creativeness with concrete-mindedness, is something peculiar to the psychology of invention. In this respect also the modern inventor and his remote precursor may join hands as of one kind. Further, as we saw, primitive invention represents, at least in the majority of cases, a deliberate utilization of an accidental discovery. This aspect, though partially disguised by the high degree of deliberateness in modern invention, is present here also. At one point or another, a modern inventor, though knowing what he wants and what he might have to use, finds himself in a situation where he must test things out, trying and trying again, in anticipation of a discovery which might come if his preparations happen to be adequate, but which nevertheless might be withheld. At any rate, he cannot know, except vaguely, what he will find until he finds it, and these are the earmarks of a discovery.

In these several respects then, which, as will be recognized, lie at the very root of the invention complex, the primitive and the modern situations are strictly comparable.

There are two further standpoints from which primitive invention needs to be examined. Impressed by the overwhelming number and capacity of modern inventions, we are often inclined to minimize the accomplishments of the primitives. We are thus prompted to forget that invention is easier when it can lean against a background of numerous other inventions. The very presence of this background, the opportunities it provides for comparative study, the stimulation of the technological faculty by observed similarities, differences, merits and defects, furnish a mighty impetus for the next invention. Everything else being equal, the more inventions there are the more will come—and the quicker.[9] From this angle, primitive inventions which occurred in a world sparsely set with inventions were infinitely more difficult. In this perspective, the incandescent lamp, in all its glory, pales before the dimmer light of the hesitant and modest flame which flickered forth from under the hands of the man who used the first fire-saw or fire-drill. Similarly, the long procession of inventions which followed upon the wheel—the cart with its road-bed, the train with its steel track, the tractor which carries its

[9] Compare the figures given by W. F. Ogburn in 'The Influence of Invention and Discovery,' *Recent Social Trends*, vol. I, p. 126. (Reprinted by permission of the author.)

PATENTS ISSUED IN THE UNITED STATES 1840–1931, BY FIVE-YEAR PERIODS		INVENTIONS REPORTED BY DARMSTAEDTER, 1450–1899, BY TWENTY-FIVE-YEAR PERIODS	
5 YEARS ENDING	NUMBER OF PATENTS	25 YEARS ENDING	NUMBER OF INVENTIONS
1845	2425	1474	39
1850	3517	1499	50
1855	6143	1524	84
1860	16,997	1549	102
1865	20,779	1574	109
1870	58,833	1599	127
1875	61,024	1624	135
1880	64,496	1649	129
1885	97,357	1674	237
1890	110,493	1699	218
1895	108,465	1724	180
1900	112,325	1759	281
1905	143,791	1774	410
1910	171,560	1799	680
1915	186,241	1824	1034
1920	197,644	1849	1885
1925	203,977	1874	2468
1930	219,384	1899	2880

Now patents, though not to be identified with inventions, are evidently correlated with them. Again, the selection of 'inventions' made by Darmstaedter must, of course, be subjective to some extent. Still, the increase of patents and inventions in the two periods selected is impressive; and, as the rate of increase also tends to increase, even though not consistently, the figures certainly suggest that the number of inventions in existence at any time is an important factor in determining the number of inventions likely to follow within a given period, more or less.

road with it—were both easier and less basic than the wheel itself. As one looks upon the wheel from the standpoint of a world in which there was no wheel, its appearance may be likened to a miracle giving wings to pedestrian creatures and opening up unlimited possibilities of further unfoldment.

And, finally, there is this one last point: Having been impregnated almost fatally with the seed of evolutionary thinking, we like to conceive of everything in the history of culture as a series of transformations. Let us not forget, then, in connexion with invention, that persistence is an equally ubiquitous and no less significant phenomenon. The basic primitive inventions are not dead—they live on among us, either as constituent parts of later inventions, or side by side with them. The lever, though not understood theoretically, was used as an empirical device among many primitives, and it still constitutes one of the pillars of modern mechanics. The sapling, bent out of its natural position to provide the dynamic factor in a primitive trap, is the remote forerunner of the spring which runs untold millions of watches and performs numerous other tasks in modern technology. The achievement of Alexander the Great in cutting the Gordian Knot, though dramatic, did not equal that other achievement—the tying of the first knot. And this knot, in the midst of an ever growing family of knots, is still with us. There are, moreover, numerous persons, mostly male, in our present society incapable of tying a single knot, and if and when they learn to do it, they learn something very primitive and very old. Knife and hammer, pot and basket, house and boat, are all primitive inventions, still used in forms essentially like those of their primitive models. By far the larger number of domesticated animals and cultivated plants were subjugated to the will and use of man before the modern age dawned. In other words, what the primitives did in bringing into the world these basic and difficult inventions was to lay the foundation for man's career as a toolmaker, to sharpen the line separating him from the animal, thus adding to culture numerous devices, material expressions of ideas, which have come to stay and continue to live on among us as important though modest elements of our mechanized civilization.

Chapter IX

DIVISION OF LABOUR AND PROFESSION

When primitive society as a whole is compared with the modern scene there is no gainsaying the fact that division of labour and specialization in particular pursuits stand out as characteristic of the modern age, whereas occupational uniformity accompanied by individual versatility is characteristic of primitiveness. Take, for example, the basic occupations of the food quest. By and large, there are in a primitive group no special providers of food for the rest of the community. The food quest is, as it were, a universal service. Take hunting as the type of most primitive economy—all the men of the group are hunters, and all the boys are trained to become such. Similarly, the needs of safety and war do not in the simplest societies lead to the differentiation of a special warrior class, such as we find in many African tribes. On the contrary, every able-bodied man is a potential warrior and is fitting himself to become a brave, that is, an outstanding warrior. In the plant-gathering pursuits of the women, again, every housewife must do her share, not merely as a cook but also as the provider of that which is to be cooked. At the same time the illustrations already mentioned reveal the presence of a division of labour of a very sweeping and significant sort. It is, after all, the man who is hunter and warrior, whereas the woman is the gatherer of the wild products of nature and the cook. There are exceptions to all this, to be sure. Here and there, men will do the cooking or even the gathering of plants, and in certain tribes, almost anywhere in the primitive world, individual women will occasionally join the ranks of hunters or warriors. In more developed societies, as are those of Africa, regiments of women —Amazons—are not unknown, as, for example, the famous feminine body-guard of the king of Dahomey, these women being especially trained for the warrior profession and acquiring sufficient expertness in it to enjoy a high reputation both for their proficiency in the art and for their ferocity.[1] Still it will be admitted that these are exceptions on the background of an opposite and widely prevalent principle.

[1] These women were known in Dahomey as 'king's wives' or 'our mothers.' Burton, writing in 1862, computed the number of female troops as 2500 (one third of these unarmed). In earlier days the Amazons consisted mostly of criminals or

This primary division of labour has significant after-effects in later phases of civilization when agriculture and herding or animal breeding develop. The primitive herder is a man, and there are good reasons to believe that domestication was man's invention. The primitive agriculturist, on the other hand—again with some exceptions—is woman, and there is equal ground for the belief—proof here is impossible—that women were the inventors of cultivation.

We must, it is true, grant that a primitive local group is more self-sufficient and more definitely dependent on its own industrial activity than is a modern local group, and that every family within such a group is not unlike an industrial unit within the tribal whole, able if necessary to take care of itself. Still, this generalization should not be carried too far. Even in industrially very primitive Australia, for example, we find a modicum of industrial exchange between local groups. The men of one local group will have a reputation for skill in the manufacture of stone knives, those of another, of spears, javelins, or shields, a fact sometimes associated with the presence or profusion in a given locality of the needed materials. On certain periodic occasions members of these tribes foregather at very crude 'markets' for the exchange of their respective products. Nor is the psychology of supply and demand wholly foreign to these natives. Thus a man who has some stone knives to exchange will be careful not to reveal to his adversary in trade just how many knives he has, hoping that an underestimate of the actual number on the part of that adversary will make him more willing to exchange his shields or spears at an advantage to the maker of the stone knives.

In other industrially more advanced societies this aspect of industry is developed much further. Thus, for example, in Polynesia expert woodworkers in general, and in particular boat-builders, represent a professional group which enjoys considerable social prestige. This is especially true of the boat-builders, whose occupation, often hereditary, acquires among these sea-minded peoples a quasi-religious halo. In Africa, again, industrial specialization goes still further. We find here not only a definite occupational and social division between herders and agricultur-

faithless wives who became warriors, at the king's pleasure, instead of being sacrificed, as was the custom. Later any unmarried woman could be chosen by the king for his body-guard. An Amazon was sworn to celibacy, a commitment frequently honoured in the breach. The usual penalty was death. The Amazons, in Burton's days, were armed with blunderbusses (a short muzzle-loading gun), muskets, and long razor-shaped knives with an 18-inch blade. In battle the Amazons were known for their courage. As tokens of their prowess they were wont to carry off human heads and jawbones. (See C. G. Seligman, *Races of Africa*, pp. 74–76.)

ists, but also occupational groups of salt-diggers, wood-carvers, fisher-men, and smiths.

The status of the smith in Africa is so interesting as to deserve special comment. Among the agricultural tribes of Africa the hoe naturally oc-cupies a central position in their economy equal to that of the weapons. The iron-smith, as the only one who can provide the metal parts of these tools, enjoys the prestige corresponding to the importance of this func-tion. The social position of the smith is not by any means always the same. In the region extending from the Zambezi to the Guinea Coast the smith often rises to the position of highest chief or king. If this privilege is denied him he may yet be used by the king as prime minister or chief adviser. In eastern Africa he also appears as a private physician to the king. In the great states of the western Sudan, where a guild-like or-ganization of crafts has developed, the chief smith occupies an especially prominent position at court. An aura of supernaturalism frequently de-scends upon the personage of the smith, who understands how to trans-form reddish ore into pure metal and this into articles of use. The entire process connected with the melting and working of iron is often sur-rounded by taboos and special observances. When, as in western Sudan, the smith also rises to exceptional prominence in the ancient secret so-cieties, his importance is at its highest.

His social position changes materially as we pass to those tribes of North and East Africa which stand under Hamitic influence. Though he maintains his status in industry he is socially despised. In the entire easternmost part of Africa, among the Somali, the Gala, and the Masai, the smith belongs to the most despised class, with which one avoids all contact. The Somali noble never enters a smithy, and the Masai warrior first rubs his hand with oil before he grips the weapon prepared by the smith. Similar conditions obtain among the Herero and Ovambo of Southwest Africa. This social inferiority of the profession of the smith transforms its representatives into an endogamous caste which inter-marries within itself. Between the two extremes of social exaltation and inferiority there are numerous transitional stages.

The situation with traders is very similar. In Australia and America the trader as a specialized profession is unknown. In Oceania, especially in Melanesia, where trade-mindedness is pronounced and a variety of exchange media are in general use, no trading class as such has emerged. In Africa, on the other hand, with its roads, markets, and a high degree of professional specialization, there are traders, known as a class among many tribes and especially developed as a profession in the western

Sudan. There are, of course, also numerous media of exchange, from cowry-shells to cattle and iron bars.

So also in the field of religion. When contrasted with the modern situation where the vast majority of people are purely passive as to religion, all primitives are active participants in the religious realm, both as experience and certainly as an institution. Personal religious experiences, though not universal, are certainly as common among primitives as they are rare among moderns, and all primitives place at the service of their religion or magic their early acquired facility in singing and dancing. Also, every primitive man or woman is to a degree a magician, not merely in the sense of believing in magic or benefiting or suffering through it, but in the more active sense of performing magical acts. On the other hand, even in the crudest communities, as in Australia, there is a special class of medicine-men who are experts in magic. They are well versed in all esoteric lore and can be relied upon to perform the relevant rituals with all the necessary care and skill. They are expert at the art either of bringing about illness or death by magical means, or of curing sickness, as the case may be. When functioning in this latter capacity they are compensated by social prestige and also, commonly enough, by payments of one sort or another. In Oceania the priest is a member of a more or less exalted profession, not a mere magical practitioner. The priests are village treasurers, in Melanesia, genealogists, in Polynesia. This differentiation is also present in North America, where among the Pueblo peoples, the southern Sioux of the eastern Plains, and the Pawnee a priest is something more than just a medicine-man. In Africa this distinction becomes quite precise in many districts. The magician here is a powerful figure, to be sure, capable of doing both good and evil by plying his craft, but he is not a priest, whose social position is beyond dispute and one of whose functions is to attend upon the recognized tribal or national deities. Here, in fact, we can find in an incipient form a phenomenon more conspicuously present in European society of the Middle Ages, namely the recognition of the magician by the priest. The latter is socially exalted but he has forgotten some of the useful techniques of his ancestors, and on occasion we find him standing in fear and trembling before his less reputable but more formidable brother, the magician or fetish-doctor, whose art is too dangerous for mere contempt.

What applies to technical work in general is true even more emphatically about craft or artistic work. Here we once more encounter the prevalent division between man and woman. Man, for example, is the

woodworker, as in Oceania, the Northwest Coast of America, or anywhere else, for that matter.[2] He is also the carver or artist of that particular technique. A Maori or Haida woman may understand the fine points
of an artistically embellished boat, club, or ceremonial pole better than
does an outsider or a White man, but she does not understand it as well
as her man does, and certainly it is not her occupation. Among the
Iroquois, where bark-work and woodwork, including the making of
masks, were man's occupations, some women have been known to practise minor woodwork or mask-making, but a woman always did this on
the sly, as it were, as something distinctly improper and not to be ad-
vertised.

Among the Eskimo, men decorate the weapons which they also make,
and they carve the very skilfully executed bone figurines so typical of
Eskimo craftsmanship. They also carve, with exquisite skill, the needle-
cases used by women to preserve their ivory needles, which may be made
by persons of either sex. Women, on the other hand, who cut to pattern
and sew the very adequately made garments of these people, are also the
artists of their trade, decorating the garments with relatively simple
patterns consisting of attractively arranged bits of hide in *appliqué*.

Among the Iroquois the men work in bark and also take care of whatever little woodwork there is, while the women embroider the garments,
which in this group of tribes and in the Woodland culture area generally
are distinguished by floral patterns, as to subject, and by an elaborate
curvilinearity, as to form.

Among the Plains Indians the more realistic painting on the tents and
shields are the work of men, whereas the characteristic and beautiful
porcupine-quill (in more recent days, bead) embroidery, coloured and
geometrical, on the shirts, moccasins and bags, is invariably the handiwork of women. When, however, a woman fashions and embroiders a
pair of moccasins for her husband or admirer, she is responsible merely
for the geometrical pattern, and the symbolism is supplied by the man.
The men, of course, take care of the horses, which they use in war and
chase and steal with zest and much accruing honour from other tribes,
but the women do all the work connected with buffalo hides: together
with men, or alone, they skin the animals, tan the skins, cook the meat,
grind the dried meat into pemmican, cut the skins to pattern, make the

---

[2] It is curious that this particular industrial activity is even more definitely
androcentric than hunting or fighting. Whether in primitive or modern times, it
would be hard to find an example of women professionally engaged in woodwork,
except, of course, in altogether individual instances.

clothes and, as already stated, decorate them with embroidery. They also use the tougher hides for tent material, erect the tents or *tipis*, and dismantle them when camp is broken.

The division of function is even more apparent in the socio-political field—I might have said fatally apparent, as far as woman is concerned. The warrior, as noted before, is of course a man, a fact of double connotation, occupational and social. The fact that the warrior or fighter, who is skilled in the wielding of weapons, is always a man, inevitably stands for a certain social pre-eminence. It is in fact likely, though difficult to prove, that one of the earliest incentives for the socio-political disfranchisement of woman came in consequence of her helplessness when confronted with her armed male brother, whose natural physical superiority was thus further enhanced in a most emphatic and—shall we say with her?—dangerous way.

Then comes leadership. Men not being born equal, one respect in which they are unequally equipped by nature is in capacity to lead. In some tribes, this leadership takes a very modest and definitely restricted form; in others, it means social pre-eminence, privilege, power. When examining leadership from the standpoint of division of functions, we encounter, for the first time, a marked one-sidedness: the plus is all on the side of man, the minus on that of woman. In economy, technology, art, there was division of labour, often between the sexes, as we saw, but no discrimination: man did his share, woman hers. The economic discrimination against woman, which threw her out of many professions and made her dependent upon man, is conspicuous among primitives by its absence. Similarly in art: the taboo against the woman artist, writer, or actress, so characteristic of the high Asiatic civilizations and of those of Europe, from antiquity almost to yesterday, is foreign to primitive society. Not so in socio-political matters. Woman's unique and irreplaceable role in the family and household saved her from demotion, within these limits, but in the wider field of social and political functioning, especially with reference to the exercise of power, she was not thus protected. At any rate, in this important sphere we find her pushed to the wall. The leader—chief, king, priest, ceremonial official, judge—is pre-eminently a man. We know, of course, of women in each and all of these positions, but these are individual instances—the opposite is the rule, which gives a peculiar slant to primitive society, from this angle, and, more broadly, lends a strange, not altogether wholesome colour to the entire history of mankind. As to power, openly and officially exercised, this has always been a man-made world. Nor should we misunderstand certain facts, in particular places, which seem to point the other way: for example, the political rights of Iroquois women or the presence of queens in Africa. True, women made and unmade Iroquoian chieftains; this in itself is important, and exceptional. But the chiefs, meaning now the 50 League chieftains, were men, nor does history or tradition record a single lapse from masculine leadership. There were here certain other chieftainships, honorary ones, bestowed for special deserts. Among such 'pine tree' chiefs there were some women. This again is significant, of course, in so far as the *relatively* high position of women among the Iroquois is thus revealed. But it must also be remembered that a 'pine tree' chieftainship (the term implying that the bearer of the title is 'as straight as a pine') was a strictly personal distinction which vanished, as a social factor, with its bearer: meanwhile things political pursued, undisturbed, their androcentric course.

As to Africa, the title 'queen' there, as we shall see further on, is applied to the mother and the wife of the king. These two personages are, of course, exalted; they possess lands, wealth, have their own retinues of slaves, servants, officials, enjoy prestige and influence. But here the matter ends. The queens do not rule, the affairs of state do not concern them, we know of no official councils at which they figure. Human relations being what they are—and by and large very much the same, wherever and regardless—it is to be assumed that here and there the queen (or queens) may have had something to say to the king—but this was family business. The fact remains that an African queen is merely her king's queen, not the people's queen. She does not rule; in matters of state she is little more than a decorative appendage. Further, the existence of a queen (or queens) among these peoples does not reflect the position of women among them any more than the queenships (in these cases, in their own right) of Elizabeth or Maria Theresa or Catherine II reflected the status of European women in their times and countries. The socio-political disabilities of African women were radical; as to the queens, they merely represented an extension of royal prerogatives to those who bore kings or were wedded to them.

Next to the political sphere, that of religion is heavily weighted against woman. There are, we know, medicine-women as well as men, also female shamans. The mediums at the shrines of African gods are often women. In Melanesia, West Africa, North America, women, in different tribes, band together into religious societies. But there is another side to all this. An African medium is, after all, not the priest; the latter is a man, always; quite as in North America, where medicine-women and sorceresses occur, but the priests, whether Omaha or Zuñi, are men. Similarly with religious societies: those of men are always more numerous, and they set the style; the women's societies are patterned after them. To this must be added those numerous instances, strikingly exhibited in Australia, where women are strictly excluded, except at most as spectators, from all the more sacred activities and rites. Of course, women are drawn into the spell of faith and rite not less fully than are men: they give as much, perhaps more, but they receive less, by way of privilege, influence, or initiative.

In connexion with religion there are two factors here. On the one hand, the limitation of woman's socio-political sphere is reflected in her partial disabilities in the national, social, ritual aspects of religion. On the other, woman is handicapped in matters sacred by the fact that she herself is not merely a human but also a woman—a peculiar creature with a distracting and at times repulsive periodicity in her life cycle, a peculiar and only partly understood relationship to the fact of birth, and a fascinating but often excessive and always disturbing influence on man *via* sex. She is, therefore, herself quasi-sacred, and often wholly unclean; she must be treated with circumspection; taboos cling to her person; to let her loose in the sacred realm might upset the whole order of things mystical as well as secular.

And finally, woman is also side-tracked in regard to property and all that pertains thereto. Among tribes lacking unilateral social units, woman's proprietary inequality is least marked or, in certain instances, absent altogether. But in sib [3] society the picture changes. Wherever the male principle dominates descent, property inheritance follows suit; in the majority of tribes where descent is maternal, inheritance of property is nevertheless through males. There are a few tribes in America and India where both descent and inheritance follow the spindle. This situation may give woman proprietary equality, but also it may not. On the Northwest Coast, where maternal property inheritance is one of the most firmly established institutions, *what* is inherited, including a large variety of religious and ceremonial prerogatives, concerns men, not women—woman passes it on, man uses it. Property, the most valuable and honorific part of it, uses woman as a medium of transfer, not as a point of delivery.

As in the case of religion, woman herself is in many instances part of man's proprietary equipment. When this is the case, she belongs to the realm of things owned (achieving distinction in this not too flattering status), rather than to the wielders and manipulators of owned things.

---

[3] A sib is a unilateral social unit, like a clan (descent maternal) or a gens (descent paternal). For particulars see p. 330.

In property, as in religion and politics, woman's status, instead of rising, tended to fall with the transcending of primitiveness. There she remained throughout history. Even today and in the Western world, with official emancipation all but achieved, real equality of status for women remains rather a hope for the future than an accomplishment of the present.[4]

In this, as in other matters, there are exceptions. Margaret Mead, the genial anthropologist whose fate it is to upset established notions, has given us a picture of a primitive matriarchate *de facto* in spite of contrary institutions *de jure*. The tribe are the Tchambuli in northern New Guinea (once German, now British), to whom the following section is devoted.

The Tchambuli

Among these dwellers of a New Guinea lake-shore who number a bare 500, life runs an easy course. The major occupation of the food quest consists in fishing, which is almost altogether in the hands of women. The excess of fish, which is almost always great, is traded, together with shell money, for sago and sugar-cane produced by tribes dwelling in the bush. The currency used in such markets consists of the *talibun*, or green snail shells. These shells themselves are derived from far away Wallis Island of the Arapesh coast and are as much objects of inherent worth as they are currency. Thus marketing with *talibun*, says the author, is 'shopping on both sides,' the possessor of the currency extolling the value of his coin as much as the possessor of the food stresses that article. Besides the fishing, women also do the weaving. The men, on the other hand, in addition to engaging in innumerable ceremonies, are the artists *par excellence*, each one having a variety of skills at his disposal: dancing, carving, painting. 'Every man's hand,' we are told, 'is occupied, etching a pattern on a lime-gourd, plaiting a bird, or a piece of a mask, brocading a house-blind, or fashioning a cassowary-bone into the semblance of a parrot or a hornbill.'[5]

The tribe is divided into patrilineal groups bearing a common name and owning strips of territory. There is a dual organization also, all the

---

[4] However, let us distinguish. Formal rights, recognized institutional leadership, are one thing; psychological situation, personal knots, tied and resolved, another. Let us remember that French women have been known to smile condescendingly upon the emancipatory efforts of their foreign sisters. 'What if we lack the right to vote?' they said. 'We have the men. They control the vote, we control them, *voilà!*' Who can tell but that they were right?

[5] Margaret Mead, *Sex and Temperament*, p. 244. (Reprinted by permission of William Morrow & Company, Inc.)

members of one gens belonging to the Sun people, those of another to the Mother people. Marriage is between these divisions, although not invariably so. When a boy is between eight and twelve, he is due for scarification. Squirming, he will be held on a log, while a distantly related maternal 'uncle' cuts patterns on his back. While he is making the best of this pitiable situation, an elaborately conceived ceremonial is taking place all about him in which he himself is, however, the least important item; in fact no one pays any attention to the boy. The one solid group upon whom he depends for support, food, and protection are the women, nor is there any split between the women of his blood group and his wife, for he marries the daughter of one of his mother's half-brothers or cousins and calls her by the same name that he also applies to his own mother, *aiyai*. On his wife or wives the man depends for his food and comfort. Not only is the business of fishing controlled by women, as already said, but the most important manufacture, namely the mosquito bags, two of which will buy a canoe, are made entirely by women. The initiative in marriage is taken by the 'weaker sex,' and it is for the man to make himself attractive and desirable. 'He will learn to play the flute beautifully, to play the flute that sounds like a cassowary, the flute that barks like a dog, the flutes that cry like birds, the set of flutes that are blown together to produce an organ-like effect.' [6]

The women's attitude towards the men, we are told, is one of kindly tolerance and appreciation. They enjoy men's games and the theatricals put on by the men for their benefit. At a certain dance the men appear in wooden masks balanced in the midst of a head-dress of leaves and flowers, in the centre of which dozens of little flowers are thrust on sticks. Some masks are male, others female; the former carry spears, the latter brooms, but the dancers are all male. The older men usually wear male masks, whereas the younger and more frivolous ones wear female masks. It is with the latter that the women flirt during their dance, trying to attract their attention and to arouse them. The solidarity of women and the unstable and brittle relationships of men are illustrated by a picture of the inside of a Tchambuli dwelling house: 'The entire centre is firmly occupied by well-entrenched women, while the men sit about the edges, near the door, one foot on the house-ladder almost, unwanted, on sufferance, ready to flee away to their men's houses, where they do their own cooking, gather their own firewood, and generally live a near-bachelor life in a state of mutual discomfort and suspicion.' [7] It is against the old men that the young men have a particular grudge. They say bitterly that

[6] Mead, *op. cit.*, p. 253.
[7] *Ibid.*, p. 258.

these 'use every bit of power and strategy which they possess to cut out their young rivals, to shame and disgrace them before the women.' [8]

It must not be imagined that the men's houses, which among many tribes are strictly taboo to women, are so here also. On the contrary, on important ceremonial occasions the women come and stay. 'For the scarification of a child, the woman who carries the child enters the men's house in state, and sits there proudly upon a stool. If there is a quarrel, the women gather on the hill-side and shout advice and directions into the very centre of the house where the debate is going on. They come armed with thick staves, to take part in the battle if need be. The elaborate ceremonies, the beating of water-drums, the blowing of flutes, are no secrets to the women.

'As they stood,' continues the author, 'an appreciative audience, listening solemnly to the voice of the crocodile, I asked them: "Do you know what makes that noise?" "Of course," came the answer, "it is a water-drum, but we don't say we know for fear the men would be ashamed." And the young men answer, when asked if the women know their secrets: "Yes, they know them, but they are good and pretend not to, for fear we become ashamed." And they add: "We might become so ashamed that we would beat them." ' And so they might indeed, for the men, when all is said, are stronger and the official institutions of the Tchambuli are with them. But the point is that they do not beat them, instead they worry about the women. 'What the women will think, what the women will say, what the women will do, lies at the back of each man's mind as he weaves his tenuous and uncertain web of insubstantial relations with other men.' [9]

Of course, the Tchambuli only number 500 people at a lake in northern British New Guinea. Also, the author in her enthusiasm may have overdrawn the picture somewhat, a point which might have become clearer had she elaborated the following chapter, 'The Unplaced Men and Women,' more fully than she does. Still, the mass of details and the care with which the picture is drawn leave no doubt of the essential correctness of the sketch. And what occurs here must evidently be regarded as no less than possible, and as such, instructive.

[8] *Ibid.*, p. 259.
[9] *Ibid.*, p. 263.

Chapter X

PROPERTY

The Ownership of Property

As everyone knows, the ownership of property, especially in the form of individual ownership, stands in the very centre of the capitalistic culture of our Western world—so much so that even the imagination has come to be completely in its grip. It is next to impossible for most of us to conceive of a state of society in which property or individual property does not exist. This more than anything else makes so many people shudder at the very idea of communism, in which property, though not eliminated, is shifted from the individual to the social or national level. As usual in such instances, ideologies readily suggest themselves which make the proprietary impulse out to be an inherent organic component of man's make-up. Owning property, striving for property, is felt to be an essential, irreducible element behind human initiative. Remove it, and the zest for life will go with it. The very meaning of human life in society seems irrevocably wedded to the sense of owning things. That this in cold fact is actually so is not by any means certain. Perhaps property with its associates is but a cultural accretion, a convention of living, and history-made, like many other artifices of its kind. A survey of primitive ideas about property is likely to prove instructive and illuminating in this connexion.

A review of the relevant facts leaves no room for doubt that property as an historic phenomenon is indeed co-extensive with man as we know him. In fact, we might, if we chose, read the beginnings of the proprietary sense into the lives of animals, where we should, as usual, be handicapped by the unavoidable thinness of our insight into the animal psyche. We do not really know in any direct way how animals feel about property or how they think about it, if they do, but we are cognizant of their behaviour. An animal will fight for the preservation of its body; the latter, however, is property only in a remote and metaphorical sense just because it is so obviously the material embodiment of whatever it is that constitutes the animal as a living and psychic thing. On the other hand, when we observe an animal fighting for its young, its food or its

146

home, the proprietary sense is manifested in a more direct way, one more relevant to our problem. Now most animals with whose habits we are familiar actually do this, and certainly all the higher animals. Over and above the general pugnacity of animal kind with reference to all but their 'friends,' there is this special behaviour when the animal is at home or in the presence of its feed. That its behaviour in these two situations reveals an attitude containing something beyond mere pugnacity or readiness to fight with strangers seems fairly obvious. It is also significant in this connexion that man's closest animal associate, the domesticated dog, who has learned from man so many other things, has so thoroughly absorbed man's proprietary inclinations. When it comes to the master's property, which in a sense is *his* property, the dog is an unmitigated egotist and an incurable snob. Man himself, with the possible exception of the landed proprietor, seldom equals in the virulence of his proprietary sense the corresponding behaviour of the watch-dog. Apparently there was here a native inclination which provided a basis on which the rest could be built up.

However this may be, man, everywhere and always, had some property. Nor is it true, as some social scientists have once supposed, that the primitives were addicted to communal or group ownership rather than the ownership of things by individuals. The patent facts do not at all support this *a priori* conception, which must be regarded as one of the *ad hoc* concoctions of the evolutionists who were looking for something less specific than individual property from which it could be derived, and found this something in communal ownership. An impartial survey of the data makes it plain that ownership by groups as well as by individuals is present everywhere. Communal ownership is most frequently found in conjunction with the territory and its resources. Hunting regions, fishing shores, agricultural fields or gardens, are apparently without exceptions owned by a group, whether it be a tribe, sib, family, or village. This is true in so many well-authenticated instances—in Australia, the South Seas, Africa, or America—that citation of individual instances is not necessary. In addition to districts owned by particular social divisions, there are frequently hunting territories or agricultural or grazing fields which constitute public or free lands or fields—free, that is, to all within a larger local or tribal group who may want or need to make use of these districts. We find this institution, for example, among the Polynesians as well as in Melanesia, frequently also in Africa, both among the agriculturists and the herders. And we find it again in America, both among some of the hunters like the Athapascans and among such agriculturists as the Iroquois.

It is fairly clear that what the primitives mean by ownership here is not by any means equivalent to land-ownership in the later periods of history. They do not really consider that the community, family, or clan own an agricultural field or a hunting region in the same sense in which a modern landlord owns his lands, or for that matter, a landlord of Egypt, Rome, or Mediaeval Europe. What is 'owned,' in these primitive communities, is the usufruct, not the land itself. The quasi-legal concept here is that individuals belonging to a particular group have the right to use certain districts for whatever they can obtain from them by way of vital stuffs.[1]

What is true of territory also applies frequently to the primary objects of physical need, first of all to food. This is also frequently regarded as a communal rather than an individual possession. With certain exceptions, when the product of the chase or the catch of a fishing expedition, or the harvest from a field, is brought in, these things are held in common by certain groups among whom the stock is distributed, often with much ceremony and with due regard to the social or relationship status of particular individuals, or in proportion to the role played by them in the hunting, fishing, or agricultural enterprise. This is often true, for example, in Australia, among the Eskimo, and the Iroquois, the Trobrianders, and the agricultural Negroes of Africa.

These communal possessions do not preclude the ownership of property by individuals. By and large, what an individual makes, wears, or uses as a tool or weapon, is owned by him. This applies both to men and to women. In this sense, individual property is universal among primitives. On the other hand, communal ownership is, of course, not unknown in modern days. I do not mean merely such things as rivers, lakes, roads, which as a rule are owned by the community, state, or nation, but also the joint ownership of stock companies and the like, with subdivision of proceeds proportionate to the investment, in this case not of effort or labour, but of capital.

The theory regarding primitive communism as a prelude to the individual ownership of later history, must therefore be rejected, at least in this drastic form. It contains, however, the germ of a truth, to this extent:

---

[1] An identical attitude, it seems, with that of the Russian peasants who, driven from the southern regions by the inroads of Mongolian hordes, migrated farther north in the course of the twelfth, thirteenth, and fourteenth centuries, and settled there. To these peasants the land as such was God's or the Count's; what they themselves claimed was the right to use it. It is for this reason that later, when vast lands were distributed by the government to individuals of the nobility, the peasants living on these lands offered no resistance, as long as they were permitted to ply their normal occupations and benefit therefrom.

in modern Western society, individual ownership has, as we know, acquired a significance and a role far beyond the importance of this institution among most primitives. Also, not a few individuals in our society own many more things than any primitive ever dreamed of. On the other hand, ownership of the essential articles needed for life or of the territories from which these are derived, in other words, just those things which in later times came to represent the most coveted forms of individual property, constitute among primitives the prerogative of the group: what is needed and used by all is held in common. To this extent, then, it may be justly said that communal ownership is exemplified in primitive society, individual ownership in modern. But let me repeat: it is a mistake to deny to primitives individual ownership. It is ubiquitous and apparently as old as man himself, or older.

Another conspicuous fact regarding primitive property is the extension of proprietary ideas to things other than material and the apparent ease with which this extension is achieved. Primitives own not only houses and boats, pots and baskets, tools and weapons, but also such things as dances, songs, stories, magical rites and formulae, individual names, and even guardian spirits. Here again individual instances need not be cited because the fact is universal. Myths, rituals, medicinal practices, dances, songs, are owned among the Pacific Coast Indians in the same sense in which they own material property; the same is true among Malinowski's Trobrianders, and what applies to these two regions is true everywhere. This spiritual or functional property, like its material counterpart, refers either to groups or to particular individuals. Thus a religious society will own its ritualistic technique, its stories, myths, dances and songs; but certain songs, dances, stories, and magical rites will also be owned by individuals.

This extension of the proprietary domain to things other than material is especially interesting in so far as it illustrates the characteristic facility with which the primitive mind travels from the material to the psychic, the relatively slight distinction it draws between things which exist as substance and others that are mere acts or ideas.[2]

[2] This is, of course, a field made familiar in more recent days by the problems arising in connexion with the right to the products of one's mind, the right of authorship with its accruing benefits, the right to an invention, both as idea and as its material embodiment, the right to a thought or an expression used in writing. The fact that there are such things in the modern world as infringement of a patent or copyright, stealing of someone's play, plagiarizing another's ideas, quoting from another's writing without quotation marks, and the further fact that these things or acts are generally condemned by the modern conscience, indicate that the concept of ownership of property other than material has gained recognition among us, or is headed that way. It may be added, however, that this entire field of our

Property Inheritance. To own property is one thing, to be born as its owner, another. The inheritance of property, in other words, is a cultural phenomenon in some respects quite distinct from the fact of ownership as such. Whatever may be said of the universality and antiquity of the latter, the inheritance of property is certainly not a pristine feature. Animals, if in a vague sense, may be owners of property but not inheritors of it, except in the still vaguer sense of just stepping into another's shoes. The inheritance of property, then, is a convention developed in history, which implies a human mind and a certain ideology.

From a psychological standpoint, the proprietary sense is a sort of extension of the sense of ego or selfhood: the ego expands beyond the limits of its mental domain to the ownership of the mind's body and beyond it to those things which are owned by the individual. This is best illustrated by the ease and universality with which ownership is claimed in things produced by one's hands, and only a little less markedly, to the things worn or used by a person. A thing that owes its existence to the labour of our hands sucks in the personality of its maker during the very process of its becoming. When it is done it is part of you, its maker. Similarly, what one wears and uses becomes part and parcel of the very spirit of the wearer or user. With less facility but an unmistakable zest, the ego expands still further, to the things a person owns.

To all this a definite and terrible limit is set by a factor beyond our control, namely the death of the individual. Thus the entire proprietary complex collapses through the removal of the very centre around which it was built up. We cannot save the individual from his fate. Not so with the proprietary complex—it might be preserved to extend beyond the individual. It is precisely this that is accomplished by the inheritance of property. The individual passes away but the property passes on. The road it takes in its passing on, moreover, is not left to accident. If I myself cannot own it, I want at least to make sure before I go that it will be owned by those whom I have conceived or fathered, and into whom I have instilled the proper regard for this property as well as the technique of its use. In this way the perpetuity of the proprietary complex is assured. In proportion to the definiteness of the limits within which this extended proprietary complex will operate, and to the certainty of the very fact of its prospective operation, is the tendency of the original

culture, as well as the fights and litigations to which it has led, would impress the primitives as very strange and perhaps incomprehensible. To them these things are perfectly obvious, and they might well be inclined to condemn us as crude, undiscerning, or unsophisticated, for making so much fuss about it.

owner to project his ego also into this future property which will live on when the individual is no longer there.[3]

In speaking about property inheritance it is necessary to distinguish between non-deliberate inheritance by custom or law, and deliberate inheritance initiated by the will of the donor. Communal property is not subject to the latter kind of inheritance; individuals pass away but the group survives, and with it goes from generation to generation the ownership of its communal property. This is often the case also with individual property. Broadly, where paternal inheritance prevails the father's property will pass on to his children; where the maternal line is followed, the same will hold for the woman's lineage. If the kind of property involved is in a given tribe man's property, then it will under maternal inheritance be passed on through a man's sister to her sons, that is, his nephews. This is, for example, the case among the Pacific Coast Indians, among whom most of the ceremonial prerogatives belong to men who alone have the right to exercise them, and are passed on as just described. The same situation is found among the Trobrianders and, of course, among any number of other tribes in all parts of the world.

In other instances an individual wills his property deliberately. Customary routine must still be observed, but not without the intrusion of personal choice. Thus in Australia it not infrequently happens that a fond father, member of a maternal inheritance group, chooses to will certain weapons or other valued articles to his son who, under the prevailing rule of maternal inheritance, is not his lawful heir. The same has been recorded among the Indians of the Pacific Coast, especially among the Kwakiutl, whose customs have been studied by Franz Boas with a great deal of care. Maternal property inheritance here is complex both in content and in mechanisms, and it partakes of the halo of semi-sanctity typical of the proprietary institutions of this region. This notwithstanding, fathers have been known, again and again, to will valued prerogatives to their sons or, for that matter, to other persons of their own choosing.

One of the indirect consequences of the inheritance of property is its accumulation in the hands of particular individuals. Even among prim-

---

[3] The psychological mechanism explained in the text is not often brought into consciousness just because it is so natural and, therefore, trite. Its operation extends not to individuals alone but to families as units, where it has become responsible for the concepts of the heirloom and the 'family estate.' It is also observable in less personal institutions such as industries when they become the hereditary property of a long succession of related individuals, gaining in self-esteem and in a kind of sanctity with each generation. In his *Forsyte Saga* the late Galsworthy has given us marvellous samples of the operation of these mechanisms.

itives an industrious or shrewd individual may accumulate considerable property by his personal efforts, as for example, in Melanesia or Africa; but he cannot accomplish as much as a succession of generations of individuals. By inheritance individual articles of property or entire proprietary complexes may converge upon one individual from different directions, leading to an impressive total accumulation.[4]

What Property Means

In the modern Western world property usually means comfort if not luxury, ability to indulge in many personal whims; it also means power, and in particular, power over people, ability to buy and control. As the landowner expands psychically in the realization that he shares with the Divine Being, as it were, the ownership over the earth, so the industrialist or banker who disposes of vast wealth divides with his superhuman prototype the control over the world's affairs. In other words, to us property as wealth means in the first place what it can be used for to acquire the comforts of life, and in the second place what it can be used for to control human beings and economic or social affairs. Among primitives these aspects of the proprietary sphere are on the whole developed much less markedly. Among the more primitive tribes in particular, and among all primitives in comparison to moderns, the habitual mode of life does not differ much as between man and man, whatever their social or economic status. All but a few, generally speaking all who can, work; work physically and along the same lines as the rest of their tribal mates. Also, all enjoy about the same kind of food and 'comfort.' This is true even of Polynesia and Africa where considerable accumulation of property is common and social distinctions are marked, and it applies in these two areas to all but the supreme chief in Polynesia or the king in Africa, and even they do not, in a strict sense, belong to what we might call a leisure class, a class, that is, whose privilege it is to enjoy life's luxuries without exerting corresponding efforts, or any at all. Then again, what wealth can buy counts for little here. At most it is the direct exchange value of one's possessions that is felt to be a privilege and an asset, that is, the ability to acquire something that someone else has and that you want more than what you happen to own. The most interesting

[4] It is perhaps worth noting that the proprietary sense tends to develop to unusual heights in those who hold their property by inheritance. To those who acquire property as a result of their efforts, it remains one of the incidents or fortunes of life; to those who inherit it, it tends to appear as part of the order of nature. They are born into it and come to regard it as an element in their personal make-up, like the bodies they are born with: they cannot dissociate themselves from it.

aspect of the proprietary sense is, however, the purely social or ceremonial setting which in more than one instance lends property all the
social worth it represents.

It has often been observed that among African herders the wealthy man
who owns vast numbers of flocks can scarcely be said to put these to
any economic use whatsoever. What he actually needs for his family and
household, ample and plural though these may be, amounts but to
a fraction of what he owns in flocks and might, if he chose, dispose of
in return for something else. This, however, he refuses to do. Instead, he
permits his flocks to multiply; in fact, he exerts persistent and not infrequently successful efforts in this direction—and lets it go at that. The
number of animals in his flocks is to the African herder and breeder
a source of joy and pride. His social prestige goes up with the size of
his herds. The fact that his cattle or sheep or goats are fine specimens
exalts his ego immensely. As a wealthy and successful herder, he is a
great and admirable man, envied by those less fortunate. But this is
where the matter ends. From our economic standpoint the whole business
represents little but waste of energy and effort; but our standpoint is not
that of the Africans.

Another case in point is the situation we find among the Indians of
the Pacific Coast. This latter instance is doubly interesting because property here reigns supreme. It has been described and should be recognized
as the dominant social value of these people. In property-mindedness they
are second to no one, not even to ourselves. Even individual names are,
among the Haida, derived from property. They talk property, live property, manipulate property, as lustily as any group of modern business
men. What property means to them is, nevertheless, something entirely
different from what it means to us. As I have already stated, here as
among most primitives the rich man and the poor man live pretty much
in the same style. The house of a West Coast chief may be a little larger
than that of an average native, and some allowance should also be made
for the accumulation, often enormous, of boxes, coppers, and blankets,
great stores of which are among his belongings, temporary though these
may be. But outside of this his life is like that of any other man. With
others he hunts, fishes, fights, trades, performs ceremonies. With them he
faces those hazards which primitive life in nature brings with it. Still,
the accumulation of property must be described as standing in the very
centre of the social values of these people. What is accumulated, however, is valuable not in its bearing on the standard of life, nor for its
worth in exchange, nor for the power it might give one to manipulate
humans. Rather does its value lie in what might be called its ceremonial

aspect. This is illustrated by the institution known as the potlatch. A potlatch is a feast given by one individual to another, or by a family, clan, or phratry [5] to another. On the occasion of such a feast, in which some participate as actors, others as spectators, the feast-giver distributes among his guests presents in the form of blankets, canoes, oil, or other valuables. Also, on such occasions, much property is neither used nor distributed but destroyed outright. For example, huge quantities of the greatly prized seal oil will simply be burned. The more generous the presents given away, the more lavish the destruction of property, the greater is the feast and the higher the esteem that thus accrues to the giver of the feast, whereas the rival to whom the feast is given suffers a corresponding drop in his social status. Nor does the matter rest there. If the former guest or guests are unable or unwilling to return the feast, their song is sung—they will never again enjoy public esteem. It is therefore incumbent upon him or them to give a return feast. At this second feast, the presents distributed on the initial occasion must be returned—with interest, which is the higher the longer the return feast has been delayed. Among the Kwakiutl the interest amounts to 100 percent, if the return feast occurs one year after the initial feast. The amount of property destroyed on this second occasion must also be correspondingly large. If the individual or group have accomplished this successfully, social prestige favours them once more, at the expense of the initial feast giver who now finds himself debased in status.

In connexion with the potlatch the so-called 'coppers' have come into use. A copper is an object hammered out of native copper or perhaps out of a sheet of the metal left behind by a White man (see Fig. 40). The intrinsic worth of a copper is nil but its symbolic or ceremonial value may become enormous. These coppers are given away at feasts and the value of a copper rises with the magnificence of the feast at which it has figured. When a copper thus given away at a potlatch is in the course of time returned to the original owner at the second feast, its value rises once more. Thus it comes about that some of these coppers are worth hundreds or even thousands of blankets (a blanket has come to be a unit of value among these Indians, amounting to about 50 cents). Each copper is known by a name which bespeaks its high ceremonial significance. Among such names are: All-Other-Coppers-Are-Ashamed-to-Look-at-It (this specimen was worth 7500 blankets), Steel-Head-Salmon (6000

[5] A phratry is a social subdivision of a tribe, which is, as a rule, further subdivided into clans or gentes. When the number of phratries is two, as among the Tlingit or Haida, they are also referred to as 'moieties' or 'dual divisions' (see p. 330).

blankets), It-Makes-the-House-Empty-of-Blankets (5000 blankets), and so on. A broken copper is even more valuable than a whole one. As a copper passes from hand to hand, certain parts of it are broken off, but the several separate parts continue to function as a unit. Finally only the T-shaped section is left whole, which is a copper's most valuable part, amounting to about two-thirds of its total value. Among the Kwakiutl a chief may break a copper and present the broken parts to his rival at a feast. Then the challenged chief might take his own copper, break it and return both broken coppers to the original owner at the return feast. This will be accompanied by the usual enhancement of prestige. Instead of doing this, however, he might throw the pieces of both coppers into the ocean. Then he is a truly great man, for no possible return can be expected from this process, whereas in instances like the preceding, when the broken coppers continue to circulate at feasts, there is always the expectation of receiving back what one has given away, and more besides.

It will now be seen that the essence of social position among these people rests in these feasts. The feasts themselves represent the most coveted and appreciated use to which wealth can be put. The social value of wealth, then, does not lie in what it does for your

FIG. 40. A KWAKIUTL COPPER. (Boas, *The Social Organization and Secret Societies of the Kwakiutl Indians*.) This copper appears in Fig. 41 (p. 156) at the extreme right of a row of coppers.)

mode of life, nor in what you can buy for it, nor in the power over other individuals which it might bring, but in the opportunity it gives you to give that accumulated wealth away as presents or destroy it outright at a potlatch. If there is accumulation here, it is in anticipation of distribution or destruction. What counts is not how much you possess but how much you can afford to part with. The feasts here are given not so much to people as against people. 'Rivals fight with property alone,' say the Kwakiutl, and the best way to humiliate one's rival is to 'flatten him out' by means of a sumptuous feast.

On account of the vast amount of property involved in a feast, even a prominent chief cannot afford to give such a potlatch alone. Usually he is assisted in such an enterprise by his family, clan, phratry, or friends. Not infrequently most of the wealth of an individual, clan, or other social division may change hands on occasion of a great feast. Property here is in constant flux. It is given away and destroyed in astounding quan-

Fig. 41. Mortuary Display of the Body of a Chief, Enclosed in a Casket and Lying in State in His House at Kasa-an, Surrounded by His Personal Effects and the Tokens of His Wealth. (Boas, *op. cit.*)

tities. And as property passes from hand to hand or disappears, the social prestige of individuals goes up or down [6] (see Fig. 41).

These customs illustrate the radical difference in the significance of property between these Indians and ourselves. The enhancement of social

[6] An interesting excrescence of potlatch psychology may be seen in the marriage practices of the Kwakiutl, among whom these ceremonial feasts have acquired such extravagant prominence. When a man wants to marry a girl he presents his prospective father-in-law with a considerable amount of property, in return for which he expects to receive not only his bride but some of the privileges of her clan, including at times the crest itself. The wife is then regarded as the first installment of the return payment on the part of the father-in-law. As children are born to the couple, further payments are made by the father-in-law. The more children, moreover, the higher the interest on these payments: for the first child, 200 percent interest, for the second and third, 300. After this the father-in-law is regarded as having acquitted himself. At the same time he has redeemed his daughter, and in consequence the marriage is regarded as annulled: she is now free to return to her parents. She may also, if she chooses, remain with her husband. Then, say the Kwakiutl, she is 'staying in the house for nothing.' The husband, however, may be unwilling to stake the continuance of his matrimonial alliance on the disposition of his wife. In such a case he will make another payment to the father-in-law, thus extending his claim upon her. This peculiar and to us ridiculous way of treating marriage, while incomprehensible if taken alone, becomes feasible enough in the light of potlatch psychology.

prestige through the distribution and squandering of wealth might at first
blush impress us not only as esoteric but as absurd. It must not be forgotten, however, that this very element is not by any means absent from
our own customs, namely those once described by Veblen as 'conspicuous
waste.' The household equipment and ways of life of one of our rich
men may within limits contribute to his comfort, luxuries, sporting proclivities, and the like. But there is also in all this an element of showing
off. He wants to display his wealth, to give evidence of its extent. It is
well known that many members of our wealthy leisure class may live
economically and even stingily in their regular daily habits, but when
it comes to a public occasion, a ball, banquet, garden or yachting party,
an excessive amount of wealth will be squandered on these. They have
advertising value. They show how much the owner can afford to waste.
Similarly the jewellery which bedecks a millionaire's wife is not so much
a measure of his personal appreciation of the lady, as of her function as
a show-window of his financial prowess: the wives of other rich men,
not so fortunate, cannot afford quite the same measure of splendour. The
wealth of the Coast natives can thus be designated as ceremonial wealth,
and the potlatch as a symbol of its extent, in a particular case. The entire
complex has little indeed to do with that basic significance of economic
goods which leads one to describe them as necessities or even luxuries of
life. On the contrary, the whole situation in which wealth here plays a
part could be more accurately characterized as conventional, symbolic,
and to a degree, playful.[7]

A Maori Feast

The complexity and efficiency of Maori gardening, as well as their
handling of one type of property accumulation, are illustrated by their
feasts, at which enormous quantities of food are amassed and distributed.
'In the northerly district of the North Island,' writes Firth in this con-

[7] This vicarious functioning of a cultural feature, which at times becomes the
source of its major local significance, can be illustrated by other instances. With
fine discernment, Wissler once pointed out that the inter-tribal wars of the Plains
Indians may well be described as ceremonial. These Indians, split into numerous
tribes though they are, are the carriers of a well-knit and relatively uniform cultural complex. Nevertheless, they have throughout known times been almost constantly engaged in internal strife, of which the stealing of horses, war raids, and
'counting coup' on one's enemies, are among the best-known earmarks. These persistent warlike activities, which mean so much to the ego of a Plains brave and to
the vanity of his bride or spouse, cannot really be compared with modern wars.
There is here neither nationalism nor imperialism, neither annexation of territory
nor economic exploitation of the weak. Instead, these activities should rather be
envisaged as a ceremonial by-play of a civilization in which military exploits have
become traditional.

nexion, 'huge stages or scaffolds were built to support the food, and tree trunks of quite large size were used in their erection. . . . It is obvious from the accounts of all the authors . . . that an immense amount of labour was necessary to construct them, measuring as they did upwards of 50 feet in height. Some were conical while others were of the shape of a triangular prism. Colenso states that the food was generally piled up in the form of a pyramid, 80–90 feet high, and 20–30 feet square at the base. A straight trunk of a tree was set up in the ground, strong poles were fixed around it, and a series of horizontal platforms was then erected to encircle the scaffolding at intervals of 7 to 9 feet. The whole structure was then filled in by baskets of provisions, and built up so as to present to the eye, when completed, one solid mass of food! At a great feast given . . . in 1849 . . . the stage was said to have been one of the largest ever put up. It was oblong in shape, 211 feet long, 18 feet wide at the base, tapering to 8 feet wide at the top. To form the framework . . . spars were raised perpendicularly, several of them being squared timbers. Five of them were from 90 to 100 feet high, topped by smaller spars 10–15 feet in height, bound firmly together by the strong *torotoro* vine, making the total height of the turret in the centre from 115 to 130 feet. From this eight other turrets, ranging from 80 to 90 feet, ran the length of the staging. On these turrets were built the platforms on which the food was laid out, at intervals of 10 to 12 feet, from the ground to the top.

'Considering the primitive tools of the Maori,' continues the author, 'and the almost entire lack of mechanical appliances to assist labour, the erection of such stages must be considered as a stupendous achievement. The mere organization of men and materials for the work was an economic feat of no mean kind. The manifest purpose of building such structures was to impress the guests and to give scope for the display of the food to the best advantage. The effect was much more striking than if the provisions had been merely heaped on the ground.' [8] The distribution and partaking of the food on such occasions was accompanied by much ceremony, magical rites, and the singing of songs.

'The fact that the natives,' remarks Firth, 'composed songs about the different kinds of food to be sung in conjunction with the ceremonial bearing of it from the ovens for consumption reveals the keenness which attended its display and the interest which was taken in the event. . . . Considerable importance was attached to the ceremony of apportioning the food, and every effort was made by the donors of it to make the

[8] Raymond Firth, *Primitive Economics of the New Zealand Maori*, pp. 310–312. (Reprinted by permission of George Routledge and Sons, Ltd.)

presentation as effective as possible. A somewhat similar psychological attitude is also indicated in the many proverbs relating to food. . . . Some foods, however, evoked much more interest than others. For instance, a saying current among the Urewera is "Should you awaken me from my sleep let it be for the purpose of eating *hinau* bread." It is clear that the interest in food was not always excited simply by the desire felt for it or as a means of appeasing hunger. It supplied the means of entertaining guests, of inducing other people to perform certain tasks, of fulfilling numerous social obligations. In short, . . . food represented potential hospitality, economic control, reputation, and social power. In virtue of this, an emotional interest only indirectly derived from its physical qualities attached itself in the Maori mind to accumulations of food. It was this which played so important a part in the determination of its value.' [9]

[9] *Ibid.*, pp. 313–314.

Chapter XI

ART AND SYMBOL

Like technology, art is coextensive with man; industrial art appears among primitives wherever a particular industry is highly developed.

Our examination of primitive technology has revealed the fact that there is little evidence here of that carelessness in execution or technical imperfection which people were wont to ascribe to the primitive craftsmen. Primitive technology may in certain respects deserve the term primitive, but much of it is far from crude. It can moreover be observed that many articles of primitive industry are made better than would be necessary for practical purposes. Consider, for example, the boats of Polynesia or its woodwork in general, the boxes or spoons of the Pacific Coast Indians (see Plate XII), the pots of the Pueblos or of the Huichol, the baskets of the California Indians (see Plate XIII) or of Guiana. It seems that the technical skill developed in industry becomes a stimulus for still higher skill. The craftsman responds to the lure of technical achievement and at times plays with the possibilities of variation presented by the technical task. Thus skill from being a means becomes an end. Skill, thus exalted, turns into virtuosity, a triumph in technique, and valuable as such. This brings us to the threshold of art.

The industrial object itself is not as passive in this context as might be imagined. Granted the aesthetic impulse, the texture and form of the object invite artistic embellishment. The flat angular or curved surfaces of blankets, boxes, boats, pots, the necks and handles of certain articles, the borders of garments and mats, the grips of tools and weapons, and the edges of all things, call for art. In one form or another features of surface and shape of industrial objects are seized upon for purposes of artistic effect and expression.[1]

[1] A word is due here to the distinction between decorative art and art as such. The distinction is like that between making an object beautiful and making a beautiful object. In the latter instance the product—picture, statue, edifice—materializes the aesthetic impulse or creative idea of the artist; nothing further is demanded. In the former, the 'art' serves the purpose of embellishment. In primitive society the close relationship of plastic and graphic art with industry reveals its prevailingly decorative nature. But decorative art did not perish with primitive-

PLATE XII.   A SET OF HAIDA MOUNTAIN-GOAT HORN
SPOONS

(John R. Swanton, 'The Haida,' *Jesup North Pacific Expedition*, Vol. V.)

PLATE XIII.   PIMA BASKETS

(California)

I say 'expression' deliberately, for the primitive artist is not by any means as passive an imitator of traditional style as he has often been represented as being. In those areas where careful studies of primitive art have been made ethnologists have always found a typical variability in the form and decoration of artistic objects. Not that the tribal style is disregarded or radically changed. This, of course, is rare (see p. 200). The woman embroiderer of the Plains, Iroquois, or Algonquin, the man carver of the Coast, the woman potter of the Southwest, the wood-craftsman of Polynesia, work along well-established lines of technique and design-pattern. But within these fixed limits, room is left for infinite variation, often minute, at times fairly radical, variation which cannot be explained by mere inaccuracy in reproduction, but only by the individual technical aptitude of the artist, a peculiarity of his imagination, or the direction of his playfulness.[2] In the Plains, for example, the units of the embroidery patterns are combined into a great variety of more complicated designs. Of course, even these composite designs follow certain tribal principles as to decorative field and the arrangement of design units, but room is left here for considerable variation in detail (see p. 173).

Design, Technique, and Material

In the absence of relevant psychological material, due to the decay of much primitive art or to our inability to penetrate into the psyche of the artist, the psychological side of primitive art must needs be reconstructed by purely speculative analysis. At times, however, the suggestive-

ness. In architecture, for example, whether Egyptian, Greek, Moslem, Gothic, or modern, an important aspect of the art lies in surface decoration. In the Italian Renaissance of the fourteenth, fifteenth, and sixteenth centuries what may be called 'free' art flourished side by side with the art of decoration. The latter, embracing what was already known as the 'minor arts,' clung closer to industry. Every article of house, palace, or church interior, every bit of attire, every object of use or luxury, called for adornment. Such artists as the della Robbia brothers or Benvenuto Cellini shone mainly as artistic craftsmen, that is, highly accomplished decorators. At the same time the partial contradiction between the two forms of art also led to a certain tension. Thus when Raphael, whose artistic genius chafed under the restrictions of merely decorative fresco, was confronted with the task of painting the antechamber of the Sistine Chapel, he started out in true fresco fashion, but presently the creative urge of the free artist gained the upper hand, and he proceeded to paint pictures with scant regard for limitations of surface or the dimensions of the chamber.

[2] In an interesting experiment Boas has shown that a group of primitive artists, when confronted with the task of reproducing a design, developed variations characterized by the author as a sort of artistic handwriting. This result could not be described as a new style, nor were the individual variations of the kind usually found within the definite style of a cultural district or area.

ness of the material itself helps one to transcend this handicap. We find, for instance, that certain rafters of Maori buildings are covered by curvilinear patterns which at first seem complex and unanalyzable. On more careful inspection, however, it can be recognized that the patterns consist, in the main, of combinations and recombinations of a simple curvilinear element, not unlike a large comma, which appears in a variety of positions (see Fig. 42a). Once this is realized it becomes easy to visualize the artist experimenting and playing, perhaps deliberately, with the effects produced by these combinations.

Industrial art, in particular, which has grown out of technical processes operating with specific materials, never wholly loses its dependence upon these elements of technique or of substance. Not that definite forms of object or decoration are invariably associated with particular materials. Such absolute dependence should not be looked for here. But the material does set certain limits to the form of the object and to the character of the art as well. Pots or other vessels made of sandstone do not lend themselves to the elaboration of form in curves or to such fine nuances of surface or shape as are observable in pots fashioned of clay, where the yielding and resisting material invites further elaboration and permits its execution. The large, at times enormous, stone statues or monuments of the Mexicans and Peruvians, and many features of their temples and other edifices, bear unmistakable evidence of the character and limitations of the structural material, namely stone.[3]

Wood allows of much greater delicacy of technique, including open work or filigree, even though the tools be crude. But woodwork, of course, must not necessarily bear this character. The skilful and highly finished art of the Northwest Coast lacks almost completely just this element of

---

[3] It is relevant to the text to remember here what is sometimes referred to as the miracle of the Gothic cathedral. In this case the limitations of the material, namely stone, were transcended by an unusual and prolonged concentration on this task of a long series of creative artists and expert craftsmen. As has been often stated, the problem here was to spirit away the stone. As Worringer put it in his *Form in Gothic:* 'All expression to which Greek architecture attained was attained *through* the stone, *by means of* the stone; all expression to which Gothic architecture attained was attained—and this is the full significance of the contrast —*in spite of* the stone.' From the standpoint of the principle of the arch, the Gothic was technically two rungs above the Incas and the Mayas. They lacked even the pre-Gothic semicircular arch of the Romanesque. In consequence, their structures, however remarkable otherwise, were heavy of exterior, and in the interior, when roofed, they lacked height—and light. The pointed arch of the Gothic cathedral, by eschewing the horizontal, solved the problem of height, and with it, by providing vast spaces for illumination from the outside, through long windows, it solved the problem of light. Before the magic of invention even stone capitulates; but also: it holds out stubbornly—to the last.

lightness. On the other hand, the delicate filigree work of Melanesian masks and ceremonial objects or of the carved boat-prows of Kamerun could scarcely be accomplished except in wood, at least not by primitive craftsmen.

Similarly, the very technique of basketry invariably lends a character of angularity to any design applied to it. Also the fact that the substance of the basket is woven and consists of interlocking strands, rhythmically revealed or covered up, provides in and by itself a pattern, or a base for a variety of patterns, which can be 'read into' the basket by a mere effort

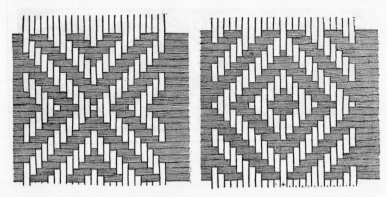

Fig. 42. ORIGINS (?) OF DESIGN IN BASKETRY UNDER INFLUENCE OF TECHNIQUE.
(Max Schmidt, *Völkerkunde.*)

Max Schmidt is a great basketry enthusiast and tends to over-stress technical determinants. A careful examination of these patterns—or an attempt to reproduce them with strips of paper—will, I think, convince the student that technique, unaided by idea, will not produce the patterns.

of the imagination even when the material is of uniform colour. As soon as the strands vary in colour—which is sometimes naturally the case, some strands being lighter than others, and can also be effected by artificial means—the pattern of the angular design can be made to stand out at will (see Fig. 42). In all such cases, however, it must also be remembered that the character of the material or nature of the technique can only affect the artist's imagination or intent but cannot in any strict sense determine it. The type of pattern he wants to represent pre-exists in his mind. Perhaps it was suggested by some other material or technique, or by an experience extraneous to art, such as the memory of a form or an animal. This he is intent on portraying or representing, and he will do so, using the facilities of the technique when possible, and overcoming it as a handicap should this prove necessary.

How varying the results can be in this interaction between object, design, and artist, can be illustrated by a juxtaposition between the wood carvings of the Northwest Coast and those of the New Zealand Maori. In both cases, as stated, wood is the medium; also, the decorated objects range through a great variety of forms. The Indian in his designs and carvings represents various animals and birds in a semi-realistic, semi-conventional form. In this process certain features are utilized which are firmly fixed and may thus serve as earmarks of the art: for example, the application of heavy lines as a sort of frame for parts of the design,

FIG. 42a. MAORI SCROLL.

the eccentricity of the curves and circles, the employment of the so-called 'eye ornament,' and the like. In his attempt to adjust the design to the object, which is frequently unsuitable for the application of the design as a whole, the artist is here led to break up the representation into segments which thus acquire a certain freedom of movement, while also preserving a formal unity of spatial arrangement.[4] The Maori artist, on the other hand, while not unmindful of the character of the surface and shape of the object, also displays a marked independence of these features. The decorations on many of his carved products make the impression that the artist was unwilling to permit the limitations of surface to affect the size or character of his design, except to a slight degree. As a result, the design often seems to extend beyond the physical limits of the object; or to put it differently, only part of the design, as visualized by the artist, is materialized in the object. One consequence of this attitude is the disregard of proportions in the design in relation to the object. What can be represented is represented, the rest is cut off by the physical edge of the object.

When a design is transferred from one material or technique to another—from basketry to pottery, for example, from wood to stone, or vice versa—the influence of medium and surface assert themselves in a

[4] For further details of Northwest Coast art see p. 179.

variety of ways. W. H. Holmes, one of the pioneers in this field, drew attention long ago to the peculiarities of pottery decoration traceable in many instances to the baskets over which pots, at least in some districts, were originally moulded. Similarly, in the case of Polynesian clubs: to these a wrapping of bark or cord strands is often applied; in other instances, a type of carving appears which mimics skilfully the wrapping that is no longer there.[5]

Realistic and Geometrical Art

Much discussion has been aroused by the problem of realistic designs in relation to geometrical or conventionalized ones. The patterns on pots, baskets, rugs, walls of caves or houses, sides of canoes, dishes, and the like, often suggest more or less realistically the forms of animals, birds, snakes, crocodiles, or of plants or objects of human manufacture. The same is true of the work in relief on pots or objects of wood, bone, or stone. On the other hand, equally numerous drawings, paintings, etchings, carvings, on similar objects are wholly devoid of any realistic suggestion but must be described as more or less geometrical, consisting of lines, straight or curved, or angular and curvilinear figures. Such geometrical designs, although bearing but the faintest suggestion of realism or none at all, are often interpreted by the makers or users of the objects as representations of animals, birds, natural features, or even abstract ideas. Sometimes the name given to the object or pattern reflects such a realistic interpretation.

In view of facts such as these, some anthropologists of the late nineteenth century, who were primarily interested in origins and laws of development, conceived a theory according to which realistic designs belonged to the beginning, geometrical ones to the end of a genetic series. Such, for example, is the theory of A. C. Haddon in his *Evolution in Art.* The earliest form of art, we are told, was realistic, but as generation succeeded generation, the influence of technique and other causes led to the introduction of geometrical forms which in time completely oblit-

[5] In modern days these phenomena can be conveniently observed in the domain of fashion. On the one hand, there is the material: stiff materials, such as lamé or brocade, call for straight or angular lines; soft and thick materials, like velvet or plush, are utilized for heavy curves and the effect called 'fullness' in the dressmaker's jargon. Soft, thin, and delicate materials, on the other hand, like chiffon or crêpe, are employed for light and airy effects. And once more, the change of material can leave its trace in the patterns and shapes produced.

The technical origin of a design can often be detected in spite of the medium, as when a carpet design appears on a linoleum rug, or a pattern originated in carved stone is utilized as a wall-paper motif.

erated the once realistic outlines of the design. The realistic origin of these designs survived in the symbolic meanings or names attached to them.

Like all such simplistic theories, this one had in its favour the advantage of a single and definite solution of a complex problem. It held the field for awhile, but could not withstand the adverse criticism born of more penetrating studies of materials and a more critical approach. It was pointed out that the very arrangement of specimens such as Haddon's in a quasi-chronological sequence was wholly arbitrary in the absence of proof that the realistic specimens really represented the earlier stages or that the other specimens were later. Such proof was necessary, if what the theory claimed was the reality of a historic sequence, not merely the presence of a variety of forms, some realistic, others geometrical, still others partaking of both characters. To arrange the specimens in a series of progressive conventionalization was to prejudge the issue.[6]

Again, instances were found, such as that of Plains embroidery, where the priority of the geometrical patterns seemed beyond doubt (see p. 176). The independent origin of such patterns is further suggested by the fact referred to above, that in basketry, for example, the requirements of technique naturally lead to geometrical lines and combinations.[7]

[6] Substituting noses for Haddon's crocodiles, one might as well arrange the persons of any locality in such a way as to make them constitute a series beginning with a diminutive pug and proceeding through many intervening gradations to a Cyrano. Surely no one would interpret the experiment as demonstrating a genetic succession!

[7] An excellent theoretical argument bearing on this point and developed on the basis of an elaborate and minute study of a definitely circumscribed set of objects, will be found in Boas's 'Decorative Designs of Alaskan Needle Cases' (*Proceedings, United States National Museum*, vol. XXXIV, 1908, pp. 321–344). The material presented in this study which, as the title indicates, deals with Eskimo needle cases, is too complex for our purposes (see Fig. 16, p. 77), but Boas's conclusion will be read with profit: 'I believe a considerable amount of other evidence can be brought forward sustaining the point of view that I have tried to develop, namely, that decorative forms may be largely explained as results of the play of the imagination under the restricting influence of a fixed conventional style. Looking at this matter from a purely theoretical point of view, it is quite obvious that in any series in which we have at one end a realistic figure and at the other end a conventional figure, the arrangement is due entirely to our judgment regarding similarities. If, without further proof, we interpret such a series as a genetic one, we simply substitute for the classificatory principle which has guided us in the arrangement of the series a new principle which has nothing to do with the principle of our classification. No proof whatever can be given that the series selected according to similarities really represents an historical sequence. It is just as conceivable that the same series may begin at the conventional end and that realistic forms have been read into it, and we might interpret the series, therefore, as an historical series beginning at the opposite end. Since both of these

The principal argument, however, is psychological. In primitive as well as in later times purely geometrical combinations of straight or curved lines, angular or rounded figures, coloured or uncoloured, carry an aesthetic appeal. This being so, the numerous occasions for the origination of geometrical patterns offered by material, technique, and accident must have been seized upon from the beginning and subsequently elaborated quite independently of any realistic antecedents.[8]

At the end of a penetrating study of the decorative art of the Golds, an Amur River tribe, Berthold Laufer arrives at certain conclusions relevant to the issues here raised. I shall reproduce his argument in greatly abbreviated form. The decorative art of this region carried out in different techniques and materials, has reached an especially high degree of development. Laufer shows conclusively that the Golds and other Amur tribes must have derived the inspiration for their art from the Chinese. This is indicated, among other features, by the fact that the complexity

tendencies are active in the human mind at the present time, it seems much more likely that both processes have been at work constantly, and that neither the one nor the other theory really represents the historical development of decorative design.' Continuing, Boas draws attention to the fact that the theory of development from realistic to conventional designs does not solve the problem of the diversity of conventional styles. The nature of these styles remains unaccounted for; nor does the introduction of the influence of technical motives quite solve the problem. Some very simple designs may be almost entirely due to the influence of technique, but it is powerless to explain the elaboration of detail. As examples Boas mentions the West African designs in woven checkered mattings where realistic figures alternate with geometrical band designs, the designs on cedar-bark mattings of the Ojibway and the North Pacific Coast, the designs in the same technique in South America. The technical conditions in all these cases are the same, but the styles are radically different. Finally, Boas refers to the important point that fundamental types of design characteristic of the styles of certain areas may yet be interpreted in a variety of ways by the people who make the designs, as well as by those who use them. In these cases it is often probable and sometimes certain that these interpretations are secondary. In many instances, however, the designs so interpreted may themselves have been borrowed from the outside, thus complicating the situation still further.

[8] To transfer to modern conditions the theoretical point here raised in connection with primitive art, I may once more refer to what occurs in the domain of fashion. When a certain type of garment establishes itself as an accepted style, the resulting fashion never consists in a slavish reproduction of the one original pattern. What actually takes place is that a great variety of garments are worn, differing in detail but similar in the points prescribed by the style. Out of these differences or through a suggestion from outside—an invention, an actress, a war—there soon arises an outline of a new style which in its turn asserts itself, leading to a similar differentiation. Now the large variety of different garments which fall between one style and the next, or certain features of such garments, could be readily conceived as constituting stages in a genetic series. But this interpretation would evidently be erroneous, for the variations in question are practically synchronous and must be regarded as expressions of creative ingenuity and individual taste disporting themselves within the limits of an accepted style.

and perfection of that art varies inversely as the distance of a particular
tribe from Chinese territory. The dominant decorative unit throughout
is the spiral with derivatives, cock and fish providing the favourite patterns. The prominence of the cock here is especially interesting in view
of the fact that these tribes until recently had never seen cocks and must
therefore have taken their motifs over from the Chinese, originally perhaps lured by what the author calls its 'artistic adaptability.' 'That such
is exclusively the case,' Laufer goes on to say, 'is seen from all the various
positions of fish and cock which are suggested solely by the tendency to
create new and aesthetically effective forms. The strongly developed
form-perception prevents the reproduction of realistic representations
. . . , as shown in the designs of numerous animals none of which have
endured in their natural forms, but rather have deteriorated into a style
of conventionality adapted to the cock and fish ornament, as the musk
deer, the dragon, and so on.'

Cock and fish appear in Gold ornaments in a vast variety of conventionalized forms, some representations being fairly realistic, others so
thoroughly conventionalized as to make the original creature unrecogniz-
able to one unfamiliar with Gold ornaments. The case, it will be seen,
is strictly comparable to Haddon's Melanesian crocodiles. This is what
Laufer has to say in this connexion: 'If we now take into consideration
the evolution of the cock and fish ornaments, we are impressed first by
the fact that differing and numerous stages of development are met with
frequently even in the same design; so that the development appears
almost to be based on a juxtaposition in space rather than on a succession
in time. In other words, the question arises, are we correct in supposing
a definite scale of gradations in the stages of development, from the
cock and fish, true to nature, down to the hardly recognizable conventional patterns? The whole series of forms does undeniably occur. These,
however, should under no circumstances be regarded as a chronological
sequence; for it is by no means true that the natural picture of the cock
or fish is sunk in oblivion, and that the conventional form has exclusively
taken its place. On the contrary, we see that the single phases of development are nothing more nor less than various forms of different kinds of
adaptation to certain spaces or given geometrical forms, mostly spiral.
This process of adaptation, constantly repeating itself in multitudinous
ways, has created a large number of varieties, still coexisting side by
side, like the varieties of a zoological species. One does not exclude the
other but each carries on its separate existence, because art indulges in
a wealth of forms and requires an abundance of varieties for building
up large fundamental compositions.'

In commenting, finally, upon the variety of attitudes in which the cock appears in these ornaments, Laufer writes: 'Here we have perhaps a primitive form from which all others have genetically originated; rather a long series of fundamental forms exist, based upon the observation of the various natural attitudes and motions of this ever-moving bird. We have distinguished a series of types, we have found standing, reclining, perching and perfectly erect cocks, some with beaks turned downwards, others with heads looking upward. All these types exist side by side without having developed one from another. The conventionalizations proper have arisen only through the influence of the fish ornament on the cock type. This is the same process which was above designated, in a more general style, as an assimilation to existing forms. Thus the cock for instance, assumes a fish body to get a spiral form more suitable for the entire ornament; or its tail is represented as a fish tail, its pinion as a spiral. Finally forms are even found in which the whole cock is composed of geometrical constituents. These have not been evolved from the form of the cock, but they are the primary element of the material from which it is constructed. This ensues from the diversity of function of the geometrical components. The spiral for instance may symbolically express all possible things. It may serve to indicate the cock's body, its pinion, its tail feathers. It may even perform two or more functions. . . . It would be absurd to infer from this that the spiral is the final result of the gradual conventionalization of purely realistic beginnings, it is rather a given prius, . . . which is employed for the symbolical expression of the most varied things since its forms are so convenient for this particular purpose.' [9]

Primitive Art and Children's Art

Another common tendency in the study of primitive art is to compare it with that of our children. The first and obvious objection to such a view lies in the fact, repeatedly stressed, that much primitive art exhibits skill, technical command, and imaginativeness of a very high order. The decorative carvings of the Maori or Haida, the carved clubs of the Marquesans and the Tonga Islanders, the painted pots of the Pueblos and those of the Chiriqui, the woven blankets of the Chilkat and the Navajo, the spun materials of Peru or India, the bone carvings of the Eskimo and those of the Sudan, the bronze castings, finally, of the African Gold Coast, all

[9] *Jesup North Pacific Expedition,* vol. IV, part 2, pp. 76–78. Even a cursory study of Laufer's monograph will greatly facilitate the understanding of the remarks made in the text.

of these and many other artistic products of the primitive world cannot be passed over slightingly as mere stepping-stones to something later and better. They *are* art, conceived in accordance with general aesthetic principles, carried out with great technical skill, in conformity with the requirements of local style, and with sufficient latitude to allow for individual artistic creativeness. No child, of course, could do such work.

In fairness to the theory, however, it must be admitted that much primitive art, whether realistic or geometrical, is crude, and that one at least of the reasons for this crudeness lies in deficient skill in handling certain tools or in the crudeness of the tools themselves, or in both. Now this, of course, also applies to children. To this extent a certain similarity is discernible between the artistic or technical efforts of children and some of the cruder work of primitives. A crude specimen is like another crude specimen, at least in its crudeness. But we may not leave the case here, for primitive art, however crude, remains distinct from the artistic products of children, in so far as the art work of a primitive tribe inevitably rests upon a background of an artistic tradition embodied in a style. However a particular local art may have originated, and however simple it may be, it has become fixed by tradition and comes to constitute an artistic convention of the group. Therefore, when the men or women of a tribe execute their art work in a certain way, it is not because they cannot do it in any other way [10] but because the work is dominated by the prescribed style, the traditional way of doing that particular thing.[11]

Whenever one is tempted to compare modern children with primitive adults, in art or anything else, one should, moreover, remember that primitives also have children and that these are related to their adults as our children are to theirs. Modern children might profitably be compared to those of the primitives—as Margaret Mead, among others, has done so successfully—but any parallel between modern children and primitive adults, while not necessarily futile, should be drawn with the strictest of reservations.

[10] The wood-carving of the Pacific Coast has, as we shall see, a very distinctive style, far from pure realism. But these natives, supremely skilled in the ways of wood-craft, can turn out remarkable specimens of realistic art, when they so choose (see Figs. 67 and 68 and Plates XXIV and XXV).

[11] One of the tasks of the modern experimental school, in which incidentally it has proved most successful, is precisely that of liberating the artistic and creative urges of the child *before* it becomes affected by the prevailing styles and techniques.

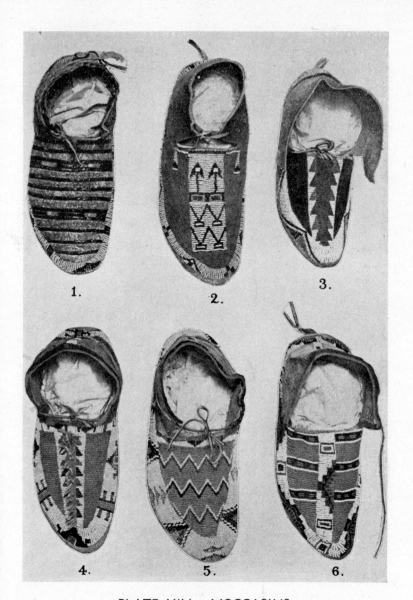

PLATE XIV. MOCCASINS

(Wissler, *Decorative Art of the Sioux Indians.*)

PLATE XV.   PIPE-AND-TOBACCO BAGS

(Wissler, *Decorative Art of the Sioux Indians.*)

PLATE XVI. GIRLS' DRESSES

(Wissler, *Decorative Art of the Sioux Indians.*)

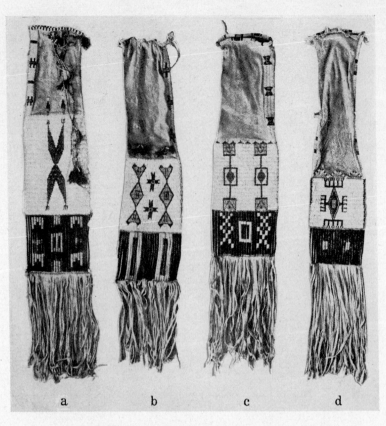

PLATE XVII.   PIPE-AND-TOBACCO BAGS

(Wissler, *Decorative Art of the Sioux Indians.*)

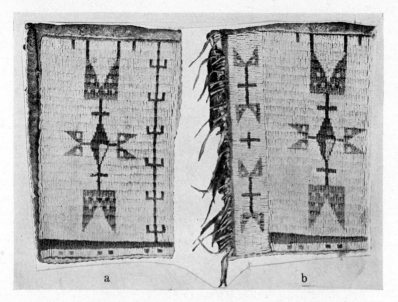

a   b

PLATE XVIII.   WOMAN'S LEGGINGS

(Wissler, *Decorative Art of the Sioux Indians.*)

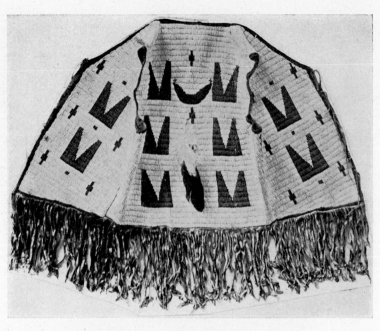

PLATE XIX.   BEADED WAISTCOAT

(Wissler, *Decorative Art of the Sioux Indians.*)

PLATE XX.   DANCE OF THE BULL SOCIETY, MANDAN

(Wissler after Maximilian.) This picture, together with that of a Kwakiutl ceremony (Plate XXVIII), give an excellent idea of the tenseness and excitement of such occasions.

PLATE XXI.   A DOG DANCER, HIDATSA

(Wissler after Maximilian.)

PLATE XXII.   MASKED PERFORMER OF KWAKIUTL
CANNIBAL SOCIETY

(Max Schmidt, *Völkerkunde.*)

PLATE XXIII.   HAIDA TOTEM POLE MODELS

(Swanton, 'The Haida.')

PLATE XXIV

CARVED FIGURE, BRITISH COLUMBIA

(Boas, *Primitive Art.*)

PLATE XXV.   HAIDA SLATE-CARVING,
REPRESENTING THE 'BEAR-MOTHER'

(Niblack, *The Coast Indians of Southern Alaska and
Northern British Columbia*.)

PLATE XXVI. CARVED WOOD-
EN CEREMONIAL RATTLE FROM
THE NORTHWEST COAST

(Niblack, *The Coast Indians of Southern Alaska
and Northern British Columbia.*)

PLATE XXVII.   NORTHWEST COAST WAR CLUBS

(Niblack, *The Coast Indians of Southern Alaska and Northern British Columbia*.)

PLATE XXVIII.   KWAKIUTL CEREMONIAL DANCE

(Boas, *Social Organization and Secret Societies of the Kwakiutl Indians.*)

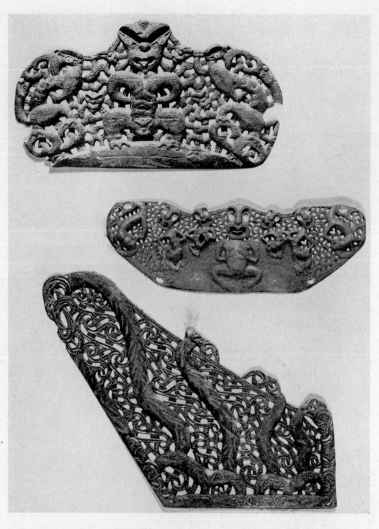

PLATE XXIX.   MAORI CARVED DOOR LINTELS (above)
CARVING ON SHIP-BOW (below)

Chapter XII

INDIAN ART

Plains Embroidery

In approaching the art of the Dakota, a Siouan-speaking tribe of the Plains area, a few words are due the general culture of the Indians of the Plains. These people in their geographical distribution spread roughly over the area once inhabited by the buffalo (see Map, Fig. 43). Their material life has always been rooted in that animal. The flesh of the buffalo was consumed in a variety of forms. Its hide was used for the

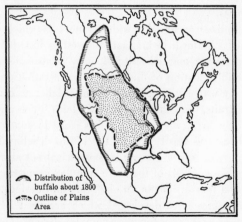

FIG. 43. PLAINS AREA AND THE BUFFALO. (Clark Wissler, *American Indians of the Plains.*)

famed Plains *tipi*, as well as for shields, garments, moccasins, and parfleches. Water transportation was little developed, although canoes were known among some of the tribes. The northern Village tribes, who had no canoes, used a bull-boat—a tub-like contrivance consisting of buffalo skins stretched over a twig frame—for crossing the Missouri River. Land transportation in ancient times was on foot, while baggage was transported on dogs with the assistance of the travois (see Fig. 7, p. 67). After the arrival of the Spaniards, the horse gradually spread through the Plains from the South northward and was thenceforth used for rid-

ing in war and chase, and as a draft animal as well, the old dog travois
having been greatly enlarged to take advantage of the larger and
stronger animal. Pottery was not manufactured here, nor is there any
basketry or true weaving, the art of the Plains taking the form of bead-
work on buffalo hide or of painting on the same material. There was
also some work in wood, stone, and bone. The social organization
varied. Whereas among the eastern tribes, a gentile organization and
dual phratries are found, the Crow in the northwestern Plains have
clans and phratries which here are not moieties, whereas the western
tribes lack sibs altogether, the primary social unit being a loose local
band, regarded by Wissler as the basic and oldest social unit of the
Plains region. There was a Camp Circle organization (see Fig. 36, p.
108), more or less developed in the different tribes, which was especially
associated with the buffalo hunt. A large number of men's societies occurred, some religious, others military. The Sun Dance had a wide distribution. There was also a ceremonial complex centring around sweat-
house observances.

The Plains Indians occupied a wide territory in which considerable
tribal differences obtained, in language as well as in culture. Over and
above this, however, a marked cultural unity is also observable, especially after the introduction of the horse. Concentration on the buffalo,
exaltation of war with its associated customs, elaborate ceremonialism,
and some other traits, were characteristic of Plains life as a whole. Along
the borders of the area, where these tribes came in contact with other
areas, cultural features less typical of the Plains developed.

The embroidery art of the women is geometrical but also symbolic in
a peculiar way. An analysis of the more complex geometric patterns reveals the fact that they are made up of simple unit designs. In this connexion pattern names have developed which are used for the simple
decorative units as well as for the more complex designs. Turning now to
the moccasins represented on Plate XIV, it should be said at the outset
that the women who were the makers of these designs asserted that their
only object in making them was purely aesthetic, that they were aiming
at beautiful moccasins. On all the moccasins we find ornamental borders
which follow the uppers along the edges of the soles. These borders consist of small geometric designs arranged symmetrically on a background
of uniform colour. The most frequent design here is the triangle with the
apex pointing upward along the surface of the moccasin. This design is
commonly referred to as the *tipi* pattern or 'tent' design. In some instances a small rectangular area appears within the triangle and upon the
base of it. This pattern is referred to as the 'door' or 'entrance' to the tent.

A variation of the triangular design is a block-like figure as in 2. This pattern is referred to as the 'cut-out' or 'step' pattern, though the whole figure is still referred to as a 'tent' design. The rectangular borders 1 and 6 are variously described as the 'bundle,' the 'bag,' or the 'box.'

While the moccasins all have this border, there is greater variation in the decorations of the instep. In 1 the transverse bands are referred to as the 'road,' 'trail,' or 'path' pattern; in brief, as 'trail' designs. The design in 2 is known as the 'three row' pattern, whereas the longitudinal band on the insteps of 3, 4, and 6 is called the 'middle row' pattern. The painted area between the middle row and the border has no special name but is simply spoken of as 'space' or the 'part between.' On 3 and 4 a series of small triangles will be seen extending down the middle row. They are designated as 'vertebrae.' Of the three designs on 2, the upper one was called the 'arrow' design, the middle one the 'box' design, whereas the lowest one remained nameless. The lateral stripes in 6 which form the background for a series of rectangles, are referred to as the 'filled-up' pattern.

It will be noted that in almost all cases the names refer to objects which are geometrically somewhat like the designs.

The simple design units here mentioned, as well as others that might have been illustrated if space permitted, comprise the following set of primary design units or patterns (see Fig. 44). The elaboration of these primary units into more complex designs can be studied on the pipe and tobacco bags of which three are reproduced on Plate XV. These bags, though used by men only, are made by women, and are regarded by both sexes as pure works of art. Ordinarily the men use plain bags, the decorated varieties being employed on special social and ceremonial occasions. Wissler thinks that these more complicated designs are less pleasing to the eye than the simpler ones and that a certain confusion of eye movements results from looking at them. This, of course, is partly a matter of taste. The Indians themselves referred to these designs as 'looking-glass' patterns or 'reflected' patterns. 'No one seemed able to give a rational explanation,' says Wissler, 'as to the applicability of this term, but it is possible that the effect of such a combination of lines and areas upon the observer was noted by the Indian and expressed in the terms given above. The experience is certainly somewhat analagous to the flashing of a mirror in the face.' [1] Wissler's interpretation does not impress me as very feasible. It may be suggested that the term 'looking-

[1] 'Decorative Art of the Sioux Indians,' *Bulletin*, American Museum of Natural History, vol. XVIII, part 3, p. 238. This discussion of Plains art is based on Wissler's study.

glass' or 'reflected' pattern derives from the fact that these designs are symmetrical both laterally and vertically, representing therefore the sort of figure that would result if half of the design, either vertically or horizontally, were reflected in water.

Let me repeat with reference to the designs so far considered that

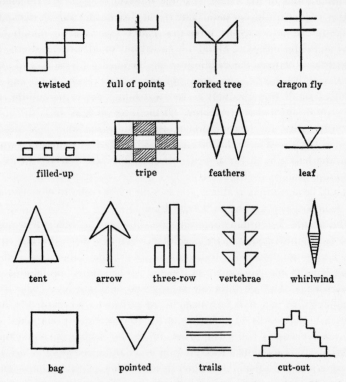

FIG. 44. PRIMARY DESIGN UNITS. (Wissler, *American Indians of the Plains.*)

while they constitute elaborations of unit elements which are either conventionalized realistic forms or geometrical shapes with realistic reference, the whole complex design is nameless and its object, according to the Indians, is purely aesthetic.

In other instances the designs vary somewhat and the symbolism acquires a different slant. This can be seen on the garments presented on Plate XVI. Garment *1* is a dress for a small girl, which is cut from a single piece folded along the shoulder line with a hole cut for the head, the sides of the skirts being sewed up. The oblong area across the shoulders, breast, and back is beaded with designs on a blue background. The women refer to this as 'blue breast beading.' The simple designs here found form a complex with symbolic significance. The U-shaped figure on the breast of *1* represents the breast of the turtle, whereas the wing-like extensions represent the sides of the turtle's shell. The large beaded area represents a lake or some other body of water in which the reflection of the sky is seen. Most designs within this area on the dress traditionally stand for reflections of objects in the sky or on the shore; the stars in this case are represented by the five-pointed star designs, the clouds by the triangular designs with their appendages. There are also four crosses which were supposed to have been put in purely for decorative effect. The small beaded area to which the strings are tied stands for the knots of the string. The beaded border is a repetition of the border in the large beaded area and is interpreted as the shore of the lake.

There is no complete harmony here between the symbolic reference determined by tradition and the attitude of the artist. A woman may tell you that she puts the designs in to 'please her eye,' but she also knows that according to tradition the designs mean 'reflections in the water' and the like.

Another interesting fact is that, according to the testimony of the women, they sometimes dream out complex designs. In the dream the design usually appears on a rock or the face of a cliff, although it will also occur that the entire specimen in its finished form appears in the dream. Such experiences are ascribed to the workings of a feminine culture heroine, who according to the story seems to have been one of twin sisters. These twins are often spoken of as two women tied or fastened together. They exercised many magical functions and are believed to have originated the art here discussed by giving instructions to a Dakota woman in a dream. The belief is that this woman dreamed out many of the designs now current. Since her death it has become common for twin sisters to dream similar designs which are always ascribed to the culture heroine herself. Women other than twins, however, sometimes dream out designs which are similarly interpreted.[2] Such designs are copied by other women and thus established patterns later to be followed by many others. Wissler says that the few designs of recent dream origin which he had occasion to examine differed in no way from other designs which were not due to dreams. Wissler is right then in saying that the dream design is not so much a distinct type of design as an illustration of the Dakotan philosophy with reference to the origin of the present style of

[2] Such an origin, or imputed origin, of design patterns is not foreign to modern experience. Our artists as well as designers not infrequently claim to have dreamed of a new pattern or combination of patterns, or even of an entire artistic composition.

art. When an association is thus established between the patterns used and the culture heroine just referred to, the art acquires a certain vague symbolic background of mystic connotation.

From what has been said already it is apparent that the symbolic meanings of the designs are more diversified than the forms of the design patterns. The designs on the four pipe and tobacco bags (Plate XVII) will serve to illustrate the varieties of symbolism. The large design in *a* represents feathers with tips; the four horseshoe-shaped figures in quill work represent horse-tracks. The other designs in this specimen are given the usual pattern names. Design *b* represents the buffalo; the bar and quill work is the tail. The divisions of the beaded design are the head, hump, and hind quarter. The other figures are purely decorative. On specimen *c* the diamond area within the central rectangle represents a butte, the rectangle itself, the grass about it. The appendages to the rectangle are a tree or a 'forked' tree. In specimen *d* the centre of the design represents a hill, and the four appendages, trees around the hill. I think it will be clear from an examination of these four designs that to think of them or any parts of them as conventionalizations of realistic or quasi-realistic designs would be arguing in the face of all probability. The symbolic meanings are so patently artificial that they must be conceived of as *ex post facto*, the geometrical patterns pre-existing and the symbolic meanings having been read into them.

This conclusion will be supported by an examination of the designs on a woman's leggings (Plate XVIII). On specimen *a* the diamond-shaped centre of the large figure is made up of red, green, blue, and yellow triangles, and is said to represent the breast of a turtle; the green lines extending from the crosses represent the four directions. The large blue areas with the small white rectangles are forks of trees struck by hail-stones. The long stripe to the right of the figure with its symmetrical projections is declared to be purely decorative. The border or side figure in specimen *b* on the left is again interpreted as forks of trees and the four directions. It is interesting to compare the designs and interpretations on the two specimens. On specimen *b* the whole large design is taken to represent a battle. The diamond-shaped centre is the body of a man. The large triangles are the tents of the village in which the battle took place. The pronged figures represent wounds and blood, and the straight lines supporting them, the flight of arrows. The cross lines to the right are also said to represent arrows and lances. Clearly, the design on specimen *b* is very similar in general style to that on specimen *a*, but the symbolic meanings are entirely different.

Similar designs, though differing in certain particulars, appear on parfleche paintings (Fig. 45).[3]

An example may finally be given of the symbolization of a more com-

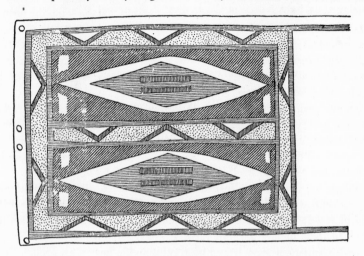

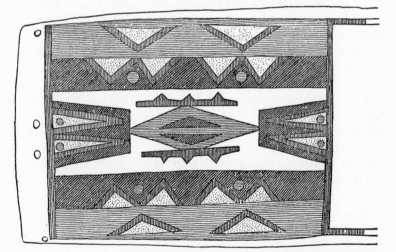

FIG. 45. PARFLECHE DESIGNS. (Wissler, *op. cit.*)

plex event as illustrated by the design on a waistcoat on Plate XIX. The background is white, implying winter. The time of the month is in-

[3] The parfleche is a common and most useful accessory of Plains material culture. In construction it is nothing but a sheet of buffalo hide folded up into a

dicated by the stage of the moon, and the colour of the moon, dark blue, signifies that the battle was fought at night. The triangular pictures of tents imply that an attack was made from the enemy's camp. The crosses on the white field represent the bodies of the fallen, a red cross meaning a wounded warrior, a blue cross, a dead one. The small red rectangles represent the number of hits that wound, the blue ones, of those that kill. The eagle feather attached to one of the crosses refers to the fact that the owner struck an enemy. At the horns of the moon are small crosses representing stars.

Colours among these people have a general symbolic value, apart from geometrical form. In connexion with military matters the significance is as follows: red means blood or wounds; blue or black, victory or enemies' camp; yellow, horse; white, snow or winter time; green, grass or summer. According to Wissler, the Sioux have a preference for blue. He also believes that blue pigment was not known to these Indians until the coming of the traders, whereupon it was promptly adopted and substituted for black. In earlier days when a war party gained a victory or killed enemies, they painted their bodies black; so when blue was substituted, it acquired the same meaning. In bead-work purple and green are sometimes used with the same significance. Yellow is the symbol of the war-horse because of the fact that tawny or dun-coloured horses were highly prized. Green is, like blue, a new colour. It may be substituted for blue and yellow and generally refers to summer. It is also sometimes used to designate a chief. All of these colours, however, vary in significance in accordance with position. Red on a coat may mean that the owner was wounded; red on a weapon, that he wounded an enemy; and the like. It is plain, at any rate, that the military symbolism differs radically from that associated with the other non-military objects previously examined. The designs used, however, are in many particulars the same. This suggests once more that these designs or patterns represent a general characteristic of the area, whereas the symbolic mean-

package somewhat like a modern envelope. The ends that have been turned over, and in some cases the narrow strips along the edges, are used for decoration. The parfleche was primarily used as a receptacle for dried food, especially pemmican which consisted of dried ground buffalo meat with cherries, pits included, ground into it. Numbers of these were stacked in the lodge and brought eloquent evidence of the industry of the family, the women in particular. The impressiveness of the pile was, of course, enhanced by the painting on the parfleches, but the women were also wont to say that the designs on the outside preserved the contents. One gathers from the traditions that the first parfleches were not painted, but that the hair of the buffalo was carefully removed without marring the pigmented layer of the skin which was dark brown in colour. The designs were produced by scraping away portions of this layer, with the resulting effect of light and shade.

ings differ according to tribes, nature of the object, position in the design, and even the sex of the person who reads in the meaning.

Carving and Painting on the North Pacific Coast

The principal technique of the natives of the Northwest Coast, including the Tlingit, Haida, Tsimshian, Bella Coola, and Kwakiutl, is woodwork, the principal materials being red and yellow cedar. These natives live in relatively large houses built of boards placed vertically and with gable roofs, also of board. Their boats, used both for ceremonial and for war purposes, reach enormous dimensions. They belong to the so-called dugout variety, a boat being fashioned out of a large tree trunk split in two longitudinally. There is no pottery here and no basketry, except in the extreme North among the Tlingit, who borrowed their basketry technique and the basis of their basketry art from their Athapascan neighbours, the Tahltan. For most of the purposes for which the Pueblos use pots and the Californians baskets, including that of cooking, the Northwest Indians employ boxes. A box of this sort consists of three principal elements, the sides, the bottom, and the top or cover. All the four sides of a box are fashioned out of one board, which is bent over hot steam to form the three corners. At the fourth corner, where the two sides meet, they are sewed together by means of the so-called disappearing stitch. Then the four sides are fitted over the bottom, which has an elevated section over which the sides of the box fit snugly, so that once this is accomplished, the sides and bottom form a solid unit, without the use of any such additional devices as pivots, sewing, or anything else. The cover of the box fits over the top of the sides in the same fashion, but less snugly.

Wood is also used for making dishes of an endless variety of shapes and sizes, baby-carrying boards, spoons or ladles (also made of horn), a variety of ceremonial paraphernalia, such as masks and staffs, and various ritualistic adornments which are made out of the soft inner bark of the cedar. Wood is employed for the totem-poles and memorial columns, some of which reach great size. Even the famous Chilkat blankets woven by the Tlingit women have a wooden component, the materials employed being mountain goat wool and the soft inner bark of the cedar. As secondary materials, bone, ivory, and horn are also employed by these Coast tribes.

The wood technique of the Pacific Coast has become the basis of their very remarkable art which takes the form of carving, in low and high relief, applied to totem-poles, memorial columns, boxes, dishes, and ladles, and of painting, also applied to boxes as well as to the walls of houses and the sides of canoes. The decorative patterns on the Chilkat blankets, although made by women and more highly conventionalized than any of the other forms of Northwest art, must also be included in the general range of wood-inspired art, in so far as a woman executes the woven design after a pattern painted on a board by a man (see Fig. 46), just as our ladies embroider and knit after blue-print patterns, or used to.

FIG. 46. PATTERN-BOARD FOR CHILKAT BLANKET. (Emmons, *The Chilkat Blanket*. Drawn by Miss Harriette Akin.)

This Northwest art is in a sense realistic, in so far as it deals with animals, birds, sea creatures, and the human figure, all of which are recognizable in their artistic versions; but in the character of its execution the art is conventional, to a greater or lesser extent. The carving on the totem-poles and memorial columns is, on the whole, the most realistic, whereas that on the boxes is often highly conventionalized, the extreme of conventionalization, as just stated, being reached in the woven designs of the Chilkat blankets.

Passing now to the art of carving and painting itself, let me note at the outset that the external inspiration for this art is provided by animals and birds whose representations in art are used as the so-called 'crests,' an object thus adorned becoming of great emotional value to the people and articulating with their social and ceremonial organization and their religious and mythological concepts. When thus represented in artistic design, the different parts of an animal or bird are not equally significant. Certain features are selected for emphasis and become symbolic of that particular animal. The little figure (Fig. 47), for example, which is taken from the model of a totem-pole, represents a beaver. A first view

of the face might suggest a human countenance, but the fact that the ears are on top rather than at the sides characterizes it as that of an animal. The two large incisors protruding from the mouth stamp the animal as a rodent, namely a beaver; the tail is turned up in front between the two hind legs, and on it there is a cross-hatching which represents the scales on the beaver's tail. This is another symbol of the beaver. In its fore paws the animal holds a stick. The nose is short and forms a sharp angle with the forehead; the large nostrils are represented by highly stylized spirals. Of these various features associated with the beaver, the large incisors, the

FIG. 47. CARVINGS REPRESENTING THE BEAVER. From Models of Haida Totem Poles Carved in Slate. (Boas, *Primitive Art*.)

cross-hatched tail, the stick, and the form of the nose are the most important. They may all appear on a particular carving or they may not. The presence of the incisors, for example, or of the cross-hatched tail, is in itself sufficient to identify the carving as that of a beaver. Thus in Fig. 48 the representation is very similar indeed, not so much in the proportions as in mode and details of the treatment. Here, however, the stick is absent. In Fig. 49, which is a spoon, all the teeth are omitted except an upper pair of incisors; the nose is also different, in so far as the spirals are omitted. The scaly tail is here too, only it appears on the back of the spoon. In Fig. 50, which is a painting from a Kwakiutl housefront, the body of the beaver has vanished, but the painting can be readily identified as that of a beaver: the incisors are there, the scaly tail appears under the mouth, the scales in this case being represented more realistically; the broken lines around the eyes indicate the hair of the beaver, another moderate touch of realism. The nostrils are large and round, even though they lack the other features mentioned before. The two clawed figures under the corners of the mouth are the feet.

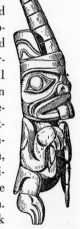

FIG. 48. CARVING OF BEAVER. (Boas, *op. cit.*)

Similarly, the symbols of the sculpin are fins and tail, which are common to it and other fish, while the specific symbols of the sculpin are two spines rising over the mouth and a joint dorsal fin.

The symbol of a hawk is a large beak, hooked and curved backward so that its slender point touches the chin or the mouth. The face here, as in many other such cases, may be altogether human, except for that unmistakable beak which identifies it as belonging to a hawk. In Fig. 51, for example, the head is that of a hawk with the usual beak. At the top of the figure is a man with a head very much like the hawk's below, except for the beak. The man is holding an animal which may be a dragon-fly. The symbol of the killer-whale, especially as represented by the Haida, is a long dorsal fin which may either be plain or have a white stripe or circle painted on it. The head is elongated, the mouth long and square in front. The nostrils are large, high, and also elongated. When represented on a totem-pole or a spoon, the head is always so placed that the long snout points downward. Fig. 52 represents killer-whales, whose symbols can be easily recognized.

Fig. 49. Carving from Handle of Spoon Representing Beaver, Tlingit. (Boas, *op. cit.*)

The bear is symbolized by a large mouth set with many teeth, often in the act of swallowing some animal or human. The tongue protrudes, as a rule; the nostrils are high and round and sometimes are represented by spirals; the paws of the bear are large and are usually provided with very long claws.

The most distinctive characteristics of the shark are a large mouth filled with numerous, often triangular, teeth and a high decoration over the forehead on which two or three curved lines, in the form of crescents, can usually be found.

The symbols of the different animals may be brought together in the following enumeration, as given by Boas.[4] Beaver—large incisors, large

[4] Boas, *Primitive Art*, p. 202. This sketch of Northwest art is based on Boas's study. I might add to this that the sketch of Northwest Coast art in Boas's book is a revised version of his essay, 'The Decorative Art of the Indians of the North Pacific Coast of America' (*Bulletin*, American Museum of Natural History, vol. XXIX, pp. 123–176), which appeared some forty years ago. In this detailed and highly analytical investigation Boas succeeded in unravelling what up to then had appeared as the mystery of Northwest art. He pointed out, in particular, that an animal or bird, as represented in this art, is often conceived as dissected, the different parts of the creature thus acquiring relative freedom of movement, limited, however, by the fact that their natural spatial relations in the animal's body must be, to a degree, preserved. The conventionalization of the different bodily parts, thus divided, henceforth proceeded separately for each part. Ultimately this led, as in the case of the Chilkat blanket, to a practically complete formalizing of the pattern, in which the animal form could no longer be identified, or only barely so. In such extreme instances a 'reading' of the design meant little more than knowing what the artist had intended.

FIG. 50. PAINTING FOR A HOUSEFRONT PLACED OVER THE DOOR, REPRESENTING THE BEAVER, KWAKIUTL. (Boas, *op. cit.*)

round nose, scaly tail, stick in the fore paws. Sculpin—two spines lying over the mouth and a continuous dorsal fin. Hawk—large curved beak with the point turned backward and touching the face. Eagle—large curved beak with the point turned downward. Killer-whale—large long head, large elongated nostrils, round eyes, large mouth set with teeth, blow-hole, and most important of all, large dorsal fin. Shark or dog-fish —an elongated rounded cone rising over the forehead, with two or three circles representing nostrils and several curved lines representing wrinkles, mouth with depressed corners, curving lines on the cheeks, set of gills, round eyes, numerous sharp teeth, and peculiar tail. Bear—large paws with long claws, large mouth set with teeth, protruding tongue (frequently), large round nose, sudden turn from snout to forehead. The sea-monster, dragon-fly, frog, and snail also have their symbolic parts and typical forms of representation.

Being equipped with the knowledge of the symbols, let us now apply it to the deciphering of the three totem-pole models (Plate VII).

On pole *a* three creatures are represented. The top one is the bear with its animal ears on top of the head and the huge claws. It is devouring a human figure, half-hidden in its mouth (an indication, by the way, that a slave was buried alive under this house-post when it was erected). The large projecting cylinder with its five segments on top of the bear's head, indicates five potlatches given by the

FIG. 51. LOWER FIGURE, HAWK; UPPER FIGURE, MAN HOLDING DRAGONFLY, PROBABLY TSIMSHIAN. (Boas, *op. cit.*)

owners of the pole. Under the bear is the shark with the usual three crescents on top of the forehead, and also a labret in the lower lip

which means that the shark in this case represents a woman. Below the shark is the raven with its beak. The belly of the raven is used for a 'filler face,' a face that is, without any particular signification, but used as an element in the design (or carving) to 'fill in' an otherwise unoccupied space.[5] Another such face appears in the lower part of the body of the shark, between the ears of the raven.

On pole *b* the top figure represents an eagle, with the typical beak, point straight, and the breast feathers, partially realistic. The second figure is a bear, with long claws on all four paws; he is holding a column of five (or six) potlatch disks. The lowest figure is a beaver, with four incisors, the round nostrils, the stick in the fore-

Fig. 52. Carvings from Handles of Spoons of Mountain-Goat Horn Representing Killer-Whales, Tlingit. (Boas, *op. cit.*)

paws, and the cross-hatched tail, with a 'filler face.'

The totem-pole *c* carries the carving of three creatures. On the top is the shark with its large mouth and triangular teeth, gills on the side of the face, and three crescent-like shapes on the upward projection of the forehead. It will be noticed that these symbols of the shark could not have been properly placed had the animal been represented in its natural position—then, of course, they would have been buried within the pole. So the face has been brought onto the top of the animal's head and appears on the pole in greatly exaggerated dimensions. Below the shark is the raven with its huge beak and the conventional wings at the sides. Below it is the killer-whale. It may be conceived as lying on its back, split in two along the

Fig. 53. Dancing Hat, Representing Killer-Whale, Tsimshian. (Boas, *op. cit.*)

[5] Such fillers—an eye-design, a whole face, a geometrical shape of some sort— are constantly used in Northwest specimens, apparently in conformity with the

belly, the head leaning far forward over the body, so as to appear on the pole. There is here the long snout, the dorsal fin split in two and provided with a white circle, the two parts of the fin appearing on the two sides of the pole, and the typical bifurcated tail of the species, which is bent over so as to cover the belly of the killer and incidentally fill the space between the mouth and the bottom of the pole. Into the large lateral spaces left by the tail the two parts of the dorsal fin are fitted. And then, the last touch! The tail itself, if represented without additions, would leave a considerable part of the bottom of the pole undecorated; so a face is carved on the top of the tail: it is merely a 'filler face.'

FIG. 54. CARVING ON WOODEN HAT REPRESENTING SCULPIN. (Boas, *op. cit.*)

It must be remembered that these symbolic parts of animals appear when the whole animal is represented, but they may also be used when the animal form has become reduced or even disappears altogether. The efforts made to adjust the representation of the animal to the shape of the object can be illustrated by a number of specimens. In Fig. 53, representing a wooden dancing hat, the body

FIG. 55. GREASE-DISH REPRESENTING SEAL. (Boas, *op. cit.*)

of the killer-whale is gone, therefore the essential dorsal fin appears on the top of the head, whereas the flippers are attached to the head, as if they were ears projecting backwards. On the wooden hat in Fig. 54 the animal, in this case a sculpin, is envisaged as split from the back. The two halves thus formed extend along the rim of the hat, the two sides of the mouth appear in front, the fin, split in two, appears on the two sides of the hat, and the typical tail of the species, on the side opposite of

principle of leaving as little space undecorated as possible. This principle is not uniformly observed in their art, but it is nevertheless conspicuous in its operation and frequently leads to curious combinations of design. It has also been responsible for a common misrepresentation, especially of totem-poles. On these a number of faces will often be seen, in addition to those of the animals represented on the pole. Early observers, erroneously regarding all faces as equivalent, were led to conceive of the totem-pole as a family tree, a sort of collection of ancestral portraits. The pole, of course, is no such thing.

the head. In Fig. 55, a grease dish representing a seal, the animal has been similarly split. Its different parts can be readily recognized. On the bracelet in Fig. 56, representing a bear, the animal is split in two altogether, except in the region of the nose, the two sides of the animal extending laterally to the left and right of the nose. The enormous mouth really consists of two profiles of the natural mouth, as seen from the right and left sides. In this specimen, it will be seen, the different parts of the animal are represented in a decidedly conventionalized form.

FIG. 56. DESIGN ON A BRACELET REPRESENTING A BEAR, NASS RIVER INDIANS. (Boas, *op. cit.*)

On the Haida painting, Fig. 57, representing the bear, the division of the animal into two parts appears even more conspicuously, the enormous mouth appearing in the centre of the design with the nose perched on the top, whereas the remnants of the two sides of the animal appear as two emaciated-looking creatures facing each other. A similar representation of the bear will be seen on the house-front in Fig. 58, and another one representing the sculpin, on the wooden hat of Fig. 59, or on the painting in Fig. 60, representing a dog-fish. In the slate carving, Fig. 61, representing the sea monster, the squeezing of a design into a given shape becomes especially conspicuous. It will be seen that the dorsal fin here is placed downward so as to conform to the vertical line of the slab. The tail is turned upward to fit into the allowed space, and the long snout is curved upward too, to fit within the range marked by the horizontal line at the top of the slate. In Fig. 62, representing a killer-whale in considerably conventionalized detail, the animal is provided with two dorsal fins. The body of the killer-whale is bent around the rim of the dish, so that the tail touches the mouth. The two dorsal fins are laid flat along the back, whereas the flipper occupies the centre of the dish.

When these carvings are compared with the Tlingit carved box represented in Fig. 63, it will be observed that the reduction of the body here has proceeded very far. In this case the eye-designs and the adjoining curves on the upper margin are 'fillers.'

The representations on the four sides of carved trays in Fig. 64 show how far the conventionalization of the different parts of an animal can go even in carvings.

FIG. 57. PAINTING REPRE-
SENTING BEAR, HAIDA (Boas,
op. cit.)

FIG. 58. PAINTING FROM A
HOUSEFRONT REPRESENTING A
BEAR, TSIMSHIAN. (Boas, *op.
cit.*)

FIG. 59. WOODEN HAT WITH
PAINTING REPRESENTING SCUL-
PIN, HAIDA. (Boas, *op. cit.*)

FIG. 60. PAINTING REPRE-
SENTING A DOG-FISH, HAIDA.
(Boas, *op. cit.*)

FIG. 61. SLATE CARV-
ING REPRESENTING SEA-
MONSTER, HAIDA.
(Boas, *op. cit.*)

FIG. 62. SLATE DISH WITH DESIGN
REPRESENTING KILLER-WHALE, HAIDA.
(Boas, *op. cit.*)

It will carry us too far to attempt to also analyze the Chilkat blanket. From the two specimens here reproduced (see Fig. 65), a good idea can be derived both of the decorative effect here achieved and of the extreme

FIG. 63. CARVED BOX, TLINGIT. (Boas, *op. cit.*)

conventionalization of the animal design. In cases such as this even experts will vary in their interpretations of a design. (See also Fig 66.)

In concluding this descriptive sketch, which does not begin to exhaust the wealth of the material available for analysis, I want to draw attention to the carved figure from British Columbia (Plate XXIV), the Tlingit helmet and mask (Figs. 67 and 68), and the Haida carving of a woman nursing a child (Plate XXV), as illustrations of the realism which these native artists can attain when they so desire. In the carved figure, Northwest style could only be recognized in the eyebrows and the figures on the cheeks. The representation of the face, hair, and long garment reveals great skill in realism. What the carver has succeeded in conveying is the sense of body under the garment. Figs. 67 and 68 are studies in facial expression. In Fig. 67, the head of an old man affected with partial paralysis is represented. The treatment here is so naturalis-

FIG. 64. CARVED TRAYS. (Boas, *op. cit.*)

tic as to lead Boas to regard this specimen as a portrait head. The blank stare of the eyes, the lateral dislocation of the nose and mouth, the contorted wrinkles on the right cheek, all tell the story unmistakably. Fig. 68 represents a dying warrior. Here we see the relaxed muscles of mouth and tongue, the drooping eyelids, the motionless eyeballs; the mask almost seems to be dying under one's very eyes. In these two specimens the artist also portrays, with some exaggeration, the typical so-called pentagonal face of the Indian, a configuration brought about by the great lateral expanse of the upper and especially the lower cheek bones. The Haida slate-carving (Plate XXV) is a realistic masterpiece. The baby clasping his mother's breast is really a bear, as revealed by the enormous paw-hands with long claws partially imbedded in the woman's breast. The woman is in agony, her head is thrown back, eyes

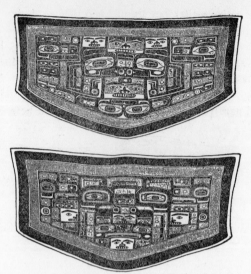

FIG. 65. CHILKAT BLANKETS. (Boas, *op. cit.*)

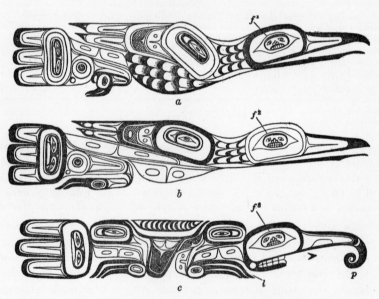

FIG. 66. HAIDA PAINTINGS. (Swanton, *The Haida.*)

These paintings are very typical of Northwest art. At first *a, b,* and *c* look very similar. In fact, *a* and *b* are birds, whereas *c* is a mosquito, as revealed by the curled up proboscis (*p*) and an extra leg (*l*). Observe also the faces within the eyes (f^1, f^2, f^3) and the less complete ones in the eye designs at base of tails.

FIG. 67. TLINGIT HELMET, REPRESENTING
PARTIALLY PARALYZED FACE OF AN OLD MAN.
(Boas, *op. cit.*)

FIG. 68. TLINGIT MASK
REPRESENTING A . DYING
WARRIOR. (Boas, *op. cit.*)

are half closed, pain and muscular tension pervade the whole figure.[6]

[6] We know, of course, that the art of certain peoples and periods was distinguished by its realism: the art of the Palaeolithic cave-dwellers of Europe, that of
the African Bushmen, that of Renaissance Netherlands. In other words, realism is
itself a style and a convention. But this apart, it must be understood that realistic
or naturalistic representation requires certain specific features in the artist's
equipment: he must be able to 'see' and to portray so as to convey the 'truth'
(about the 'reality' portrayed) and carry conviction. Not everyone can do this,
whatever the style or convention. It could probably be shown, if the data were
available, that among primitives, where art, as we know, is an accomplishment of
the many, there is more difference between the best and the less good when the
art is realistic than when it is geometrical, or at least, that fewer individuals are
capable of producing the best.

Chapter XIII

INDIAN ART (Continued) AND THE WHARE WHAKAIRO

Pueblo Pottery

Before we pass to an examination of Pueblo pottery, a few words are due the general culture of these peoples. The Pueblos certainly possessed one of the highest cultures, if not the highest culture, of all the American Indians north of Mexico,—especially material culture. This is in part accounted for by the cultural relationships and contacts with the Aztecs of Mexico. At any rate, we find in these two areas marked parallelisms, not only in language but also in the utilization of stone for buildings (in Zuñi mostly adobe, in Hopi, stone), the prevalence of agriculture, the high development of pottery, a complex cosmogony connected with an elaborate ceremonialism. In contrast to most other North American tribes, the people of the Pueblos were specialists in more than one form of craft and art. We find here not only the best-made pottery in North America, but also excellent baskets and weaving. Even though hunting, as usual, played its part in the domestic economy, agriculture constituted the essential material base of life, with the additional feature that men, not women, were the agricultural labourers; women, on the other hand, were the pottery makers. Agricultural technique was characterized by the presence of a system of irrigation, essential in this arid region.[1]

[1] Some authors make much of the physical environment of the Southwest in trying to account for the peculiarities of this culture. 'Certain physical surroundings,' says Goddard in his *Indians of the Southwest* (p. 15), 'also in a large measure influence art, religion, and man's conception of the universe as a whole. In the Southwest is an atmosphere wonderfully clear through which one sees with great distinctness the sculptured mountain peaks and ridges and the variously coloured flat-topped terraced mesas. The violent storms with terrifying thunder and frequent rainbows which mark the seasonal rains; the mirage, the shimmer and the whirl-winds of the dry season have produced results which we find reflected in songs, formulated prayers, and pictorial art. Only in the Southwest do the gods travel with rainbows and lightning and wrap themselves in clouds tied with sunbeams. So pronounced are these features that one feels, from whatever unknown source came the people themselves with their language and original customs, that many features of their arts, their mythology, and their religion could only have

192

In this discussion of Pueblo pottery, as technique and as art, I shall follow in the main the careful and discerning study of Ruth L. Bunzel, *The Pueblo Potter*, which carries the significant subtitle, *A Study of Creative Imagination in Primitive Art*. Miss Bunzel's book comprises an examination of the pottery of four Pueblos: Zuñi, Acoma, San Ildefonso, and Hopi.

Among the Zuñi the clay for the pottery is secured from a rather distant place on the top of Corn Mountain, where a dark grey shale abounds. The access to this spot is difficult, and so a journey for pottery clay becomes quite an expedition accompanied by religious rites. When the clay has been secured it must be crumbled, cleaned, and spread out for a couple of days, before it can be used. Pulverized potsherds are used for tempering. Fragments of broken household pots or sherds lying about the ruins are ground to fine powder on a metate or grinding stone, and mixed with the fresh clay. In mixing the paste, comments Miss Bunzel, the natives are guided by their tactile sense of the proper proportions, developed by experience; they are quite unconscious of what these proportions are in numerical terms.[2]

The texture of the clay used in the Pueblos included in Miss Bunzel's study differs as between one Pueblo and the others. She found that the Acoma ware was the best. The paste here is light in colour and very hard, and the texture is fine. The surfaces are very smooth and the walls almost as thin as an eggshell. In spite of this slightness of build, the vessels are strong and water-tight. Zuñi pottery, while good enough for practical purposes, is heavy and coarse. The walls of the vessels are thick,

arisen and could only continue to exist in the Southwest.' Like other such interpretations of culture, this one should not be taken too seriously. But it must also be admitted that the fitness of the culture to the environment is apparent enough.

[2] One woman in Acoma, we are told, gives the following recipe: two cups of tempering to each cup of clay. This recipe, comments the author, seems impossible. The same applies to the process of mixing the clay with water, the next stage in the proceedings. Here also there is no sense of any quantitative relation between liquid and solid parts. It would in fact be practically impossible to arrive at such a ratio, we are told, for it would depend upon the rapidity with which the clay is worked, the aridity of the climate requiring a constant compensation for evaporation. This kneading is a difficult task; cleaning is continued while the clay is being mixed, the gritty particles being removed as the soft paste passes through the fingers.

This factor in the technique, namely an effective procedure combined with unconsciousness of the particulars, to which the author draws attention, has an important general bearing on the psychology of craft (compare p. 411). In a situation such as this the material and its moulder are almost equivalent factors in an interacting whole. Granting the aim of the worker, which of course is to produce a fit clay, the rest is a matter of mechanical pressure by the paste on the fingers and by these on the clay. In this mechanical complex the fingers play almost as automatic a part as does the clay.

though not as thick as those of the Hopi. The surfaces of the ware, when not slipped, are rough. Also, the vessels are inconveniently heavy. The paste here is dark brownish. The ware of San Ildefonso is also heavy. In texture it is smoother than the Zuñi and is hard and strong; it is, however, not water-tight: as soon as the vessel is filled with water, the beautiful black surface becomes dull and streaked, a fault that cannot be remedied. Hopi ware is even worse—the walls are thick, the paste soft and coarse. It is rendered smooth by polishing but becomes scratched and flaked. The fragile vessels often crumble when first filled with water. The author found that these types of ware, as technique, are definitely localized and constant within each group at any given time, although as time passes, changes come about.

The next problem is the moulding of the vessel described by Miss Bunzel, in substance, as follows. First a lump of clay is worked with the hands. By hollowing this out or pressing it flat, a cup- or disk-shaped base is formed, which is then placed in a low mould, made either of the bottom of a broken pot or of a saucer or pie tin filled with clay and sprinkled with sand. Carefully, the base is pressed into the mould, then rounds of clay are added to build up the walls. The clay is rolled between the hands or on the floor into thin long strips, about an inch in diameter, and from two to three feet long, which are added to the top of the vessel. The strips are always placed inside the finished wall and pressed into place with the fingers. In rolling and joining care must be exercised not to permit air spaces to remain, for this would cause the vessel to break during the firing. In making small vessels the shaping is begun after the walls have been built up to the full height, except for the neck; in larger vessels, preliminary shaping accompanies the building. All shaping is done from the interior, except when the outer surface is being smoothed. The only tools used are fragments of gourd shell, pieces of different curvature being used for shaping the different parts of the vessel. When a Zuñi vessel, usually a large water jar, is built up to a point somewhat below the shoulder, it is set aside for a few hours to become firm enough to support the upper walls. During this time the upper edge must be kept constantly wet. An important additional point is that the lower part of the vessel is set in its final form before the upper part is moulded. As no corrections are possible after the half-finished vessel has been set aside and dried, it is evident that the entire form must be clearly visualized before this occurs. And here again, as in the case of clay mixing, the final form is not a matter of trial and error, 'adding a little there and taking off something here'; on the contrary: 'the operator is guided by a very definite sense of proportion, no less rigorous because it is unconscious.' [3]

When the pot has been given the desired form it is still far from ready. There remains the laborious process of preliminary finishing, slipping, and polishing. When the vessel is thoroughly dried, the rough finishing begins. The whole surface is moistened and scraped, inside and out; all roughness is worn down, the ridge formed at the top of the mould is eliminated, the walls are further thinned, and the rim is made smooth and regular. The tool employed in this process is a plain knife, the top of a baking powder tin, or a rough stone. At Zuñi, this rough finishing is done very hurriedly and carelessly, with the result that the jars show many irregularities of surface. At other places the same technique is used with much greater care. If any imperfections of structure are noted at this stage in the proceedings, such as cracks, air bubbles, or pieces of gritty material imbedded in the clay, which would cause the pot to break during the firing, the vessel is destroyed and the same clay used for another vessel.

The next process is the application of the slip, which is a thin solution of very fine clay containing no tempering. With a smooth cloth it is evenly applied to the surface of the vessel. Three or four coatings are the rule. The colour of the slip varies with the Pueblos. At Zuñi, Acoma, and Laguna it is chalky white. The bases of the pots remain unslipped at Zuñi, whereas at Laguna and Acoma they are slipped with bright orange-red. At Hopi the slipping is done with the same clay that forms the paste for the pot. This clay, which is a clear light grey before firing, turns yellow during the process, shading from pale ivory to a deep buff tinged with rose. A bright red slip is used at San Ildefonso. If the fire is smothered at the right moment, the slip turns to a deep lustrous black.

The last process is polishing, which is begun while the last coating or slip is still damp. The surface is rubbed lightly with a very smooth stone.

---

[3] Impressed by the similarity of proportions in a number of San Ildefonso vases, a similarity so great 'that they might almost have been cast from the same mould,' Miss Bunzel drew the potter's attention to one relation, namely that of the base to the neck, which is almost invariably 2:3, whereupon the pot-makers agreed that they had never thought of this before. Here as before, then, these crafts-women did not think of form in terms of numerical relations nor were they guided by the number or size of the strips of clay used. When pressed for some guiding principle, all the potters 'without exception' stated: 'It must be even all around, not larger on one side than another, the neck must not be too long; the mouth must not be too small.' Though not numerically cognizant of the problem of form, the native potters are nevertheless highly sensitive to it, as shown in the uniformity of vessels in any one village, as well as in the very critical attitude shown by the women

This use of the polishing stone requires great skill: to obtain a high polish without scratching or pebbling the surface, the pressure must be just right. At San Ildefonso, where the polish is the chief source of ornament, it is done with even greater care than in other places. After a high polish has been secured with the stone, the surface is further rubbed with a greasy rag. All this requires meticulous care. If a single scratch or irregularity is observed, a fresh coating of clay is applied and the whole process is repeated.

Now the pot as such is finished, but it is still no more than a base for the design, to an examination of which we shall now proceed.

As between Pueblo and Pueblo, there is much difference in form, design, and the relation of the former to the latter. Among the Zuñi there is a definite break structurally between the foot and body of the pot, and then again between the body and the neck. These three parts are treated separately, not merely as to form but also in the decoration applied. This formal separation in the three structural parts scarcely ever occurs in the three other regions, while in the Acoma pots the decorator completely disregards them, the entire surface being treated as a unit. Among the Zuñi a definite line must be drawn between sacred and secular decoration. 'The cleavage between household and ceremonial objects in regard to form and decoration is so complete,' writes the author, 'that it is difficult to believe that two such different ceramic types belong to the same age and the same people.' [4] In the sacred bowls, apart from differences in form, the decoration inside and out consists of any or all of the following designs: serpent, frog, tadpole, and dragon-fly. These designs are applied without any regard for decorative style. They are painted directly on the white background without any reference to one another. The requirements of a carefully integrated structure, such as is always found in the household pottery, are disregarded here. The workmanship of these sacred paintings, moreover, is crude and hasty, from which, as the author correctly notes, it may be inferred that the purpose of the artist here is to depict rather than to adorn, and that the development of these patterns was not guided by aesthetic standards, or only slightly so. [5]

towards any deviation from accepted form. 'For them all problems of form of which they are conscious are semi-technical, the attainment of perfection within imposed limits. The creative process itself lies deeper than consciousness.' (Ruth L. Bunzel, *The Pueblo Potter*, p. 11; compare below, p. 199.)

[4] *Ibid.*, p. 23.

[5] This characteristic of religious art is not confined to the Pueblos but may be regarded as a general feature of such art in many different places, as Boas has long ago pointed out. He says '. . . we find a considerable number of cases which demonstrate the fact that the decoration of ceremonial objects is much more realistic than that of ordinary objects. Thus we find the garments for ceremonial

Of the secular designs only two approach the realism of these ceremonial patterns; these are the deer and the bird. The deer design, evidently taken over from the religious art, becomes stylized in the secular ware through the addition of graceful scrollwork, by which it is always surrounded, thus transforming it into a pattern rather than a picture. The birds also show the influence of style; the conventional effect is enhanced by the fact that this design is always used within narrow, clearly defined borders. The butterfly and dragon-fly patterns, when used on secular ware, are highly stylized and so is the medallion, which is referred to as sunflower, the one plant-form used.

The decorative scheme of the secular pots of the Zuñi rests on a considerable number of geometrical pattern units. Of these the author lists and reproduces some 200 which she succeeded in securing from an exceptionally gifted woman informant. These unit designs are combined into more complicated patterns which vary somewhat as between pot and pot, although considerable likeness between one pot and another is also frequent. In the Acoma pots, on the other hand, as we saw, the pot is treated as a unit: the whole surface is covered with a design. Here there is scarcely anything corresponding to a background, by contrast with the Zuñi, among whom a background is deemed essential. Although a sophisticated modern student could readily enough resolve the Acoma designs into a number of pattern units, if not as many as among the Zuñi, these units are not distinguished by the Acoma themselves. In the San Idlefonso ware, finally, the main element is the perfection of finish. Here it is felt that the ornament is valuable mainly in so far as it brings out the deep lustre of the polish. While the Acoma are great colourists, the Zuñi and Hopi women regard the line of their design as more important than the colour. When these latter women speak of their efforts to reconstruct

dances of the Arapaho covered with pictographic representations of animals, the sacred pipe covered with human and other forms, while the painted blankets for ordinary wear are generally adorned with geometric designs. Among the Thompson River Indians ceremonial blankets are also covered with pictographic designs, while ordinary wearing apparel and basketry are decorated with simple geometrical motifs. On the stem of a shaman's pipe we find a series of pictographs while an ordinary pipe shows geometric forms. Even among the Eastern Eskimo, whose decorative art, on the whole, is very rudimentary, a shamanistic coat has been found which has a number of realistic motifs, while the ordinary dress of the same tribe shows no trace of such decoration.' (Boas, 'Decorative Art of North American Indians,' *Popular Science Monthly*, vol. LXIII, 1903.)

In addition to the relatively unaesthetic character of decoration in religious art it is also characterized by unusual conservatism. The normal and universal tendency of patterns to become standardized and to resist further change is here enhanced by the halo of sanctity which everywhere rests on ceremonial objects. Here change is not only undesirable but sacrilegious; therefore, it will, by and large, not occur.

the ancient designs from diminutive potsherds, they refer to this as 'getting the line of the design.' Instead of the Zuñi clarity of conception, emphasis on structural lines, and recognition of the decorative value of white spaces, the author finds among the Acoma what she calls 'an almost Gothic exuberance of ornament, filling without break the whole surface of the jar from rim to base.' Another contrast betwen the Acoma and the Zuñi is that, whereas the latter, as we saw, emphasize line, the Acoma are more concerned with the treatment of surfaces which paves the way for an exuberant use of colour. 'We have three kinds of designs,' said an Acoma informant to the author, 'the red, the black, and the striped designs.' [6]

Although the principles of decoration are thus seen to be as definitely fixed in the mind of these natives as those of form, and are also seen to vary as between Pueblo and Pueblo, the women are no more conscious of these principles than they are of those underlying form. At the same time these primitive artists seem to be agreed that the design is a thing more significant as well as more difficult than the mere form. 'Anyone can make a good shape,' they say, 'but you have to use your head in putting on the design.' 'I have the whole design in my head before I start to paint,' says one Hopi woman, and another adds, 'Whenever I am ready to paint I just close my eyes and see the design, and then I paint it.'

Even though the relative uniformity of designs in each district might make the impression of routine, they are not conceived as such by the pot-makers themselves, who dream these designs (as, it will be remembered, the Plains women also do), see them before them, think of them even when doing other things, object to copying, avoid making the same design twice. 'We paint our thoughts,' they say.

The relative uniformity of these art products, then, when looked at in the light of modern standards, does not prevent the native potter from regarding her task as that of a creative artist. 'Even at Zuñi,' says the author, 'where the inventive faculty is at low ebb and where choice of design is narrowly circumscribed by prevailing taste, in spite of all this, each pot is approached as a new creation, the decoration of which is evolved only after much thought and inner communing. However much theory and practice may be at variance, there can be no doubt concerning the theory. And strangely enough, it is at Zuñi where the ideal is stated with the deepest conviction that it is most frequently violated.'

[6] From this standpoint the contrast between the Zuñi, on the one hand, and the Acoma, on the other, is like that between the painters of Florence and those of Venice in the Renaissance, where the former were the master draughtsmen, whereas the latter specialized in colour.

This conflict between ideal and practice comes out in other connexions. A woman will apply three design units to a pot, will do so again and again. Yet when asked how many units she prefers, she will answer, 'Four.' Again, the women will use certain particular rim designs in association with certain body designs. The choice here is unfailing, but the potter is not aware of making it. When her attention is drawn to the fact she will say: 'Yes, that is right; we always do it that way, but I never thought about it before.' 'As a matter of fact,' remarks the author sagely, 'however much she may rationalize, she has probably never thought about the design, its structure, or its elements, at all. She has experienced it unanalytically as a configuration, just as she has experienced the forms of her vessels. The design is a constellation of which the essential part is a relationship. The various elements may later be abstracted, as words may be isolated from the sentences of a naïve speaker, who for many years has been correctly speaking his native tongue, though innocent of the simplest rules of grammar. In art, as in language, it is not difficult to bring into consciousness these unexpressed feelings for formal relationships. . . . Here as elsewhere, sensation and intuition play a larger role than intellect in the creation of design.' [7]

Without being able to make her conclusion wholly convincing, the author believes that some elements inherent in a decorative style may encourage or inhibit originality. Thus at Zuñi, where the style is very uniform, individual differences appear mainly in technique. With increased variability of design, the way is open for the creation of individual patterns or even styles by gifted persons. The author finds that individual originality has reached its peak at San Ildefonso, where Maria Martinez and her brother, Julian, execute such strikingly individual work and where pots almost equally original are made by Bonita Cruz and her husband, Juan. In Acoma too the author discovered two potters whose work could be identified with certainty, one specializing in archaic forms, while the other preferred highly complex modern pieces. At Hopi also some creative spirits were to be found, of whom Nampeyo, the author's star informant, was one.

Miss Bunzel is full of admiration for the artistry of Julian mentioned above. She found his pots to have the simplest designs at San Ildefonso. Sometimes these merely consist of a row of scallops or dots around the rim of a large bowl; but the execution approaches technical perfection. 'He needs no pattern book,' we are told, 'no poring over the archaeologist's tray of sherds. He has created a style in which he can operate blindly, feeling his way like a cat in the dark.'

[7] Bunzel, *op. cit.*, p. 53.

This man Julian and his sister, Maria, were responsible for the artistic revival in San Ildefonso.

While at work at the Santa Fé Museum and at archaeological diggings, Julian became familiar with many kinds of pottery. From these he borrowed designs and suggestions, subsequently to introduce them in his village. Hopi (Sikyatki) designs enjoyed his special favour. Then, in 1921, a new factor entered the situation. In that year Maria Martinez invented a process by which designs in dull black paint could be applied to the polished black surface which had long been a favourite at San Ildefonso. The new ware took the first prize at the Santa Fé fair and was eagerly bought by traders and tourists. Presently other potters began to imitate it, and now it represents the principal ware of the Pueblo, having displaced other types. This revolution in technique also had an effect on style, which became simpler in response to the demands of the new technique. What has happened here, I may add, may and must have happened in other places too, in America and elsewhere, if only the facts were known.

Another artistic revival, so striking as to be called a re-creation, took place at Hopi. The heroine of this incident was Nampeyo, the wife of a Hano man who was one of the workers for Dr. Fewkes at the excavations he was conducting at Sikyatki in 1895. During her frequent visits to her husband, Nampeyo was struck by the character of the ancient designs on the pottery brought to light in the excavations. She began to imitate these designs in her own work, presently to be followed by other potters. When Miss Bunzel visited the First Mesa in 1924, she found that the new ware had completely displaced the other types.[8]

The Technique of Peruvian Weaving

The Peruvians, of the Andean coast of South America, of whom we shall hear more as we proceed, were distinguished for weaving a variety of textiles, certainly superior to any others found in America and fully the equals of those of India. The principal materials they employed for

---

[8] This curious instance of a specially gifted native artist being inspired to new creativeness by the ancient art products of her ancestors can be paralleled by what happened at the dawn of the Italian Renaissance in the fourteenth and fifteenth centuries. With the fall of the repressions and constraints of the Middle Ages, the attention of the Italians of that period was drawn to the products of Greek and Roman art which were lying about their cities and cemeteries. Inspired by these ancestral achievements, they were stimulated to create their own art which was as firmly rooted in the past as it was prophetic of the future. In marked form this is true, for example, of the work of Donatello, but even Michelangelo, deep in the sixteenth century, may be cited in illustration of the same tendency.

this purpose were cotton and wool, although a number of supplementary substances were also used. Of the different varieties of cotton present in Peru or the neighbourhood, *Gossypium Peruvianum* is the one best fitted for the purposes for which it was employed by the Incas of Peru, and for this reason was greatly preferred by them. The length of its fibres, ranging from an inch to almost two inches, and the presence of tiny hook-shaped projections along the fibres, giving this cotton the 'rough' quality for which it is noted, were some of the traits appreciated by these ancient craftsmen. In addition, this particular variety of cotton is not annual but perennial: it can live and bear for as long as 20 years.

The wool employed by the Peruvians all came from certain animals indigenous to that country and belonging to the order of *Camelidae*, four of which were available to the Incas: the guanaco, llama, alpaca, and vicuña. Of these the guanaco is the least important as a wool-bearer, the llama with its coarse wool coming next; the wool of the alpaca is finer in quality and noteworthy for the range of its natural colours, including white, bluish-grey, tawny orange, red, and dark brown. The vicuña, which was never domesticated, furnished by far the finest and most highly prized wool of all.[9]

Of the secondary raw materials used by the Peruvians, the nearest approach to linen was the bast fibre derived from the maguey plant. No fine fabrics were made from it, but the fibre was employed for making ropes, cords, and coarse threads. It was sometimes used for sandals, for network, and for a kind of burlap-like cloth in which mummies were wrapped.

The cotton or wool threads used by the Peruvians for high-quality materials were of a high degree of perfection, though the methods at their disposal were technically crude. After being picked from the bolls, cotton was rid of seeds by hand, as was done everywhere before the days of the cotton gin. This seeded cotton was then bundled into convenient lots which were carded in order to straighten the fibres and to lay them approximately parallel to one another. Just exactly how this was done in ancient days is uncertain. Some believe that the necessary raking motion was performed by the fingers. Others hold that the combs of different degrees of fineness which are common in Peruvian burial-grounds were carding combs rather than hair combs.

Having been seeded and carded, the cotton was ready for the distaff.

---

[9] The original habitat of the *Camelidae* was North America, from where one branch of the order moved southward, giving rise to the four animals just mentioned. The other moved into Asia, where it evolved into a number of beasts of the camel variety.

This apparatus was a slender stick, less thick than a finger and about a foot in length, with a small ring at one end not quite closed at its upper extremity. Into this an appropriate amount of cotton was fitted, the two ends of the mass being somewhat fluffed out to ensure easy fingering. The lower end of the distaff was held in the spinner's left arm pit or in her left hand. Sometimes the whole mass of carded cotton was held in the left hand without the assistance of the distaff.

The cotton was now ready to be transferred to the spindle in the form of one-ply thread. The spindle was a much used and admired tool among the Peruvians, and so we usually find it carved or painted, while the whorls or weights which surrounded the shafts to give them steadiness of motion and momentum were richly ornamented, the materials of which they were made being pottery, stone, bone, or wood.

The preparation of woollen thread is quite like that of cotton. Having been removed from the animal, the wool was washed in water, but not so thoroughly as to wash out all of its natural oils. The latter, combined with spinner's saliva, helped to give the woollen thread, especially that of the vicuña, a moist pliability and smoothness.

Woollen threads, though naturally less fine than those of cotton, were here of extraordinary fineness when compared to modern standards. Means states that he saw a specimen of single-ply vicuña wool with a thread fine enough to give a weft count of 240 to the inch. More usually the best woollen threads of ancient Peru ranged from 200 to 180 for one-ply thread and 190 to 130 for two-ply. The finest modern woollen threads made of vicuña wool, we are informed by the author, give a weft count of between 90 and 70.[10]

Peruvian looms were hand looms, all the operations being performed by the hands and fingers of the weaver. Although of the type commonly known as vertical, this tool when in use assumed almost a horizontal position. In any case the warps were maintained at proper tension by the

[10] M. D. C. Crawford, who has made a minute study of Peruvian weaving, is full of admiration for the skill of these ancient craftsmen. Commenting upon a particularly fine piece of weave, he writes: 'Here is a highly complex design built up one pick of weft at a time, requiring 780 picks to complete it. Each crossing of weft over or under warps, causing a minute spot of colour on face or reverse, had to be considered in advance of each pick. It is perfectly woven, in no instance does weft go over or under warp more or less than the design required. How such weaving was possible without some form of draft or diagram to go by is most extraordinary. . . . No doubt the conventional geometric figures, which appear to be the common property of other advanced textile races, and the realistic representations peculiar to Peru, were well-known to each weaver, but the mechanical structure of each fabric had to be thought out by the worker almost independently of every other.' ('Peruvian Fabrics,' *Anthropological Papers*, American Museum of Natural History, vol. XII, p. 151.)

pull of the heavy lower loom-bar. This was sometimes attached by a belt to the weaver's body so as to enable him or her to increase the tension by merely leaning backward. When large pieces of cloth were made, a hand loom of somewhat different type was used. Two bars about as thick as a person's forearm were fixed to sticks driven into the ground, the bars being parallel and at a distance of 4½ or 5 feet from each other. The warp was stretched on these bars in a horizontal position, and as the weaving progressed, the cloth was wound up on the bar nearer to the weaver. There were also other varieties of the loom, including the small looms, some measuring only a half inch in width, which were employed for such very narrow fabrics as girdles, fillets, slings, and binding-bands.

The use of dye-stuffs was another important element in this art. In order to give depth and fastness to the coloured designs, these craftsmen had to use mordants. The function of the mordant was to corrode the fibres to a slight extent, thus rendering them somewhat rough and porous, with the result that they became greatly receptive to the dye and retained it after application. In Peru silicate of chalk, aluminium, silicate of aluminium, and oxide of iron were used as mordants. Means tells us that M. Valette, a French expert who ascertained these facts by an analysis of Peruvian specimens, also found that cochineal, an animal substance, was used for red shades and that some of the blue ones were derived from indigo. Many of the shades were obtained by using the materials in their natural colours, as has already been stated in the case of cotton. Nearly all of this dyeing was done in the thread rather than in the piece.[11]

The lower classes used for their garments and other needs a cloth made from the lowest grade of llama wool. For floor covering and bedding a thick and heavy stuff was used, somewhat like thick felt. The aristocracy of the Empire wore *cumpi*, which was made of the fine wool of the vicuñas, lambkin being preferred. Probably most of the fine woollen tapestry common in museum collections is *cumpi*. The weavers of *cumpi*, according to Father Cobo, were usually men, but the *aclla-cuna* or Chosen Women were the finest makers of *cumpi*, which in this case was mixed with the soft hair of the vizcacha, a chinchilloid rodent of the South

---

[11] A particularly interesting form of dyeing is the so-called 'resist' dyeing for which the Punjab (India) is also noted. 'In resist dyeing,' says Crawford, 'the fabric is so treated that when put in the dye pot, only certain portions of it absorb the colours. One form of this craft was to tie little bunches of cloth with a cord either soaked in clay or wax or spun from fibre which has no affinity for the colours and then dip the tied web in the pot. This tying was done in such a way as to produce design by the small circles or rough squares covered by the cord and therefore left undyed. By tying different knots while leaving the original in place and starting with the lightest shade for the first immersion, it is possible to produce designs of many colours.' (*Ibid.*, p. 153.)

American pampas, and of the bat. Even more distinguished than *cumpi* was a cloth, usually cotton but sometimes wool, which was densely covered with numerous tiny and many-coloured feathers. This covering was so thick that the fabric of the cloth was practically invisible. The finest cloth of all was the material called *chaquira*, which was adorned with gold, silver, and burnished copper in the form of either tiny bells or spangles.

Thereto hangs a tale. One of the numerous legends referring to the origin of the Inca chiefs is known as the Shining Mantle story and it runs as follows: Mama Siuyacu, whose name means Gradually Widening Ring, perceived and lamented the misery, bestiality, and ignorance in which the people throughout the highlands were living. Being an audacious woman and richly endowed with initiative, she determined to improve matters for the benefit of all, including her own kindred. She arrayed her beautiful son, Roca, in a specially prepared costume of fine cloth shining with closely sewn bangles of gold. Then she placed him in a certain cave in the hill-side overlooking Cuzco. The lad was instructed to appear, at a certain time, at the mouth of the cave and to announce himself as the Son of the Sun and as the one sent by his Father to rule over the land. All went as Siuyacu had calculated. The youth appeared at the mouth of the cave, the rays of the sun fell upon his spangled garment and caused it to flash and glitter. When the people beheld this marvel, they believed what they had been told concerning the divine origin of the boy. Such is the tale of the origin of the great Inca chieftain, Inca Roca.

It may be added here that the garments of the Incas, those of the ordinary folk and of the nobility as well, were of extreme simplicity, not unlike those of the Greeks. The distinction between the style of the lowly and that of the exalted was not in cut or amplitude, but solely in the quality of the stuffs employed and the profusion and kinds of adornments. The chief peculiarity of Incaic costume, however, was the head-dress known as *llautu* or *masca-paicha*, which was the distinctive head-gear of the Inca and of the imperial and noble classes. It consisted of a narrow and thick braid bound several times around the head, so as to form a band four or five inches wide. At its lower edge was a fringe which hung down to the eyebrows and ran from temple to temple. There were many variations in the colour and arrangement of this adornment, each class and tribe having its distinguishing form. On ceremonial and other special occasions ornaments of flowers and feathers were added to the *llautu*. Both sexes wore sandals; the soles of these were of leather and sometimes also the straps, but according to Cobo, the cords which held the sandals in place were usually of soft finely wrought wool with delicate patterns worked into them.[12]

Space and the limitations of a book such as this do not permit me to prolong this sketch so as to include other remarkable products of the Peruvian looms, equally distinguished as technique and as art. But enough has been said, I trust, to show what heights an essentially primitive technique can reach, at its best. It is equally interesting that here, as among the Maori, the highest achievements of technique as of art were not prompted by economic motives, the requirements of comfort, or any other 'needs,' but by the self-perpetuating and self-enhancing processes of craft, spurred on by a widespread appreciation of things skilful and things beautiful, and exploited as well as fostered by the pride of class.

The *Whare Whakairo*, Meeting House of the Maori

As a fitting conclusion to this section on art, let me comment briefly on an elaborate sample of primitive technical skill and artistic taste, resting, in this case, against the background of a highly sensitized culture, namely that of the Maori of New Zealand. In 'agriculture' and economy, in seamanship, boat-building, and numerous other crafts of land or sea, in military valour and the arts of fortification, in poetic imagination, and, finally, in what for short might be called a gift for living, the Maori were second to none among the peoples of Polynesia.

The anthropologist, when confronted with the cultures of Tahiti, Hawaii, or New Zealand, is likely to become aware, somewhat painfully, of the awkwardness of the term 'primitive,' even when used in the neutral way of science, that is, in the sense of pre-literate. Literacy, one is reminded, is not yet culture, but merely a condition for its attainment, nor does the absence of literacy preclude high cultural achievement.

The most conspicuous building in the public square, or *marae*, of a Maori village is the *whare whakairo*, a house of imposing dimensions, elaborately carved, which is the public meeting house of the villagers. From a strictly technical standpoint a house of this sort required careful planning, structural skill, and the co-operation of many individuals. The hauling and setting up of the large timbers used for the ridge-pole and the central pillars, though not requiring skilled labour, demanded organization and supervision. There was room here for timber-dressers, thatchers, carvers, as well as experts in panelling reed-work. Though the

---

[12] Philip Ainsworth Means, *Ancient Civilizations of the Andes*, pp. 450–482. The preceding sketch is based on Means's study.

workers were not paid in our sense, presents were given them, and the continued presence of so many persons in one spot necessitated the accumulation of considerable quantities of food. It was, in other words, a major enterprise. The building of such a house often took five years, in one somewhat doubtful instance of a house at Te Oriori, even as long as eight years.

As native buildings go, some of the *whare whakairo* were of great size. One was 85 feet long, 30 feet broad, and 20 feet high, and could hold as many as 1500 people. Another was 75 feet long, 32 feet broad, while its ridge-pole, 16 feet from the ground, was so bulky as to have been originally supported by four pillars. The carving alone of such a house took between three and four years.[13]

The adornment of the building was beautiful and lavish. There was wood carving on door-jambs and lintel-shield, on the architrave of the windows, on the slabs along the inside of the veranda, on the ends of the deep large boards, and on the supporting posts. From the apex of the gable arose a finial in the form of a sculptured human figure or a grotesquely shaped head. Nor was the interior decoration neglected. Broad wooden slabs, heavily carved, set off the low walls, the slabs alternating with reed-work panels, finely laced. The skirting board and frieze panels were often carved in low relief. The huge ridge-pole, itself graven or painted, was supported by one or more pillars, each hewn from a whole tree trunk. At its base each pillar was worked into the semblance of a human figure, almost natural size. The rafters also were covered with patterned scrolls and red, white, and black decorations. As might be expected, the social affairs in these great houses were accompanied by much etiquette. The section allotted to guests was on the right side of the entrance, right under the window. Opposite, near the front of the house, the chief men of the village were located. The highest chief had his own sleeping place near the central pillar, which could not be occupied or even touched by persons of lesser degree, such acts being interpreted as an insult to the chief. No food was permitted in the house, as this would destroy the taboo or sacred character of the house itself and of the people within.

Among the Maori the appreciation of carving was general and profound. This fact alone, if there were no others, would account both for the pains expended on the meeting house and the awe it aroused when completed. Firth here cites a story which illustrates what heights some of

---

[13] Firth justly draws attention to the fact that at least among the Maori great skill and much artistry were expended on objects other than those needed for primary economic purposes: carved houses, war canoes, the famous greenstone neck ornament (*heitiki*), and the *taniko* cloak with its elaborate border.

the Maori art products could attain. The chief Tangaroa once paid a visit to such a meeting house which was ornamented with carved figures. After greeting the host, also a chief, with the customary salute of nose pressing, Tangaroa saw in the dim light a tattooed figure standing at the side of the house and was about to greet him in the same fashion. To his amazement, however, he discovered that it was a wooden slab carved by the host himself into the likeness of a tattooed chief. 'So was Tangaroa deceived.'

The exalted sentiments aroused by these carvings were enhanced by some of the subjects represented in the carvings. The broad slabs supporting the walls of the interior were carved into a semblance of fabulous monsters, deities, and human beings. Of the latter there were two types. One showed a distorted and conventionalized form, a huge head with staring eyes in rakishly slanting sockets, a wide gaping mouth, out-thrust tongue, bowed legs, hands either gripping a weapon or with fingers clasped on the stomach. The other type was more realistic though not lacking in certain marks of conventionalization—the face was that of a human being in repose and was delicately and intricately tattooed as that of a chief. Here the proportions of the human body were more closely adhered to. Either of these two types of carving generally bore the name of a deity, a famous tribal ancestor, a mythical eponymic hero, or of a man once renowned for his deeds who perhaps had given his name to a *hapu*. At the present time all such eminent personages, human or divine, are indicated by names. In former days this was neither necessary nor possible, but each was readily recognized by some distinguishing mark— a flower, a mountain, two ropes to one of which the sun was attached, and the like. It may be added to this that only the dead, not the living, were represented, nor was there any attempt at portraiture. What was aimed at was to awaken the memory of a famous deed or of personal greatness, and these features were suggested by some detail in the representation.

'The *whare whakairo* was thus a centre of communal life, a place literally crammed with tribal associations, its very name redolent with tribal feeling or significant of some episode of note. In this way it tended to provide a focus for the sentiment of the people. In its material structure and type of adornment it gave a means of expression for aesthetic interests, offering a field of display for the highest branches of wood-carving and of reed-panel technique. It gave the village people, their relatives and guests an opportunity of appreciating the art of the carver; it provided a "gallery for display" and a "public" before whom the artist could place his work for criticism and admiration.' [14] (See Plate XXIX.)

[14] Raymond Firth, *Primitive Economics of the New Zealand Maori*, pp. 82 seq.

Chapter XIV

MAGIC AND RELIGION

In tracing the history of the human mind in its emergence from the animal, I took occasion to point out that the faculty of imagination shares with intellect as such, as a rational faculty, the distinction of being specifically human. Perhaps the most outstanding and certainly the most historically significant achievement of this faculty is supernaturalism. It is to this man-made realm—first conceived and fed by man, then to feed and inspire him—that we shall turn in these chapters on religion. In discussion and example we shall survey magic and religion, taboo and *mana*, the practices of medicine-men, the origins of new religions, supplementing these analytical sections with a few detailed expositions of primitive divinities, a sketch of a remarkable primitive cosmology, and another of the ceremonial cycle of a relatively advanced 'primitive' group.

What Is Magic?

Among primitives magic is ever around the corner. The bone-pointing of the Australian bushmen; the malevolent as well as benevolent activities of the ubiquitous medicine-men; the trances and tricks of the shamans of the Northwest Coast and Northeast Siberia; the 'black object' symbolizing sin among the Eskimo, which frightens away the animals; the *intichiuma* ceremonies of the Arunta, intended to multiply the supply of totem animals; the fetishism of the West Coast of Africa (is not a fetish a magical battery?) ; the miracle-working 'medicine-bundles' of the Plains; [1] the automatic penalization of broken taboos in Africa or Poly-

---

[1] The object of such a bundle was to secure control over the evil spirits and other hostile powers which bring sickness and misfortune. The possessor of a medicine-bundle could count upon health and a long life, he was also able to confer these blessings upon others. The following is a partial inventory of the contents of a Winnebago medicine-bundle: three paws of a black bear used as bags and containing herbs; a little bone tube stuffed with small feathers wrapped in the skin of an eagle's head and neck which, in turn, is enclosed in a pouch made of an otter skin; an otter skin containing dried bird's flesh and a bunch of feathers and fastened at the mouth with a piece of eagle's skin; two cane whistles; a paint bag in the form of a tiny embroidered moccasin with legging attached, containing

nesia—all these and innumerable other instances here unmentioned represent magic as it appears in primitive society.

To these must be added the beliefs in sympathetic magic popularized by Frazer, beliefs which are well-nigh universal. Have in your possession someone's hair, nail-shavings, a piece of skin, or a garment, and he or she is in your power. For better or worse, their fate is in your hands. If a wound is inflicted by a weapon, the application of the weapon may also cure it. The very mention of the name of a dead person may spell disaster.

herbs and closed by a bunch of buffalo hair; four snake skins; a white weasel skin containing herbs and a cane whistle; a brown weasel skin containing herbs; two snake vertebrae; a bone whistle; a cormorant head; a woodpecker head; a black squirrel skin; two small wooden dolls tied together; a dried eagle claw clasping a little pack of herbs, and a feather dyed red; an eagle claw clasping a pack of herbs, and a bunch of eagle quills painted red and green; an animal's eye; a horse chestnut and a tooth enclosed in a woven sack; a diminutive wooden bowl and spoon; eight woven and five rolled pouches containing numerous dried herbs (from a description by M. R. Harrington). Compare with this the witches' charm in Macbeth:

> Round about the cauldron go
> In the poison'd entrails throw.
> Toad, that under coldest stone,
> Days and nights hast thirty-one
> Swelter'd venom sleeping got,
> Boil thou first i' the charmed pot

> *

> . . . . Fillet of a fenny snake,
> In the cauldron boil and bake:
> Eye of newt, and toe of frog,
> Wool of bat, and tongue of dog,
> Adder's fork, and blind-worm's sting,
> Lizard's leg, and owlet's wing,
> For a charm of powerful trouble,
> Like a hell-broth boil and bubble.

> *

> . . . . . Scale of dragon, tooth of wolf;
> Witches' mummy, maw and gulf
> Of the ravin'd salt-sea shark;
> Root of hemlock, digg'd i' the dark;
> Liver of blaspheming Jew;
> Gall of goat, and slips of yew,
> Sliver'd in the moon's eclipse:
> Nose of Turk, and Tartar's lips;
> Finger of a strangled babe,
> Ditch-delivered by a drab,
> Make the gruel thick and slab.
> Add thereto a tiger's chaudron
> For the ingredients of our cauldron.

> *

> Cool it with a baboon's blood
> Then the charm is firm and good.
> (*Macbeth*, Act IV, Scene I.)

Bronislaw Malinowski in his *Argonauts of the Western Pacific*, as well as Raymond Firth in his Maori book, have emphasized another somewhat different type of magic associated with economic and industrial activity. As we had ample occasion to note, the technical aspects of primitive economics and industry are quite precise and often elaborate. But technique and skill do not quite solve the problem, or do not do so in every case. Whether in war, chase, fishing expedition, trading enterprise, the erection of a communal building, the giving of a feast, or the sowing of seed, the matter-of-fact processes mean that this much has been done in the direction of success. But does 'this much' suffice? The animals or fish may come or they may not. The seed will sprout into an ample harvest, if sun and rain co-operate, but not otherwise. The trading expedition may bring fortune and security, or failure and disaster. And so on all along the line.

It is here that magic steps in. Magical rites performed before and after such important acts or occasions supplement the technical effort, bring assurance where there was only hope, extend control into the very realm of chance. The role of magic in this connexion is of tremendous importance, even though it can be exaggerated, as has to some extent been done by the authors just referred to. The psychology of the situation may be stated in Malinowski's own words: 'An interesting and crucial test is provided by fishing in the Trobriand Islands and its magic. While in the villages on the inner Lagoon fishing is done in an easy and absolutely reliable manner by the method of poisoning, yielding abundant results without danger and uncertainty, there are on the shores of the open sea dangerous modes of fishing and also certain types in which the yield greatly varies according to whether shoals of fish appear beforehand or not. It is most significant that in the Lagoon fishing, where man can rely completely upon his knowledge and skill, magic does not exist, while in the open-sea fishing, full of danger and uncertainty, there is extensive magical ritual to secure safety and good results.' [2]

---

[2] 'Magic, Science and Religion,' a section in *Science, Religion and Reality*, ed. Joseph Needham, p. 32. (By permission of The Macmillan Company, publishers.) *Cf.* further Malinowski's carefully weighed words bearing on the relative role of magical and matter-of-fact interpretation: 'Nowhere is the duality of natural and supernatural causes divided by a line so thin and intricate, yet, if carefully followed up, so well marked, decisive and instructive, as in the two most fateful forces of human destiny: health and death. Health to the Melanesian is a natural state of affairs, and unless tampered with, the human body will remain in perfect order. But the natives know perfectly well that there are natural means which can affect health and even destroy the body. Poisons, wounds, falls, are known to cause disablement or death in a natural way. And this is not a matter of private opinion of this or that individual, but it is laid down in traditional lore and even in belief, for there are

Magical Beliefs in Modern Days

Magic has often been represented as the very essence of the savage out-look on life, this attitude being embodied in such terms as 'magic-ridden savage,' 'in the throes of magic,' and the like. To this notion is related Lévy-Bruhl's view that savage mentality is essentially magical and pre-logical in contrast with the objective rationality of the modern mind. In a certain sense all this is, of course, true. In many technical and economic pursuits, from which all magic, supernaturalism, and even subjectivism are strictly excluded in the modern scene, magical beliefs and rituals play an important part in all primitive communities. It is also true that magi-cal notions and practices are more regularly and systematically employed among primitives than they are today and that the associated beliefs enjoy a more respectable and generally approved status among these peoples.

To say this, however, is one thing, to whitewash modern man com-pletely as to matters magical is another. The fact is that magical ways of thought are far from unknown in societies other than the primitive. Frazer and Mannhardt found inspiration for highly elaborate and pictur-esque accounts in the 'superstitions' current among the peasantry of mod-ern Europe. In the traditional beliefs of these folk, spirits, ghosts and demons, spooks and apparitions, visions, dreams, and omens continue to hold undisputed sway in the face of the centuries-old teachings of Chris-tianity, which seem quite powerless to dislodge these more ancient and deep-rooted attitudes.[3]

considered to be different ways to the nether world for those who die by sorcery and those who meet "natural" death. Again, it is recognized that cold, heat, overstrain, too much sun, overeating, can all cause minor ailments, which are treated by natural remedies such as massage, steaming, warming at a fire, and certain potions. Old age is known to lead to bodily decay and the explanation is given by the natives that very old people grow weak, their oesophagus closes up and therefore they must die.

'But besides these natural causes there is a vast domain of sorcery and by far the most cases of illness and death are ascribed to this. The line of distinction be-tween sorcery and the other causes is clear in theory and in most cases of practice, but it must be realized that it is subject to what could be called the personal perspective. That is, the more closely a case has to do with the person who con-siders it, the less will it be "natural," the more "magical." Thus a very old man, whose pending death will be considered natural by the other members of the community, will be afraid only of sorcery and never think of his natural fate. A fairly sick person will diagnose sorcery in his own case, while all the others might speak of too much betel nut or over-eating or some other indulgence.' (*Ibid.*, pp. 32–33; *cf.* also the entire section, pp. 30–35.)

[3] In the early writings of the Russian satirist, Gogol, which deal with the peasant life of South Russia, we find a picture of the beliefs and customs of these peasants which are thick with magical notions and rites, and might, in this re-

Even in our cities, amid schools and universities, the faith in charms persists unabated side by side with the belief in lucky and unlucky days and the evil eye.[4]

In the fold of institutionalized Christianity itself we discern attitudes towards the objective symbols of the divine which are heavy with magical connotations. So are the beliefs in other than natural healing which render medical charlatanism so common and profitable, and feed the fame of certain holy places, 'shrines of salvation,' which were numerous and popular in Czarist Russia, and are known to exist and thrive in France and Canada.[5]

Everyone knows of the great popularity of such modern magicians as Wagner or Thurston, who amazed and delighted vast audiences in the midst of a matter-of-fact world. 'But what bearing has this on magic?' someone might exclaim. 'Surely everyone knows that these magicians are merely tricksters.' True enough; but we do not know how they perform their tricks, and our reactions to the emergence of a rabbit out of a silk hat or to the levitation of a magician's female companion until she hangs suspended in mid-air are visual experiences which for the time being are accepted as facts, not tricks. It is to this that our amazement is due. Many frank persons have confessed to a feeling of distinct uneasiness when watching such performances, plausibly due to a recognition on the part of these persons that at the time and place they found themselves accepting as true something they would under other conditions reject as impossible.

spect, be favourably compared with the supernatural equipment of any primitive community.

[4] Over 20 years ago, when I was teaching anthropology at Barnard College, I once chanced to ask my students, distinguished as a group for their 'modernity' and sophistication, whether they carried on their persons any objects to which they ascribed magic-working properties, such as rings, amulets, lockets, necklaces, and the like. I called for written statements, unsigned. As a result some one-half of the students present confessed to one or another sort of relevant belief or practice. In commenting upon these confessions to the class I remember having stated that some 50 percent of them had admitted their partial submergence in magical idiosyncrasies, whereas the other 50 percent had not had the courage to do so. Nothing has happened in my teaching experience in the interim to change my judgment in this matter, apart from a possible shift in percentages.

[5] Note in this connection the following news item: 'Templemore, Ireland. An incessant stream of pilgrims from all parts of Ireland continues to pour into Templemore to visit the home of Thomas Divan, where it was recently asserted miraculous cures were being effected through the medium of sacred statues, said to have shed blood mysteriously last week.

'The neighbouring towns and villages are overflowing with people unable to get into Templemore. . . .

'Further remarkable cures are claimed today.' From *The New York Times*, August 25, 1920. (Reprinted by permission.)

It is especially interesting that a disclosure of sleight-of-hand in a magician's performance—and such disclosures have been frequent—does not seem to stem his popularity or weaken the gullibility of his audience. Houdini, a great trickster and 'magician' in his own right, spent much time and effort in exposing his less sincere colleagues. His books were read by many, but the magicians, undismayed, continued to ply their trade in miracles. Another striking instance connected with the modern stage and bearing on this point is to be found in the movies of the Mickey Mouse variety. These pictures represent the magical universe in its most undistilled form. We have here the same disregard of space and time; the typical magical shifts in size and shape; humanizing of animals, birds, and other natural features; transformation of men into animals and vice versa; accomplishment of impossible feats of speed and strength. And what is our reaction? When a huge monster hides his portly figure behind the trunk of a sapling, or when a cow smashed to bits by bullets presently becomes whole again, we are not outraged but delighted. The whole performance does not impress us as either ludicrous or absurd, but as fascinating and, for the moment, convincing. Apparently our minds follow this tabloid magic without any effort whatsoever, delighted to travel along these ancient trails. In such moments we are ourselves magicians, or magical devotees, pure and simple. It is, moreover, to be noted that the line between the merely improbable and the impossible is not carefully drawn in the pictures, nor is it clearly realized by the beholder.

Nor is the domain of secular life free from the incursions of magic. This includes medicine, notoriously the most matter-of-fact of the professions. The status in modern society of medicine and its representative, the physician, is by no means devoid of a certain magical flavour. To be sure, the physician's knowledge and experience count for much in determining his reputation, but they do not count for all. What is uppermost in the mind of the public is success: a few conspicuous cures, however accidental and unforeseeable, contribute more to the good repute of a practitioner than a prolonged period of efficient but drab medical toil. A successful physician walks in a halo which is not wholly unlike that of the shaman. His appeal is at least in part that of a man whose powers are extraordinary. Nor are they felt to be reducible to mere knowledge and experience. It is felt that there is something here beyond the reach of ordinary individuals and perhaps of most other physicians. Many of us, I suppose, would be loathe to aver this, although some few do so; the rest experience the reaction but are not frank or discerning enough to admit it.

The belief in dreams is no longer 'good form' in our midst, but how many are there who can claim complete emancipation from the tendency to ascribe to dreams at least a certain power to transcend space and time? A woman dreams of her mother and upon awakening finds the news of the mother's sickness or death in her morning mail; she 'had not thought of mother for days,' 'had no idea that she could be sick,' and 'why just the night before the letter came?' and 'can it be only a coincidence?,' and so it goes. Let only the 'coincidences' multiply, and the staunchest doubter begins to waver in his or her scepticism.

Among the examples of latter-day supernaturalism few are more striking than the persistent belief that the psychic or other experiences of a pregnant woman may exercise a specific effect on the child. We hear of children born during the French Revolution with the revolutionary emblem on their chests or backs; or again a mother frightened by a frog gives birth to a child with a birth-mark resembling a frog. Another child whose mother had broken her wrist while in pregnancy is born with its wrist broken or weakened in the same place; and so on indefinitely. In a book published some years ago (*Sex Antagonism*, by Walter Heape), a collection of such instances is brought before the reader as worthy of belief. The author happens to be a professional animal fancier, whose day-by-day experiences inevitably acquaint him with facts suggesting interpretations through 'inheritance by magic' (Kroeber). As Jacob could not resist the temptation of interpreting by a mechanism like the above the peculiar and varied colouration of his sheep, no more can the modern fancier overcome the suggestion derived from the many instances in his experience where an interpretation through prenatal influence might be made—and he makes it forthwith. Many persons who would reject such reasoning with a shrug of the shoulders prove equally positive in their claim that should the expectant mother engage in voluminous reading, the literary proclivities of the offspring might be stimulated; or should she frequent concerts, its musical gifts would be similarly enhanced. In principle, of course, there is no difference between the two kinds of cases. Add to this lucky and unlucky days, magic numbers, black cats, nuns, umbrellas opened indoors, knocking on wood, three candles (or cigarettes) lighted by one match, open pen-knives, the number 13 (still omitted in many hotels), starting things on Monday, wishing good luck to a hunter (which is supposed to be an ill omen), breaking a dish, or any untoward happening at a ceremony or other emotionally significant occasion, and the impression becomes inescapable that modern society is, after all, not so far removed from a belief in other than natural causes. When an average modern, moreover, tries to be most 'scientific,' he would often prove, upon analysis, to be furthest removed from rationality. Thus, when he is found declaring that this or that is done by electricity, without understanding what it is or how it operates, electricity to him, psychologically speaking, is but another *mana*, a power other than natural, working in mysterious and incomprehensible ways—in brief, accomplishing the impossible.

Not infrequently one may hear a person remarking: 'I am superstitious.' In this form sincere persons give expression to their recognition of the fact that, though rational in intent, they are unable to resist the temptation to react in a special way in certain situations. It may be observed, I think, that the proclivity of people to be 'superstitious' in this sense is proportionate to the degree to which their profession or occupation stands in the control of unforeseeable factors. Here the gambler comes first. From day to day, from moment to moment, his future is uncertain. He may be a mathematician and as such fully aware of the unreasonableness of the concept of luck; yet, no sooner does he fall under the spell of the green lawn, the green table, or the tape, than the psychology of chance has him in its power; like his brother, primitive man, he is under the spell of luck magic. Next to the gambler comes the hunter or fisherman; he may be a master of his craft, but legion is the name of unforeseeable factors which at least co-determine his success. Hence his acute sensitivity towards omens, dreams, prognostications, well-wishing, and other like premonitions. Here also belongs the actor. Actors and actresses enjoy a deserved reputation for superstitious inclinations far above the average. Once more this tendency may be brought into relation with the capriciousness of their fate. Apart from talent, training, or even former favours on the part of the public, the life of an actor, including his contract and ultimately his dinner, depends from night to night on the appeal of a particular performance to the audience. We all know the elusiveness of public taste, and actors and actresses know it only too well. One cannot bank on it, hence the constant suspense. Such being the case, the host of omens, good and bad signs, and other representatives of the magical family, appear upon the scene.[6]

[6] Another recent profession subject to unusual concatenations of unforeseeable and menacing factors is that of the aviator, and the usual result *in re* magic is much in evidence. A well known scout-pilot was known to wear five charms hung around his neck. Whenever he took the air these were to be in place. One was the famous 'square 13' engraved upon a thin gold plate, another was a locket which he was never seen to open, the third was a bit of lace presumably from the edge of a handkerchief, the fourth was a tiny drawing on a square of heavily oiled silk, and the fifth was some sort of metallic object, perhaps a ring, sewn into a small cloth sack.

There was one charm known to pilots of the British Royal Air Force, few of whom were fortunate enough to possess it. It was a small gold horse-shoe, made

Some Problems in the Study of Magic and Religion

A number of topics in the field of primitive religion have been claiming the attention of anthropologists for a long time. Some of these topics are significant and real, others less so, but they should not be passed over in silence, if only for the reason that they have already been discussed so much. In this connexion we shall now consider briefly the following subjects: the relations of magic to science and religion, and the relations of the individual to the social element in religion.

Magic and Science. Among the many scholars who have written on and about magic, J. G. Frazer stands out as the one who has in his *The Golden Bough* covered the entire enormous range of magical phenomena and brought them to a common denominator. In the course of his analysis Frazer also examines magic in its relationship to religion and to science. Frazer conceives of the magical universe as closely akin to that of science; in fact, he refers to magic as primitive science. Magic, he says, is definite and precise. Its mechanisms, the 'acts' of magic, operate uniformly to achieve uniform results. These results, moreover, follow automatically or mechanically. So far, Frazer's analogy seems feasible enough. On closer examination, however, this characterization of magic proves to be

in two parts, similar to two shoes fitted together; on the inner sides of these halves the words 'faith and hope' were inscribed. The crack pilot of the British Central Flying School outside London carried one of these talismans and managed to survive more bad crashes than any other man in the station. One Polish pilot had a small box built into the side of his ship close to his right hand; in this he arranged a comfortable nest for his mascot, a snowy white imperial Peking drake, who went out with him on every flight.

Many pilots were superstitious about the number 13, some regarding it as a bad, others as a good omen. The most widely recognized jinx, however, was that of the 'last-flight' man. The record seems to show that more good pilots were killed while making what they knew to be their last flight at a certain field, or the last flight before being discharged, than on any other occasion, even including the hottest days of the war. Armistice Day claimed a large number of flyers, one of whom was 'Hobie' Baker of Princeton, who was killed while celebrating the end of the war.

Another common superstition carrying a good-luck connotation was that of seeing the shadow of one's ship in reduced detail upon the surface of a summer's-day cloud. Under such conditions the billowy white banks of moisture always produce a fairy-like rainbow encircling the tiny picture. The effect is of an exquisite miniature painted in silhouette upon ivory. The vision is always fleeting: just for an instant is the aeroplane in exactly the right position between the sun and the ground. Some thoroughly sophisticated pilots have been known to laugh over 'the rainbow's good luck,' but the majority felt otherwise—and they 'knew.' (These airmen's superstitions are gleaned from the *New York Times Magazine* for November 7, 1926.) A primitive overcome with awe at the sight of White man's technical accomplishment in the aeroplane would appreciate these touches of the common human in his modern brother.

more nearly correct than significant: it leaves out that which is of the essence of magic, namely the belief in the transcendent or supernatural power of the magical act and, behind it, of the will that controls it, that is, the will of the magician. Furthermore, the failure of any particular magical act in no way affects the faith in magic or even in the efficacy of the act that has failed. No, the failure is accounted for by another magical act exercised by someone else, perhaps more powerful, which frustrates the initial act. In other words the magical act or performance is proof against the lessons of experience and ensured against change consequent upon failure.

If this is magic, the analogy with science evaporates. In the centre of scientific operations stands the willingness of the scientist to profit by adverse experience, to revise his acts in the light of failure or incomplete success, thus ultimately to achieve the desired result and the implied control. There is similarity, then, between magic and science in so far as both possess precision and a teleological character; but the similarity is more apparent than real. The magician's precision, his hard-and-fast magical recipe, is after all, nothing but a sanctified routine; the precision of the scientist aims at accuracy, measurement—these are, of course, quite beyond the magician's pan. And again, whereas the magician wields a tool that remains unchangeable, for experience cannot touch it, the tool of the scientist—his hypothesis or experiment—is plastic: it is ready to change at the bidding of experience.

Magic and Religion. Frazer's view of the relation of magic to religion is even less satisfactory. We are told that religion involves the conception of a superior deity, and the particulars added by the author leave no room for doubt what particular deity he has in mind. Short of this there is no religion, only magic. Consequently the Australians, for example, though magic-ridden, are innocent of religion. In the light of such a conception of religion a vast number of primitive tribes would fall into the category of the Australians: magic—no religion. This attitude reminds one of the notion against which E. B. Tylor had to fight in his day: the notion, namely, that the most primitive peoples were utterly devoid of religion, a conclusion made possible by a trick of terminology—the religion of these folk was disposed of as 'superstition.' But 'superstition,' as everyone knows, is merely a religion one does not believe in. Frazer's attitude represents the same kind of reasoning.

When we say that magic may not be excluded from religion, this should not imply that it may not also be differentiated from religion. Wherein, then, lies the common element of magic and religion, and what are the earmarks of magic as such? The common element lies in the immersion in supernaturalism. In conception, in mode of behaviour, in the implied emotions, the supernatural constitutes a realm apart. Experiences with the supernatural are accompanied by a peculiar exaltation, a *religious thrill*. It is true that in religion or magic, as actually practised even by primitives, this thrill is not always there. This is due to the tendency of such emotions to 'evaporate' (Marett) when the procedure becomes habitual and formalized, a mere something to be gone through and over with. But the 'live' religious or magical situation is characterized by the presence of these emotions; the atmosphere is charged with mystic potency, and man responds. In this, then, lies the common ground of magic and religion.

The peculiarity of the magical situation, on the other hand, lies in the attitude of the magician when contrasted with that of the religious devotee. Both pursue certain ends, often practical ones, and both operate within the supernatural realm, but whereas the religious devotee prays or sacrifices, the magician controls—he performs his act and the result must follow. The orientation of the will, then, is different. In the first case (religion) there is submission or dependence, in the second (magic), self-determination and control.

Connected with the typical technical complications of the magical act is the further fact, stressed by Malinowski, that magic tends to develop technical experts or professionals, whereas religion, though equipped with priests and religious leaders, remains free to all and for all. This interpretation of magic and religion gains in plausibility when viewed in the light of later historic developments. Both religion and magic are rooted in subjectivity, but whereas magic tends in its later stages to crystallize into a ritual or spell, pure and simple, religion, though never free from ritualism, hence standardization, remains amenable to subjective elaboration and reinterpretation.[7]

---

[7] In connexion with the argument developed in the last two sections, consider the following quotation from Malinowski. 'Science, even as represented by the primitive knowledge of savage man, is based on the normal, universal experience of everyday life, experience won in man's struggle with nature for his subsistence and safety, founded on observation, fixed by reason. Magic is based on specific experience of emotional states in which man observes not nature but himself, in which the truth is revealed not by reason, but by the play of emotions upon the human organism. Science is founded on the conviction that experience, effort, and reason are valid; magic on the belief that hope cannot fail nor desire deceive. The theories of knowledge are dictated by logic, those of magic by the association of ideas under the influence of desire. As a matter of empirical fact, the body of rational knowledge and the body of magical law are incorporated each in a different tradition, in a different social setting, and in a different type of activity, and all these differences are clearly recognized by the savages. The one constitutes the domain of the profane; the other, edged around by observances, mysteries, and

The Individual and the Social Factors in Religion. All students of
religion recognize the importance for an understanding of religious phenomena of two factors: the individual and the social. The phenomena of
conversion, the lives of prophets, saints, messiahs, or such subjective records as William James succeeded in bringing together in his *Varieties of
Religious Experience,* served to draw attention to the individual and personal in religion. The role of ritual, on the other hand, the force of religious traditionalism and dogma, the ubiquity, finally, of suggestion and
imitation in religious movements, as described, for example, by Otto
Stoll, in his *Hypnotism and Suggestion* (in German), tended to throw
light on the participation of society in determining the content and form
of religion. Withal, it remained for Émile Durkheim, in his *The Elementary Forms of Religious Life,* to construct a purely sociological theory
of religion, in which society is made to function not merely as the moulder
and preserver of religion, but as its source and prototype, of which religion itself is but a subjective reflection.

The fundamental fact of all religion, according to Durkheim, is the
bifurcation of culture into two realms, the sacred and the profane. The
real problem to him is to find an answer to the questions: Whence the sacred? What experiences have engendered it?

By way of introduction to this doctrine, Durkheim argues that the natural and supernatural, as intellectual categories, cannot be clearly distinguished by the primitives. Having no precise sense of the natural, he
says, the primitives cannot have a clear idea of the supernatural. Durkheim also rejects the attempt made by Spencer and Tylor to derive the
basic religious concepts and attitudes from the experiences of ordinary
perception, supplemented by dreams and visions. Such experiences,
thinks Durkheim, might indeed lead to mental aberrations, to errors of
judgment, but they cannot account for the categorical character and the
irresistible impact of religious faith. This faith is too real to have been
engendered by an illusion. Rather must it be rooted in a reality as solid
as religious experience itself. This reality Durkheim finds in Society (note
the capital). He observes that the profane or secular realm in primitive
Australia—the major subject of his book—embraces most of the private
or individual activities, whereas the Sacred or religious realm is represented by myths, ceremonies, and rites, all of which are group affairs.
On these latter occasions, the individual undergoes a radical psychic
transformation. When in the throes of ritual-induced ecstasy he is beyond
himself, his energy seems well-nigh inexhaustible, his senses and percep-

taboos, makes up half of the domain of the sacred.' (*Op. cit.,* p. 80. By permission
of The Macmillan Company, publishers.)

tions function abnormally. Whether leader or led, he lives for the time being on a different level. What makes the individual behave this way, argues Durkheim, is nothing else but Society itself—stirring and irresistible, it dominates the individual psyche, thus giving rise to the sense of the Sacred. The Sacred, then, is but a subjective reflection of the social 'categorical determinant.' Religion, as experienced by the individual, is the symbol of Society.

However ingenious as a theory, Durkheim's position must be regarded as extremely one-sided and psychologically inadmissible. The division of experience or life into a sacred and a profane realm is a valid enough conception, applicable to modern as to primitive society. What is inadmissible is the identification of the profane with the individual, the sacred with the social. In economic pursuits and industry, in the ideas and customs clustering about the family or kinship, social factors figure at least as prominently as individual ones, without, however, assuming a halo of sanctity. In the religious realm, on the other hand, the individual often finds himself 'alone,' in more than a literal sense. The very essence, in fact, of the religious situation may at times reside in this aloneness and aloofness of the individual, his only companion, in this context, being the supernatural itself. To say that the social factors in rites and ceremonies tend to fortify and crystallize the religious emotion is one thing, to regard them as its only or basic source, another. It is true that religious dogma and the traditionalism of religious forms, obviously social factors, are ever present in the realm of the sacred. But society here remains, after all, a fortifying or precipitating agency, not a germinating force. Grant the religious emotion, and society can do wonders with it! But it cannot manufacture it out of whole cloth, nor out of itself. Society, of course, finds in religion a useful helpmate, and religion, in turn, leans heavily upon society. But this is another story.[8]

[8] For a much more elaborate presentation and criticism of Durkheim's position see my 'Religion and Society' (*Journal of Philosophy*, 1916; now reprinted, with slight changes, in *History, Psychology, and Culture*). After some hesitation, I decided to include this brief résumé and critique of Durkheim in this book at the risk of its being snubbed as 'dated.' Durkheim's very remarkable book continues to be read by students and laymen, and frequently I find them enthralled ('taken in' is the right word) by just those of his ideas which are most questionable.

Chapter XV

FAITH AND THE SUPERNATURAL

Mana or Impersonal Supernatural Power

Our analysis of religion and magic makes it clear that the idea of super-natural power is common to both and represents the basic concept under-lying the religio-magical world view. On the emotional side an equally fundamental factor is the *religious thrill*.

The idea of supernatural power assumed a central position in the dis-cussion of primitive religions with the introduction of the *mana* concept. The recent career of this concept is so instructive as to invite a slight historical digression.

Mana was formally introduced to ethnologists by R. H. Codrington in his book, *The Melanesians* (1891). By means of numerous illustra-tions, Codrington showed that among the various tribes of the South Seas, *mana*, as a religious concept, occupies a distinct and clearly defined po-sition: it indicates power which is supernatural and impersonal. *Mana* itself is not an animal or a human being, nor a ghost or spirit. It is just power, magical potency. Although impersonal in itself, it can work its effects with equal facility through natural objects or beings, or through men, spirits, or ghosts.[1]

Writing about *mana* in his book, *Polynesian Religion*, E. S. C. Handy says: 'The *mana* of the individual was believed to be concentrated in the head which, according to Polynesian philosophy, was associated with the superior, divine aspect of nature. . . .

'A prophet or diviner, who was the oracular medium of a spirit or god, had little or no accretion of personal *mana* because of his inspirational talent—his *mana* was but that of the spirit or god he served. . . . On the other hand, the ritualistic priest was a personal embodiment of acquired *mana*, who exhibited his power in the efficacy of his ritual, and in his knowledge of occult influences and power to interpret omens. . . .

---

[1] It may be noted in passing that in this area the ideas of ghost and spirit are sharply distinguished. A ghost is always the spirit of a deceased individual, whereas a spirit is a spiritual entity which either exists in detached form or dwells in a thing or being.

'In the case of a man of learning, such as a teacher of sacred law, accuracy of memory, extensive knowledge, and keenness of mind, were the evidences of his *mana*. In the Marquesas Islands any person who was an adept at any occupation was a *tuhuna*, a master. Every *tuhuna* possessed *mana* for the particular activity in which he was skilled. But there were rare individuals whose learning and ability extended to all the departments of man's activity: knowledge, ritual, arts and crafts. Such an adept, whose *mana* was so great that he was second to none in the tribe in sacredness, was honoured with the title of *tuhuna nui*, great master or adept. The ability, talent or capacity possessed by *tuhuna* appears to have been regarded as in part due to natural endowment, but more particularly to education, consecration, and experience. A Marquesan youth who could not memorize the ancient law was spoken of as being "without *mana*"; but anyone who had great ability, showed sufficient persistence in learning from his teacher, and submitted to the required consecratory rites could become a master bard and ceremonial priest (*tuhuna oono*). Such a scholar grew in power and prestige as he demonstrated the superiority of his knowledge and wit in contests that were from time to time held between the wise men of different tribes; but if in such a contest with other *tuhuna*, he proved incapable of meeting his opponent's sallies, or to be ignorant or in error, he was considered in some way to have lost the *mana* he once possessed. With his defeat, his prestige and power were dissipated, he was no longer recognized as a master, and it was sometimes even believed that his defeat would cause his death. The mental darkness or blindness that would lead to such a downfall might, according to native ideas, result from the man's having come under a spell of witchcraft of an opponent or enemy, or from psychic defilement or broken *tapu*.

'Another type of *mana* was that evidenced in physical prowess. . . . In the Marquesas it was through personal prowess that a tribesman became a war chief. The warrior was thought to embody the *mana* of all those whom he had killed, his own *mana* increasing in proportion with his prowess. In the mind of the native, the prowess was the result, however, not the cause of his *mana*. The *mana* of the warrior's spear was likewise increased with each death he inflicted. As the sign of his assumption of his defeated enemy's power, the victor in a hand-to-hand combat assumed his slain foe's name; with a view to absorbing directly his *mana*, he ate some of his flesh; and to bind the presence of the empowering influence in battle, to insure his intimate rapport with the captured *mana*, he wore as a part of his war dress some physical relic of his vanquished foe—a bone, a dried hand, sometimes a whole skull.' [2]

[2] *Bulletin*, Bernice P. Bishop Museum, vol. XXXIV, pp. 31–32.

Among these South Seas natives, *mana* was identified with procreative power, with the male principle in nature, with the divine, with life and light.

Quite independently of Codrington's researches, primitive concepts, similar to *mana* were discovered in North America. Of special interest in this connexion are William Jones's article, 'The Algonquin Manitou,' [3] and J. N. B. Hewitt's 'Orenda or a Definition of Religion.' [4] Both writers are of Indian descent, William Jones belonging to the Algonquin-speaking Sauk and Fox Indians, while Hewitt is a Tuscarora Iroquois.

By means of ethnological and linguistic evidence Jones shows convincingly that the Algonquin concept, *manitou*, implies supernatural power, in itself impersonal, which may or may not manifest itself through objects, beings, and natural phenomena. The term may appear either with or without a personal prefix, in accordance with the meaning intended. Among other illustrations of the application of the idea, Jones mentions the practice of eating the heart of a slain warrior in order to partake of his *manitou*, or supernatural potency. The practice, it will be seen, as well as the ideology, are strictly comparable to those recorded by Handy among the Polynesians.

Hewitt's argument is based wholly on a linguistic reconstruction. He traces the root vowel of the term *orenda* in a large number of terms referring to things, beings, or actions connected with supernatural power. Taking this as his starting point, Hewitt constructs an ancient Iroquoian religion built around the idea of *orenda*, impersonal supernatural power. While this procedure is not wholly unobjectionable from a theoretical standpoint, it is quite certain that the term *orenda*, with all its derivatives, carries a mystical connotation, and that the implied concept is related to the Algonquin *manitou* and the Siouan *wakan* or *wakonda*. While the cultural diversification of these tribes, as well as the cultural gulf separating these Indians from the Polynesians, would preclude any identity in the specific terms employed or the denoted ideas, *manitou*, *orenda*, *wakan*, and other such concepts—for instance, among the Kwakiutl and Eskimo—must certainly be regarded as closely related to *mana*.

Presently still another field was drawn into the discussion. In a volume on certain natives of the West Coast of Africa, between the deltas of the Congo and the Niger, Pechuel-Loesche [5] brought further contributory evidence. This is the classical region of fetishism. In his book *Fetishism* (in German), Heinrich Schurtz, now some seventy years ago, defined

---

[3] *Journal of American Folk-Lore*, vol. XVIII, 1905, pp. 183–190.
[4] *American Anthropologist*, vol. IV, New Series, 1892.
[5] *The Loango Expedition* (in German), vol. III, 1907, pp. 347–349.

fetishism as the religion of the fetish, a small (usually artificial) object through which an indwelling spirit is believed to be operating. As a result of his painstaking researches, including a linguistic analysis, Pechuel-Loesche arrived at a different interpretation. He claims that the conception underlying the fetishistic beliefs of this area (in particular, of the Bafioti) is not that of an indwelling spirit. To him a fetish is an artificial object made in a certain way or prepared in accordance with a standardized recipe, which possesses a specific power, or in some instances, several such powers.[6] If the shape of the object is changed or the recipe carelessly followed, the power is lost or modified. The underlying idea is that of power, in itself impersonal, definite qualities and quantities of which can be secured under certain highly specific conditions. Once again, then, the idea involved seems similar to *mana*.

In its wider bearings, Pechuel-Loesche's position may be one-sided. The idea of an indwelling spirit is so common in Africa and elsewhere that there can scarcely be any doubt of its occurrence in this western region of the continent. However this may be, the author's stand with reference to West African fetishes seems well taken.[7]

Thus the *mana* idea was established on a fairly wide geographical basis. There followed a rich harvest of theory and discussion. In this phase of the problem, the main stimulus came from Marett's essay, 'Pre-animistic Religion,'[8] in which he used the *mana* concept to supplement the ideology of animism which was still in complete possession of the field of primitive religion. Marett argued, moreover, that the idea of impersonal power was in its very nature more simple than that of spirit and that it should, therefore, be regarded as more primitive. Marett's contribution came at an auspicious moment; presently his little essay became the crystallization-point for a new philosophy of primitive religion. At the Third International Congress of Religions, held at Oxford in 1908, the subject of *mana* and 'animatism' (Marett's term for the pre-animistic

---

[6] A substance or object, in itself, has only one specific power; but by combining several substances or objects a composite fetish ('revolver fetish,' the author calls it) can be produced which will wield the combined powers of its parts. Pechuel-Loesche distinguishes two grades of fetishism, a lower and a higher. What he designates as low-grade fetishism appears to be nothing more than common magic: to cure a thorn sore, rub the thorn over the wound; to protect yourself against elephant or hippopotamus, carry with you parts of its body. Hoofs, horns, claws, hair, nails, skin-shavings, of animals or men, can all be similarly used, for offence or defence. High-grade fetishism, on the other hand, implies esoteric knowledge and expertness; it is the prerogative of medicine-men or magicians to know the recipes and possess the requisite skill.

[7] For a careful summary of beliefs in souls and spirits in Africa, see Ankermann in *Zeitschrift für Ethnologie*, vol. L, 1918, pp. 89–153 (in German).

[8] *Folk-Lore*, 1900. See also Marett's book, *The Threshold of Religion*.

religion) was the principal topic of discussion in the section devoted to primitive religion.

In subsequent writings *mana* became identified with magic and in this form its use became still further extended. Hubert and Mauss, two faithful students of Durkheim, made a sweeping application of the *mana* concept in their treatise on magic,[9] T. K. Preuss skilfully wove the *mana* idea into his analysis of the beginnings of religion and art,[10] while Durkheim in his great book identified *mana* with the religious core of totemism.

Thus the dogma of animism, of a spirit-infested world, was supplemented, in fact, came near being replaced by another dogma, a world swept by *mana*, or impersonal magic power.

In retrospect, the *mana* idea must be welcomed as a genuine addition to our understanding of early religion, nay of all religion. There is, of course, no point in juxtaposing *mana* and spirit, as to chronological priority; what is important is to realize that the idea of spirit must be supplemented by that of power (*mana*), if primitive religion, or any religion, is to be understood. *Mana* supplies the dynamic principle, whereas spirit, as such, is but a concept of form or being. When James T. Shotwell defines religion as 'a reaction of mankind to something which is apprehended but not comprehended' [11] he omits to state that the something to which there is a reaction is not merely a form, substance, or being, but a power. From this it follows that the idea of supernatural power—impersonal, formless in itself, but withal, a power and supernatural—must be coupled with spirit in all interpretations of religion. Indeed, if the signs of the times are to be trusted, may I not suggest that the more dynamic and vaguer idea may outlive its more precise and static companion? [12]

[9] 'Sketch of a General Theory of Magic' (in French), *Année Sociologique*, vol. VII, 1904.
[10] 'Origin of Religion and Art' (in German), *Globus*, 1904–1905.
[11] *The Religious Revolution of Today*, p. 101.
[12] A brief formulation of the relations of *mana* to religion, magic, and animism will be found in my article 'Spirit, *Mana* and the Religious Thrill,' *Journal of Philosophy*, vol. XIII, 1915 (reprinted, with revisions, in *History, Psychology, and Culture*). In this somewhat abstract essay I made an attempt to show that, from a psychological and epistemological standpoint, *mana* must be regarded as a projection or objectivation of what, on the subjective side, is the religious thrill: *mana is that which causes the religious thrill*. Now, if the religious thrill is accepted as the basic emotional root of religion, then *mana*, a psychologically basic *mana*, underlying its varied historic forms, becomes the fundamental idea of religion. *Mana* is but a term for an emotion, projected as a 'something' into the supernatural realm. Such emotions, religious, aesthetic, sexual, luminous as experience, defy more precise analysis.

The All-Father

During recent years certain primitive ideas have been reported from different fields of investigation which seem to differ not only from the cruder animistic beliefs, but also from the zoomorphic conceptions of early mythology. These ideas are usually discussed as the All-Father beliefs. The Aranda or Arunta of Central Australia, for example, believe in a great moral being, Aljira. He is conceived as a very large, strong man, with red skin and light hair which falls on his shoulders. His legs are like those of an emu. He is decorated with a white forehead-band, a neck-band, and a bracelet, and he wears a hair loin-girdle. His many wives, the Beautiful Ones, also red in complexion, have dogs' legs. Of his many sons and daughters, the former have emu legs, the latter dogs' legs. Handsome men and beautiful women frequent his neighbourhood.

Aljira never dies. He lives in heaven, which has existed from the beginning. The Milky Way is a great river with inexhaustible reservoirs of sweet water; tall trees, tasty berries, and fruits abound here. Great flocks of birds enliven Aljira's domain and different animals, such as kangaroos and wild-cats, seek his enormous hunting grounds. While Aljira follows the game, his wives gather edible herbs and other fruits which grow in abundance at all seasons. The stars are the camp-fires of Aljira.

Aljira is the supreme deity of the Aranda, known by men as well as women, but his reign is restricted to heaven. He is not the creator of man, nor is he concerned about him. No *churinga*—sacred stone or wooden slab—are consecrated to him. The Aranda do not fear him nor do they like him, but they do fear that some day the heaven, which rests upon piles or stone legs, will collapse and kill them all.[13]

What Strehlow says about Aljira agrees closely with the accounts about the All-Fathers of Southeast Australia collected by Howitt.

Thus the Narrinyeri believe in a supreme being who is said to have made all things on earth, to have given man his weapons and taught him ceremonies. When asked about the origin of a custom, they reply that the supreme being has instituted it. The Wotjobaluk, as well as the Kulin, speak of Bunjil, who is represented as an old man. He is the heavenly head-man of the tribe, and has two wives and a son, the Rainbow, whose wife is the Little Rainbow, the faint duplicate of the rainbow sometimes visible in the sky. He has given the Kulin their art, and according to at least one legend, he instituted the phratries and originated the law of

---

[13] This account of Aljira is based on C. Strehlow, *The Aranda and Loritja Tribes of Central Australia* (in German), Part I.

exogamy. Howitt stresses the fact that among these tribes the All-Father is endowed with distinctly human, rather than animal, traits.

Among the Kurnai, knowledge about a supreme being is almost entirely restricted to the initiated men, although the older women know at least of the existence of this being. The novices are initiated into the mysteries of the All-Father lore at the last and most sacred session of the initiation ceremonies. At this time they learn that long ago he lived on earth and taught the Kurnai how to make implements, nets, canoes, and weapons. The individual names which the people inherit from their ancestors were first bestowed by the supreme being. He also established the secret rituals. When someone revealed these ritualistic secrets to the women, the supreme being was full of wrath. In revenge he sent down his fire, the *Aurora Australis*, which filled the whole space between the sky and the earth. Men went mad with fear, brothers killing brothers, fathers their children, and husbands their wives. Then the sea rushed over the land and almost all mankind was drowned. Some of those who survived became the ancestors of the Kurnai, while others turned into animals, birds, reptiles, and fish. Tun Sun, son of the supreme being, and Sun's wife, became turtles. Then the supreme being left the earth and ascended to the sky, where he still resides.

All the tribes which attend the *kuringal* ceremonies of the Yuin people believe in a great being, Dara-Mulun, who once lived on earth with his mother. At first the earth was bare and, 'like the sky, as hard as a stone.' Land extended to where the sea is now. There were as yet no men or women, but only animals, birds, and reptiles. Dara-Mulun made the trees. Then he caused a great flood which covered the entire coast country, so that no people were left except some who crawled out of the water onto Mount Dromedary. Then Dara-Mulun ascended to the sky where he still lives, watching the actions of men. He made the bull-roarer—a *churinga* which, when swung around on a string, makes a noise remotely resembling the roaring of a bull—the sound of which is still believed to be his voice. He also gave the Yuin their laws, which ever since have been handed down by the old men. When men die and their spirits leave them, Dara-Mulun is there to meet them and take care of them.

Upon first analysis, these beliefs strongly suggest the possibility of missionary influence. The flood, its relation to the animal kingdom, the escape of some humans to a mountain, the moral character of the supreme being, and other traits strongly suggest the influence of White teachers. The problem, however, cannot be settled so easily. We cannot be sure what savages might think until we find them thinking it. Beliefs in a su-

preme being, more or less similar to those described, also occur among
some of the Negro peoples of the Gold Coast of West Africa, and cognate
notions seem to be present in North America and northeastern Siberia.
'Our Woman' of the Bella Coola, and Katonda, the creator and 'father of
the gods' among the African Baganda, clearly belong to the same category
of divine beings. It is especially notable that the supreme being is often
conceived as remote and detached from the affairs of men, although in
some instances he is believed to have created them. These two attributes,
the fact that the supreme being does not now actively participate in the
affairs of men, and the further fact that he is superior to other deities,
are the most consistently recurring ideas with reference to the All-
Father.

I shall cite two further instances of a somewhat different type. 'Among
the Kagaba [Colombia, South America],' writes Radin, 'we encounter a
female supreme deity and a profession of faith that should satisfy even
the most exacting monotheist.[14]

' "The mother of our songs, the mother of all our seed, bore us in the
beginning of things and she is the mother of all types of men, the mother
of all nations. She is the mother of the thunder, the mother of the streams,
the mother of trees and of all things. She is the mother of the world and
of the older brothers, the stone-people. She is the mother of our younger
brothers, the French, and the strangers. She is the mother of our dance
paraphernalia, of all our temples and she is the only mother we possess.
She alone is the mother of the fire and the Sun and the Milky Way. She
is the mother of the rain and the only mother we possess. And she has
left us a token in all the temples,—a token in the form of songs and
dances."

'She has no cult, and no prayers are really directed to her, but when
the fields are sown and the priests chant their incantations, the Kagaba
say, "And then we think of the one and only mother of the growing
things, of the mother of all things." One prayer was recorded. "Our
mother of the growing fields, our mother of the streams, will have pity

[14] The problem of the All-Father should not be confused with that of early
monotheism. A critical discussion of the problem was first undertaken by Andrew
Lang in his *The Making of Religion* (now 'dated'—and out of print), while a
systematic review of all relevant data and theories will be found in Father Schmidt's
work, *The Origin of the Idea of God* (in German). In all the instances cited in
the text—and the same is true in many other cases—the All-Father, it will be
observed, was not by any means the *only* supernatural being or deity. Thus the
generalization of Father Schmidt with reference to the original monotheism of the
pygmies (*cf.* his work *The Pygmy Tribes*, in German) must be placed on a distinct level from the discussions of the All-Father.

upon us. For to whom do we belong? Whose seeds are we? To our mother alone do we belong." ' [15]

'I refer to the very marked monotheism of the Amazulus of South Africa as described by Bishop Callaway,' writes Radin in his book. ' "Unkulunkulu," so their creation-account runs, "is no longer known (i.e., no memory of him exists). It is he who was the first being; he broke off in the beginning (i.e., sprang from something). We do not know his wife and the ancients do not tell us that he had a wife. Unkulunkulu gave men the spirits of the dead; he gave them doctors for treating disease, and diviners. The old men say Unkulunkulu is (i.e., was a reality); he made the first men, the ancients of long ago."

'There are a number of suggestive features about this Unkulunkulu. The name itself means the "old-old one," and his other designations imply priority and potential source of existence. But what is his relation to mankind? There the versions differ, some regarding him as having created men, others as having begotten them. It is likewise quite difficult to decide often whether he is regarded as the direct ancestor of man or as a true creator. What has happened seems clear. The Amazulus are ancestor-worshippers, worship the spirits of the departed, and this has influenced their conception of the supreme being to the extent of transforming him into the mythical ancestor of his race. Something of the irresponsible Transformer still clings to him at times as the following story indicates. He sends a chameleon to say, "Let not men die," but the chameleon lingers along the road and he then dispatches a lizard to say, "Let men die." Thus it is that death came into the world. But such traits are unimportant. When, indeed, it is recalled that the spirit of the deceased ancestor is predominantly evil and has to be propitiated, the fact that the partial transformation of Unkulunkulu into an ancestor has in no way affected his ethical and benevolent activities lends additional corroboration to the well-nigh universal moral nature of the supreme being among primitive peoples. Whatever else may happen, his ethical nature apparently can in no way be contaminated.' [16]

In concluding this sketchy presentation of the All-Father idea I cannot

[15] T. K. Preuss, *Religion and Mythology of the Uitoto* (in German), vol. I, p. 170. Unfortunately Preuss's book was not accessible to me at the time of this writing. I am therefore reproducing the above passage from Paul Radin's book, *Primitive Man as a Philosopher*, pp. 357–358. (Reprinted by permission of D. Appleton-Century Company.)

[16] Bishop Callaway, *The Religious System of the Amazulu*, pp. 1 seq. This book also was not available to me, and I once more reproduce Radin's statement on pp. 351–353 (*loc. cit.*). Note that Radin does not always differentiate between the idea of a supreme being and monotheism.

do better than quote once more from Radin's conclusion in his pro-
vocative book. In my judgment this anthropologist has thought more
deeply on this difficult topic than anyone else. This is what he writes:

'If we are right in assuming the same more or less fixed distribution of
ability and temperament in every group of approximately the same size,
it would follow that no type has ever been totally absent. I feel quite con-
vinced that the idealist and the materialist, the dreamer and the realist,
the introspective and the nonintrospective man have always been with us.
And the same would hold for the different grades of religious temperament, the devoutly religious, the intermittently, the indifferently religious
man. If individuals with specific temperaments, for instance the religious-
aesthetic, have always existed we should expect to find them expressing
themselves in much the same way at all times. And this, it seems to me,
is exactly what we do find. The pagan polytheistic religions are replete
with instances of men—poets, philosophers, priests—who have given ut-
terance to definitely monotheistic beliefs. It is the characteristic of such
individuals, I contend, always to picture the world as a unified whole,
always to postulate some first cause. No evolution from animism to monotheism was ever necessary in their case. What was required were individuals of a certain type. Alongside of them and vastly in the majority have
always been found others with a temperament fundamentally distinct,
to whom the world has never appeared as a unified whole and who have
never evinced any marked curiosity as to its origin.

'Such, too, is the situation among primitive peoples. If anything, the
opposition of the two types is much clearer. All the monotheists, it is my
claim, have sprung from the ranks of the eminently religious individuals.
Its precise formulation is due to those specifically religious individuals
who happen to be thinkers at the same time. It is in the ritualistic version
of the original myth, for example, that Earthmaker [17] is depicted as a supreme deity who definitely creates the other deities and the culture-
heroes; it is in the ritualistic version of the culture-hero cycle again that
a nonmoral, buffoon-like hero, whose acts are only incidentally benefi-
cial to mankind, is transformed into an ethical, intelligent, beneficent
creator. No other explanation for the characteristics of the supreme deities, as I have attempted to sketch them, is indeed conceivable except upon
the assumption that they reflect a definite type of temperament, examples
of which we know actually exist in every primitive group. Such people
are admittedly few in number, for the overwhelming mass belong to the
indifferently religious group, are materialists, realists, to whom a god,

[17] God-Creator of the Winnebago, among whom Radin has spent many years of
fruitful research.

be he supreme deity or not, is simply to be regarded as a source of power. If men of this type accept such a god, he is immediately equated with the more concrete deities who enter into direct relations with man, and as a result contamination ensues. It is thus that that particular type of creator arose, where a marked admixture of attributes belonging to the culture-hero and transformer was manifest.

'On such a hypothesis a really satisfactory explanation of the existence and of the dominant traits of the monotheism among primitive peoples can be given. Monotheism would then have to be taken as fundamentally an intellectual-religious expression of a very special type of temperament and emotion. Hence the absence of cults, for instance, the unapproachability of the supreme being, his vagueness of outline, and his essential lack of function. Whatever dynamic force he possesses for the community is that with which the realists invested him. In so doing they frequently converted him into a cult deity, into a creator of gods; made him but one among many. This is merely monolatry if you wish, but this in no way detracts from the possibility that the faith of the religious man himself may have been different, may have been essentially explicit monotheism. Yet even if we should not care to press this claim, the existence of monolatry and implicit monotheism must constitute a definite challenge to the views still current as to the development of the concept of a supreme creator.' [18]

By way of comment on this passage, I might add that, though it suffers from the confusion of monotheism with the notion of a supreme but not sole deity, the idea of connecting kinds of religious orientation with types of temperament seems to me a capital one. Also, it chimes well with what in recent years we have come to know about individual variability among primitives.

Taboo

Another concept and institution, religious in essence and more impressive in its sweep than almost any other aspect of primitive culture, is taboo. In the notion of taboo the polarity or ambivalence of religion comes to the fore. It represents a merging of the notion of sacredness with that of uncleanness, and with this goes the further trait of infectiousness. A tabooed thing, animal, or person may not be handled, killed, eaten, spoken to, or if it is, can be so dealt with only under certain specially defined conditions. It has the tendency to radiate its holy but dangerous essence, its tabooness as it were, to surrounding things and persons

[18] Radin, *op. cit.*, pp. 365–367.

which in consequence may also become taboo, at least for a time. It is for this reason that rites exist among most primitive tribes for the removal of taboo. What has been rendered sacred or unclean by a proscribed act or even an accidental association with a thing tabooed, can once more be drawn into the realm of normal things if certain rites are performed.

Among the most common taboos, found practically everywhere, are certain food prohibitions which become associated with people of a certain age, status, or condition, for example with young boys or girls before a certain age is reached, or with women during pregnancy, the menstrual period, or after childbirth, or with hunters and warriors before the chase or a war raid, or with individuals in search of a religious experience, like the Indian youth during the period preceding the guardian-spirit vision. Exalted persons, such as chiefs, are often taboo by dint of their high status.

The notion of taboo in its varied ramifications will become clearer when illustrated by concrete examples taken from different areas. One of the most widespread applications of taboo is in connection with totemic tribes (see p. 324), where the sacred animal, bird, or plant may not be killed or eaten by the members of a sib with whom it is in one or another way associated. Among the Australians this prohibition is universal. No Australian is permitted to partake of or kill his taboo creature, and if such instances do occur, it is in a special ceremonial setting and under strictly prescribed conditions such as those of the magical *intichiuma* ceremonies (see p. 324).

Not all food restrictions, however, are associated with totemism, even where it exists. In Australia, for example, where the totemic taboo, as stated, is universal, there are also numerous other eating restrictions. In the Kakadu tribe, for example, a boy after one of the initiation rites finds himself greatly hampered in his choice of foods. From now on and for some time to come he is forbidden to eat a variety of yams, the goanna lizard, a variety of snakes, flying fox, the female opossum, emu, white crane, female turtle, and about twice as many more animals and birds. These prohibitions are so comprehensive that the things that the poor fellow may partake of also require to be specified, and so they are. Among the same tribe, if a dog catches a goanna lizard, no boy or young man may eat it; if he were to do so, he would be seized with severe pains in the back and his fingers would rot away. This last feature, namely the automatic magical penalty for the transgression of a taboo, is characteristic of that institution and vouchsafes its supernatural character. The transgression of a taboo thus appears not merely as a social offence but as a sacrilege, and the penalization is therefore administered through supernatural channels. In the case of the boy and the goanna, as in other such cases, the consequences of a transgression of a taboo can be removed by means of certain prescribed techniques. An old man takes the bones of a goanna caught by a dog. He powders them up and mixes them with a substance of a certain yam, also powdered. Of this concoction the young man must partake, whereupon the taboo is removed.

Similarly, women during childbirth or in pregnancy are forbidden to eat a variety of birds and snakes, as well as certain plants. In this case the penalty for infraction is visited upon the child. If a pregnant mother partakes of the forbidden spur-winged plover, the child is born with sores under its arms; if she partakes of the flying fox, the child will have sore feet and tongue; if she eats a jungle-fowl, a spirit will take the child away and bury it in the mountain nest of a jungle-bird. If the mother eats a rock-snake, the navel string will become twisted around the child and it will die in the womb. During this same period the woman must not eat anything that is cooked in an oven. The native oven consists of a hole in the ground lined with stones, previously heated on a fire; the food is placed on the stones, covered with paper bark or leaves, and cooked, under an additional covering of earth. It is food thus prepared that the woman may not touch; anything she eats must be cooked on an ordinary fire above the ground. Even after the child is born and while it is still young, the mother must submit to further restrictions. She may not drink out of a deep water-hole, having been warned by her husband that if she does so the child will die. Nor may she eat fish out of a deep water-hole: if a child were to see its mother drinking out of a deep water-hole, its spirit would leave the body, run to the water-hole, and drown or be swallowed up by a certain snake. Still, as in other cases, there is a way out. Should the mother by any chance break this rule, father, mother, and child, accompanied by a medicine-man, go to the water-hole. The father gives the mother a little water in a bark basket. The spirit of the child is thus induced to come up and is caught by the medicine-man, who alone is able to see it. He places the spirit in the mother's head from which it descends into her breast; the child, which is at once put to the breast, drinks in its spirit with the mother's milk and is thus saved for the living,[19]—a simple and salutary process.

Anything out of the ordinary is likely to be dangerous and fenced in by taboos, for example, the dead or any things or actions connected with them. Thus we find among the Salish-speaking tribes of British Columbia that after the death of a person his or her name may not be used, some-

[19] Spencer and Gillen, *Native Tribes of the Northern Territory of Australia,* pp. 342 seq.

times for as long as a year. Not only this, but any other word of which the name may be a constituent part, is also excluded from use. To illustrate this in English: it is as if after the death of Mary, the name itself, as well as the words 'marriage,' 'mariner,' 'marionette,' were to be excluded from use for a year.

In certain instances such prohibitions seem curiously artificial, perhaps only on account of our ignorance of their origin. Thus, among the Siouan Omaha of the Plains, who are divided into gentes with animal and bird totems, the Eagle people are not allowed to touch a buffalo head; the people of a certain sub-gens, the name of which may be translated as 'To-carry-a-turtle-on-one's-back,' are allowed to touch or carry a turtle but not to eat it; in the Buffalo Tail gens, the Keepers-of-the-Pipe do not eat the lowest buffalo rib, while the Keepers-of-the-Sweet-Medicine may not touch any calves; and so on and on.

In Polynesia the institution of taboo has reached an unusual degree of development and importance. It applies to many things but to none more emphatically than to the person and acts of an hereditary chieftain. Beyond all other things, he is taboo, as the embodiment of the divine and the instrument of the *mana* or supernatural power of his divine ancestors. Thus he is doomed to be fenced about with numerous taboos designed to protect him and through him his ancestors from any disgrace and consequent loss of *mana*. The head of every person here is taboo, especially so the head of a chief, for it is there that his *mana* is believed to be concentrated. The height of disgrace in Polynesia is to touch a chief's head or to pass something common or unclean over it, or to insult it by comparing it to a profane thing. This is so serious an offence that wars, in certain instances, have been known to break out for no other reason than the commission of such an act. And here as always, the taboo radiates from the chief to all things with which he comes in contact, such as clothing, houses, personal possessions, canoes, land, his food, and all vessels or processes associated with its preparation and consumption.

A taboo was imposed upon whole communities on important occasions such as birth, marriage, the sickness or death of a chief, religious festivals, war, fishing expeditions. On such occasions all members of the tribe were subjected to a taboo on all common everyday activities. Those not actively engaged in the particular enterprise involved were yet passively parts of it by engaging in no other activity. All noise was forbidden, people were restrained from moving about, no fires were lighted, and no food prepared or eaten. New objects or first fruits were subject to a taboo: a crop about to be harvested, food recently collected and ready for consumption, a catch of fish, were taboo, until a small proportion had been offered to the gods whose *mana* had been utilized in the enterprise. This offering of first fruits to the gods 'raised' the taboo and set the stuffs free (*noa*) for general consumption.

Another kind of Polynesian taboos, sometimes distinguished as *rahui*, were arbitrary prohibitions instituted by chiefs or other proprietors of trees, lands, or fishing grounds, for the purpose of keeping away trespassers or reserving the food supply for some particular occasion. When a chief was imposing a *rahui* on a crop or a kind of fish, he would do so by calling upon the priest to invoke the support of the gods, promising them a share of the food when it was harvested. In New Zealand a chief who desired to place a *rahui* upon a piece of land or a stream could do so by erecting a post and hanging a piece of cloth upon it, while uttering a curse against trespassers. Among the Marquesans the same effect could be achieved by the chief giving the land his own name or calling it his head. As among the Australian Kakadu, we find among the natives of Tahiti that a pregnant woman who insists on partaking of forbidden food endangers her child. Handy tells of a boy who had claw-like hands as a result of the fact that his mother when pregnant partook of some crab meat. Club-feet, mottled skin, and other deformities were similarly accounted for.[20]

In the economic life and ideas of the Maori the influence of taboo was all-pervasive. Forests, for example, were believed to stand under the guardianship of the god Tane, who protected the trees, rats, birds, and all woodland products from unauthorized interference. A taboo lay upon them. Hence Tane had to be placated and the taboo raised before a Maori would venture to put any of these things to his own use. We find among the Maori a whole series of *whakanoa* rites, ceremonies devised to make sacred or forbidden things 'common,' before they could be made available for ordinary use. Thus, the erection of a carved meeting house was surrounded by much taboo. While the work was in progress only authorized persons, such as the priest and the builders, were allowed within. No food could be taken inside nor could the chips and shavings from the timber be used for cooking food or for any ordinary purpose. When the building was finally completed, there was no further necessity for stringent taboo; however, it still clung to the completed structure and had to be removed by special ceremony, which finally freed the finished house from any taboo restrictions and made it available for common use.

The concept and nature of taboo, as operative among the Maori, is

[20] E. S. Craighill Handy, *Polynesian Religion*, pp. 43 seq.

best understood by associating it with the correlated notion of a non-material core or 'life-principle' (*mauri*) which was connected with all things in nature and gave them their vitality, in fact their very existence. In the case of a forest, for example, its fertility and productive power depended upon its *mauri*. The fruiting of trees, the abundance of birds and rats, all hinged upon the preservation of their *mauri* intact. The same applied to fisheries. Firth correctly notes that this *mauri* was an intangible and imponderable essence, impersonal in character. It should not be confused with the notion of an indwelling spirit. In the various economic undertakings of their daily life the Maori, while using the resources provided by their environment, were careful not to interfere with the *mauri* of these things, thus contaminating them. Hence the taboo regulations. A system of protective magic was instituted. This was made possible or more readily workable for the reason that the *mauri* of a thing could be isolated from its normal physical base and localized in a particular spot or a small material object, such as a stone. This could easily be hidden away in some obscure spot where it would be safe from prying eyes, thus ensuring the life principle and productive powers of the forest.[21] The term applied to such a material depository of the life power of something else being also *mauri*, one should be forewarned against confusion in interpretation. The *mauri* stone is generally concealed at the base of a tree, buried in the ground or sunk in the bed of a stream.[22]

In addition to these relatively passive measures for the protection of natural resources, more active ones were taken on occasion, which consisted in the setting up of a *rahui*. The procedure was, in brief, like this. A post, termed *rahui*, was set up in the ground on the edge of a forest, the bank of a stream, or other spot which was to be protected. To this post was attached a *maro*, consisting of a lock of hair or a bunch of grass.

[21] Raymond Firth, *Primitive Economics of the New Zealand Maori*, pp. 234 seq. Aptly enough, Firth here refers to the well-known Russian fairy-tale in which a giant hides his life or soul in an egg which he carefully conceals; thence he is impervious to bodily assault and continues on his cheerful and wicked course, until one day the egg is found and broken. Thereupon the giant perishes.

[22] The *mauri* of the fisheries of the Mokau River reposes in a large hour-glass-shaped stone (perhaps of great antiquity, as according to tradition it had been the anchor of the ancestral canoe, Tainui). This stone was once carried away by a European, but had to be restored by the government at the natives' earnest request, the latter claiming that their fish had deserted the river. 'Recently,' continues Firth, 'hearing that it was proposed to remove the stone for safe keeping at a museum, the local natives assembled, dug it out from its resting place in the sands of the river, and concealed it, subsequently revealing it again to the public view by imbedding it in a concrete base for protection. They feared lest again the "rock" of the fishing grounds depart.' (*Ibid.*, p. 246, note 1.)

Then a priest proceeded by means of magical incantations to 'sharpen the teeth of the *rahui,* that it might destroy man.' To overcome the protective power of the *rahui,* counter-devices, also magical, were known, which an ill-wishing intruder might employ to neutralize the power of the *rahui.* Whereupon he might use his spell to hurt the fertility of the forest. Such an eventuality was, in fact, foreseen and measures were taken against it: a false *maro* was attached to the post, whereas the real one impregnated with the destructive magic against an intruder, as well as the *rahui* stone, were concealed. As a consequence, the misled intruder, when he tried to direct his arts against the *rahui* post, would fail to neutralize its magic: on the contrary, it was still there and would work to his destruction should he attempt to meddle with the *mauri* of the forest.

The infringement of a *rahui,* as will be seen, was a serious matter. When a *rahui* was equipped with a dangerous spell, a breach of it was believed to be punished automatically, the culprit being afflicted with a wasting disease. In case no spell had been performed over a *rahui,* its infringement was penalized by means of witchcraft exercised by the owners of the forest or fishery. When a *rahui* was imposed by a chief on behalf of his tribe, transgressors were slain in punishment. In some historical instances, hostilities between two tribes or *hapu* broke out on account of an infringement against a *rahui.*

It will be clear from these instances of Maori taboo how close, on occasion, can be the relationship between taboo and magic. It seems then that Marett knew well whereof he spoke when he referred to taboo as 'negative magic.'

Chapter XVI

THE SPIRIT WORLD

Chukchee Animism

Like that of all primitives, the world view of the Chukchee is an animistic one. Every object here can act, speak, and walk. Everything that exists has its own 'Voice' or 'Master.' Reindeer skins have a Master of their own. In the night-time they turn into reindeer and walk to and fro. The very shadows on the walls live in tribes in their own country where they have huts and subsist by hunting.

Interesting beliefs are entertained about Mushrooms and Mushroom-Men. Mushrooms, when they grow, are so powerful that they split whole trees. These Mushrooms appear to be intoxicated men in the shape of humans, resembling their real shapes in some particular. Thus one may have but one leg, another a very large head, and so on. The number of Mushrooms that appear to a man varies in accordance with the number of mushrooms he has eaten. The Mushroom-Men lead the dreamer through the world and show him real and imaginary things. They take him to places where the dead live, through which they travel along many intricate paths.

Wooden amulets in a bag become Herdsmen and go out at night to protect the herd from wolves. Black and polar bears, eagles, small birds, sea mammals, all have countries of their own and live like humans. They can turn into human beings, while preserving some of their own qualities. Mice-People live in underground houses, using a certain root as their reindeer. They have sledges made of grass. Off and on, they become transformed into real hunters, with regular sledges, and hunt polar bears.

According to one story, a dried skin of an ermine transformed itself into a real ermine, which later turned into a large polar bear. Boulders are regarded as petrified creatures. They represent the first attempt of the Creator to make man. As they were very clumsy, he transformed them into stones. After this, animals and men were created.

Forests, rivers, and lakes have their own Masters; the same applies to various classes of animals and trees, which must thence be treated with

238

circumspection. The only exception among trees is the birch, which men handle as their 'equal.' Sledges, shafts of spears, and the like are made of birch wood. Native sketches of spirits collected by Bogoras show that these resemble, to a degree, the animals to which they belong. Thus the Master of fish and of mountain brooks has a long thin body and a face covered with hair. The Master of the forest has a body of wood without arms or legs. His eyes are on the crown of his head and he rolls along like a log of wood.[1]

Pitchvutchin is an especially important Owner or Master of wild reindeer and of all land game. He lives in deep ravines, or stays near the forest border. When amiable, he sends reindeer to the hunters, but when he is angered, he withholds the supply. He is the guardian of all ancient customs and sacrifices connected with the hunt. Any neglect of these angers him. In size he is reported to be not larger than a man's finger, while his footprints on the snow are like those of a mouse. According to the beliefs of the Maritime Chukchee, Pitchvutchin has power over sea game also. At times one may see him passing the door of a house in the shape of a small black pup, but on inspection the footprints will prove like those of a mouse, revealing his identity. As soon as this is discovered, the people offer him a sacrifice, believing that in the following year a large whale will drift to that part of the house. Pitchvutchin's sled is very small and made of grass. Instead of reindeer, he drives a mouse, or a certain small root. In fact, he himself is sometimes represented as the root driving a mouse. The lemming is his polar bear. He kills it and loads it on his sledge. On the other hand, he is believed to be very strong, can wrestle with giants, and upon occasion can load a real polar bear upon his sledge. He takes no solid food, living on odours.

Three classes of spirits called *kelet* are especially prominent in Chukchee belief: evil spirits which, walking invisibly, carry disease and death and prey on human bodies and souls; blood-thirsty cannibals who live on distant shores and fight Chukchee warriors; and spirits which are at the call of shamans and help them in their magic.

Among spirits of the first variety are the Ground Spirits. They have the forms of different creatures, fish, dog, bird, fox, insect, but are very

---

[1] This has an interesting bearing on Spencer's theory that the spirits populating the world in the animistic age were, at least in origin, human spirits. This part of Spencer's theory, incidentally, was rejected by Tylor, who held that each order of creatures or things in nature had its own kind of spirits from the beginning. The Chukchee evidence supports Tylor's view. But there are, of course, numerous instances where the spirits of animals, plants, etc., *are* human spirits. It seems thus that both Tylor and Spencer were right in their individual versions of the theory, wrong in rejecting each other's versions.

small.[2] In proportion to their size, they always have a very large mouth, set with many strong teeth. The *kelet* do not like to stay in their own villages. They prefer to visit human settlements, and are believed to be constantly wandering about in search of human prey. But they themselves live like human beings, and are considered a tribe like other tribes: they marry and have children, occupy villages and camps, and travel about the country with reindeer and dogs. Their young boys and girls go hunting and fishing, while the old men sit at home and try to read the future by the aid of divining stones. They always hunt man, whom they call 'Little Seal.' Their divining stone is a human skull, while men often use animal skulls for that purpose.

If the *kelet* can catch a human soul, they chop it to pieces, cook it in a kettle and feed it to their children. The *kelet* and the shamans are hostile to each other. In their encounters, victory does not always rest with the *kelet*. Animals of peculiar form are sacrificed to the *kelet*, such as reindeer with unusual antlers, white reindeer with black ear-points, or new-born fauns with misshapen mouths. Natural death is unknown to the Chukchee. When a man dies, he is supposed to have been killed by a spirit, or by the charm of an evil shaman.

The second variety of supernatural creatures are the Giants, who live on earth but far removed from human habitation. They are always represented as very poor. They can be fought with ordinary means.

The third variety of spirits are those appearing to shamans. At shamanistic performances, they usually figure as the 'spirit-voices' of the shaman produced by the latter by means of ventriloquism. Shamanistic spirits may appear as wolves, reindeer, walrus, whales, birds, plants, icebergs, utensils, pots, needles, and needle-cases. The shamanistic spirits are very mean to the shaman in case he commits any irregularities, but if his behaviour is unobjectionable, they are always at his call. Also, these spirits seem to engage in constant quarrels with each other, and then the shaman plays the conciliator.

The Chukchee personify the 'directions' of the compass, of which they recognize twenty-two, including the Zenith and the Nadir. Of these the Mid-Day and the Dawn are the most important and to them most of the sacrifices are made.

The sun, moon, and stars are also conceived as men of different kinds.

The Chukchee believe in a number of indefinite beings whose character and shape remain vague. Among these are the Creator, the Upper

---

[2] The diminutive character of many of the Chukchee spirits is paralleled by a similar trait of some Northwest Coast spirits. Why this should be so, is, as so often, not easy to see.

Being, the World, the Merciful Being, the Life-Giving Being, and the Luck-Giving Being.[3]

The Zenith, Mid-Day, and Dawn are often represented as identical with the creator of the world. Among the baptized Chukchee, the Christian God has a place assigned to him side-by-side with these vague superior beings.

A special group of spirits are the House Spirits. They are regarded as permanently associated with the house, their very names being derived from a stem meaning 'absence of motion.' These spirits live like the Chukchee themselves. They stay in pairs and have children. Their children get sick and die. When a spirit child dies, the spirit may make friends with another spirit and allow it to have relations with his wife, a custom current among the Chukchee.

Among the many charms of the Chukchee those of the household are of special interest, and among these, particularly, the hearth itself. Bogoras's statement on this subject deserves to be quoted verbatim: 'The chief place among the sacred things of the household belongs to the hearth itself. At every ceremonial, the hearth-fire is fed by a new spark from each of the hereditary fire-tools. Each family has a fire of its own and interchange of fires is strictly prohibited. Families whose fires are derived from different lines of ancestors, even though they may be living for years in one camp, will carefully guard against any contact with their fires. To borrow a neighbour's fire is held to be one of the greatest of sins. If a camp is pitched on a spot formerly occupied by another family, the Chukchee woman, in order to start a new fire, will not avail herself of the coal or wood that was left. Even when encamped on the treeless tundra, she will break up the sledges for firewood rather than take a single splinter bearing marks of an alien fire. Interchange of household utensils connected with the hearth—like kettles, dishes, lamps, receptacles for meat, etc.—is also strictly forbidden. It is even considered sinful to warm at one hearth a piece of cold meat which has been boiled at another. All these restrictions, however, refer only to the "genuine fire," obtained for a native hearth by means of a wooden drill and the sacred fire board.'

[3] Bogoras believes that these vague deities represent an indefinite transformation of the creative principle of the world and may be compared to the *manitou* or *wakan* of the American Indians. On the basis of Bogoras's own statement about these beings, this analogy seems doubtful. The talented author's opinion is adduced here for what it may be worth. It may be noted in passing that while Bogoras has few peers as an observer, his interpretations, mostly omitted here, are often arbitrary. The data on Chukchee animism are taken from W. Bogoras, *The Chukchee*, I: 'Religion' (*Jesup North Pacific Expedition*, vol. VII).

The Guardian Spirit in American Indian Religion

Of all religious phenomena in North America, the most general as
well as varied are the beliefs and practices centring in the cult of the
guardian spirit. In essence, these cults are rooted in a faith in supernatural power, personal or impersonal.

To acquire a guardian spirit is the Indian's most sacred quest. When
a boy approaches maturity, when 'his voice begins to change,' he repairs to the woods, where he builds for himself a crude hut or tent. Here
he lives in isolation, takes frequent purgatives and eats sparingly. His
thoughts are bent on the supernatural experience he is about to face.
When he has reached a high state of purity, physically and spiritually
('so the spirits can look through him,' says the Indian), the desire of
his soul is realized: the guardian spirit appears to him in a dream or
vision. The spirit may appear in animal, bird, or human shape, or it may
be a monster creature told about in myth. The guardian spirit bestows
upon the novice a supernatural gift or several such and, having given
him advice as to a proper life to lead, disappears. Henceforth, the youth
stands in an intimate personal relation to the spirit, appeals to it for
protection, and is warned by it when danger impends. If the spirit is an
animal or bird, the youth may have to abstain from eating or killing
individuals of that species; this taboo, however, is not found in all Indian
tribes.[4]

This generalized representation of the guardian-spirit quest does scant
justice to this central cult of the North American Indians and its many
cultural ramifications. It may be of interest, therefore, to dwell somewhat more fully on the particular forms assumed by the guardian-spirit
cult among several representative tribal groups.

The southern Kwakiutl of the Northwest Coast are divided into a large
number of clans, each of which traces its origin to a mythical ancestor
whose adventures are connected with the crests and privileges of the
clan. In the course of his adventures, the ancestor meets the sacred creature of the clan and obtains from it supernatural powers and magical

---

[4] A suggestive account of the acquisition of a guardian spirit is found in Paul
Radin's 'An Autobiography of a Winnebago Indian,' *Journal of American Folk-
Lore*, 1913. In this case, the supernatural protector is the Earth Spirit, with whom
the somewhat sophisticated Indian repeatedly fails to enter into rapport. The
entire account bears the stamp of genuineness and is particularly interesting as a
portrayal of the transition between blind faith and mild scepticism characteristic
of some modern Indians. For an excellent account of a highly elaborate and
picturesque vision I want to refer to *Black Elk Speaks*, the life story of a 'holy man'
of the Ogalala Sioux, as told to John G. Neihardt, pp. 20–47 ('The Great Vision').
Unfortunately the account is too long for reproduction here.

objects, such as the magic harpoon which ensures success in sea-water hunting, the water of life which resuscitates the dead, and the like. He also receives a dance, a song, a distinctive cry—each spirit having a cry of its own—and the right to use certain carvings. The dance consists of a dramatization of the myth in which the ancestor acquires gifts from the spirit. Some of these spirits are animals, such as the bear, wolf, sea-lion, killer-whale; others are fabulous monsters. To the latter class belongs Sisiutl, a mythical double-headed snake which often assumes the shape of a fish. To eat or even see it means death: all joints of the culprit become dislocated and his head is turned backwards. Another monster is the cannibal-woman, Dzonoqwa. Both Sisiutl and Dzonoqwa are dangerous when hostile, but when their goodwill is assured they become useful, and the powers they bestow are greatly sought after.

Among the Kwakiutl all these spirits with their gifts tend to become hereditary clan privileges. In some instances an individual may transmit some of these valuable possessions to his own descendants; but more often a set of guardian spirits with their gifts are hereditary in a clan, and all individuals of the clan may obtain supernatural powers from these spirits. Some spirits appear only in the ancestral tradition, others may still be obtained by Kwakiutl youths. Prominent among spirits of the latter class is Making-War-all-over-the-Earth. With the assistance of this spirit, a youth may obtain three different powers: mastery over the Sisiutl, the capacity to catch the invisible Dream Spirits, and insensibility to pain and wounds. With the assistance of The-First-One-to-Eat-Man-at-the-Mouth-of-the-River, another spirit, nine powers may be obtained. The spirit Maden is a bird and gives the faculty of flying. Various ghost spirits bestow the power to return to life after having been killed.

The spirits appear only in the winter, the season of the 'secrets.' During the winter ceremonial, the people are divided into two main bodies: the initiated ('Seals') and the uninitiated ('Sparrows'). The latter are divided into groups consisting of individuals who expect to be initiated at about the same time. There are ten such groups or societies—seven male and three female—and most of them bear animal names. Throughout the ceremonies the two groups are hostile to each other. The Seals attack and torment the Sparrows, who try to reciprocate to the best of their ability. The object of a number of ceremonies performed by each society is to secure the return of the youth who has been taken away by the spirit protector of the society. When the novice finally returns he is in a state of ecstasy, and other ceremonies are performed to restore him to his senses.

Among the Haida the guardian-spirit idea finds its clearest expression

in the beliefs about shamans. When a supernatural being takes possession of a man, speaking and acting through him, the man becomes a
shaman. While thus possessed, the shaman loses his personal identity
and becomes one with the spirit. He dresses as directed by the spirit
and uses its language. Thus, if a supernatural being from the Tlingit
country takes possession of a shaman, he speaks Tlingit, although otherwise ignorant of that tongue. The personal name, also, is discarded, and
that of the spirit substituted, and as the spirit changes, the name is also
changed.

The Tlingit shamans were even more powerful than those of the Haida.
Whereas the Haida shaman usually owns only one spirit and no masks,
his Tlingit colleague can boast of several spirits and masks. The representations of subsidiary spirits, to be seen on some masks, are expected
to strengthen various faculties of the shaman. The shamans, as well as
ordinary individuals, can increase their powers by obtaining the tongues
of a variety of spirit animals, especially those of land-otters. These
tongues are mixed with eagle claws and other articles and are carefully
stored away. Shamans often perform merely for display, or, when de-
sirous of demonstrating their superior powers, they may engage in imaginary battles with other shamans many miles away.

It will thus be seen how deeply the belief in guardian spirits has
entered into the lives and thoughts of the people of British Columbia
and southern Alaska. Reared on the fertile ground of an all-pervading
animism, guardian spirits manifest themselves through the medium of
many things and creatures. By means of art, the realm of magical potentialities becomes further extended—when the representation of a spirit
protector is carved on an implement, weapon, or ceremonial object, the
thing itself becomes a carrier of supernatural powers. Among the Kwakiutl, the guardian-spirit idea stands in the centre of a complex system
of secret societies and initiation rites. With the approach of winter, the
guardian spirit, like a ghost of the past, emerges from its summer re-
tirement and through the medium of names transforms the social organization of the people.[5] Among the Haida and Tlingit the belief in the
magical powers of supernatural helpers has engendered a prolific growth
of shamanistic practices. The Tsimshian, Haida, and Tlingit have woven
the guardian spirit into their family and clan legends, the incidents of
which receive dramatic embodiment in the dances of the secret societies.

[5] For details about this unique seasonal transformation of the Kwakiutl consult
Franz Boas, 'The Secret Societies and Social Organization of the Kwakiutl Indians,'
Proceedings, United States National Museum, 1895, from which study the details
about Kwakiutl guardian spirits are gleaned.

The guardian spirit also figures as a standard of rank. The vaster the powers of a supernatural guardian, the greater respect does its owner command, while the secret societies rank according to the powers of their members.

In the Plateau area, the guardian-spirit phenomena have been studied with particular care among the Thompson River Indians, the Shuswap, and the Lillooet. Among the Thompson River Indians, every person acquired a guardian spirit at puberty. The spirits were not inherited, except in the case of a few powerful shamans. All animals and objects possessed of magical qualities could become guardian spirits. The powers of such spirits had become differentiated, so that certain kinds of spirits were associated with definite social or professional groups. The shamans had their favourite spirits, including natural phenomena (night, fog, east, west), man or parts of the human body (woman, young girl, hands or feet of man, etc.), animals (bat), objects referring to death (land of souls, ghosts, dead men's hair, bones and teeth, etc.). Warriors had their set of spirits, so did hunters, fishermen, gamblers, runners, women. Each person partook of the qualities of his or her guardian spirit. Among the spirits peculiar to shamans, parts of animals or objects were not uncommon, such as the tail of a snake, the nipple of a gun, the left or right side of anything, and the like.[6] Although the range of animals, natural phenomena, inanimate objects, which could become guardian spirits, embraced a large part of nature, certain animals lacked magic power and never figured as guardian spirits.[7] Such were the mouse, chipmunk, squirrel, rat, and butterfly. Few birds and scarcely any trees or herbs ever functioned as spirit protectors.

When the Shuswap lad began to dream of women, arrows, and canoes, or when his voice began to change, his time had arrived for craving and obtaining a guardian spirit. Similarly, the young men of the Lillooet acquired guardian spirits, and at the instigation of their elders, performed guardian-spirit dances during which they imitated their supernatural protectors in motion, gesture, and cry. In some of their clan dances masks were used, which sometimes referred to an incident in the clan myth. The dancer personified the ancestor himself or the guardian spirit. Powerful spirits enabled the shaman to perform wonderful feats. Among the Lillooet weapons, implements, and other objects were

---

[6] Compare this variety of spirits with Frazer's 'split totems.' (*Totemism and Exogamy*, vol. IV.)

[7] In Australia, where the larger part of animal and bird nature is drawn upon for totemic service, there are certain animals and birds which, for one reason or another, never function in this capacity.

often decorated with designs representing guardian spirits. Similar figures were painted or tattooed on face and body.

Among these tribes, the common people were divided into societies.
Membership in most of these was not strictly hereditary, while in others,
such as the Black Bear, the hereditary character was more pronounced.
Among the twenty-nine protectors of the society, twenty were animals,
while the rest included plants, natural phenomena, inanimate objects, as
well as hunger and famine. Some of these societies were regarded as
closely related and the members of these were permitted to use each
other's dances and songs; but as a rule each society claimed its own distinctive garments, ornaments, songs, and dances.

Some of the ceremonies could be performed at any time, but the favourite ceremonial season was the winter. During the dances the moose, caribou, elk, deer, and other protective spirits were impersonated. The actors
dressed in the skins of these animals, the scalp part hanging over their
heads and faces. Some had antlers attached to the head and neck. The
dancers went through all the actions of the animal impersonated, imitat-
ing the incidents in the fishing, hunting, snaring, chasing over lakes in
canoes, and final capture or death of the animal.

In the Plains area, the form assumed by the guardian-spirit experience
is that of a transfer of a possession, material or spiritual, natural or supernatural, from one owner to another. The transfer may be from man to
man, or from a guardian spirit to a novice. The medium of transfer is
usually a dream. The pattern of the entire procedure has become so
highly standardized that students find it hard to distinguish between an
original guardian-spirit acquisition and an account of a transfer of a
spirit from individual to individual. What is peculiar here is the role
played by the medicine-bundle. Having secured a vision, or dream, the
initiate prepares a medicine-bundle, a bag made of otter skin, filled with
various small articles, such as pieces of skin, small pebbles, quartz,
or animal or vegetable matter (p. 208, note 1). While the intrinsic value of
these objects is nil, they acquire in this context the significance of charms
carrying supernatural power. A medicine-bundle may thus be likened to
an electric battery, charged with potential current, from which great
quantities of dynamic force can be extracted at will. Contrary to the
customs of the Plateau area but in line with those of the Northwest,
medicine-bundles and even guardian spirits tend to become hereditary
among some Plains tribes. It must be noted, however, that this process
of hereditary transfer, when unaccompanied by a personal guardian-
spirit experience, may not continue indefinitely without a consequent
loss of power. It may go on for two generations, but at the third transfer

the power gives out—the dynamo must be recharged by personal contact with a supernatural source if it is to continue doing work along magical lines.

It is characteristic of the guardian-spirit cult in the Plains that the supernatural vision is sought, not at puberty, but by adults. In details, the cults differ greatly from tribe to tribe.[8]

Among the Winnebago, who in their guardian-spirit customs are a typical Plains tribe, there is one peculiarity in so far as the guardian spirits are conceived as being localized. These spirits, which may be designated as guardian prototypes or originals, reside in definite places, in a valley or mountain fastness, or behind a certain rock.[9] The guardian spirits which appear to the searchers for power are but reflections or spiritual representatives of these permanent reservoirs of magical potency. There is striking resemblance between this conception and the ideas of the Chukchee and Koryak of northeastern Siberia, where a similar relationship obtains between the so-called supernatural Masters and their animal representatives on earth.

Among the Iroquois, guardian spirits—whether of animals, birds or objects—almost always appear in human form. This is in keeping with the highly anthropomorphic character of Iroquoian religion, mythology

---

[8] The following condensed statement of the local peculiarities of guardian-spirit cults in the Plains is abstracted from Ruth Benedict's *The Concept of the Guardian Spirit in North America.*

The Arapaho use self-torture to induce the vision. All adult males seek it, and it depends wholly on the power given him at that time whether the suppliant becomes a shaman or a warrior. The Dakota mark off the laity—shamans fast once to obtain a guardian spirit and have a vision of an elaborate nature; the laity, on the other hand, fast on every occasion, with extreme self-torture, the fast being not for the guardian spirit but for help from the Sun in some particular and immediate undertaking. The Crow, again, require a guardian spirit as a part of the equipment of every ambitious man, and the suppliant becomes a 'child' of his vision-adopted 'father.' The formula of the procedure in this tribe is rigid and distinctive.

The Blackfoot use no torture except hunger and thirst to induce the vision. Here the pattern permits and almost demands that the vision be bought and sold. The Blackfoot make no distinction between the visions they have bought and those for which they have themselves fasted. To invest in other men's visions is a necessary qualification for social prestige; the medicine-bundles, which are the visible insignia of possession, form the basis of their economic system.

Among the Hidatsa the idea of inheritance was elaborated. They paid sufficient heed to the Blackfoot scheme to require that payment be made for all such inherited things. Also they behaved in accordance with general Plains theory in insisting that before inheriting one must see the vision. Hence, it became necessary for the head of a family to exercise supervision over the novice in order that the proper family spirit might appear to him. In spite of all this, however, the tribal pattern required that the medicine-bundle descend from father to son.

[9] *Cf.* p. 284, where a similar belief is reported among the African Baganda.

and cosmology. A number of societies also occur here which are more or less clearly associated with supernatural protectors.

The guardian-spirit beliefs of the North American Indians thus present an interesting illustration of a cultural feature, indigenous in an immense area and evidently of great antiquity, which in a multitude of forms and cultural associations appears in all the major areas and probably in every tribe of the vast continent. A possible exception are the Eskimo, but even here the spirit helpers of the *angakut* almost certainly belong to the same category of spirits, on a par with the spirit assistants, messengers, and the like of the shamans of northeastern Siberia.

Guardian spirits are not unknown in Australia, and cognate beliefs have been described in some of the Island groups of Melanesia as well as in the Malay archipelago. In a wider sense, beliefs in guardian spirits or spirit protectors are common throughout Africa and among primitive tribes in general, but in North America alone have these beliefs with their associated practices entered into an extraordinary number of cultural associations, thus affecting the personal religion, as well as the religious institutionalism, mythology, totemism, and even some aspects of the social organization of the Indians. It is in this sense that one might well speak of the guardian-spirit cults as one of the central features of the religion of the North American Indians.

Chapter XVII

SHAMANS AND RELIGIOUS ORIGINS

Medicine-Men Among the Chukchee and Others

Some family rituals of the Chukchee are in some respects like shamanism. Almost any Chukchee will from time to time sit down in the outer room with the family drum, and while drumming energetically will sing songs and perhaps even try to commune with spirits. In this sense it can be said that many people act as shamans. The real shamanistic performances, however, always take place in the sleeping-room, at night, and in darkness.

Shamans among the Chukchee are essentially 'those with spirits.' Both men and women may be shamans. It is in fact probable that true shamanism is more common among women than among men, but the higher grades of shamanistic powers and performances are restricted to men. The bearing of children has a bad effect on shamanistic power. The same is true of anything in any way connected with birth, the evil influence extending both to men and to women. There is, however, one feature which is entirely beyond the reach of women shamans, and that is ventriloquism.

True shamans among the Chukchee, as in northeastern Siberia generally, are people of a distinct psychic cast. 'The shamans among the Chukchee with whom I conversed,' writes Bogoras, 'were as a rule extremely excitable, almost hysterical, and not a few of them were half crazy. Their cunning resembled the cunning of a lunatic.'

The future shaman may be discerned at an early age. His gaze is directed into space and his eyes are unusually bright, so bright, indeed, claim the people, that he can see spirits in the dark. During a shamanistic performance, the shaman is extremely sensitive ('bashful'). He is afraid of strange people and objects and shrinks from ridicule and criticism. The spirits themselves are also believed to be bashful 'unless the audience is such as to favour their appearance.' [1]

---

[1] This setting should be compared with that of modern spiritualistic séances which, as a rule, take place in utter darkness, the major performer or medium

Bogoras states, in agreement with his predecessors in Siberian ethnology, that this hypersensitiveness of the shaman is restricted neither to this class of magicians, nor to the Chukchee region, but is a psychological characteristic of this entire Siberian area. Even the Russian creoles are not immune from it. Men of the latter class have been known to die when threatened, or when their death was foretold in a dream.[2] While disharmony with the *kelet* may occasion the death of a shaman, he is otherwise regarded as 'very tough.' Normally 'hard to kill,' then, a shaman is, under certain conditions, 'soft to die.'

When the call to shamanism comes to a young boy, spirits appear to him. Strange objects lie across his path, of which he makes amulets, and the like. For a time he may resist the call, for persons do not usually want to become shamans.[3] When the youth finally becomes a shaman and has practised for a number of years, he may discard his art, without fear of angering the spirits.

The 'gathering' of shamanistic powers is a prolonged and laborious process. 'For men, the preparatory stage of shamanistic inspiration is in most cases very painful, and extends over a long time. The call comes in an abrupt and obscure manner, leaving the young novice in much uncertainty regarding it. He feels "bashful" and frightened; he doubts his own disposition and strength, as has been the case with all seers, from Moses down. Half unconsciously and half against his own will, his whole soul undergoes a strange and painful transformation. This period may last months, and sometimes even years. The young novice, the "newly inspired," loses all interest in the ordinary affairs of life. He ceases to work, takes little food and without relishing it, ceases to talk to people, does not even answer their questions. The greater part of his time he spends in sleep.

'Some keep to the inner room and go out but rarely. Others wander about in the wilderness under the pretext of hunting or of keeping watch over the herd, but often without taking along any arms, or the lasso of the herdsman. A wanderer like this, however, must be closely watched, otherwise he might lie down on the open tundra and sleep for

being usually in a high-strung condition. Here, too, the audience is expected to be 'friendly' or 'willing'—sceptics are not welcomed—for latter-day spirits also tend to be 'bashful,' unless unusually shameless.

[2] It has been reported about Pacific Coast shamanism that here too a shaman, threatened with destruction by a rival, has been known on occasion to collapse or even to die.

[3] Contrast this with the frantic zeal displayed by the searchers for visions and guardian spirits in North America.

three or four days, incurring the danger, in winter, of being buried in drifting snow.'⁴

Hard as is the shamanistic initiation, it must at least in part be gone over again before each performance, nor may the shaman resist the call; when the inspiration is upon him, he must practise. Should he resist, his suffering becomes acute. He may sweat blood, and his actions become those of a madman, or epileptic.

These performances require considerable physical exertion. Even the beating of the drum, without which no shamanistic performance takes place, requires skill and physical endurance. The same applies to the capacity of passing rapidly from a state of frantic excitation to one of normal quiescence. All this requires prolonged and strenuous practice. For this reason shamanism is on the whole a young man's profession, and when a man reaches the age of forty, he usually lays down his art, sometimes passing it on to another. The latter act is achieved by blowing into the eyes or mouth of the novice, or by stabbing one's self and then the latter with a knife. Whatever the novice gains in power is lost by the shaman, and the loss is irretrievable.

While the typical Chukchee shaman is a neurotic, shamans occur whose psychic mould is very different. Thus Bogoras refers to a shaman who was a 'good-looking, well-proportioned man, of rather quiet manners, though an ill-advised word might throw him into intense excitement. He excelled in shamanistic devices, which apparently required great physical strength and dexterity. At the same time, however, he declared that he did not consider himself a shaman of a high order, and that his relations with the "spirits" should not be taken too seriously. To explain this, he said, that when he was young, he suffered from syphilis. To heal himself, he had recourse to spirits, and after two years, when he had become skilful in shamanistic practices, he was completely restored by their help. After that, he maintained intercourse with the *kelet* for several years, and was on the point of becoming a really great shaman. Then suddenly his luck was gone. One of his dogs bore two black pups; and when he saw them both sitting side by side on their haunches, looking into his face, he took it as a sign that the time had come for him to withdraw from shamanistic practice. He suffered a relapse of his illness, and his herd was visited by hoof disease. Fearing that worse things might happen, he dropped all serious pursuit of shamanism, and practised only the tricks which were completely

---

⁴ W. Bogoras, *The Chukchee*, I: 'Religion' (*Jesup North Pacific Expedition*, vol. VII), p. 420. Bogoras is our authority for this sketch of Chukchee shamanism.

harmless. As far as I could learn, he had been a magician employing especially the powers of evil, or practising the black art; and after the return of his disease he abandoned those practices, considering them detrimental to his health and well-being.' [5]

That the shamans practise deceit in the course of their performances is obvious enough. Not infrequently, in fact, this is observed even by a native audience, but the traditional prestige of shamanism overcomes the sporadic moments of scepticism. In compensation for their services, the shamans receive presents of meat, thongs, skins, garments, live reindeer, or 'alien food.' 'Shamanistic advice or treatment,' says the native practitioner, 'when given gratuitously, amounts to nothing.' [6]

The most common aims pursued at a shamanistic performance is the cure of the patient through the invocation of advice from spirits, or the bringing back of the patient's soul, abducted by hostile spirits, or the foretelling of future events after consultation with the same source.

The following is a description of a typical shamanistic performance: 'After the evening meal is finished and the kettles and trays are removed to the outer tent, all the people who wish to be present at this seance enter the inner room, which is carefully closed for the night. Among the Reindeer Chukchee, the inner room is especially small, and its narrow space causes much inconvenience to the audience, which is packed together in a tight and most uncomfortable manner. The Maritime Chukchee have more room, and may listen to the voices of the spirits with more ease and freedom. The shaman sits on the "master's place" near the back wall; and even in the most limited sleeping-room, some free space must be left around him. The drum is carefully looked over, its hide tightened, and, if it is much shrunken, it is moistened with urine and hung up for a short time over the lamp to dry. The shaman sometimes occupies more than an hour in this process, before he is satisfied with the drum. To have more freedom in his movements, the shaman usually takes off his fur shirt, and remains quite naked down to the waist. He often removes also his shoes and stockings, which, of course, gives free play to his feet and toes.

'In olden times, shamans used no stimulants; but at present they often smoke a pipeful of strong tobacco without admixture of wood, which certainly works like a strong narcotic. This habit is copied from the Tungus shamans, who make great use of unmixed tobacco as a powerful stimulant.

---

[5] *Ibid.*, p. 428–429.

[6] This reminds one of the attitude of modern psychoanalysts who insist on the therapeutic value of the financial sacrifice made by the patient.

'At last the light is put out and the shaman begins to operate. He beats the drum and sings his introductory tunes at first in a low voice. Then gradually his voice increases in volume, and soon it fills the small closed-up room with violent clamour. The narrow walls resound in all directions.

'Moreover, the shaman uses his drum for modifying his voice, now placing it directly before his mouth, now turning it at an oblique angle, and all the time beating it violently. After a few minutes, all this noise begins to work strangely on the listeners, who are crouching down, squeezed together in a most uncomfortable position. They begin to lose the power to locate the source of the sound; and, almost without any effort of imagination, the song and the drum seem to shift from corner to corner, or even to move about without having any definite place at all.

'The shaman's songs have no words. Their music is mostly simple, and consists of one short phrase repeated again and again. After repeating it many times, the shaman breaks off, and utters a series of long-drawn, hysterical sighs, which sound something like "Ah, ya, ka, ya, ka, ya, ka!." After that, he comes back to his song. For this he draws his breath as deep as possible in order to have more air in his lungs, and to make the first note the longest.

'Some of the tunes, however, are more varied, and are not devoid of a certain grace. Not a few are improvised by the shaman on the spot; others are repeated from seance to seance. Each shaman has several songs of his own, which are well-known to the people; so that if anybody uses one of them, for instance, at a ceremonial, the listeners recognize it immediately, and say that such and such a man is using the particular song of such and such a shaman.

'But there is no definite order for the succession of the songs, and the shaman changes them at will, sometimes even recurring to the first one after a considerable interval has elapsed. This introductory singing lasts from a quarter of an hour to half an hour, or more, after which the *kelet* make their first appearance.' [7]

While the shaman does all the singing, he expects someone from the audience to support him by means of a series of interjections. Without such 'answering calls,' a Chukchee shaman considers himself unable to perform his calling in a proper way.[8] Therefore, novices, while trying to learn the shamanistic practices, usually induce a brother or sister to respond, thus encouraging the zeal of the performer. Some

[7] *Ibid.*, p. 430.

[8] Compare the 'answering calls' of our congregations or the similar behaviour of audiences at evangelical meetings.

shamans also require those people who claim their advice or treatment
to give them answering calls during the particular part of the performance which refers to their affairs. The story-tellers of the Chukchee
also usually claim the assistance of their listeners, who must call out
the same exclamations.

'Among the Asiatic Eskimo, the wife and other members of the family
form a kind of chorus, which from time to time catches up the tune
and sings with the shaman. Among the Russianized Yukaghir of the
lower Kolyma, the wife is also the assistant of her shaman husband,
and during the performance she gives him encouraging answers, and
he addresses her as his "supporting staff."

'In most cases the *kelet* begin by entering the body of the shaman.
This is marked with some change in his manner of beating the drum,
which becomes faster and more violent; but the chief mark is a series
of new sounds, supposed to be peculiar to the *kelet*. The shaman shakes
his head violently, producing with his lips a peculiar chattering noise,
not unlike a man who is shivering with cold. He shouts hysterically
and in a changed voice utters strange, prolonged shrieks, such as "O
to, to, to, to," or "I pi, pi, pi, pi," all of which are supposed to characterize the voice of the *kelet*. He often imitates the cries of various
animals and birds which are supposed to be the particular assistants.
If the shaman is only a "single-bodied" one—that is, has no ventrilo-
quistic powers—the *kelet* will proceed to sing and beat the drum by
means of his body. The only difference will be in the timbre of the
voice, which will sound harsh and unnatural as becomes supernatural
beings.' [9]

The traits characteristic of Chukchee shamans are shared by them,
often to a striking degree, with the Koryak, Kamchadal, and Yukaghir.
More remotely, the Chukchee shaman is related culturally to the *angakut*
of the Eskimo and the shamans of the American Northwest.

For comparison with the above let me reproduce an account of a
similar performance among a people called by Miss Czaplicka 'Neo-
Siberian' (she designates the Chukchee as 'Palaeo-Siberian'). She has
borrowed her story from the Russian writer Syeroshevsky. In his book,
Twelve Years in the Land of the Yakut (in Russian), he describes the
performance of a shaman among the Yakut. It runs like this: 'When the
shaman who has been called to a sick person enters the *yurta* (hut), he
at once takes the place destined for him on the *billiryk agon* (seat for
honoured guests). He lies on his white mare's skin and waits for the

[9] W. Bogoras, *The Chukchee* etc., pp. 433–435.

night, the time when it is possible to shamanize. Meanwhile he is entertained with food and drink.

'When the sun sets and the dusk of evening approaches, all preparations for the ceremony in the *yurta* are hurriedly completed: the ground is swept, the wood is cut, and food is provided in larger quantity and of better quality than usual. One by one the neighbours arrive and seat themselves along the wall, the men on the right, and the women on the left; the conversation is peculiarly serious and reserved, the movements gentle.

'In the northern part of the Yakut district the host chooses the best latchets and forms them into a loop, which is placed around the shaman's shoulders and held by one of those present during the dance, in order to prevent the spirits from carrying him off. At length everyone has supper, and the household takes some rest. The shaman, sitting on the edge of the *billiryk*, slowly untwists his tresses, muttering and giving orders. He sometimes has a nervous and artificial hiccup which makes his whole body shake; his gaze does not wander, his eyes being fixed on one point, usually on the fire.

'The fire is allowed to die out. More and more deeply the dusk descends on the room; voices are hushed, and the company talks in a whisper; notice is given that anybody wishing to go out must do so at once, because soon the door will be closed, after which nobody can either go out or come in.

'The shaman slowly takes off his shirt and puts on his wizard's coat, or failing that, he takes the woman's coat called *sangyniah*.[10] Then he is given a pipe, which he smokes for a long time, swallowing the smoke; his hiccup becomes louder, he shivers more violently. When he has finished smoking, his face is pale, his head falls on his breast, his eyes are half-closed.

'At this point the white mare's skin is placed in the middle of the room. The shaman asks for cold water, and when he has drunk it he slowly holds out his hand for the drum prepared for him; he then walks to the middle of the room, and, kneeling for a time on his right knee, bows solemnly to all the four corners of the world, at the same time sprinkling the ground about him with the water from his mouth.

'Now everything is silent. A handful of white horsehair is thrown on the fire, putting it quite out; in the faint gleam of the red coals the black motionless figure of the shaman is still to be seen for a while,

---

[10] Another Russian writer, Gmelin, speaks of special embroidered stockings which the shaman dons in the *yurta*.

with drooping head, big drum on breast, and face turned towards the south, as is also the head of the mare's skin upon which he is sitting.

'Complete darkness follows the dusk; the audience scarcely breathes, and only the unintelligible mutterings and hiccups of the shaman can be heard; gradually even this sinks into a profound silence. Eventually a single great yawn like the clang of iron breaks the stillness, followed by the loud piercing cry of a falcon, or the plaintive weeping of a sea-mew—then silence again.

'Only the gentle sound of the voice of the drum, like the humming of a gnat, announces that the shaman has begun to play.

'This music is at first soft, delicate, tender, then rough and irrepressible like the roar of an oncoming storm. It grows louder and louder and, like peals of thunder, wild shouts rend the air; the crow calls, the grebe laughs, the sea-mews complain, snipes whistle, eagles and hawks scream.[11]

'The music swells and rises to the highest pitch, the beating of the drum becomes more and more vigorous, until the two sounds combine in one long-drawn crescendo. The numberless small bells ring and clang; it is not a storm—it is a whole cascade of sounds, enough to overwhelm all the listeners.——All at once it breaks off—there are one or two strong beats on the drum, which, hitherto held aloft, now falls to the shaman's knees. Suddenly the sound of the drum and the small bells ceases. Then silence for a long moment, while the gentle gnat-like murmur of the drum begins again.

'This may be repeated several times, according to the degree of the shaman's inspiration; at last, when the music takes on a certain new rhythm and melody, sombrely the voice of the shaman chants the following obscure fragments:

"Mighty bull of the earth. . . . Horse of the steppes!

"I, the mighty bull . . . bellow!

"I, the horse of the steppes . . . neigh!

"I, the man set above all other beings!

"I, the most gifted of all!

"I, the man created by the master all-powerful!

"Horse of the steppes, appear! Teach me!

"Enchanted bull of the earth, appear! Speak to me!

"Powerful master, command me!

"All of you, who will go with me, give heed with your ears! Those whom I command not, follow me not!

"Approach not nearer than is permitted! Look intently!

[11] All these sounds are produced by the shaman by means of ventriloquism.

"Give heed! Have a care!

"Look heedfully! Do this, all of you . . . all together . . . all, however many you may be!

"Thou of the left side, O lady with thy staff, if anything be done amiss, if I take not the right way, I entreat you—correct me! Command! . . .

"My errors and my path show to me! O mother of mine! Wing thy free flight! Pave my wide roadway!

"Souls of the sun, mothers of the sun, living in the south, in the nine wooded hills, ye who shall be jealous . . . I adjure you all . . . let them stay . . . let your three shadows stand high!

"In the East, on your mountain, lord, grandsire of mine, great of power and thick of neck—be thou with me!

"And thou, grey-bearded wizard [fire], I ask thee: with all my dreams, with all comply! To all my desires consent. . . . Heed all! Fulfil all! . . . All heed. . . . All fulfil!"

'In the ensuing prayers the shaman addresses his *ämägyat* [ancestral spirit] and other protective "spirits"; he talks with the *kaliany* [mischievous familiar spirits], asks them questions, and gives answers in their names. Sometimes the shaman must pray and beat the drum a long time before the spirits come; often their appearance is so sudden and so impetuous that the shaman is overcome and falls down. It is a good sign if he falls on his face, and a bad sign if he falls on his back.

'When the *ämägyat* comes down to a shaman, he arises and begins to leap and dance, at first on the skin, and then, his movements becoming more rapid, he glides into the middle of the room. Wood is quickly piled on the fire, and the light spreads through the *yurta*, which is now full of noise and movement. The shaman dances, sings, and beats the drum uninterruptedly, jumps about furiously, turning his face to the south, then to the west, then to the east. Those who hold him by the leather thongs sometimes have great difficulty in controlling his movements. In the south Yakut district, however, the shaman dances unfettered. Indeed, he often gives up his drum so as to be able to dance more unrestrainedly.

'The head of the shaman is bowed, his eyes are half-closed; his hair tumbled and in wild disorder lies on his sweating face, his mouth is twisted strangely, saliva streams down his chin, often he foams at the mouth.

'He moves round the room, advancing and retreating, beating the drum, which resounds no less wildly than the roaring of the shaman himself; he shakes his jingling coat, and seems to become more and more maniacal, intoxicated with the noise and movement.

'His fury ebbs and rises like a wave; sometimes it leaves him for a while, and then, holding his drum high above his head, solemnly and calmly he chants a prayer and summons the "spirit."

'At last he knows all he desires; he is acquainted with the cause of the misfortune or disease with which he has been striving; he is sure of the help of the beings whose aid he needs. Circling about in his dance, singing and playing, he approaches the patient.

'With new objurgations he drives away the cause of the illness by frightening it, or by sucking it out with his mouth from the painful place: then, returning to the middle of the room, he drives it away by spitting and blowing. Then he learns what sacrifice is to be made to the "powerful spirits" for this harsh treatment of the spirits' servant, who was sent to the patient.

'Then the shaman, shading his eyes from the light with his hands, looks attentively into each corner of the room; and if he notices any-thing suspicious, he again beats the drum, dances, makes terrifying gestures, and entreats the "spirits."

'At length all is made clean, the suspicious "cloud" is no more to be seen, which signifies that the cause of the illness has been driven out; the sacrifice is accepted, the prayers have been heard—the ceremony is over.

'The shaman still retains for some time after this the gift of prophecy; he foretells various happenings, answers the questions of the curious, or relates what he saw on his journey away from the earth.

'Finally he is carried with his mare's skin back to his place of honour on the *billiryk*.' [12]

Medicine-men are, of course, ubiquitous in the primitive world. But in other localities their traits are only in part like those of the magic-working practitioners of Northeast Siberia and of northwestern and northern North America. According to Koch-Grünberg, men and women practitioners occur among the Guana, Tuppi-Ymba, and Yekuana of South America. Among the Chiriguama and many other tribes studied by Nordenskiöld, both men and women practitioners have a 'comrade' in the other world who renders assistance to them. The 'comrades' of men are women, those of women, men. Both Dobritzhoffer and Hyades-Deniker state that old women are often held responsible for death. According to the same authors, definite separation does not always exist between the offices of chief and medicine-man, at least to the extent that

---

[12] M. A. Czaplicka, *Aboriginal Siberia*. (Reprinted by permission of The Clarendon Press, Oxford.)

some of the prominent chiefs were also known as medicine-men. In his work on the Arawak-speaking peoples, Max Schmidt refers to some traits, physical and psychic, on the basis of which boys were selected for the profession of medicine-men. Among others, he mentions epilepsy, various physical peculiarities, such as hemorrhage of the breast, and general nervousness. Payments for medicinal services are mentioned constantly and seem to be as common as they are in Siberia. In some districts medicine-men belonging to a different tribe, or even to a different village occupied by the same tribe, are regarded as evil, whereas the practitioners of one's own tribe and village are thought to be helpful and benevolent.[13]

In some South American tribes the profession of a medicine-man requires long preparation, sometimes extending over months, or even years. Enforced fasting and various forms of self-castigation are common characteristics of the period of apprenticeship. Some of the things the apprentice is expected to learn from his expert preceptors are monotonous singing, ventriloquism, imitation of animal voices, sucking out of poison, the habit of drinking narcotics and poisons, the swallowing of small animals, the swallowing and expectorating of small pebbles and pieces of wood. This list of professional accomplishments, not radically different in South America and Northeast Siberia, brings home the fact that the medicine-man, if he is a mountebank, takes great pains to be a good one. In extreme cases, we are informed, magicians will not hesitate to take violent measures rather than endanger their prestige. Thus, Von den Steinen relates about the Bororo healers that when the death of a sick child has been foretold by one of them, he will try to help matters along by strangling it with a thread.

In Australia, the medicinal functions of magicians are so characteristic that Howitt, in speaking of the southeastern district of the continent, defines the medicine-man as 'one who causes or cures death by projecting into bodies, or extracting from them, quartz crystals, bone, wood or other things.' And he continues: 'The belief in magic in its various

---

[13] This psychologically plausible attitude occurs frequently in different parts of the world: magicians of other tribes are regarded either as evil or as more powerful. A number of such instances have been recorded in Australia, and in North America the Haida, at least, show an extraordinary respect for the shamans of the Tlingit. In modern days, also, people who disclaim any faith in magic, do yet lend an eager ear to a Gipsy soothsayer and an equally responsive eye to a Hindu fakir. In a more sophisticated realm we find the common tendency of importing a physician or consultant from another city, or country—if one can afford it —although in sheer objectivity those available in the 'home town' may be just as good.

forms—in dreams, omens and warnings—is so universal and mingles so intimately with the daily life of the aborigines that no one, not even those who practise deceit themselves, doubt the power of other medicine-men, or that if they failed to detect their magical purpose, the failure is due to an error in the practice or to the superior skill or power of some adverse practitioner.' [14]

The *kunki*, magicians of the Dieri, hold intercourse with supernatural beings, and with their assistance interpret dreams and reveal the identity of those responsible for death by magic. Howitt relates the case of a magician who cured a man who was about to expire. The magician stepped outside and caught the spirit of the man just as it was proceeding towards the other world; then, lying down on the top of the half-dead man, he thrust the spirit into him, thus bringing him back to life. As simple as that!

In other instances, knowledge rather than magic is used, but the two kinds of cures are taken by the natives very much in the same spirit. Thus, a woman who was bitten by a snake was cured by her husband, not a regular magician, in the following way: he secured a cord, tied it above the knee of the bitten leg, twisting it tighter with a stick, then he picked up a quartz pebble, cracked it in two, and with the sharp edge cut a circle right around the leg, severing the skin. The blood oozed out, and though the woman at first became drowsy and ill, she gradually recovered.

Among the Kurnai, there is a separate variety of harmless magicians who go up to the spirit world to learn songs and dances, then come back and teach them to the people.

While marked elements of similarity must have been noted between the magical practitioners of Northeast Siberia and those of South America and Southeast Australia, it must be remembered that the general character of the individuals who engage in magical cures in these regions, is not by any means the same. The shamans of Siberia and North America are high-strung and often neurotic individuals. This is also true of South America, though less markedly so. The magicians of Australia, on the other hand, are perfectly normal people, distinguished rather by common sense and shrewdness than by the qualities of a so-called 'psychic.' Their 'fitness' is more like that of chiefs and leaders in industrial pursuits. Together with the latter and the old men generally, they guide the younger generation by their example and their teaching.

[14] A. W. Howitt, *Native Tribes of Southeast Australia*, p. 356. (By permission of The Macmillan Company, publishers.)

The Ghost-Dance Religions of the North American Indians

While the origin of religion is a psychological or even a psycho-biological problem, the anthropologist is primarily concerned with the forms religion takes in particular tribes, as well as with the appearance of religious features in a group, either as spontaneous inventions or as borrowed traits. A variety of forms taken by religious belief and practice in different tribes have been described in the preceding pages. To find examples of religious origins, on the other hand, is not so easy. It is for this reason that the data available on the Ghost-Dance religions of the Indians present a more than ordinary interest.

The common cause of these religious revivals is to be sought in the abnormal conditions arising out of the contact of White man's civilization with the religious and ethical traditions of the Indians. The mode of origin of these so-called revivals in the different tribes is strikingly similar, while the irresistible spread of revivalist fervour from tribe to tribe presents an astounding picture of religious receptivity, as well as of the rapidity with which a trait-complex may travel, under favourable conditions.

One or two concrete examples will make clear just what it is that took place here.

The great revivalist prophet, Smohalla, was a member of a small tribe related to the Nez Percé Indians. The date of his birth falls between 1815 and 1820. After frequenting a Catholic Mission among the Yakima, the youth achieved renown as a warrior, and later as a medicine-man. As his fame as a magical practitioner grew, he became involved in an acrimonious dispute with Moses, a rival medicine-man and chief of a neighbouring tribe. The affair came to an open fight in which Smohalla was worsted and nearly killed. He was, in fact, left for dead on the battle-field. Reviving, he managed to drag himself to a boat, and was carried down the current of the Columbia River, until picked up by some White men.

His recovery was slow. When his strength ultimately returned, he showed no inclination to rejoin his people, among whom, he knew, he was regarded as dead. So he started on a prolonged period of wanderings. He made his way along the coast to Mexico, and from there he travelled back north through Arizona and Nevada. While on this trip, he began to preach the new doctrine. He averred that after his body had died he had visited the spirit world, and that he was now preaching by divine command. When he arrived among the tribes who had heard of him before his unlucky fight, his tale was accepted as true, for he had been thought dead, and it was known that his body had disappeared. His doctrine centred in the prophecy that Indian life, as it was in ancient days, would return, that the buffalo would come back, and White man withdraw from the land. In the ceremonies which accompanied his preaching, the evidence of the impact of the rituals of the Catholic Church was unmistakable. The new doctrine also contained a rigid code of ethical behaviour, which exerted a remarkable influence on the tribes that fell under its sweep.

Smohalla knew well how to enhance his prestige by little tricks, such as the foretelling of eclipses.[15] He was enabled to do this by using an almanac and gleaning some additional items from a party of surveyors. This particular trick, incidentally, almost cost him his reputation. It so happened that at the expiration of the year he was unable to secure another almanac, with the credible result that his reputation for prophetic prowess went into a sudden decline.

It seems that Smohalla was subject to cataleptic trances and that his alleged supernatural revelations came to him while he was lying prostrate in an apparently unconscious condition. The somewhat naïve remarks quoted by James Mooney from MacMurray are of sufficient interest to be reproduced here:

'He falls into trances and lies rigid for considerable periods. Unbelievers have experimented by sticking needles through his flesh, cutting him with knives and otherwise testing his sensibilities to pain without provoking any responsive action. It was asserted that he was surely dead, because blood did not flow from his wounds. These trances always excite great interest and often alarm, as he threatens to abandon his earthly body altogether, because of the disobedience of his people. . . . It is this going into long trances, out of which he comes as from heavy sleep, and almost immediately relates his experiences in the spirit land, that gave rise to the title of "Dreamers," or believers in dreams, commonly given to his followers by the neighbouring Whites. His actions are similar to those of a trance medium, and if self-hypnotization be practicable, that would seem to explain it. I questioned him as to his trances, and hoped to have him explain them to me, but he avoided the subject, and was angered when I pressed him. He manifestly believes all he says of what occurs to him in this trance state. As we have hundreds of thousands of educated White people who

---

[15] It will be remembered that the early Ionian Greek philosopher, Thales, also enhanced his prestige by foretelling eclipses.

believe in similar fallacies, this is not more unlikely in an Indian subjected to such influences.' [16]

Further on the same author continues to describe one of the ceremonial occasions on which Smohalla preached the new religion and made converts.

'Smohalla invited me to participate in what he considered a great ceremonial service within the larger house. His house was built with a frame work of stout logs placed upright in the ground, and roofed over with brush, or with canvas in rainy weather. The sides consisted of bark and rush matting. It was about seventy-five feet long, by about twenty-five feet wide. Singing and drumming had been going on for some time when I arrived. The air resounded with the voices of hundreds of Indians, male and female, and the banging of drums. Within, the room was dimly lighted. Smoke curled from a fire on the floor at the farther end, and pervaded the atmosphere. The ceiling was hung with hundreds of salmon, split and drying in the smoke.

'The scene was a strange one. On either side of the room was a row of twelve women, standing erect, with arms crossed and hands extended, with finger-tips at the shoulders. They kept time to the drums and the voices by balancing on the balls of their feet and tapping with their heels on the floor, while they chanted with varying pitch and time. The excitement and persistent repetition wore them out, and I heard that others than Smohalla had seen visions in their trances, but I saw none who would admit it, or explain anything of it. I fancied they feared their own action, and that real death might come to them in this simulated death.

'Those on the right hand were dressed in garments of a red colour with an attempt at uniformity. Those on the left wore costumes of white buckskin, said to be very ancient ceremonial costumes, with red and blue trimmings. All wore large round silver plates, or such other glittering ornaments as they possessed. A canvas covered the floor, and on it knelt the men and boys in lines of seven. Each seven, as a rule, had shirts of the same colour. The tallest were in front, the size diminishing regularly to the rear. Children and ancient hags filled in any spare space. In front on a mattress knelt Smohalla, his left hand covering his heart. On his right was the boy bell ringer in similar posture.' [17]

Another great prophet or messiah was Wovoka, probably a Paiute

[16] James Mooney, 'The Ghost-Dance Religion and the Sioux Outbreak of 1890,' *14th Report*, Bureau of American Ethnology, pp. 719–720.

[17] *Ibid.*, p. 726.

Indian, born about 1856. It seems that his father had been a minor prophet, so that Wovoka grew up in an atmosphere suggesting his future calling. He received his great revelation at the early age of fourteen. 'On this occasion "the sun died" [18] . . . and he fell asleep in the daytime and was taken up to the other world. Here he saw God, with all the people who had died long ago engaged in their old-time sports and occupations, all happy and for ever young. It was a pleasant land and full of game. After showing him all, God told him he must go back and tell his people they must be good and love one another, have no quarrelling and live in peace with the Whites; that they must work and not lie or steal; that they must put away all the old practices that savoured of war; that if they faithfully obeyed his instructions, they would at last be reunited with their friends in this other world, where there would be no more death, or sickness, or old age. He was then given the dance which he was commanded to bring back to his people. By performing this dance at intervals, for five consecutive days each time, they would secure this happiness to themselves and hasten the event. Finally, God gave him control over the elements, so that he could make it rain or snow or be dry at will, and appointed him his deputy to take charge of affairs in the West, while "Governor Harrison" would attend to matters in the East, and he, God, would look after the world above. He then returned to earth and began to preach as he was directed, convincing the people by exercising the wonderful powers that had been given him.' [19]

Wovoka was a powerful magician. He had five songs by means of which he could control rain and snow. The first song brought mists or clouds, the others, each with its specific power, brought snowfall, shower, rain or storm, and clear weather. The ceremonial aspect of the dances produced by Wovoka were of the usual kind, embracing frenzy, fits, and visions.

The mythology of the doctrine can be briefly stated in the words of Mooney: 'The dead are all arisen and the spirit hosts are advancing and have already arrived at the boundaries of this earth, led forward by the regenerator in shape of cloudlike indistinctness. The spirit captain of the dead is always represented under this shadowy semblance. The great change will be ushered in by a trembling of this earth, at which the faithful are exhorted to feel no alarm. The hope held out is the

---

[18] The reference is to the eclipse of that year, an event which always arouses great commotion among Indians, as in any other community. It seems that the sickly youth was thrown into a fit, accompanied by a rather elaborate hallucination.

[19] *Ibid.*, pp. 771–772.

same that has inspired the Christian for nineteen centuries—a happy immortality in perpetual youth. As to fixing a date, the Messiah is as thoughtless as his predecessor in prophecy, who declares that "no man knoweth the time, not even the angels above." ' [20]

The ethical code embraced such maxims as, 'Do no harm to anyone; do right always,' 'Do not tell lies,' 'When your friends die, you must not cry'—a reference to the elaborate, expensive, and often cruel burial rites practised by these tribes. But the most important maxim was, 'You must not fight.' The effect of this ethical code, in its setting of a revivalist doctrine, seems to have been remarkable, in so far as it fostered friendliness among tribes that had previously been almost perpetually at war.

A religious upheaval similar to the Ghost-Dance religions of the West swept over the Iroquois tribes of the Great Lakes region in the beginning of the nineteenth century. Here the prophet was Sganyadaiyu, 'Handsome-Lake,' the brother of a renowned war chief. So far as known, his life to the age of sixty was in no way unusual, and if he achieved any distinction, it was by his rather wild and disorderly habits. Then he fell sick, his ailment being pronounced hopeless. While on his death-bed he had an elaborate dream accompanied by a vision, usually referred to as the vision of the 'four angels.' In this dream and vision he claims to have received the message on which he built his doctrine. Christian influence in this episode is obvious: there were the 'four angels' and an implied belief in one supreme god, a belief foreign to aboriginal Indian religion. Handsome-Lake's teaching rejected some of the ancient beliefs and ceremonies of the Iroquois as heathen and evil. At the same time many of the pre-existing beliefs and practices were incorporated in the precepts of the new doctrine. Here also the new teaching had an ethical flavour—it prescribed peace, truthfulness, and sobriety, and comprised certain educational maxims.

The doctrine of Handsome-Lake received wide acceptance among the Iroquois tribes, and to this day, on many of the Iroquoian reservations, some Indians belong to one or another Christian denomination, while others, not always the minority, are followers of Handsome-Lake and prefer to be designated as 'deists.' [21] There are still a number of men

[20] *Ibid.*, p. 782.

[21] The reference is to my friend and one-time informant, the late Chief John Gibson and his followers. An outstanding personality and leading expert on all matters Iroquoian, this remarkable man was during the last years of his life the principal representative of the Handsome-Lake doctrine. Notwithstanding his total blindness, he travelled yearly to the different reservations, accompanied by his brother, in order to preach the doctrine. He it was who objected to the term

living who know the entire doctrine and preach it on the different reservations. This process, when accompanied by explanations, takes all of three hours' preaching a day for five days. It is remarkable, as has often been noted, how thoroughly the older beliefs of the Iroquois were extirpated after the emergence and spread of the new religion.[22]

The Ghost-Dance religions of the western Indians and the doctrine of Handsome-Lake call to mind parallel phenomena in modern times. The numerous Russian sects, which in the course of the last three centuries have split off from the Greek Catholic Church, present many features of striking resemblance to those reviewed above. The conflicting interests and customs of the Whites and the Indians, which provide the socio-psychological background for American Indian revivalism, find their analogue in the ruthless pressure exerted by the Orthodox Church upon the religious ideas of the ethnically complex population of the Russian plains. Once more we meet the prophets, wonder-workers and messiahs, or earthly representatives of *the* Messiah. The new religions are accompanied by ceremonialism, often of a secret nature. One hears of visions and fits. There is, finally, an ethical code with the usual drastic demands on the stolidity and altruism of the devotees.[23]

The religious transformations of early society are veiled in darkness. It is doubtful whether we shall ever possess authentic material to fill in this chapter in human history; but one may be permitted to conjecture that religious revivals, when they did occur, came at periods of emotional stress and strain, perhaps precipitated by inter-tribal con-

'heathen' used in Canadian Government reports to designate those Indians who had not become Christians. He undertook a special trip to the Indian Office in Ottawa to present his case in favour of the term 'deist.' He won the case, and the term is now officially used in the Canadian Government publications.

[22] In his study, *The Prophet Dance of the Northwest and its Derivatives*; *The Source of the Ghost Dance* (1935), Leslie Spier, with extensive documentation, defends the thesis that later Ghost-Dance religions (beginning in 1890) leaned against the background of the Prophet Dance, in many ways similar to the Ghost Dance in content, but much older as well as nearer to the original native culture. The author shows on a map the relative distributions of the Prophet Dance, the Ghost Dance, as represented by the Smohalla cult, and the modern Shaker cult, a christianized form of the Ghost Dance. The geographical distribution shows the Prophet cult to be by far the most widespread, extending south, east, and north beyond the Ghost Dance, thus indicating, with the support of chronology, that the latter developed on the older foundation laid by the Prophet cult. The Shaker cult extends along the border of the Pacific, from the northern fringe of southern California to Puget Sound. It represents a western extension of the older native cults.

[23] The statements in the above paragraph refer to nineteenth-century Russia. For lack of data I am unable to say what has become of the sectarians under the present régime.

flict or the impact of incompatible idea-systems, and that in their nature, mechanism and progress, these revivals were not unlike the Ghost-Dance religions of the American Indians or the heretical creeds of the Russian sectarians.

Chapter XVIII

GODS AND RITUALISM

The Supernatural World of the Bella Coola [1]

The views of the Bella Coola about the Other World and its relation to the earth are elaborate and unusually systematic. Altogether, they say, there are five worlds, one above another. In the middle is our own world. Above it extend two heavens and below, two under-worlds. In the upper heaven resides the supreme female deity, who is relatively little concerned with the affairs of mankind. In the centre of the lower heaven stands the House-of-the-Gods in which reside the Sun and all the other deities. The earth is an island floating upon the ocean. The first under-world is inhabited by the ghosts who are at liberty to return to heaven, whence they may be sent down to earth again. A ghost that dies for a second time sinks to the lower under-world, from which there is no return. The female deity who rules in the uppermost heaven is referred to as Our Woman or Afraid-of-Nothing. This uppermost heaven is a prairie without any trees. To reach it one must go up the river from the House-of-the-Gods in the first heaven, or one may also reach it from the first heaven by passing through a rent in the sky. The house of Our Woman stands in the far East where a gale is continually blowing over the open country, driving everything towards the entrance of her house. Near the house itself, however, calm reigns. In front of the house stands a post shaped like a large winged monster. The entrance to the house is through its mouth. A spot in front of the house is cov-

---

[1] The Bella Coola Indians inhabit the coasts of two long and narrow fjords in British Columbia. This tribe occupies a peculiar position among the peoples of the Northwest Coast. Analysis of their language and traditions proves that they are relatively recent immigrants into the region which they now inhabit. The language of the Bella Coola is Salish, and they must have once lived in the immediate proximity of other Salish-speaking tribes farther down the coast. In their physical appearance the Bella Coola have undergone changes due to their intermarriages with the northern coast tribes as well as the Athabascans of the interior, so that at present they differ considerably from their relatives to the south. The same is true of their customs and beliefs, which have become greatly modified through the influence of their northern neighbours. From this latter standpoint the Bella Coola, though differing from the typical Pacific Coast tribes in many particulars, must be regarded as forming a subdivision of the Northwest Coast area.

ered with gravel of three colours: blue, black, and white. Behind the
house is a salt-water pond in which the goddess bathes. In this pond
lives Sisiutl, variously described as a snake or a fish. Sisiutl sometimes
comes down to earth. Wherever it moves the rocks burst and slide down
the mountain-sides.

In the beginning, it is said, the mountains were of great height. These
mountains are supposed to have been human beings. Our Woman made
war upon the mountains, and having vanquished them she made them
smaller than they were before. During this fight she broke off the nose
of one mountain, as can still be seen, say the Indians, when one looks at
the mountain. When it is called by name, it answers. At the head-waters
of the Bella Coola River there are two mountains, one of which had
a fire burning in its house. This fire warned the mountain god of the
approach of enemies. When Our Woman was making war upon the
mountain, the fire forewarned its master. When she approached, coming
down the river in her canoe, he broke the canoe, and she returned to
heaven. The canoe turned into stone and may still be seen at the foot
of the mountain. Our Woman visits the earth now and then, bringing
sickness and death with her. She is described as a great warrior.

In the centre of the first heaven, as was said, stands the House-of-the-
Gods. It is also referred to as the House-of-Myths or Where-Man-Was-
Created, or the House-from-Which-People-Come-Down, or the House-
to-Which-People-Go. In front of the house stands a post painted with
representations of different birds, a white crane sitting on the top of
the post. The master of the house is the Sun, also referred to as Our
Father or The-Sacred-One. This god, the Sun, is the only one to whom
the Bella Coola address their prayers. They also make offerings to him.
There is also another deity, as important as the Sun, who lives with
him in the rear of the House-of-the-Gods. Near the fire is a third deity,
an old man who formerly ruled the House-of-the-Gods but has ceded
his place to the other two deities. These two are the rulers of mankind. It is believed that they have created man, but curiously enough,
they are also thought to be seeking the destruction of mankind. A number of inferior deities also reside in the House-of-the-Gods, whose
functions all refer to the great winter ceremonial of the Bella Coola
known as the *kusiut*. The various rituals performed during the *kusiut*
are dramatic representations of the myths referring to different deities,
particularly those in the House-of-the-Gods, and masks representing
these deities are used in the ceremonies. One of these deities ordains the
deaths of men and animals; its particular duty is to kill those who ·
transgress the laws of the *kusiut*. Another deity sits by itself in one

corner of the House-of-the-Gods, and its function it is to prevent those who are not initiated in the secrets of the *kusiut* from approaching the house. Then there is a deity in the form of a fabulous monster. Still another is a boy who performs *kusiut* dances all the time, and when the gods resolve to send a new dance to the earth it is conveyed by this boy. In addition to these, there are other deities of similar functions and still others whose concern is not the *kusiut* but the affairs of man and the world. One of these is associated with the Sun, who is the creator of man. Thus the Sun is held responsible for the creation of new-born children, whereas his assistant gives a child its particular features. A female goddess takes charge of children before they are born by rocking them in a cradle. After she has done this they are sent down to the world. She does this also with the children of animals, ordaining at the same time that their skins and flesh shall provide clothing and food for man. Another deity is the Mother-of-Flowers. Every spring she gives birth to all the plants in the order in which they appear. In this work she is assisted by two old women and a shaman.

While the Sun and his assistant deity are seen to play an important part in determining the fates of men, they do not do so personally but through the intermediation of four brothers who carry out their thoughts. The names of three of these brothers are The-One-Who-Fin-ishes-His-Work-By-Chopping-Once, The-One-Who-Finishes-His-Work-By-Rubbing-Once, and The-One-Who-Finishes-His-Work-by-Cutting-Once. With the brothers lives a sister; together they inhabit an elevated room in the rear of the House-of-the-Gods. They are engaged in carving and painting and are supposed to have given man his arts. They taught him to build canoes and houses, to make boxes, carve in wood, and paint. They taught him the art of hunting and some say that they made the fish. The Bella Coola believe that when a carving is made by them, the idea for the design is suggested by the four brothers. Although most of the Bella Coola will say that the Raven also lives in the House-of-the-Gods, there seems to be some doubt about this.

In addition to all these deities there are nine brothers and a sister even more particularly concerned with the observation of the *kusiut*. Each one of these deities is painted with a certain design, two with that of the full moon, two with that of the half-moon, two with a design representing stars, two with the rainbow, another with the salmonberry blossom, still another with the kingfisher, and the last with a sealion bladder filled with grease. The last one, who is the sister, wears rings of red and white cedar bark.

In the rear of the House-of-the-Gods there is a special room in which lives the son of the deities, whom we might designate as Cannibal-Maker. Whenever the Sun and his assistant desire to destroy a visitor, they send him past the door of Cannibal-Maker's room. The latter rushes out and devours the visitor. It is he who initiates the Cannibal into the society of that name. According to the tradition of one of the Bella Coola tribes, they acquired membership in the Cannibal Society in the following way:

Cannibal-Maker came down to a certain mountain where he met the son of the first member of the tribe. He conducted him to the House-of-the-Gods, took him to his room, and bestowed a name upon him. He put a snake into his body which enabled him to pass through water. When the youth applied his mouth to the body of a person, the snake tore pieces of flesh from the body and devoured it. Cannibal-Maker took the youth to the uppermost heaven, passing through the rent in the sky and into the house of the supreme deity, Our Woman. The two were blown towards the house by the strong gale which, as we saw, is prevalent in this heaven. They found Our Woman sitting in front of the house. She said to Cannibal-Maker, 'Why don't you come in? You wish that your friend should obtain great supernatural powers. Bring him to my house and I will give him what you desire. Stay for a short while where you are and I will show you what I am doing. Watch closely when the post of my house closes its eyes.' In a while the post closed its eyes, but at once it grew dark and the two visitors fainted, but soon recovered. When the post opened its eyes it grew light again. The visitors remained sitting on the ground, and suddenly a strong wind arose and rolled them over the prairie to the door of the house, and then it calmed down. They remained sitting on the ground near the doorway, when Our Woman said, 'Watch closely when the post of my house closes its eyes.' Sitting opposite each other, they were watching the post. When it closed its eyes they were transformed into stone, but soon regained human shape. Then Our Woman asked them to come in; she took the youth's blanket and gave him another made of bearskin set with fringes of red cedar bark. She told him the blanket was to keep him warm and direct his course. Then she brought some water from the salt-water pond behind her house. She sprinkled it over the faces of her visitors and told the youth to sing about his experiences in the upper-most heaven when he was to perform the Cannibal dance. Had she not sprinkled the face of her visitors with water they would have died. She said to the youth, 'Your country is not far away. Do not be afraid of the dangerous road that you have to pass. Later on there shall be many

Cannibals like you. Do not be afraid to touch the food another Cannibal may offer you. You are strong because you have seen me.' Then
she sent him back to the first heaven. Here the gods placed him on the
back of a bird which carried him down to the sea. As soon as the bird
reached the water, it uttered its cry, and then the young man uttered
the cry of the Cannibal. The people heard it and they said, 'That must
be the boy whom we lost some time ago.' They connected many canoes
by means of planks and paddled to the place where the bird was swimming about. They covered their canoes with red cedar bark and eagle-
down and tried to capture the youth, but as they approached the bird
swam towards the village. They surrounded it with their canoes, but
the bird flew up and disappeared in the sky. At the same time
the youth flew towards the village. When the people landed he
attacked them, taking hold of their arms. And the snake which was
still in his body tore pieces of flesh out of their arms. In order to
appease him people sang songs and beat time. Such is the tradition
of one Bella Coola tribe as to the manner in which they acquired membership in the Cannibal Society.

The sky is believed to be in the care of twenty-four guardians. According to tradition the sky must be continually fed with firewood. Once upon
a time the guardians put too much firewood into the sky and it burst.
All the pieces except one fell down to the earth. The fragments of the
sky hit the faces of the twenty-four guardians and distorted them. They
tried to mend the sky but did not know how to do it. Then they went down
the river and came to the four brothers, whose assistance they asked.
The brothers gathered up the pieces and glued them together. Up to
that time the Sun had been dwelling in the East, but now he began to
travel on his daily course, and it is at that time that the four brothers
built a bridge over which the sun can be seen proceeding every day.
They placed a wedge in the opening of the sky into which the twenty-four
guardians have to put the firewood. This opening is called Mouth-Kept-
Open-by-Means-of-a-Wedge. The four brothers said: 'The sky shall not
burst again, this wedge shall keep its mouth open.'

The supernatural world below the earth is the Ghost Country. Descriptions of it are principally obtained from shamans, who believe
that they visit the Ghost Country in their trances. According to the
statement of an old woman who had done this when she was a little
girl, the entrance to the country of the ghosts is through a hole situated
in each house between the doorway and the fireplace. The Ghost Country stretches along the sandy banks of a large river. Behind the village
stands a hill the base of which is covered with sharp stones. When it is

summer here, it is winter in the Ghost Country. When it is night here, it is day there. Ghosts do not walk on their feet, but on their heads. Their language is also different from that spoken on earth. When human souls reach the lower world they receive new names. The ghost village is surrounded by a fence. They have a dancing-house there in which they perform the *kusiut*. This dancing-house is just below the burial-place of each village. It is very large and long and has four fires. The women ghosts stay on the floor of the house while the men sit on an elevated platform. The house has doors, but the ghosts upon first leaving the lower world enter it through the smoke-hole, aided by a rope ladder placed in the smoke-hole. Two men stand at the foot of the ladder. Once a person has entered the dancing-house there is no return to earth. Their souls, however, are free to return to the first heaven by ascending the rope ladder. Those who thus ascend to the first heaven are sent back to earth by the deities to be born as children in the same family to which they belonged. Those who enjoy life in the Ghost Country and do not return to heaven die a second death, whereupon they sink to the lowermost world from which there is no return.

As a sample of Bella Coola myths I shall now reproduce one about the Raven, as recorded by Professor Boas.

There was a widow with a beautiful daughter. The Raven married the widow, but soon began to covet the daughter, and to think how he could get possession of her. Now he had devised a plan. He did not light a fire in his house for two days, until the girl began to complain of the cold. Then he offered to go to get firewood. First he went to the Alder, made a cut in its bark, and asked, 'What do you do when you are thrown into the fire?' The Alder replied, 'I burn very quietly and steadily.' Then the Raven retorted, 'You are not the one whom I want.' Next he went to the Pine, made a cut in its bark, and asked, 'What do you do when you are thrown into the fire?' The Pine retorted, 'My nose runs and the fire crackles.' 'You are not the one whom I want,' said the Raven. He went to the Red Cedar, made a cut in its bark, and asked, 'What do you do when you are thrown into the fire?'

Then he planned what to do next. At this time a certain bird living on the mountains invited all the people to a feast. The Raven was not invited, and he planned how to obtain the food that they were preparing. He pretended to be sick, and said to his two children: 'It is ridiculous that this bird pretends to be a chief. He has nothing but leaves to eat. But you had better go and see what kind of food he is preparing.' Then the two young ravens went, and saw that he was broiling meat. When the food was almost done, the Raven arose, and crept stealthily behind the house in which all the guests were assembled. By this time the meat was done, and the people were placing it on long planks. Then he cried, 'Wina, wina, wina, wina! exa, exa, exa, exa!' Then the people stopped, and said, 'Who is crying there?' But the Raven ran home as quickly as possible, and lay down by the side of the fireplace. He asked his children to strew ashes over his body so as to avert suspicion of his having left the house.

Now the people sent two messengers to the Raven's house, in order to see if he might have uttered the cries; but they saw him lying down near the fireplace, and noticed that he was covered with ashes. Then the messengers returned, and reported what they had seen. The people discussed the meaning of the cries, and finally resolved to send to the Raven, who was renowned on account of his experience, and to ask his opinion. Two messengers went to see him. When they asked him, he said. 'Those cries mean that your enemies will come to kill you. Escape while there is yet time. Don't stop to take your food along, but run away.' The people followed his advice. He said, 'I cannot join you because I am sick. It does not matter whether the enemies kill me or whether I die of disease.' As soon as the people had left, he arose, took all the meat, and hid it near his own house. On the following morning the people returned, and saw that the village was undisturbed, only the meat had disappeared. They looked askance at the Raven, suspecting that he had stolen their meat.

On the following day the Raven thought, 'I will go to visit the Deer.' He went there, opened the door of the Deer's house, and said, 'At what season are you fattest?' The Deer replied, 'At the time when the people have dried all their fish.' Then the Raven left him, and returned at the time when all the fish had been dried. He said, 'Lequmai, come! I want to speak to you. Let us go up the mountain, and let us tell about our ancestors.' They went up the mountain; and the Raven said, 'Here is the place where I am accustomed to sit and to bask in the sun. Let us sit down here.' It was a meadow near a steep precipice. The Raven induced the Deer to sit down near the precipice, while he himself sat down a little farther back. Now he supported his head on his hand, and began to cry, 'How long your fore legs are, how long your fore legs are!' Then the Deer began to cry, and sang, 'How grey your nose is!' And the Raven retorted, singing, 'How long your nose is!'

Thus they continued for some time. When they had finished crying, the Raven asked, 'How long have you been in this world?' The Deer replied, 'It is a long time that I have been here. Tell me first how long you have been here.' Then the Raven said: 'I became a man when the mountains began to rise.' The Deer retorted, 'That is not so long. I am older than you are. I became a man before the Sun gave the world its present form.' Then they began to cry again; and this time the Deer sang, 'How ugly his foot is! His foot is all covered with scars.' Then the Raven grew angry, pushed the Deer, and threw him down the precipice. Then he assumed the shape of the Raven, and flew down the mountain, crying, '*Qoax!*' He ate part of the Deer's meat, and concealed the rest under the stones.

Then he returned home and lay down. He thought, 'What shall I do next?' He made up his mind to travel. After some time he reached a house, the door of which was open. He stepped in and looked about. He saw that the house was full of dried fish, which was moving as though women were working at it; but he did not see anybody. Then he went out and called his sisters, Crow, Mouse, Gull, and Rat. He told them what he had seen, and asked them to help him carry away the provisions. He said, 'I do not see any people; but implements moving by themselves are at work on the provisions.' They entered the house, and the Raven took the fish down from the drying-frames, and asked his sisters to pack it into baskets and to carry it away. After he had thrown all the fish down, he descended to the floor of the house, and intended to go out; but he felt himself held by arms and feet, and was beaten without mercy. His sisters were treated in the same manner. . . . Then he found that the Echo inhabited this house.

He returned home, and thought what to do next. He was hungry, and was glad when after a little while a small Waterfowl invited him to his house. He accepted the invitation, and sat down near the fire. Then the fowl took a box, held his foot over it, and cut his ankle with a stone knife. At once salmon-eggs fell down into the box, filling it entirely. The Raven ate, and carried home to his sisters what was left over.

On the next morning a woman named Young Seal invited him to a feast. He sat down near the fire, and she took a dish. She cleaned it, placed it near the fire, and held her hands over it. Then grease dropped down into the dish, filling it entirely. She gave it to the Raven, who ate heartily, and took home to his sisters what was left over.

On the following day a Bird invited him to a feast. He placed a box near the fire and sang. . . . At once the box was full of salmon-berries. The Raven ate, and carried home to his sisters what was left over.

Now he resolved to invite the Waterfowl. On the following day the bird came. Then the Raven took a box, put his foot into it, and cut his ankle, but nothing came out of it. And he said to the Waterfowl, 'Go back! I have nothing to give you.' In the evening he made up his mind to invite Young Seal. He felt his hands all the time, to see if fat were dripping from them. On the next morning he invited her. He placed a mat for her near the fire, took a dish, cleaned it, and placed it on the mat. Then he held his hands over the dish, but not a particle of fat dripped out of them. His hands, however, were burnt to a crisp by the heat of the fire. Then he said to Young Seal, 'Go back! I have no food for you.' Then he invited the Bird. He placed a box near the fire, and tried to sing the Bird's song; but there was only a single berry in the box. He continued, but did not succeed any better. Finally he sang, 'Menk,' and the box was full of excrements.

On the following day he made up his mind to marry the Sockeye Salmon. He said to his sisters, 'Let us go to the Salmon country. I want to marry the Sockeye Salmon.' His sisters went with him in his canoe. They travelled westward. When they reached the country of the Salmon, he told his sisters that he intended to carry away the chief's daughter, and he ordered them to make holes in the canoes of all the Salmon by pulling out the filling of the knot-holes. Then they went up to the house where he was invited, and feasted. After they had eaten, the Raven prepared to carry to his canoe the food that was left over. He said to the chief's daughter, 'Will you please help me to carry my food to the canoe?' She did so, accompanying him down to the beach. He went aboard, and asked the girl to step into the water, in order to reach the canoe more easily. He induced her to step farther and farther, and finally took her into his canoe. Then his sisters struck the sides of the canoe with the palms of their hands, and it went off by itself. The Salmon rushed to their canoes in order to pursue them; but after they had gone a short distance, their canoes foundered.

The Raven and his sisters carried away the young woman, and reached their home safely. The woman had beautiful long hair. Her husband asked her, 'Where did you get that long hair?' She replied, 'I pulled it and made it grow.' Then the Raven said, 'Oh, please pull my hair too, and make it grow!' 'No,' she said, 'I don't want to do it. If I should do so, your hair would become entangled in the salmon there drying over the fire, and you would pull them down.' But the Raven insisted. Finally she grew angry, and said, 'Well, I will pull your hair.' She did so, and the Raven found that it reached down to his shoulders; but he was not satisfied, he wanted to have it longer. Then she pulled it until it reached down to his waist, but still he was not satisfied. He insisted, until finally she made it as long as her own hair. Then the

Raven arose, intending to show himself to the people. While he was going out of the house, he moved his head from side to side, so that his hair flew about. When he passed under the drying salmon, they became entangled in his hair. He tried to pull it out, and finally succeeded. Then he went out and showed himself to the people. Soon he re-entered; and since he was still moving his head from side to side, his hair again became entangled in the salmon. He tried to disengage himself, but found it very difficult. Then he grew impatient, and said to the salmon, 'I don't want to catch you a second time,' and threw them out of the house. Then his wife arose and said, 'I refused to make your hair long, but you insisted. I knew that you would maltreat the salmon.' With this she jumped into the water, and all the salmon followed her. They swam back to the country of the Salmon, and the Raven lost his long hair. Then he was very sad.[2]

As already stated, the Bella Coola Olympus is extraordinarily elaborate and systematized. Boas is inclined to explain this feature by the fact that the Bella Coola were stimulated towards this elaboration of their ideas about the supernatural world by the impact of new beliefs and thoughts which overwhelmed them when they reached their new coastal home, and he offers the suggestion that the process of systematizing their mythology may have taken place 'very rapidly.' This is, of course, a conjecture, but if true it would account for this unusual effort of the imagination. Boas also suggests that the endogamy of the Bella Coola villages could be accounted for by the social factors that came into play after the Bella Coola migrated to the coast. Having developed a high regard for the clan traditions of their neighbours, they may have felt the need to preserve these in the local units which constituted the basis of their social organization. Taking into account the habits of the Bella Coola, Boas believes that this purpose was attained by them by placing a prohibition on marriage outside of the local group, that is, by endogamy.[3]

[2] Franz Boas, 'The Mythology of the Bella Coola Indians,' *Jesup North Pacific Expedition*, vol. I, pp. 90–95.

[3] Boas notes here that the southern Kwakiutl, who also were originally organized upon the basis of village communities, later adopted the institution of exogamy. He accounts for this difference in solving the problem by the pre-existing difference in the organization of the village communities among the Bella Coola and the Kwakiutl. Among the Bella Coola we generally find four ancestors in each village, three men and one woman. While these generally are referred to as brothers and sisters, they were separately created by the Sun and need therefore not be considered as blood relatives. Among the Kwakiutl, on the other hand, the village community is regarded as descended from a single personage. Consequently, among the Kwakiutl the village-mates are all relatives and therefore forbidden to intermarry, whereas among the Bella Coola they are not relatives and

Baganda Deities

Our next sketch of a tribal religion refers to the Baganda, an African tribe situated in the proximity of the equator in the eastern section of the continent. Like many of their Bantu-speaking neighbours, the Baganda engage in both agriculture and herding; their crafts are highly diversified and specialized, and include smelting and use of iron, characteristic of many African tribes. The political organization of Uganda-land is centralized, with a king at its head, as we shall see in the sequel.

The religious ideas and customs of the Baganda were elaborate. Here we find gods, both local and national, fetishes, ghosts, amulets and other 'medicines.' Among the religious officials were priests whose duties were usually associated with the temples of the national gods, and medicine-men who plied their craft somewhat aside from the established religious routine.

The worship of the national gods stood in direct control of the king, and the principal function of these gods was the protection of his person as well as of the Uganda state. In hours of need the king sent messengers to the gods to consult and propitiate them. At the same time, when a particular god displeased him, he would, with truly royal temerity, send out his emissaries to loot the god's temple and estate. Each of the national gods had a temple dedicated to it which was usually situated on a hill-top on one of the gentile estates. The headman of the gens owning the estate was in charge of the temple with its allotment of lands. Sometimes this man was also the chief priest of the temple and as such responsible for the safety and good conduct of the attendant slaves, the cattle, and the god. In some of the temples there were as many as four priests. One of the duties of the chief priest was to receive the persons who wanted to commune with the god, accept their offerings, and bring their message to the god himself. The god's answer took the form of an oracle given through a medium (of this more presently). Though each priestship was hereditary within a gens, a son of a priest did not always succeed his father; instead, the successor was appointed by the gens, subject to approval or rejection by the king.

Both the priest and the medium were sacred personages and any offence committed against them was punishable by death. They had a house situated in the neighbourhood of the temple in which they kept their sacred regalia and where they robed and disrobed, rather elaborate performances surrounded by considerable decorum and sanctity.

are free to intermarry. Though conjectural, this explanation makes the situation comprehensible.

The god's choice was gathered from the following symptoms: The person in question was suddenly possessed (presumably by the god). He or she began to utter secret things and predict future events, positive evidence that the god was within the person. This possession was called 'being married to the god,' while all subsequent possessions were referred to as 'being seized by the head.' As a rule, each god had only one medium, but in the case of Kibuka and Nende, the gods of war, there were several mediums, so that one or more could absent himself at any given time. The method used by a medium in anticipation of possession is described by Roscoe in the following words: 'When a medium wished to become possessed in order to give the oracle, he would smoke a sacred pipe, using in most instances the ordinary tobacco of the country. Sometimes a cup of beer was also given him before the pipe was handed to him to smoke. He sat in the temple, near the fire, and after smoking the pipe, remained perfectly silent, gazing steadily into the fire or upon the ground, until the spirit came upon him. During the time that a medium was under the influence of the god he was in a frenzied state, and his utterances were often unintelligible to anyone except the priest, who was the interpreter. A priest often had to tell the medium afterwards what he had been talking about. As soon as the spirit of the god had left the medium, he became prostrated, and was allowed to sleep off the effects. When a woman was chosen to be the medium, she was separated from men, and had to observe the laws of chastity for the rest of her life; she was looked upon as the wife of the god.' [4]

In most temples there were a number of young girls who were dedicated to the god. Their most important duty was to keep guard over the sacred fire, which had to be kept burning day and night. They also had to keep the material paraphernalia of the temple in good working order. The persons of these girls were sacred and they were not to be trifled with. These girls were brought to the temple when they were weaned, and represented the offering of parents who had prayed to the particular god for children, promising to devote them to his service if their request was granted. Such a girl remained in office until puberty, whereupon the god decided whom she was to marry. Presently she was removed from the temple, because no woman was permitted to enter a temple or have any dealings with the god during her period of menstruation. It is for this reason that the office of temple virgin was restricted to immature girls. When the medium was a woman she was not

[4] J. Roscoe, *The Baganda*, p. 275. (By permission of The Macmillan Company, publishers.)

permitted to perform her temple duties during her menstrual period.

The medicine-men of the Baganda, though not connected with either temples or gods, constituted an influential group and were much feared; their power in fact was greater than that of the priests and mediums, even though its exercise was not associated with the pomp and formality amidst which the priest performed his functions. A number of medicine-men were connected with each gens. These men were distinguished by their skill and cunning; they were good judges of human character and expert in the practice of their secret arts. They could diagnose illness, prescribe for the sick, and in particular could deal with cases of sickness caused by ghosts. They were also reputed for their surgical prowess. They manufactured fetishes and amulets which they sold to the people; and as the demand for such things was great, a medicine-man was a busy individual. As already stated, medicine-men were generally feared, even priests sharing in this attitude.

Turning now to the gods themselves, I shall describe the principal ones among them. The highest god in Uganda was Mukasa. He was a good and kindly god; no human sacrifices were offered to him, the god being satisfied with animal gifts which were made to him at the yearly festivals or whenever the king or a chief wished to confer with him. He was regarded as the god of plenty who assured ample food, cattle, and children to the people. From an examination of Baganda legends one might conclude that Mukasa, like some of the other Baganda gods, was once a human being reputed for his benign character, who on that account came to be regarded as a god. The historicity of these legends should, however, not be taken too seriously, as Roscoe seems inclined to do. Mukasa's temple was situated on Bubembe Island in Lake Victoria Nyanza, but there were also smaller temples dedicated to him in different parts of the country. In these temples Mukasa's sacred emblem was a paddle. The chief temple on Bubembe, however, had no such paddle; instead, it is said, there was once a large meteoric stone in that temple which was turned to the east or the west according to the faces of the moon. The chief priest of Mukasa was the one associated with the Bubembe temple, to which only the king, a leading chief, or the followers of the god on the island itself could come for aid.

According to tradition, as I said, Mukasa was once a man. The story of his life, of which several varieties are told, runs about like this. 'Mukasa, we are told, was the son of Wanema, whom the people on the island call Mirawa; . . . his younger brother, Kibuka, became the famous war god. Wanema was also a god, though of little note in comparison with his sons, Mukasa and Kibuka. Before his birth, Mukasa's mother, Nambubi, is said to have refused to touch any food except a special kind of ripe plantains, . . . cooked food she would not eat. When the boy was born she gave him the name Selwanga. When he had been weaned, he refused to eat ordinary food, but ate the heart and liver of animals and drank their blood. While still a child, he disappeared from home, leaving no trace behind him as to his whereabouts, but subsequently he was found on the island of Bubembe, sitting under a large tree near the lake. Some people saw him as they passed the place, and told the elders of the village, who went to see him and to find out who he was; they concluded that he had come from Bukasa, and called him a 'Mukasa' (that is, a person from the island of Bukasa), and this name attached itself to him from that time.

'One of the men who went to see him, named Semagumba, told his companions that he could not leave the boy on the shore all night, so he carried him to the garden and placed him upon a rock, until they could decide where he was to go. The people were afraid to take him into their houses, because they said that he must be superhuman to have thus come to their island; so it was decided that a hut should be built for him near to the rock on which he was seated, and that Semagumba should take care of him. They were at a loss what to give him to eat because he refused all sorts of things which they brought to him; at length they happened to kill an ox, and he at once asked for the blood, the liver, and heart, though he refused any of the meat which they offered him. This confirmed the people in their opinion that he was a god, and they consulted him about any illness, and sought his advice when they were in trouble. Semagumba became chief priest, while Gugu and Sebadide, who had been his assistants, also became priests; the names of these men became the official names of later priests. For many years (according to the statements of some people, for 14 generations), Mukasa continued to live in the hut which they had built for him, and the priests cared for him. He married three wives. . . . There are differences of opinion as to the end of the god; some say that he died and was buried on the island, in the forest near the temple, while others affirm that he disappeared as suddenly as he had come.' [5]

There were three priests connected with Mukasa's temple: Semagumba, who was the chief priest, Gugu, and Sebadide. When one of the priests died the remaining two instructed the new incumbent in his duties. When either of these priests officiated his attire consisted of

[5] *Ibid.*, pp. 291–292.

two well-dressed bark cloths, one knotted over each shoulder. In addition he had nine white goat-skins tied around his waist. The priests shaved their hair, each of the three having his own coiffure. Semagumba left a patch of hair on the right side at the back of the head which was allowed to grow long and into which coloured beads were plaited. Gugu allowed his hair to grow long on the top of his head and wore it plaited with beads and cowry shells. Sebadide wore his hair like Semagumba only that his unshaved tuft was smaller and no ornaments were plaited into it. In connection with the temple there were two sacred drums, the larger one of the two having human bones for drum sticks. The method of procuring these bones was as follows: 'A chief named Sekadu was sent from the island Busiro with a canoe to the mainland, to a place named Sango, between the islands Zinga and Busi. On his arrival there, the canoe was beached and a bunch of ripe plantains was placed on the prow, as though the canoemen were about to ship them; the men then went off to the gardens, leaving one of their number in hiding to watch the canoe. If a man came and took some of the fruit, he was caught, bound, and placed in the canoe; if a woman came and attempted to take the fruit, she was driven away by the man in hiding. After capturing their prisoner, the men were obliged to row to the island Kibi without stopping; here they might spend the night, and on the following day they rowed to a small island Kaziri, where the captive was landed and put to death by having his throat cut. The body was left lying on the ground with a guard to protect it against crocodiles or birds, until the flesh decayed. When the shin-bones were quite clean and bleached, the guard took them to Bubembe, and handed them to the priest Semagumba, who beat the drum two or three blows with them and then handed them to Sendowoza, the man in charge of the drum. The drum (Betobanga) was beaten for the annual festival, on which occasion the rhythm had to be kept up at intervals by day and by night until the end of the festival; the drum also announced the appearance of the new moon, warned the people of the monthly cessation from work, and made known when any special festival was to be held, as for instance, when the king sent to consult the god.' [6]

The medium of Mukasa was a woman. When she was about to become possessed she dressed like one of the priests except that she had eighteen instead of nine goat-skins around her waist. She smoked a pipe of tobacco until the god came upon her; then she began talking in a shrill voice and announced what was to be done. While giving the oracle she sat over a sacred fire, perspiring very freely and foam-

[6] J. Roscoe, *The Baganda*, pp. 296–297.

ing at the mouth. Upon the delivery of the oracle and after the god
had left her, she lay prostrate for a time, very fatigued. While giving
the oracle she had a stick in her hand with which she struck the ground
to give emphasis to her words.

Next to Mukasa the most important god was Kibuka, who, as we already know, was once a brother of the real Mukasa. He was the god of
war. His temple stood on Sese Island, where Kibuka had once lived.
In this temple were preserved the jaw-bone, the umbilical cord, copper
ax, spear, and a number of other things which had once belonged to the
real Kibuka. Kibuka's temple was very luxuriously fitted out, as this
god was very wealthy. The temple was surrounded on three sides by a
thick forest, whereas the fourth side faced a large open space. All around
it for some distance lay the gardens of the priests and of the god's
retainers. The king and his most powerful chiefs were constantly offering him men and women slaves. Whenever the king wished to consult Kibuka, he sent a present of slaves and cattle. The slaves sent by
the king to Kibuka were prisoners who had presumably committed
some offence. They were given an opportunity to state their case before
the god, although there is no record of their ever having been acquitted. After visiting the temple, these persons were taken away by
the head of the police, named Sabata, to a tree near by on which their
outer clothes were hung; then they were given a special kind of doc-
tored beer to drink so as to prevent their ghosts from injuring the
king. After they had drunk the beer they were led to the sacrificial
place where they were either speared or clubbed to death, their bodies
being left to lie where they fell for the wild beasts and birds to do
the rest. In certain instances when Kibuka was particularly incensed
against a prisoner, the latter was put to death at once in the temple—
the medium, still possessed by the god, seized the spear and ran it
through the man as he knelt pleading his cause.

There were many other gods: Nende, the second god of war;
Kaumpuli, the god of the plague; Dangu, the god of the chase; and Katonda, also called the Creator. It is interesting to note that this last god,
who was referred to as 'the father of the gods' and was believed to have
created all things, was yet treated with relatively scant attention. Offerings of cattle were occasionally made to him, some of which might be put
to death, but the majority were decorated with a bell around the
neck and were allowed to roam about during the day, while at night
they were brought to one of the huts.[7]

[7] This god apparently belongs to the category discussed by us as the All-Father;
at any rate, Katonda combines the two traits characteristic of All-Fathers: he is

Still other gods were Kitaka, the earth god; Musisi, the god of earthquakes; and Wamala, to whom human sacrifices were made. The victims were clubbed to death on the lake-shore and speared and thrown into the lake. It is said that the waters used to turn crimson with the blood of the victims by the time the sacrifices were ended. There was also Walumbe, the god of death. The king alone made offerings to this god, at the bidding of the other gods, to prevent Walumbe from killing the people.

The story is told about a man, Mpobe, who was following a rat with his dogs, until he was led into a hole into which the rat had fled. There he met Death, who permitted him to return to the surface on condition that he should not tell anyone of what had occurred to him. When he came home he at first refused to speak, but his mother insisted on hearing his tale, until finally he agreed to tell her a little provided that she would not tell anyone. In the evening when it was dark Mpobe heard someone calling him, 'Mpobe! Mpobe!' and he replied, 'I am here. What do you want?' Death said, 'What did I tell you?' Mpobe said, 'You told me not to tell what I had seen in this place, and, Sir (*sic!*), I have only told my mother a little.' To which Death responded, 'I will leave you then to settle up your affairs. You must die when you have expended your property.' After a while Death called to him and asked if he had consumed everything. Mpobe said he had not and tried to hide away in the forest, but Death said: 'Mpobe, why are you hiding in the forest? Do you think I cannot see you?' He tried to hide in all sorts of places, but Death always discovered him. Finally Death came to him and asked, 'Mpobe, have you finished your wealth?' and he replied, 'I have finished it all.' So Death took him. Hence comes the saying, 'Being worried into telling a secret killed Mpobe.'

In addition to the gods there were various spirits connected with animals, rivers, and hills. Certain hills regarded as sacred were associated with the lion spirit; others with the leopard spirit. Not even the king nor any of his messengers might venture upon these hills. It is for this reason that whenever the king sent his men to rob or plunder the people, they would escape to one of these hills and wait there until the king's party had withdrawn.

A fetish was usually an artificial object, or sometimes a natural one

the most important of all gods, in so far as he has created all things, but also not much is known about him; he steers clear of any dealings with humans, and practically no worship is extended to him.

of uncommon shape. Ordinarily the mere possession of a fetish was sufficient to ward off evil. Hence numbers of such fetishes were kept in a certain place in each house and had drink placed before them daily by the owner's wife. Some fetishes were made of wood or of clay mixed with other substances after a recipe known to the medicine-men and to them alone. These fetishes were moulded into different shapes by which they were known to the people. Some were kidney-shaped, others shaped like crescents, while still others were large disks with a hole in the centre. A warrior had his fetish and so had a huntsman, each with its special powers. Even a thief had his fetish, which enabled him to enter undetected any house which he wished to rob. Some of the more elaborate fetishes enjoyed a more than local prestige.

Ghosts were universally believed in. The ghosts of humans were thought to be patterned after the bodies of those whose ghosts they became. As a consequence people stood in great horror of being mutilated, for in addition to suffering the attendant pain and indignity, one had to anticipate that one's ghost would be similarly disfigured. Some people said that they preferred to die with a limb rather than to live without it, thus losing their chance of possessing full powers in the other world where the ghosts dwelt. Ghosts were not by any means uniformly hostile; they had their likes and dislikes and could be appeased by kindness and made angry by neglect. One could not, therefore, disregard them. A favourite place of ghosts was among the trees in the gardens, where they liked to amuse themselves, especially at noon when the sun shone brightly.[8] For this reason children were warned against going out to play in the gardens in the heat of the day, and even adults were careful not to do so unless they could not help themselves.

A ghost, it was thought, never lost its taste for the particular body it had once inhabited. Ghosts tended to hang about the graves in which the bodies lay buried, nor would they go far away from the spot unless the body or part of it were removed. The part with which they were particularly associated was the lower jaw-bone. If this was taken away the ghost would go with it to any distance, and remain there, if properly honoured. On this account the lower jaw-bones of men have for generations been treated by the Baganda as a privileged part of their anatomy. The jaw-bones of men who lived nearly a thousand years ago were still

---

[8] This idea of the predilection of ghosts for the noon-time hour strikes us as peculiar because our ghosts seem to prefer the hour of midnight. It is, however, to be noted that the association of the noon hour with ghosts is also widely prevalent among the Mediterranean peoples of Europe.

preserved by members of the gens to which these men once belonged. The jaw-bones of kings were, of course, treated with particular care and handed down from generation to generation.

The ghosts of ordinary people received less consideration, but they also played their part in the life of the community. The belief was that all ghosts first went to Tandu, a place where they had to give an account of their doings in the flesh. After they had paid their respects to Walumbe, the god of death, they were permitted to return to their own burial grounds. As a rule ghosts were not malevolent; on the contrary, they were wont to assist the members of the gens to which they had belonged. Only the ghosts of a man's sisters were regarded as troublesome, especially with reference to his children. Here a medicine-man came in good stead. After consulting an oracle, he was able to discover which particular ghost was the source of the trouble and what methods should be used to appease it. If a ghost's grave had been neglected, an offering of a goat or even of a cow had to be made in extenuation of the slight. These animals were not killed but were permitted to live and roam about in the vicinity of the ghost's shrine. They could not be sold. When a house was haunted by a ghost, a medicine-man was able to remove it. He would arrive equipped with an empty vessel and a bag of fetishes by means of which he was able to induce the ghost to enter the vessel. As such a domestic ghost always resided at the highest point of the house, it had to be brought down. The medicine-man, working in the dark, emitted sounds which seemed to come from the ghost on the top of the house, and later from the vessel. Then he would carry the captured ghost off to some wasteland, leaving it there to be burned by the next grass fire, or he would throw the vessel with the ghost into a stream and permit it to perish in this way.

It seems that animal ghosts were not general, but some animals like lions, leopards, and crocodiles, were believed to turn into ghosts after their deaths, and these were worshipped in certain localities. Sheep also had their ghosts. The method of killing sheep was therefore different from that used in the case of goats, whose throats were cut. A sheep was led by a man to an open space, while another man stood behind it. When it was not looking, it was struck on the head with the handle of an ax and stunned, whereupon its throat was cut. The reason given for this procedure was that, if a sheep saw the man who was about to kill it, the sheep's ghost would cause him to fall ill and die.

There were certain places which had for generations been devoted to human sacrifices. There were thirteen such places in the country, each with its peculiar usages with reference to the ways the victims were

put to death. All sacrificial places had their custodians, while some
also had temples with priests and retinues. The custodian always kept a
large pot which was usually distinguished by a number of mouths. When
victims were sent in for sacrifice, this pot was brought out, full of medi-
cated beer which the victims were forced to drink, it being considered
that this gave the king control of the victim's ghost, or prevented it from
coming back and haunting or hurting the people or the king himself.
Two methods were employed to supply the sacrificial places with victims. Some of these were men or women who had committed some offence and had been apprehended, but others were innocent people who
had been caught in the open road 'by order of the gods,' so as to make
up the number of persons required for the sacrifice. The office of executioner was a very popular one, for there was an opportunity for enrich-
ment at the expense of the possible victims, some of whom were spared,
for a price; others were promised to be dispatched without undue pain
or torture. At the sacrifices specifically ordered by the king, the number of people thus done away with varied from two to five hundred. The
relatives of a condemned man might try to influence the king to release
him. If the request was accompanied by an offering of a good-looking
girl or a large number of cattle, the gift might prove acceptable, and
the prisoner was released. The sacrificial place, Nakinzire, on Seguku
Hill in Busiro, had its temple and a medium who was the son of a prin-
cess and as such should have been put to death, according to the amiable
Baganda custom. This medium was possessed by a leopard. When under
the influence of the leopard ghost, he growled and rolled his eyes. The
victims were either clubbed or speared to death. If they were tortured,
their flesh was cut off with splinters of reeds which were sharp and cut
like razor-blades. The flesh was pinched up and cut off over the body.
Afterwards the victims were killed. These executions at times extended
for a whole week because the executioners became weary and went off
to drink beer and talk things over. The bodies of the victims were never
removed from the places where they fell, but were permitted to remain
for wild animals or birds to feed upon.

Sometimes an ordeal was used to test the guilt of a person. This
method of ascertaining guilt deserves attention on account of its widespread use in Africa and, incidentally, in Mediaeval Europe. The priest
attached to Kibuka's temple administered the poison test. He gave to
each of the two disputants a cup of a drug obtained by boiling the root
of the datura plant, then made both sit down at a little distance, while
the drug was taking effect. Then he called to the two men to get up, step
over a plantain stem and come over to him. If one of them was able to

do this, the case was decided in his favour; if both failed, they were pronounced equally guilty; if both succeeded, they were deemed innocent. Another test was to use a heated piece of iron or the blade of a hoe. Each disputant brought with him a bunch of grass which the priest passed over a hot iron. If one bunch was burned and not the other, the one whose bunch was burned was considered guilty. Or again the priest would make the disputants sit down and pass the hot iron down each man's leg from the knee to the foot. The man who was burned was the guilty one.[9]

Ceremonial and Religious Life of the Incas

Before broaching the state ceremonialism of the Incas, it will be fitting to cast a brief glance at their family.

Bachelorhood and spinsterhood in persons past marrying age were almost non-existent among the Incas; practically everyone was married at least once and many were married repeatedly. Polygyny was practised, and in the upper classes it was general. The first woman whom a man married or received, either in the ordinary course of things or as a reward for valour, became his wife-in-chief and such she remained until his death. She was the only woman whom he married with any pomp, provided, of course, he belonged to the upper class. Having received his bride at the hand of the Inca or his representative official, he led her to the house of her father, accompanied by a throng of his kinfolk. At the father's house the bride's relatives were waiting; in the presence of the two groups of relatives, the father now handed her over to the groom. Then the young man knelt down and shod his bride's

---

[9] Like the Baganda political organization (see p. 387), the organized religion of these people bears evidence of a cultural situation made possible by a vast population and the great power of the king and his henchmen, rendered relatively safe by their retinues of body-guards. It will have been observed how intimately the person and influence of the king are associated with the highly ramified and localized forms of this religion. The same applies to the methods of treating victims and other executions so common in Uganda. As between torture and torture, the difference may perhaps not be significant. Still, the constant placing of human lives at the call of a king's whim is a feature not to be found in more primitive societies which are usually greatly concerned with the preservation of their numbers, and whose chieftains, being in more constant and direct contact with their subordinates, are more sensitive of public opinion, and could not afford, even if they chose, to try the patience of their subjects further than just so far, without forfeiting their prestige or their very office. In this respect, to repeat, as in certain items of their socio-political organization, these African customs differ from those of more primitive groups and come closer to the social conditions characteristic of later historic cultures, with their barbarisms, privileges, and despotisms.

right foot with a sandal of wool, if she was a maiden, or with one of *ichu* grass, if she was a widow. After the ceremony which signified that the bridegroom accepted the bride as his wife-in-chief, he led her to their future home, which had by this time been prepared for them, the relatives following after them. Having arrived there, the bride took from her girdle a shirt of fine wool, a fillet, and a breast ornament, which she handed to her husband, who donned them forthwith. From this moment until night was well advanced the young people were separated and kept busy by elder persons of their sexes who were expected to instruct them in the meaning and obligations of marriage. When the two parties reunited the festivities began which in due time tended to become an orgy. A woman so wedded, let me repeat, could never be repudiated nor abandoned, and while her husband lived, she remained his chief wife. It is also of interest that the ceremony was purely secular, no priest participating in it. When a man's first wife died, the man after a prolonged period of mourning was expected to take another chief wife from women outside of his household, this event also being accompanied by ceremonies similar to the preceding. Many writers on the Incas consider this a salutary custom, in so far as the secondary wives of the man had no occasion to quarrel among themselves as to who would become his next chief wife, for none of them could expect that this privilege would be bestowed upon them.

There were various methods of acquiring secondary wives. The sons of high-born parents were placed in the care of nursemaids, who attended to their needs while they were still young, and later on initiated them into the mysteries of sex. When the wards married, these nursemaids remained as their concubines. If an orphan boy was given in to the care of a childless widow whose duty it was to bring him up, it was customary for her also to become, in due time, one of his concubines. Women captured in war were other candidates for this position. The Inca himself was wont to confer upon valorous fighters such secondary wives, whom he drew from the imperial supplies of women, which were always ample.

While such were the customs in the upper classes, the inhabitants of the provinces were dealt with less ceremoniously. The official in charge of each village periodically assembled the youths and maidens of marriageable age into two groups and then paired them off into couples. It is, however, made clear by the Spanish writers that personal inclination was not altogether left out of consideration, and that couples who had previously been attracted by each other were given a chance, on these occasions, to have their unions socially sanctified.

The period of childhood, in so far as it can be disentangled from a maze of incomplete data, was not a happy one. Children were treated either with excessive severity or with equally excessive indulgence. By and large, the facts were about as follows: When a woman was at the point of giving birth, she and her husband fasted, the wife also making a confession of her transgressions and proffering propitiatory prayers to the minor deities. When the time for birth was at hand, the woman went into isolation for a brief period, and gave birth without as much as the assistance of a midwife. With the new-born infant in her arms she was expected presently to proceed to the nearest stream and wash herself and the baby, no matter how cold the air or water might be (a practice which persists in this region until the present day). The infant was permitted to feed at the breast only three times a day, early in the morning, at noon, and at sundown, the Incas having noted that animals suckled their young at fixed times, and holding that greater frequency of feeding would induce vomiting and make the baby gluttonous when it grew up. Wet-nursing was resorted to only in cases where the mother's health made it necessary. During the nursing period the mother had to abstain from sexual intercourse, for fear that this would have a bad effect on her milk and render the baby anaemic. When the baby was able to crawl it took its meals kneeling at one side of the mother's breast while the latter bent over it, and whenever it wanted to feed from the other breast it had to crawl around the mother on its hands and knees, for it was never permitted on her lap. It was customary for a mother to carry the child on her back, swathed in a shawl together with its cradle, a custom probably even less pleasant for the infant than it was for the mother. When the child outgrew its cradle it was wrapped in any cloth that lay handy and placed in a hole dug in the ground which came up to its arm pits; there it was left to jump and kick as well as amuse itself with whatever toys the mother may have left within its reach. The ceremonies which graced the early childhood years, such as the first cutting of its hair and nails by means of sharpened stones, or the name-giving ritual, were as secular as the rites of marriage, no person of priestly station officiating on these occasions.

We may now pass to a consideration of the more elaborate public ceremonials of the Inca state.

Ritualism, as we saw, provides one of the universal settings of religion. It is to be observed in addition that in highly centralized societies, either primitive or modern, ritualism tends to run high. Such was the case among the Peruvians. The state festivals of the Incas were known according to the months into which they fell. During the month

Intip Raimi, beginning with the June solstice, was held the great Feast-of-the-Sun. At Cuzco, where the ceremonies were naturally most imposing, the rites were in part conducted by the Sapa Inca himself, as the Sun's first-born, and in part by the *Villac Umu*, high priest of the Sun, who was the Inca's uncle or brother. Provincial officials from all parts of the Empire, each one attended by an impressive retinue, assembled at Cuzco to pay homage to their chief divinity. Those from certain mountain districts came in robes fashioned from puma-skins; from the East and North came others adorned in gorgeous raiments of brilliant bird plumage; from the coastal states came still others attired in finely woven cotton cloths of many colours. The outstanding visitors among all were the chiefs, who came rigged out in condor costumes provided with outstretched wings. This highly picturesque company foregathered in the capitol from which all strangers of low degree were temporarily expelled. The rituals themselves took place in the *Huaca Pata* (Holy Terrace or Great Square), where the Inca himself participated, while persons of lesser station held similar rituals on the *Cusi Pata* (Joy Terrace) from which the major ritual on the Holy Terrace could easily be observed. On this occasion a black llama was formally sacrificed. It was placed with its head to the East; while four Incas sat upon it to keep it still, its left side was slashed open by the officiating priest, who plunged his hands into the wound and drew forth the still living heart, lungs, and gullet, all of which had to be removed entire and without cutting. These entrails were supposed to have great prognostic value. If the lungs, in particular, were still palpitating when separated from the victim's body, the omen was regarded as favourable and the ceremony proceeded with enhanced zeal. After the sacrifice of the black llama, many other animals were offered to the Sun, their flesh being subsequently distributed and consumed by people in widely separated districts. It was held that the fire used for the sacrifice should be new and derived directly from the Sun. For this purpose a large bracelet called *chipana* was employed, like those usually worn on the left wrist. The bracelet held by the high priest had on it a highly polished concave plate about the diameter of an orange. This was held at an angle towards the Sun to permit the reflected rays to concentrate on one point where some cotton wool had been placed, which presently became ignited. At the conclusion of the more sacred rites and after ample food had been partaken of, drinking began, which started in an orderly enough fashion but presently gathered momentum, usually to assume the character of an orgy before much time had elapsed.

The second month (July 22 to about the same date in August) was mainly devoted to brewing and to cleaning or repairing the irrigation ditches. The third month, *Yapaquiz* (August 22 to September 22), was the month of sowing, during which a festival was held called *huayara*. On this occasion fifteen brown llamas were sacrificed, the animals being selected from the flocks of the Sun and those of the Inca. In this month the farms belonging to the Sun were ploughed with special rites by priests and priestesses. As they worked they were accompanied by a white llama with golden ornaments in its ears, and a great quantity of maize beer was sprinkled over the fields in its honour. When the sowing was completed a great sacrifice was held, consisting of the selfsame llamas and large numbers of other animals, the aim of the sacrifice being to propitiate the air, water, ice, and thunder, in order that they might favour the crops.

The fourth month, or *Coya Raimi* (September 22 to about October 22), was devoted to the Moon cult, which was intended, among other things, to ward off sickness and other evils connected with the annual rains. On this, as on all similar occasions, all provincial persons, all individuals suffering from physical defects, and all dogs were cleared from the city of Cuzco, the first because they were not descendants of the moon, the second as unworthy to observe the festival, and the third because they were apt to bark or howl at untoward moments. During the ceremony that followed a great urn of gold was set up in the centre of the Temple Square into which, within the sight of all, quantities of maize beer were solemnly poured. Around this urn were stationed 400 warriors in full war regalia, each group of 100 facing towards one of the cardinal points. Then, as the new moon made its appearance in the heavens, all present burst into loud cries: 'All sickness, disaster, misfortunes, and perils, go forth from the land!' This cry was taken up in all parts of the city, and at that very moment the four groups of warriors began running rapidly in the directions they were facing, crying out while they ran: 'Go forth, all evils! go forth, all evils!' The warriors sped beyond the boundaries of the city into the country where the provincial folk were camped; they took up the shout, which was thus made to spread into the far-flung regions of the Empire. A little later the four groups of warriors, having run the appointed course, plunged into certain rivers which were known to flow into regions beyond the confines of the Inca state. There they bathed under the new moon's beams, so that the waters might carry evils and misfortunes out of the country. At the same time the whole populace were expected to bathe with appropriate rites to purify themselves for the coming year.

Towards the close of the festival the provincial folk, who had been chased out of the city at the beginning of the festivities, were invited to come back. In groups of kindred they assembled on the Joy Terrace to observe the closing ceremonies of the season. Thirty spotless white llamas brought from every part of the Empire were now sacrificed on a fire composed of thirty bundles of saffron-scented quishular-wood. The fleece of these animals, which had never been shorn, and their flesh were used for various ceremonial purposes.

Passing by the next two months, not so notable by way of ceremonies, we come to the seventh month or *Capac Raimi* (December 22 to about January 22). This was one of the most important months of the year, especially for the youths of the imperial castes of either sex, as in it were held the ceremonies which marked the entrance of boys into manhood. These rites, called *huarachicu*, were a sort of an ordeal, the purpose of which was to test the virility, endurance, strength, and discipline of the youths. The ceremony was preceded by a course of instruction in the arts of war, the making and management of weapons, the manufacture of sandals and other equipment, which instruction was administered by elder Incas of ample and varied experience. At the conclusion of instruction and upon completing the examinations, the lads fasted for six days, during which time they took no nourishment save raw maize and water, after which they partook of ample food and were ready for the next act, which consisted of a race from Huanacauri Hill to the plain on the northern side of Sacsahuamán. Upon a hill in the neighbourhood of the latter place certain animals were segregated, a falcon, a vicuña, a fox, a humming bird, a vulture and an ostrich, the purpose and meaning of these creatures not being altogether clear to us. As the runners approached, they could see the Inca and his court sitting to the right upon seats carved in the living rock. The first ten runners were commended by the Inca, whereas those who came last were met with scorn and derision and were expected henceforth to wear a breech-clout of black cloth instead of the white ones trimmed with gay feathers which were donned by their more successful competitors. Then came a sort of sham battle; in this the youths successful in the race were divided into two armies, of which one held and the other attacked the fortress of Sacsahuamán. The next day their roles were exchanged. These exercises were regarded as part of their military training and were a mere preliminary to the principal rite called *huarachicu*.

Finally the day of the major rites arrived. The Sapa Inca himself played the leading part in these. The crowning moment of the performance was the piercing of the lads' ear-lobes (or at least the ceremonial piercing, as the actual act had been performed two months previously by the Inca himself, who used golden pins for the purpose). To keep the holes open, ear-studs were fitted into them, which were subsequently exchanged for larger and still larger ones, until by the time the boys had reached manhood, their ear-lobes became greatly enlarged because of the weight of the studs. It is for this reason that the Spaniards after the conquest were wont to designate members of the Imperial caste as *orejón* or big-ears. At the conclusion of the piercing rite each novice passed on to other officials, who dressed him in breech-clout and sandals, and furnished him with weapons. At the same time the youths were garlanded with *cantut* flowers, shaped like lilies and coloured yellow, purple, and red, and with *chihuayhua* plumes, which resemble yellow carnations. Upon their brows the lads wore wreaths of a plant called *uiñay huayna*, meaning 'ever young.'

In the eighth month, or *Camay* (January 22 to about February 22), other military ceremonies were held; these included sham fights with slings (fruit being used as missiles), also hand-to-hand combats, probably a sort of wrestling, the purpose of which was to test the arm muscles of the contestants. The costumes worn during these proceedings consisted of black tunics under tawny-coloured mantles, and of headgear made from the white plumes of the *ttucu*, a kind of owl. On the day of the new moon a great number of old llamas from all four quarters of the realm were assembled in the Great Square and there their ears were pierced by persons appointed thereto; after this these animals became known as *apu-rucu*, or 'chief who is old.' On the day of the full moon, or the fifteenth of the month, a great multitude of people assembled in the Great Square, before whom ten llamas of all colours were sacrificed to ensure the health of the Inca. This was followed by a night-long dance performed throughout the city and terminating at dawn in the Square where ten costumes of the finest red and white cloth were burned, two each being offered to the major gods: *Viracocha*, the Sun, the Moon, Thunder, and Earth. Finally, two white baby llamas were sacrificed for the health of the public at large. On this, the sixteenth day of the month, the priests brought to the Square the images of all the gods, both major and minor, as well as the mummies of the illustrious dead, all of which were arranged in certain places in the Square. At the same time another and most remarkable object was brought into the Square, a very long thick cable braided from wool coloured black, white, red, and yellow. This cable was known as *huascar*, meaning 'cable' or 'rope,' or *muru-urcu*, or 'spotted male.' This rope was used in the following fashion, according to Means: 'The men lined up along one side of the *huascar* and women on the other, both sexes grasping it all along its great length in such a way that a long serpentine group of people was formed, with the brightly coloured rope running down the middle, its forward end being a large ball of red wool, like a head. In this quaint formation the group solemnly marched around the edges of the square, partly no doubt to get the *muru-urcu* stretched out to full length. As they passed in front of the idols and the Inca, the dancers made low obeisances which must have imparted an interesting undulation to the group, as it moved along. Then, having surrounded the Square, the dancers gradually began to form a coil, slowly drawing in the convolutions as closely as possible. When this process was completed, they dropped the *huascar* upon the ground and went away from it, leaving it all curled up on the pavement like a monstrous serpent. Of all the rites of the Incas this dance of the cable must surely have been one of the most charming. The famous "golden chain" which was made towards the end of the Incaic period, to celebrate the birth of the ruler known as Huascar, was merely a rope such as that here described but one adorned most lavishly with strands of gold.' [10]

The ninth, tenth, eleventh and twelfth months also had their ceremonies which, however, were not so important, nor have the relevant details been as carefully ascertained.

After surveying these state ceremonies of the Incas, one is prompted to ask when the people had time to do anything else. The answer, of course, lies in the fact that participation in these rituals was largely restricted to the upper classes, often to those of the Imperial caste. The people at large, in the different parts of the Empire, knew of them only as occasional eyewitnesses or merely by hearsay.

[10] Philip Ainsworth Means, *Ancient Civilizations of the Andes*, pp. 383–384. (Reprinted by permission of Charles Scribner's Sons.)

Chapter XIX

SOCIAL GROUPS AND THEIR FUNCTIONS

Groups of Status

Man is a social animal. No matter how far down we go in culture there is society, always, and also some form of organization. In a sense, indeed, society antedates the individual. It is difficult to see how some of the more distinctive attributes of man, such as speech, and perhaps religion, could have originated in the absence of a social setting. Further, social submergence of the individual belongs to the very beginnings of human life on earth.

If there is a social organization, there must be a basis on which it rests. Some writers are wont to ascribe the institution of social forms to the foresight and vision of wise and powerful men. It may be true, within limits, that deliberate intervention and control have played their part in socio-political history, but the basic forms of society have certainly not arisen in this way. Here we must turn to the natural factors implied in man's relations to his physical and social environment. The process, moreover, was as spontaneous as it was unconscious. Whatever later transformations may have occurred in society and politics, they were rooted in these basic forms—some of which are as old as man, or older.

Local Groups. What then were the factors in primitive life upon which the different forms of social organization were built? The first is *locality.* Man has always lived somewhere.[1] Perpetual vagrancy is not

---

[1] Here, as so often, man has been anticipated by animals. This is what Julian Huxley has to say about birds. 'Territory in some form or other is of prime biological importance in the life of birds (and probably of other groups as well). The first sign of sexual activity . . . is in most species seen in the instinct of the males, not, as has usually been assumed, to seek out the females, but to find, occupy, and defend a territory. So far as there is choice of mates, in monogamous species, it is by the females, who seek out the males; but they only compete for those males who are in possession of territory. Even when the pair is established in the area, the occasions when the female is the primary object of the male's actions is only during the so-called courtship, whose function is to stimulate the female psychically and bring her to the condition in which pairing may be accomplished; but both male and female, singly and as a pair, still react to the fact of territory, and are always active in its defence. Mr. Howard quotes an

primitive. The restless mobility of modern Gipsies seems to be correlated with the permanently fixed habitats of a higher civilization. Neither the Gipsy of fact nor the Wandering Jew of fancy belongs to the beginnings of history. Whether in the snow-built villages of the Eskimo, in the woody recesses or grassland villages of African tribesmen, in the cave dwellings of prehistoric Europe or the sparse camps of the Australians, man, however primitive, always lived somewhere. There was some locality or a number of localities which he regarded as his home. If he did not live permanently in one place, neither did he wander from place to place indefinitely, but returned periodically to certain places within a more or less limited district. This is true, for example, of the Chukchee and Koryak of northeastern Siberia and the Indians of the Pacific Northwest, whose habitats pulsate with the seasons between the sea- or river-shores and the interior.

A home is not only a physical fact; it is also a psychological one. To have a home is to know one's physical environment, to foresee the habitual climatic changes, cold and heat, drought and storm. It is to know the animals and plants available in the neighbourhood, to be familiar with their habits, to learn to avoid them as dangerous, to seek them as food or as friends. A home, moreover, comprises a human group; it implies a common habitation, common adjustments and knowledge, as well as familiarity with one another. People who live together know each other's behaviour. They learn to understand each other's gestures and physiognomy, and in some cases, as in Central Australia, they can tell each other's footprints. There is a spirit of neighbourhood. No matter what other forms of political or social organization may exist, there is always co-operation, mutual helpfulness, on the part of the members of a local group. And there is a readiness, if not an organization, for protection against climatic dangers as well as against the dangers from beasts and hostile men.

Human nature being what it is, to know about people is to want to know more about them. Gossip is one of the universal institutions of mankind, and it is specifically associated with the local group, a circumstance from which many an ethnologist has greatly profited. In condi-

illuminating observation: he saw a weasel passing through the territory of a pair of reed-buntings, who were pursuing it in rage. Another male of the same species of bird approached. But instead of welcoming it as an aid in driving off the intruder, the male whose nest was actually in danger, several times left the pursuit of the weasel to attack the other reed-bunting!' Huxley makes this statement in the course of an exposition of a book by H. Eliot Howard, *Territory in Bird Life*, in his *Essays in Popular Science*, pp. 182–183. (Reprinted by permission of Alfred A. Knopf, Inc.)

tions where the written word is absent and the spirit of systematic investigation as yet unborn, gossip is an important source of dissemination
of knowledge, especially of personal and intimate knowledge, and
the professional gossip, the unofficial historian of primitive days, is the
ethnologist's great friend.

A phase of primitive life in which both prescriptive and proscriptive
regulations abound is marriage. As will presently be seen, the control
of marriage is a function of more than one type of grouping. Where
local exogamy prevails, the control of marriage is a function of the
local group—no marriage within one's own village. This form of marriage regulation occurs, for instance, among the Blackfoot Indians, a
number of the coastal tribes of Australia, and among many of the island
tribes of Torres Straits and Melanesia, where localized clans are the
rule. From the standpoint of culture, as such, another item deserves
emphasis here: the local group is the smallest unit of cultural specialization. In details of custom, daily habits, rituals, and often dialect, a local
group differs to some extent from every other local group. Cultural
changes are rooted in local variants.[2]

Relationship Groups. Another basis of social organization is blood-
relationship. The importance of blood-ties in primitive life has long
been understood. Relationship here underlies a variety of groupings.
Of these only the *family*, though varied in form, is universal. Contrary to
a widespread notion, for which anthropologists are in part responsible,
the family, consisting of husband, wife, and children, is found everywhere. There may be more than one wife, and here and there, more than
one husband; the average duration of matrimonial ties may fall short
of modern standards; the household may embrace other related individuals in addition to the immediate family. The fact remains, the
family is there as a distinct unit. It is there, whatever other social units
may coexist with it. Moreover, it antedates them—where no other social
forms are found, as in the most primitive tribes, the family can always
be discerned. It may be noted incidentally that in the crudest cultures,
for example among the Andamanese or the African pygmies, monogamy
is more generally the rule than among somewhat more advanced tribes.

[2] It is scarcely necessary to add that the basic character of locality as a social
classifier has never been transcended. Among the fixed groupings of modern
society, local determinants loom large. State, city, village, quarter, street, block,
are territorial units the significance of which is physical as well as socio-
psychological. And as ever, there liveth the spirit of the neighbourhood with its
grotesque twin, the spirit of gossip. It is interesting to note in this connection that
in the most recent socio-political experiment on a gigantic scale, in the Soviet
Union, territorial as well as industrial groups function as the primary electoral
units, the former in rural districts, the latter in urban ones.

The family controls the individual in a variety of ways. Its influence is especially pronounced during the earliest years of education and the immediately succeeding period of industrial apprenticeship.[3] Even marriage in its many varied forms—that ubiquitous and all-important social usage—is in many instances controlled by a member or members of the immediate family, more often than not by the mother. The family often functions as a unit upon the ceremonial occasions connected with pregnancy, birth, marriage, death, and burial.[4]

Important though these functions are, the most significant role of the primitive family remains to be mentioned. Everywhere and always, the family serves as the principal point of cultural transfer from one generation to another. It must be remembered that culture consists not only of material things but also of ideas, attitudes, customs, and the like, the latter accounting for by far the larger part of its content. Even material things, as a part of culture, are not passed along automatically; their uses must be explained, the implied techniques learned. As to spiritual culture, including language itself, there is no other way in which it can be communicated, among primitives, except by verbal explanation and teaching, and the direct absorption by the learner of what is being said and done. It is evident that most of what boys or girls learn in this way, especially during the important formative years of childhood, is brought to them through the medium of the family. There are other agencies through which they learn, but in the earliest years the role of the family

[3] It must not be understood by this that the family everywhere enjoys a monopoly of these functions. Among the maternally organized tribes of northwestern Melanesia, the mother's brother, who belongs to a different household than that of his sister, usurps many of the functions more commonly exercised by the father; he, rather than his sister's husband, is the chief guardian of her children and the person largely responsible for their education.

[4] An interesting, though rare, form of family organization has been described by F. G. Speck among some eastern Algonquin tribes. The tribe here is subdivided into a number of families, each including certain relatives in addition to the primal nucleus of parents and children. The pre-eminence of the father is marked. Associated with each family is a hunting territory of varying size in which its members claim exclusive hunting privileges, the latter being extended to strangers only by special arrangement. The boundaries of such hunting territories are marked at varying intervals by natural or artificial sign-posts. The Indians have a very clear idea of the expanse and limits of their respective territories. Professor Speck was able to secure from his informants a series of maps, drawn under his direction, on which the boundaries of family territories are indicated. (Cf. his 'Family Hunting Territories and Social Life of Various Algonkian Bands of the Ottawa Valley,' Memoirs, Geological Survey, vol. LXX, Ottawa, Canada.) Such territorial organizations, delimiting hunting and other prerogatives, are not unknown elsewhere in North America, and have also been reported from Australia, but the association of the institution with a family system seems peculiar to Dr. Speck's tribes.

is overwhelmingly preponderant. The significance of *the family as a transfer point of culture* cannot be overestimated. It serves as a bridge between the generations, between 'fathers and sons.'

The family, in this basic sense, is, of course, universal among more advanced historic peoples, but it will be seen from the above that it is also ubiquitous and important among primitives.[5] History, we know, is rich in special and local forms of the family. For example: the patriarchal family, centring about its male master, as among the Hebrews; or the highly institutionalized and sanctified family, which becomes the base of a lusty and picturesque ancestor worship, as in China and Japan. These types of the family, however, belong to conditions very different from the primitive.

Another form of blood-relationship bond is discovered in the amorphous *group of blood relatives*, consisting of individuals, male and female, who are designated by different terms expressing kinship: mother, father, brother, sister, uncle, aunt, cousin, etc. Such groups of blood-kindred, with their adhering 'in-laws,' exist among all peoples, primitive and modern. Any discussion of blood-relatives must include the in-law group, as the two kinds of kinship constantly intertwine, both sociologically and terminologically. Of this the primary unit itself is an illustration, as the children are related by blood both to mother and father, whereas the parents may be and often are related merely by marriage, thus introducing two in-law groups into the blood group. From this angle, a family is a social knot through which two potential in-law groups become such in fact.

Primitive relationship terms are often designated by the somewhat misleading term 'classificatory.' By this is meant that a kinship term is used to designate not merely an individual related to one in a certain definite way but also other individuals related to one in a different way. Thus the term 'mother' will not only be used to designate one's own mother, but also the mother's sisters and her first cousins and perhaps still other women even more remotely related to the speaker. The term for 'father' may be used in a similar fashion to designate one's own father, the father's brothers, his first cousins, and so on. Or again, the mother's brother and the father's sister's husband will be covered by one term, or the father's sister and the mother's brother's wife. Or one term may be used for the father's sister, her daughter, her daughter's

---

[5] Apart from the utopian society of Plato's *Republic*, and setting aside the somewhat aberrant experiment of Sparta after which the *Republic* was partially patterned, we must look to modern conditions to find a society in which the family seems to have 'outlived its usefulness,' not, as some think, hopelessly and permanently, but sufficiently so to require a radical revamping.

daughter.[6] A great many such extensions in the uses of relationship terms are found throughout primitive terminologies of relationship. In contrasting these kinship systems with our own, for example the English, the term 'classificatory' is justified for the former only in so far as the terms for the immediate family—father, mother, brother, sister, son, daughter—are always used by us to designate a relative standing to the speaker in one particular degree of relationship, whereas just these terms are in primitive systems most frequently extended to cover entire classes of relatives. On the other hand, such terms as 'uncle' and 'aunt' are used by us in a classificatory way to designate father's or mother's brother, father's or mother's sister, whereas in primitive terminologies 'aunt' is often used for father's, not mother's, sister, 'uncle' for mother's, not father's, brother, the terms 'uncle' and 'aunt' being in such instances used in a descriptive, not a classificatory way. At the same time it is important to remember, as bearing upon the status of the family, that in many primitive tribes the terms used for the immediate members of the family are either distinguished from the same terms in their extended uses by the addition of some particle, or terms corresponding to 'own' are used, or a distinction is implied in the context of the conversation. Family is family, whatever the system of relationship or uses of terms.[7]

It must not be imagined that these extensions in the use of terms represent but terminological issues. Far from it. First of all, relationship terms are often employed in place of our personal names, the latter being reserved for special, generally ceremonial, occasions.[8] Then again, special rules of behaviour, proscriptive and prescriptive, often apply to certain relatives. Apart from the multifarious and, of course, ubiquitous functions of parents towards children and the only less numerous ones of children towards parents, the mother's brother is a relative who, particularly in maternally organized societies, occupies a place of special prominence, often above that of the father. In such tribes, as already noted, it is the mother's brother, not the father, who stands in the very centre of the social complex in all matters pertaining to rituals, education, inheritance, and control of property. Again there

---

[6] While this subject cannot be discussed here in greater detail, compare the section on Australian classes and sub-classes (pp. 343 seq.).

[7] An interesting illustration of this occurs among the Iroquois, where, as we shall see, a nephew (sister's son) and a younger brother are the most common successors to a chief's office. Both these terms are used by the Iroquois in a classificatory sense. Still, in the vast majority of cases, it is the *own* sister's son or *own* younger brother who succeeds a chief.

[8] It was shown in the section on religion how important it is for an understanding of primitive attitudes to appreciate this reluctance to use personal names too freely.

is the so-called mother-in-law taboo, a widespread custom in many cultural districts according to which all familiarity and even conversation are forbidden between son-in-law and mother-in-law. Less stringent regulations control not infrequently the relations of daughter-in-law and father-in-law. In Melanesia, as both Rivers and Malinowski have shown, the connexion between social behaviour and particular relatives is especially frequent and important. In Australia, again, the right to marry, in fact almost the duty to do so, belongs to certain groups of related individuals within phratry, class, or sub-class limits, who are from birth on designated as 'husbands' and 'wives.' Here definite duties are assigned to groups of relatives at ceremonies; also, when the hunters return from the chase, food is apportioned to individuals in accordance with their relationship status.

An interesting and amusing form of behaviour between relatives is the so-called 'joking-relationship' of the Plains Indians. Dr. Lowie in a recent book, *The Crow Indians*, gives some illustrations of the custom among this people. A joking-relationship obtains between the sons and daughters of fellow-clansmen (descent here is maternal). The particular behaviour might take a humorous turn. Thus, 'if a man recognizes a wagon outside a house as his joking-relative's, the fancy might seize him to reverse front and rear wheels. Under ordinary circumstances the owner would show resentment, but not as soon as he discovers the identity of the joker: then he must not get angry, he merely bides his chance for getting even.' [9] When a man or woman has committed an objectionable act, the joking-relatives have the privilege of publicly jeering at the person. There are also other regulations of behaviour between relatives. With his own brother's or clansman's wife a man is on terms of greatest familiarity; he may treat his wife's sister with utmost freedom and she will reciprocate in kind.[10] Brothers-in-law may speak to one another lightly on impersonal matters, but any kind of obscenity, in act or word, is forbidden. A brother and a sister may discuss important matters together, but are enjoined from chatting or being together by themselves. I might add to this that in certain parts of Melanesia where the brother-sister taboo is pronounced, sentiment runs so high on these matters that one of twin siblings is often put to death as soon as born on account of their objectionable intimacy in prenatal life.

While in Australia the matrimonial correlates of relationship are exceptionally conspicuous, in view mainly of their prescriptive character, relatives of varying degrees were prohibited from intermarriage or sex

[9] R. H. Lowie, *The Crow Indians*, p. 22.
[10] *Ibid.*, p. 28.

contact among all peoples and at all times. Among these prohibitions some are particularly general and drastic: mother and son, father and daughter, brother and sister, in the order named, stand at the head of the list. Not one of these sex taboos, categorical though they are, has remained wholly free from infraction—outside the law, and even, in certain exceptional instances, inside the law, as among the Pharaohs of Egypt or the kings of Bantu Negroes—but barring these exceptions, it must be said that these particular taboos are everywhere reinforced by the so-called 'horror of incest,' an emotional reaction of somewhat mysterious origin, which is by no means restricted in its range to these primary sex taboos, but readily extends at least to the major sex prohibitions prevalent in a given community.[11]

The two kinds of relationship groups so far discussed—the family and the comprehensive group of blood-relatives and 'in-laws'—different though they are, have certain elements in common: both are biological and bilateral. The individuals of a relationship group are united by actual ties of blood, and these ties branch out in both lateral directions, through the mother as well as the father. This represents in an extended form the basic fact that the family itself is bilateral, in so far as the parents are related to their children by actual bonds of blood, and the children are related to each other through both parents. Husband and wife, on the other hand, need not be related to each other except in tribes where cross-cousin marriage is general or obligatory (as in Australia).[12] In general, however, it may be remarked that in small communities—provided exogamy does not prevail—all individuals of the local group soon become interrelated. Then, of course, all marriages constitute a sort of inbreeding, married couples being, if only in a remote way, related by blood.[13]

[11] It seems hardly fair to doubt that psychoanalysis will ultimately furnish a satisfactory psychological interpretation of this 'horror of incest.' Freud has shown all but conclusively that incestuous tendencies represent one of the most deeply rooted impulses of the individual. If then culture brings with it a negative attitude towards incestuous unions—and here further psychological and perhaps sociological sounding is required as to the *why* and *how*—it is to be expected that these attitudes would become reinforced by most formidable barriers which become buttressed by powerful emotions, a 'horror' of incest.

[12] Cross-cousin marriage is marriage between the children of a woman and those of her brother, and conversely.

[13] This is what Boas has to say in this connexion, with special reference to the Eskimo of Smith Sound in North Greenland. 'From all we know, it seems extremely unlikely that this community ever consisted of more than a few hundred individuals. . . . [It] has been cut off from the outer world for very long periods; and while there may have been accessions of new individuals from outside once each century, on the whole it has remained completely isolated. It is

The blood-groups now to be considered are of a different order. They are neither purely biological (with one exception) nor bilateral. These groups are the clan, gens,[14] dual division (or moiety), the maternal or paternal family (biological), and the Australian class. From a biological standpoint it is justifiable to class all of these groups in the category of blood-relationship, in so far as all of them contain nuclei of blood-relatives, while the maternal or paternal family comprises only actual blood-relatives. There is, moreover, additional reason for classing these social units with the relationship category—psychologically, in the minds of the people themselves, the individuals in these social units *are* related. This status does not depend on the presence or absence of actual blood-ties, but is psychological—a 'legal fiction.' These groups, with the exception of the maternal family, may thus be designated as pseudo-biological, in so far as their biological character is at least in part fictitious.

Of the groups just enumerated the *clan* and *gens* are by far the most important. A clan can be defined as follows: it comprises individuals partly related by blood and partly conceived as so related; it is hereditary (a person is born into a clan); it is unilateral (the children belong to the clan of the mother). Without including them in the definition, two additional features must be added, for completeness: a clan almost always has a name, and more often than not it is exogamous, that is, there is no marriage within the clan. The definition of a gens is the same, except that the children follow the father.

Sibs have a far-flung distribution in the primitive world. As one surveys these units in different geographical areas, scores of differences appear, in size, number, and functions. In North America, for example, the Iroquoian Mohawk and Oneida have only three clans each, while the other tribes of the League have at least eight each. The adjoining Algonquin Delaware have three clans, among the southern Siouan tribes the Omaha have ten gentes, while the other similarly organized tribes— the Iowa, Kansas, Osage, etc.—have more than ten each but less than twenty-five. The Winnebago have twelve clans. As contrasted with this, the Tlingit and Haida have fifty or more clans each, while the southern Kwakiutl seem to have had considerably more than that. In the Southwest, the Hopi, Zuñi, and other tribes have at least as many clans as the Tlingit and Haida, and some have more, and the same applies to some

therefore obvious . . . that all the individuals [of this group] must be interrelated through their remote ancestry.' (*The Mind of Primitive Man*, p. 82.)

[14] Dr. Lowie has introduced the term *sib* to cover both clan and gens. Whenever the difference between the two is not important, it is a convenient term to use.

tribes in the Southeast. In those Californian tribes which have gentes the number of these units seems somewhat limited, perhaps falling below the North Pacific Coast figures. In Africa, with the thirty-odd Baganda gentes, some tribes of the Centre and East have more than one hundred clans or gentes. Granted similar populational conditions, the multiplicity of these social units is, of course, correlated with a relative paucity of individuals in each. In Africa, where population is much denser than in America or Australia, single gentes may comprise many thousands of members, scattered over a wide territory.

The variability in functions is equally conspicuous. There are great differences in the way a sib system is interwoven with the rest of culture. The variations are striking. Among the Tlingit and Haida the clan system enters actively into nearly all aspects of life—art, mythology, economic pursuits, politics, ceremonialism. Among the Iroquois the clans are the carriers of the all-important socio-political functions of the League. The Zuñi clans, as Kroeber has emphasized, merely stand for a method of counting descent. In Africa, barring occasional industrial specialization of gentes, these units often represent little more than very wide and loose groups with a common name and a common taboo. The sibs of Central Australia, finally, have become almost purely ceremonial in character; they are magic-working associations, having shed all other functions, if they ever possessed them.

When one compares the clans of two areas in greater detail, contrasts stand out even more strikingly. Thus, among the Iroquois, the clans, in addition to having a bird or animal name, control exogamy, own cemeteries and perhaps fields for cultivation, elect ceremonial officials, and play a definite part in the election of federal chiefs; whereas the clans of the Tlingit and the Haida have local names and elect clan chiefs, own hunting and fishing territories, and are distinguished from each other by a series of ceremonial and mythological prerogatives—a clan myth, a clan carving or set of carvings, clan ceremonial dances with accessories, a clan song or set of songs. The clans here are also exogamous but merely as parts of the major units, the moieties, which are the real carriers of the matrimonial functions. Perhaps the greatest contrast between the Northwest Coast and Iroquois clans lies in the fact that in the former area the clans have different rank in accordance with the privileges and supernatural powers claimed by the component individuals; whereas among the Iroquois a clan is a clan, no less and no more, notwithstanding the fact that some of the clans comprise maternal families with hereditary League chieftainships, while other clans, though comprising maternal families, have no such chieftainships. Different as the clans of the Haida and Tlingit may be from those of the Iroquois, the clans of both groups appear relatively similar when contrasted with, say, the gentes of the Baganda with their double or triple totems and their caste-like specialization in industrial functions and in services to a king.

Correlated with some of the differences in the functions of clans is the relation of a clan system to the family system in the same tribe. Thus, among the Tlingit and Haida, once more, the family is divided against itself by the intrusion of the clan principle. The inheritance of property and privileges glides along the edges of the family, as it were, the main line of transfer being from maternal uncle to nephew or from father-in-law to son-in-law. In the old days of clan feuds, moreover, clan allegiance here counted for more than family allegiance: fathers and sons met in deadly combat prompted by bonds stronger than those of the family hearth. Among the Zuñi, on the other hand, the family is but little impressed by the clan division within its midst—for here also clan members do not intermarry—and attends to its many economic, educational, and domestic functions almost wholly undisturbed by the presence of another social grouping.

A comparison of sibs in different geographical areas, it will be seen, discloses striking dissimilarities and even contrasts in the number of sib units in a tribe, in the number of individuals in each unit, in sib functions, in their relative importance as carriers of the group culture, in their relations, finally, to the family.

The impression might thus be conveyed that the sib represents a wholly fictitious category corresponding to no one reality, that it is but a term, more useful in the scientist's study, with its abstractionist inclinations, than realistic in connotation or univocal in meaning.

Fortunately, it is not necessary to accept so extreme a conclusion. Whatever the differences, clans and gentes, wherever found, have certain traits in common. Among these we can recognize the traits indicated in the definitions of clan and gens: the fiction of blood-relationship, the hereditary character, the unilateral aspect, as well as a sib name.

The characteristic of having a name might be thought artificial and trivial; who or what in this world does not carry a name? And yet, there is significance in this trait. It will be noted that of the social groupings here enumerated only two almost always have a name: the local group and the sib.[15] Families, in primitive society, usually remain nameless; the maternal families of the Iroquois or the paternal ones of Ontong-

[15] To these must be added those strictly Australian units, the class and subclass, which also have names.

Java have no names; relationship groups are always nameless; so are, as a rule, age, generation, and sex groups. Even dual divisions and phratries, while named at times, are often nameless. But the local group and the sib have names, with but rare exceptions. In the case of the latter units, moreover, the name carries with it certain sociological implications which are absent in the case of the local name. An individual from a local group with a name wanders off and marries elsewhere. His children and grandchildren may still refer to or at least know of his local provenience; but barring exceptions, his great-grandchildren and their children will have forgotten it. The imported local name disappears from the new locality. It is different with a clan or a gens. These survive as long as any persons are left—male in gentile, female in clan society—to pass on the sib name. In cases where patri-local residence is combined with paternal descent, or matrilocal residence with maternal descent,[16] the survival of a sib in a locality is assured as long as procreating individuals are left, male in the former case, female in the latter. Where descent and residence are not of one type, a sib can more readily disappear from a locality, but it will continue—somewhere, through its name, under the conditions already stated.

Four cultural features deserve attention here, all linked with sibs in their geographical distribution: blood-revenge, adoption, exogamy, and totemism. Not that any of these features are invariable companions of sibs or never occur without them. The opposite is true. In other words the statement just made should be understood to mean that the association or linkage of these features with sibs is so frequent as to constitute an 'adhesion' (Tylor).

Before launching upon the subject of exogamy, a few words about blood-revenge and adoption. In its broadest aspect blood-vengeance has, of course, nothing to do with sibs or any other kind of social unit. This custom represents one of the most widespread and probably one of the earliest reactions of mankind, of the nature of eye for eye. Specifically, it means here death for death. The punishment for murder is death, and the punishment is not exercised by society through any representative or legal agency, but by those most closely affected by the death of the victim, his kin. In this form then, blood-vengeance acquires a social character. One step further, and we find the principle of communal responsibility entering the situation. The death of the victim is avenged by the killing not necessarily of the culprit himself but of anyone of his kin. In this form the custom is widespread in connexion with sibs: a

---

[16] When residence is patrilocal, the wife joins her husband at his village; when residence is matrilocal, the husband joins his wife at her village.

sib-mate for a sib-mate. But it also occurs in families, especially in societies beyond the primitive. We find it functioning today among the mountaineers of the Caucasus, as well as those of Kentucky.

Adoption also is in its base independent of and, perhaps, antecedent to the emergence of sibs. Its psycho-sociological roots must probably be seen in the desire, socially sanctified, to take care of unattached children and of adults without a social passport. Particularly in cases of the latter type the benefit is mutual—the adult thus adopted finds in the new relationship a social security which he badly needs, whereas the adopting group enhances its man-power, an important consideration in primitive conditions. This latter aspect is well illustrated by the custom, common among American Indians and elsewhere, of adopting prisoners of war to compensate the group for its own losses in killed and captured. This kind of adoption is in its typical form administered by a sib. After submitting to the ritual of a blood-covenant, the adopted member becomes part and parcel of the sib community. In the course of this rite the blood of the outsider is in many instances actually permitted to mix with that of a member of the adopting sib, a blood-vessel being slit open in an arm of both for the purpose. The sense of blood kinship in a sib is well exemplified by this custom. It must also be remembered that families, clans, and even larger groups of people, such as tribes, could be and were thus adopted, on occasion, as when the Delaware Indians were adopted by the Iroquois, in this case in the capacity of 'assistant cooks,' symbolized by a corn-pestle, a hoe, and petticoats. This incident, be it noted, had about it nothing humiliating to the Delaware, contrary to the statements of writers who misunderstood the custom.

The association of sibs with exogamy and totemism is much more striking. Exogamy is an all but universal associate, while totemism is an extraordinarily common one. Leaving totemism for later consideration, let us first turn to exogamy.

Clan and gentile exogamy—the rule to marry outside one's own sib unit—is so general a feature that it may here be assumed to be practically universal. But there is a difficulty. In cases like those of the Crow and the Delaware clans, or the clans of the League Iroquois, or the *gotras* of India and the African gentes, the exogamous issue is clear: a sib member is prohibited from marrying in his or her own sib unit, and must look for a mate outside, in one of the other sibs.

The situation becomes more complex when other tribes are considered. Among the Tlingit and Haida, for example, there is no marriage within the clan, but on further inspection it appears that the exogamous rule really applies to the moiety: marry outside your own moiety and into the other one. As the clans are comprised in the moieties and no clan is found in both moieties, it follows that there is also no marriage within one's clan. A similar situation obtains in Australian tribes organized like the Dieri.

In all such instances the moiety is the real exogamous unit, while the exogamy of the clans may be designated as *derivative*. This becomes clear when one considers that the rule which prohibits marriage in one's own clan also applies to marriage with *any* clans of the same moiety, thus:

$$\left.\begin{array}{l} \text{Moiety } A \\ \text{(comprising} \\ \text{clans } a_1,\, a_2, \\ a_3 \ldots) \end{array}\right\} \text{marries} \left\{\begin{array}{l} \text{Moiety } B \\ \text{(comprising} \\ \text{clans } b_1,\, b_2, \\ b_3 \ldots) \end{array}\right.$$

An a_1 man may not marry an a_1 woman, nor may he marry an a_2 or a_3 woman; he marries *any* woman of moiety B; etc.

It is as if one were to say that in a football game a Harvard freshman is pitted against a Yale junior. Even though objectively correct, the statement would be misleading, in so far as the groups pitted against each other are the *college teams*, whereas the classes do not figure as units in the game, but merely indirectly as subdivisions within the college body.

Further complications arise upon an analysis of tribes organized like the Australian Kamilaroi or Warramunga. Here both the negative and the positive marriage regulations are drastically determined, whereas the clans or gentes, while exogamous *de facto*, do not appear as units in either connexion. Take the case of the Kamilaroi—the tribe is divided into two phratries or moieties, each moiety is subdivided into two 'classes' and also into a number of clans, thus:

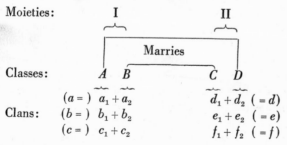

Moieties: I   II

Classes: A B C D

Clans: $(a =)$ $a_1 + a_2$ $d_1 + d_2$ $(= d)$
         $(b =)$ $b_1 + b_2$ $e_1 + e_2$ $(= e)$
         $(c =)$ $c_1 + c_2$ $f_1 + f_2$ $(= f)$

Marriage follows class: A marries D, B marries C. Now class A contains a_1, b_1 and c_1, which are parts of clans a, b, and c. Similarly, class B contains a_2, b_2 and c_2, which are the other parts of clans a, b

and *c*. And so also with classes *C* and *D*. As to marriage, then, the clan sections a_1, b_1 and c_1 of clans *a*, *b* and *c* have common obligations and restrictions: they marry *D*, but may not marry *B* or *C*. The same holds throughout. So that the matrimonial regulations referring to section a_1 (clan *a*) are quite different from those for a_2 (clan *a*); the first marries *D*, the second, *C*. From the standpoint of marriage regulation, on its positive side, the clan is divided against itself. As to the negative side, the situation is the same, as can be easily figured out. This is what is meant by saying that the clan here is not an 'exogamous unit,' either positively or negatively.[17]

From an examination of all such tribes—and their number is large—one might derive the impression that the alleged universality of sib exogamy represents but another superannuated dogma, that clans and gentes, while exogamous in many instances, have in others no connexion whatsoever with matrimony.

This conclusion would be erroneous. Of the functional characteristics of sibs, exogamy must still be regarded as the most persistent. But how, it will be asked, can this proposition be reconciled with the complications outlined in the foregoing? A glance at the world picture of sib exogamy furnishes the answer. First, there are tribes where sibs appear as exogamous units. Then come other tribes where the presence of exogamous moieties or phratries prompt one to describe the exogamy of the minor units as derivative. Finally, there are still other tribes—primarily those of Australia—where each sib comprises sections with their own positive and negative matrimonial regulations. But one fact holds true: with only such exceptions as all social 'laws' are subject to, *intermarriage within a sib is nowhere permitted*. One is forced to conclude that in the absence of moieties, phratries, and classes, sib exogamy would still obtain, just as it does when these social units stand alone. In other words, it is in the nature of sibs, as groups of blood-relatives, actual or assumed, to function exogamously—in the negative sense of a taboo on intermarriage within the unit—and in all but very few instances they do so.[18]

It must be noted here that while the family and local group are basic in modern as in primitive society, relationship, age, and sex groups, though more important among primitives, persist in an attenuated form

[17] For further details on Australian social divisions see pp. 343 seq.

[18] For particulars the student is referred to the ample literature on exogamy. Here only this should be added: Though specifically congenial with sibs, exogamy also occurs in connexion with other social units, such as phratries and moieties (frequently) or local groups (less frequently).

in modern civilization, whereas clans, gentes, maternal families, moieties, phratries, and 'classes' are peculiar to primitive society. In other words, the unilateral hereditary principle, in the drastic form in which it operates in these groupings, is foreign to the spirit of our social life. The principle itself is, of course, present in connexion with the inheritance of property and the family name, but it does not figure as a basis for the formation of a definite hereditary group into which an individual is born and to which he belongs until death—or beyond, in defiance of marriage ties and local residence.

Of these unilateral primitive groups the sib is the one having the widest distribution. It is therefore not surprising that sibs should have been regarded as not only characteristic of primitive society but as universal, at a certain stage. This, of course, is not the case.

Dual divisions or moieties, such as those of the Tlingit and Haida, Iroquois, Winnebago, Omaha, etc., as well as numerous Australian and Melanesian tribes, are like sibs in many ways. They are hereditary and unilateral, either maternal or paternal. Usually but not always, they have names. They also comprise blood relatives, real and assumed, although the sense of relationship here is weaker than in the smaller kin unit. The moiety is a much more populous group; the very fact, moreover, that it is, as a rule, subdivided into minor units with strong relationship bonds, is apt to weaken this element in the moiety.[19]

Functionally, moieties are no more uniform than are clans. Among the Iroquois the phratries, which here are also moieties or dual divisions, attend primarily to ceremonies. Games, such as ball and lacrosse, are also played between phratries. The phratries have the obligation of burying each other's members. Also, the phratric groups of clan chiefs are the two bodies to which the name of the candidate for chieftainship is submitted by the matron of a maternal family, before the name is passed on to the council of the League for final ratification.

Among the Tlingit and Haida the moiety plays a distinctly different role. There is a moiety chief, an official unknown among the Iroquois. In so far as the moieties are named after birds and animals—Eagle and Raven among the Haida, Raven and Wolf among the Tlingit—the

---

[19] From moieties such as the above two other types of social divisions must be distinguished. Dual divisions have been described among the Yuchi Indians, but here these groups are purely ceremonial and instead of comprising clans, crosscut them, so that each clan contains members of both divisions. Dual divisions of this type have no connexion with blood relationship.

Then there are phratries like the six of the Crow or those of some Southwest tribes. These groups also comprise clans as subdivisions but have, once more, no connexion with blood-relationship. Many phratries, no doubt, represent secondary associations of clans, on a ceremonial, mythical, or some other basis.

mythologies and traditions of the two halves of the people are very different. Among the Tlingit the moieties have one important ceremonial function, as the potlatches are here given between the moieties, never in the same moiety. There is also, as among the Iroquois, reciprocal burial. But the principal function of the Northwest moieties is the control of marriage—they are rigorously exogamous.

In Central Australia the moieties are connected with intermarriage in so far as no unions are permitted within a phratry. They also figure as a basis of local grouping in camping. In preparation for the *intichiuma* ceremonies members of the opposite phratry announce the time at which a ceremony is to be performed; and, as part of the ritualistic routine itself, members of the opposite phratry are charged with the very serious task of painting the dancers and of adorning them with bird-down.

Not only are reciprocal functions common in moieties, but the dual division of the tribe seems to stimulate a tendency to emphasize contrasts with reference to the two moieties. One moiety is believed to be of local origin, the other to have come from elsewhere; or they are supposed to represent different physical types; or the names are contrasting, as for example, in the case of the widespread Australian moiety names, Eaglehawk (white) and Crow (black). The infection occasionally spreads to the investigating ethnologist, who tends to take the local theories seriously or invents some similar ones of his own. In some instances, of course, the ethnologist, and even the natives, may be right.[20]

Two further blood-relationship groups are the *maternal* or *paternal family* and the Australian *class*. The latter will be discussed in a special section (see pp. 343 seq.), but a few words are due to the former.

The maternal or paternal family occupies an intermediate position between a family, in the ordinary sense, and a clan. It is like the bilateral family in that it comprises only actual blood-relatives. Also, it frequently remains nameless. Therefore there attaches to it that vagueness of outline as a social unit which is characteristic of all groups of blood based on remembered relationships. What is merely remembered may also be forgotten. A name settles such difficulties with one stroke. Now a person's status is fixed at birth, in fact in advance of birth, by the hereditary transmission of the group name, and with it as a tag, mem-

---

[20] It is curious how well a dual division lends itself to all occasions where games, conflicts, or political issues are involved. It has often been remarked that in democracies either there are two parties or the rest tend to group themselves about the two leading ones, in connexion with elections, parliamentary debates, voting in important issues. To an Eaglehawk a Crow seems blacker than ever, whereas to an outsider both may well appear as sparrows—and grey.

bership in the group is both guaranteed and enforced. But the unilateral family, like the bilateral family, has no name.

The unilateral family, then, is like a clan or gens. It is, however, a
much smaller group, as a rule at least, and where it is combined with a
sib organization, as among the Iroquois, there are several unilateral
families in each sib.

Being in principle so nearly like a sib, the unilateral family has
often been identified and confused with that unit by investigators. After
what was said, it will be clear that the two units are distinct—the unilateral family is an actual blood group, maternal or paternal, whereas
a sib, we know, involves a fiction of relationship.

Chapter XX

SOCIAL GROUPS AND THEIR FUNCTIONS
(Continued)

Groups of Function

As we survey once more the array of social forms now passed in review, one fact stands out with great clearness: *society has seized upon a large number, if not all possible relations, spatial, temporal, and biological, of man to nature and of man to man, and on the basis of these relations social divisions have grown up.* First, there is the spatial relation, implied in the habitat of a human group. This is the foundation of local groups, villages, towns, tribal territories, and states. Then there is the biological relation, which appears in two forms, actual blood-relationship and assumed or fictitious blood-relationship (pseudo-biological). Actual blood-relationship is represented by the parent-to-child and child-to-child bond in the individual family, bilateral; also by the maternal or paternal family, both unilateral; and by the group of blood-relatives with its adhering system of relationship terms, bilateral. Fictitious or assumed blood-relationship is represented in such groups as the clan, gens, dual division (in some instances), and the Australian classes and sub-classes, all unilateral. Then there is the grouping based on sex. And finally come the two forms of temporal relation of man to man, as expressed in the principles of age and generation.

Age, Generation, and Sex Groups. Three kinds of grouping still remain to be considered. They are of a different order from the preceding in so far as the limits of these groups cannot be fixed with the precision attainable in the case of the family, sib, local group, or even a set of relatives united by demonstrable bonds of kinship. These groupings are based on age, generation, and sex.

In all primitive societies *age* is an important factor; in some it stands out very prominently. Generally speaking, the following rough classification of individuals obtains practically everywhere. First come the infants or babies, who are important enough in their immediate families, particularly in relation to their mothers, but not in the society beyond. Before a name is ceremonially bestowed upon an infant, it is, in many primitive groups, practically outside the society; its life counts for as

little as does its death.[1] The next class is that of children. These count
in many ways. They are subject to instruction in the affairs of the household, in the arts and crafts, the accomplishments of the hunt and the
gathering of the products of wild nature. During this period, the children usually begin to participate in some at least of the ceremonial activities of the group, and in tribes such as the Trobrianders they become
acquainted, in the rough, with the elements of sex and the lures of sex
attraction. It is in general characteristic of primitive conditions that
relatively young children, say of the age of eight or nine, have already
absorbed most of the fundamental industrial techniques, a great deal of
the ethics and etiquette, and much of the traditional lore of the group.
The next class is that of young men and women, just before and through
the period of puberty. At this time the girls become full-fledged and
active members of the household, while the boys learn to excel in the
arts of the chase, and to pay heed increasingly to the political and
religious teachings of the old men, chiefs, and medicine-men. About
this time also the first important initiatory ceremonies are performed,
wherever these are present, ushering the young people—male more
frequently, female less so—into the early stages of the ceremonial cycle
and the esoteric knowledge of religious or secret societies. By this
time the girls and boys have grown into young men and women. This is
the time for marriage. The youth is now a warrior, the maiden not
merely a helper but an independent housewife. In the arts and crafts,
the social rules and amenities of the tribe, they are now thoroughly at
home, but in matters of religious, ceremonial, and political import
they may still have to cede first place to the older men and women.

The class above this is that of mature men and women. They are full
members of the tribe, participating in all industrial, religious, social,
military, and educational activities and forming the backbone of family
life. The last and in some respects most important and influential class
is that of old men and, in some tribes, old women. While these take a
less active part in the day-by-day activities, their leadership in ceremonial and political matters is pronounced, and they do everywhere
constitute the great depositories of tradition, figuring as the mouthpiece,
as it were, of the conservative *status quo*. They know the past, in fact,
all there is to be known, and see to it that this knowledge is passed on
without much loss—or addition.[2]

---

[1] This is one of the reasons why newly born infants can so readily be done away
with, as they often are for magical or other motives.

[2] The role of the 'fathers' in the conflict of generations has been well brought
out in the works of Mrs. Elsie Clews Parsons, who has dealt with this topic in

The rigidity with which these age classes are separated—and this separation is, of course, always flexible to a degree—varies among different tribes. Thus the old men are not by any means everywhere as influential, in fact all-powerful, as they are in the Australian gerontocracy,[3] nor are the infants always as unimportant and negligible as they seem to be among some Melanesian tribes.[4]

The principle of generation never appears with any great distinctness, but it might be described somewhat as follows: From the standpoint of the mature men and women, they themselves represent the present generation, below this is the generation of their children, and below this the incipient generation of the grandchildren. Above the present generation is that of the mothers and fathers, and above this the waning generation of the grandparents. This rough classification of the generations is especially noticeable in the study of relationships, where terms are often used to cover individuals of one or both sexes belonging to one generation, although, in other instances, relationship terms also transcend the generation level.[5] In the course of ethnological field work it has also been observed that the memory of informants runs most naturally along horizontal generation lines. In obtaining information of the basis of genealogies, therefore, it is usually preferable first to group the questions around individuals who belong to the same generation, rather than to begin by following up each line of

a great many articles as well as in most of her popular books. *Cf.*, for example, *The Old Fashioned Woman* and *Fear and Conventionality*.

[3] The exaggerated prestige of old age is one of the earmarks of primitive culture. While the life-wisdom, sophistication, and balanced outlook of ripening years continue to command respect in modern society, the prestige of old age, as such, has been shaken by the growing artificiality and vicariousness of knowledge and the ever-increasing demands which social life makes upon the energy and vigour of its carriers. In a young, boisterous, and hurried community, like that of the United States, age at times seems definitely outclassed. In the United States, industrial executive positions and educational and academic as well, go in increasing proportion to young people. In family life, also, the prestige of the highest age group is visibly on the decline. In the eyes of the young, the omniscient Solons of former days are turning into old fogies.

It is curious to note that in villages and on farms, where life approaches that of more primitive communities, the prerogatives of old age continue to hold their own.

[4] Economic conditions, here as always, play their part. Among the Eskimo, for example, where subsistence comes hard, the sick and the old are an intolerable burden. And so we find that the former are not infrequently abandoned to their fate, should they collapse on a journey, whereas the old people, when they reach an age and physical condition precluding self-support or co-operation with others, are abandoned in a snow house, often self-built,—to die from starvation.

[5] For example, among the Crow, where one's father's sister's son is called 'father,' and one's mother's brother and even one's mother's mother's brother are 'elder brothers.'

descent, perpendicularly upwards and downwards, to the limit of the informant's memory.[6] This principle obtains to a degree also in modern society. Men and women of the same generation share certain elements of knowledge, habit, and attitude which create a bond separating them vaguely from preceding and succeeding generations. A young man begins his career in the generation of his fathers and ends it in the generation of his children.

The one remaining grouping is the one based on *sex*. While this principle of classification has often been exaggerated—by Schurtz, for example, who built upon it his entire theory of social organization—it is undeniable that the sex division gives rise to a set of formal and functional distinctions in society, and that this is on the whole more emphatically true of primitive than of modern communities. It is equally notable that certain forms of behaviour and attitude resting on sex-distinction, for example the entire social complex growing out of the discrimination against women,[7] are more pronounced in later cultures than in most primitive ones.

The social units based on these different principles all perform functions in society. The cultural status of a social division represents, in fact, no more and no less than the sum total of its functional relations in society—a social unit is what it does. For this reason it has often been felt that it would be both scientifically justifiable and convenient if social units could be defined by their functions. This, unfortunately, cannot be done for the simple reason that specific functions are not monopolized by one rather than another kind of social unit. Some functions, in fact, such as the ritualistic ones, occur in connexion with all the social units here enumerated. Economic functions are exercised by families, sibs, phratries, tribes or groups of tribes. And so it goes through the entire list of possible social functions. Thus the idea of differentiating social units terminologically, on the basis of function, must be given up except in special instances.[8] It becomes clear, furthermore, that in their cultural status, which depends on function, different kinds of social units may be equivalent. A clan in one tribe may stand for what a family represents in another, a local group here may mean

---

[6] On the genealogical method in field work, see above, p. 49.

[7] On the disabilities of women, *cf.* the section 'Division of Labour and Profession' (pp. 142 seq.).

[8] It was shown that economic functions are more particularly the business of local groups; matrimonial and ceremonial ones, of moieties; matrimonial and totemic ones, of sibs; and so on. But all this is relative: in no instance do we find an *exclusive* association of a specific function with a particular kind of social unit.

the same that a phratry or dual division means there, a tribe or group
of tribes may function in one place as a clan or a village or an age
group functions in another.

One must be careful, therefore, not to accept too literally this analytical presentation of social units. The lines of demarcation between the
different units are not by any means distinct, either when identical units
are compared in different tribes or even when different units in one
and the same tribe are juxtaposed. The analytical distinctions are nevertheless significant, in so far as they aid us to discern the principal forms
of social units, in so far also as they disclose the basic natural roots of
social structure.

This does not complete the survey of social units. Primitive society
knows still other social groups which, unlike those enumerated above,
are *purely* functional.

Industrial Groups. Some groupings are based on industrial association. I have previously referred to the fact that under primitive conditions industrial specialization is relatively inconspicuous. Each family
here resembles every other family in its industrial functioning, and
large numbers of individuals in a tribe perform the same round of economic functions. By way of emphasizing the contrast between modern
and primitive society, this picture may stand. It must, however, be remembered that industrial or economic specialization always exists. It is
coextensive with society itself.

The economic or industrial division of labour discussed in the section 'Division of Labour and Profession,' implies specialization. We
saw that among the Haida and Tlingit, all men are woodworkers, just
as all women are potters among the Zuñi or Hopi, basket-weavers among
the Maidu. In tribes such as these a distinction arises between average
workers and those who have become experts, and, to that extent, there
is an incipient specialization of an industrial group, over and above
the specialization which follows sex. Even in the much cruder industrial conditions of Australia, it has been noted that men of certain localities excel in the manufacture of one or another weapon. In certain
Australian tribes messengers constitute a class by themselves. In more
advanced communities, such as the Negroes of Africa or the Polynesians, industrial differentiation has proceeded much further. Among
many of the Bantu-speaking Negro tribes, the agriculturists and the
herdsmen are separated into veritable social classes. There also one
finds, as we saw, salt-diggers, iron-smiths, merchants. In Polynesia the
boat-makers constitute an ancient and honoured class.

Apart from instances of communal work which implies social and even personal intimacy, groups of industrial specialization develop bonds based on common knowledge and skill, a variety of common interests, perhaps a common supernatural protector, and last but not least, a certain mutual understanding, a feeling of belonging together. All this is strikingly true of the Hindu castes, where industrial specialization is associated with social status, matrimonial rules, and rules of etiquette (with special reference to food), in addition to the numerous factors involved in the work itself which make men alike and bring them together. In the Indian castes these features are developed to an extraordinary degree, but they are present, in one form or another, wherever industrial specialization occurs.[9]

Societies or Associations. Another type of functional grouping is represented by the various kinds of *societies* or *associations*, religious, military, medicinal. Such societies are widely distributed in the primitive world. Among other places, they thrive in Northwest Melanesia, in West Africa, and in a number of wide tribal areas in North and South America. The societies—for usually there are several—may be purely male or purely female or mixed. They may comprise most of the members of a tribe or only a small esoteric group, may be based on age, guardian-spirit initiation, or payment by an individual or a group. The societies may be equivalent in status or more or less rigidly graded into lower and higher ones. The functions of the societies may be purely religious and ceremonial, as is most frequently the case; or medicinal in addition, as for example among the Iroquois and Zuñi; or military, as in certain well-known Plains organizations; or juridical, as in Melanesia and West Africa. What is characteristic of all such organizations is that the bond between the members is not one of status but of function—remove the common functions and the organization based upon them becomes a mere shell. This applies not merely to the 'societies' just mentioned but to groups of industrial specialization as well—where common function is the *only* basis of group formation, the elimination of the function would carry with it a dissolution of the group.

Birth Groups. Still other groups are based on *birth and inheritance*

---

[9] The best-known and most typical example of industrial specialization combined with social solidarity is, of course, that of the guilds. These groupings—economic, craft, commercial, religious, esoteric or secular, hereditary or otherwise, legal or subversive—flourished in old China; they were not unknown among the ancients of the Mediterranean basin, and during the Middle Ages their development reached extraordinary exuberance. During the Renaissance decay began to set in. Thenceforth the guilds pursued a downward course, until the Industrial Revolution finished them, at least temporarily. In recent years a certain revival of the guild spirit is observable, both in theory and in practice. (For a brilliant though not always reliable sketch of the guilds see Peter Kropotkin, *Mutual Aid in Evolution.*)

of privileges, or *birth and occupation.* An illustration of the birth-and-privilege grouping is found on the Northwest Coast, where the hereditary prerogative of chieftainship, with all its accruing distinctions, belongs to the class of nobles. The same is true of many groups in Polynesia. The reverse situation is found in the case of slaves. This institution is more widespread in primitive society than is generally supposed, being common in Polynesia, Africa, and America. Barring special instances in which a slave or a descendant of a slave may pass into another social class, a man born a slave dies a slave, and with this status go the inevitable restrictions on social participation.

The best known example of the working of the birth-and-occupation principle is found in the Hindu castes cited above in connexion with industrial specialization. Here the different occupational groupings have become hereditary, and with this status go privileges and restrictions, social, ceremonial, matrimonial (a caste is endogamous, it marries within itself). Caste-like traits are also observed, for example, in the Baganda gentes, with their hereditary specialization in different industrial occupations related to the needs of the royal household.

In connexion with hereditary or acquired privileges, the principle of *rank* makes its appearance. Rank may be static, as when different social classes are firmly fixed by birth and are kept apart with greater or less stringency. Rank may also be mobile, as for example, in the graded societies of the American Plains or of Mota (Banks Islands, Melanesia), where rank is something to be striven for and attained, by complying with certain conditions.

Property Groups. Wealth—not always in the modern sense, as we saw—may become the mark of a group with somewhat fluctuating outlines, as happens among the herd-owners of Africa or the reindeer-breeding Chukchee, Koryak, or Tungus of Northeast Siberia.

When one compares these purely functional groupings with those based on spatial, temporal, or biological factors, it becomes apparent why these two kinds of groups could be distinguished as *groups of status,* on the one hand, and *groups of function,* on the other. The groups of status are based on principles which flow directly from certain relations between man and nature and man and man. Culture here figures as a mere background, while man's proclivity to fall into groups on the basis of such lines of cleavage is taken for granted. Groups of function, on the other hand, emphatically presuppose culture. The funtions are really the dynamic aspects of culture itself, and the groupings become social units on the basis of such common functions. Groups of status are *social units by composition*—people of one locality, common blood, one sex, same age—while the range and depth of their penetration into a culture depend on the functions they exercise; whereas groups of function are *functional* and cultural *in the first place,* and become social units *as* groups of common functions.[10]

In the concrete, the distinction between the two kinds of groups often becomes obliterated. A clan exercising a ceremonial function like that of a religious society, in the same or another tribe, is to that extent equivalent to that society. A family or a local group specializing in an industrial pursuit, is equivalent to a corresponding industrial group without foundation in status. The blurring of the distinction between groups of status and those of function is further enhanced by the fact that both kinds of groups tend to assume new functions or lose some of their old ones. In any case, a comparison of groups of status with groups of function serves to disengage a sociological principle, which is this: *social divisions of whatever provenience tend to exercise cultural functions and to assume new ones; functions, on the other hand, tend to attach themselves to pre-existing social units or to create new ones.*

In concluding this survey of social groups and their functions we must further note that a primitive tribesman participates at any given time in a number of such units. He is a family man and a clansman, a member of a local group and of a religious society or of several such societies; he functions as part of an age, sex, generation, and relationship group, and he may also share in the privileges and obligations of an industrial or a hereditary-rank group. Thus the intellectual and emotional orientation of an individual becomes highly complex. On the social side again he finds himself enmeshed in a network of multiple, varied, at times contradictory, rights and duties, prescriptions and proscriptions. We shall see in the sequel how these 'participations' (Lévy-Bruhl) are reflected in the life and thought of primitive man.

Totemism

The socio-religious institution called totemism is of more than ordinary interest. Its distribution is wide and the forms it assumes are many and varied. Few primitive topics have aroused such general interest or provoked such heated controversy. Spencer, Frazer, and Andrew Lang, Rivers, Laurence Gomme, and N. W. Thomas, Thurnwald, Graebner, and Father Schmidt, Van Gennep and Durkheim, Wundt and Freud, all

---

[10] Obviously, all birth groups—of privilege, occupation, rank—were originally purely functional. When these functions became hereditary, groups of status arose —blue blood.

of these and many others have contributed their share to the discussion of this well-nigh inexhaustible subject.

What, then, is totemism? What is its nature and its distribution in the primitive world?

One speaks of totemism when a tribe comprises a social organization, usually of the sib pattern, combined with a peculiar form of supernaturalism which, in the more typical cases, consists of certain attitudes towards species of animals or plants or classes of natural objects.

The geographical distribution of totemic tribes is extraordinarily wide. In North America totemism occurs in the Northwest, among such tribes as the Tlingit and Haida; among the Zuñi, Hopi, and related tribes of the Southwest, in the Southeast (Natchez, Creek, etc.), among certain California tribes, as well as among such Woodland tribes as the Algonquin Delaware, and, in attenuated form, among the Iroquois-speaking tribes of the League. In the Plains, the so-called Southern Siouan tribes (Omaha and others) have totemism. Our South American material is still full of gaps, but totemism has been described by Im Thurn, in British Guiana, some of the Indians of Brazil certainly are totemic, and it does not seem unlikely that, on further investigation, totemism will be found as prevalent in South America as it is in the northern continent. In Africa, the tribes of the Mediterranean littoral must be eliminated as belonging to a distinct cultural layer, nor is totemism found at the extreme southern end of the continent, among such tribes as the Bushmen and Hottentot. But in the enormous intervening area, among the Bantu and the Sudanese Negroes, totemism is very general if not universal. Ankermann's presentation, moreover, suggests that further totemic tribes are likely to be discovered in this region (see p. 465). In aboriginal India the more developed forms of totemism do not seem to occur, but many of the *gotras* or clan-like social groupings of that area have some form of totemism, while others seem to have had it in the past. Australia is the totemic continent *par excellence*. Here all the tribes are totemic with the possible exception of the southeastern and northwestern tribes, and even among some of these the evidence for former totemism is not unsatisfactory. Among the islanders of the Torres Straits and in Melanesia totemism occurs sporadically, and when it does, it is often highly developed. For Polynesia the evidence is doubtful, but it is not improbable that some of the western island clusters had totemism in the past.

This enormous geographical distribution of totemism, wide but discontinuous, can only be interpreted in one way. A single historical acci-

dent, followed by diffusion, could not account for it.[11] Totemism must
have originated independently, at least once in each of the major areas of
its distribution. Among the tribes, moreover, to whom totemism was
brought by their neighbours, there must have been a marked receptivity
for this institution. In other words, the complex of ideas, attitudes, and
practices which make up totemism is congenial to primitive mentality
and therefore characteristic of it,[12] especially so, as we shall see, in all
those instances where a tribe is organized on a sib basis.

As one analyzes totemic tribes on a broad geographical basis, a
variety of beliefs and practices with reference to totems come into view.
The totemites, or members of a totemic group, trace their descent from
an animal or bird or thing, or they regard themselves as in some other
way related to the totem; totem and totemites share physical and psychic
traits; the totem protects the totemites against danger; the totem is represented in art and figures as a sacred symbol at ceremonies; the totem
is taboo—it may not be eaten or killed or seen or touched; the totemic
sib is named after the totem; ceremonies are performed by the totemites
to multiply the supply of the totem animal. These are only some of the
positive and negative rules observed by totemites with reference to their
totems. In addition to this it must be noted that the totem is scarcely
ever some one animal or plant or thing (although this happens); in the
overwhelming majority of cases the totem is a species of animal or class
of things.

It must not, however, be imagined that any or all of these features are
invariably present wherever totemism occurs. Such is by no means the
case. Totemism is one of those cultural complexes which, though distinctive enough when understood, are not distinguishable by content alone.

[11] The attentive reader might well ask, 'Why not?' All indications are that
totemism is very old; its distribution, we saw, is world-wide if not universal;
moreover, it comprises a whole complex of features—social, religious, ceremonial,
etc. A complex such as this cannot be picked up casually. When therefore one
finds it in hundreds of tribes, this can only be explained by assuming that a certain congeniality exists between totemism and the many tribal cultures which
have it. This being so, the very conditions favouring the borrowing of totemism
from without would invite its development from within. It follows that many
totemic tribes must be assumed to have developed it independently, unless indeed
borrowing can be demonstrated. The burden of proof, at any rate, rests upon
those who would uphold a singular origin for totemism.

[12] Therein lies the justification for the procedure adopted by L. Gomme (*Folk-
lore as a Historical Science*), É. Durkheim (*Elementary Forms of the Religious
Life*), W. Wundt (*Elements of Folk Psychology*), and R. Thurnwald (*Psychological Foundations of Totemism*, in German) who discuss totemism in the perspective of a mentality characteristic of primitive groups.

Discarding the differences between minor totemic districts, broad continental areas are clearly differentiable, from the standpoint of totemism. In North America the artistic side of totemism is often developed, and among the tribes of the Northwest Coast this is highly marked. The totemic sib name is common but not universal, and the same is true of the totemic taboo. Where totemism is richly developed it becomes associated with the beliefs in guardian spirits. Then again, there are tribes like the League Iroquois and many tribes of the Southwest where the only discernible features are sib exogamy and the animal or bird name of the sib—barely enough to justify the designation 'totemic,' perhaps scarcely enough.

In Africa, the totemic sib name is often absent and so are, in many instances, the artistic representations of the totem. Double totems occur, as among the Baganda, where most of the gentes have two totems. The idea of descent from the totem is very rare; instead, stories of varying pattern are told among the different tribes to explain how the totems first made their appearance. The typical trait of African totemism is the taboo—the prohibition to eat or kill the totemic creature. The very term for totem among many Bantu-speaking tribes means 'that which is forbidden.' The punishment for the transgression of this taboo is severe; the current notion is that nature herself takes revenge upon the offender: he or she is afflicted with a skin disease, the natives believe, which is interpreted as a partial transformation of the culprit into the tabooed animal.

In Australia the number of totemic sibs in a tribe is frequently very large—much larger than in Africa or North America—and the number of individuals in each sib is correspondingly small. The totemic sib name is universal and so is the taboo. The conception is common that the totemites are closely related to their totem. General also is the idea that the totemites are in one way or another descended from the totem. Totemic art, where it occurs, is peculiar in so far as identical designs are used by the different sibs of one tribe as well as by sibs belonging to different tribes; but each sib interprets these designs in accordance with its own totemic ideas. In Central Australia individuals of one totem and locality perform magical ceremonies believed to bring about the multiplication of the totemic species.

This characterization of the three continental areas will suffice for our purpose. It will be seen that what we may call the 'totemic complexes' of these areas differ considerably in the number of totemic features and in the relative prominence of certain features. Thus, in

Central Australia the magical aspect predominates; in Africa it is the taboo aspect; in North America the guardian-spirit aspect; on the Northwest Coast, finally, art is the predominant feature.

If we cared to push our analysis still further, we might note that the extent to which a culture is saturated with totemism also varies. Thus, among the Northwest tribes almost every aspect of culture is touched by totemic flavour: religion and myth, social organization, ritualism and property, industry and art. Among the Omaha, material culture seems wholly free from totemic connexions, and ritualism almost entirely so; here totemism is relegated largely to the domain of religion and myth. In Africa, again, totemism is often little more than a system of food restrictions. In the Iroquois or Zuñi, finally, we see marginal samples of totemism, where the zoomorphic clan name alone points to unrealized totemic possibilities.

It is, however, possible to overemphasize these differences at the expense of equally fundamental similarities. In the first place, some features are much more common than others. Whereas magical ceremonies to multiply totems are, perhaps, unknown outside of Australia,[13] while totemic art is nowhere developed so prolifically as on the Northwest Coast, other traits occur with fair uniformity in most or all of the main totemic areas. Among such widely diffused attributes are totemic sib names, taboos, and the idea of some form of relationship with the totem. Nor is this all. Exogamy of the totemic sib is an almost universal trait of totemism. Whether one holds with some that exogamy is of the very essence of totemism, or with others that both exogamy and totemism, being sib attributes, become interrelated secondarily, the fact remains that the prohibition to marry one's totem mate is almost coextensive with totemism itself. And now we come to still another totemic trait which deserves emphasis because it has often been misunderstood. While most of the totemic attitudes and practices belong to what Durkheim would call the 'sacred' rather than the 'profane' realm, totems as such are not worshipped. Totems are not gods, rather are they intimates, more or less sanctified. Animism, magic, the worship of nature, are not totemism. The universality of these features in all tribes, totemic or otherwise, shows that totemism nowhere exhausts the content of a tribal religion.

The distinctive thing about totemism is not the vehemence of the religious attitude toward the totem—that, as just noted, is not discernible—

---

[13] *Cf.* p. 341, note 15.

but the way totemic ideas and rites are interwoven with a social system.[14]

It would be wholly satisfactory to regard this peculiar relation of mystical ideas and acts to a social system as *the* most distinctive trait of totemism, if not for one circumstance which, at first sight, seems not a little disturbing: our diagram would serve as well to illustrate a tribal set of religious societies. In the latter case, namely, a tribal pattern of traits also appears in a variety of concrete forms, a different one for each society. It thus becomes necessary to stress with added emphasis the character of the social skeleton underlying a totemic complex. *The skeleton is always a social system.* It may be a tribal set of families or local groups, but in a large majority of cases it is a sib system. The totemic complex, without doubt, lends the social system whatever cultural significance it has, but were the complex removed, the skeleton would remain; there would still be a social system. This, as we saw, is characteristic of groups of status as contrasted with groups of function. The social system underlying a totemic complex consists of social units

[14] The following diagram may serve to illustrate how a totemic complex fits into a social organization:

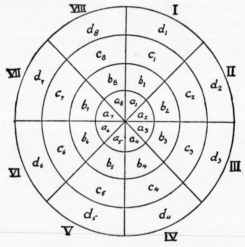

Here the segments I, II, III, . . . are social units (in totemism generally clans or gentes), while a, b, c and d are totemic features, say taboo (a), name (b), relationship (c), and artistic representation (d). Now $a + b + c + d$ is sufficient to characterize the totemic complex, if one notes in addition that in each segment these features appear in somewhat different form (a_1, a_2, a_3, . . . b_1, b_2, b_3, etc.), for each totemic unit has a different animal or bird or plant or thing for its totem, and to that extent its taboo, its relationship, its artistic representation, are different in their concrete aspects from the corresponding features in the other totemic units of the complex.

The sibs—I to VIII—are, totemically speaking, not identical but homologous.

which are not merely functional—they are groups of status, namely sibs.

Thus it appears that neither the socio-psychological nature of totemism, nor its geographical distributions, nor its historic role can be
understood without a proper appraisal of the underlying social skeleton.
This, in a majority of cases, will be found to be a sib system. Socio-
psychologically this means that there is some delicate correspondence,
some *fitness*, between the supernatural aspect of totemism and clan or
gentile systems. Geographically this means that wherever clans or
gentes occur, there also totemism is likely to be (although there are
exceptions).[15] And historically this means that totemism had its share
in at least some of those elements of primitive life expressed by clans
and gentes, as well as in some of those they brought into it. Finally,
let me add this, as not subject to *any* exceptions: an exuberant totemic
complex is never to be found except in association with a sib system. It
must be remembered that, whereas families and local groups are shared
by primitive and modern culture, sibs—and with them totemism—occur
only among primitives. And again, the most primitive tribes lack both
sibs and totemism. Like sibs, then, totemism, as an historic phenomenon,
belongs to the middle range, between the most primitive and the 'historic' societies, in the narrow sense.

If a further formulation of the totemic situation were to be attempted,
it would run about like this. We note three tendencies characteristic
of clusters of social units, especially so when these are sibs: a tendency
to become associated with cultural features, homologous as between sib
and sib; a tendency towards exogamy; and a tendency towards certain

[15] Exceptions, in history as in grammar, prove the rule, unless numerous enough
to offset it. Each case here must be judged on its merits. In the instance of sibs
and totemism, then, have we 'adhesion' (in Tylor's sense) or mere accidental coexistence? There can be no doubt as to the answer. Totemism always implies a
social system. The cases in which such a system consists of groups of families or
local units are *very rare:* in the vast majority of instances the social system
underlying a totemic complex is a sib system. On the other hand, families or local
groups are in all but a few (*very rare*) cases not connected with totemism,
whereas sibs are *much more frequently* totemic than not, as anyone familiar with
Australian, African, or American data, will have to concede. Have we then
adhesion or not? If we have, it is an historical fact or process (Tylor's 'adhesion'
is an historical concept), and the point of view adopted is an *historical* point of
view, as contrasted with a purely analytical one. This much is to be said in answer
to Dr. Lowie's stricture upon this position (see his *Primitive Society*, pp. 144–
145). For the benefit of those interested in the broader aspects of scientific theory,
I might say that in totemism we can see a fine example of the applicability of
the standpoint of *Gestalt* or *configuration*. As a configuration—one of many characteristic of primitives—it stands out very much a specific and clearly defined
thing. As such it can, of course, not be proved but only apperceived, like all
configurations. When this is achieved, there arises the further problem of placing
this 'thing' historically—this is what I have attempted to do.

mystical attitudes with reference to creatures and things in nature. All three tendencies are present in historic society (including the modern), but are much more pronounced in primitive conditions. These three tendencies—which in their origins and psycho-sociological nature are disparate and in and by themselves not in any sense 'totemic'—find in primitive sib systems, with which they are so frequently associated, a fertile soil for mutual interpenetration and further elaboration. Thus spring up totemic complexes in their many forms and varieties.[16]

Before we leave the subject of totemism, two further queries must be met: Has totemism and all it stands for been left definitely behind? Or can certain adumbrations of it be discerned in modern society? It can be shown that neither the supernaturalism involved in totemism nor the peculiar form of socialization implied in it is wholly foreign to modern life.

While plants and inanimate things have long since been relegated to the realm of the matter-of-fact, animals still inhabit a region where fact and fancy are peacefully wedded together. As between the animal and its human master, verbal usage reveals a common range of physical and psychic qualities. One thinks of the eagle eye, the leonine heart, the bull's neck, dogged perseverance, catty behaviour, piggish manners. Some of us are 'stubborn like a donkey,' others 'sly like a fox,' still others 'pugnacious like a rooster.' Current metaphor—half in earnest, half in jest—has introduced a fairly representative zoo into the human scene: fox and beaver, bear and rabbit, cat and cow, hog and ass, ape and shark. Some mothers treat their children with an affection we think ape-like, while others make children of apes, and of cats, dogs, and parrots as well. And it is typical that psychic qualities—intellect, affection, understanding, sensitiveness—are wont to be ascribed to these creatures just by those masters who may at times refuse to grant such traits to some humans.

From the days of Lavater's physiognomics to those of Lombrosian criminology, note was taken of animalistic suggestions in human countenances, balanced perhaps less commonly by the reading of human features and expressions into the faces of animals. Marguérite Audou's delightful book, *Marie Claire*, abounds in such observations, while Georgette Leblanc's 'dog book' will supply still others.

---

[16] *Cf.* my 'Form and Content in Totemism' (*American Anthropologist*, 1918), also 'Totemism, an Analytical Study' (*Journal of American Folk-Lore*, 1910) — reprinted with revisions in my *History, Psychology, and Culture*—which falls short of a complete formulation, in so far as I was then unaware of the historical perspective emphasized in the present discussion. As a general guide to totemic literature consult Van Gennep's *The Present State of the Totemic Problem* (in French).

We moderns also bestow animal or bird names upon esoteric societies, game terms, political parties. Similarly, certain groups among us are wont to project their sense of solidarity into a symbol, a college pin, party emblem, national flag, regimental banner or mascot. We do, however, lack sibs. In the absence of this congenial gathering point, our totemic proclivities, rather than blossoming into totemic complexes, remain disjointed cultural fragments.[17]

[17] It is generally known that the United States as a nation has a bird emblem, the bald eagle—less generally, that the separate states also have their birds. The perhaps incomplete list of birds thus far chosen by the states would run as follows:

Alabama	Flicker	Nebraska	Western Meadowlark
Arizona	Cactus Wren	Nevada	Mountain Bluebird
Arkansas	Mockingbird	New Hampshire	Purple Finch
California	Valley Quail	New Mexico	Road Runner
Colorado	Lark Bunting	New York	Eastern Bluebird
Delaware	Cardinal	North Carolina	Carolina Chicadee
District of Columbia	Wood Thrush	North Dakota	Western Meadowlark
Florida	Mockingbird	Ohio	House Wren
Georgia	Brown Thrasher	Oklahoma	Bob White
Idaho	Mountain Bluebird	Oregon	Western Meadowlark
Illinois	Cardinal	Pennsylvania	Ruffed Grouse
Indiana	Eastern Cardinal	Rhode Island	Bob White
Kansas	Western Meadowlark	South Carolina	Carolina Wren
Kentucky	Cardinal	South Dakota	Western Meadowlark
Louisiana	Brown Pelican	Texas	Western Mockingbird
Maine	Chickadee	Utah	California Gull
Maryland	Baltimore Oriole	Vermont	Hermit Thrush
Massachusetts	Veery	Virginia	Robin
Michigan	Robin	Washington	Willow Goldfinch
Minnesota	Goldfinch	West Virginia	Tufted Titmouse
Mississippi	Mockingbird	Wisconsin	Robin
Missouri	Eastern Bluebird	Wyoming	Western Meadowlark
Montana	Western Meadowlark		

Some of the state birds were selected for their beauty, others for the quality of their songs, for their economic value, or for their role in local tradition. Thus Utah chose the gull, which is credited with having saved her crop from insects in 1848. The flicker or 'yellow hammer' was adopted by Alabama because her cavalry in the Confederate army were nicknamed 'yellow hammers' from the colour of their uniforms. And so on.

If confronted with this list, a primitive totemite would experience a warm feeling of congeniality towards his White brethren. Upon reflection, he might group Kansas, Montana, Nebraska, North Dakota, Oregon, South Dakota, and Wyoming together as belonging to the Western Meadowlark clan. Similarly, Delaware, Illinois, and Kentucky would constitute the Cardinal clan, with possibly Indiana, with its Eastern Cardinal, as a sub-clan. He might inquire whether New Yorkers sang like Eastern Bluebirds and the people of Maryland like Baltimore Orioles. He might also comment on the exclusive selection of birds as totems, although, if he happened to be a Melanesian, this feature would not surprise him. He might even express surprise at the fact that a North Dakota man is permitted to marry an Oregon woman, or even a North Dakota woman. At any rate his mind would be stimulated along congenial lines. He would feel passably at home in this scene.

Chapter XXI

SIBS AND OTHER SOCIAL UNITS

The Tlingit

The two northern tribes of the Northwest Coast of America, the Haida and Tlingit, have social systems identical in most respects. For the sake of brevity I shall, in the main, restrict this sketch to the Tlingit. There are two main social divisions or phratries among the Tlingit known as Raven and Wolf. The principal function of these phratric groups is to control intermarriage, no marriage being permitted within a phratry.[1] Descent is maternal, the children belonging to the phratry of the mother. In addition to controlling intermarriage, the phratries exercise certain functions with reference to each other which may be called reciprocal. Thus the members of the two phratries assist each other at burials of their members and the building of houses. Also, the principal feast or potlatch of the year is given by one phratry to the opposite phratry.[2]

The phratries are subdivided into clans: twenty-eight in the Raven phratry and twenty-six in the Wolf phratry. These clans are known by local names and all evidence points to the fact that they originally constituted local divisions or villages. The local character of these social units is pronounced even today. Thus, of the Wolf clans, one is prominently represented in four localities, one in two, while two clans occur in three localities. The remaining twenty-one clans are almost wholly restricted to one village. Of the Raven clans, one predominates in four

---

[1] Earlier writers spoke of a third social division, very small numerically and represented in only one locality, with which members of both phratries were permitted to intermarry. More recent investigations have thrown some doubt on the importance and, perhaps, the very presence of this third division.

[2] The difference in this item between the Tlingit and Haida provides an interesting illustration of local differentiation between these two culturally so closely related tribes. Among the Haida also a potlatch may on occasion be given to a member or group of the opposite phratry, but the main potlatch of the year is always given to members of one's own phratry. Their neighbours, the Tlingit, feel very keenly on this subject. To have a potlatch given to one is to be placed under very serious obligation, they argue; it is therefore distinctly in bad taste to inflict such a feast on the members of one's own phratry, most of whom are close relatives of the feast-giver.

villages, one in three, and one in two. The remaining twenty-five clans are in the main restricted to one village.

Being subdivisions of the phratries, which are exogamous, the clans are also subject to this rule. As already pointed out a while ago, the abstention from marriage within the same clan is here felt to be a phratry, not a clan, matter. Seeing that a member of a clan is prohibited from marrying not only the woman of his clan but also those of *any* clan of his own phratry, it is obvious that the clan here cannot be called an exogamous unit—its exogamy is secondary and results from the fact that the clan is a subdivision of an exogamous phratry. A Tlingit clan, as well as a Haida one, is in the main a ceremonial unit, distinguished by a variety of prerogatives hereditary in the clan. Every clan owns its special ceremonial features, such as dances, cries, and decorative paraphernalia. The clan's most cherished prerogative, however, is the right to carve or paint as its crest a particular animal, bird, or supernatural creature. Among the Tlingit each clan owns one crest, whereas among the Haida many of the clans have several crests each. These crests consist of carvings on totem-poles and memorial columns which are executed and owned by the families or individuals comprised in the clan. Crests, in whole or in part, are also carved on boxes or ladles, or painted on the sides of canoes and the front walls of houses, as well as on the faces of individual clan members. From the artistic angle I have already discussed these crests in the chapter on Indian art.

Every clan has a tradition in which a human ancestor of the clan comes into intimate association with the animal, bird, or supernatural creature which thenceforth becomes the crest of the clan. Some people belonging to the Desitan family, we read in Swanton's *Tlingit Myths*, captured a small beaver, and, as it was cunning and very clean, they kept it as a pet. By and by, however, although it was well cared for, it took offence at something and began to compose songs. Afterwards one of the beaver's masters went through the woods to a certain salmon creek and found two salmon-spear handles, beautifully carved, standing at the foot of a big tree. He carried these home; and, as soon as they were brought into the house, the beaver said: 'That is my make.' Then something was said that offended it again. Upon this the beaver began to sing just like a human being and surprised the people very much. While it was doing this it seized a spear and threw it straight through its master's chest, killing him instantly. Then it threw its tail down upon the ground, and the earth on which that house stood dropped in. They found afterward that the beaver had been digging out the earth under the camp so as to make a great hollow. It is from this story that the

Desitan claim the beaver and have the beaver hat; they also sing songs composed by the beaver.[3]

Another story quite similar in form, it will be noted, though different in content, is told by the Kiksadi of Wrangel, who use the frog crest. 'A man belonging to the Stikine Kiksadi kicked a frog over on its back; but as soon as he had done so, he lay motionless, unable to talk, and they carried his body into the house. Meanwhile his soul was taken by the frogs to their own town (arranged, by the way, exactly after the mode of human towns) where it was brought into the presence of Chief Frightful-Face. The chief said to the man, "We belong to your clan, and it is a shame that you should treat one of your own people as you have done. We are Kiksadi, and it is a Kiksadi youth who has done this. You had better go to your own village. You have disgraced yourself as well as us, for this woman belongs to your own clan." After this the man left Frog-Town, and at the same time his body at home came to. He told the people of his adventure. All the people were listening to what this man said, and it is because the frog himself said he was a Kiksadi that they claim the Frog.' [4]

Another crest tradition, apparently of different pattern but at bottom very much the same, comes from the Chilkat. George T. Emmons, to whom we also owe an admirable study of the Chilkat blanket, has devoted a little monograph to the whale house of this Tlingit tribe.[5] In the course of his description of the house—a big one, incidentally, measuring some 50 odd feet front by 53 feet deep—he mentions a carved post inside of the house standing to the left of a remarkable ornamental screen. This post is named Tlukeassagars, 'Wood-Worm Post.' The large upper figure on the post represents Kakutchan, 'the girl who fondled the wood-worm,' which she holds in front of her body with both hands. Over her head are carved two wood-worms whose heads form her ears. Beneath appears a frog and the bill of a crane. The whole post symbolizes a tree in which the wood-worm lives. The crane lights on the outer surface, while the frog lives underneath among the roots.

'It is said that in early days, in a village that would seem to have been near Klawak, on the west coast of Prince of Wales Island, there was a chief of the Tlowonwegadi family whose wife was of the Konnuhtadi. They had a daughter just reaching womanhood. One day after the members of the household had returned from gathering firewood, the

[3] Swanton, *Tlingit Myths*, p. 227.
[4] *Ibid.*, p. 231.
[5] 'A Whale House of the Chilkat,' *Anthropological Papers*, American Museum of Natural History, vol. XIX, Part I, pp. 1–33.

daughter, picking up a piece of bark, found a wood-worm which she wrapped up in her blanket and carried in the house. After the evening meal she took it into the back compartment and offered it some food, but it would not eat, and then she gave it her breast, and it grew very rapidly, and she became very fond of it, as if it were her child, and as time went on her whole life seemed to be absorbed by her pet, which she kept secreted. Her constant abstraction and absences grew so noticeable that the mother's suspicions were aroused and one day she detected her fondling the worm that had now grown as large as a person. She called the chief and they wondered greatly, for no one had ever seen anything like it. As she played with the worm, she sang to it all the time. . . .

'The father told the uncle, and he sent for his niece and set food before her, and while she ate he stole away to see the worm which she had hidden behind the food chests in the back apartment. That evening the uncle called the people together and told them that his niece had a great "living creature," Kutzeceteut, that might in time kill them all, and they decided to kill the worm. Another reason given for the destruction of the creature was that it was held accountable for the loss of much food that had been mysteriously disappearing from the grease boxes for some time past.

'The following day the aunt invited her to come and sew her marten-skin robe, and in her absence the men sharpened their long wooden spears and going to the house killed the worm. Upon her return she cried bitterly and said they had killed her child and she sang her song night and day until she died. Then her family left this place and migrated north. In commemoration of this event the Tlowonwegadi family display the tail of the worm on their dance dress, pipes, etc., as they attacked that part, while the Konnuhtadi display the whole worm figure, as they killed the head, which was the most important part.' [6]

Although the clans and phratries are maternal among the Tlingit and their southern neighbours, the Haida and Tsimshian, the position of women in these communities is not high, by which is meant that they are deprived of most of the ceremonial prerogatives and do not figure except inconspicuously in the customs clustering about the beliefs in guardian spirits.[7]

[6] *Ibid.*, pp. 30–31.

[7] See pp. 242 seq. It is interesting in this connexion that the relatively inferior position of woman is here associated with the maternal organization of group descent and property inheritance. Among the Iroquois tribes of the East, on the other hand, who also have maternal descent and inheritance of property, women stand very high, both socially and politically. In modern days when the ancient custom

The Iroquois

By contrast with the tribes of the Coast, the phratries of the Iroquois of the Great Lakes and vicinity were in the main ceremonial units, whereas the clans were exogamous with important ceremonial functions. The social organization of the Iroquois was as follows: The five Iroquois tribes—Mohawk, Oneida, Onondaga, Cayuga, and Seneca—were organized into a League or Confederacy. This event took place some time around the middle of the sixteenth century. Later another Iroquois tribe, the Tuscarora, who had been living farther south in North Carolina, came north and joined the League. The formation of the Confederacy, which cost the component tribes some of their rights as sovereign groups, resulted in an enormous enhancement of the military power of the Iroquois, who proceeded to make use of this in their far-flung plans of military conquest. The ideology of this 'historic mission' has a strangely familiar ring to modern ears. The chiefs of the Iroquois claimed that their purpose was peace, and that they intended to incorporate in the League all the tribes of American Indians, thus establishing a reign of peace among the Indian tribes. In fact they designated the League metaphorically as the Great Peace. In other contexts it was also referred to as the Long-House, meaning the spacious long-house in which the League ceremonies were held and where the chiefs met for council. In pursuance of these peaceful intentions the confederated Iroquois adopted a method familiar to later historic periods, namely that of 'fire and sword.' They would offer membership in the League to a tribe and, if there was no opposition, incorporate it in a position somewhat inferior to that of the Iroquois. This, however, did not happen very often. As a rule a tribe thus approached would refuse in no equivocal terms. Then the Iroquois proceeded to attack it and, having proved victorious, dealt with it as they pleased. The military successes of the Iroquois were remarkable and continued until they chanced upon their own relatives, the Cherokee of the South, who finally put an end to this pacific land-slide.

There were fifty chiefs in the League whose functions and authority extended not merely to a chief's own tribe but to the entire population of the League. In other words, they were federal officials. These fifty

of blood-revenge, once practised by the Indians, was discontinued and a fine substituted, the different valuation of women on the part of the two groups of tribes found expression in the relative size of fines. In the Northwest the penalty for killing a woman was only half of that imposed for killing a man, whereas among the Iroquois the reverse was the case—the penalty for killing a woman was double that exacted for killing a man.

chiefs came from the five original tribes. The Tuscarora chieftains also sat at the deliberations of the League chiefs, but their role was purely consultative; they were not permitted to vote on the measures passed by the council. The Iroquois explained this partial disfranchisement of the Tuscarora by saying that they were thus penalized for entering the Long-House through the side wall (obviously an irregular form of entry), thereby forfeiting their claim upon full membership in the League. The apportionment of chiefs to the five tribes was as follows: the Mohawk sent 9; the Oneida, 9; the Onondaga, 14; the Cayuga, 10; and the Seneca, 8. Each chief had a dynastic name, which he assumed on being 'raised' to chieftainship and on laying aside his individual name which he had received earlier in life. These dynastic names were the prerogatives of certain clans, so that each federal chief was, on the one hand, a federal official, on the other, a chief elected by a certain tribe and clan.[8] As a rule the chiefs declared war and made agreements of peace. They also sat as a court of judges in certain instances of major crimes, such as murder, and, in more recent days, of litigation about land and property. As individuals the chiefs exercised a wide influence, both in their places of habitual residence and in their occasional travels, even though their functions in this connexion were not formal but personal. They functioned as teachers of the young, familiarizing them with the nature of the Confederacy, reciting at length the elaborate traditions of the founding of the League, and instructing the young braves in the behaviour proper in peace, war, and on ceremonial occasions. The Iroquois, like other peoples, had their own ideas of what a chief should be. First and foremost, a chief must not lie; second (a more recent specification made necessary by the inroads of White civilization), he must not drink; and third, he must be imperturbable—a chief's temper must never be ruffled. 'A chief's skin,' said the Iroquois, 'is seven thumbs thick,' meaning that it could not be pierced. That many of these chieftains lived up to these requirements is evidenced by their reputation among the Whites, both English and American.[9]

Each Iroquois tribe was divided into two phratries, which among

[8] The ultimate units in which these chiefs were both hereditary and elective were the *maternal families*, about which see pp. 361 seq.

[9] In addition to the traits here mentioned a chief was, of course, expected to be thoroughly versed in the traditions, stories, social regulations, and ceremonial techniques of the Iroquois. Old Chief Gibson, a Seneca of the Turtle clan, with whom I spent many fascinating hours some 20 years ago, possessed all these qualifications. He was both informant and interpreter, a good Indian and as good a White man, well-versed in the cultures of both. Although totally blind from his thirtieth year on, he continued to serve as a chief on the Grand River Reservation in Ontario until his death at the age of 64. I regard this Indian parliamentarian as one of the truest

these people had no names; however, the clans which were comprised
in one phratry referred to each other as Brother clans and to those of
the opposite phratry as Cousin clans. Descent in the phratries was maternal. The principal phratric functions were ceremonial. On ceremonial
occasions, such as those of the great seasonal festivals, the members of

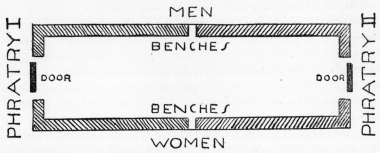

FIG. 69. SEATING ARRANGEMENT IN IROQUOIS CEREMONIAL LONG-HOUSE.

the two phratries sat facing each other at the opposite ends of the Long-
House (Fig. 69). The ceremony, usually conducted by two chiefs, one
on each side, was performed as between the two phratries. At all public
games the contending sides divided according to phratries, for example,
at the lacrosse game, at target-shooting, ball games, or the snow-snake
game.[10]

The phratries were further subdivided into clans; the number of
these, never very large, differed in the different tribes. Thus the Mohawk
and Oneida had only three each,[11] the other tribes eight or more. Among
the Seneca the clans were named and grouped as follows:

Phratries:	I	II
Clans:	Bear Wolf Turtle Beaver	Deer Snipe Heron Hawk

friends I ever had, and I shall never forget the dignity and wisdom of the man
and his tragic faith in Iroquois culture. Tragic because futile—and he knew that too.

[10] This game was played with long sticks, an inch or so wide and perhaps a
quarter of an inch thick, pointed at one end and with a slight groove at the butt
end into which the index finger was placed when the stick was thrown. It was
played on snow which, for this purpose, was smoothed over a long narrow strip,
usually at a slight incline. The stick was either permitted to remain rough or was
polished, in accordance with the condition of the snow. When skilfully thrown,
such a stick, travelling along an incline, would cover a half mile or more before
it came to a stop. When striking an uneven spot on the way, it would jerk, jump,
slightly change its direction and speed, thus calling to mind the movements of a
snake—whence the name.

[11] The clans in these two tribes were Bear, Wolf, and Turtle, all of which belonged to one phratry, the second phratry thus being absent. Whether this arrangement represented the original condition among the Mohawk and Oneida it is
impossible to say.

The clans were not local units, although it is not improbable that in early conditions this may have been the case. Members of one clan lived in more than one village. Each clan was more or less closely associated with one or more long-houses, the long, narrow bark structures in which the Iroquois lived, and the majority of individuals in such a long-house probably belonged to one clan.

Unlike many other peoples of their type of social organization, the Iroquois showed no regard whatsoever for the animals and birds from which the clans took their names. The Iroquois hunted and ate them freely; they were not looked upon as the ancestors of the clan-mates, nor was worship of any sort extended to them. So far as we can see, in fact, no special relationship whatsoever obtained between the individuals of the clan and their eponymous animal, the animal, that is, from which the name of the clan was derived. Each clan owned its own cemetery where the members of the clan were buried, and it is probable that a clan in earlier days owned its own agricultural field or fields, although this is not quite certain. The clans were exogamous, no man or woman of a clan being permitted to marry his or her clan-mate. Each clan possessed the right to use for its members certain individual names which were the property of the clan, or more accurately, of the women of the clan. No other clan was permitted to use these names, nor would two living individuals of one clan bear the same name at one time. These names were semi-ceremonial in character and were scarcely ever used for purposes of appellation or reference, relationship terms being employed for this purpose. At any given time the individual names of a clan were in charge of a woman called Keeper-of-Names, who knew which names were in actual use. When a person died, his or her name became available for use. The Keeper would then 'put' such a name 'away in a box' until it was called for. When a child was born to a woman she would visit the Keeper-of-Names and ask her for the list of available names, those, that is, that were not at that time used by anyone else. From these she could make her selection. The name was not officially bestowed upon the child until the next Green Corn Festival, held in September, on the second day of which women whose children were born within the year would bring them along for the naming ceremonial. This name, as already stated, remained largely a decorative possession of the individual, as it was scarcely ever used in conversation. Most individuals, in fact, soon forgot their personal names, although the mothers as a rule remembered them, as well as the Keeper-of-Names.[12]

---

[12] The latter was also called Keeper-of-the-Faith. Among the names were *Otetiáni* ('Always-Ready'), *Owígo* ('Floating Canoe'), *Gaháno* ('Hanging Flower').

Australia

Before proceeding to the social organization of the Australians let me make a little digression. It will be remembered that the French sociologist, Émile Durkheim, while hunting for the origins of religion, chose Australia as his particular theme for the alleged reason that these tribes, whose social system is rooted in a clan organization, must needs be truly primitive [13]—a quaint notion in view of the details of this social organization, which leave nothing to be desired in the way of definiteness, elaboration, and complexity. It has, in fact, taken much of the time of two generations of anthropologists to work them out with sufficient clarity.

In the second place, we find here an interesting instance of what might be called a disharmonious development of the different aspects of a culture (cf. pp. 522 seq.). In comparison with the Eskimo, for example, the technology of the Australians is exceedingly crude, both in the number of objects and devices and in the technical fitness of that which exists; by the side of the Eskimo, the Australians appear as poverty-ridden. A similar contrast comes to view, when one compares their technical arts with those of their 'neighbours' of the vast Pacific area, the Melanesians and Polynesians. The technical skill and the elaborateness of the arts among the latter are such as to entitle them to a place among the most highly developed primitives in this particular domain, whereas the Australians are certainly among the crudest in this respect. In social organization, on the other hand, the Australians loom far above the Eskimo and are at least the equals of the South Sea Islanders in the elaborateness and logical consistency of their system.

In the following sketch I shall eliminate, for the sake of brevity, many interesting details and stress only the salient features of the social groupings of the Australians. Underlying the many local differences in the other aspects of social structure, we find the small local group or horde (Radcliffe-Brown's term, as used here), which is ubiquitous. Such a horde, probably never exceeding 100 individuals in size, occupies a certain territory, the boundaries of which are known to its members and

When a boy reached maturity his childhood name was put aside and a new name selected for him. When he became a chief, as already mentioned, this second name was also discarded to be replaced by the chief's name. Sometimes a clan would 'lend' one of its names to a person of another clan; when the latter died, the name reverted to the original clan.

[13] The reference is to this author's *Elementary Forms of the Religious Life*, a book greatly to be recommended for its penetrating observations and astute reasoning.

within the limits of which these members exercise proprietary rights over whatever products—mineral, vegetable, or animal—may be available. Membership in a horde is hereditary in the paternal line, regardless of the character of descent in the other social units associated with it. Radcliffe-Brown, who is second to no one in his familiarity with Australian tribes, states that he knows of no instance or locality in which a man could leave his own horde and be adopted by another, not in the sense, of course, that he cannot temporarily absent himself from it, but in the sense that he belongs to it. 'As a normal thing,' he says, 'the male members enter the horde by birth and remain in it till death.' The horde is frequently exogamous and wherever this rule is not enforced, the majority of marriages are still outside the horde. A woman at marriage leaves her parental horde and joins that of her husband, marriage thus being patrilocal.

The Australian tribe, as a functional group, is weakly developed; territorially it comprises districts occupied by its component hordes. The kinship groupings are represented by phratries, sibs, classes, subclasses, and groups of blood-relatives, own and classificatory.

This enumerative presentation of the social organization of Australia seems excessive in its detail and a little bewildering. However, let us proceed, beginning with the sib systems. Each tribe is divided into a large number of clans or gentes uniformly named after animals, birds, or in rare instances after some other natural things. The members of a sib are not segregated in one locality but distributed over a number of local groups or hordes. In the central tribes and some others, the sib members regard themselves as spiritually associated with a number of ancestors, half-human, half-animal, who lived in the *alcheringa*, the mythological period. These ancestors, the stories tell us, once travelled about the country performing magical ceremonies or, in other versions, they were pursued by hunters. At certain places they stopped exhausted and disappeared into the ground. Thereupon a sacred tree, rock, or water-hole arose upon the spot. These sacred spots or *oknanikilla* are ever since being haunted by the spiritual descendants of these distant semi-human semi-animal ancestors. The central Australians believe that a woman, when passing by one of these charmed spots, will be entered into by a spirit child or *ratapa*, and that the human child born of the woman will be a spiritual descendant of the mythological creature which once entered the ground at that particular spot. Our chief authorities here, the English investigators, Spencer and Gillen, and the German missionary, Strehlow, are not quite agreed as to the exact nature of these spiritual bonds. It is clear, however, from the evidence of both accounts, that some sort of genetic relationship obtains between individuals now living and their mythological ancestors.

The sib members treat their eponymous animal with consideration and respect. They are forbidden either to kill or eat it. Their attitude, however, cannot be strictly designated as one of veneration. Instead there is the belief that the animal or bird is a relative or intimate of the sib-mates. Each sib has the power of increasing the supply of its sacred animal or totem by means of a magical ceremony, the *intichiuma*. Once a year, at the end of the dry season, natives from many tribes and localities congregate for the performance of these ceremonies. The members of each sib (or rather its male members—for women are strictly excluded except in the capacity of spectators), properly decorated with bird-down and ochre, perform specified dances and songs, in the course of which the movements and cries of the totemic creatures are skilfully dramatized. There is some blood-letting; the blood drawn from the arms of several participants by means of a sharp stone is permitted to flow over the ceremonial ground and is then spilled over the surrounding rocks. It is in this special rite that the power resides to precipitate the multiplication of the totemic animal. On this occasion one member of the totemic species is killed, and after having been tasted by the head-man of the sib, it is then partaken of sparingly by the other members. This is the only occasion on which sib-mates may eat of their totem. The old men who function throughout as the ceremonial officials produce the sacred *churinga*—made of stone among the Arunta but among other tribes more frequently of wood—and manipulate them in a variety of ways. These sacred slabs, which between ceremonial periods are kept out of sight at the sacred spots referred to before, are believed to be connected by spiritual bonds both with the totemic ancestors of the *alcheringa* and with the human representatives of the clan. Each individual has such a *churinga* assigned to him at birth and also stands in a certain not clearly defined relation to another *churinga*, namely that of his or her mother. As already stated, these elaborate ceremonies are performed by the natives at the end of the long period of drought and immediately preceding the season of torrential rains. Soon afterwards the plants and animals of the region do indeed begin to thrive and proliferate, and the landscape is transformed as if by magic. In this case, then, the natives have good reasons grounded in experience for preserving their belief in magic.

The totem of each sib stands in a certain relation to other animals or birds, the so-called 'associated totems,' which, though not as important as the principal totem, have a sacred character of their own. In the mythological tales these animals and birds figure at the side of the main totem as participants in the plot. It will be seen that the sibs of this region—central Australia—have come to function as magic-working associations. If they have any other functions, these must have eluded the observers.[14]

It is interesting to note that this magical complex of the central Australians can be duplicated elsewhere, for example, among the Yuchi Indians of Oklahoma.[15]

[14] In connexion with the history of anthropological thought, these magical practices of the central Australians seem also to have had the effect of fertilizing the mind of Sir James Frazer. As is well known, this author has described the *intichiuma* performances with their associated ideology as a system of 'co-operative magic' in which the sib-mates of the different sibs exercised magical powers (altruistically!) for the benefit of sibs other than their own; for they themselves, as we already know, are not permitted to partake of the animal the supply of which they have magically fostered. In this presentation, the magical rites of the Australians appear as a sort of fertilization complex, both economic and altruistic in character. Now apart from the facts themselves, this particular interpretation seems to derive from the fertile mind of Sir James. A study of native attitudes brings no evidence of a system of planned economy furthered by co-operative altruism. If the natives themselves, then, are not aware of this, the supposed beneficent results of the magical rites can at best be regarded as a purely factual incident, if it is one, but not as part of a cultural complex with a definite psychological connotation.

[15] Professor Speck in his book, *Ethnology of the Yuchi Indians of Central Oklahoma*, describes Yuchi clans in the following words: 'The members of each clan (descent here being maternal) believe that they are the relatives and, in some vague way, the descendants of certain pre-existing animals whose names and identity they now bear. Their animal ancestors are accordingly totemic. In regard to the living animals, they too are earthly types and descendants of the pre-existing ones, hence, since they trace their descent from the same sources as the human clans, the two are consanguineously related.

'This brings the various clan groups into close relationship with various species of animals, and we find accordingly that the members of each clan will not do violence to wild animals having the form of any of their totems, for instance, the Bear clan people never molest bears; nevertheless they use commodities made from parts of the bear. Such things, of course, as bear hides, bear mats, or whatever else may be useful, are obtained from other clans who have no taboo against killing bears. In the same way the Deer people use parts of the deer when they have occasion to but do not directly take part in killing deer. In this way a sort of amnesty has been obtained between the different clans and their different kinds of animals [shades of Frazer!], while the blame for the injuries of animals is shifted from one clan to the others. General use could consequently be made of the animal kingdom without obliging members of any clan to be the direct murderers of their animal relatives.' (*Op. cit.*, p. 70.)

The Indians also perform certain clan dances 'having for their object the placation of clan totems. The dancers imitate the motions of their totemic animals with their bodies and arms.' (*Ibid.*, p. 112.) Here also men are the exclusive or at least the principal participants in these dances, only a few privileged women being admitted to the earlier more sacred part of the ceremony. 'The feeling of the dancers seems to be,' continues Speck, 'that they are for the time in the actual form of the

In addition to belonging to a particular sib a central Australian boy, before he becomes a full-fledged member of the community, also passes through a series of stages which define his tribal status; his entry into such a stage is marked by initiation ceremonies. As one after another of these ritually marked stages are left behind, there opens up before the boy an ever-widening range of tribal functions, ritualistic activities, and other forms of participation in the esoteric knowledge and practices of the male members of the tribe. In the matter of diet, for example, he starts life under a heavy pressure of eating taboos, most of the available foods being forbidden to him. When the boy reaches maturity, these food restrictions are gradually reduced, finally to be lifted altogether, or almost so, at the approach of old age.

The most important of the initiation ceremonies which completes the ritualistic cycle is the *engwura,* which comprises an elaborate series of rites usually participated in by more than one tribe. The principal rites performed on this occasion are initiatory,[16] but in addition the totemic ceremonies and other important rituals are gone over, as if in rehearsal, by the novices. The purpose of these latter rites is to impart to the young men a thorough command of the complicated ritualistic techniques, a task accomplished, as usual, by the old men. On this occasion the novices are profusely decorated with ochre and bird-down, just as were the participants in the magical ceremonies previously described. There is, however, this difference: in the *engwura* no relation whatsoever obtains between the totem of the individual and the design used in his decoration. In other words, the ceremony is a tribal one and, as such, has no reference to the totems or sibs, the customary totemic symbols being used here as neutral decorations.[17]

---

totem, and they carry out in quite a realistic way the effect of the imitation entirely by their motions and behaviour. . . . Besides those dances which are functionally clan dances, there are others which are addressed, in the form of worship and placation, to various animals which furnish their flesh or bodies for the use of man. Then there are also others which are directed to the spirits of animals which have the power of inflicting sickness, trouble, or death upon the people. These are imitative, similar in general appearance to those already described.' (*Ibid.,* p. 113.)

[16] In the course of the ritual a strange-sounding voice is heard emanating from the bush. This, the women believe, is the voice of Twanyirika, the great spirit, who calls to the initiates; but the men know, and the boys are soon to know, that the presumed spirit is really an old man who, hidden in the bush, swings about a *churinga* attached to a rope. The weird sound produced by this operation was likened by some imaginative Englishman to the roaring of a bull, whence the apparatus just mentioned became known as a bull-roarer. As this voice resounds, the initiates are one by one spirited away by the old men and taken to the bush where the more esoteric part of the ritual takes place.

[17] It may be presumed that a certain halo of sanctity clings even to these decorations, but it is no more than the sanctity of all totems in a totemic community.

As is usual with sibs, those of Australia are exogamous in the sense that no intermarriage takes place within the sib, barring exceptional or irregular instances.[18]

The social units more specifically concerned with intermarriage are the phratries, classes, and sub-classes. From the standpoint of this aspect of the social system the tribes of Australia may be divided into three main types. The first, represented by the Dieri and other tribes farther south, is characterized by two phratries subdivided into sibs. Here exogamy is associated with the phratries and secondarily with the sibs. The second type is represented by the Kamilaroi and other eastern tribes, where the two phratries with their sibs, in this case clans, are further subdivided into two classes each. Here the classes control intermarriage in such a way that a member of one class of a phratry must marry a member of a particular class of the other phratry. The third type, finally, is represented by the Warramunga and other tribes of the Centre and North, where the two phratries with their four classes are further subdivided in such a way that each class is split into two sub-classes. Here marriage is controlled by the sub-classes—a member of a sub-class of a phratry must marry a member of a particular sub-class of the opposite phratry.[19]

---

[18] Such an instance, by the way, is exemplified by the very tribes of central Australia with which we are here concerned. Owing to the fact that the totemic membership of a child is determined by the woman's encounter with a spirit at a sacred totemic spot, children are frequently born into wrong totem groups, as it were. As a result of this again it will occur that members of one totemic sib may occasionally be found in both phratries. In consequence of this, they are permitted to intermarry—an altogether irregular procedure. While this is so among the Arunta, other tribes, for example their neighbours the Kaitish, have provided against such occurrences. Their belief is that the proper kinds of spirits follow the women around wherever they go, and so when they are impregnated in the way described, it is the right spirit that is responsible. Thus the children manage to be born into the proper totemic sibs, which among these particular tribes are those of their fathers.

[19] The conditions obtaining in the three types of cases may be visualized as follows, assuming for simplicity that the phratry throughout consists of three sibs. The actual number of clans or gentes in a phratry is always much greater.

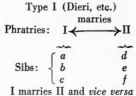

Type I (Dieri, etc.)

marries

Phratries: I⟷II

Sibs: { a   d
        b   e
        c   f

I marries II and *vice versa*

Here the children follow the phratry and clan of the mother (or the gens of the father).

Nor is this all. Marriage regulation is rendered even more precise, as we shall presently see, by the relationship system with its terminology, the truly orthodox kind of marriage in Australia being between cross-cousins, that is between the children of a brother and those of his sister (own or classificatory).

Type II (Kamilaroi, etc.)

Phratries: I   II

Classes: $\overbrace{A \quad B}$ $\overbrace{C \quad D}$

Sibs:
$$\begin{cases} (a=) & a_1 + a_2 & d_1 + d_2 & (=d) \\ (b=) & b_1 + b_2 & e_1 + e_2 & (=e) \\ (c=) & c_1 + c_2 & f_1 + f_2 & (=f) \end{cases}$$

It will be seen that the phratries (I and II) are so subdivided into classes, on the one hand, and clans, on the other, that each class—A, B, C, or D—contains part of the members of several clans, while each clan contains members of two classes. Class A, for example, contains members a_1, b_1, and c_1, of clans a, b, and c, while clan a contains members of a_1 (class A) and a_2 (class B), and so on.

The intermarriages and descent of the children as to class can be represented as follows (the children always belonging to the phratry and clan of the mother):

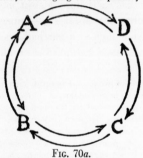

FIG. 70a.

That is, A marries D, children are C; C marries B, children are A; and D marries A, children are B; B marries C, children are D.

Type III (Warramunga, etc.)

Phratries: I   II

Classes: $\overbrace{A \quad B}$ $\overbrace{C \quad D}$

Sub-classes: $\overbrace{1 \quad 2}$ $\overbrace{3 \quad 4}$ $\overbrace{5 \quad 6}$ $\overbrace{7 \quad 8}$

Sibs:
$$\begin{cases} (a=) & a_1 + a_2 + a_3 + a_4 & d_1 + d_2 + d_3 + d_4 & (=d) \\ (b=) & b_1 + b_2 + b_3 + b_4 & e_1 + e_2 + e_3 + e_4 & (=e) \\ (c=) & c_1 + c_2 + c_3 + c_4 & f_1 + f_2 + f_3 + f_4 & (=f) \end{cases}$$

Here, then, the condition obtaining in type II is further complicated in such a way that each sub-class contains parts of the members of all the sibs of one phratry, while each sib comprises members of all the sub-classes of one phratry. Thus, sub-class 1 contains members a_1 (sib a), b_1 (sib b), and c_1 (sib c), etc., while sib a contains members a_1 (sub-class 1), a_2 (sub-class 2), a_3 (sub-class 3) and a_4 (sub-class 4), and so on. The marriages and descent of children as to class, sub-class and phratry can be represented as follows (as a rule, the children here belong to the gens of the father, but in some central tribes the gentes are not hereditary, so that membership becomes irregular):

In addition to their matrimonial functions the phratries, classes, and sub-classes also figure as units on ceremonial occasions. The camp on such instances is usually divided into two territorially distinct halves, each associated with a phratry. In preparation for the ceremonies, members of one phratry function, as a rule, as the decorators of the other, rigging them out in the usual way with bird-down and ochre. The classes and sub-classes function in a similar way, the members of each, as such, having certain specific duties assigned to them. At the more or less formal distribution of food at the end of a major hunting expedition these social divisions are also distinguished by the order in which they are served and the quantity or part they receive.

In relation to the phratries it is interesting to note that their names, when translatable, prove to be those of birds or animals, as for example, in the case of the widespread phratric couplet, Eaglehawk and Crow. The reason why the names of phratries are often untranslatable, not only to ethnologists but also to the natives, lies in the fact that these names are archaic, the natives themselves being unable to analyze them. This feature, among others, bespeaks the antiquity of the phratric institution in Australia.

In passing now to the consideration of the relationship systems, I shall first note some of their other features besides the matrimonial ones. All of these systems represent the so-called classificatory type in an extreme

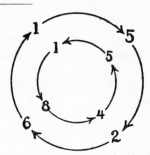 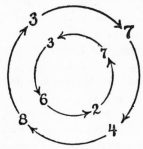

Fig. 70b.

That is, 1 marries 5, children are 2; 2 marries 6, children are 1; 5 marries 1, children are 8; 8 marries 4, children are 5; and 3 marries 7, children are 4; 4 marries 8, children are 3; 7 marries 3, children are 6; 6 marries 2, children are 7.

It will thus be seen how indirectly the clan or gens in Australia is connected with exogamy in its positive aspect, for among the tribes of type III each sib contains four groups of men and women whose matrimonial proscriptions and prescriptions are quite different; among the tribes of type II each sib contains two such groups of men and women; while even among the tribes of type I it is clearly not the clans or gentes, a, b, d, f, etc., which define the matrimonial rules on the negative or the positive side, but the phratries: the law is, no marriage in your own phratry, always marry into the opposite phratry.

form of development, the result of which is that all the individuals of a local group are not only interrelated but are so in a definite way, allowing or rather demanding the application of particular relationship terms. Now these terms, here as in other places, are far from being mere verbal expressions. On the contrary, definitely prescribed forms of behaviour, both positive and negative, are associated with the terms. This is a matter of such great importance in the life of the natives that an Australian does not feel comfortable unless he knows with whom he is dealing, as far as relationship is concerned. Radcliffe-Brown tells the following curious story from his own experience. Once when he was travelling in native territory, with a young Australian as his guide, they came to a camp. The anthropologist proceeded in the usual way to make preparations for a night's stay in the camp. The boy, however, balked in this instance, and decided to sleep outside the camp. Naturally interested, Radcliffe-Brown questioned him on the morrow and discovered that the peculiar behaviour of the youngster was due to the fact that he had in this case been unable to ascertain in what relationship he stood to the different individuals in camp. This meant that he knew neither how others would act towards him, nor how he should behave towards them. Under such circumstances the boy, apparently a wise one, decided to camp on his own.

Now it will be well to examine what Radcliffe-Brown calls the 'basic principles of classification' in the relationship systems of Australia:

1. A man is always classed with his brother and a woman with her sister (own, not classificatory), these relationships being covered by the same term. Our author calls this the 'principle of the equivalence of brothers.'

2. Relatives by marriage are drawn into a circle of consanguinity. Thus the wife of any man one calls 'father' is one's 'mother,' and the husband of any woman called 'mother' is called 'father.'

3. The third principle referred to by Brown is the absence of any limitation to the range of classificatory terms, with the result that these terms, extended without limit, come to embrace the whole of the society.

Brown groups the relationship systems of Australia into two types, as represented by the Kariera of the West coast and the Aranda or Arunta of central Australia. The Kariera type is characterized by the prevalence of cross-cousin marriage in three forms: bilateral, where a man may marry his mother's brother's daughter or his father's sister's daughter; matrilateral, where a man may marry his mother's brother's daughter but not his father's sister's daughter; and patrilateral, where a man may marry his father's sister's daughter but not his mother's brother's daughter. In the systems of the Kariera type (to be referred to as system 'K') two classes of males and two classes of females are distinguished in each generation, an additional distinction being occasionally made between younger and older relatives. In a person's own generation there are two terms for men, namely brother and mother's brother's son, and two for women, namely sister and mother's brother's daughter, a distinction being also made between older and younger brothers and sisters on the basis of actual age. In the first ascending generation four relationship terms are used: father, mother's brother, mother, and father's sister. The term 'father' covers own father, father's brother, mother's sister's husband, father's father's brother's son, mother's mother's brother's son, and so on. The term 'mother' covers own mother, mother's sister, father's brother's wife, mother's mother's sister's daughter, etc. The term for mother's brother covers the brother of anyone called 'mother' and the husband of a sister of any man called 'father.' The term for father's sister covers the sister of any man called 'father' and the wife of any man called 'mother's brother.'

In the second ascending generation the four terms are: father's father, father's mother, mother's father, and mother's mother. The term for father's father also covers the father's father's brother, the husband of the father's mother's sister, and the brother of the mother's mother. The term for father's mother also covers her sister, the wife of a father's father's brother, and the sister of the mother's father. The term for mother's father also covers his brother, the husband of the mother's mother's sister, and the brother of the father's mother. The term for mother's mother also covers her sister, the wife of a mother's father's brother, and the sister of the father's father. There are, moreover, two special features here. First, the mother's mother's brother is identified with the father's father, and the father's mother's brother with the mother's father. And second, the grandparent-grandchild relationship is reciprocal, as a result of which the same term is applied to one's father's father as to one's son's son. All persons in the first descending generation are covered by four terms: son, daughter, sister's son, and sister's daughter.

All in all, the Kariera distinguished twenty-two kinds of relatives including the distinction made between older and younger brothers and sisters. For this purpose they utilize eighteen terms, the discrepancy between the number of terms and the kinds of relatives being due to the grandparent-grandchild reciprocity.

Among the Aranda (system 'A') certain relatives grouped together in system 'K' are separated into two groups. Thus:

' K'	'A'
1. father's father	father's father mother's mother's brother
2. father's mother	father's mother mother's father's sister
3. mother's father	mother's father father's mother's brother
4. mother's mother	mother's mother father's father's sister

All of these terms have, of course, their extended meanings, in addition to the primary ones, as already indicated. The actual number of terms used by the 'A' to cover the eight kinds of relationship is, however, not

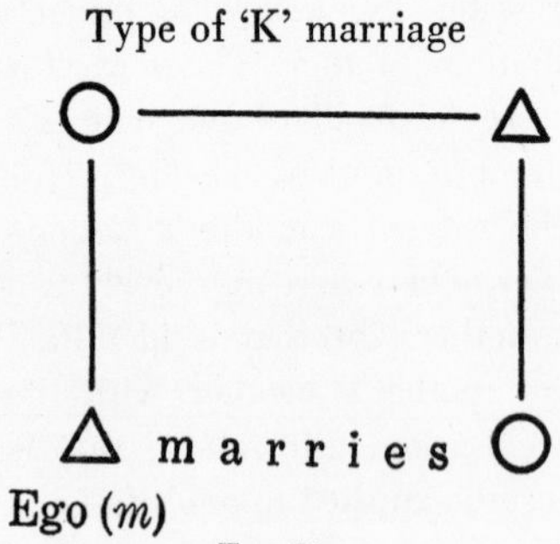

Type of 'A' marriage

Type of 'K' marriage

Fig. 71a.

A man marries his mother's brother's daughter.

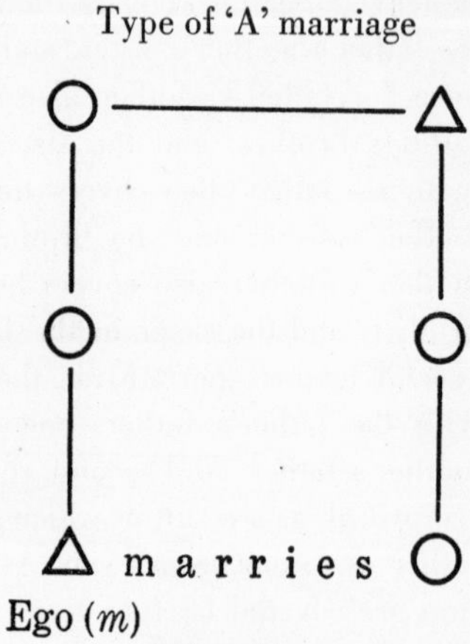

Fig. 71b.

A man marries his mother's mother's brother's daughter's daughter.

eight but four, for the reason that the same term is employed to cover a male relative and his sister, as for example, the father's father and his sister. Further reduction in the number of terms when compared to the kinds of relatives results from the fact that certain terms are reciprocal, as in the 'K' system, and that the same terms are used for grandparents and grandchildren.

From the standpoint of marriage, we find that a man in the 'A' system may not marry first cousins; he may marry four kinds of second cousins, namely, a mother's mother's brother's daughter's daughter, a father's mother's brother's son's daughter, a father's father's sister's son's daughter, and a mother's father's sister's daughter's daughter. There are also certain third and fourth cousins whom an 'A' man may marry.

All those relatives an 'A' man may marry, a 'K' man may also marry; but the reverse is not true: the women marriageable to a 'K' man are divided by an 'A' man into two groups: marriageable and non-marriageable. For example (see Fig. 71 opposite):

Now, the woman the 'A' man marries (or a corresponding relative in the Kariera tribe) would also be marriageable to a 'K' man, a mother's mother's brother's daughter's daughter being here classifiable with a mother's brother's daughter. But an 'A' man could not marry the woman the 'K' man marries (or a corresponding relative among the Aranda), because he may not marry a first cousin.

Among the Kariera, with their four classes, the relationship terms and the corresponding relatives would fit into the class system in the following way:

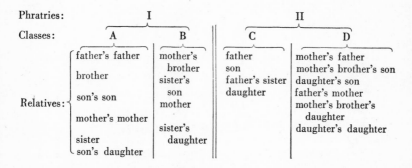

Phratries: I   II

Classes: A   B   C   D

Relatives: father's father   mother's   father   mother's father
            brother   brother   son   mother's brother's son
                              sister's   father's sister daughter's son
            son's son   son   daughter   father's mother
                              mother   mother's brother's
            mother's mother   daughter
                              sister's   daughter's daughter
            sister   daughter
            son's daughter

It will, of course, be understood that the terms designating the relatives here enumerated are used in the sweeping way already described, with the result that the table as here given will cover all the individuals in the tribe. A similar table, indicating the correspondence between the sub-classes and the relationship terms, could be constructed for the northern Aranda and the other tribes with an eight-sub-class system. For the sake of brevity, I shall omit it here, as well as the further interesting details given by Radcliffe-Brown. But enough has been said, I trust, to indicate

what is meant by saying that in the last analysis marriage in primitive
Australia is controlled by relationship,[20] and that the class and sub-class
systems, as Cunow and Boas long suspected, really represent relationship groupings crystallized into formal social units.

[20] Though distinguishing a larger variety of social systems in Australia than
those formerly recognized, Radcliffe-Brown was able to show that the regulation of
marriage is of one of the two types here described—'K' and 'A.' In some instances,
two neighbouring tribes, though identical in social type, may yet differ in relationship type and marriage regulation, for example, the Ngaluma and Mardudhunera,
which belong to the four-class type, but the former having the 'K,' the latter, the
'A' type of relationship system. This discussion of relationship systems in Australia
is based on A. R. Radcliffe-Brown's study, 'The Social Organization of Australian
Tribes,' *Oceania*, vol. I, pp. 34–63, 206–246, 322–341, 426–456.

Chapter XXII

SIBS AND OTHER SOCIAL UNITS
(Continued)

The Baganda

In passing to the gentile organization of the Baganda we are confronted with a different world from that of the Iroquois, Tlingit, or Australians. The social scene we find in this African tribe includes cattle-breeding, agriculture, populous cities, roads, and taxes. The greater density of population, never approached in America except in Mexico and Peru, makes many things possible here and some necessary which could not be thought of in a sparsely populated region. The Baganda are divided into thirty-six gentes or *kika;* most of the gentes have two totems, and a few have even three. These totemic creatures are sacred to the members of the gens and are neither killed nor eaten. All the members of a gens trace their descent back to one human ancestor— putatively, that is. The gentes are exogamous with the sole exception of the Lung-Fish gens, which is divided into two branches, differentiated by their second totems, between which intermarriage is permitted. When a Baganda woman marries she preserves her own totem, following in this the regular procedure of peoples with sibs; but in addition she also adopts her husband's totem. Baganda mothers have been known to urge their children to show some respect to the maternal totem, apparently with indifferent success.[1]

---

[1] The fact that a woman here adopts her husband's totem and the further fact just mentioned about the propaganda conducted by mothers among the children in favour of the maternal totem, are obviously traits incompatible with a strongly felt gentile principle. In an orthodox totemic or even non-totemic community with sibs such an infringement of the unilateral hereditary principle could not be thought of. Facts such as this offer evidence that the gentes of the Baganda, like those of many of their Bantu-speaking brethren, must have originated long ago under conditions more like those of regular sib societies and at a time when the population was not so dense and the membership of gentes less populous. These conditions have been left far behind. What we find now is a gentile system in the process of transmutation from its more primitive and regular pattern to one more nearly compatible with a vastly greater population and the requirements of a centralized political system (see pp. 387 seq.).

351

Each gens is subdivided into a number of local divisions, *siga,* widely scattered over the territory of Uganda, so that the *siga* of one gens are often separated by great distances. Each local division is once more subdivided into a varying number of minor units or *enda.*

Each gens is represented in the concrete by its component *siga,* which are really estates, often situated on hills covered with gardens and extending down into a valley. These estates are in charge of local chieftains who are responsible to the gentile chief for the conduct of their *siga* members. Although the gentes worship their own gods, a number of the gentes take charge, in addition, of one of the national gods. In such a case the god's temple is situated on the estate where resides the gentile chief who officiates in the temple as a priest.

In addition to the *siga* lands each gens also owns a varying number of other bits of territory acquired by having not less than three generations of a branch of a gens bury their members in that locality. The land then is regarded as having passed into the ownership of the gens. This custom is frequently taken advantage of by members of a gens eager to appropriate certain bits of land desirable for garden purposes. For this reason the chiefs are actively opposed to these localized burials. When the members of a gens have once succeeded in securing their right to a plot of land, the gentile ghosts are believed to watch over its integrity, and even the king himself would hesitate to incur their wrath. Each gens owns a set of names bestowed upon individuals which no other gens is permitted to use. These names, which constitute part of the hereditary equipment of a gens, are seldom employed, however, other less socially distinctive names being used instead. In fact, there seems to be a widespread reluctance on the part of individuals to admit their gentile allegiance unless a particular situation makes this unavoidable.[2]

The minor local subdivisions of a *siga,* the *enda,* have their own petty

---

[2] We saw a while ago that among the Iroquois also the individual names (comprised in a clan set and bestowed upon individuals at a public ceremony) are not actually employed in address or conversation generally, relationship terms being used instead. This custom, then, is not local; it is, in fact, common among primitives. While in particular tribes and localities it may be due to certain specific conditions, the general and most common cause for this avoidance is to be found in magical beliefs. In communities where a personal name may be used in a magical rite directed against its bearer, it is dangerous business to be too closely identifiable in wide circles of people. As a matter of self-preservation, the symbols of individuality are preferably kept under cover. These avoidances, characteristic of societies addicted to magic, are comparable to certain habits prevalent in our own economy-ridden society. People do not usually advertise and often disguise their incomes, holdings, or bank accounts, for fear of being imposed upon.

chiefs who are held responsible for the behaviour of the members of their local group. All the chiefs in this hierarchy—*enda, siga,* gens— bear fixed hereditary titles which are bestowed upon them when they take office. These titles are traced back by tradition to the original holders of these offices. The various chieftains are given to identifying themselves with these original holders of their offices, even to the extent of referring to their apocryphal travels and other exploits as having been undertaken by themselves.[3]

I shall now give some illustrations of certain customs associated with the gentes, including their political functions.

The Leopard gens is forbidden to eat the meat of animals scratched or torn by a wild beast. This gens is in charge of a temple situated on Maganga Hill, where the mythological King Kintu is believed to have resided. No member of this gens may become an heir to the throne. The daughters of a Leopard man are permitted to marry the king, but the sons issuing from such a union are doomed to strangulation. This gens owns four estates in one of the districts of Uganda, nine in another, two in still another, and one each in three other districts. The Leopard gens supplies the king with his chief butler, also with the man in charge of the king's drinking-water, who is put to death when the king dies.

The members of the Otter gens make bark-cloth for the use of the king; from this gens comes one of the king's wives whose duty it is to make his bed; like other quasi-political functions, this duty is hereditary in the gens. After the king's death this particular one of his wives is supposed to retire to the king's temple and remain there while she lives. On Nsoke Hill stands a temple dedicated to the deified ghost of the mythological ancestor of the gens, referred to as Father. The priest associated with this temple must belong to the Otter gens.

The Elephant gens people own fifty-one estates. They are chief herdsmen to the king and also supply the royal household with a favourite variety of fish as well as a particular kind of bark-cloth they manufacture. The butter used in the embalming ceremony of a king is also prepared and supplied by members of this gens.

The Lung-Fish gens, the one subdivided into two sub-gentes claiming

---

[3] This hierarchy of chiefs, each with his hereditary office and localized functions, is another symptom of the historic development undergone by these African tribes. There is little doubt that the original chiefs were gentile officials. With the multiplication of the population and a progressive expansion of the territory, the necessities of local leadership and administration led to the emergence of several varities of subordinate chieftains. All of this is symptomatic of a society in a state of transformation from kinship groupings to territorial subdivisions subject to a centralized hierarchical political control.

descent from one Father but permitted to intermarry, owns as many as seventy estates in different sections of Uganda.

The Mushroom gens has two other totems, a snail and a small ivory disk. This gens is overburdened with duties referring to the royal household. The temple of Mende, the second god of war, is in charge of the Mushroom people. The royal drum is taken care of by this gens, it being the duty of a Mushroom man to carry this drum daily to the royal enclosure and back again. The royal stool is also in charge of this gens. From members of the gens come the king's gate-makers as well as the keepers of the gates, including that highly important personage the Chief-Keeper-of-the-Gates. He enjoys free access to all parts of the royal enclosure, which enables him to keep careful watch on the minor gate-keepers. At the accession of a new king it is the duty of the Elephant gens people to deliver twenty cows to the royal enclosure; of these the Chief-Gate-Keeper captures and keeps ten. He also appropriates one-third of the first lot of tribute delivered to the new king. When the first chiefs arrive to pay their respects, the Chief-Gate-Keeper captures one of them and does not release him until after exacting from him a payment of ten women for the king's use. The king's gourd or drinking-cup is also taken care of by this gens. The king's gate-keepers, as well as those of the king's mother and of two of the highest chiefs, are Mushroom people. From this gens also comes one of the king's wives whose duty it is to dig the first sod for the royal garden, whereupon the people are free to take up the cultivation.

The other gentes have similar totems, taboos, temples, and duties with reference to the royal household.[4]

Clans, Moieties and Totemism in California

The social systems of California have been so frequently represented as belonging to the family-village type and lacking any of the unilateral hereditary groups, that it may be worth while to deal briefly with the more recent findings which have revealed the presence of such groups, in more or less developed forms, in a number of the California tribes.

[4] Vast territories, a dense population, and political centralization can obviously not be regarded as primitive features. These things arose in Africa in the course of a long process of historic growth. While this development was proceeding, we may conjecture, the original gentes were drawn into the rising political system, gradually assuming a variety of functions with reference to the official standing at the top of the political organization, namely the king. For further details on this exalted personage see pp. 389 seq.

The material here presented deals with the Miwok and a number of tribes further south.

The Miwok were divided into two moieties with paternal descent, which were exogamous theoretically, although the rule was broken fre-

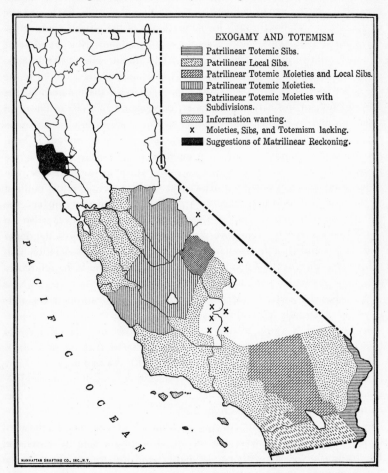

EXOGAMY AND TOTEMISM

- ▭ Patrilinear Totemic Sibs.
- ▨ Patrilinear Local Sibs.
- ▨ Patrilinear Totemic Moieties and Local Sibs.
- ▥ Patrilinear Totemic Moieties.
- ▨ Patrilinear Totemic Moieties with Subdivisions.
- ▨ Information wanting.
- x Moieties, Sibs, and Totemism lacking.
- ▬ Suggestions of Matrilinear Reckoning.

FIG. 72. EXOGAMY AND TOTEMISM IN CALIFORNIA. (Kroeber, *Handbook of the Indians of California.*)

quently enough in practice. It was thought that nature was divided into water and land or a dry and a wet half, which corresponded to the two moieties: Kigua and Tunuka. While the meaning of Tunuka is not clear, Kigua is derived from *kiku*, water. The two halves are also jokingly referred to as Frog people and Bluejay people, sometimes also as Frog and Deer, or Coyote and Bluejay. The northern division of the Miwok uses a word derived from *walli*, land, in place of Tunuka. These moieties are not themselves subdivided. Associated with each moiety is a long list of animals, plants, and objects. The natives, in fact, believe that everything in the world belongs to one or the other side. Each member of a moiety is related through his name to one of the objects characteristic of his moiety. This name, given to him in infancy by a grandfather or other relative and retained through life, refers to one of the animals or objects belonging to his moiety. This relationship may, therefore, be described as faintly totemic. Another peculiarity of these names is that they do not, in the majority of cases, correspond to the word for the totem animal itself but indicate some action or condition referring to it. This reference is also vague, in so far as no specific animal is indicated, but any number of animals might be meant. Thus there are two names, one of which denotes the yawning of an awakening bear, the other, the gaping of a salmon drawn out of the water. There is nothing in the name to indicate what animal is meant; in this case, in fact, the two animals belong to opposite moieties. It must, however, also be noted that the specific reference was known to the bearers of the name and their families and associates. In other words, the association was subjective, whereas the 'totemic' name was noncommittal in its reference. The same applies to any number of other names.[5]

A. L. Kroeber, who is our authority on this California material, ventures the abstractly possible suggestion that these names might represent a survival of a pre-existing gentile system; but he presently rejects this hypothesis, and justifiably so, on the ground that no hereditary principle seems to be present in connexion with the names, a child not being named after the same animal as its father, except in so small a number of instances that these may be attributed to accident. From the author's enumeration of the animals and birds divided according to the two sides, Land and Water, it appears that all the water animals with their associated phenomena are on the appropriate side, whereas the Land side is not so logically carried out. The Miwok do not regard these 'totem' animals as their ancestors. There is here, of course, the common Indian belief that all animals were once human or quasi-human and occupied the earth before true humans emerged, thus being the predecessors of mankind. This belief in and by itself, however, as the

[5] This reminds one of the equally passive part, as to totemic implication, played by art in Australia, where a design on the ground, for example, might mean any number of totems, according to the clan membership of the one who interprets the design.

author notes, is not equivalent to totemic descent, nor is there any apparent association among the Miwok between a 'totem' animal and a guardian spirit. A man named Bear, for example, may acquire a bear for his protector but he might also seek and adopt any other animal. Moiety exogamy, as already stated, though definitely formulated as a principle by the Miwok, does not seem to have been strictly observed by them, at least not for some time, even though the natives state that marriage within one's moiety evoked protest—but no active interference. At the present time, among the central Miwok, one marriage out of four is not exogamic. As is so often the case in other tribes, the moieties compete with each other in games and also assist each other at funerals, mourning anniversaries, and adolescent observances.

The social organization of the Yokut, whose habitat is situated south and west of that of the Miwok, is in some respects similar and in others different from that of the latter. Here also there were two moieties, exogamous and paternal. Marriage, however, was matrilocal, meaning that a husband lived with his wife's people. Here, as among the Miwok, certain animals were associated with each moiety, but among the Yokut they were also transmitted from father to child and son's child. In view of this and of the further fact that the Mono to the east and probably also the Salinan Indians to the west had a similar organization, the Yokut may be regarded as more definitely a part of this system than are the Miwok. Only a limited number of animals are associated with each moiety. Each of these functions as a hereditary totem of a paternally descended family. While the names of the people in this line of descent have no connexion with the totem animal, every member of the family regards his inherited family totem as his 'dog,' the one term applied by the Indians to any domesticated animal or captive pet. The lines of paternal descent with the same totem do, however, not constitute gentes, in so far as they bear no group names. While there is no intermarriage within these groups, exogamy, as already stated, is really controlled by the dual division. The dual divisions of all the Yokut tribes are regarded as equivalent, so that a man who marries outside of his tribe feels obligated to marry into the opposite moiety from his own as he would had he married in his own tribe.[6] The Yokut in the neighbourhood of the Miwok also identify their moieties with those of the latter, the Yokut 'Upstream' division corresponding to the Miwok Water half, whereas the 'Downstream' corresponds to the Miwok Land moiety. The representative animal of the 'Downstream' division is the eagle, with which are as-

[6] This equivalence of moieties, as between tribe and tribe, is also found on the North Pacific Coast and in Australia.

sociated the raven or crow, bluejay, road-runner, and killdeer, among the birds. The bear is most common among quadrupeds, while the fox, wild-cat, jack-rabbit, beaver, and antelope also belong to this half. The most prominent animal of the 'Upstream' division is the coyote, and with him are found the falcon, buzzard, several varieties of hawks, the owl, quail, and skunk. In the legendary traditions tales occur of contests between animals in which the dual grouping is reflected, for example struggles between the falcon and the raven or the coyote and the eagle, or the eagle and the condor. In all such cases, except where the falcon is one of the contenders, the 'Downstream' animal is victorious, although the coyote is successful in one war of the 'Uplanders' against the lake people. This 'totemic' connexion with animals seems to loom considerably in the minds of the people. When a Yokut addresses a stranger, he does not ask to what moiety he belongs, but queries, 'What is your dog?' One should, however, not be tempted to identify these moiety animals with the guardian spirits of the shamans, who also, on occasion, refer to their guardian spirit as 'the dog.' The Yokut definitely distinguished between the hereditary totemic animals which they sometimes kept in captivity but which did not confer distinctive power on the owners, and the various animals, spirits, and monsters which figured in the dreams or trances of shamans. As among the Miwok, the moieties would take sides in formal games and at the mourning rites the divisions acted reciprocally. Each moiety also had its distinctive style of body paint. As moiety descent was unilateral, the children of a brother and those of his sister belonged to opposite moieties. This, the author suggests, may have contributed to the permissibility of cross-cousin marriages among the Miwok, and the same type of marriages were, perhaps, valid among the Yokut also, although definite information in this regard is lacking.

The western Mono, at least those on the San Joaquin and probably some of the local groups on other streams, had totemic moieties. In one respect these were different from those of the Miwok and Yokut. They were not exogamous: marriages took place within a moiety as well as between moieties. Descent was paternal, and a set of animals were associated as 'pets' or 'dogs' with each moiety. These animals, especially the birds, were sometimes reared in captivity. When they grew up, they were either despoiled of their feathers by their masters or permitted to go free unharmed. The personal name here was of the Yokut rather than the Miwok type. It was inherited, usually meaningless, and carried no totemic connotations. As among the Yokut, there were two chiefs, each identified with a moiety. The chief of the one represented by the eagle had precedence over the other. One of the moieties corresponded to the Miwok 'Land' and the Yokut 'Downstream,' the other, to the Miwok 'Water' and the Yokut 'Upstream.' The first had two subdivisions. Its totemic animals were eagle, crow and chicken-hawk. The other moiety also had two subdivisions, and its totemic animals were buzzard, coyote, a variety of hawk, and the bald eagle. It seems probable, as the author suggests, that Mono totemism was even looser than that of their neighbours. It is said that here it was even permitted to change one's moiety.

Among the Serrano, considerably farther south, we have once more the exogamous and totemic moieties of the Miwok and Yokut type. Associated with these is a series of bands or local subdivisions. One moiety is called Wild-Cat, after its chief totem; as its other totems it has the puma or mountain-lion, wild-cat's older brother, and crow, its kinsman. The other moiety is referred to as Coyote, and its other totems are the coyote's older brother, wolf or jaguar, and its kinsman, the buzzard. The word for totem means 'my great-grandparent.' The institution of moieties is traced to the Creator. Moiety members are on joking terms with each other. Members of the Wild-Cat moiety are reputed to be lazy and dull, those of the Coyote moiety, swift and perhaps unreliable. The precise status of the subdivisions or local divisions or bands is not determined with precision. Rather than being sibs, these bands seem to correspond to the village communities of northern and central California. Each band owned a creek and an adjacent tract. Its most permanent settlement or 'village' was usually situated where the stream emerged from the foot-hills. The band tended to be rigidly exogamous. There was a strong tendency for particular bands to intermarry. Each band belonged either to the Wild-Cat or the Coyote moiety. As to exogamy, the determining element seems to have been band rather than moiety membership, since some of the bands which regularly intermarried belonged to the same moiety. Each band had its hereditary chief, *kika*. Associated with each *kika* was an assistant chief who had ceremonial functions. The moieties, at least in some instances, had certain common religious functions, while in others they figured in a reciprocal way. Each moiety tended the dead of the other moiety before the cremation. In some instances also one moiety cooked and served food to the other on ceremonial occasions.

Among the Cupeño, whose social organization has undergone recent changes, there were two moieties, here too called Coyotes and Wild-Cats, the first containing four, the second three gentes. The moiety totem was called 'great-great-grandparent,' but the belief in descent was lacking. A certain playful opposition existed between members of the two moieties who frequently taunted each other with being unsteady or slow-witted. Mourning ceremonies were a moiety matter, but the opposite moiety always participated. The nature of the gentes is not clear, although it is said to have been chiefly religious.

The social organization of the Cahuilla, neighbours of the Luiseño, has been relatively well preserved and it may perhaps be regarded as corresponding to the former organization of the Luiseño, who have disintegrated too far to permit even a tentative reconstruction. The Cahuilla have moieties that are patrilineal, totemic, and exogamous. The names, as among the Cupeño, are Coyote and Wild-Cat. The exogamous rule is, at least at present, observed imperfectly. The number of gentes is large, while the membership of each is small. They are associated with localities or named after places. All members of a gens trace their descent in a male line from a relatively recent ancestor. Two or more gentes might inhabit one village, and the members of one gens may be found in different villages. On account of the paucity of data, Kroeber is uncertain whether these 'gentes' are actually such, or rather represent what we should call paternal families comprising only actual blood-kindred. The totemic associations of the moieties are observable in ritual and myth. The images for the mourning anniversary are made by each moiety for the other.

The Diegueño are divided into exogamous gentes. The totemic moieties, however, are lacking. The gentes are definitely associated, at least in the minds of the natives, with localities. The gentile names, when translatable, seem to be place names. Marriage here is patrilocal.

The Mohave, the easternmost of these tribes, comprise exogamous nameless gentes of totemic reference. All the women born in a gens bear one identical name, although they may in addition also be known by nicknames or other epithets. These names are inferentially totemic, though not identical with the word used to designate the totem itself. The gentes have no religious functions.

To reduce this abbreviated sketch of the unilateral systems of California to a common denominator, I append a map on which the distribution of the different types of social systems is indicated. (Map, Fig. 72, p. 355).[7]

---

[7] This sketch is based on A. L. Kroeber's *Handbook of the Indians of California*, pp. 453–744.

Chapter XXIII

UNILATERAL FAMILIES

The Iroquois

As already intimated a while ago, the real unit in the inheritance and election of chiefs among the Iroquois is not the clan as such but a smaller unit comprised within the clan, the so-called *maternal family*. This social group is second to no other in importance in the socio-political organization of the Iroquois, and we must now clarify its structure and functioning. The term 'maternal family' is, strictly speaking, a misnomer, for the group is not a family in the accepted sense of the term. Instead of being bilateral, as is the family, it is unilateral like a clan. An Iroquoian maternal family comprises a woman, her children —male and female—the children of her daughters, of her daughter's daughters, and so on. The number of generations in a maternal family may be three or four but seldom more than five, and the number of individuals comprised in one may reach fifty but seldom more than that (see Fig. 73, p. 362). It will be seen that in a genealogy pivoted in one woman there will be individuals who will not belong to that woman's maternal family, namely her son's children with their descendants, her daughter's son's children, and so on. These persons will belong to other maternal families, namely those of their mothers. The situation, therefore, is like that encountered in a sib, when accompanied by exogamy.

In general it may be said that the maternal family represents a sort of prototype of a clan, in so far as it is unilateral, comprising individuals related through the mothers. The difference between a maternal family and a clan, on the other hand, consists in the fact that whereas in a clan, as we saw, some or even many persons are not related by blood, though assumed to be so related, in a maternal family all the component individuals are connected by genealogically traceable ties of blood relationship. Another feature which distinguishes a maternal family from a clan is the greater readiness of the former to break up, thus forming new maternal families, a phenomenon which has been known to occur also in clans, but not so frequently or typically. The head of such a

361

family is a woman, the oldest one in the group, who in the typical and original form is the actual biological progenitor of the group, in a true sense, a group-mother. With reference to the Iroquois it is customary to designate her as the 'matron' of the maternal family. When a matron dies she may leave a number of daughters differing, more or less, in age. The rule is that the oldest of the daughters becomes the new matron of the family. But suppose this oldest woman is less popular or wise or

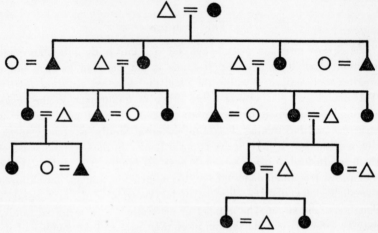

FIG. 73. MATERNAL FAMILY.

In this sample of a small maternal family, the component individuals are marked by black circles (women) and black triangles (men). Those represented by white circles and triangles do not belong to this maternal family.

otherwise fit for leadership than the next sister, who is a little younger. In such a case it might happen, and did in fact occur, that either the older sister will be side-tracked in favour of the younger one, or some of the members of the original maternal family, perhaps the direct descendants of the oldest sister, will cling to her, as the rightful heir to leadership, while others, perhaps the direct descendants of the younger sister, will prefer to submit to the latter's leadership and will split off from the original maternal family with the younger sister as their matron. In such a case two maternal families will be the result. Such instances, as I have said, have actually occurred among the Iroquois, as well as other forms of splitting off from a maternal family.

The major function of the Iroquois maternal family is a political one, in so far as each of the fifty chieftainships of the League is a hereditary prerogative of a maternal family. This chieftainship, though hereditary, is also, within the limits of the maternal family, elective: theoretically, that is, *any* man within the genealogical tree of maternal descent may succeed to the chieftainship, after the death of the former incumbent. Thus a younger brother may succeed his older brother or a sister's son may succeed his mother's brother (that is, in our terminology, a maternal nephew succeeds his maternal uncle), or a sister's daughter's son succeeds the mother's mother's brother (that is, in our terminology, a maternal great-nephew succeeds his maternal great-uncle). As a matter of fact, however, by far the most frequent successions among the Iroquois were from older to younger brother or from maternal uncle to maternal nephew.

The matron of a maternal family had everything to do in connexion with the selection of the successor as well as his appointment as a chief. When a chief died, a messenger was sent out with the news. He would run from village to village emitting the traditional call, *gwā-á! gwā-á! gwā-á!* Then the people knew that a chief was dead. When the precise facts were ascertained, the matron of the deceased's maternal family—who, it will be remembered, was frequently his own mother—determined upon the successor, say her next younger son. Thereupon she called a meeting of her maternal family, which comprised, in the first place, the women and men of that group, but was also attended by other members of the clan of which the maternal family was a part. All informants are agreed, however, that at such meetings the controlling voice was that of the maternal family of the deceased and, within the family, that of the women of the group rather than the men. Then the matron presented the name of the candidate to the gathering which, at least in ancient days, invariably ratified her choice. In more recent days, when the prestige of the matron began to wane, sharp differences of opinion have been known to arise on such occasions, or even more violent conflicts, perhaps leading to a splitting up of the family. When the candidate suggested by the matron was thus ratified, she was constituted a walking delegate, and in this capacity called individually upon all the chiefs of the clans belonging to the phratry of the deceased, that is, the chiefs of the so-called Brother Clans. Upon ratification of the candidate by these, she then called individually upon the chiefs of the clans of the opposite phratry, that is, of the Cousin Clans. When these also had ratified her choice, the name of the candidate was next presented by the matron to the council of League chiefs for their ratification. In this final instance ratification was taken for granted, as apparently it was invariably accorded. At the same meeting the council of League chiefs determined upon the date of the formal or ceremonial 'raising' of the new chief, an event much heralded and accompanied by elaborate and impressive proceedings, in the course of which the names of all the chiefs of the League were publicly recited, and the new chief was reminded of the functions and duties of an Iroquois chieftain. After this he started upon the exercise of his chiefly functions.

The chief's dependence upon the matron was not at an end, even then. Jealously she continued to watch over his activities and behaviour. If these were deemed satisfactory, nothing further happened, and in time her vigilance became relaxed. On the other hand, if the new chief deviated in any way from the behaviour expected of an Iroquois chieftain—if, for example, he was guilty of prevarication, or permitted himself to lose his temper, or worse still, if he became involved in any treacherous dealings with the League's traditional enemies, such as the Algonquin—the matron proceeded to take steps to warn the derelict, and ultimately to depose him. After the first offence she called upon him and in ceremonial tones reminded him of his unworthy behaviour, concluding with a warning that, in case his misbehaviour continued, she would call on him once more and then again for the last time, accompanied by a warrior chief, and would then depose him. As human matters go, if the chief was the sort of a person who would offend once, he was likely to do it again. Then the matron, true to her warning, called on him for the second time and, standing before him in formal posture, delivered the following standardized address: 'I am now admonishing you again to desist from your evil ways, and should you further refuse to accede to and obey this request, then I shall call upon you for the third and last time accompanied by a warrior chief. I shall take the deer's horns [symbol of chiefly rank] from off your head and with a broad-edged stone ax I shall cut the tree down [meaning that she will depose him from his position as a chief of the Confederacy]. Then your duties as chief of our family and clan will cease and you shall be chief no longer.'

If the behaviour of the chief remained unsatisfactory, the matron in due time carried out her threat. She called upon him, accompanied by a warrior chief who went through the motions of taking the deer's horns from off the chief's head and handing them to the matron. After this act the chief was regarded as deposed and the matron presently informed the chiefs of the League of what had occurred. In cases such as this the League council would meet in special session, as hurriedly as possible, and instead of initiating the usual procedure of nomination and election of a new chief, they would appoint a successor at that very session.

It will be clear from what was said that even though no woman, so far as known, ever occupied the position of a regular chief in the Iroquois Confederacy, women were more influential than men both in the election of chiefs and in their deposition. In other words, the public opinion of the clan and maternal family was involved in the limited choice of these chieftains, and that public opinion was more significantly that of the women than of the men of the group.

The available data on the relation of the maternal family to the old long-house residences of the Iroquois are not by any means satisfactory. While some authors continue to state that a long-house in olden days was the home of a maternal family, or that the members of a maternal family occupied a single long-house, there is no certainty that this was actually the case. In point of the specific individuals constituting the household of a long-house, the assumption of a one-long-house—one-maternal-family arrangement is certainly incorrect. We saw a minute ago that the children of the matron's sons, for example, did not belong to her maternal family; but we know that they lived in her long-house. What seems to have been the fact, however, is that certain long-houses were identified with particular maternal families, in so far as the larger number of the members of such a family lived in the house, and in so far also as the majority of the residents of the house belonged to one maternal family, and in so far, finally, as the dominant tone of the household was determined by such considerable overlapping between it and a maternal family. There is good reason to believe that a number of ceremonial functions were associated with maternal families, although here, once more, more precise data are unavailable, except in one matter. The preparation of the famous medicine *ga'nōda*, which according to tradition was made up of the constituent parts of many animals and had the property of curing a large number of diseases, was an hereditary prerogative of certain maternal families. Fifty maternal families comprised chieftainships, others did not. But the social status of all was the same.

The matrons of all the maternal families of the League, as a group, also functioned as a unit in a socially constructive direction, by exercising as a body a restraining influence upon the behaviour of the young warriors whenever such restraint seemed to them desirable. Considering the ease with which warfare could break out under the old conditions of traditional enmity, say between the Iroquois and Algonquin, many a devastating war must have been averted by the wise counsel of the matrons, who would warn the young and impetuous warriors, before it was too late, against dangerous attacks or discourtesies and thus prolong the duration of peace. It will be easily understood that

Iroquois braves, many of them potential chiefs, could ill afford to disregard the opinion or counsel of the matrons on whom their chances of
attaining chieftainship so largely depended.[1]

The Patwin

Another sample of the unilateral family, in this case paternal, has been
found among the Patwin, a southern branch of the Wintun Indians of
northern California. This is what McKern says of blood relationship
among these people: 'It was regarded paternally. While blood affinity
in the female line of descent was known to exist as a fact in nature,
tradition was here the defining factor rather than natural law. Traditionally, then, one's maternal relatives were not regarded as one's folk
in a consanguineous sense. Nor were they entitled to family privileges.
This was true to the degree that a man might marry his cross-cousin, the
daughter of his mother's brother, but it was taboo for him to marry the
daughter of his father's brother. The family accordingly consisted,'
continues the author, 'of the patriarch or headman, his brothers (he
being the elder), his sisters and sons and daughters, his son's children,
his brother's sons, and much other paternal descendants as he might
have.' By all signs then we have here a typical paternal family in composition, a fact further stressed by the author's statement that a woman
belonging to such a family would not lose her traditional membership
in it after marriage.

Certain kinds of personal property were passed on by inheritance
along the paternal family line. Almost invariably, these things were
willed to the incumbent before the death of the owner, and the recipient
was 'the next in the paternal line of descent.' Among the things so willed
might be included, for example, a ceremonial costume or pipe, a feather
belt, some shell beads, a magical stone, or a secret medicinal formula.
A paternal family possessed no house or houses it could call its own,
nor did it constitute one household, but that portion of a dwelling house
in which some of the members of one paternal family resided was the
joint property of that family, as well as such household utensils as

---

[1] Some fifteen years ago, when the predecessor of this volume, *Early Civilization*, first appeared, it was justifiable to regard the Iroquois maternal family as
an exceptional phenomenon. Since then parallel instances have been discovered in
more than one tribe and territory. What then had seemed an exception and almost
an unicum, now appears to be a fairly common tendency of primitive social organization. It should not surprise me, in fact, if within the next few years the
unilateral descent group or lineage should be found to constitute a frequent functional unit among primitive tribes (for further examples see below).

food baskets, mats, mortars, pestles, cooking and eating utensils, and also the granary. When the head of a household died, these articles of property, of which he was merely a custodian, descended into the keeping of the next person in line of paternal descent whose household might use or need these articles. The headman of the paternal family, some of the members of which belonged to the household of which the head had died, determined upon the individual who was to replace the deceased headman. It should be understood then that the head of the household was merely a custodian of the. properties owned as an hereditary privilege by the paternal family some members of which formed part of the particular household. Upon the death of the last male representative of the paternal family which owned these objects, they were buried, burned, or destroyed in some other way. Individual names, as among the Iroquois, were the property not of individuals but of a group, with the difference that whereas among the Iroquois the clan, not the maternal family, owned the names, among the Patwin it was the paternal family. Each person, male or female, received the name of the nearest deceased paternal relative. After the death of an individual, the name was returned to the family store of unclaimed names (the Iroquois, it will be remembered, called this 'putting the name away in a box'), to be used by the nearest paternal male relative when born.

Though the headmen of paternal families were important and influential, the village chief stood above them. As his position and functions were interrelated with those of the family headmen, a few words must be said about the village chief. His position was hereditary and whenever possible passed from father to son. A very definite system of primacy existed among paternal relatives who could succeed a chief. The order was: elder son, younger son, elder brother, younger brother, elder brother's sons, younger brother's sons, father's elder brother, father's younger brother, elder son's sons, younger son's sons, father's elder brother's sons, father's younger brother's sons, brother's son's sons, and finally, father's brothers' sons' sons. If there were several persons in any of these categories, they belonged to the line of succession in the order of their ages. Though relationship to the dead chief was a primary qualification for succession, ability and popularity also counted, especially in the following situations: when there were two candidates of equal paternal affinity to the deceased chief; when the deceased chief was the last representative of his line; and when a new village unit was being organized.

The power of a chief was great; deposition was out of the question, and when a chief resigned in favour of his son, he did so voluntarily.

Anyone who disobeyed him was forced to leave the village. If disloyalty was shown by a group rather than an individual, such a group would leave the village, and if sufficiently strong, might establish an independent community. Even in such extreme cases, moreover, the chief elected to head the new village was, if possible, a paternal relative of the former chief. The elders participating in councils were chosen by the village chief from the oldest and most respected family headmen. At all such councils the final word belonged to the chief. When an important political or territorial matter was due for discussion, the chief was notified. If he felt that the occasion so warranted, he would then call a council of elders or family heads. 'Meeting at the chief's house, they would build a great fire on the hearth place, close the door and smoke-hole with skins or mats, and "sweat." While they were sweating, the question would be brought up and discussed lengthily. The chief usually took very little part in such discussions. Nor would he, as a rule, announce his decision at the conclusion of the meeting. When the chief declared the council at an end, the members would run out of the house and plunge into the river. After a swim they would return to their respective homes. This council meeting was designated by the natives by a term meaning "they who meet together by sweating." '

The chief, who was expected to be familiar with the local centres of food-supply and the proper time for harvesting, divided the nut-, fruit-, and seed-producing localities belonging to the villages into sub-areas, which were assigned by him to the various families during harvest-time. These 'picking-grounds' were reassigned each season, in accordance with the relative sizes of the various families. Meat products also, such as fish, flesh, or fowl, provided they were of sufficient quantity, were brought to the chief, who distributed them to the various households. At the beginning of the fish-spawning season, the chief announced a certain day to be devoted to fishing by the entire community; on that day all were obliged to fish, nor was anyone permitted to fish before the appointed time. Daughters or sisters of a chief enjoyed special social distinction— children were forbidden to laugh in their presence and adults treated them with respect. A chief's wife, apparently, was not thus honoured, indicating that the prestige implied followed the lineage.

The author refers to the paternal family groups as 'functional families.' Each functional family was the possessor of an esoteric ritual or medicine. These were family property inherited by it as a unit, so that its individual members living in different villages had no exclusive claim to their use. Individuals also owned their personal charms, provided

they were 'active' members. These charms, like other personal possessions, were inherited in the male line.

In his study McKern classifies these functional families into ceremonial, trade, shamanistic, and official families. A family in possession of certain secret medicines and individual charms was qualified
to perform a specified ceremony. In such cases the ceremony and the
family were known by the same name. These ceremonies or dances were
held once a year in the ceremonial house and witnessed by all members of the family, but the active participants were men only. It should
be noted that the family 'secret' here was not the ceremonial activity
as such, dance-step and the like, but rather the medicine and its preparation. This family prerogative had to be exercised before the ceremony
could be performed.

Each trade family was fitted for the performance of a particular
economic function by the possession of inherited charms or medicines.
Thus one family specialized in salmon-fishing, another in the making
of arrow-points, still another in goose-hunting or duck-trapping. Other
families prepared salt, or manufactured ceremonial drums. (These
drums were hollowed-out sycamore logs from six to eight feet in
length; they were placed upside down in the dance-house and beaten by
the drummer with his feet.) There was also a family which specialized
in making ceremonial head-dresses. All these trade families exercised
their functions through the men only. When, as in the case of the canoe-
basket family, the actual craftsmen were the women, the descent of
these techniques was passed on as usual in the male line, that is, not from
a woman to her daughter but to her brother's daughter. Shamanism was
always the function of a shamanistic family. In addition to the inherited
right of certain charms and secret rites connected with shamanistic
practices, a man of such a family was prepared for his art by a paternal
instructor, himself a shaman, who exercised his own supernatural powers
to induce the spirits to commune with the novice and to listen to the
latter's incantations. A village might have several shamanistic families,
each independent of the others and with its own ritualistic secrets and
medicines. The shamans were always men.

In an official family, the actual family function was exercised only
by one member at a time, although the family prestige extended to all
members. For example, the fire-tender in the so-called *hesi* dance belonged to a family in which that function was hereditary. He was a
possessor of a charm and a secret magical formula which ensured his
success in the performance of this function. The functional families had

names some of which can no longer be translated; those that can are descriptive of the family functions.

It is interesting to note what the author says about the practice of adoption. Some of the families of the Patwin apparently had no traditional functions. These, we are informed, contained exclusively individuals who were actually related by descent. They were, then, paternal families in the strict sense. Those families, on the other hand, which had functional peculiarities, apparently the majority, often included individuals of assumed rather than actual relationship to the family: such were the persons adopted into a family. 'If a shaman,' writes the author, 'had no near paternal relative upon whom to bequeath the charms and secrets of his practice, or if the proper paternal descendant lacked ability or interest, a youth with no consanguiniary claim to the privilege but credited with mental capabilities and a receptive attitude might be selected by the shaman to be his successor. For this privilege he would pay the adopting shaman a standardized sum. He would be given a name from the supply pertaining to the shaman's family and would then serve an apprenticeship under his benefactor's instruction. Thenceforth he would be considered a regular member of that particular shamanistic family, not only the possessor of the family's charms and medicines, but as the undisputed blood descendant of his predecessor and instructor.'[2] When a shaman was in especially high repute, it was customary for several ceremonial families to adopt him, in which case he was regarded as related by descent to all such families. 'Thus the element of adoption in no way weakened the importance of paternal descent as the basic element in such institutions,' concludes the author. 'Descent might be true and might be fictitious, but it was always essential.' It will be readily seen that families with such adopted members were really gentes in miniature.

If for one reason or another, some individual did not care to or did not regard himself as fit to exercise a family function, he was at liberty to refuse the inherited prestige. Such individuals were the non-active members of a functional family. As between the charms and medicines which belonged to a family function, the charms were always the property of individual members, whereas the medicines were common property of all active family members.

To understand fully the social status of these functional families it must also be remembered that they were not in a strict sense profes-

[2] W. C. McKern, 'Functional Families of the Patwin' (*University of California Publications in American Archaeology and Ethnology*, vol. XIII, p. 253). The Patwin data are gleaned from McKern's study.

sional groups, since the hereditary family functions did not constitute their sole or even chief occupation; in addition to exercising these functions, the functional families also participated in all the other social, economic, and political activities of the tribe.

Ontong-Java

Another instance of the paternal family is found among the Ontong-Javanese, inhabitants of an island group situated to the northeast of the Solomon Islands. The latter, of course, are Melanesian, but the natives of Ontong-Java are Polynesian. The social organization of these people is anything but simple. In addition to the family or household we find here a 'canoe-owning or fishing group' which consists as a rule of a group of brothers led by their father, and a 'house-owning group,' which is a group of women connected by maternal descent, the house belonging to a mother, her daughters, etc. Without pursuing any further these interesting groupings, let me proceed directly to an examination of the so-called 'joint family' which is the paternal family of the Ontong-Javanese. The joint family comprises individuals connected by paternal descent with an ancestor usually not more than six generations removed. The members of such a group, which, as will be seen, strictly corresponds to the maternal family of the Iroquois, own in common a patch of land on which coco-nuts are grown. When misfortune of any sort overtakes a member of a joint family, he turns for comfort or assistance to his group-mates. A number of religious rites are carried out by the joint family as a unit. The leader or headman of a joint family is its oldest living male. The gathering of coco-nuts takes place under his supervision, and he also functions as a ceremonial official at a number of joint family rituals. Among his other duties is that of co-operating with the grandparents of the younger folk, if indeed he is not one of them, in teaching the former the traditions of the tribe; they in turn owe him obedience. All the main villages are divided into strips of land which are owned by joint families. Some of these are poor and own only one such strip. The wealthier ones may own several and, in fact, an entire island. The houses which stand on such strips can in no sense be brought into relation with joint families, for as just explained, the house-owning group is matrilineal, whereas membership in the joint family is patrilineal. Thus it is only by chance that any person will find himself living in a house situated on a strip belonging to his own joint family.

Among the common duties of the members of a joint family is the defence of any of its members against attack, such, for example, as is likely to occur when a member of the group has offended someone of another joint family and an act of vengeance is being anticipated.

Every joint family owns a song of its own called *hamaha*. In these songs, performed on various occasions, for example at the burial of a joint-family member, the deeds of the founder of the group are recounted or some dramatic event in its history, such as a famous fight, is extolled.[3]

The Dobuans

Another highly interesting instance of the unilateral family has been described by R. F. Fortune among the Dobuans, the island of Dobu belonging to the same archipelago east of New Guinea to which also belong the Trobriand Islands, so carefully and exhaustively studied by Malinowski. A description of Dobu society may well begin with a plan of a Dobu village as given by the author (see Fig. 74). In the centre of the village there is a clear space with only scattered croton shrubs. Here are buried the maternal ancestors of the villagers: their mother's mother's brothers, maternal grandmothers and their brothers, and so on for many generations back. To these the village once belonged. Now it is owned by their maternal descendants, the present villagers. The paternal ancestors of the villagers are buried in the villages of other clans, those of their mothers and female ancestors. Each villager, male or female, owns a house site and a house. But the woman's house and site are inherited by her from her mother, or her mother's sister. It is therefore situated in this instance in the village to which the woman's maternal ancestors belonged. Marriage being matrilocal, the husband comes from another village. His house, therefore, is situated elsewhere, in the village of his maternal ancestors.

This gives one an idea of the two dominant units in Dobuan society and their relationship. One unit is a maternal family, the kernel of which here is a man, his sisters, and his sisters' children, but it extends of course to his sisters' daughters' children, and so on, but not to his sisters' sons' children, and so on. This group is called a *susu*. In each village there is a small number of such *susu*, from four or five to ten or twelve, all claiming common female ancestors and an unbroken descent from her through females. This relationship is, of course, theoretical, as the actual named relationships do not go back further than four or five generations. The term *susu* itself is also that for mother's

[3] For further details see Ian Hogbin, *Law and Order in Polynesia*.

milk. The other group is a marital one. A household consists of a man, his wife, and their children. Each marital group, as we saw, owns two such houses, one belonging to the husband, the other to the wife, each in their respective villages. The couple with their children live alternately in the woman's house, in the village of her matrilineal kin, and in the man's house, in the village of his matrilineal kin. These migrations take place periodically, usually once a year, although some couples move more frequently than this. When a couple resides in the wife's village, the husband belongs to the group designated by the author as 'Those-resulting-from-marriage,' or in common parlance, the 'in-law' group. Owners of the village use personal names when speaking to

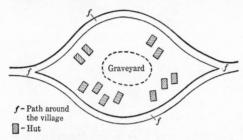

FIG. 74. VILLAGE PLAN. (Fortune, *Sorcerers of Dobu.*)

each other, although to elders they prefer to use relationship terms. Those-resulting-from-marriage are not permitted to use the personal names of any one of the owners down to the smallest child, excepting in the case of a father to his own child; they must use a term of relationship. Those-resulting-from-marriage, if they are men, are always uneasy about their wives' fidelity. There are many other men about, and in case of a quarrel the man knows that as an outsider he will receive but little support. Besides, he is jealous. When the women work in the gardens, in fact, children are usually enlisted as watchers and informers.

There is a great deal of friction between the two groupings, the *susu*, on the one hand, and the marital grouping, on the other. This friction takes the form of accusations of sorcery and witchcraft, and also expresses itself in terms of jealousy, quarrels, attempted suicides, and what the author calls 'village incest,' meaning irregularities between close relatives in the village. A corpse of a person belongs to his *susu*. At the burial of the deceased the private mourning takes place within the house in the presence of the members of his or her *susu*; the spouse, on the other hand, though he or she also mourns, kneels on the ground outside the house, away from the corpse and not looking upon it. After the mourning period is over, a year from its beginning, comes the final rite. If the surviving member of the family is a widower, the wife's sisters' sons and her brothers lead him by the hand to the farthest eastern point of the island. There they will wash off his body-coat of charcoal in the sea, then cleanse him, anoint his body with oil, replace his body-ornaments, which were removed during the mourning period, and place fragrant herbs in his armlets; then they will lead him by the hand to his own village. He may never enter their village again.

After the mother's brother's death, a man succeeds to his property and status and from this time on, he calls his mother's brother's son 'my son,' instead of cross-cousin. This is only one of the instances of change in terminology after a death, so common among the Dobuans, an interesting subject which cannot be pursued here any further. What thus passes from a man to his sister's child is his village land, his personal name, his skull, his status, his village palms and fruit trees. None of these things may a child inherit through the father—they must come from the mother's brother. A canoe descends within the *susu*, so also fishing-nets, stone adzes, ornamental valuables and all movable personal property, as well as the crop of the deceased's garden gathered in during the gardening season in which the death took place. As between the marital grouping and the *susu*, it will be seen, the gains from the social system are weighted heavily in favour of the *susu*. The tensions and frictions arising from the tugging and pulling between the two institutions are too serious to be taken lightly. The destructive and murderous magical procedures, so numerous and ubiquitous among the Dobuans, are allocated reciprocally to members of one or the other of the two groups, the *susu* or village owners, and Those-resulting-from-marriage. The magical arrows thus kept flying, from day to day, and especially at night, are usually between members of these two social groupings. (See Plate XXX.)

PLATE XXX. THE INTERIOR OF THE GREAT DOBU DAIMA OF URAMA, NEW GUINEA

The warriors live in the small cubicles on either side of the long hall. Their families dwell in small detached houses, and no woman or child is permitted to cross the threshold of the warriors' clubhouse. (Captain Frank Hurley, *Pearls and Savages*. By permission of the publishers, G. P. Putnam's Sons.)

Chapter XXIV

CHIEFS AND POLITICAL ORGANIZATION

The Eskimo

I have had occasion to point out before that leadership, in one form or another, not only is omnipresent in human society but goes back to conditions among animals. Leadership among men is reducible to two factors, one psycho-biological, the other more purely social. Certain individuals are 'born leaders,' as the saying goes; they possess those qualities of will, character, sang-froid, ambition, which mark them for positions of dominance or control. And again, social institutions, if they are to function, require some sort of organizational centre as well as an edge of power, however small, which position, from earliest times on, was filled by appropriate individuals almost spontaneously or automatically. Presently the leader becomes surrounded with emblems and traditions of authority, and a little later his position is further enhanced and fortified by the principle of succession of office.

In range of power and the social prominence of their class or individual position, chiefs among different primitive tribes vary greatly. Among such tribes as the Eskimo, for example, we can only discover the irreducible minimum of leadership. Among many tribes of American Indians, chieftainship, though more pronounced in authority, is limited by tribal councils (generally of elders), men who accept the supreme authority of the chief but also limit it by their own influence, thus providing a sort of balance wheel of political power. Among the more highly organized American tribes, such as the Iroquois or Dakota, the supreme chiefs, supported in these cases by the principle of inheritance, rise to a status of considerable personal authority and social influence. Among the most advanced American tribes, finally, namely those of Mexico and Peru, the power of the supreme chief becomes very great if not absolute.

In Australia, where political organization is amorphic, individual chieftains nevertheless stand out as the agency which keeps social things going smoothly, and at times, by dint of personal merit and character, some may rise to a position of marked influence which, on occa-

375

sion, reaches beyond tribal boundaries. The chiefs of Polynesia are representatives of a ruling class or at least a class from which rulers come. Their authority is backed by great religious sanctity, and it is provided with a cutting edge of great range and power in the institution of taboo which the chief can impose at will on anyone or anything. In Africa, finally, the supreme chief is frequently a king, surrounded by the elaborate paraphernalia of authority and power, and combining in his person the functions of ruler, judge, and military leader. In the exercise of his duties or prerogatives he is assisted by a standing army or at least a body-guard, as well as by a galaxy of other officials whose power is second only to that of the supreme ruler himself. In order to draw the lines of the chief's authority more precisely and define more accurately his relation to political organization, we shall now examine a number of typical forms of leadership in the setting of various political systems.

It is fitting here to begin with the Eskimo, who, as I said, lack chieftainship in the narrower sense. In the normal run of life, from day to day, there is here no constituted authority, excepting only that inevitable prestige attaching to those who lead their mates on certain particular occasions. The expert hunter will take charge when reindeer or walrus are to be chased, the man of high military valour will command his fellows on the rare occasions of inter-tribal strife. Their authority is not greater than that normally granted to the expert, although it may become considerable if the situation is particularly stringent. As soon as the emergency is over, the prominence of the leader of yesterday presently fades and he relapses to the more modest status of an average Eskimo performing the routine functions of daily work at the side of his companions. It follows from this that no extension of authority beyond the span of an individual life is to be found here. A man leads in the field of his special capacity, but the mantle of authority is his alone. His son, for example, is neither slated to take his place, nor will he occupy it unless he proves himself deserving, as an individual.

If any authority of a more permanent nature is to be discovered here we must turn from the secular leaders to the men of religious prestige, namely the *angakut* (singular, *angakok*). By dint of their command of superearthly power, these magicians are at all times respected and feared, and on special occasions they come to occupy the very centre of the social situation—for example, when a taboo or sacred prohibition has been transgressed. The mammals of the sea, we know, and all activities connected with them must not collide with other equally important activities centring about the reindeer. According to tradition, the sea-mammals have originated from the fingers of Sedna, the supreme female deity and ruler of the sea and its creatures and of the winds as well. In view of this supernatural derivation of sea-mammals, atonement must be made for every animal killed. When a seal is brought in, all work must be stopped until it is cut open. When the animal killed is a ground-seal, walrus, or whale, there follows an enforced rest, or partial rest, lasting three days: no new sealskin articles may be made during this time, but previously made articles may be repaired. No deerskin obtained in the summer may be touched until the first seal is killed with the harpoon. Later, when the first walrus is caught, the work on deer must stop once more. These last regulations represent aspects of the taboo cycle just referred to which separates the activities centring around the deer from those concerned with sea-mammals; the two sets of functions must be kept strictly apart (and so strict are these injunctions that in certain localities even dogs are not permitted to gnaw deer bones during the seal season and *vice versa*). Again, deer bones must not be broken during the period when walrus hunts are organized, and so on. Special sets of taboos of a nature common in primitive societies are imposed upon women before and after childbirth or during the menstrual period. They are not permitted to eat raw meat, they must cook in separate pots, and they are enjoined from participating in festivals.

Strict though these taboos may be, they are not always obeyed. Transgressions, though rare, are known to occur, accidentally in some cases, wilfully in others. According to Eskimo ideas, the transgression of a taboo takes the form of a black object which attaches itself to the culprit. This 'object,' though invisible to ordinary humans, can be seen by the animals as well as by the *angakut*. When a hunter transgresses a taboo, the animals, frightened by the black object, will avoid him, thus preventing him from killing them. The dire result may be a famine from which all the people will suffer. To forestall so great a calamity the culprit is expected to make a public confession,[1] whereupon his guilt is regarded as wiped out and normal conditions are restored. Should confession be withheld, however, famine or disease will ensue. It is here that the *angakok* appears upon the scene. In fact, one of his principal functions is to save the situation in grave emergencies such as this. When the crisis has become acute and no confession is forthcoming, the *angakok* summons a public gathering and by means of his

---

[1] This feature is particularly interesting on account of the rarity of the confessional in North America, the only authentically known other instance being the confession of 'sins' which takes place among the Iroquois in conjunction with the sacrifice of the white-dog ceremony.

magical powers detects the culprit who, when thus identified, stands in serious danger of his life, or at least did so stand in ancient conditions.

Australia

In Australia, authority is divided between the old men generally and the magicians and chiefs in the narrower sense. Of these three sources of authority that of the old men is perhaps the most uniformly distributed among Australian tribes. It penetrates into every corner of native life. The respect for age, symbol of experience and wisdom, is universal here. Instances are extant where men of extreme age, though no longer in possession of their physical prowess or mental capacity, continued to be revered on account of their age alone. The old men here are the accredited teachers of the young. During the periodic initiation ceremonies at which the younger folk are inducted into an ever-widening circle of ceremonial and religious participation, the old men are invariably the ceremonial officials who, in addition to their educational and supervising functions, also perform whatever surgical or magical rites may be involved. At the *intichiuma* ceremonies, as we saw, they stand in the very centre of the situation, handling the sacred *churinga*, performing the ceremony of blood-letting, and partaking, first among those present, of the substance of the totemic animal. It is the old men, again, who are thoroughly familiar with the location of the secret totemic spots where the *churinga* are kept, each one manufactured, if surreptitiously, by an old man. They also constitute the councils which decide on expeditions of revenge, and are at least called into consultation by the tribal chieftain when he resolves upon holding one of the occasional 'markets' for the exchange of local specialties in manufacture.

The Australian magician has not a monopoly of magical knowledge or technique. In this sense every Australian, male or female, is a magician; but the professional ones among them are experts. They know a larger number of magical formulae and are skilled in the execution of the various techniques. More often than not, a magician achieves the height of his fame only after reaching an impressive old age. At the same time many of the most influential old men are also magicians, and it is they who initiate the younger men into the relevant esoteric knowledge and tricks of the art.

Over and above these more or less prominent individuals, there are the accredited chieftains of local groups, sibs, and, in some instances, tribes. They also exercise important ceremonial functions and raise their voices prominently at local or tribal councils. The prominence to which some of these headmen attain among the people is illustrated by Howitt's account of Jalina-Piramurana who in the early sixties of the last century was headman of a totemic sib and the recognized leader of the Dieri tribe. 'He was described,' writes Howitt, 'as a man of persuasive eloquence, a skilful and brave fighting man and powerful medicine-man. From his polished manner Whites called him the "Frenchman." He was greatly feared by his own and the neighbouring tribes. Neither his brothers (both of them inferior to him in bravery and oratorical power) nor the elder men presumed to interfere with his will or dictate to the tribe except in minor matters. He decided disputes, and his decisions were received without appeal. The neighbouring tribes sent messengers to him with presents of bags, red ochre, skins and other objects. He decided when and where the tribal ceremonies were to be held, and his messengers called together the tribes from a radius of one hundred miles to attend them, or to confer on inter-tribal matters.

'His wonderful oratorical powers made his hearers believe anything that he told them and always ready to execute his commands. He was not by nature cruel or treacherous, as were many of the Dieri, and when not excited was considerate, patient, and very hospitable. No one spoke ill of Jalina-Piramurana but on the contrary with respect and reverence. This is understood when Mr. Gason adds that he distributed the presents sent to him amongst his friends to prevent jealousy. He used to interfere to check fights, even chastising the offender, and being sometimes wounded in doing so. On such occasions there would be great lamentation, and the person who had wounded him was not infrequently beaten by the others.

'As the superior head-man of the Dieri he presided at the meetings of head-men, sent out messengers to the neighbouring tribes, and exercised his privilege of giving away in marriage young women unrelated to himself, separating men from their wives when they could not agree, and of making fresh matrimonial arrangements.

'He periodically visited the various hordes [Howitt's term for local groups] of the Dieri tribes from which he also periodically received presents. Presents came to him from localities a hundred miles away, being passed on from tribe to tribe.

'He was one of the great medicine men but would only practise his art upon persons of note such as heads of totems [meaning sib chiefs] or his personal friends.

'He was the son of a previous head-man who was living during Mr.

Gason's residence in the country and who, although too infirm to join in the ceremonies, gave advice to the old men. He boasted that he had the command of his tribe when his son acquired it. He was believed to be proof against magical practices such as striking ["pointing"] a bone. 'Jalina-Piramurana succeeded to and indeed eclipsed his father.'[2]

The tribal councils of the Dieri consisted of the heads of local divisions, medicine-men, fighting men, and the more influential of the old men. From time to time these met in council, the deliberations being held in secret. This last feature, in fact, was held to be so important that whosoever was found guilty of revealing to an outsider the subject of a council's deliberations was doomed to die. The usual topics of discussion at such councils were death by magic or other forms of murder, breaches of the moral code, especially in relation to the marriage regulations, and the revealing of council secrets to women or other uninitiated persons.

In connexion with the political organization of these tribes the institution of messengers is of interest. Messengers are used by the headmen, councils, and other groups in authority to communicate to particular individuals, local groups, or tribes such information as that a ceremony is to be held and when, that a meeting is to take place for the purpose of barter, that a *pinya* party (expedition for blood-revenge) is on its way, or that the people are to gather for a communal feast. A messenger is usually equipped with a so-called messenger's stick with a varying number of notches cut into it, which are used as a sort of mnemonic device to impress the nature of the message on the mind of the particular incumbent.

In some tribes messengers are especially selected on each occasion, in others there are particular men in each locality who are widely known as messengers and are permitted to pass unmolested through the territory of any tribe in that district, even though some of these may be at war with the senders of the messenger. Among the Kamilaroi each sib claimed its own messenger. When messengers are to be sent to a hostile tribe, and on other occasions where danger is involved, women are chosen for the purpose. Whenever possible, the women selected belong to the tribe to which they are to be sent. Such a delegation, if successful, indulges in a period of licence in which the members of the delegation and the local tribesmen participate. On such occasions no resentment is shown by the women of the tribe to which the delegation was sent. The tribe which sends the messengers is, in its turn, equally insistent that

[2] A. W. Howitt, *Native Tribes of Southeast Australia*, pp. 297–299. (By permission of The Macmillan Company, publishers.)

the period of licence be properly observed. Such at least is the case among the Dieri. Should the women shirk this obligation, they do so at the risk of death upon their return. The return of a feminine delegation of this sort is described by Mr. Gason in the following words: 'The head-man and the principal old men received them kindly and congratulated them upon their safe return, but appeared anxious and clutched their spears in an excited manner. No one but the head-man spoke to the women immediately upon their return; but when all the men were seated they were questioned as to the result of the mission. The result was at once communicated to all the people in the camp, who rejoiced if it were favourable but who became fearfully excited and seemed to lose all control over themselves if it had failed, rushing to and fro, yelling, throwing sand into the air, biting themselves, and brandishing their weapons in the wildest manner imaginable.' [3] While Mr. Gason's report may be somewhat exaggerated, it is obvious that the persons involved felt very keenly on the subject.

Among the Dieri a messenger announcing a *pinya* wears a net on his head with a wide band around it in which a feather is stuck; he is painted with ochre and pipe-clay and in the string girdle at the point of his spine a bunch of emu feathers is stuck. With him he carries part of the beard of the deceased or some balls of pipe-clay taken from the heads of the mourners.

The Maori

As an illustration of a more highly developed form of chieftainship let us examine the position and functions of a chief among the Maori of New Zealand. To discourage hasty generalization, let me say at the outset that the Polynesian chief, though always representing one of the more marked forms of personal prestige and exaltation in primitive society, varies in the degree of his eminence and in other particulars in the different island groups of Polynesia. Thus chieftainship in Samoa or Tahiti should not without further ado be identified with chieftainship among the Marquesans nor with that of the Maori. The following sketch, therefore, must be taken as applying specifically to the latter people.

The social groupings of Maori society were in brief as follows: The smallest well-defined social unit was the *whanau*, or extended family. The human composition of this group was not always the same. Sometimes a man, his wife, and his children occupied a house by themselves, thus constituting a small *whanau*. Or again, several brothers with their wives and families might compose such a group. More frequently still,

[3] *Ibid.*, p. 299.

a group consisted of an old man and his wife with their children and grandchildren. It will thus be seen that numerically the *whanau* was not a very large group, although Best mentions one rare instance of a *whanau* that comprised ninety-two persons. This group was of utmost importance in social and economic affairs. Besides occupying a common dwelling house or sometimes several such houses, they performed field work, under their headman, on one or more plots held by the family as a unit. Small eel-weirs and canoes were owned by a *whanau*. On account of its small size this social unit was well adapted to communal work such as rat-trapping, fishing from a canoe, or building small eel-weirs on a branch stream.

The next wider group was known as a *hapu*, a group comprising some two or three huhdred people the members of which traced their descent from a common ancestor. These groups sometimes bore the name of their ancestor, or they might adopt that of a woman of rank, or they might be called after some special incident. The *hapu* was not an exogamous group; marriage was in fact encouraged within its limits, but neither did the practice of endogamy constitute a requirement. What is even more important for the understanding of a *hapu*, sometimes wrongly designated as a clan, is that it was not in a true sense a unilateral group. It is true that descent through one parent was sufficient to establish membership in a *hapu*, but in tracing such descent both the maternal and paternal lines were utilized. When the parents belonged to different *hapu* the children claimed membership in both; when the parents' *hapu* was the same, the children were tied to it by the bonds of double relationship. This fact should be kept in mind, in the face of the tendency among the Maori to trace one's main line of descent from one important ancestor, following if possible the male line alone.

The relationship between the *hapu* and a local group or village was not precise. Frequently, perhaps more commonly than not, a village was held by a single *hapu*, but then again if the village was large, several *hapu* might occupy it together, their quarters being delimited by small fences or palisades. In other instances a number of small villages might be occupied by members of a single *hapu*. In all these cases there were, of course, some members present in a village or local group who came from other *hapu* and had married into the one claiming ascendancy in the village. In persons who had married into another *hapu* and continued to reside in its village for several successive generations, the kinship bond with their own *hapu* tended to weaken. In the course of time, they or their descendants came to regard themselves as members of the *hapu* in which they resided.

The largest kinship group, which included several *hapu*, was the tribe, or *iwi*. All the *hapu* comprised in an *iwi* traced their descent from the common ancestor of the latter.

There was, finally, a further bond, even wider in scope, which united a number of tribes into a unit of kinship, or more accurately, quasi-kinship. This latter grouping was based on the traditional arrival in New Zealand about the year 1350 of a fleet of canoes from Tahiti and Raratonga. Even though these immigrants, when they arrived, found a large resident population which had accumulated as the result of previous voyages and the natural multiplication of the settlers; and even though, furthermore, marriage between the older and more recent arrivals was general, a definite social value came to be attached to the arrival of the later immigrants. The names of the principal canoes which then appeared in New Zealand waters were Tainue, Arawa, Takilimu, Matatua, Aotea, and Tokomaru. These names continue to recur in Maori poems and stories. The tribes of the Maori trace their descent from the crews of these vessels, several tribes claiming this lineage with each of the canoes. Thus arose another grouping called, after a canoe, *waka*. The *waka*, in this latter sense, is then a group of tribes whose ancestors formed the crew of one of these famous fourteenth-century canoes. Even today any native knows to which canoe he belongs, and in many a modern meeting house a drawing will be found, on a rafter or a wall slab, representing the ancestral *waka*. To repeat, then, in descending order: first comes the *waka* consisting of several tribes, which, as a social bond, is rather weak; then the *iwi*, or tribe; then the *hapu*, a loosely unilateral kinship group; and finally, the *whanau*, or extended family.

Many authors have maintained that the individual family such as ours, consisting of father, mother and children, did not, except in a primary biological sense, exist among the Maori. This, however, is contravened by more authoritative opinion based on a minute examination not merely of the recognized groupings but of the actual behaviour of the people. When looked at from this standpoint, the individual family emerges. Individual marriage, though complicated by frequent instances of polygyny, was an established institution, and many marriages were of long duration, extending on occasion even to a lifelong union. The relations of parents to children were more often than not characterized by intimacy and affection, the father in particular playing a prominent role in guiding the education of the child. In economic matters, though greatly overshadowed by the functions of the *whanau*, the individual family was also characterized by a certain independence. In the stories one finds references to wives grumbling at the failure of husbands to provide sufficient food, and to husbands complaining about wives negligent in cooking or the weaving of garments. In other words, the individual family, though clearly the least prominent functional group in Maori society, was there nevertheless, not merely as a biological unit but as a socio-psychological one, with at least certain common social and economic functions.

Over and above the kinship and territorial groupings, we find among the Maori a social stratification into chiefs, commoners, and slaves. Within the class of chiefs a further distinction must be drawn between the *ariki* and the *rangatira*. An *ariki* was a high-born chief, descendant of first-born children in a continuous elder line; the *rangatira*, on the other hand, were the junior relatives of the *ariki*. The commoners were people of relatively low social standing due to a constant descent from younger members of junior branches of a family or to the intermarriage of people of relatively low rank with slaves, or to the loss of prestige through being the offspring of persons redeemed from slavery.[4]

Personal relations between the people and their chiefs, though respectful, were not such to any exaggerated extent. Acts of submission, like crouching or other obeisances, were unknown, nor were any special terms of respect used in addressing a chief in ordinary conversation, beyond those prescribed by etiquette as due to married people or aged persons generally. In other words, the special position of a chief expressed itself in his functions rather than in the people's treatment of him. Best enumerates the following eight *pu manawa*, or 'qualities of man,' which a chief was supposed to possess: he must be industrious in collecting food; able in settling disputes; brave; a good leader in war; expert in carving, tattooing, and ornamental weaving; hospitable; clever in building houses, *pa*,[5] and canoes; learned in tribal boundaries.[6]

Even though birth was the main determinant of a chief's prestige, the Maori, it will be seen, had a proper regard for such personal quali-

---

[4] In addition to these classes distinguished by their rank, social prestige was attached to other groups such as priests, wizards practising black magic, teachers of traditional lore. These people, though they generally came from the families of chiefs, owed their status to training rather than to birth. Similarly, expert tattooers, carvers, specialists in a variety of economic activities, and also warriors, owed their position to skill, that is, personal qualification rather than birth. To all these individuals the term *tohunga* was applicable. A *tohunga* of whatever birth is an expert. This sketch of Maori society is based on the study by Raymond Firth, *Primitive Economics of the New Zealand Maori*, pp. 96–117.

[5] A *pa* was a fortified village. Such fortifications consisted of huge earthworks in the form of ditches, ramparts, scarps, and terraces, topped with palisades. An unfortified village was called *kainga*.

[6] This list may be profitably compared with the qualifications of an Iroquois chief (p. 335).

fications as character, foresight, initiative, and general ability in organization and command. When the first-born lacked any or all of these, the leadership of the tribe would pass him by to be vested in a younger brother, if capable, or in the nearest male cousin, usually in the paternal or even in the maternal line. An illustration is the following concrete instance: Te Hira was by birth the hereditary chief of Te Taou, *hapu* of Ngtiwhatua, but neither he nor his brother were men of force or character. Hence the father passed his authority on to his nephew. To this man the *hapu* now looked for guidance. He became the recognized political head, conducting the affairs of the people until his death.

But Te Hira could not be deprived of the prestige of birth or of his status as an *ariki*, the lineal heir. 'In certain magical and ceremonial performances,' writes Firth, 'he and he only could officiate. Thus in the imposing and lifting of *tapu*, the carrying out of ritual observances, as at the birth of children, hair-cutting, fixing of boundary marks, defining tribal territory, the recital of curative magic and the like, no one else could take his place. The reception of visitors; speech-making on state occasions, if for the tribe as a whole; the recital of genealogies, and the giving and receiving of presents, were all the privileges of Te Hira. To him also belonged the right of bestowing names on children and of asking for female children of other tribes as the betrothed wives of the younger men of his own people. With him rested the guardianship of the tribal heirlooms and of the talismans of fisheries and forests. All this centred around him as the *ariki*.' [7]

It will be seen then that the hereditary *ariki*, though deprived through personal incompetence of his authority as leader of the tribe, still retained numerous functions belonging to him alone. The tendency, moreover, was for later more competent descendants of such a noble to recover the functions lost by their unfortunate forebear.

One common mark of a chief was the number of slaves he had in his household. The majority of these slaves represented prisoners taken in war. The slave class, it should be noted, was rather mobile in its composition, since especially the women of that class tended to intermarry with low-rank free people, and the resulting offspring were free. The children of slave girls, taken as concubines or secondary wives by a chief, though always bearing a certain stigma of their parenthood, frequently rose to positions of power and influence. The status of slaves, here as among many other primitive peoples, was relatively good. Their relations with the master were fairly pleasant. Though slaves were, of course, expected to do the menial work, they were well fed and

[7] *Op. cit.*, p. 93.

adequately housed. On the other hand, it must not be forgotten that, unprotected as they were by any social rules, they stood at the mercy of their master, and were on occasion called upon for a human sacrifice or even to provide the relish at a feast.

In order to maintain his position, a chief, in addition to birth, also needed wealth. Every man of rank was expected to proffer hospitality to travellers, relatives, and other visitors. Every chief aimed at acquiring a reputation for liberality. The story is told about one chief who, when his gardens were destroyed by swamp hens and caterpillars, composed a song in which he expressed his shame and grief at there being nothing to offer to any prospective guests, and announced his intention to flee to his more remote settlements. About another noted ancestral chief it is related that on one occasion, when his supplies were all exhausted, he was visited by a large body of relatives-in-law. His shame was great. 'He could not open his mouth to say a word, he felt so disgraced at not having any food to set before his guests.' That very night he left his village and departed far away to seek a new home. In addition to entertaining strangers and visitors, it was incumbent upon a chief to distribute wealth freely as presents among his own followers. The chief was also expected to assume the initiative in the construction of large public buildings, boats, and the like.

What is said here should not be interpreted as implying that the Maori chiefs represented a rich or well-to-do class distinguished by their wealth. This was by no means the case. A large part of a chief's income accumulated from presents received from his own people and from visitors, and more was provided by his own labour as well as that of his wives, slaves, and other attendants. This explains the great role which labour, largely that of others but in part his own, played in the life of a chief. Though he was not as continuously busy with numerous kinds of occupations as were his subjects, he was not in any sense a gentleman of leisure. Generally he occupied himself with carving, the making of weapons and ornaments, as well as the direction of more important economic enterprises.

As already stated, the Maori had a consummate appreciation of experts in such undertakings as the planting of the *kumara* or sweet-potato, or the construction of a new house. The direction and leadership of the work were undertaken by a *tahunga*, or expert, skilled in the technique of the craft, and versed in magical spells and other rituals necessary to secure the favour of the gods. On such occasions also the chief provided the initiative. He exercised his oratorical gifts to stress the importance of the work or its value as an enhancement of tribal prestige.

Much of the power, prestige, and social position of Maori chiefs, and of Polynesian chiefs generally, is implied in the statement that the chief had *mana*, supernatural power, which was believed to reside in him, particularly in his head. Of all the things—and they were many—through which *mana* could operate, the head of the chief was the most exalted, symbolizing the acme of strength and refinement of *mana* power. This explains the fact that the chief in this area was so often associated with priests who were also genealogists. These men were experts in the conduct of sacred rites, past masters in the recitation of traditions and magical formulae, as well as connoisseurs of genealogical records which connected the great chief with his even greater ancestors, remote descendants of supernatural beings.

The Baganda

Now let us return to the Baganda, whose sib system we have already examined, to inquire into the nature of their political organization and kingship. The supreme power in Uganda is centred in the king, who is forbidden to marry any woman but a Muganda. No woman may occupy the royal throne, nor any person other than of royal blood. Thus the sons and grandsons of a king are his successors. At the same time the totems of the king's sons (or princes) are those of their mothers, while the royal totems connected with the lineage from which kings may come—the Lion, Leopard, and Eagle—are seldom mentioned. Next to the king the most exalted persons in the kingdom are the two queens: the king's wife (generally he marries his sister) and his mother. Princesses are not permitted to marry (the penalty once was death); princes, on the other hand, are encouraged to marry so that the supply of heirs may not become exhausted. When sons are born to the king, the king's brothers surrender to his sons their principal estates, situated in different parts of the country, and accept smaller estates in their stead. The king's brothers, after having surrendered their estates, are still eligible to the throne, but their sons are debarred.

The king and all the chiefs own individual drums, which are distinguished by their beats. Curiously enough, the eldest son of the king may not reign; instead he is expected to take care of his brothers. These princes are a source of constant uneasiness to the king, and many were the instances when princes were put to death as soon as the successor to the throne was assured. The princes, provided they survive, are represented by their own chiefs in the districts where their estates are situated. Although the king may express his own wishes with reference to the successor to the throne, the decision rests with three of his chiefs: Katikiro, the prime minister; Kimbugwe, who has charge of the king's umbilical cord; and Kasuju, who is guardian of the heirs-apparent.

When a king dies, the prospective heirs arrive in the capital, accompanied by certain ones of their chiefs. Pointed rivalries are common on these occasions, and so the chiefs and their followers come prepared to fight. One of the chiefs then confronts the princes drawn up in a row and, pointing at the one expected to reign, says, 'So-and-so is king,' and then adds, 'Those who wish to fight, let them do so now.' Should an alternative aspirant be present, spears are passed around and a fight ensues between the rival princes and their supporters, which continues until one of the princes is either wounded or killed. The victor is declared king.[8] One of the king's sisters is chosen queen on this occasion.

At the termination of this ceremony the king and his queen make a peregrination to the hills of Budo, the fetish, which is guarded by three chiefs who live in houses without fences for fear that these might be used as hiding places by a rival prince. Before the king is admitted to the temple a sham battle is enacted. There follows what is, in fact, a coronation ceremony extending over two days. The details of this procedure are too numerous to be reproduced here. The last phase is described by Roscoe in the following passage: 'The King and the Queen were carried from the enclosure down the hill to a place where some trees were grown for making spear shafts; one of these trees was cut by the priest, and handed to the King with the words: "With this overcome your enemies." The procession went forward to another place where a species of creeper was grown for making baskets; the priest took a few pieces of the creeper, and handed them to the King, saying: "May your life be like a basket which, when it falls down, does not break as an earthen vessel does." They passed on to another place where some wild plantains grew; a few seeds were taken from the trees and handed to the King with the words: "May you surpass your subjects in wisdom and understanding." *Semanobe* accompanied the King to the next hill named Sumba, and presented him to the priest *Mainja*, after which he took leave of the royal party, and returned to Budo. The ceremony called "Eating the country" was now complete, and the King was from that time looked upon as the legally appointed sovereign. From the temple of *Mainja* the party was conducted by the chief *Sebwami* to the place appointed for holding the ceremonies of mourning for the deceased King.

---

[8] When the rightful heir is a minor or for some other reason proves unacceptable to the chiefs, the prime minister appoints a regent, a post always filled by a man, for a woman cannot be tolerated on the throne even temporarily.

Each new King sent the son of the chief *Kasuju* to the god Mukasa with a large present, to announce his accession to the throne. This present took a peculiar form, and consisted of either nine, or ninety, specimens of whatever was offered. During the journey the messenger travelled alone in the royal canoe *Namfuka*, and took his meals alone; he wore two bark-cloths, as though he were a prince, and entered the temple wearing a white goatskin apron, the dress of the priests.' [9]

While the dead king's body is being embalmed with much ceremony, the new king goes into mourning. This usually lasts for some six months, during which time a temporary residence is erected for the king in the proximity of Budo, where he henceforth lives surrounded by the residences of numerous chiefs, many of whom are soon to be deposed and replaced. At some time during this period the queen and the king's mother take possession of their hereditary estates, which up to this time had been occupied by the late king's sister and mother, who now receive smaller estates in their place. When the period of mourning comes to an end the king beats his drum to make the fact known. Presently the chief of the Grasshopper gens arrives in the king's enclosure, bringing with him a gazelle. The king chases the animal and kills it. Meanwhile the king's men scan the public roads in search of anyone wearing his bark-cloth tied in a roll and swung over his left shoulder. When two such men are found, they are captured and brought to the royal enclosure. One of these men is spared while the other is strangled and his body thrown into a river under the papyrus-roots so it can never be found.

After this the king selects his permanent residence. To quote from Roscoe's picturesque description of a royal enclosure in the making: 'The workmen were soon busy erecting houses on the site chosen by the King. Each district-chief had the duty of providing for his royal master some special house which had its particular place inside the enclosure. Each district-chief had also to build some portion of the high fence which enclosed the royal residence. There was one plan followed, which had been used by the kings for years without variation. The enclosure was oval shaped, a mile in length, a half mile wide, and the capital five or six miles in front and two miles on either side. The part which was called the back was reserved for the King's wives, who had large estates there for the cultivation of plantain trees. The King also had his private road to the Lake through these estates, by which he might escape, if in danger from rebellion or sudden war: several canoes were also kept in readiness, in case of emergency, for flight to the islands of the Lake,

---

[9] J. Roscoe, *The Baganda.* (By permission of The Macmillan Company, publishers.)

where he could form his plans and restore order. The top of the hill was reserved for the King's own residence; the chiefs built dwellings around the royal enclosure according to their rank and the part of the country to which they belonged. There was one principal entrance with a wide gateway and a house to guard it, and eight other small gateways on various sides of the enclosure, which latter were private for the use of the King or his wives. Each gate had its guard houses both inside and outside; the gates were kept fastened and were only opened to those who had the right to pass them. The interior of the enclosure was divided up into wide blocks of houses with wide roads between them with gates and gate-keepers to guard each block, so that even within the enclosure it was impossible for the women to pay visits with one another without permission, or for other visitors to pass in or out without special leave. . . .

'On the road from the main entrance to the council chamber stood the best houses and there the strongest guards were stationed. The roads were lined with retainers who guarded the King and were ready for any emergency. These retainers lived in tents made from cow hide, as less inflammable than grass, in order to diminish the risk of fire in the royal houses, which were entirely constructed of reeds and grass, so that when once a fire broke out, it was a serious question whether any of the buildings could be saved. The chiefs who were acting as guards to the King had to provide their own tents during the months that they were in office. The Sovereign's retainers wore a special dress of antelope-skins slung over the right shoulder, passed over the left arm, and tied round the waist with a plantain-fibre girdle. Their wants were supplied from the King's own lands . . . they were on duty in relays for a month at a time. . . .

'As there were no lamps or candles for night work, torches were made from dry reeds; the manufacture of these reed torches became quite an industry and enabled the King to have the forts lighted up every night. Bark-cloth trees were planted near the main entrance by the priests of each principal deity, at the time when the King's houses were built, and offerings were placed under each of them for each particular god. The trees were carefully guarded and tended because it was believed that if they grew and flourished so the King's life and powers would increase.' [10]

The enclosures of the queen and the king's mother were situated at some distance from the royal residence and separated from it by a stream of running water. 'Two kings cannot live on the same hill,' said the people. The royal residence was connected with these enclosures of the

[10] J. Roscoe, *The Baganda*, pp. 200–202.

queen and the king's mother by straight roads lined on both sides with homes of important chiefs, so that communication could always be maintained without fear of attack by wild animals.

The newly elected king sent to each of the important deities presents consisting of female slaves, animals, cowry-shells, and bark-cloth. He returned the royal spear to Budo and sent with it an offering of women, cows, goats, nine of each; nine loads of cowry-shells and of bark-cloth, together with one of the deceased king's widows, who became Budo's wife. This woman was given the title *Nakato*, the name of Budo's first wife, who after giving birth to her child caused the sacred well *Nansove* to spring forth on Budo Hill. Within the royal enclosure a vast army of cooks was always kept busy, the cooks being mostly women servants and slaves who worked under the supervision of one of the king's wives. Twice a day baskets of food for the entire retinue were placed before the king for inspection. He himself ate alone, served by one of his wives who was not permitted to look at him while he was engaged in eating. 'The lion eats alone,' said the people. If anyone happened to come in and surprise the king while he was busy with his meal, he was promptly speared by the ruler, and then the people said, 'The lion when eating killed so-and-so.' The remnants of the king's repast could not be touched by anyone but were given to his favourite dogs.

In the course of this early period of the king's reign a number of other ceremonies took place, in connexion with one of which some unsuspecting passers-by were seized on the high road and put to death—to invigorate the king.

Of the twelve principal chiefs of Uganda, ten presided as district-chiefs over the ten districts into which the country was divided; the remaining two chiefs, who in some ways were more important than any of the others, were the ones we are already familiar with: Katikiro, prime minister and chief justice, and Kimbugwe, of the umbilical cord. These two chiefs had no districts of their own but, like the king himself, they owned estates in the different districts. These administrative subdivisions of Uganda had their boundaries marked by a stream of water, a small wood, or some other natural feature.[11]

[11] In addition to the divisions of Uganda proper certain tributary countries should be mentioned here which were in part subject to the Baganda. In the north lived the Bosoga, from whom a regular tribute of goats, cows, and slaves was expected. The country to the southwest of Budu belonged to the people of Koki, who paid tribute in iron hoes and cowry-shells. These people had a king of their own but they were not powerful enough to withstand the raids of the Baganda. To the west lived the Ankole, who kept peace with the Baganda at the cost of periodic contributions of herds of cattle. The Kiziba, who occupied the

The enclosure in which Katikiro, the prime minister, had his residence resembled the royal enclosure with its courts and gate-keepers. Only friends, important chiefs, and other specially privileged individuals could reach him freely. In his capacity of chief justice he settled the cases which were beyond the competence of the other chiefs. His decisions, however, were not regarded as final until confirmed by the king himself. Minor courts were held by chiefs inferior in rank to the prime minister as well as by sub-chiefs. A considerable variety of crimes were recognized. A distinction was made between murder and homicide, the former involving malicious intent. For homicide the fine consisted of cows, goats, bark-cloths, and women, twenty of each. In other instances only part of the fine was paid on the spot, the rest remaining unpaid, perhaps for years, until the man owing the fine could bring some charge against the one in whose debt he stood; when the case was tried, he would excuse the man from paying the fine, on condition that he forgave him his own debt.[12]

The chiefs had to spend a large part of their time at the capital nor were they at liberty to leave for their own districts unless permitted by the king. In their absence the administrative duties were performed by temporary officials.

All the land was regarded as belonging to the king, excepting only the freehold estates of the gentes, over which the king had no direct control. These estates, however, were not exempt from the payment of taxes and the furnishing of labour to the state. The chiefs residing on such estates, moreover, could be deposed by the king at will. If no of-

district south of Budu, sent tribute of cowry-shells and trade goods which they themselves obtained from tribes living still farther south.

[12] Roscoe throws interesting sidelights on the probity of the courts and the character of some of the punishments. 'If a man thought that he was losing his case, he would endeavour to bribe the judge; if he proposed to give him a slave, he would place his hand flat upon the top of his head as if rubbing it, when no one but the judge was looking; this signified that he would give the latter a man to carry his loads. If he proposed to give him a woman or a girl, he would double up his fist and place it to his breast, to represent a woman's breast; if he proposed to give him a cow, he would place his fist to the side of his head, to represent a horn, etc.' (*Ibid.*, p. 261.) The judges, we are told, were not immune to such suggestions. As to the penalties, there were such as these: A man convicted of adultery was usually put to death; if spared, he was maimed: a limb was cut off or an eye gouged out. A seduced woman was compelled by torture to name her seducer or to describe a personal peculiarity or some mark on his body. If a man of this description was found, he was fined or put to death. 'In order to arrive at the truth,' a man who denied a charge made against him might be stretched out with his arms and feet tied to stakes driven firmly into the ground. A piece of bark-cloth was fastened to his body and set smouldering. As the fire reached the body, the man would, of course, 'confess'—anything. Then he was fined, or killed. It seems that our 'third degree' had its worthy precedents.

fence could be shown against a chief turned out of his estate, he was permitted to take his wives and cattle along with him; if, however, he was guilty of some misdeed, the cattle and wives were appropriated by the king—provided he was able to find them. In the minor estates the sub-chiefs were masters and in local affairs their control was absolute, but in all matters referring to state work they were expected to consult their district-chiefs.

Each district-chief had to maintain a road about four yards wide leading from the capitol to his district, and the sub-chiefs had to maintain similar roads connecting their sections with the residence of the district-chief. In cases where the roads led over swamps, the road-builders' task was an arduous one; frequently bridges had to be erected to span the streams. If the stream proved too wide for a bridge and the detour to a bridgeable place was too great, papyrus stems were broken over their roots, and in this way a precarious crossing was secured. If in crossing such a bridge anyone slipped, he was doomed. No attempt was made to rescue him, as it was believed that he had been claimed by the spirits of the river, whose vengeance was feared in case a rescue was attempted.

In the capital itself roads about twenty yards wide were maintained. The labour required for the erection of residences, enclosures, fences, and roads had to be supplied by the entire country, and it was the duty of the prime minister to see to it that this was done expeditiously. Every household called upon for workers was also expected to furnish twenty-five cowry-shells. Of the large quantities of shells thus amassed, two-thirds went to the king while the Katikiro claimed one-third, which he divided as follows: one-third was given to the chiefs who had supplied the labourers, one-third to the overseers, and one-third the prime minister kept for himself. When work was in progress upon a road, any passer-by could be stopped and forced to help for awhile, before he was permitted to proceed.

To defray the cost of various state enterprises taxes were imposed by the king. This procedure is described by Roscoe in the following words:

'When the time to collect the taxes was growing near, the King, the Katikiro, and the Kimbugwe fixed the exact date and it was then announced in the council that the taxes would be collected on such and such a date. Special tax collectors for each district were appointed by the King. To these district collectors, the Katikiro, Kimbugwe, the Queen, and the King's mother added their own representatives, one each, and the district-chiefs also added a representative. The six men thus appointed to a district went to each part of it; the principal sub-chiefs

were first visited by them in person, then they chose and sent messengers
to each of the less important chiefs. The King's tax-collector and his
associates then returned to the district-chief's enclosure where they were
entertained while the work was being carried out by their men. The first
thing to be done was to count the houses in each sub-district and to ascertain the number of the inhabitants; the tax collector would then settle
with each chief what amount he was expected to send to the King. One
cowry-shell was brought by the collector's assistant to represent each
cow, and after these had been counted the assistants went back to collect the tax. The amount usually demanded was a fixed number of cattle from each sub-chief and a fixed number of bark-cloths and one hundred cowry-shells from each peasant; of the smaller chiefs, each paid a
number of goats and also a few hoes. It frequently took two months or
more to collect the tax, because the bark-cloth and hoes had to be made
and the cattle collected. When this was accomplished, each servant took
his amount to the district-chief on the appointed day; the cowry-shells
and bark-cloths were counted and tied up in bundles, while the cattle
were sent on. The King's tax-collector took the whole amount to the
Katikiro, who had to examine it and hear the details as to the number of
houses and people in each sub-district and as to how many bark-cloths
and cowry-shells had been collected from them. If the amount was correct the Katikiro took the whole to the King; if it was wrong, the tax
collector was required to return to the district and to gather what was
missing according to the instructions from the Katikiro. The chief of
the district received a portion of the taxes for himself and for his sub-
chiefs; the King took half for himself, while the Katikiro, the Kimbugwe, the Queen and the King's mother also had their portions. Each
sub-chief was given a small portion of the amount which came from his
own district; the King, the Queen, the King's mother, the Katikiro, and
the Kimbugwe kept the whole of what came from their own estates in
addition to the portions they received from the taxes of the whole country. The tributary states paid their tribute through the chiefs under
whom they were placed, making their payment with cattle, slaves,
ivories, cowry-shells, salt, hoes, and the like.' [13]

For minor services the king was wont to secure young boys and girls
from people in different parts of the country. Relevant statistics were
obtained by representatives of the king whose task it was to induce the
people to supply information about their neighbours and acquaintances.
Then an arrangement was made with the district-chiefs, whereupon the
children were furnished. The king kept for himself the boys and girls

[13] Roscoe, *op. cit.*, pp. 244–245.

he liked best, turning the others over to his mother, the queen, the Katikiro, and the Kimbugwe. A great many individuals throughout the land lived on the private estates of chiefs, working and on occasion fighting for them as compensation for tenure.

The Incas

Our last sketch of chieftainship and political organization, in this case primitive only in the loosest sense of the word, is to comprise the state of the Peruvian Incas, which was situated in the littoral region of the Andes of South America, just south of the sources of the great Amazon. The history of the rise and spread of the Inca Empire in a continuous series of military conquests presents one of the most dramatic accounts known to us of the expansion of a state by means of war. In the eleventh century A.D. the Inca state, as it became known to later history, was as yet non-existent. The unit of political organization among the tribes of the Andean highlands was the *ayllu*, or tribe. These tribes were ruled by petty chiefs known as *sinchi* ('strong men') who were war-time leaders chosen by the heads of households in an *ayllu* for purposes of directing military operations against unfriendly neighbours. Of these tribes the one fated to become the Inca Empire was only one among others. The first partly historical figure among the leaders of this tribe was Sinchi Roca, who was chief during a large part of the first half of the twelfth century. It was he who initiated the systematic war-like policy of the tribe, beginning with the consolidation of his authority in the immediate vicinity of Cuzco, the administrative seat of the tribe. It is around the personality of Roca that the first steps centred in the direction of developing that ritualistic setting and royal pomp for which the later Incas were so famed. The military equipment of the Inca leader may be gathered from the fact that the fourth Inca, Mayta Capac, who ruled in the second quarter of the thirteenth century, was able to assemble an army of some 20,000 men. With the rule of this Inca dates the beginning of their practice of transferring whole communities of conquered peoples to districts already permeated with Inca rule and ideas. This practice was supplemented by another, namely having considerable numbers of well-educated persons settle down in newly conquered regions to promulgate there the principles of the Inca state. When forced colonists of the type just mentioned were transferred to districts of the Inca state, the rulers were careful to assign to them locations conforming, wherever possible, to their original geography and climate. Thus mountaineers were not placed on the coast, or *vice versa,* nor were people from hot countries forced to submit to the rigours of a cold climate.[14]

At the death of the fourth Inca, the state already comprised a district of some 120,000 square miles. With the rule of the fifth Inca, Capac Yupanqui, begins the systematic and more rapid expansion of the Inca state, accompanied by a development of their peculiar system of political and economic organization, this process going on at an accelerated rate until the reign of the tenth Inca, Tupac Yupanqui, who ruled in the third quarter of the fifteenth century, just preceding the arrival of the Spaniards.

During the period preceding the systematic expansion of the Incas and in the early centuries of that process, there were many states in the Andean region of different degrees of size and organization. The simplest ones of these were those mentioned before, which consisted of a mere *ayllu* or tribe under the leadership of a *sinchi*. More advanced states consisted of a combination of several *ayllu* under the rule of a permanent chief or *curoca*, whose authority was hereditary. Still other states were formed through a combination of several curocadoms. These finally grew into still larger kingdoms of a feudal character, examples of which are still to be found both on the coast and in the highlands. It seems almost certain that in all these states the land of an *ayllu*, or the tribal land, was owned not individually but by the group as a whole, the usufruct being distributed among the heads of the households. As the Inca state developed, the land of each *ayllu* was divided into three portions, one for the Sun or the state religion, one for the Inca or the state, and one for the inhabitants of the *ayllu*. It is certain, at any rate, that no one was permitted to sell or buy land, and also that if an *ayllu* or household happened to find itself in possession of more land than was needed for its purposes, the residual land reverted to the state. The chiefs of the *ayllu* made an annual distribution of lands among the heads of the families, each receiving as much as was required for the support of the individuals comprised in it. The fields were tilled by the man to whom the land was granted, with the aid of his neighbours and other fellow-members of the *ayllu*, this work extending also to the fields of men who were absent in the army or on other business.

Out of this ancient social organization, which was fluctuating in its administrative functions and varied as to the size of the holdings by the different *ayllu*, the Inca forged a remarkably compact and strictly symmetrical organization and an equally well-proportioned administrative system. Under the Incas, then, the old *ayllu* was converted into a

[14] However, *cf.* p. 404.

pachaca, a social group composed of 100 households with an official at its head. The administrative pyramid just referred to came to comprise the following officials: the lowest ones were in charge of 10 households; above them stood those in charge of 50 households. These two officials came from the common people. The next higher official was in charge of 100 households. Above him were officials in charge of 500, of 1000, and of 10,000 households. The officials of these four classes belonged to the order of *curoca* or noblemen. Of the two topmost classes of officials the lower ones were in charge of districts containing 40,000 households, and the higher ones, four in number, presided over the four quarters of the Empire. The officials of the last two categories were high nobles, often of royal blood. At the top of the entire pyramid, finally, stood the Sapa Inca himself. In general, each official was appointed by the next higher official.

Of this large group of officials, belonging to several categories, the two lowest ones, who themselves were of the people, naturally came into closer contact with the population than did the others. They supervised the labour of the heads of households under them, were responsible for the adequate supply of food for the people in their charge, maintained discipline, and administered punishments, such as flogging or stoning for 'minor' offences, while graver ones were reported to their superior officers. They also kept a record of vital statistics in their groups, of which they were expected to furnish accurate reports to the higher officials.

This entire socio-economic system was in its essence an organization for production of which the unit was not the individual but the household. Nevertheless, as the actual work was done by individuals, people were classified, from the standpoint of their capacity for work, into the following categories: (1) babe newly born and still in arms; (2) child able to stand (about 1 year old); (3) child between 1 and 6 years old; (4) 'bread receiver'—6 to 8 years; (5) 'boy playing about'—8 to 16 years; (6) 'coca-picker,' doing light manual labour—16 to 20 years; (7) 'almost a youth,' aiding his elders in their tasks—20 to 25; (8) 'able-bodied man,' head of household and payer of tribute—25 to 50; (9) 'half old,' doing light work—50 to 60; (10) 'old man sleeping'—60 and upwards.

As the Empire grew, the Inca was no longer able to supervise personally the operations of the mass of officials; this task now fell to certain extra-hierarchical officials who functioned after the nature of the secret police of modern dictatorships. Quite in line with the ideology of such institutions, these officials are variously designated by the old

Spanish writers as 'guardians' or 'shepherds.' We are told that their activities were 'as a rule' benevolent but also that they had the power to become 'terrible,' a privilege exercised whenever they deemed it necessary.

A *pachaca* of the later period contained perhaps from 500 to 1000 individuals. Continuing the computation on this scale, each of the four quarters of the Empire ultimately contained between 4 and 8 millions of persons, and the whole state between 16 and 32 millions, the former figure in each case being, perhaps, nearer the truth. It will be seen from this that in the case of the Inca state we are dealing with population conditions entirely beyond the range of those otherwise encountered among the American Indians, with the sole exception of the ancient Mexicans.

In addition to the classes of people already described, we also find references to another, still lower class, the so-called *yana-cuna*, whose social status approximated that of slaves. It is certain, at any rate, that they were not comprised in the regular social system, and their standing and well-being must have reflected this condition. By contrast with this lowest class, the heads of households were counted upon to perform two of the important state functions, namely the collection of tribute and the carrying on of war, whether for expansion or defence. It may be added here, incidentally, that manual labour stood very high in the estimation of the Incas, and that all individuals comprised within the state—including the nobles, persons of royal blood, and the Inca himself—were expected to participate, to some extent, in the labour performed in the state. Another important point is this: the appointment of officials which, as stated, was in the hands of the next higher officials, was regulated by considerations of ability, not of descent, a circumstance which, without doubt, had its share in the success of the Inca organization.[15] The power of the Inca himself was, theoretically at least, absolute. He was limited by no restrictions whatsoever excepting only those which every tyrant or dictator must heed, as a matter of wisdom or self-preservation.

As will be apparent from the systematic application of the hierarchical principle in the Inca state, this organization had an aristocratic flavour. Ever since the time of Inca Roca, there was a College at Cuzco for the teaching of the sciences. According to a rule laid down by the first Incas, these were to be taught to the nobles but not the common

---

[15] Compare this condition with that found among the Maori, where the principle of descent was of the highest importance but was also balanced by a regard for ability (p. 384).

people, 'lest the lower classes should become shrewd and endanger the commonwealth.' In this College or *yachahuasi* (House of Teaching) lived the *amauta*, or philosophers, and the *haravec*, or poets; both types of scholars enjoyed great esteem among the Incas. With them lived many disciples, mostly persons of royal blood.

Each of the households was, in the main, self-supporting. Most or all of the food and clothing needed by it were obtained from its own territory and by its own work. The houses of the common people consisted of a rectangular, generally windowless structure with a thatched roof containing one room, sometimes two or three rooms; the floors were of trodden earth. If there were windows, no closure device was provided, and there were no chimneys. The lower-class dwellings were perhaps more commodious, being made of sun-dried brick or adobe and provided with better ventilation. The houses of the rich and noble differed from these largely in their size and luxurious adornment; but they also were crude by way of comfort and almost barren of furniture. Most of the house-work was done by women, who took care of the cooking, spinning, and weaving. Cotton or wool was used for textiles and the workmanship, we saw, was fine. The household gadgets, almost entirely of home manufacture, comprised vessels of pottery, stone, or wood; wooden spoons; gourds of various shapes and sizes, and perhaps some minor articles. The well-being of a family largely depended upon its size and the number of working hands.

Although the family or household was, as stated, in the main self-sufficient, this principle could not, of course, be carried out fully; room was left for acquiring commodities available in one family or locality but not in others. This function was taken care of by markets, both small and large, at which commodities were exchanged in kind. Our authority, Philip Ainsworth Means, when mentioning these markets, refers to a description by the Spanish writer, Father Cobo, which I shall reproduce, in part:

The Indian women place all their merchandise or a part of it, which is fruit or something of that sort, in a row of little piles before them, . . . or if it is meat, in rows of pieces, and in like manner with other kinds of goods. The Indian woman, who comes to buy with maize instead of money, sits herself down very slowly close to the seller and makes a little pile of maize wherewith she thinks to buy what she desires, neither woman speaking to the other the while. She who sells fixes her eyes upon the maize, and if it appears to her little, says nothing nor makes any sign other than to continue looking, and so long as she continues thus it is understood that she is not contented with the price offered. Meanwhile, she who buys has her eyes fixed on the seller and all the while that she sees her remaining unmoved she keeps adding a few grains more to her pile of maize, and this goes on little by little until she who sells is content with the price and declares her approbation, not by word—for from beginning to end they say nothing to one another even though the bargaining lasts for half an hour—but by the act of extending her hand and gathering the maize to herself.[16]

To this it may be added that, most of the basic articles of food or wear being amply provided by each household for its own use, almost if not all of those disposed of at markets belonged to the category of luxuries. Thus the coast contributed cotton (not an article of luxury since it was in universal use), many vegetables, fruits, fish, sea-shell, algarroba and balsa wood. The highlands yielded the metals; wool (of which that of the vicuña was a luxury); various vegetables, such as maize, potatoes,[17] and a variety of tubers; fresh and dried meat; and fine building stones. The forests brought timber, coca, medicinal plants, dye-stuffs, and coloured feathers.

Passing now to the methods employed by the Inca masters in their attempts to keep the political organization going, the one deserving first mention is the use made of statistics, which provided the ruler with all relevant information concerning the material wealth of each district as well as its man-power. In this connexion the principal, perhaps the only, tool used by the Incas was the *quipu*, which was employed as a mnemonic device for purposes of computation.[18]

---

[16] Philip Ainsworth Means, *Ancient Civilizations of the Andes*, pp. 315–316. This description is quite interesting in its psychological implications. It is fairly obvious that no such form of bargaining could represent a natural or spontaneous phenomenon. On the contrary, these practically-minded people must have learned from experience the futility of the vociferous transactions of the market place. In addition they seem to have recognized that the only way to check the market-woman's spontaneous explosions is to shut her up completely. It is notable also that the two women thus engaged abstain not only from talking but also from looking at each other—the buyer looks at the seller, the seller at the maize, which adds point to this comment.

[17] We are told that 'no less than a dozen species of potatoes' were in existence in the Andean highlands. See the essay by Carl Sauer, 'American Agricultural Origins: A Consideration of Nature and Culture,' *Essays in Anthropology* (in honor of Alfred Louis Kroeber), p. 290. Sauer's thought-provoking study contains *inter alia* a brief account of an investigation of the places of domestication of cultivated plants in America conducted by the scientists of the Russian Institute of Applied Botany and Plant Breeding. To judge by the information given by Sauer, the results of this investigation promise to prove little short of epoch-making in this much-debated field. The evidence, by the way, seems to point to a plural origin of agriculture in native America.

[18] The common form of *quipu* consisted of knotted ropes, the numerical value of the knots being indicated by their position on the rope, as in Fig. 75. Rope complexes

Another even more important technical device was the road system. There were two main highways, both passing through Cuzco, which bound the coast and the highland zone to the capital. Supplementary to these was an intricate network of secondary roads. All of these roads

---

like that below would constitute a unit in much more complicated *quipu*, but the principle remained the same. This accomplished the counting. What was counted had to be carried in the mind.

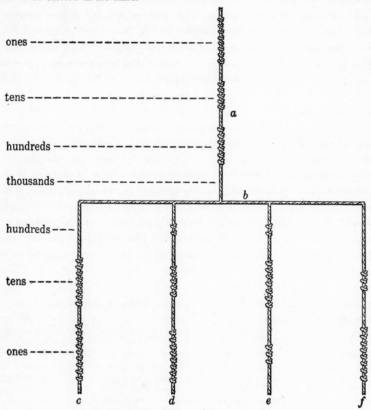

ones

tens

a

hundreds

thousands

b

hundreds

tens

ones

c   *d*   *e*   *f*

FIG. 75. INCA QUIPU, USED IN COUNTING.

On the ropes *c, d, e, f,* suspended from rope *b,* the knots indicated the number of whatever was counted; the knots on rope *a,* attached to *b,* indicated the total of the numbers denoted by *c, d, e, f.*

Thus, in the above example:

c has 9 ones, 8 tens, no hundreds	= 89
d has 8 ones, 5 tens, 2 hundreds	= 258
e has 3 ones, 7 tens, 2 hundreds	= 273
f has 8 ones, 3 tens, no hundreds	= 38
	Total = 658

a has 8 ones, 5 tens, 6 hundreds, no thousands = 658

ran, whenever possible, in straight lines. Those in the mountains were
frequently paved and stepped, those on the coast were surfaced with
sun-baked earth and lined with bowls of adobe, or with large wooden
posts set at intervals. The roads were always kept neat and in good
repair. Along the coast roads long stretches set with shade trees could
be seen, while on the mountain roads there were numerous turnouts
used as rest-places. In view of the tendency of roads to run straight,
there arose the necessity for causeways and bridges, the most interesting
ones of the latter being the famous suspension bridges constructed in
the following way. Three aloe-fibre ropes, about a foot thick, were
thrown across a chasm and securely fastened to massive masonry piers
on the banks. On these ropes was laid a flooring of sticks firmly lashed
together and covered with strong coarse matting. This provided a foot-
way from 6 to 8 feet wide and frequently as much as 100 or 150 yards
long. Along the sides of the foot-way ran two thick fibre ropes of the
same size, which were securely lashed to it, thus forming a sort of balus-
trade. The dramatic and somewhat terrifying character of these bridges
came from the inevitably steep pitch from the bank to the centre of the
hanging bridge, and from there to the other bank. Also, the whole bridge
would swing distractingly at the slightest wind, a feature which could
be mitigated somewhat by ropes tied to the centre of the bridge and attached diagonally to secure points on the shores. This method was at
times adopted. Another less common type of bridge consisted of a
single aloe-fibre rope upon which a large basket was slung which was
drawn across by means of smaller ropes. There was also a famous bridge
across the Desaguadero River, near Lake Titicaca, which was built of
planks resting on reed pontoons.

These roads were used not only for travel but also for post-runners.
These were specially trained men who could run at full speed for about
4½ miles on flat country. For the use of these men post-houses were
erected in which the couriers on duty were stationed. Two, four, six,
or more couriers took turns in watching the road, so that no time should
be lost if a message came by in either direction. When one of these men
saw a messenger approaching from the next station on either side, the
runner whose duty it was to relieve him would go out to meet him and
would run along with him long enough to learn the message, usually
brief, or to receive the *quipu* with any words that might accompany it,
or to relieve the runner of his burden. All these things were accomplished without any diminution of pace. 'So well was the running performed,' quotes Means from Cieza de León, 'that in a short time they
knew at a distance of 300, 500, and even 800 leagues [that is, 900, 1500,

and 2400 miles] what had passed or what was needed or required. With such secrecy did the runners keep the message that was entrusted to them that neither entreaty nor menace could extort from them a relation of what they had thus heard, although the news had already passed onwards. The roads passed over rugged mountains, over snow-covered regions, over stony wildernesses and forests full of thorny thickets, in such sort that it may be taken as quite certain that the news could not be conveyed at greater speed with swift horses or mules than by these foot-posts. For the men on foot had no impediments, and one of them could do more in a day than a mounted messenger in three. I do not mean one single Indian, but one running for a half league and another for the next, according to the established order. It must be understood that neither storms nor anything else prevented the due service of the posts in the wildest parts, and as soon as one started another arrived to wait in his place.' [19]

In addition to the towns and villages through which the roads ran, so-called 'royal apartments' were erected along the roads at intervals of 12 or 18 miles. These were served and provided by the provinces in which they stood. At these places the Inca or his nobles could enjoy their rest, and here also ample provisions were available to replenish the supplies of any expedition, however elaborate.

It must be remembered that these admirable Peruvian roads with their accessories did not represent means of communication, in the ordinary sense, but rather arteries of government, in that they were meant and used almost entirely for officially approved journeys. Along these far-flung roads passed armies, couriers, colonists, officials, burden-bearers and employees of the state. The Inca himself travelled frequently, and when he did so it was always an affair of great complexity and pomp. We are told in the words of Cieza that 'when the Incas visited the provinces of the empire in time of peace they travelled in great majesty, seated in rich litters, fitted with loose poles of excellent wood, long and enriched with gold and silver work. Over the litter there were two high arches of gold set with precious stones, and long mantles fell around all sides of the litter so as to cover it completely. If the inmate did not wish to be seen, the mantles remained down; they were raised when he got in or came out. In order that he might see the road, and have fresh air, holes were made in the curtain. Over all parts of these mantles or curtains there was rich ornamentation. On some were embroidered the sun and the moon, on others great curved serpents, and what would appear to be stags passing across them. These were borne as insignia of arms. The

[19] *Op. cit.*, p. 333.

litters were raised on the shoulders of the greatest and most important lords of the kingdom, and he who was employed most frequently on this duty was held to be most honoured and in highest favour.' [20] Around this imperial litter marched the cañari guard to the number of 2000, who always surrounded the monarch's person. In addition to these, 5000 slingers marched in front of the litter, and it was followed by 2000 warriors of the Inca caste.[21]

The high development of land transportation among the Incas implies an accurate geographical or topographical knowledge on the part of the rulers or their advisers. In this connexion our author quotes on the authority of Sarmiento that the Inca Pachacutec 'ordered the visitors to go through all the subdued provinces with orders to measure and survey them and to bring in models of the natural features in clay. This was done. The models and reports were brought before the Inca. He examined them and considered the mountainous fastnesses and the plains. He ordered the visitors to look well to what he would do. He then began to demolish the fastnesses and to have their inhabitants moved to plains country, and those of the plains were moved to mountainous regions so far from each other and each so far from their native countries that they could not return to it. Next the Inca ordered the visitors to go and do with the people what they had seen him do with the models. They went and did so.' [22] It will be seen from this quotation that the Incas pos-

[20] Means, *op. cit.*, p. 337.

[21] It is interesting that the art of navigation was in comparison little developed among these people. A type of dugout was made of the hardwood of the mountainous regions where it was used on the rivers. Along the coast similar dugouts were made of the strong light wood of the *ceiba* tree. These dugouts were swift and manageable whether with paddles or with sails, but they capsized easily. In ancient days these boats varied in size from little ones for two or three people to enormous vessels 50 or 60 feet in length capable of holding thirty persons. In addition to this, pontoon-rafts were in use. One type common on the southern coast was fashioned of two sealskins held together by a wooden platform. The other type also consisted of a wooden platform supported by a number of sealskins, and was used principally as a ferry on the rivers. On Lake Titicaca *totora*-reed boats were in use, which were pointed at the ends and provided with matting sails on unstable A-shaped masts. A rather distracting peculiarity of these boats was the fact that when they reached saturation point they sank—without notice. Until this point was reached, however, they were practically unsinkable although never dry. A not very fit craft, it will be seen. There was, finally, the great raft of the northern part of the coast, which consisted of seven to eleven and even more logs made of the light balsa wood, so arranged that the central log was longest and the others were shorter and shorter, as one approached the outer edge of the raft. A wooden platform, sometimes with a crude roof, stood in the middle, and near the bow was a mast with a cotton-cloth sail; sometimes there was a second mast at the stern. This clumsy contraption was steered by means of paddles.

[22] Means, *op. cit.*, p. 342.

sessed the art of making relief maps and knew how to use them, even though at times for strange purposes.

Man, we know, is addicted to regimentation. It is possible that he may never learn to get along without a modicum of it. It is, however, equally true that too much regimentation goes against man's grain. Wherever, as among the Incas, regimentation is carried to an extreme, provision is invariably made for supplementing counsel and training with a strong hand and one or another form of ferocity. So among the Incas. Consider, for example, their institutions for dispensing justice. This state activity was in the hands of the various officials with whom we are now familiar, each having jurisdiction over his immediate environs. In case of serious crimes such as treason or *lèse majesté*, the Inca took charge personally, or at any rate his council of four major chieftains did so. The punishments meted out were always severe and often ferocious. Thieves were publicly flogged or stoned for their first offence. For the second they were subjected to various torments described by our author as 'ingenious and spirit-corroding.' And for the third offence they were slain 'lingeringly.' Vagabonds, gossip-spreaders, and all persons who had failed in their appointed duties were lashed with a sling or, in cases of particularly heinous offences, hanged by the feet until they were dead. In regard to robbery, the law, curiously enough, differentiated between an act of forethought, for which the culprit was chastised, and one committed for need of food or for some other necessary thing, when the punishment was inflicted upon the official who should have forestalled the need. Certain crimes of passion, such as a rape of a chosen virgin or sodomy, were punished by the violent death of the guilty parties as well as the obliteration of their villages and the slaughter of all living things therein. With reference to the upper classes, corporal punishments were on the whole avoided and psychological ones, involving loss of prestige, were substituted in their place. In view of the rigour of the state organization of the Incas, treason and disobedience were especially dreaded by them. To suppress such crimes the Inca, Tupac Yupanqui, had built in the neighbourhood of Cuzco a subterranean dungeon with numerous blind doors and tortuous passages; in this attractive place a great number of wild beasts were kept—pumas, jaguars, bears—and among the flints upon the pavement there were toads, vipers, and vermin. All traitors and disobedient persons were thrust into this dungeon.

Before closing this sketch of Inca policy, a word about the great hunts periodically instituted in the state. Our author describes one such hunt conducted in the presence of the Inca himself:

'A great throng of men was assembled in the chosen locality to act as beaters, there being usually from ten to sixty thousand men in this throng. The tents from which the Inca was to watch the spectacular display were set up in a place from whence a wide view could be enjoyed of a stretch of the country some twenty or thirty leagues in circuit. A vast circle was formed by the beaters who at the beginning stood at some distance from one another. But, when they advanced shouting and making a fearful din by every known method, they gradually drew closer and closer together, driving all the animals within the circle before them. At length the yelling beaters were close enough together to take hands, each with his neighbour, and so they proceeded under the observant eye of the Inca, the circle drawing ever closer and closer, until it became necessary to form two or more concentric rings of beaters. As the wall of human beings closed in upon the frightened, struggling animals of many kinds, the racket and confusion grew ever greater and greater, until at length the signal was given for the slaughter to begin. Whereupon certain especially trained slayers, armed with *bola*,[23] clubs and sticks, plunged in among the prey and set about seizing and slaying the poor terrified beasts. Females were always spared.' [24] Not infrequently from twenty to forty thousand head were taken in these hunts, in addition to vast quantities of pumas, bears, foxes, and wild-cats, which were slaughtered because of their harmfulness to useful animals. Each one of the four provinces was divided into four hunting areas, one of which was hunted in turn every year under the auspices of the Inca or one of the great chieftains. These hunts, it must be remembered, unlike the luxury hunts of European royalty and nobility, were intended to furnish ample supplies of food, furs, feathers, and other articles, to be subsequently stored in numerous places in cities and along the roads provided for the purpose, and ultimately to be distributed among those who happened to stand in need of provisions or other necessities.

[23] A *bola* is a missile consisting of two or more stone or iron balls attached to interconnected ropes. It is thrown at large game animals so as to entangle their legs. It is still used on the South American pampas, and a similar device is known in certain parts of Africa.

[24] Means, *op. cit.*, p. 350.

Chapter XXV

PRIMITIVE LIFE AND THOUGHT

Culture and 'Primitive Mind'

Broadly speaking there is no such thing as a primitive mind; primitive man is potentially like modern man or any other kind of man. Still, from another angle, the concept 'primitive mind' is not a figment but a reality. In many situations the mind of the primitive behaves differently from the modern mind. If primitive mind is not to be interpreted in terms of biology, if primitiveness is not a matter of birth, then these differences in mental operation, as between modern and primitive, must be reducible to the cultural setting. Primitive mind is primitive because it is rooted in a primitive culture.

What, then, in summary, are the characteristics of primitive culture?

Though populational conditions in the primitive world differ greatly —from the relative sparseness of Australia to the almost modern denseness of Africa, Mexico, or Peru—the primary local unit of cultural life is numerically small. More often than not, it is measured not by thousands but by hundreds. Even in Africa, moreover, where the denseness of population occasionally approximates modern conditions, the closely knit local group, which is also the primary cultural unit, is small.

This numerically slight local unit is also isolated geographically. Not that inter-tribal or inter-local contact is ever completely absent. On the contrary; here, as everywhere, people travel, visit, and trade; others, whether on sea or land, lose their way and find themselves in strange surroundings. But withal, intercommunication between separate groups is here less frequent, less regular, less rapid, and more hazardous than under later historic conditions. In this relative isolation we must see one of the reasons for the marked individuality of local cultures among the primitives, a trait with which we have become familiar.

Another cause of the individuality of local groups lies in the deficient plasticity of primitive culture. Its patterns are set in a rigid frame. Primitive culture is stiff-jointed and the number and kinds of movements it can make at short notice are limited.

Relatively again, the group is cut off from its own past. In primitive

communities the continuity of cultural life from generation to generation is attained in two ways: by the objective persistence of material
things, and by tradition passed on through education. The material
equipment of a group persists by its own inertia, as it were: baskets,
pots, tools, weapons, and canoes pass from the past into the present as
do trees, sea, or sky; each growing generation simply finds these objects
there to be picked up where they were left by their fathers. As to tradition, it is communicated by word of mouth, in non-deliberate example,
conscious instruction, or tribal initiation. What does not persist or is
not passed on in one of these ways must vanish.[1]

Primitive tradition, then, is shallow, and the historical inquisitiveness
of the primitive is slight. The world of fathers, grandfathers, and great-
grandfathers remains relatively concrete and therefore significant; it
may be brought to bear on things of today and tomorrow. Back of this
lies semi-historical tradition, still interesting but no longer so relevant
to day-by-day experience. Beyond this, tradition soon passes into myth,
a thing of the imagination, perhaps helpful as dogma and entertaining
as play, but no longer relevant as an objective background for life.

The knowledge of facts and events, historically so thin, is, as we saw,
equally limited geographically. The width of the cultural span is no
less restricted than its depths. With the human, animal, and material
factors of its immediate environment, the tribe is thoroughly conversant.
Outside of this a very fragmentary and unreliable set of data is available, referring to people, and customs with which some sort of contact
is maintained. There the world of humanity ceases. Beyond is the
void, or at best the realm of imagination with its grotesque figures and
fantastic happenings.

In a society where personal observation and the absorption of tradition are the only sources of knowledge and wisdom, age is a tremendous
advantage. A man who has passed through the different age-periods,

---

[1] The importance of the spoken word in primitive times deserves some emphasis
here. For the modern man whose culture is tied to the past by threads without
number, it is difficult to visualize the conditions of a primitive group in which
the stark persistence of material things is supplemented by tradition alone. The
spoken, living word here becomes the principal vehicle of culture. The past comes
to the present as things or as words; what is neither seen nor said nor remembered
vanishes beyond recovery. This process of self-obliteration applies on occasion to
language itself, as has come to the attention of those lucky ethnologists who chanced
to come upon a last living representative of a language. They knew that what
they were thus enabled to pick up from someone's lips was the last and only
source in which this particular human tongue was preserved. If the chance were
missed or no such occasion had arisen, the language spoken by no one would be lost
beyond redemption. In modern times when all survives, deservedly or otherwise,
these conditions seem strange and barely comprehensible.

has been initiated, one by one, into the secular or sacred groups of his tribe, who has been a bachelor, a married man, a father and father-in-law, a warrior and leader in the chase, who as an elder has taken part in the deliberations over war and peace and internecine strife, who has composed songs and told and retold stories, who has faced the tragic emergencies of primitive life—famine, pestilence, flood, and drought— and above all, one who has had time and opportunity to talk to his own elders, and pick up from their lips whatever knowledge and experience in fact or lore they themselves possessed—such a man comes to personify the tribal culture. In him the others find a veritable treasure-trove of knowledge and a fount of wisdom as well. He is admired and revered. To him one turns for advice in perplexity and danger. What he says holds and goes. Thus everywhere in primitive society the elders are in the saddle. It is the fathers' generation that rules and the fathers, here as always, are the bulwark of law and order. They stand for established routine, a fearful avoidance of the new, a sagacious management and occasional exploitation of the young.

This conservative trend is reinforced by other factors. Apart from esoteric groups—clubs, societies, and the like—which in point of knowledge and practice almost constitute a world unto themselves, division of labour and specialization are, as we saw, not unknown in primitive life. Even so, the group is in the main strikingly homogeneous from a cultural standpoint; a great number of individuals within a tribe and locality feel and act along similar lines, and not a few activities and experiences are participated in by nearly all the tribesmen. This is folk culture. Under such conditions the control exercised by public opinion and customary routine is well-nigh absolute. The individual here is but a miniature reproduction of the group culture, and the latter but a magnified version of the individual with his knowledge, attitudes, and behaviour. Any conspicuous digression from the set norm of thought and action is resented, ridiculed, and repressed, either as a breach of custom or in certain instances as a flagrant violation of the very essence of group culture, as an unnatural act. Then the punishment comes from nature herself in the form of an automatic chastisement, Marett's 'negative magic,' which threatens the transgressor of a taboo.

Nor does this exhaust the factors which stand for conservatism. Contrary to what is found under modern conditions, the primitive group lives in close communion with nature. We have learned either to control environment or to protect ourselves against the immediate consequences of deficient control. With relative impunity we cherish the illusion of an actual mastery over the forces of nature. How different in early conditions! Here every breath of cultural life is dominated by natural things and events. Such adjustment to physical environment constitutes a genuine and vital problem in every primitive group. No stability is reached until it is solved. After this there is little incentive for change. Owing to deficient familiarity with other cultures and the consequent lack of comparative cultural material, no conscious idea of progress can develop. Under such conditions the economic adjustment is taken almost as a fact of nature. It may be sorely inadequate, but it works after a fashion and is accepted as final.

Such then is the general background of primitive life. In this setting the economic pursuits and techniques, religion, social structure, and art co-operate in fashioning the mind of the primitive.

Industrial Life

It was shown before that economic and industrial experience come to stand for matter-of-factness and knowledge. There is familiarity with the forms, habits, and behaviour of plants and animals, with certain of the more obvious and humanly significant movements of the celestial bodies, with the exhilarating and distracting peculiarities of local climate. To this equipment must be added a thoroughgoing acquaintance with the materials available for industry as well as with the industrial processes themselves. In the techniques of industry, moreover, motor habits (Boas) develop which are rooted in knowledge and fed by experience, often of a personal sort, soon to become mechanized by practice. Other bits of information, perhaps less objective but equally relevant and significant, accumulate about the ways of man himself. In this vast domain of culture, then, there is abundant evidence of knowledge and common sense, persistent observation, and at least incipient generalization. Here also logic rules within limits, and invention on occasion sows its germinating seed.

It must here be noted that in industry, technique, and matter-of-fact activities generally, the individual is alone with some aspect of physical nature. He may, to be sure, be engaged in a communal enterprise. In hunting and building, in agriculture and herd-tending, one frequently finds co-operation, group labour, not uncommonly accompanied by those rhythms of communal work, in act and sound, of which Buecher wrote so eloquently—rhythms which, operating through psychic channels, greatly further the activities and joys of labour. But even so, the individual, technically speaking, remains alone with his task. When engaged in manufacturing a pot, basket, or blanket, tilling the soil, hunting or fighting an animal, man faces an individual technical task. In industry he must overcome the resistance of the material, master the mechanical difficulties; in war, raid, or chase, he must become expert in a great variety of movements and tricks by means of which the prey or enemy are to be sought, captured, or killed. The worker, hunter, or warrior here faces natural conditions with an implied willingness to learn from experience. As a consequence he does learn, acquires knowledge, becomes familiar with effective ways of using it. In all this the individual functions alone; others may provide a setting, example, stimulation, but no more. Experience, learning, acquiring skill, are personal, individual matters. The only active companions of the individual here are the objective conditions, and these pull him along towards matter-of-factness, sober thinking, and effective action.

It is, however, equally important to realize that the intellectual harvest of industry and such like pursuits does not extend very far. Reason here is incidental and evanescent, not unlike the 'intellectual acumen' of the bee, ant, spider, or beaver. The logic observed in early tools and appliances is but the logic of nature, of the objective relationship of things. Things and processes are what they are. If one wants to forge ahead in their midst, they must be heeded. Thus guided, the mind of man glides into an attitude of sober objectivity so smoothly and inevitably that consciousness and deliberate thought are all but excluded.

It is of course inevitable, with man, that deliberation and therefore awareness will here and there break into the course of the industrial process. But the spark of intellectual discernment flickers but for a moment, presently to go out again. What is passed on to the following generation is the objective result, not the intellectual insight. This is so because these pursuits, one and all, are direct and pragmatic. What is aimed at is achievement, not understanding. The realm of matter-of-factness in primitive life is a hunting-ground for the pragmatist, not an abode for the pursuit of 'idle curiosity' (Veblen). What is wanted is that a thing should work, and if and when it does, further changes are deferred, perhaps indefinitely so. Henceforth the tools and inventions, these condensed depositories of reason, are accepted traditionally as are other things that come from the past; they become part of the technical equipment of behaviour, not of thought and understanding.

This explains at least in part why the objective experience in primitive life failed to bring its full intellectual harvest. True, observation, knowledge, and invention are all there, but they remain in solution, as it were, in the psycho-physical flow of behaviour. Hence their relative barrenness in the intellectual level. Not until centuries later,[2] under totally different conditions of life and inquiry, do these precious fragments of knowledge and insight become precipitated as clear-edged crystals of science and critical thought.

While the intellectual aspect of technique is thus seen to be limited, certain other aspects are furthered by primitive conditions of life and labour. One of these is skill. In industry, warfare, or the chase, things can be done well and less well. There is room here for the emergence of skill. Skill is furthered by rivalry, and the stage is set for rivalry wherever many persons are engaged earnestly or playfully in the same pursuits. Now this, of course, is exactly what we find in all these primitive situations. The group here functions as a community of experts, a setting calculated to spur the individual on to the utmost of effort and skill.

Another factor is lack of hurry. Art is long, in primitive as in modern conditions, but there life is not so short, for time is not at a premium. The span of work is determined by the technical necessities; an article is not done until it is finished, and so when finished, it is done well.[3]

Above all else it must be remembered, once more, that in industry and allied domains of the matter-of-fact, the primitive faces nature, experience, craft, as a learner. Being willing to learn, he does so.

It would, however, be an error to assume that such an attitude is typical of the average person in the primitive tribe. Far from it. Someone has explored and learned, difficulties have been overcome, skills achieved, innovations made. Now all this forms part of the tribal pattern. It is learned from one's elders and must be followed to the letter.

---

[2] The reader should not be confused by the fact that the peoples of whom I treat are 'our primitive contemporaries' (Robinson). If these peoples were assisted in their rise, or still better, left alone, instead of being doomed to corruption and decay, they would some day experience the intellectual illumination hinted at in the text. Similarly, our own ancestors, of whom we know a little but might know more, must have once lived under conditions like those here described.

[3] There is a great contrast here between primitive and modern handiwork. Apart from the articles made by highly skilled craftsmen whose work may, in certain respects, be superior to the corresponding products of early man, many modern things are made in slipshod fashion. One of the reasons for this lies in the fact that the individuals who make the things are surrounded by others who have no knowledge of the techniques. Illustrations are provided by modern household amateurs as well as by servants attached to incompetent masters. Again, it is generally understood and almost proverbial that the pressure of time kills the craftsman. Of this our culture brings abundant evidence, while Japan can furnish other striking instances.

Whatever individual variation occurs—and variation is, of course, inevitable both physically and psychologically—remains within closely set limits. Primitive society, as we saw, is not a friend of the nonconformist or innovator, and primitive education sees to it that no tribesman becomes one. This applies emphatically not only to faith, rite, morals, mores, etiquette, and the like, but also to economic, industrial, and military pursuits.

The Individual. The question naturally arises: what then is left of the individual? Is there such a thing among primitives as individual freedom, or the sense of it? Paradoxically enough, there is. Society can prescribe a form, set a pattern, preside over a process, but the actual dynamics of it all eludes society. When all is said, the day's work and play are in the hands of individuals, particular persons. Baskets, pots, and canoes, traps, dances, songs, and rituals must be such and such, and as a means society offers or prescribes traditional techniques. Thus the limits are set, and they are narrow indeed. But within these limits, the processes remain plastic. Anyone familiar with techniques knows that there can be no absolute standardization. It is like the rules and skills of a game; these are given, but then there is the game itself, consisting of a series of events or acts which can neither be foreseen nor determined in advance. So also with industry, hunting, or fighting. The individual starts out with his patterns, but within these limits he must meet the emergencies of time, place, and event. It is the difference between learning how to shoot and shooting to wound or kill, the difference between knowing how a pot is made and how to make a pot, the difference between shadow-boxing and a prize-fight.

There is this to be said, further: All in all, the patterns of primitive culture are set down categorically and, speaking with reservations, apply to the whole group or a very large part of it. This is true, first of all, of visible and audible things and activities. Whether one turns to crafts and economic pursuits; to tools, weapons, and fighting; to dances, songs, and myths; or to rules of social and ceremonial behaviour; the network of pattern is always there, and enmeshed in it are most of the individuals of the group. This applies equally to thought and attitude as exhibited in a world view—the ideas about things—or in moral judgments.

So far, however, we have only presented an objective view, a picture of the culture as beheld by an observer or student from the outside. To all this there is a subjective side, an inside view as experienced by the natives themselves.

Here we must first of all dispose of the notion that primitive man, as

put aside by me

an individual, views his culture, his patterns, as a whole which he can contemplate, analyse or juxtapose to himself. It is certain that nothing of the sort occurs, at least not in the case of an average person, which means the vast majority. To him his culture is a much more particular and intimate thing. It comes as experience, or rather as numerous experiences, in education, training, work, ritual, chase, war, social contacts. In each and all of these situations, patterns knock at the door of the individual. But now note this: the pattern has two aspects—a negative and a positive. In its negative capacity a pattern excludes the unacceptable and therefore proscribed; in its positive capacity it prescribes and delineates the acceptable—the pattern is its model. A pattern in a given sphere is then a taboo on anything outside the pattern, as well as an invitation or command to reproduce the pattern itself. From the latter standpoint the pattern sets a task; it indicates what one is expected to do.

Now there is no occasion for us to snub the primitives with their patterns, for patterns continue to dominate culture and no doubt always will. Still, in the complexity and relative individuality of modern life there is often much latitude; there are alternative patterns ('just as good'), or the pattern may be transcended or simply left alone. When confronted with a categorical pattern, like that of traffic regulation, we are thus prone to stress its limiting aspect, to feel it as pressure, to resent it as an imposition. Not so among primitives. In the absence of criticism and choice, the pattern here is scarcely ever thought of or felt as a limit; rather is it a model. There is no frustration of impulse, merely guidance and direction. The pattern defines a task, concrete and complete. It points the road one is to travel. When we say, therefore, that primitive life is weighed down by patterns, the metaphor is unfortunate; rather should we say that it is carried by them.[4]

---

[4] Returning once more to the objective aspect of pattern, it is further to be observed that in its negative or limiting capacity, pattern lays another stamp on certain aspects of primitive culture. When pattern is categorical, of course, checks development or change. When a design, type of garment, ritual, magical formula, technique, persists with but slight change, as it so often does, pattern functions in its most compelling form. It simply insures its own perpetuation. But pattern is not always so narrow; at other times room is left for development within the pattern. What takes place then may be described as a multiplication of pattern or a development by *involution*. This leads to an undue, seemingly absurd complexity in a cultural trait or institution. This feature has often been commented on by observers of primitive life. The all-pervading ceremonialism of the Todas, the interminable exchanges of presents attending Trobriand marriages, the minute apportionment of a hunting booty among the central Australians (just such and such a piece to such and such a relative), the elaborateness of Maori or Marquesan art (arts that overreach themselves), the ravages of taboo in Polynesia (taboo run

All these pursuits, moreover—technique, war, chase, and so on—are activities. What you do may be socially prescribed, and to a degree how you do it, but the doing is your own and it brings a thrill and a sense of selfhood.

In primitive life this latter feature is enhanced by two further factors. The primitive has to deal with a whole task, not with fragments, and he is versatile. It is *his* pot, *his* canoe, *his* chase, *his* fight. He plans it, executes it, and winds it up. The result is a whole thing, a complete experience. The primitive may and does identify himself with it. If it stands out, so does he, and his pride or vanity is gratified.[5]

If the primitive did not identify himself with his achievement, he could not be vain, and that of all things he is, as writers from Spencer to Lowie have pointed out. 'Man is a peacock,' remarks the latter; 'he loves to excel; social approbation and prestige are his dearest rewards.' And in proportion to his achievement, or at times out of proportion to it, is his vanity.[6] And then there is versatility. While division of labour and specialization are always present, each person, man or woman, engages in a great variety of activities. He is a craftsman, hunter, fighter, story-teller, dancer, singer, and perhaps magician, while his mate is similarly accomplished. Such many-sided activity, however dominated by pattern, cannot fail to enhance the ego and heighten the sense of life.

In other spheres of experience, routine is relieved by the personal equation. When an Indian youth goes forth into the hills or forest to seek a guardian spirit, the content of what he experiences conforms more or less fully to tribal pattern, but the religious thrill belongs to the youth and 'the memory lingers on.'

It must finally be remarked that the thoroughgoing way in which tribal norm and tradition are absorbed by the primitive negates any

amuck)—all of these and many similar cultural traits exhibit development by involution. When all constructive change or evolution is thwarted by pattern tyranny, a cultural feature, like a seedless orange, breeds within itself, resulting in what might be termed a cultural monstrosity.

[5] In another place it was suggested how decorative art may develop out of industrial technique. The very possibility of such sublimation implies that the craftsman's imagination has been quickened. If his task were dull and his self wholly excluded, art could not have been thus conceived. The modern factory worker might, in his private capacity, be an artist, but it is hardly conceivable that his mechanical task, like Chaplin's tightening of a bolt in *Modern Times*, could blossom forth into an art.

[6] This phenomenon is not foreign to modern civilization, wherever similar conditions obtain. Thus hunters and fishermen, craftsmen and actors, athletes and soldiers, are at one in their rivalries and pointed exhibitions of skill, their vanities and their bragging. And even in the domain of thought, the sensitiveness and vanity of the platform lecturer contrast strangely with the austerity and detachment of the closet philosopher.

sense of servitude or submission. Society is there and it imposes itself even more thoroughly than nature. The latter can be modified by tools and magic; not so society—it is simply accepted. To put it even more strongly: society, one's culture, is lived, whereas the problem of accepting, rejecting, or modifying it does not arise at all.

It is true that primitive culture also knows its nonconformists, offenders, heretics. These persons may have the courage—or weakness—to deviate from the norm, but they do not, except most rarely, entertain any thought of changing the existing order. And certainly all the rest, the great conforming majority, accept their society as an unchanging element, as something given, and without quite knowing what it is they are accepting. A weight one is not aware of is only half a weight. Even as the animal bends its instinctive nature to an existence full of excitement and gusto, so does the primitive, while bowing to the pattern, lead a life rich in content and animated in tempo.

Now we must return to our main thesis, namely the remarkably slight extent to which the great achievements of industry are translated into rational thought. I have in part accounted for this result, but there are further contributory causes.

Religious Life

In the section on religion it was pointed out that supernaturalism comprises three main aspects: emotional, ritualistic, and intellectual. It is this latter aspect, the concepts of supernaturalism as affecting primitive thought, which will detain us for the moment. Now we must recall that supernaturalism, as a system of ideas, is perfectly natural. It is supernatural only in its claims or tenets but not in its psychological roots—these are natural. Granted the limited knowledge and theoretical naïvety of original man, and his ideas about the world follow almost inevitably. This insight, it may be added, has already been reached by Spencer and Tylor, whose ideas on this point were in better accord with the facts than those of such later thinkers as Durkheim or Lévy-Bruhl. A world of spirits, magical powers, transformations of substances and beings into each other, are conclusions forced upon the untutored mind by the data of experience. Do we not observe similar tendencies even today in those whose mental processes are not thoroughly buttressed by theoretical safeguards, and to a certain extent at least, in all of us? These primitive ideas, I must insist, were not arrived at by a deliberate act of reason. They were not conclusions resulting from a conscious and rational attempt to answer questions or solve problems. Rather were they direct and intuitive. As Wundt and Lévy-Bruhl have insisted, the intuitive adjustments which experience elicits here take the form of an *instantaneous solution:* a moment of puzzlement, an ideational friction with facts, a direct automatic response, and the adjustment is made. To investigate, under the circumstances, rather than to accept such an instantaneous solution, would be a highly indirect procedure, impossible until much later in the advance of civilization. We must, finally, accept the concept of the 'omnipotence of thought,' formulated in this connexion by Freud: mental states are projected into the material world, thoughts turn into things, wishes and fears into objective reality.[7]

[7] To quote from my *Robots or Gods:*
'In all their essential traits, supernatural beings, born of mind, are like mind. Like mind, their creator, they exist in minds alone. Like mental images, they have form but no substance, at least none to speak of. They may appear in space, as images also seem to do. Their relationship to space, however, is at best insecure and transitory. We saw, in fact, that this spacial elusiveness of supernatural things and creatures is of the very essence of their make-up. They may be sensed, heard or seen, as images are, but always they evade the human touch—the final and convincing test of substantiality—for, however else they may exist, touch reveals them as non-existing, at least in the sense in which matter or substance exists. Like mental images, the supernaturals scoff at time. The yesterdays, todays and tomorrows mean but little to them. They do not age, for time does not touch them. They can see the future, as does mind in its intuitive flights, for what was and what is and what will be is all the same to them.
'Like mental images, once more, the supernaturals can change their shape. At one moment the human form may harbour them, then again it is the form of an animal, or again they may be like a cloud or just a vibrant something which is more like nothing except for its potency. Qualities, to be sure, they possess, but these, as we saw, when ascribed to the gods, are but projections of human fears and desires.
'Now, what is it that makes spirits and gods divine? Patently it is the fact that, on the one hand, they are like mind: as forms and as functions they are mental in origin and nature. On the other hand, they lack the qualities of substance which holds mind enthralled. They are, therefore, disembodied minds, minds freed from the limitations of substance, of bodies. Mind relieved of substance, removed from space and time, and projected as a disembodied spirit into the universe, becomes a divinity. Is not mind itself, then, a divinity, the divine principle residing in man under the limitations of space and time and substance?
'That mind may eventually prove to be the only divinity need not here concern us. All I claim is that if the gods created by mind unto its likeness are recognized by us as divine, then mind, their moulder and creator, belongs to the realm of the divine. Is divine:
'I sent my Soul through the Invisible,
Some letter of that After-Life to spell:
And by and by my Soul returned to me,
And answered, "I myself am Heav'n and Hell." '
Omar Khayyám.
A. Goldenweiser, *Robots or Gods.* (Reprinted by permission of Alfred A. Knopf, Inc.)

On the skeletal framework of these basic notions the systematizing thought of the priest weaves its elaborate and multi-coloured fabric; rapturously the story-teller plays with it. In this realm human imagination, unchecked by criticism and objective reference, reaches marvellous heights of complexity and virtuosity. Myth-making is a self-fertilizing pursuit. Nurtured in the medium of extraneous motives and purposes, it presently becomes an end in itself. Wundt was emphatically right in dwelling at length on the wondrous ways of myth-building fancy. The supernatural, moreover, although spun out of mind stuff, is more than a mere mental pastime to be played with in hours of leisure. Far from it. Emphatically it is put to work in the service of man in his everyday pursuits and, as will presently be shown once more, it fills in the gaps and blank spots left by industry, at best only partially effective.

Supernaturalism, once established, becomes firmly entrenched. Why indeed should it not persist? Under primitive conditions of life and knowledge no ground is forthcoming for rejecting any of its conclusions or theories. They are neither unreasonable, nor uninteresting, nor unaesthetic. On the contrary, the figments of supernaturalism are aesthetically attractive. They have beauty of thought, form, and movement, and abound in delightful samples of logical coherence. Last but not least, supernaturalism seems to work even better than does industry, for all its common sense and ingenuity.

Granted the tenets of supernaturalism are not true—but what is truth? Shielded by the warm intimacy of psychological reality, supernaturalism may well dispense with the truth of objective verification.

In supernaturalism as in science, experience and imagination are wedded together. In supernaturalism imagination works upon experience accepted in faith and naïvety; in science, experience utilized by imagination is critically sifted with reference to its objective verifiability. The way towards a world view adopted by supernaturalism is the easier way; it follows the spontaneous tendencies of the mind, it operates with experience accepted without question, with smoothly working associations, with automatic projections and objectifications of mental states, with the play of fancy born of an unencumbered imagination. The way towards a scientific world view, on the contrary, is devious and hard to tread. The spontaneous tendencies of the mind, which here also are in operation, must now be constantly controlled to satisfy the demands of criticism, merciless logic, objective reference. An attempt at such refinements, if essayed in primitive conditions, would fail; but no such attempt is made. For the time being the riddles of the universe are solved without residue by supernaturalism.

Supernaturalism, it is true, cannot altogether escape occasional conflicts with objective reality. From these it invariably emerges victorious, for it refers its failures to the same mechanisms by which it achieves its successes. If magic fails, it is magic that is held responsible for the failure.

In primitive life, as we saw, conformity is the watchword. Here, even more markedly than elsewhere, the organized community is despotic in act and dogmatic in thought.[8] The full weight of tribal dogma is invoked in support of supernaturalism. The offender in act, word, or thought is here not merely a crank or nonconformist but a heretic. His offence is not merely a social transgression but a sacrilege. In cases of such gravity, dogma invokes the gods themselves to take up arms in self-defence. And so they do: when a taboo is transgressed, the punishment is automatic and magical.[9]

---

[8] To illustrate how social rule may interfere with the 'freedom of thought,' one example. Among the Trobrianders (Northwest Melanesia) a mother and her children are of 'one body'; the father, on the other hand, is a 'stranger,' and is regarded as having nothing to do with procreation. This notwithstanding, the natives claim that children never resemble their mother, each other, or, in fact, any of their blood-relatives. When such resemblances are pointed out to them, they deny the fact and are shocked and offended. To say 'thy face thy sister's' to a Trobriander is to offend him mortally. The children, it is claimed, do resemble the father. The fact that he is always about and with the mother is held accountable for the resemblance: 'It coagulates (moulds) the face of the child; for always he lies with her, they sit together.'

Thus the resemblance to the father is always claimed even though contrary to fact (for such is the social theory), but arouses no thought of his part in procreation (for this is contrary to social theory). The resemblance to the mother, on the contrary, or to any maternal relative, is 'not seen,' though often apparent. Thus all thought of the relation of blood to physical resemblance is effectively checked.

In this way observations are prevented or perverted, and what might have become a source of fruitful biological speculation is nipped in the bud. (Malinowski, *The Sexual Life of Savages*, vol. I, pp. 203 seq.)

[9] The early emergence of theological dogma is striking but feasible. As stated elsewhere, attitudes and ideas born of imagination and sustained by faith require dogma to insure them against doubt, and the dogma is supplied by the organized society.

The crux of the situation lies in education. The truths of industry are demonstrable. The parents or old men may, therefore, discuss them and give real reasons. Supernaturalism cannot be demonstrated, or at best, only casually so. Here one can only proffer 'good reasons.' Dogma is by far the most comfortable way out. Do we not find that in matters where adequate reasons fail, as in religion, morals, politics, etiquette, modern educators either provide such 'good reasons,' that is, rationalistic fictions *ad hoc*, or they take recourse to dogma?

Thus firmly entrenched on the intellectual side and fenced in by social imperatives, supernaturalism is further enhanced by powerful emotions.

When dealing with religious origins or revivals, I placed due emphasis on the psychology of conversion. Stirring personal experience with the divine, it will be remembered, is crucial here. Matter-of-fact experience with natural things and events, though constant and continuous, takes place in an atmosphere of emotional casualness. The supernatural, even among primitives, comes in spurts, but when it comes it does so with a bang. Typical here are the guardian-spirit cults of the American Indian. The setting in which they occur is calculated to arouse the emotions to the utmost. The youth is alone, starved, expectant. For days and nights the atmosphere about him has been athrob with mystical potency. Finally the vision comes. The emotional thrill is tremendous. It burns its way into his very soul, leaving an indelible mark.[10]

And once more there is a social side in the form of ceremonialism. Ritual punctuates the life of the individual, marking critical periods: war and the chase, initiation, death, burial. Rhythms, dances, songs, symbols, decorum. Surrounded by his mates, fuming with fervour, the individual is overwhelmed. What transpires here is beyond argument or doubt. The sacred, the 'secrets,' hold sway.[11]

Congenial as a vision and effective as practice, supernaturalism, then, is also stirring to the emotions. In the face of the mystic complex, reason and objectivity, though invited by matter-of-fact experience, could not take firm root in the mind of man. Successful in the level of industry and certain other forms of behaviour, reason capitulated in the domain of thought before the more direct, more brilliant, and more sweeping conquests of supernaturalism.

It will be seen that technique, on the one hand, and religion and magic,

---

[10] On the whole, the conditions of primitive life favour supernaturalism, for the mystical world view thrives on traditionalism, whereas the materialistic world view imbedded in industry with its rationality and matter-of-factness, is served best by change and mobility.

[11] The conservatism of ritual cannot be sufficiently stressed. In ritual, a conservative society is present as a crowd. Its crowd character reacts upon its conservatism, enhancing it. No deviation is possible here. Not possible, because it will not be tolerated. Not possible, also, because in a performance—and a ritual is one —each item interlocks with the rest. Omitting a song, changing a dance step, misplacing a participant or an object, makes the whole thing go wrong. With good reason difficult parts of a ritual are always carefully rehearsed.

Now a ritual, as we saw, carries a message which lies in its meanings. This message is as clear-cut and precise as its vehicle. The relation between life and ritual, as a system of meanings, is reciprocal: ritual mirrors life; then life, turning reflection to its own image, is guided by ritual.

on the other, present from one angle the opposite poles of the primitive attitude. Industry stands for common sense, knowledge, skill, objective matter-of-fact achievement. Religion stands for mysticism, a subjective translation of experience, a substitution of mental states for external realities and a reification of such states into presumed existences in a realm which in part is 'another' world but in part also belongs to 'this' world, in so far as the two worlds interpenetrate. It is this latter feature which deserves to be noted here.

Industry cannot wholly escape the intrusions of mysticism. Not only that industrial undertakings—the building of a house or canoe, the beginning or conclusion of field work—are accompanied by rituals, sanctions which place a halo about particular techniques and render them immune to change; but also: thinking about techniques tends to merge with other thinking about strange and puzzling things—it becomes mystical. The construction of an arrow is guided by the lessons of experience, and so it is a good arrow; but the proffered explanation of its effectiveness is magical.

We must not forget that in any given society at any given time, the vast majority of devices and techniques are used not by those who invented them but by individuals who were taught the use of these pre-existing techniques and devices. In a world full of strange things these concoctions of man are among the strangest. Failing to discern the shrewdness of man behind the tool, the primitive credits it to the divine.[12]

Social Life

The role of social organization as a determinant of thought and attitude is more elusive. I need not again emphasize the prevailing conservatism of the primitive group except in one respect: the sub-division into families, clans, secret societies, and the like, still further enhances conformity and strengthens authority. Inside these smaller units, the patterns and idea-systems (Teggart) of the tribe do not encounter opposition, as is frequently the case in modern society. On the contrary: consisting so often of 'brothers' in blood, fiction, or function, these social units constitute groups of cultural conformity within which the principle of authority holds easy sway. This applies especially to the social phase

---

[12] This need not surprise us. When watching the legion-handed performance of a printing press in operation or sensing the invisible work of an electric power station, immaculate and ominous, do we not exclaim: 'It is like magic!' And this term describes our state of mind more accurately than we should care to admit. If the machine were to do something not merely strange but impossible, the beholder, unless properly equipped, would not be able to tell the difference.

of life, in the narrow sense, such as morals, rituals, mores, social customs, etiquette. In other domains, it is well to repeat here, social imperatives slacken somewhat. In economic pursuits and industry, as well as in artistic techniques, conformity, as we saw, is possible only within limits. For here the individual must reckon with the results of his personal experience. These must be heeded, society or no society. And further: hunting, fishing, building, pottery- or basket-making, crafts in general, are less uniform and conservative than the ideas about these things; military techniques are less conservative than the notions about war. Religion, from one angle, must be classed with morality, social functions, and the rest, for the techniques of religion—magical acts and the like—are proof against objective experience.[13]

Granting the mystic proclivities of the primitive mind, social organization furnishes a fertile field for the expression of such proclivities. We saw how in religion psychic relations become, through projection, objective fact. Thus the association of things in idea easily passes into ascription of objective bonds or even attribution of common nature. Things, beings, acts, which occur together in time or in space, things that are in contact or form parts of a whole, interpenetrate, become as one. A man is identified with his totemic animal, and both, as in Australia, are one with a wooden slab. A weapon which inflicts a wound may also heal it. The nails, hair, picture, name, of a person cannot readily be detached from him; unless special equally magical precautions are taken, their fates are linked for good or evil. A thing sacred or unclean radiates its essence—infection spreads from it. It may not be touched, seen, spoken of, except in strictly prescribed ways.

All this we know. What, it may be asked, is the connexion with social units? It lies in their functions. A clan, for example, will in its functions have reference to property, art, ritual, medicinal rites, a species of animal. All these things and processes are brought together as functions of a social unit. In the minds of the component individuals, they interpenetrate and merge. This psychological association is translated into objective relationships. Thus there comes into being what Lévy-Bruhl calls a 'cycle of participation.' This mystic complex promptly becomes traditional. Spontaneous tendency is reinforced by dogma. The outlines

---

[13] A critical reader might take exception to the proposition that ideas are more conservative than acts or arts. 'Is it not true,' he might remark, 'that in modern days such "arts" as agriculture or housekeeping are still conservative, whereas ideas, here and there at least, tend to be free?' Though true, this does not contradict the statement in the text. Cultural conditions apart, ideas are more plastic than arts. They can go further, in both conformity and heresy, than the arts which can be neither wholly conforming nor wholly free.

of each cycle of participation, moreover, are brought into relief by juxtaposition to other similar cycles clustering about the other social units in the tribe.[14]

And, as in religion, the final touch is added by ceremonialism. Periodically, in a setting of thrill, ecstasy, and terror, the human battery is recharged, ideationally and emotionally. More effectively, perhaps, than any other single factor, this ritual reliving of the cycle of participation places it far beyond the range of analysis, doubt, or criticism. To this effect a share is contributed by symbolism, more often than not the symbolism of art. In the whirl of ritual colours, shapes, patterns, masks, tunes, rhythms, and words, all carry their vicarious message, and the message, once more, is the cycle of participation, the mystic complex. Concrete, tangible, visible, and audible to all, the art-symbol radiates back to the tribesmen the thoughts and emotions it had once absorbed from them in the contacts of life.

Artistic Life

This brings us to the consideration of art. Art as technique appears at the edges of skill, expertness, virtuosity. The conditions of primitive life, as we saw, favour the emergence of these achievements and the latter again pave the way for art. This applies to the plastic arts but also to song, dance, and story. When Havelock Ellis said that the primitives danced their way through life, the exaggeration was pardonable. In dance and song they find exercise and enjoyment, but also a periodic outlet for pent-up emotions—a safety valve against a society which at best fits a bit tightly over original nature [15]—as well as ample oppor-

---

[14] We saw a while ago a striking example of this in totemism. But totemism here figures but as one of a class. Families, local groups, religious societies, fulfil similar functions.

It is also to be noted that the difference between primitive and modern is here one of degree rather than of kind. In religion, law, politics, we observe how things, persons, acts, become sanctified through association with exalted institutions; while social groups—families, colleges, political parties—continue to preserve the emotional values of society, thus enhancing their consolidation and interpenetration.

[15] Two institutions common in primitive society are illuminating in this connexion. One is the orgiastic licence which often follows upon a ritualistic period, the other is the feature of clowning which occurs in secret societies. Both may be envisaged as a protest against constraining and excessive standardization. In the post-ritualistic sexual orgy, as for example in central Australia, the natives freely transgress the otherwise rigid sexual taboos. These prohibitions are set aside during a moment of communal licence (it must, of course, be remembered that, were the forbidden not pleasurable, hence desirable, it would not have to be forbidden). Similarly in the case of the clown—his function is to break the rules. In attire, move-

tunity for skilled performance, gratification of vanity, stimulation and
satisfaction of the sex urge. On such occasions there are performers and
spectators, not always carefully separated. Together the group experiences a physical, aesthetic, and emotional enhancement of life. _theatrical_

In all these forms of art—plastic, vocal, narrative, histrionic, choreo-
graphic—the pattern exacts conformity to a 'harnessed art' (Von den
Steinen's *gebundene Kunst*). But here as in other primitive situations,
the negative aspect of pattern must not be overestimated; the norm may
be rigid, but it is accepted as something given, therefore beyond question
or dispute. Within the norm, ample opportunity is provided for individuality, skill, and achievement.

As will have been gathered from what was said about ceremonialism,
the intellectual aspect of primitive art centres in symbolism. Properly
speaking symbolic art ceases to be art in the true sense. Functioning no
longer as 'significant form'—significant, that is, in and by itself—it now
lends itself to vicarious and vehicular purposes. From the moment when
art becomes the carrier of a message, what counts is no longer the carrier
but the message it carries.[16]

Primitive mind, as already revealed in religion and ritual, lends itself
admirably to the administration of symbolic functions. The difficulty
the primitive experiences in shaking off associations of any sort, as well
as the ease with which he passes from the subjective to the objective, real
or presumed, conspire to make him symbol-minded. With a facility surprising to us, he is wont to see or hear one thing and experience another.
As a result primitive culture is shot through with symbolic connexions.
War and the chase, property and sex, status, rank and personal valour,
are all linked up with these eloquent signs which, vocal at all times and
vociferous in ritual, bind value to value and man to man by bonds of
common meaning and shared emotion.

Primitive Culture as a Whole

Turning at last to primitive life and thought in its totality and rooted
in a local culture, we find it differing in certain respects from the more
complex and less restricted civilizations of history. Like a plant rooted

ment, language, he does the opposite of the prescribed and proper. Everyone is
shocked—into amusement, however, not protest. The clown's behaviour is a vicarious
gesture of the group, a gesture of liberation from the pressure of exacting routine.
He is a sort of a positive scapegoat.

[16] It may be noted in passing as possibly significant, that from primitive times onwards, the highest and most perfect products of art in materials, movements, story,
or drama, are found outside of symbolism.

in its soil, a primitive culture grows up in its locality and becomes firmly entrenched in it. By innumerable bonds of interest, knowledge and interaction, it is tied to that bit of the natural scene which happens to be its home. In the light of other standards and a superior sophistication, the native may be an ignorant person, but he is well versed in his immediate surroundings. His knowledge is empirical—much of it is error— but it suffices for the purposes of life. It permits him to obtain from nature what he wants and, within limits, when he wants it. Such a relationship to be effective must be dynamic, and so it is. It consists of activities, of efforts purposefully exercised. All members of the group, barring only the small children, the very aged and the sick, share in these efforts. The business of physical living is here an active, continuous, day-by-day affair. Much of the available time and human energy is absorbed in it. This also is the domain of skills. Primitives know how to use their bodies and their tools. Though arduous, many of these activities are also pleasurable. They keep one on the alert. This aspect of life, so often reduced to a minimum in our own vicarious living, is here developed to the full.

Primitive culture is compact. We know how restricted are its geographical and historical horizons. Though notorious for its limitations, localism has its compensating virtues. Living in familiar surroundings, dealing with familiar things, seeing familiar faces, may not be conducive to intellectual breadth or adventurousness of spirit, but attitudes are genuine, convictions strong, knowledge is solid. Reading about the 'far away' in newspapers and the 'long ago' in books may lend the average modern a certain veneer of sophistication. The spread is wide but the substance thin, the resulting knowledge little more than presumption and affectation. There is little sham in primitive culture. The native's world is compact and thick with content. What it means it means, and the primitive is very much of one piece with it.

As a process, we can see, primitive culture is dynamic and vibrant; as content it is traditional. Preservation is the watchword. Radical changes are as rare as are criticisms of the *status quo* or visions of improvement. In attempting to evaluate this cultural situation, it is, however, easy to go astray. In a culture quickened by progressive outlooks, individual traditionalism becomes reaction, perhaps betraying an ignorant or callous indifference to some precious values of the group. Not so where traditionalism is the order of the day. Here it becomes the goal for much ardent endeavour. It must be known. It will be understood. It is accepted as wisdom. If properly wielded, it becomes a source of power. The tribal old man, steeped in tradition, is an artist, after a fashion, and an art critic. He is an expert in form and a keen censor of the

ANTHROPOLOGY

fitness of things. Those familiar at first hand with traditional cultures know the charm of such a personage; there is wisdom here and dignity, considered judgment, inflexible conviction, a matured sense of values. One immersed in the modern world where change is common and the necessity for change a favourite slogan, knows only too well that many current values are not worth preserving, but he is likely to forget that the sense that existing values are worth preserving is a great asset; it is itself a cultural value. Living for the future breeds enthusiasm and keeps one on the go; but it is likely to detract from one's appreciation and enjoyment of the present in which, when all is said, one must live. The primitives live by the past but also in and for the present. Theirs is a restricted life and a small world. Space and time have cut it to a slight scale, but it has wholeness, this world of the primitives, and depth, and the wholesome feel of immediacy. With an ardour unmarred by criticism or vision, the primitives make the best of the here and now. Comparisons are invidious. Something is lost, something is gained. Viewed without prejudice, it *is* a life, not unworthy of humans and possessing a charm all its own.

Chapter XXVI

THE WHITE MAN'S BURDEN

> There are two sides in all situations,
> that of the driver and that of the mule.
> *An old adage.*

What Civilization Does to the Primitives

At different times in the history of civilization and in many different places individuals and groups belonging to a higher culture have come in contact with their primitive contemporaries. When such contacts were restricted to casual visits by merchants or travellers or seekers for the exotic, they were innocent of cultural consequences. Neither the primitives nor the moderns were to any marked degree influenced or affected by such contacts. This, however, belongs to the past generations. Today White man's civilization is everywhere encroaching upon primitive domains. The territories of the primitives, whether in Australia, the South Seas, Asia, Africa, or the two Americas, have simply been taken possession of by peoples and nations who could command irresistible tools of conquest. Almost invariably, these conquests were bloody, conscienceless, and devastating to the natives. The higher Indian civilizations of Peru, Mexico, and Yucatan have gone down before the fire-arms of armoured Spaniards. With minor variations, a similar process took place in the conquest of Siberia by the Russian Cossacks, the occupation of Australia by English colonists and convicts, the dismemberment of native Africa, the 'winning' of North America by the English and French settlers of the United States and Canada, or the partitioning of the islands of the South Seas between the French, British, German, Dutch, and American nations.

The prime object and major outcome of these expansions of White civilization was, as everyone knows, the economic exploitation of these territories, which contained untold wealth in raw materials, as well as cheap or free labour. While this was happening on a world scale, another and older process was also taking place, namely, the settlement in different native domains, and for more or less prolonged periods of residence, of missionaries whose function it was to carry the Gospel

427

to the heathens and wherever possible to baptize them. The net outcome of these historic events represents perhaps the ugliest and most shameful chapter in the history of mankind. Natives were massacred, exploited, pauperized, and speaking generally, they have been permitted or induced to lose their culture and to degenerate physically.

Some aspects of this tragedy were, perhaps, unavoidable, for example, the ease with which natives in different parts of the world fell prey to White man's diseases, such as measles, scarlet fever, diphtheria, tuberculosis, and the like. While the problem of immunity is still very much of a puzzle to the biologist and physician, the facts of crude experience indicate beyond a shadow of a doubt that new diseases are especially devastating to a population. This factor has invariably been magnified by the inadequate medical provisions characteristic of colonial affairs. But there were other aspects, for example alcoholism, which was everywhere imposed upon the natives notwithstanding the overt professions and regulations to the contrary.

This is, however, a text-book of anthropology, not a treatise on international morals. I cannot, therefore, pursue any further the morbid tale of the particular ways in which White man conceived of his burden and the price the primitives were made to pay for the privilege of knowing and worshipping a true God. What interests us here as anthropologists is more particularly the cultural degeneration of the natives. Minor variations in cultures, when they appear and function in the historical contact of peoples, seem to be among the most powerful incentives of development and progress. But there is a limit to the cultural disparity between two groups in contact which can be resolved with relative safety. When the disparity is extreme, as in this case, there is danger. This refers to both parties concerned. It is often forgotten that the degeneration of natives in colonial territories runs parallel with the deterioration of the Whites, who more often than not 'go native,' lose their moral stamina, self-respect, and whatever other items of humanity they may have possessed. It was easy to overlook this factor in view of the fact that the contacts here involved took place in native territory and the number of Whites participating in them was relatively slight in comparison to the masses of native population.

But this aspect also we may let pass to turn to the major problem, namely the cultural deterioration of the natives themselves. The introduction of White man's manufactures and tools invariably led to the demoralization and ultimate decay of native crafts. White man's devices proved so alluring, were so handy, and on the whole so cheap, that natives everywhere fell upon these innovations with zest. When a

good tool or a handy article can be had without effort and for a very
small cost, the laborious and time-consuming techniques of the primitives naturally recede. The same happens to the social and political
aspects of the native culture. The chiefs, medicine-men, and other leaders
and dignitaries of the primitives cannot maintain their prestige in the
presence of colonial officials or missionaries whose might is supported
by the armed power and moral authority of the White stranger. A boss
who has a boss over him is no boss at all, and so the chiefs became mere
figureheads utilized by the foreigners for their own purposes but no
longer enjoying the confidence or respect of their own brethren—
especially not of the young, who naturally are most easily influenced and
begin to fall away from their old ways and allegiances. They themselves,
however, come to live a life strangely devoid of content, ambition, or
purpose. Racial prejudice or its twin, social snobbishness, bars the
way to their adequate participation in the culture of the White intruders.
Their own culture, on the other hand, no longer offers them any ob-
jectives worthy of effort or sacrifice. Thus they find themselves in a
cultural vacuum, serving the White master for whatever little favours
or emoluments may fall to their share, and wasting their lives and
their substance in dissipation, an existence not so much immoral, perhaps, as amoral, for a cultural in-between has no morality.

Similarly with religion. The beatific aspects of Christianity must
everywhere have appeared strangely remote to the natives. To them,
at any rate, the Garden of Eden, though at times accepted as a matter
of superficial faith, must have seemed a very remote and unreal place.
The imposition upon natives, still half immersed in their own traditional
attitudes, of a system of belief and worship which could establish no
contacts with their behaviour, interests, or understanding, constitutes
perhaps the most stupid act of racial pride and cultural snobbishness
ever perpetrated by White civilization. Many individual representatives
of the Christian religion have, of course, functioned to the benefit and
help of the natives, but these are mere exceptions in the totality of this
wasteful and absurd process of mass conversion imposed upon a world
of 'heathens.'

Nor is this all. Paraphrasing the familiar saying, the natives might be
pictured as uttering, 'Let us eat, drink, and be merry, for short of this
we are dead already.' When life offers nothing, its little petty pleasures
and excitements may at least be exploited while physical existence persists. Now precisely this has been observed and recorded again and
again from all corners of the earth. When Rivers mournfully refers to
the Melanesians as 'dying from boredom,' when we hear about the

native migrants of Siberia that they are losing their zest for life, when the American Indians, especially the men, are represented by government officials as lazy, indolent parasites devoid of all stamina and ambition, these are merely different formulae for the same fundamental fact that life in a cultural void is no life at all for man, and this is precisely the tragic setting bestowed upon the natives by the intrusion of White man and his civilization.

The 'Essential Kaffir' at Bay. To particularize for a moment. The 'instinctive' because 'primitive' socialism of the South African Kaffir must be distinguished—Sarah Gertrude Millin correctly holds—from the 'self-conscious' and 'deliberate' socialism of the modern European. The land of the native camp or *Kraal* belongs to the community. The chief is no more than its trustee. Under this system destitution is impossible: whosoever needs assistance receives it unquestioningly. A fellow-tribesman is a 'brother' and is treated as one. At the same time the tribe is responsible not merely for the well-being and security but for the misdeeds of its members. 'Owning things,' as an individual, is not part of the native Kaffir's ambition.

The intrusion of the European changes all this. As 'the Kaffir drives the animal,' we are told, so 'the European drives the Kaffir.' When the Kaffir goes to town, to seek employment, the European way of life creeps up on him with his job. He no longer accepts his country brother as an equal. The latter, again, looks down upon the town Kaffir for performing menial tasks for his foreign masters.

Though the black tribesmen continue to increase in number, the lands assigned to them have shrunk. Being incapable of mastering intensive agriculture in a hurry, the Kaffir finds himself confronted with economic dearth. Literally driven to the city, he is now dependent upon *any* employment that may be thrown open to him. There he may be seen as one of a motley crowd of job-seekers dressed in discarded European clothing, 'the unrelated, the filthy, the unsightly rags that not the most degraded white man would wear.' To the average European these disinherited natives are 'niggers,' a human variety of a half-domesticated animal. Here, as in other regions where white and native are brought face to face, there seems to be no escape from this tragic predicament, nor a remedy for it. No remedy, that is, short of a recognition on the part of the European that 'the white man's burden' presents an opportunity for cultural achievement which would require not intelligence alone, but sympathy, understanding, and patience, infinite patience.[1]

---

[1] The Kaffir material is gleaned from Sarah Gertrude Millin's enlightened book, *The South Africans*, pp. 237–244.

'*School-boy*' *Superiority Complex*. Much has been said in these pages
about the role of education, for good or evil. In his book, *Must England
Lose India?* Lieutenant-Colonel Arthur Osburn, not a radical nor an
Indian nationalist, but an English official who wants England to keep
India, holds the English school system, especially the institution of
boy-prefects, responsible for the behaviour of Englishmen in India and
the ensuing problems. Writes the Colonel:

'Young men who have recently left Public Schools and Universities
admit that their outlook, and especially their attitude towards those
they are afterwards called upon to govern, is influenced by what may be
called the School-prefect mind—it is, in fact, "cheek" for anyone not
of the same race or antecedents to question their opinion or action.

'This complex of "cheek" remains fixed throughout the lives of very
many ex-Public School men. Orders, however rash, unreasonable, or
unjust, or however brusquely or even insolently given, must be obeyed,
or the offending one will be treated with insult or with the physical
violence which a prefect of an English Public School—who is himself
little more than a child—may inflict on a somewhat smaller child—
some third-form boy who dares to question his authority, or whose
manner he dislikes, or who is not sufficiently submissive and subservient
to satisfy the *amour propre* of his lordship the prefect.

'The English upper classes, even from their earliest years, are thus
taught to exalt Authority—even when it is wielded by a school-boy
in his teens—and abase Reason. Unfortunately other races have the
temerity to imagine that Authority that is intolerant of Reason is not
an Authority to command moral support or respect, even though it be
backed up by the prefect's cane, or the boot of an irritable official.

'As a result of this early training, we have now got to the stage when
we consider it to be "cheek" for a Belgian or a Hindu or a member
of some weaker race than our own to demand social or economic equality or to argue against our decisions. One hears the word "cheek" used
frequently whenever any weaker or smaller power lays claim to some
disputed island or territory. We have, in short, the prefectorial-complex
—a state of mind quite incompatible with the theory embodied in the
Covenant of the League of Nations.

'The [printer's] "proofs" of these incidents were submitted to several
young men who have recently left Eton and Harrow and other Public
Schools, some of them as prefects. They were returned with the admis-
sion that they exemplified the prefectorial attitude—the school-boy's
domination-complex. It is supposed that the playing of games and the
much belauded discipline of team work acts as an antidote. But why

do we deny that one of the main objects of games is to defeat—and just that much humiliate—our fellow-men, and so proportionately increase our own pride and self-confidence, qualities by no means already lacking in the average young Englishman of the Public School class. The team spirit—so unattractive to us when it shows itself in the discipline of the wolf-pack or in the combination of a gang of cat burglars —has of course its good co-operative side, it also works as a form of *esprit de corps* against inconvenient questions in the House of Commons, as we discovered during the Irish Rebellion.

'The maxim concerning "Never hit a man excepting your own size" has, since the Boer War, become unfashionable. It would hardly suit the Public School system where a prefect, himself little more than a child, and at the most neurotic, irritable and erotic period in his life, is allowed to flog and to "discipline" the smaller children. Anyone who has been himself a prefect at a Public School knows that the system— if it can be called a system—saves the schoolmaster a good deal of trouble. The schoolmaster will tell the parents that it has a good "hardening" effect. Not long ago the House of Commons was informed by an ex-Harrovian Prime Minister that when the Almighty had anything "hard" to be done he found an Englishman to do it. The spectacle of an old Harrovian of the upper middle classes rendering a kind of "first-aid" to The Creator of the starry Universe would not, of course, raise a laugh at Harrow—perhaps after two thousand years of gloom a Pharisee may have laughed in the Underworld.' [2]

Indian Administration Under Commissioner John Collier

It is not possible here to review the ugly and humiliating record of American official dealings with the Indians in the past. Only a word as to the land tenure of the Indians before the General Allotment Act of 1887. Previous to this time Indian reservations were owned in common, title remaining in the tribe. Every member of the tribe could own as much land as he could beneficially use. His house and other improvements passed on to his heirs but he could not alienate and dispose of a square foot of tribal soil. Those reservations which escaped allotment have as much and frequently more land than they contained 60 years ago. Through the General Allotment Act the Government proceeded to break up the reservations to attach to each Indian there living a tract of land as his individual property, and to throw the part of the reserva-

[2] Lieutenant-Colonel Arthur Osburn, *Must England Lose India?* (Reprinted by permission of Alfred A. Knopf, Inc.)

tion not used in this individual land distribution open to White settlement. Thus the Indian was to become an individualized farmer and assume all of White man's burden with a comparatively small trust period during which the privilege of mortgaging and selling his land was denied him.

After allotment the individualized land began to slip out of the Indian owner's hand at high speed. When the trust period expired and the Indian was declared 'competent,' he disposed of his land in short order, spent the proceeds, and went to live with his relatives, and when an allotted Indian died, the usual impossibility to make an equitable partition of the land forced the sale, not to Indians but to those who had the money to buy, to the waiting White people. Thus allotment dissipated and continues to dissipate the Indian estate.

In 1887 the Indians were owners of 136,340,950 acres of the best land. In 1933 they were owners of 47,311,099 acres of which a full 20,000,000 acres were desert or semi-desert. The surface value of the Indian owned lands had shrunken 90% in 46 years. Of the residual land, 7,032,237 acres (the most convertible of the remnant) were awaiting a 'knockdown sale' to the Whites—a sale conducted by the Government itself usually without reference to Indian choice—and of the usable land still owned by the allotted Indians a full three-quarters was already possessed and used by Whites under the allotment-leasing system. Such land is tax-exempt, and when it was seized (by cattlemen, sheepmen, farmers, and grain corporations) they reaped the benefit of tax-exemption. Since 1837, 150,000 Indians have been rendered totally landless. The existing law—the practices mandatory or administratively inescapable under it—ensured the dispossession of the remaining allotted Indians within the present generation.

In his *A Bird's Eye View of Indian Policy, Historic and Contemporary* (submitted to the Subcommittee of the Appropriation Committee of the House of Representatives, December 30, 1935), Commissioner Collier writes, in substance, as follows: The general Allotment Act of 1887 was ostensibly to lead the Indians into the individualistic property system of the White man and thereby, automatically, into the White man's civilization and economic life. Actually, and intentionally also, it was put into law as a mechanism whereby, under cover of legality, the Indians could be gradually divested of the lands inviolately secured to them through treaties and through valid grants.

On its face a purely economic measure, the allotment law actually was a weapon for cultural destruction as well. Allotment was intended as a tool to destroy community and family ownership by individualizing the land, and to destroy Indian community and family life by scattering the Indians on to their individual (never their family) allotments.

A colour of protection was thrown about the allotted Indians through the provision of a twenty-five-year trust period before the allottees could get absolute fee patent. The theory was that in these twenty-five years the Indian allottees would become hard-working and hard-boiled, propertied individual citizens. But this beneficent theory was not implemented in action. There has never existed and there does not fully exist today, an adequate juvenile or adult educational system to fit Indians to become farmers, stockmen, woods-workers, or rural workers of any type. No sufficient provision of capital, equipment, housing, or livestock, through credit or through the wise use of Indian tribal and individual monies, was made in all these past years to enable Indians to wrest their livelihood from the soil.

The Indians did not, in fact, successfully become individualized property owners. Their effective property sense was, and largely it remains, a tribal, group, and family property sense. As a result of the allotment system, during less than a half century, they have lost about 90,000,000 acres of their lands. That is two-thirds of all their land in area; four-fifths, at least, in value. They have lost it through the sale of their fee patented allotments, through the sale by the Government of their inherited allotted lands, and through the cession to, or seizure by the Government, for settlement by Whites, of the so-called 'surplus' lands, namely, the lands that were supposedly not needed by the Indians after each member of the tribe had his allotment, usually a meagre allotment of grazing land.

The evils of allotment were not confined merely to the loss of land, as recorded by diminishing total quantities of land. Allotment and subsequent alienation checker-boarded many reservations to the extent of making the land unusable by Indians and forced its leasing to White cattlemen or farmers. Whatever excuse there may doubtfully have been for the allotment of good agricultural land, there was no justification whatever for the allotment of grazing and timber lands, which generally can be productively managed only in large blocks.

The Indian Reorganization Act of June 18, 1934, strikes at the vicious system of land ownership by allotment. As to those tribes who have accepted it (176 in all) the further allotment of land is debarred. The remaining unentered, ceded land is restored to the Indians on whose reservations where such land still exists and where a public school is served thereby.

The Commissioner holds that the blocking of further losses is not a complete solution of the Indian land problem; he feels that much of the land must be restored to tribal ownership and additional land provided.

In tribal constitutions adopted pursuant to the Reorganization Act, provision is made for revesting allotted and heirship lands back in tribal ownership. The revestment is wholly voluntary. This revestment is especially needed in the case of grazing and timber lands, where tribal ownership is essential to good land management and to the use of the land by Indians instead of by Whites. Moreover the Reorganization Act sets up a land purchase program with a view to blocking up shredded reservations and ultimately to providing land for at least a part of the one hundred thousand landless Indians of today. The $2,000,000 land purchase authorization of the Reorganization Act permits only a snail's pace when it is considered that the Indians need at least $60,000,000 of additional land merely for a subsistence agriculture, and another $70,000,000 to come up to rural White living standards. Far greater land values have been taken from the Indians through the allotment system in the last forty years.

Through the credit section of the Reorganization Act a further step towards restitution is taken. This section authorized the appropriation of $10,000,000 as a revolving loan fund to promote the economic development of Indian tribes and their members.

'The fund will prove to be too small,' adds Mr. Collier, 'but it is a beginning. The credit system thus created may well turn out to be a better system than White agricultural credit, because repayment of loans will be secured not by the mortgage system *per se* but by the making of careful farm management plans and by an advisory follow-up service which will keep the plans operating; above all, by the use of the group principle for the insuring of a thrifty use and a faithful repayment of loans. Indian service experience already has proved that Indians, so guided and organized, are good credit risks, and can put their capital to work and repay it.' [3]

The new Indian policy, through the Reorganization Act and otherwise, seeks to reinstate the Indians as normally functioning units, individual and group, into the life of the world. It makes them equal partners in Indian administration. It permits the adoption of tribal constitutions, which when approved by the Secretary of the Interior and ratified by the tribe, cannot be arbitrarily revoked or altered. It provides further for the chartering of Indian corporations, compounded to pro-

[3] John Collier, *A Bird's Eye View of Indian Policy, Historic and Contemporary* (1935).

mote economic enterprises and to enter into contracts with counties and states whereby they may receive the local public welfare services accorded to other American citizens. These charters are safeguarded through being made irrevocable except by act of Congress.

The response of the Indians to this opportunity for home rule has been enthusiastic, even overwhelming. That response was first indicated by the revolutionary step of submitting the proposed draft of the Reorganization Act to the Indians themselves, so that their objections and suggestions could be taken into account in the final draft. And the Act itself, even when passed, was not forced upon the Indians. Its adoption was made optional. Up to December 31, 1935, elections on adoption or rejection have been held by 263 tribes, of which 176 accepted the Act, 75 rejected it, and 12 elections are in doubt. The enthusiasm of the Indians for home rule is indicated by the fact that on some reservations practically 100% of the eligible voters, men and women, turned out to vote; on all the reservations which have voted, an average of 63% turned out, which is far above the usual turn-out of White voters in a Presidential election. Up to December 31, 1935, 21 tribal constitutions had been ratified; 5 had been rejected and were being worked over for resubmission; and a number of charters of incorporation were at various stages towards submission for ratification.

Here again, the Reorganization Act seeks to get to the root of the problem, in two directions. In effect, it creates a special Indian Civil Service by permitting the Secretary of the Interior to set up standards for Indian employees and to appoint Indians who come up to these standards without regard to the Civil Service system. This provision is not intended, nor will it be administered in a manner, to lower the standards of administration; but it does open the door to qualified Indians who are equipped through character and experience to take a dignified and responsible part in the guidance of their own people.

But it is not enough merely to open the door. Indians must become systematically qualified to enter the door, as well as to enter into the professions and vocations of the White world. To that end, the Reorganization Act authorizes a loan fund of $250,000 a year for the vocational and higher education of Indians. Similar but much more limited loan funds have existed for some years.

During the present year, 250 Indian students are in universities and colleges with the help of these funds and 125 are in vocational schools. Of this total, about two-thirds are studying subjects such as teaching, engineering, social service, business and business administration, agriculture, and forestry, that will fit them for future posts in and out of the

Indian service. It should be noted that in the operations carried out through emergency grants (Public Works Authority, Indian Emergency Conservation Work, Roads and Soil Conservation) Indians not only have done practically all of the rank-and-file work, but have been used to an extent heretofore unknown in the facilitating and supervising posts.

With these funds, when they are released by the Comptroller-General, it is proposed to concentrate on a number of demonstrational rehabilitation projects, in which groups of qualified Indian families will be launched on small-scale farming, stock-raising, and other rural industries.

Coupled with this, the Indian Service now has, for the first time in its history, through the co-operation of the Soil Conservation Service of the Department of Agriculture, adequate help to begin making systematic, integral, long-range plans on a number of reservations, for economic and social rehabilitation as a factor in the saving of the soil. Included in this planning will be reorientation of Indian education to the needs of soil conservation and conservation land use. Substantial progress in this direction is already being made at the new day schools and community centers of the Navajo reservation and among the Pueblos elsewhere.

Closely connected with the rehabilitation program are the Emergency Conservation Work and the Soil Conservation program on Indian Reservations. The Emergency Conservation Work among the Indians— the Indian part of the Civilian Conservation Corps—has made enormous strides in the betterment of the Indian estate—through water-development, fencing, range- and forest-improvement, truck trails, erosion-control, and similar work.

The Soil Conservation Service, during the past two years, has made great headway against the critical erosion and overgrazing problem on the Navajo Reservation, and it is initiating similar work among the New Mexico Pueblos and on the Wind River Reservation of Wyoming— work which will probably be extended later to still other eroded reservations. Probably half of the whole area of Indian land is badly run down through overgrazing, erosion, and the overcutting of timber. The Indian Reorganization Act makes mandatory the permanent good management of these lands, in order to stop the depletion of their natural resources. The Game Co-ordination Act of 1934 likewise makes mandatory the permanent wise management of the wild-life resources of the Indian Reservations. In this item we have made only the slightest beginning as yet.

In a nutshell, the new land policy may be summed up as: prevention of further land loss, increase in land holdings, reintegration of tribal holdings, conservation and upbuilding of the soil and its products, and use of the soil and its products by and for the Indians.

In a section of his report entitled 'The Right of Indian Culture to Live,' the Commissioner gives expression to what might be called his credo as to Indian policy. He writes: 'On the purely cultural side, only sheer fanaticism would decide the further destruction of Indian languages, crafts, poetry, music, ritual, philosophy, and religion. These possessions have a significance and a beauty which grew patiently through endless generations of a people immersed in the life of nature, filled with imaginative and ethical insight into the core of being. To destroy them would be comparable to destroying the rich cultural heritage of the Aryan races—its music and poetry, its religion and philosophy, its temples and monuments. Yet through generations the Government did deliberately seek to destroy the Indian cultural heritage; and only because the roots of it lay so deep in the Indian soul, and only because age-old, instinctive modes of thought and expression are so much less destructible than individual life itself, has the Indian culture stubbornly persisted.

'The new Indian policy seeks to preserve these unique cultural values through the Indian schools and otherwise. Through the recently enacted Indian Arts and Crafts Act, which creates a permanent Indian Arts Commission, the Government now is setting out to preserve, enrich, and protect from factory made imitations the rapidly disappearing and unique Indian crafts. Their long-abrogated constitutional rights of religious liberty have been restored to the Indians. But while protecting the Indian culture from violent up-rooting, the new policy seeks also to give the Indians the full advantage of modern education and of science, and thus fit them for modern life.' [4]

Juxtaposing, in conclusion, the historic policy of Indian administration with the present policy, the Commissioner writes:

'The historic policy: That Indian property must pass to Whites; that Indian organization must be repressed and prevented; that Indian family life must be dismembered; that Indian cultures must be killed; and that Indians as a race must die.

'The present policy: That Indian property must not pass to Whites; that Indian organization must be encouraged and assisted; that Indian family life must be respected and reinforced; that Indian culture must be appreciated, used, and brought into the stream of American culture

[4] John Collier, *op. cit.*

as a whole; and that the Indian as a race must not die, but must grow and live.' [5]

I need hardly add how deeply I sympathize with the efforts of the present administration. I must however say, to my regret, that I do not share the implied optimism as to the possibility at this late date of saving the culture and the creativeness of the Indians along the old lines. The material aspects of the situation can certainly be relieved and built up, the self-respect of the Indian can be restored, but the idea of native cultures existing safely, happily, and creatively in our midst somehow does not fit into my view of the nature and possibilities of our civilization. I hope that I am wrong and that John Collier is right.

[5] All the information utilized in this section was very obligingly sent to me upon request, from the Commissioner's office. Most of the facts here stated and comments made are directly reproduced from the official publications; so much so that I have omitted the customary quotation marks and instead merely express my appreciation of the Commissioner's co-operation.

By way of recollection I might add that when some thirteen years ago, during one of my class hours at the Walden School in New York, I first met John Collier, a pale, sensitive, and enthusiastic young man, absorbed in the problems, the culture, especially the art of the Indians, I should never have believed that under our system of administration he would one day be placed in a position to guide and determine the Indian policies of the nation. That this has occurred shows that scepticism can sometimes be overdone.

PART III

THE WAYS OF CULTURE

Chapter XXVII

CULTURE AND ENVIRONMENT

In the course of our discussion of the different aspects of primitive cultures we have come across many similarities, as well as equally numerous and conspicuous differences. As one contemplates similarities in things, customs, or ideas, comprised in the cultures of different times and places, the thought of the psychic unity of man forces itself upon the mind. How much the same, after all, is man wherever and whenever found! The differences, on the other hand, invite another thought: how varied and multiform is human culture! Confronted with this dilemma, we are prompted to search for some general and simple explanation of the similarities and, perhaps, for an equally sweeping one of the differences. That such a general explanation can and will be found is doubtful indeed, and it is more than doubtful whether, if found, it would prove simple. The fact remains that the history of human thought abounds in efforts to find precisely such an explanation. We are already familiar with the racial theories of culture calculated to reduce cultural similarities and differences to inborn racial characteristics. It has been amply shown, however, that these interpretative attempts will not hold water. Do not the cultures of racially identical or related stocks abound in differences, whereas the cultures of peoples of different stock reveal equally patent similarities? The purpose of racialism, moreover, was rather to set certain broad limits to racial capacity, to define cultural possibilities, than to account for the similarities or differences in particulars such as are revealed, for example, in this volume.

Another similar approach may be seen in the attempts to reduce culture to physical environment, or one or more of its aspects, such as geographical position, climate, flora, or fauna. What renders this approach so attractive is its apparent matter-of-factness due to the objective solidity of the physical environment. It is describable and measurable, if not calculable. Culture reduced to such a determinant would lose its elusiveness and for once become amenable to law and order. It should cause no surprise, therefore, to find inquisitive spirits adopting this point of view on more than one occasion. Montesquieu in his *Spirit of*

Laws advocated an environmental interpretation of cultural differences.[1] The talented historian, Taine, once aroused considerable attention by his attempt to reduce culture, especially in its artistic and literary aspects, to geographical factors, the *milieu*. The English historian, Buckle, though not as narrow or dogmatic as is often assumed, was inclined to stress environmental determinants in his unfinished *History of Civilization in England*. Ratzel, geographer and anthropologist, argued the case with a greater regard for the niceties of scientific method. In his famous essay, *Der Staat und sein Boden* (*The State and Its Territory*), he made a systematic effort to correlate forms of political organization with differences in physical environment. In his better-known work, *Anthropogeographie* (rendered into English and revised by Miss Helen Churchill Semple), the same thesis is discussed on a broader basis of a comprehensive comparative material. Aside from Miss Semple, the most enthusiastic of modern environmentalists is perhaps the geographer, Ellsworth Huntington, author of *The Pulse of Asia* and *Climate and Civilization*, whose environmentalism takes a peculiar slant in so far as he tends to subordinate other factors in the environment to climate.

---

[1] Space is lacking here for an analysis or criticism of Montesquieu's famous book, but the reader might enjoy pondering awhile over one or two references: Montesquieu holds that the inhabitants of cold countries tend to be brave, vigorous, insensible to pain, devoid of sex passion and possessed of relatively strong physical frames and phlegmatic temperaments. The people of warm climates are weak, timid, apathetic towards physical exertion, vivacious, sensitive to pleasure or pain, inordinate in their sexual indulgences and utterly lacking in mental ambition (*cf.* F. Thomas, *Environmental Basis of Society*, referring to *Spirit of Laws*, bk. XIV, ch. II). As to sensitivity to pain, in particular, Montesquieu has this to say: '. . . now it is evident (*sic!*) that the large bodies and coarse fibres of the people of the north are less capable of laceration than the delicate fibres of the inhabitants of warm countries; consequently the soul is there less sensible to pain. You must flay a Moscovite alive to make him feel.' (*Ibid.*) Environmentalism apart, compare with this the following sketch of a sub-racial stock, namely the Huns, written over one thousand years earlier (around the middle of the sixth century) by Jordanes, a Gothic historian: 'By the terror of their features they [the Huns] inspired great fear in those whom perhaps they did not really surpass in war. They made their foes flee in horror because their swarthy aspect was fearful, and they had, if I may call it so, a sort of shapeless lump, not head, with pin-holes rather than eyes [*sic!*]. Their hardihood is evident in their wild appearance, and they are beings who are cruel to their children on the very day they are born. For they cut the cheeks of the males with a sword, so that before they receive the nourishment of milk they must learn to endure wounds. Hence they grow old beardless and their young men are without comeliness, because a face furrowed by the sword spoils by its scars the natural beauty [*sic!*] of a beard. They are short in stature, quick in bodily movement, alert horsemen, broad shouldered, ready in the use of bow and arrow, and have firm-set necks which are ever erect in pride. Though they live in the form of men, they have the cruelty of wild beasts.' (Jordanes, *The Gothic History*, English version by Charles Christopher Mierow, pp. 86–87. My attention was drawn to this passage by my wife.)

As a sample of the climatic approach combined with a highly specula-tive use of the concept of natural selection, I offer the following excerpt from Huntington's *The Character of Races*. In this case the subject of his analysis is the American Indian, whose 'racial characteristics' he is endeavouring to explain. 'On their way from Asia to America,' we read, 'almost every stream of migrants, no matter what its original racial characteristics, probably passed through the regions where Arctic hys-teria is most prevalent, and where life often depends on sheer passive endurance rather than on energy, activity, or inventiveness. There for perhaps thousands of years they may have been subjected to a selective process which weeded out those who were of the more nervous, active types, the kind who lead, who invent, and who are largely responsible for human progress. Thus the American aborigines, whatever their race, may have acquired a certain uniformly dull, passive quality. They did not, to be sure, lose all capacity for improvement, as their achieve-ments abundantly prove. Moreover, among them as among any race new mutants may have arisen, and may yet arise, possessing qualities sur-passing those of the original Asiatic stock. Nevertheless when once a certain quality has been acquired by a species or race, laws of heredity make it very difficult to get rid of that quality. So it would seem that the Arctic environment may have stamped upon the people of America a certain lack of originality, a certain tendency toward stoicism, a great ability to endure privation; and may have weeded out much, though not all, of the alertness, curiosity, and inventive faculty which are so essential to progress. This may perhaps help to explain some of the qualities which distinguish the American race, if race it is, from the races of Europe and Asia.' [2] This excerpt from Huntington's attempt to interpret the 'characteristics' of the American race, 'if race it is,' in terms of its climatic past and under the shadow of Arctic hysteria, presents a good sample of what happens when a student, laying aside the impedi-ments of method, seeks to deduce cultural traits from the vicissitudes of climate. Though a detailed analysis of this passage would furnish interesting material for a study of method, logic, psychology, and tem-perament, I shall resist the temptation to carry it out, leaving this enter-taining task to the reader. Instead, let us glance at the facts.

It is clear enough that of the different aspects of culture the material side is most intimately related to physical environment. People eat, dress, build, and move about in accordance with the requirements of the en-vironment and by means of the facilities and materials provided by it.

[2] Ellsworth Huntington, *The Character of Races*, pp. 71–72. (Reprinted by per-mission of Charles Scribner's Sons.)

Industry, always matter-of-fact and pragmatic, is ever carefully attuned to the materials it uses. What can be made out of wood cannot be made with equal facility, if at all, out of bark or bone or hide. Nor is earth the same as clay, nor clay the same as stone. Each kind of material, though plastic to a degree, sets limits to its use by its inherent properties; and industry, if it is to be effective, must take cognizance of this fact. While all this should be granted, unprejudiced inspection of the actual state of affairs presently introduces a variety of complications. What nature offers merely indicates what is there to be used, but not that it must or will be used; and what it does not offer, at the time and place, may yet be secured by stepping outside of one's immediate environment and borrowing from another. Any naïve spirit, when first confronted with the wood-industry of the Northwest Indians, would immediately conclude that these natives were doomed to become expert carvers. What would you expect, one might exclaim, when nature on all sides offers such excellent material? This argument, at first apparently unanswerable, presently collapses if one shifts one's attention farther south and observes that in the region occupied by the Indians of California an equal if not greater sylvan opulence fails to result in a similar proclivity towards woodwork. Among the California Indians, in fact, wood-industry has not developed in any form, basketry taking its place. An equally instructive example is offered by the distribution of pottery in North America in its relation to the materials available in the environment. Broadly speaking, the clay necessary for this industry is more or less available in all parts of the continent, but pots are only made among certain tribes, as we saw. The fact, moreover, that the tribes with pottery, as well as those without it, cluster in continuous geographic areas, suggest the presence of another factor, namely the spread of pottery technique from tribe to tribe. Or, consider this fact: the Iroquois or Creek use pots; the California or Thompson Indians, baskets; the Pacific Coast peoples, finally, use wooden boxes for practically the same purposes, including that of cooking. The need is there throughout and it is essentially the same; to satisfy this need, advantage is taken of whatever material is available. What is culturally of significance here is that for cooking, for example, vessels are used. One way of making the water in the vessel boil or at least rise in temperature, is to throw stones heated on fire or coals into the water. Now this is done in all the areas here mentioned, while the material for the vessel varies in accordance with what is available or customary.

Another striking example in point is provided by the Eskimo. What is more plausible, one might ask, than that the Eskimo should build snow houses? Is not this material abundantly provided for by nature almost all year around, and does it not lend itself admirably for structural purposes—as illustrated, for instance, by the fact that wherever snow occurs at all, children, if not adults, engage in structural experiments in snow? For once, then, the environmentalists seem to stand on firm ground—until a glance across Bering Strait reveals the cultural status of the Chukchee and Koryak. These two Arctic peoples live under physical conditions differing in no essential respect from those of the Eskimo. Here, as in Arctic America, snow is almost continuously available; but there is no evidence of snow houses. Instead we know that these people construct large, clumsy tents, made of hide over heavy wooden supports, and that they have persisted in this custom in the face of their seasonal migrations during which they drag these clumsy contraptions along with them. A similar contrast obtains between these two groups—the Eskimo, on the one hand, and the Chukchee and Koryak on the other—with reference to the use made of the reindeer. This animal plays an important role in Arctic America as well as in Northeast Siberia. The Eskimo use it for food, they employ its hide for various purposes, and even the deer's antlers are, as we saw, made use of as a feature of the sledge. The deer is thus seen to play an important role in the life of the Eskimo, but not in front of the sledge, for the latter is driven by dogs, even though the reindeer, as a faster and stronger animal, would have done much better in this capacity. Among the Chukchee and Koryak, on the other hand, the reindeer is used to pull their sledges. The obvious immediate reason for this difference lies in the fact that among the Siberians the reindeer has been domesticated and is therefore available for transportation purposes, whereas among the Eskimo domestication has not occurred, nor have they had any opportunity to learn this art from their neighbours, the Indians, among whom domestication, always excepting the dog, is also unknown.[3]

Is it not clear then that what is culturally utilized is only part of what is available as raw material, and also that a similar or identical environmental feature will be used differently in different places, thus leading to a variety of cultural forms? To this it must be added that even in primitive conditions the limitations of one's immediate environment are often

[3] The reindeer is especially well adapted to the Arctic; even in very low temperatures it loses but little body heat for the reason that it perspires through the tongue instead of the skin, and as a consequence its hide does not become moist. For riding the reindeer is not particularly suitable; of the different herders of Siberia the Tungus alone use it for this purpose. When they do so, the rider is taught to sit on the neck of the animal instead of its back, for fear of injuring this weak link in its anatomy.

transcended to secure an object of use or even one of luxury. In the decidedly crude conditions of Australia we find that the Dieri of the Lake Eyre region send a yearly expedition to a region in central Queensland to secure a supply of the *pituri* root which they like to chew. The *pituri*, it will be observed, is not a food, nor otherwise a necessity; but they like to have it, and they have found a way of securing it. The country traversed by this expedition is, moreover, inhabited by hostile tribes, so that the men thus engaged must be a choice lot, armed and prepared to give battle. When reaching the point of their destination, they usually encounter opposition from the tribes inhabiting that district, but they generally succeed in collecting and carrying off large quantities of the coveted delicacy. The homeward journey invariably proves more peaceful, for now the Dieri are in a position to pay for their passage, as it were, with some of their supply of *pituri*. The residue is in part consumed at home and, in part, it is bartered off to other tribes farther south. Similar expeditions are sent out by the Dieri and neighbouring tribes to the South coast to obtain ochre which, it will be remembered, is used for ceremonial designs on the ground and for decorating the bodies of dancers.

The Todas of southern India provide another illustration. These people, as we already know, are great dairymen; their dairies, in fact, stand in the very centre of their socio-ceremonial life. Dairies require pots, and the Todas might be expected to supply this article of need. They do not do so, however, relying instead upon their neighbours, the Kota, for whatever earthenware they may need, as well as for a variety of iron objects. Nor is this case exceptional in southern and southeastern Asia, where such dependence upon one's neighbours for useful and even essential articles is a common and frequently noted phenomenon.

In Africa with its trade and markets, in Oceania with its well-regulated trading expeditions by sea, the relation of a tribe to its physical environment and its dependence upon it is constantly and inevitably broken into by its contacts with other tribes.

All these instances and any number of others that might be quoted are but special cases of the universal fact that any local culture, however firmly rooted in its own physical environment, depends upon other cultures for numerous articles of need, use, or luxury, brought in through barter, war, or chance, as well as for ideas, customs, rituals, myths, and what not, which percolate from individual to individual, or from tribe to tribe, in the course of their historic contacts, whether regulated or not. In primitive life, it is true, this aspect of culture is relatively less important than it is in modern days. It is, however, present and its significance should not be underestimated.

The environmentalist, often argumentative, does not leave these considerations unanswered. It is true, he admits, that things and ideas penetrate into a tribe from without, but then, he asks, where do these things or ideas come from? In their ultimate home it is the physical environment that controls their origin and development. It will be apparent from the preceding that this last assertion does not correspond to the known facts; still, for argument's sake, it may be granted. What is of interest in the environmentalist's argument is the logical flow. This tendency to go back to ultimate origins is a very common device of thinkers, I mean bad ones, in such matters. It might be designated as the 'reduction-to-the-amoeba fallacy.' The point is that things and ideas which reach a tribe from another tribe, *however* these ideas or things may have originated in the first place, are, in the second place, borrowed elements in the tribe that receives them, and with reference to this tribe they function as cultural traits, as part, therefore, of its cultural environment. If then they exercise an influence, as we know they do, this influence comes from culture, and to this extent this complex of events cuts into the dependence of the recipient tribe on its physical environment.

Still, it must be admitted that in primitive conditions every tribe or local group tends to utilize in its material culture at least part of the natural resources provided by its physical environment, and also that its culture is more significantly and constantly attuned to its immediate environment than it is to the contacts with other tribes. This, as we saw before, accounts for the relative autonomy and individuality of primitive cultures. In modern conditions all this is changed. The division of labour between social groups and within them, local industrial specialization, the enormous range and capacity of modern means of transportation and communication, the emergence of large and populous urban centres, the highly perfected system of credit in trade, all these and many other like factors have completely transformed the environmental orientation of civilization. In what it eats, wears, buys, hears, or knows, almost any modern hamlet finds itself in touch with the world, whereas its relationships to its own physical environment may be of the thinnest.[4]

[4] A stray example from the show-window of a drug store: A bit of gentian root from the mountains of south or central Europe; some seeds of nux vomica extracted from an orange-like fruit raised in Bombay, India; some roots of rhubarb grown in Tartary in the interior of China; some drops of aloes which flow from the cut piece of a plant in the Cape of Good Hope; a dose of peppermint herbs and bicarbonate of soda, native to the United States—all of these, combined in proper proportion, go to

Most important of all is to realize that in its relation to material culture, nature can set limits and furnish materials, but it cannot do more. If a thing is not there, its use may be precluded or at least rendered difficult and therefore, to a degree, unlikely; if it is there, it may be used—but need not. At most nature provides what Wissler calls the 'brick and mortar' of culture, merely the structural materials, not the plan. Now culture is, in essence, plan crystallized into pattern. Things are not what they are made of, but what they are used for, or even what they look like. A table is not a piece of wood but a table, unless used for feeding a fire, when it becomes fuel. An ax is not a bit of steel but an ax, unless it is discarded to become scrap iron. Skyscrapers have walls, we think, and most of us would feel uncomfortable if we realized they had not. But in fact the walls of skyscrapers, though appearing to be such, are not walls, strictly speaking, but steel frames, like those of bridges, stuffed with hollow porous brick and faced with thin sheets of marble, granite, or what not. Whatever as to substance and structure they may be, they *look* like walls, which in this case is sufficient unto the day. Similarly with automobiles. The base of a car, as well as its most important part, is the chassis plus the motor. Of course, there must be provision for the driver and the passengers, but also for their social ego. The car must look like a car, solid, comfortable, luxurious, and expensive. Now, the part of the car which to the beholder makes the car is the least solid, almost ephemeral part of it, and in a sense a subterfuge. Still, this is what sells the car. To the technician, the mechanic, the car is what the materials and processes that go into its making are; to the buyer, it is what it does and looks like. Culturally the one is as important as the other. And yet, what the car looks like, *in re* 'class,' is pure psychology and convention, an imponderable, wholly out of reach of physical determinants. And again, a stylish American car or boat might look stiff in England; a similar English car, rakish in America. What is true of a car would hold of a Polynesian boat and ultimately of all things cultural. Environment merely offers the opportunity to choose between possibilities, and that only in the rough. Culture supplies pattern, style, worth.

Many an advocate of the environmentalist creed would object to all this on the ground that the discussion is off the point. Is it not true, he might say, that the primitive agriculturist, the modern European peasant, the American farmer, are true children of the soil and all that hangs on to it—weather, the seasons, insect pests? These things constitute the

the making of certain digestive tablets. These, we might add, may be and probably are eaten, with profit or otherwise, in New York, Chicago, Oshkosh, or in the mountains of Kentucky.

very breath of the agriculturist's life. The tasks and preoccupations imposed upon him by nature are written all over him. Such is the agricultural complex, and its ear-marks are unmistakable. True enough! But the question is: are the roots of agricultural life in the *ager* or in culture? A smooth wide plain, thick with lusty vegetation, is, to be sure, inviting to the agriculturist, provided he already is one. If he is not, he might prefer to use the plain for chasing the buffalo, as did the Plains Indians, or the guanaco, as did the Indians of the Argentine pampas. It will be remembered, in fact, that some of the Plains Indians who had once practised agriculture shelved this occupation in favour of a more whole-hearted immersion in the exciting pursuit of the buffalo. On the other hand, if the agriculturist not only is but intends to remain one, he does not wait for the *ager* but makes it. So did our Western immigrants when suitable fields were not at hand: they transformed a forest into a field, and let it be at that. And the primitive Iroquoian agriculturists did the same when they put huge trees to the stone ax and cleared (that is, made) the fields for agriculture. Similarly, the Pueblo Indians and others turned a desert into a granary by means of artificial irrigation ditches. The agricultural Finns had to carry their soil from the valley on to the mountain slopes before it would bear fruit, while the natives of the Philippines transformed the rolling hills of their landscape which, as such, did not look good for anything, into the curvilinear zig-zags of fertile rice fields.

The same argument applies to all attempts to interpret the tone of a culture by its physical setting, whether the latter be plains, mountains, or the shores of the ocean. One would not expect the natives of a Tibetan plateau to become mariners or love the sea or rave about it in their folklore and traditions, but neither does the proximity of sea or ocean make mariners. The Dutch became such, but only when the time was ripe for exploration, discovery, and trade. The primitive Australians, wherever they live by the ocean, seem to be supremely indifferent to it. Their mode of life and daily preoccupations are not, in any essential way, different from those of the tribes of the interior. They accept what the sea brings them, but they do not go forth towards it for either food, battle, or adventure, whereas their primitive neighbours to the north and east, the Melanesians and Polynesians, are among the most inveterate mariners on the face of the earth. Reams of pages have been written about the gloomy temperament and hard uncompromising ways of mountaineers. There may be such, I admit, but not in Switzerland with its neat, gay, and boisterous towns and its yodelling, beer-loving inhabitants. Yet these very mountains and vastnesses must have seemed gloomy and forbidding indeed to the legions of Hannibal or the Russian soldiers of General Suvorov. The whole business is silly. Nature does not make man. Man uses nature to make himself, as he sees fit. Someone might want to classify the material cultures of the primitive tribes of the globe from the standpoint of the materials they employ in their industries. The result would tally somewhat with a similar classification of the floral and faunal aspects of the world's surface, but it would throw little light on the different cultures of the primitives, unless we also knew what they did with these materials.

What is true of economic life and industry—food, clothing, boats and houses, tools, weapons, and utensils—holds more emphatically of the other aspects of culture—social and political organization, religion, art, morality, and the rest. Take, for example, religion or art. To some extent both use natural features as *dramatis personae,* as it were, but no more than that. The realistic artist will draw or paint or sculpture what he sees, but this something is not what makes him an artist, nor does it determine his selection, emphasis, or style. From this standpoint it is a matter of utmost indifference just what it is he uses for the concrete subject-matter of his art. Similarly in religion. That to the Eskimo the mammals of the sea wear a halo of sanctity, whereas the South Africans worship as ancestors the crocodile or leopard, may stand to reason. But how much insight does the species of animal worshipped give us into the character of a religion? What counts here is what a god is or what is thought of him, not what shape he happens to assume.

In former days students of politics often stressed environmental determinism. Political structure was represented as a function of topography. The restricted valleys of Greece, encircled by more or less forbidding mountain chains, determined, we are told, the city-states, whereas the vast unbroken plains of European Russia were responsible for the sweep of autocracy. But do we not find that Mediaeval and Renaissance Italy, as well as Germany before the Franco-Prussian war, bore a similar character of political pluralism without corresponding environmental accessories? On the other hand, the imperial expanse of Russia had a parallel in that of Rome, which had to overcome all the obstacles of seas and mountains; not to speak of the vast domains of Great Britain, an empire coextensive with the earth, or at least its choicest spots.

That the physical environment may not be disregarded in a study of culture or history is obvious enough, also that even today we are not in a position to assert that we have nature licked to a standstill. It has its storms and cyclones, its droughts and torrential rains, its inundations and earthquakes, its tidal waves. It would take incurable optimism to expect that these powers will ever be thoroughly harnessed. And so, in particulars, at a time and a place, nature will assert her prowess and ascendancy over man. But also, it should not be forgotten that in all these instances nature thunders against man as an animal and at his culture as material things. No more. The wrath of Zeus was formidable, but whenever it struck, it left man thinking and feeling and acting pretty much as before. Nature's errors cannot reach the mind of man nor the imponderables of culture. Nature unaided would have been powerless to create culture, as it is powerless to undo it or even change it significantly. In the last analysis, if all man's material goods and techniques were destroyed or removed, man, if he lived, could still have culture and in the highest sense. To this argument nature has no comeback.

In view of all this, it need occasion no surprise when different civilizations are found in similar environments, as in the case of continental Europe, and similar civilizations in different environments, as in England, the United States, and Canada. 'Do not talk to me about environmental determinants!' the philosopher Hegel is reported to have exclaimed. 'Where the Greeks once lived, the Turks live now, that settles the matter.' In the meantime, the Turks, without materially changing the nature or range of their territory, have moved signally in the direction, if not of Greece, at least of a culture quite different from that of the old empire of Abdul Hamid. That all this should be as it is becomes obvious when nature and culture are compared in their essential quality. All things considered, culture is dynamic, a thing of growth and development, whereas nature, as environment, is relatively inert and static.

It has, it is true, been asserted that this very stability of the environment constitutes a dynamic factor in culture. But surely cultural changes cannot be traced to an unchanging environment! To this the rejoinder is made that environment does in fact change, in so far as it contributes further and further elements to culture, as the latter itself changes and learns to discover and utilize heretofore unknown or neglected elements of its environment. So far, so good. But does this not mean that culture, as it changes and exacts more and more from its environment, does in fact make its own environment according to its capacity?

One more example: the pre-Iroquoian Algonquin once hunted in the forests on and about Manhattan Island; later the Iroquois cut the forests and cultivated the soil; still later the White settlers applied more intensive agriculture to the same soil, thus extracting new riches from it, and also began to utilize the waterfront as a harbour; the modern New Yorker, finally, transformed the island into a great metropolis and learned to make such excellent use of the harbour facilities as to call into being a tremendous congestion of commercial activity in lower Manhattan, which necessitated the erection of skyscrapers made possible by the utilization of steel frameworks, and so on. These changing relations between culture and environment cannot be traced to the characteristics of the environment, which have remained the same. The alternative, and obviously true, interpretation, points at culture with its expanding interests and technical facilities which enable it to know more about a given environment, see more in it, and make more exhaustive use of its resources.

Before we leave this topic there is one more point to be made. Environment may not, does not, determine *what* adjustment culture will make but it calls for *some* adjustment. The Indians of the Plains, for example, made an adjustment to the buffalo, the North Pacific Coast Indians to the salmon and cedar, the Eskimo to the Arctic, the Pueblo to the desert, and the South Sea Islanders to an archipelago. Such an adjustment, when made, tends to persist (Wissler). It crystallizes into a relatively fixed pattern of economic life and technical activity and, as a rule, calls forth a supporting idea-system (Teggart). By and large, such a pattern of economy and technique will tend to spread to the approximate limits of the same or similar environment, as Wissler has also pointed out. This feature spells conservatism, thus playing its part in the often noted stability of a local culture. And conversely, when a human group prompted by environmental pressure, political exigency, or the lure of foreign lands or conquests, moves from its former residence, takes to the road, and ultimately settles down in a different territory, conservatism slackens, the old habits tend to break down, idea-systems waver and become transmuted. There is some truth, therefore, in Teggart's contention that migration is one of the great liberators of history. The point, of course, should not be overworked, for sooner or later those who remain at home are also shaken out of their lethargy; there is, moreover, a conservatism of the road to match that of the hearth.

Chapter XXVIII

THE SPREAD OF CULTURE

It was shown in the preceding chapter that every culture, modern or primitive, comprises some traits imported from outside. This fact, we argued, suffices to refute the theory of the exclusive dependence of a local culture on its physical environment. The imported traits, coming from outside the group, are evidently independent of its environment. But we must go further. If all local cultures comprise objects and ideas coming from other cultures, then any study of culture must include in its scope an investigation of such objects and ideas, of the reasons and occasions for their wanderings, of their distribution, their rejection or acceptance by foreign cultures. Such a study, then, would deal with the diffusion of culture, to which we must now turn.

Varieties of Diffusion

It appears, from the outset, that certain features of culture have a universal distribution: they are found wherever man is found. This applies, first of all, to culture itself: it is a generic trait of man—man is a cultured animal. The major aspects of culture share with it this universality. While opinions may differ as to the precise scope of the 'universal culture pattern' (Wissler), the fact remains that everywhere culture comprises certain aspects, such as religion, socio-political structure, a material equipment, art, morality, and the like. This fact is so trite as usually to be taken for granted. Mistakenly so, for it is not at all *a priori* obvious: there might be tribes without morality, for instance, or without religion; and the fact that all human groups manifest these aspects as well as the rest of culture, is a discovery, not a deduction from principle.

We find further that certain subdivisions within the major aspects of culture are also ubiquitous. Religion, for example, comprises animism, magic, ritual, myth; social organization includes local groups, families, relationship systems, marriage regulations; material culture embraces tools, weapons, habitations, clothes or body ornaments, means of transportation; and so on with the rest.

The reasons for this universality of distribution are not far to seek. They are, in brief, as follows:

First, *the psychic unity of man:* man is everywhere the same, a creature with certain capacities and urges which make culture possible and make it what it is. Once man is taken for granted, the second reason follows: *the basic needs of life are also identical.* To supplement his inadequate instincts and physical limitations, man in his quest for food, comfort, and safety, needs tools which he is able to invent and construct. Broadly speaking, this covers his entire material equipment. Social life does not run by itself; to ensure order, safety, and parity, it calls for social divisions, regulations, and powers; these, also, man is able to realize, administer, and supply with adequate ideational and emotional props, thus taking care of his socio-political, socio-economic, and moral needs. Being eager, imaginative, and impatient, man, not quite at home in the world, craves some psychic reinforcement beyond that provided by his technical equipment, something that would bring intellectual peace, emotional balance, and an enhanced sense of power; this need he fills by conjuring up a supernatural world of beings, forces, and values; this is religion. And, finally, *man's physical environment is,* broadly speaking, *always the same,* in so far as it everywhere furnishes, in one form or another, the conditions and materials for the technical equipment, and makes social life possible; and in so far also as it everywhere provides occasion for those experiences out of which the stuff of religion is spun.

There are other features, such as agriculture and pottery, which, while widely distributed, are far from universal. Pottery is found in an enormous, practically continuous area in America; it is general throughout most of Africa south of the Sahara, except in the extreme South; it occurs throughout India, although some Indian tribes, like the Todas of the South, do not themselves manufacture the pots; in Australia there is no pottery; neither is any made in Polynesia, while in Melanesia it occurs sporadically. Agriculture is distributed in America in an area coextensive with but somewhat narrower than that of pottery; it is carried on in Africa in large territorial blocks of the expanse south of the Sahara and north of the desert of Kalahari; it does not occur in Australia, but is found in the form of garden culture in Melanesia and Polynesia.

It will be seen from these distributions that neither pottery nor agriculture is essential to culture: man can and does get along without

them. But it will also be gathered that both inventions are of high usefulness and, once achieved, will be eagerly borrowed from tribe to
tribe. The distributions, moreover, are interesting: both pottery and
agriculture are found in wide continuous areas and are absent in other
large areas, also continuous, as in America, where both features are absent in wide adjoining districts in the South and East of South America

Fig. 76. Map of Types of Clothing in America. (Wissler, *The American Indian.*)

and the West and North of North America. Leaving possible interconti-
nental contacts aside, for the present, such distribution suggests singular
invention or, at most, a very few independent inventions within each area
of continuous distribution and subsequent spread.[1] Were we to assume
repeated independent invention within the areas of distribution, the absence of the feature in equally large areas could hardly be accounted for
except by some environmental factor, such as the presence or absence of
suitable grains or materials. But no such environmental factor is extant
in these or in many other similar instances.

[1] With reference to agriculture, see above, p. 400, footnote 17.

Cultural features, when more narrowly circumscribed, show distributions similar in type but less sweeping in range. From Wissler's map (see p. 457) of types of costume in the two Americas it appears that tailored clothing cut to pattern (as among ourselves) occurs in a wide area in the North; textile clothing is distributed in the North American Southwest, through Mexico and Central America and along the western districts of South America down to Peru; while robes are worn in the central area of North America, the Northwest Coast, and the entire South American continent except the textile area in the West.

Or again, to follow Ankermann's African map (see below), fur and

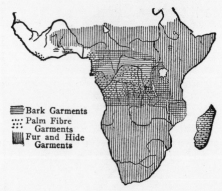

Bark Garments
Palm Fibre
    Garments
Fur and Hide
    Garments

FIG. 77. MAP OF TYPES OF CLOTHING IN AFRICA. (B. Ankermann, 'Kulturkreise und Kulturschichten in Afrika,' *Zeitschrift für Ethnologie*, vol. XXXVII, 1905.)

hide garments occur practically throughout the entire expanse of Africa south of the Sahara and east of the western states of the Gulf of Guinea, excepting only a large area embracing most of the watershed of the Congo and its tributaries; garments made of bark are worn in an area starting with a broad base on the Gulf of Guinea and around the lower Congo and extending eastward across the continent in a gradually narrowing wedge which reaches over to the island of Madagascar. Through part of this area the distribution of fur and hide garments overlaps with that of bark garments. Again, clothes are also made of palm-fibre in parts of the Congo area where fur and hide garments do not occur, as well as throughout Madagascar and in a few smaller districts in the West of the mainland. Similarly, Ankermann's map (see p. 459) of types of huts in Africa shows more or less wide distribution of certain types as well as an occasional overlapping along the boundaries.

In all such instances the continuous distributions and particularly the overlappings along the fringes point unmistakably to the spread of a feature through inter-tribal diffusion. It would be going too far to assume

invariably the singular invention of a feature within each area of continuous distribution (although in particular instances the assumption
might prove correct), but the number of independent inventions of such
a feature must certainly have been strictly limited, else the distributions
would be inexplicable.

Still more particular features have even narrower distributions, while
details of technique and pattern, finally, are localized in small groups
of tribes or even in individual tribes. Wissler's study of Plains shirts,
for example, shows a differentiation of pattern from tribe to tribe, and

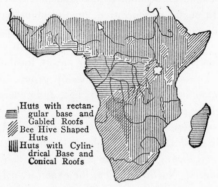

Huts with rectan-
gular base and
Gabled Roofs
Bee Hive Shaped
Huts
Huts with Cylin-
drical Base and
Conical Roofs

Fig. 78. Map of Types of Huts in Africa. (B. Ankermann, 'Kulturkreise,' etc.)

the guardian-spirit cults of this area are, as we saw, similarly differentiated.

To take another illustration from the domain of art. While Oceania
as a whole is noted for artistic woodwork, the art-work of Melanesia,
taken as a unit, can be easily differentiated from that of Polynesia. Open
work or filigree, so characteristic of Melanesia, is almost unknown in
Polynesia, except among the Maori of New Zealand who are marginal
to both areas; the use of colour, almost universal in Melanesia, is absent
in Polynesia, again with the exception of the Maori who differ from other
Polynesians in using colour and from the Melanesians in the colour they
use (red) and in the way they use it: contrary to Melanesian practice,
entire objects—poles, boats, houses—are here painted one solid colour:
red. Further, animal figures constantly occur in Melanesia in fairly
realistic or semi-conventional form, while in Polynesia the human figure
alone is used, and the conventionalization is almost always extreme.
The polishing of wooden objects, finally, which in Polynesia has reached
a high degree of perfection, is almost unknown in Melanesia.

And once again, a more detailed study of the crafts of Oceania reveals unmistakable local peculiarities. The pottery of Fiji, the shields and spear-throwers of New Guinea, the wooden gongs of the New Hebrides, the open-work totemic columns and masks of New Ireland, the clubs and wooden foot-rests of the Marquesans, the spears set with shark-teeth of the Gilbert Islands, the feather-work of Hawaii, the great stone figures of Easter Island, and the grotesque jade neck ornaments of New Zealand —all of these are highly distinctive features each one of which may serve as a diagnostic trait of a locality.

The facts of distribution are less readily discernible in a survey of religious phenomena, on account of the greater elusiveness of the religious content. In social organization, on the other hand, distribution once more stands out clear-cut and convincing. Certain forms of social organization are ubiquitous; others are distributed in wide areas, more or less continuous; still others represent purely local variants.

Thus the local group, family, relationship group, differentiation of one sort or another on the basis of sex, age, and generation, are found everywhere, including modern society.

In primitive societies, social organization of the family-village type— meaning by this that clans, gentes, phratries, and the like, are absent, and the family and local group alone are found—is somewhat restricted in its distribution. In North America, for example, a line drawn from Greenland to the coast of Southern California [2] would roughly divide the continent into two triangles, the northwestern being characterized by the family-village system, barring only the tribes of the Northwest Coast, the southeastern, by clan and gentile systems. In Africa, at least some of the more primitive tribes of the extreme South and the great forests of the upper Congo, are organized on the family-village basis. In Australia, some relatively non-numerous tribes along the southern, southeastern, and western coasts have the same type of organization. In Melanesia, many tribes conform to the family-village type, while in Polynesia, this form of organization seems universal, at least within more recent times.

Sib systems, while more widely distributed than the family-village type, are not found everywhere, as appears from what was said in the preceding paragraph. In addition to the areas in North America where sibs prevail, and equally large although at present not as clearly defined areas in South America,[3] gentes are widely distributed, in solid blocks,

[2] With reference to California, see pp. 354 seq.

[3] For a distribution map of sibs in the two Americas, the most complete to date, see Ronald L. Olson, 'Clan and Moiety in Native America,' *University of California Publications in American Archaeology and Ethnology*, vol. XXX (facing title page).

in the whole of Africa between the Sahara in the North and the Kalahari in the South, while clans occur here and there within this area. In Australia alone are clans and gentes well-nigh universal, barring only the relatively few tribes noted above as having the family-village system. In Melanesia clans appear sporadically, while in Polynesia they may have once occurred in the western island-groups.

Some other forms are much more restricted in their distribution. The Australian classes and sub-classes are not found anywhere else. The maternal family, like that of the Iroquois, as well as the paternal family, once thought exceptional, are now known to have a fairly wide distribution in primitive societies (pp. 361 seq.), but data are not available for a more precise statement. Dual divisions are present in several large areas in North America, in some tribes of the northern interior of South America,[4] in almost the whole of Australia and in parts of Melanesia, but are probably absent and certainly quite exceptional in Africa and India.

Now, as soon as any functional specifications are added to these purely formal divisions, the area of distribution of each becomes more and more restricted. The clans of the Northwest Coast are not those of the Crow nor those of the Iroquois. The dual divisions of the latter are not those of the Omaha, nor those of the Tlingit and Haida, and all of these are markedly different from the dual divisions of Australia. Magical totemic ceremonies are an exclusive functional peculiarity of the sibs of the Arunta and some neighbouring tribes. Differentiation in forms of hair-cut among boys is peculiar to the gentes of the Omaha. Definite association of families with hunting territories is apparently nowhere as clearly developed as it is among some of the eastern Algonquin tribes. And so on, throughout the entire line of social divisions in their functional capacity.

Again, in political organization, the geographical factor is definitely recognizable. First come political features characteristic of wide areas, either as universal within such areas or as frequent there but not elsewhere: federated tribes and the limitation of the power of chiefs, as in America; the centralized state and high status of the king, as in large parts of Africa; relative vagueness of the political unit combined with prominence of the old men, as in Australia; socio-religious prominence of chiefs with the power of imposing taboos, as in Polynesia. Within these wider geographical districts further subdivisions are discernible. In North America, a comparison of those groups characterized by relatively high political organization, such as the Zuñi, Dakota, Iroquois,

[4] See Olson's map referred to above.

discloses differences of structure and function. In Africa, the political organization of the Yoruba differs from those of the Herrero, Zulu, Massai, or Baganda, and these differ among themselves.

It will be seen, then, that certain forms of social organization belong to the common-human: their distribution is universal; their congeniality to human society is such that no amount of historic caprice seems capable of side-tracking them. Other forms of social or political organization are widely distributed but not by any means universal. While these forms must also be regarded as singularly well adapted to the purposes they fulfil, their uniform distribution in certain areas and absence from others strongly suggest diffusion through historic contact as an explanatory factor. More specialized forms of social units and the functional peculiarities of corresponding units in different tribes, have as a rule a limited distribution; while still more minute peculiarities are restricted to single groups. Here there can be only one interpretation: just as variants in industry, art, religion, arise in particular localities, so also does social organization fluctuate with the specialized conditions of individual tribes and local groups. Some of these specialized forms prove congenial to an ever-widening circle of neighbours, and the new form or function may thus reach a wider distribution; other specialized forms remain restricted to a narrow area or even an individual tribe.

Local Cultures in the Light of Diffusion and Invention

The insight gained from this analysis may now be applied to concrete samples of primitive culture, selecting those most frequently referred to in the preceding pages, such as the Eskimo, Iroquois, Haida and Tlingit, the central Australians, the African Baganda, the Melanesian Trobrianders, the Polynesian Maori, and some others.

All these cultures will be readily recognized as primitive in the sense explained in the chapter, 'Primitive Life and Thought.' Beyond this, however, each of these tribes shares some elements of its culture with tribes of a much wider area, at times continental in scope. Thus the Iroquois, however different in various ways from the Eskimo or Haida or Crow, share with these certain characteristics, positive or negative, that are American, such as the guardian spirit, absence of domestication, definite limitation of the power of chiefs, high local development of particular industries. The Trobrianders share with the Samoans certain Oceanic characteristics: high development of navigation, wood-industry, domestication, complex proprietary ideas and customs. The Baganda are

African (always excluding the extreme North and South) in so far as they practise both agriculture and herding associated with separate social classes; represent politico-economically a bureaucratic state with a king, taxes, markets, roads; have a typical system of legal procedure; possess the art of smelting metals. And so on with the rest.

Each tribe, again, forms part of a culture area—in the narrow sense, an area, that is, with certain more or less defined cultural characteristics. The Iroquois belong to the Woodlands, the Crow to the Plains, the Haida to the Northwest Coast, the Trobrianders to northwestern Melanesia, the central Australians to that continent, the Chukchee, with the Koryak and Yukaghir, to northeastern Siberia, and so on.

Each of the tribes, or tribal groups, finally, has certain traits that are its own and can serve to identify it. Thus the Haida are revealed, among other traits, in their horn spoons, the Eskimo in their composite bow or snow house, the Iroquois in their bark houses or corn mortars, the Baganda in their industrially specialized gentes, the Bushmen in their cave paintings, the Todas in their dairies, the Chukchee in their tent or shaman, the Trobrianders in their secret societies or trading, the Hawaiians in their feather-work. It must be understood, of course, that while one or two traits are here cited as characteristic of each tribe or tribal group, the actual number of diagnostic traits is large. In a sense, in fact, such traits are innumerable, for the process of local particularization, if carried to its logical and objective limit, culminates in individual variability. To take only one instance: the Haida, while typical of the Coast and still more closely allied to the Tlingit, are yet distinguishable from the latter in many ways: they speak a different language; the artistic finish of their woodwork has been carried a shade further; the tendency to multiply clan crests is strong among the Haida, weak among the Tlingit; the reciprocal functions of the phratries are less definitely fixed among the Haida than among the Tlingit; the majority of individual names among the Haida refer in various ways to property, among the Tlingit they are derived from animals and birds; the potlatch among the Haida is more elaborate than among the Tlingit; and so on.

In the final analysis, what we find is this: *Every primitive culture is in certain respects like all cultures; in certain others, like all primitive cultures; then it is like the cultures of certain very large geographical areas, perhaps continental in their sweep; it is further like the cultures of a more restricted area; and, finally, it is like unto itself: in certain local peculiarities, individual and unique.*[5]

---

[5] This passage (or its equivalent in *Early Civilization*) was quoted with commendation by Clark Wissler in his chapter, 'Recent Developments in Anthropology' (in

The above formulation can be restated differently and more simply if attention is focussed on the two basic processes implied in the statement: *Man, as man, has culture; culture develops through the origination of new features in local groups* (tribes), *and the spread of such features from locality to locality* (tribe to tribe). The latter proposition, moreover, bears on the former, in so far as the origination of new features in local groups is constantly fostered as well as supplemented by the reception of other features from without, from other groups; and the former bears on the latter, in so far as diffusion is almost always accompanied by one or another kind of transformation, pointing to origina-

Recent Developments in the Social Sciences by various authors). After quoting the passage, the author remarks (p. 84) : 'A careful reading of this will show that what is stated is geographical distribution, for if one takes the culture traits found in function within a given tribe and plots their distributions one by one, the result will be in the concrete exactly what is here stated in the abstract as a general law. And a valid one it promises to be, since everywhere one looks in the world he finds just this kind of distribution, even in our own culture.' This 'general law' Wissler designates as 'the law of diffusion.' To my regret I must note here that the author's enthusiastic endorsement implies a radical misunderstanding of the intended meaning. When I say 'every primitive culture is in certain respects like all cultures,' this, in the view here formulated, is attributable to the psychic unity of man as revealed in culture which, in certain essentials, is everywhere the same. When it is further said that every primitive culture is 'in certain other respects like all primitive cultures,' clearly no diffusion of any sort can be meant, but only a phase in the historic process. Whatever we may think of social evolution (pp. 507 seq.), it is certain that writing was preceded by culture without writing, and that there was primitiveness before it changed into—something else. Only when I speak of every primitive culture as 'like the cultures of certain very large geographical areas' and 'like the cultures of a more restricted area,' is there implication of diffusion, emphatic in the latter statement, vague in the former.

A little reflection will show that the explanations of the several propositions do not lie in one level. The basic similarity of all culture is rooted in psychology; man is man, and the world about him is everywhere sufficiently alike to account for the broad general similarity of his adjustment to it, through culture. Not so with primitiveness. We know that it cannot be explained either racially or environmentally. Nor does psychology give any clue, for man primitive, we now know, is like man civilized, except for the primitiveness of his culture. The explanation here is historical. We may not know *why* certain cultures have remained primitive, but we do know that we call them primitive because certain things or processes have appeared or occurred in their culture-history making them what they are, while certain other processes or things, with associated ideas and attitudes, which would have raised them above primitiveness, have not occurred or appeared—a matter of history, then. The reasons for the similarity of cultures in certain very large areas and in certain smaller areas must also be sought in history, more specifically in diffusion, even though we do not know, as a rule, how and when it has taken place. Cultural individuality, finally, while it rests, once more, in psychology, as does culture in general, points more particularly to human creativeness. To say here, 'man is man,' is not enough or too much; rather must we say 'man is creative,' for cultural variations are rooted in innovations or inventions, and inventions, whatever the setting, are man-made—they are creations.

tion or invention. These two processes—*origination* (or invention) *and spread* (or diffusion)—are equally fundamental and omnipresent.

Discontinuous Distribution: Diffusion versus Independent Development

In the instances of diffusion so far considered, the distribution of a trait was continuous or nearly so. The more difficult aspects of the dif-

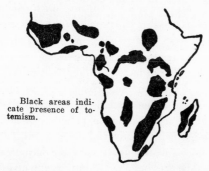

Black areas indi-
cate presence of to-
temism.

Fig. 79. Distribution of Totemism in Africa (B. Ankermann, 'Verbreitung und Formen des Totemismus in Afrika,' *Zeitschrift für Ethnologie,* vol. XLVII, 1915, p. 180.)

fusion problem arise when the geographical distribution of a trait is discontinuous.

In some cases of discontinuous distribution what may be called the geographical physiognomy of a trait may furnish an answer to the prob-lem. In Ankermann's map (see above), for example, the distribution of totemism in Africa is represented. As this map dates from 1915, it is no longer accurate in all particulars, but it will do for our purposes. It is provokingly discontinuous. Now totemism, as shown before, is a frequent feature of primitive cultures: without being ubiquitous, it is world-wide in distribution. In the absence of historical evidence to the contrary, it must be assumed, therefore, that it has originated independently more than once. This notwithstanding, it would be straining probability to assume a separate origin for each of the totemic areas in Africa, espe-cially so in view of the similarities, general and specific, in the totemic practices and beliefs of African tribes. Even in the absence of confirma-tory historic evidence—to make an assumption contrary to fact—one would, therefore, conclude that historic contact had taken place between at least some of the disconnected totemic areas, making spread by diffu-sion possible; or that there once existed connecting links of totemic tribes among which totemism had subsequently fallen into decay. While this last conjecture might fit the facts in particular cases, it should be used with caution, unless there is at least some confirmatory historical evidence. For obviously, if the absence of a trait makes as good a case as its presence, the procedure is methodologically worthless. As an alternative hypothesis, leaning on the far from exhaustive state of African exploration, one might allow that some cases of totemism in the intervening districts may have been overlooked.[6]

There are other instances where an answer proves more difficult. Religious societies, for example, occur in North Melanesia, in West Africa, and in several areas in North and South America. Shall we assume historic contact here, or a remote common origin, or are separate historic origins to be assigned to the societies of each region? The answer will depend upon a number of factors. Unless the similarities between the societies in the several areas are so striking as to preclude independent origins—which is certainly not the case here—we shall have to inquire how common religious societies are in primitive tribes. Finding them fairly frequent, though neither universal nor general, and distributed in widely separated areas, we should favour the hypothesis of repeated independent origins. Hence, before committing ourselves to an explanation through diffusion between any two of the separate regions, we should pay heed to the probabilities or even actualities of historic contact. The case, it will be seen, is no longer simple.

As a further illustration let us consider certain carved objects of New Ireland (North Melanesia) when compared with similar carvings from the Northwest Coast of America. In both areas the art objects in question consist of decorated wooden poles, while the painted carvings represent superimposed figures of animals and birds intertwined in various ways. In both localities these poles have symbolic significance and figure in religious ceremonies. Such are the similarities. But there are differences. The totemic poles of New Ireland are relatively small ceremonial objects, usually some three to five feet in height, the carving being carried out in open work or filigree, lace-like in effect. The familiar totem poles of the Northwest Coast, on the contrary, are gigantic posts looming above the roofs of the houses, while the carving is in high or low relief. There is no open work. The New Ireland poles are Gothic in effect, one might say; the Northwest ones, Egyptian. On the Coast, again, as explained before, the animals are often conceived as dissected in an

---

[6] Since this was first penned (in 1921), the last hypothesis has been vindicated in a number of instances. I might repeat at this time that further totemic finds are still to be expected in Africa.

altogether peculiar fashion, and this is reflected in the carvings; also, certain parts of the creatures receive preferential treatment, figuring as symbols by means of which the otherwise indistinguishable crests can be identified. None of these features occur in New Ireland. On analysis, then, the differences outweigh the similarities, or are, at least, equally striking.[7] Once more, therefore, independent origin or common origin or borrowing by diffusion swing in the balance, unless indeed historic evidence were forthcoming, in which case there would, of course, be no further problem.

Before going any further, it must be noted that in one respect the hypothesis of diffusion is more favourably situated than that of independent origin. Diffusion can often be demonstrated. Not so, independent origin. When we say that a feature—object or idea—developed independently in a given tribe, this is a negative proposition scarcely amenable of proof. To furnish such we should be able to put the finger on that feature at the very time and place of its origin, in addition to being fully conversant with its cultural antecedents within the tribe—a condition too unlikely for serious consideration. On the other hand, when we say that diffusion is demonstrable, we do not mean that it can be demonstrated in each and every case. Far from it, as was shown in the preceding. In the absence of historic evidence, which alone can furnish conclusive demonstration, diffusion must be balanced against independent development on the scales of probability. It is precisely in those numerous instances where this is the only possible course, that the issue between independent development and diffusion becomes a problem.

[7] In connexion with the weighing of probabilities the following point may be noted. Perhaps the most striking similarity between the New Ireland poles and those of the Northwest is the superposition or partial intertwining of the carved figures. Though 'striking' at first sight, and in so far negatory of independent development, this feature appears in a different light when the technical side of the situation is taken into account. Granted that poles are to be decorated, or any long and narrow surface, and that the decoration consists of realistic or semi-realistic units (usually, if narrow, not so long), and superposition becomes a natural and therefore no longer striking solution. Hence we may expect it to appear in other instances, outside the two areas in question. And this is what we actually find. In the carvings on the doorposts and other kinds of posts of the Maori (New Zealand) and on the doorposts of western Kamerun (West Africa) the same problem is met in the same way. The Gothic architects of the Middle Ages proceeded in analogous fashion when they decorated the arches of cathedral doorways (and other similar places) with superimposed carvings of saints. It will be seen from this that in weighing probabilities, in certain instances, cognizance must be taken of the limitation of technical possibilities.

Critical Use of Diffusion

The difficulties we encounter in recognizing and evaluating similarities in cultural traits should serve as a warning against the uncritical use of the principle of diffusion. The partisans of independent development as well as the partisans of diffusion (let us designate them *ID* and *D*) are interested in cultural similarities which constitute the starting-point of their investigations or interpretations. Similarities being, as we saw, more or less elusive, they can easily be underestimated or overestimated. Both the *ID* and the *D*, being interested in similarities, are likely to over-estimate them. This is particularly true of the *D*. If at all reasonable, the *ID* knows that his similarities might easily prove 'too good' for his needs: for, all else being equal, the greater the similarity, the less likely is independent development. The *D*, on the contrary, cannot have enough of similarity: for, all else being equal, the greater the similarity, the more likely is diffusion. It is among the *D*, therefore, that one is apt to en-counter an excessively keen perception of similarities. When this is the case, anthropologists call them 'diffusionists.' [8]

A critical use of the principle of diffusion, on the other hand, may bring most gratifying results. A striking instance will be found in Ber-thold Laufer's essay, 'The Potter's Wheel.' [9] As is generally known, among most primitive tribes pots are made by hand. Among tribes on a somewhat higher level pots are often turned on the wheel, a more expe-ditious and efficient method. Laufer's problem is to discover the proveni-ence of this device. The potter's wheel, argues Laufer, is distributed through a well-defined area. It is found only in the Old World: in An-cient Egypt, the Mediterranean and western Asiatic civilizations, Iran, India, and China with her dependencies. In this area the distribution of the potter's wheel has remained practically unchanged for millenniums. Primitive tribes, on the other hand, do not seem to adopt it even when surrounded by more civilized groups which have it. Thus, the Veddhas of Ceylon fashion pots by hand, while the neighbouring Singhalese use the wheel. The African Negroes, who might have learned the use of the wheel

---

[8] It would carry us too deep into the jungles of ethnological theory to discuss here the works and ideas of the leading diffusionists: Fritz Graebner, W. H. R. Rivers, and G. Elliot Smith. The interested student is referred to my *History, Psychology, and Culture* (pp. 80–83, 132–143), where he will find relevant discussions and bibliographies. A much more detailed analysis of the diffusionists as such is under-taken by Roland B. Dixon in his *The Building of Cultures*.

[9] In his monograph, 'The Beginnings of Porcelain in China,' *Anthropological Series*, Field Museum of Natural History, vol. XV, No. 2, pp. 148–177.

from the ancient Egyptians or later from the Arabs, seem never to have been acquainted with its use. The Yakut of Northeast Siberia continue to produce pottery by hand, notwithstanding their intermarriages with the Russians and the fact that wheel-turned Russian pottery is for sale at Yakutsk. Now, hand-made pottery, argues Laufer, is as a rule woman's work, the participation of men in this pursuit being always strictly localized and limited. The potter's wheel, on the other hand, is the creation of man. It must therefore be regarded as an entirely distinct invention which entered the field of pottery from the outside, as it were, and when it came, man came with it and took over the pot-making industry.

This historic distinctness of the two methods of pottery-making is reflected in the customs current in different countries. In India and China the division of ceramic labour sets apart the thrower or wheel potter and separates him from the moulder. The potters of India who work on the wheel do not intermarry with those who do not; they form a caste by themselves. Also, different uses are made of the two kinds of pots. And, most important of all—wherever the potter's wheel is in use, it is manipulated by men, never by women.

Technically speaking, the potter's wheel is nothing but a primitive cart-wheel turning on its axle. The existence of the potter's wheel therefore presupposes the existence of the wheel adapted to transportation. In accordance with this, it is found that in all civilizations with the potter's wheel, the cart-wheel is also in use. Further, wherever the potter's wheel occurs while the wheeled cart does not, the former is known to have been introduced from a different culture. To Japan, for example, which had no cart, the potter's wheel was introduced from Korea, while the Tibetans, who also lacked wheeled vehicles, adopted the potter's wheel from the Chinese (who still enjoy a monopoly of handling it in Tibet). And contrariwise, where the potter's wheel does not occur, the wheeled cart is also absent. In other words, in all cases where original conditions have remained undisturbed, the wheeled cart and the potter's wheel either do not exist or coexist.[10]

It is thus clear, concludes Laufer, that we may not regard the potter's wheel as an evolutionary stage in the development of pottery technique. There is no feature in hand-made pottery from which the potter's wheel could be derived. It belongs, on the contrary, to a distinct and strictly

---

[10] Laufer's handling of this feature—the concurrent existence or non-existence of the potter's wheel and the wheeled cart—is particularly instructive. It shows how far-reaching may be the conclusions that can be reached, even in the absence of historical evidence, on the sole basis of distribution, provided it is handled without malice or favour.

localized civilization. Like its prototype, the cart-wheel, it was the invention of man; and so, when the wheel came into the potter's industry
'from the outside,' man came with it.

With mere scraps of historic evidence as guide-posts, but mainly on
the basis of technological comparison and distributional facts, critically
harnessed, Laufer here succeeds in building up an all but unanswerable
case for a chapter in the history of technique. Incidentally, interesting
sidelights are thrown on evolution and the division of labour.

The Problem of Cultural Similarities in Relation to Diffusion

Clearly, then, the problem of cultural similarities is closely related
to that of diffusion. Before the distribution or diffusion of a trait can be
studied, we must identify it, must make sure that it is this particular trait
and no other. But why should this be a problem? In our discussion of
diffusion, so far, we took similarities for granted. But there are similarities and similarities. Some are measurable, others are not. Some would
be recognized by anyone, others lead to differences of opinion. Also,
some similarities, though recognizable and unmistakable, are to be dis-
counted because 'they are to be expected,' others become significant because they are 'strange' or 'suspicious.' Let us look at the situation somewhat closely, starting with a familiar illustration.

A teacher is reading a set of examination papers. In many respects they
are all similar, in content as well as in some of the expressions used.
This does not surprise the teacher. He knows that the students acquired
their knowledge of the subject from him, the teacher. Most of them have
not supplemented this by any independent reading. He therefore expects
many similarities in the answers, and finds them, without surprise. But
suppose he discovers in two papers a number of identical turns of phrase
which, moreover, are not among the expressions used by the teacher
himself. His suspicion is aroused. He follows up the clue, presently to
discover that one of the two students has habitually used these expressions in his former papers, whereas the other has used them for the first
time. The teacher's suspicions become keener. And note this—the more
curious or individual the expressions in question, the greater the alarm
of the teacher. He is now prepared to discard the hypothesis of independent development in favour of diffusion, in this case, copying. Should
he have any further doubts, these are resolved when he finds that the
second student was seated right behind the first where he could conveniently scan the latter's copy. The teacher is now as sure that copying has

taken place as if he had actually seen the process in operation, and he acts accordingly.

In this case the identification of the similarities is easy, but their evaluation requires some attention. Some similarities deserve no notice because 'expected,' others arouse suspicion because the resemblance is 'too close,' still others confirm the suspicion because certain expressions are habitual with one student but not with the other. And the argument for diffusion is clinched with the discovery of geographical proximity and consequent ease of intercommunication. If the two students were not located thus conveniently (for copying) but were found to be seated at opposite ends of the classroom, the geographical evidence would be less satisfactory. The teacher, of course, knows that students will copy their own papers or paragraphs and slip a saving sheet to a friend in need wherever seated, but he also knows that this is a dangerous process, eschewed by most students, otherwise willing, because of the risks involved. Therefore, if the teacher had found that the two students under suspicion were seated unfavourably (for copying), he would have hesitated with his verdict, *unless* the other evidence, taken alone, was absolutely damning.

As to the similarities themselves, there is a radical difference between material objects and everything else. The former can be compared, bit by bit; they can be measured. Here not only similarity but identity is possible, as between two bullets from one gun or from two guns of the same make and calibre. Not so with other traits of culture: art, religion, mythology, social systems. Here the observation of similarities is no longer so simple. The graphic or plastic arts, being from one angle material, present less difficulty than the other traits. Two patterns, for example, can be measured, compared in part and in whole, and superimposed. Similarity, of any degree, can thus be ascertained. That such similarity is always equally significant, does not necessarily follow, as every student of art knows. Take, for instance, the problem of copies and originals. The objective similarity, as to measurements and the like, may be striking or even absolute, but there are other items to be noted— minute shades of colour, lightness or heaviness of touch, the character of the brush stroke, as continuous or jerky, etc. Some of these cannot escape the sensitive eye of the expert, others can only be distinguished under the microscope, still others require chemical analysis. The problem of similarity becomes complex and is removed from the range of ordinary observation. Still, in their bearing on diffusion, some of these items would not count. If the objective similarity is sufficient to preclude independent origin, the rest would not matter. Which was the copy, which the original, would be irrelevant here, so long as one could be certain that one of the two was a copy of the other. Should we become interested in the *direction* of diffusion, however, then the identification of the original would at once become a major issue.

In social or religious matters, comparison—the discernment of similarities and differences—becomes increasingly difficult. The psychological aspects which rise into prominence here are not readily amenable to judgments of difference or similarity. Conclusions, therefore, must be based on indirection: names, presence of certain objective features, organizational items, etc. And when this much is accomplished, other difficulties arise. To illustrate: Moieties occur among the Tlingit and Haida, but also among the southern Siouan tribes of the Plains, such as the Omaha, Ponca, Kansas, etc. In each of these areas moieties occur in a number of contiguous tribes where a common historical source can scarcely be doubted. The situation changes when interest is directed to the two areas—Northwest and Eastern Plains—and the question is asked: have the moieties developed independently in the two areas or is there a common historic source? Moieties are moieties, that is, dual divisions—there is then similarity. But few students will accept this as sufficient evidence of diffusion. Certain reciprocal moiety functions are common to both areas, but this also scarcely suffices as a diagnostic trait for diffusion. The Iroquois moieties also have reciprocal functions, and so have the moieties of Australia. A trait apparently so characteristic of moieties generally loses its value as a clue to diffusion when discovered in moieties of two particular areas. And so it goes! A comparison of similarities in two areas broadens into a comparative ethnographic inquiry, with what result? Usually the problem remains unsolved even then. The persistent student might, at this point, shift his search towards historical evidences of diffusion—a very different kind of investigation.

Two additional points claim our attention here. Some cultural traits are natural or basic in man—no history is needed to account for them. Other traits are more or less derived, leaning against a historical background. Again, some traits are simple; they allow of no dismemberment or analysis, except in psychological terms. Other traits are complex; they can be broken up into a series of traits. Let us take an example of a simple trait from the domain of religion, where similarities are elusive and unconvincing, and of a complex trait from material culture, where similarities are tangible, thus carrying a more definite message: the belief in spirits (animism) and a Gothic cathedral. The belief in spirits is a basic, natural trait; people believe in spirits almost as naturally as they love and hate. No history is required here, once man is taken for granted. Also, it is a simple trait; it cannot be analyzed any further (except psychologically). Not so a Gothic cathedral—it is highly derivative and complex. It is derivative, because people do not naturally build Gothic cathedrals but come to do so as a result of a specific and elaborate historic process. It is complex, because it is analyzable into an enormous number of traits: height, flying buttresses, cross-like ground-plan, long narrow windows with pointed arches, coloured glass window panes, ribbed arched ceilings, fluted columns, and so on to any length. Suppose then we take tribe A with its animism, and, at a great distance from A, tribe B with its animism. All the intervening tribes, of course, also have it (animism being universal). There is, therefore, continuous distribution. This notwithstanding, we shall not dream of attributing animism in B to animism in A or the reverse. As the animism of the intervening tribes patently does not affect the argument, they may be eliminated, and the distance between A and B shrunk to a neighbourhood; A and B are now contiguous. But our stand will remain the same—we shall persist in ascribing the animism of each of the two tribes to independent development. The geographical factor, it will be seen, counts for naught here. Yet, our position *may* be wrong; for, after all, it is conceivable and possible that A acquired its belief in spirits from B or the reverse; but nothing will convince us that this was actually the case, short of a minute comparison of the detailed content of the belief in A and B, probably supplemented by at least an inkling of the actual historic process of the transfer.

Consider, by way of contrast, a Gothic cathedral in A and another in a neighbouring spot, B. Let us assume, in addition, that the observer, though of normal intelligence, is thoroughly ignorant of European history, including the *how* and *where* of Gothic cathedrals. What will he conclude? Without a moment's hesitation, he will ascribe the numerous specific similarities to a common history. Nor will he waste his time probing into the contacts between A and B. The contiguity of the spots being thus irrelevant to the argument, we might just as well assume that A and B are separated by a great distance, perhaps continental in scope. Also, the intervening region may be thickly crowded with Gothic cathedrals or be completely devoid of them. This will not alter the conclusion. In this case also the inspection of the similarities suffices to carry conviction: the geographical factor does not enter at all. And once more, the conclusion *may* be wrong: it is after all possible, though only barely conceivable, that the two cathedrals came into being independently; but the probability of this event is so infinitesimal that no one will consider it seriously, *unless* a complete historic demonstration of independent development were produced which, in this case, would have to consist of a full historic and archeological record of the two cathedrals and their architectural antecedents *in loco*, supplemented by a mental history of the builders, as well as by a similar historical, archeological, and psychological reconstruction of the entire intervening region in which, presumably, no links of any sort with either *A* or *B* would be discovered. If such a demonstration could be made, the miracle of an independent evolution of Gothic in *A* and *B* would have to be conceded. There is no arguing with history. Historic evidence, when mobilized in force, is unanswerable.

It will, I trust, be understood that no such exhaustive investigation as is here assumed could actually be carried out anywhere, for lack of data; and if it were, the improbability of independent development in our instance is so overwhelming that a lurking suspicion would always remain that some sort of contact had after all occurred (perhaps the other way around the world). This example shows that in extreme instances of similarity, particularly when a feature is derived and complex, the verdict for diffusion or historic unity is categorical—and unchallengeable.

These imaginary examples teach a number of lessons. In relation to similarities between cultural traits, in their bearing on diffusion, the following propositions will hold: if the traits are natural or basic (psychologically primary), the presumption, all else being equal, is in favour of independent development; if the traits are derived (presupposing a historic background), the presumption, all else being equal, is in favour of diffusion. The same applies to simple traits when compared to complex traits (or trait complexes): the simpler the traits, all else being equal, the greater will be the presumption in favour of independent development. In our examples we took extreme cases where the inspection of similarities sufficed to induce a conclusion. Here then geographical factors need not enter. In the vast majority of actual instances the situation is not so simple: no definitive judgment can be reached on the basis of the similarities alone. Then the geographical factor must be taken into account. In the absence of historic evidence, and all else being equal, proximity, ease of communication or knowledge of its actuality, favour diffusion; remoteness, difficulty of communication or absence of evidence of it, favour independent development. In many instances, the resulting conclusion will remain in terms of probability. Then recourse must be taken to historic evidence. If it can be produced, the case is clinched; there is no more problem.

Chapter XXIX

THE SPREAD OF CULTURE (Continued)

Culture Areas in North America

An interesting phase of distribution and diffusion is revealed in the *culture-area* concept as developed and used particularly by American students. It was observed, in the first place on museum specimens arranged for exhibition in a museum, that these objects fell into groups by means of which certain geographical areas could be characterized. What was true of the objects held also for the art of which some of these objects were the material carriers. Later the idea was extended to the non-material aspects of culture, with equal success. When the cultures of the North American Indians were re-examined and reclassified from this point of view, the result was a division of the continent into nine culture-areas, each characterized by a complex of traits. These areas were designated as: (1) Eskimo or Arctic, (2) MacKenzie, (3) North Pacific, or Northwest Coast, (4) Plateau, (5) Plains, (6) Eastern Woodland, (7) Southeast (or Gulf), (8) Southwest, (9) California.

We need not go here into a complete characterization of each one of these areas; [1] but let us examine two, by way of illustration: the North Pacific and the Plains, as given by Wissler (with slight changes). Most typical of the Coast culture are the Tlingit, Haida, and Tsimshian (*cf.* the sketches of their culture in the different sections of this book). Here we find the following traits: sea food most important, supplemented by mainland hunting, and large use of berries; staple food consists of dried fish (especially salmon), clams, and berries; cooking in boxes and baskets, hot stones being thrown into the water to heat it; large rectangular houses of cedar planks placed on end, with gabled roofs, carved posts and totem-poles; travel mostly by water in large sea-going dugout canoes (occasional sails); no pottery or stone vessels (except mortars); checker baskets (excellent twine baskets only among Tlingit), no coil baskets; plenty of cedar-bark mats and soft bags; elaborately woven blanket of soft cedar bark and goat hair (a Chilkat [Tlingit] specialty); rather

[1] A detailed enumeration of the cultural traits of the areas will be found in Wissler, *The American Indian*, pp. 206–227.

scanty clothing, mostly of skin, and a wide basket hat (unique on the continent); occasional skin moccasins and leggings (otherwise feet bare); bow, club, and peculiar dagger, no lances, slat, rod, and skin armour, wooden helmets, no shields; chipped stone tools rare, but nephrite or greenstone used; some work in copper (probably borrowed from Whites), no smelting of ore; woodwork highly developed, splitting and dressing of planks, peculiar bending of sides of boxes, joining by concealed stitches, carving technique high; remarkable decorative art, semirealistic with marked conventional features on carved totem-poles, houseposts, memorial columns, and other objects; when applied to flat surfaces unique dissection of animal forms; some geometric art on baskets, realistic tendency in woven blankets; two tribal moieties (four, among Tsimshian), with exogamy and maternal descent; chiefs, nobles, common people, slaves; the potlatch and coppers; religious societies centring about guardian-spirit initiation; Raven legends. The tribes farther south, such as the Kwakiutl, Coast Salish, Nootka, show most of the above traits in aberrant or attenuated form, and lack some of the traits.

Compare with this the trait complex of the Plains. The more typical tribes here, according to Wissler, are the Assiniboin, Arapaho, Blackfoot, Cheyenne, Comanche, Crow, Gros Ventre, Iowa, Iowa-Apache, Sarsi, and Teton-Dakota. They are distinguished by the following traits: Dependence of food, clothing, tents, etc., upon the buffalo, roots and berries used sparsely; no fishing or agriculture; the *tipi*, movable tent; transportation only by land, with dog and travois (horse for travois and riding, after contact with Whites); no pottery, basketry, or true weaving; special bead technique; high development of skin-work; special rawhide worn (parfleche, cylindrical bag, etc.); circular shield; wood-, stone-, and bone-work weakly developed; geometrical art with weakly developed symbolism; social organization based on family and land; camp circle; men's societies; sweat-house; scalp dances. On the eastern, western, and northeastern borders of these central tribes other tribes are located which share with the former all of their most typical traits but also have some traits the central tribes lack most of which can be identified as typical of one or another of the adjoining culture areas.

Similar characterizations can be made of the other culture-areas of North America.

From the standpoint of diffusion the culture-area concept, as here applied, presents a number of points of interest. Each trait in the above lists must be conceived as having spread by diffusion to all the tribes of the culture area, or, more accurately, to all the tribes that have it (for, as noted before, not all the traits of a trait complex are found in all the tribes of a culture-area). Whether such a trait originated in one of the more typical tribes, or in one of the less typical ones, or even in a tribe outside the culture area (as the horse in the Plains and, perhaps, copper technique on the Coast), can but seldom be ascertained; but of whatever origin, the trait must have travelled from tribe to tribe. To assume that such a trait originated more than once, independently, within a closely knit group of geographically contiguous tribes, would be arguing against all probability. From this standpoint, then, a culture-area comprises a complex of traits each of which, at one time or another, spread from tribe to tribe within the area.

It will be observed that so far we have dealt with culture-areas from the outside, as it were, as a statistician might do: our characterization was an enumeration of objective traits. But there is also an inner side to the picture, a psychological one. The objective description of traits gives merely a static view, it presents a culture as if it had stopped in its tracks. The psychological view makes the picture dynamic; the culture moves again, it comes to life. Now, as must have become apparent from preceding discussions, this psychological side consists of 'meanings' which include the interrelations of the traits comprised in the culture complex. Through their functions the social units—families, clans, phratries—become tied up with religion, myths, ritual, economic ideas. The art, in its symbols, becomes saturated, as in the Coast tribes, with most of the other traits of the tribal culture. The potlatch is not merely a phase of economy; it articulates with society, etiquette, ritual, legal ideas. And so on, with the rest. It is the same in the Plains and in the other culture-areas. In this way the culture of an area becomes a whole of interlocking and interacting parts.

On a map of culture-areas the linear outlines are their boundaries—beyond are other culture-areas. Here the thoughtful student is prompted to ask: What cuts an area short with such seeming abruptness? What keeps it from spreading beyond the boundary? The answer is that it is not cut off thus abruptly and does spread beyond, to a degree. The tribes at the boundaries are marginal tribes comprised in cultural districts distinguished as *marginal areas*. A marginal area, then, is characterized by a culture complex which combines traits of two or more adjoining culture-areas. Thus the Wind River Shoshoni and some of the Ute are marginal to the Plains and Plateau; the Plains Ojibway and Plains Cree, to the Plains and Woodlands; the western Shuswap, together with the Carrier, Chilcotin, and Lillooet, to the Plateau and Northwest; the Tahltan, to the Northwest and Plateau. Similarly, the Eskimo tribes adjoining the Tlingit in the West and those adjoining the eastern

Algonquin in the East, are marginal—the former to the Northwest, the latter to the Woodlands.

In connexion with the marginal areas, the distinction between the objective and the psychological approach becomes especially significant. The areas are truly marginal only from the objective angle, in so far as they comprise traits which are indigenous in or typical of two or more other areas. Psychologically, on the other hand, a marginal area is a culture-area like any other, comprising, as it does, an organically integrated complex of cultural traits.

The presence of marginal areas also brings home the fact that there is a certain artificiality in the choice and delimitation of culture-areas. After all, these areas represent but one of several possible and even significant groupings. As I had occasion to point out before, moreover, every culture area is itself a part of a still wider geographic-historical complex, perhaps continental in scope.

The Seneca, Omaha, or Tlingit, while on the one hand representing the Woodland, Plains, and Pacific Coast areas, have also certain traits in common—some positive, some negative—which stamp these tribes as American. As such they can be distinguished from any group of African or Melanesian tribes. And further, within a culture-area we discern the more minute differentiations into sub-areas—northern and southern groups of tribes, on the Coast; eastern, western, central, and village tribes in the Plains—and, finally, into individual tribes. As was shown before, the latter differ more or less markedly. In the Plains, for example, the tribes even of a sub-area can be distinguished from each other by the symbolism attached to the embroidered designs, less easily by the designs themselves, by the presence or absence of certain societies or the details of a ritual, by the number of gentes (if any), or their precise functions, etc. In the perspective of a culture-area these tribal differences are negligible, they become minor variations; but in the eyes of the tribesmen themselves these differences are anything but negligible. The tribal sense of 'doing things right,' the 'local patriotism,' attaches itself precisely to such peculiarities of culture. It must never be forgotten that the true unit of cultural life, its locus par excellence, is not the culture-area but the individual tribe.

It will be seen from all this that culture-areas do not represent the only, nor even an essential, classification of tribes, but they do embody a grouping of tribes based on certain objectively valid facts as well as on certain other facts, psychological in nature, which are, perhaps, more elusive, and as such, become a convenient accessory in a more systematic study of a larger area, such as North America.

If this is so, the questions arise: Why North America? Are culture-areas something peculiar to the northern continent of the New World? Certainly not. Unless culture-areas are to be regarded as a questionable idiosyncrasy of American ethnologists, they must possess general validity as a classificatory concept in the study of culture. In conformity with this, attempts to isolate culture-areas have been made in other districts— South America, Africa, Australia.[2] If the results to date are not as definite as in North America, this is to be ascribed to the relative imperfection of our descriptive knowledge (as in Africa and South America), or the relative uniformity of a continental culture (as in Australia) which manifests itself in the comparatively weak individuality of the several tribal complexes.[3]

Before we leave the culture-areas, one further circumstance calls for explanation. What is it that holds a culture-area together, ample time being thus provided during which the various features of a local culture can interpenetrate? For, as we have noted, the culture complex of an area presents the aspect of quasi-organic cohesion. A full answer to this question would take us far; it is moreover, doubtful whether an altogether adequate solution of this problem could be given at this time. I may, however, point to one factor which is certainly operating in the desired direction. Every local culture, especially every primitive culture, must solve its environmental problem. To make life possible and reason-

[2] Cf. such attempts by Father W. Schmidt, M. J. Herskovits, and F. Graebner. It should be added to this that only the African areas of Dr. Herskovits are comparable, at least in intent, to those of North America, whereas the procedures of Schmidt and Graebner will be found vitiated by certain principles of selection and grouping which these scholars share as diffusionists.

[3] We do not speak of culture-areas in the modern world, but they are there, patently enough. The same definiteness, moreover, as well as the relativity observed in the primitive field, are found here also. The national states, France, Germany, England (not including Ireland), Italy, clearly qualify as culture areas. Again, Sweden, Norway, and Denmark, each a culture-area from one angle, can also be combined into a Scandinavian culture-area, to which Finland may be added as somewhat marginal. Similarly, Germany and the new Austria (post-War) form a fairly well-characterized culture area. Switzerland, a marked culture-area on its own account, is yet marginal to Germany, France, and Italy. The countries of the Continent may be combined into a culture area when contrasted with England, and the Continent plus England into a still wider culture-area when juxtaposed to the United States. Each one of these groupings is, in part, realistic and objective, in so far as based on certain objectively valid facts; in part, again, these groupings are subjective, in so far as the choice of a particular grouping is dependent upon the interest of the student and the direction of his research. The situation is the same, it will be seen, as we found it to be in the primitive field. If there is a difference, it bears not on the theoretical validity but on the heuristic value of the culture-area concept in the two fields. This difference lies in the more marked individuality of local cultures (or areas) in the primitive world.

ably secure, a working balance must be established with the available features of the physical environment. This is accomplished primarily by the material equipment and the attendant economic pursuits. Not that the environment forces a particular technique and economy upon a tribe (or tribal complex)—far from it! To almost any environment a variety of adjustments might be made.[4] The point is: *one* adjustment *is* made; and having occurred, persists. The agricultural complex of the Iroquois, the buffalo complex of the Plains, the fishing and woodwork complex of the North Pacific Coast, what might be called the Arctic complex of the Eskimo, represent such adjustments. With this technical and economic base, the other aspects of culture—social, artistic, religious, ceremonial —articulate more or less closely. All sorts of associations, interpenetrations, symbolizations, take place. The culture is welded into a semblance of unity. A marked dislocation of one aspect would now threaten a general disruption of the culture. This puts a premium on the preservation of the *status quo*. What happens then is this—a local culture (or the culture of an area) is anchored to its physical environment; the anchor is the techno-economic equipment and procedure; the other aspects of the culture crystallize around this anchor.

As I have just remarked, this explanation is far from complete, nor will it fit all cases equally well. The more drastic the environmental solution—as in the Arctic or in the Plains, for example—the better will our scheme correspond to the concrete situation. At any rate, it helps us somewhat to understand an otherwise puzzling state of affairs. So let it suffice, for the present.

How Cultural Traits Travel

When contact and communication are established between two or more tribes, there is no holding the process of diffusion. So Graebner, the diffusionist, once expressed it: where one trait goes, others will follow. In the light of culture history, as envisaged by Graebner, any other view seemed absurd. Now it is, of course, true that between two cultures in contact cultural features will spread until, in extreme cases, a complete transfer of a culture, or identification of the two cultures, may come about. We know, for example, that the Salish Bella Coola, whose culture once belonged to the Plateau type, have become thoroughly permeated with the elements of the Coast culture of the Northwest. Again, the Athapascan Navajo and Apache have undergone a similar process of acculturation to the Southwest. Both of these instances are, however, quite

[4] See p. 454.

extreme. The Bella Coola, as well as the Navajo and Apache, having left their original home and environment, were confronted with the problem of adjustment to a new environment, and while thus engaged, succumbed to the overwhelming influence of well-established local patterns. What we find here is a decay of cultures, torn away from their accustomed moorings and ill-fitted to survive in their new surroundings, and a substitution of the dominant local cultures. Such is frequently the fate of immigrant cultures and peoples, in primitive as well as modern conditions.

The process of cultural diffusion between two locally attached and normally developing cultures reveals very different aspects. Let us here call to mind what happens in marginal areas. A marginal area, as we saw, comprises some of the traits of, let us say, two areas to which it is marginal. *Some* of the traits, not all. Some traits of the adjoining areas spread to the marginal area, others do not. Passing from areas to tribes, we find a similar situation. The Tlingit have not become identified with the Tahltan, nor the latter with the former, but the Tahltan took over some features of Tlingit social organization, while the Tlingit learned their basketry technique from the Tahltan. The maternal descent and inheritance of the northern Coast tribes have influenced the Kwakiutl, whereas the religious societies of the latter have at least moulded the societies of the more northern tribes. Some of the eastern Algonquin tribes in contact with the Iroquois have partially adopted the socio-political organization of their politically-minded neighbours, but they have not taken over their long-houses nor many another, abstractly speaking, equally available feature.

A true picture of trait-diffusion is secured when, instead of taking culture-areas or individual tribes as our starting-point, we turn to the traits themselves as units of investigation. The distribution of single traits has been frequently plotted by students. A book like Wissler's *The American Indian*, for example, contains a number of maps of this kind, showing the distribution in the two Americas of kinds of food, types of clothing, animal transport, varieties of canoes, types of basketry or pottery, clans and gentes, etc. The African monographs of Frobenius and the various articles by Ankermann contain similar maps dealing with Africa. In comparing such distribution maps of one continent we find the distributions of some traits more or less comparable, of others, somewhat overlapping, of still others, altogether distinct. The total result of the comparison is to the effect that each trait has its own distribution. When we examine a culture trait as enmeshed in an area or tribal culture, its individuality is marred by the numerous functional, symbolic, and such like associations into which it enters with other traits of a local culture. When it comes to travelling, however, the individuality of a trait is restored. Nor need it occasion surpise that this should be so.

What takes place in such cases may be accounted for by two reasons. The cohesion of a local culture is constituted by the functional relations of its traits. This is a purely psychological matter, a system of meanings. These meanings, intellectual in part but heavily weighted with emotion, are valid only for those of whose experiences they are part, and who therefore can understand them. This does not apply to an outsider. To him the culture will have no meaning, or its meanings will be flat, de-emotionalized; or he might, at best, attach a new meaning to it. The cohesion expressed in the original meanings does not exist for him, but merely an objective conglomerate of traits. To those who participate in a culture the loss of a trait, such as occurs under conditions of subjection or forced acculturation, leaves a gaping void, and the void aches like an amputated limb with a pain projected by the nerve centres into what seems the missing part. An outsider can take or leave any part of a strange culture without experiencing any emotional disturbance. Under conditions of diffusion, then, cultural cohesion lapses, and the separate traits, disengaged from the local complex, are thenceforth free to follow their individual fates as travellers in foreign parts.

And now note this! The conditions of borrowing and diffusion are not the same for all traits. Most readily taken is something that is lying loose, can be easily acquired, and adopted without causing dislocation or disruption in the recipient medium. Thus minor social customs will travel more readily than a social system, individual myths or incidents more readily than a mythological scheme,[5] objects more readily than techniques, material things more readily than standards or ideas. Things and processes that can be handled or observed will spread more readily than traits that will be understood, implying, for example, a knowledge of the language. Thus, rituals or dances will travel more readily than ritualistic concepts, symbols more readily than symbolic meanings.

It will now be understood why cultural features which in their local homes develop constraining intimacies and loyalties, should behave,

[5] This should not be misunderstood to mean that a more general pattern may not be more widely distributed than its variants, for this is precisely what frequently occurs. Wissler, for example, found that a common pattern underlies the types of dress in the Plains—a pattern centring in the 'concept of a two-skin garment'—whereas variants of the pattern, though common to several contiguous tribes, are not as widely distributed. (A point of this nature is best understood when tested by personal inspection, in this case of the reproductions and diagrams of garments in Wissler's 'Plains Costume,' *Anthropological Papers*, American Museum of Natural History, vol. XVII, pp. 41–91.)

when travelling, with the irresponsibility of detachment, and display in their distributions all sorts of individualisms and peculiarities.[6]

The Psychology of Diffusion, Adoption, and Assimilation

When a cultural trait finds its way to a new home what occurs is not merely physical transplantation—there is also a psychological aspect to the process. This applies to the positive as well as to the negative phase of borrowing or, in other words, to borrowing and to non-borrowing. As between individual and individual, so between tribe and tribe, much is not taken that could and might be taken. Apart from specific instances, this is apparent from the very fact that cultures differ. As cultures in general differ, neighbouring cultures, more or less, must also differ. We know from experience that they do. Now neighbours are by and large familiar with each other's cultural equipment; and, of

[6] If the particularization of cultural features, in diffusion, is to be regarded as a general trait of culture, it should apply to modern conditions. And so it does, conspicuously. We often refer to the modern Western world as a unit. Patently, for good reason. In many ways Occidental culture has become one. Central status of the family, prevalence of legalized monogamy, technological advance led by science, competitive industrial capitalism, urbanization, education universal and secular, social hygiene rooted in medicine and bacteriology, rapid emancipation of women— these are only some of the traits common to the Western world. On so level a plateau of culture, diffusion might be conceived as a wholesale process. This, however, is by no means the case. While scientific facts, wherever discovered, seem to spread with great speed and facility, technological inventions do not travel quite so fast, unless they happen to constitute a matter of general interest, such as radio or the automobile. While some books and authors have become internationalized, others— not necessarily inferior in quality or significance—remain more or less localized, nationally or linguistically. While the West as a unit has closed its doors upon political autocracy, the varieties of democratic rule are many, nor do they seem to be readily communicable from nation to nation. The cultural individualism of the Continent makes painfully slow headway in England and the United States, while the socio-political individualism of England seems entrenched—in England. Politics, law, and the politico-legal aspects of economy are national matters, nor do they spread beyond national frontiers, unless a deliberate effort is made by outsiders to learn 'how the Germans are doing it' or 'how the Americans are doing it.' Though the European sources of American culture are, historically speaking, not so distant, we also hear of the more recent 'Americanization' of certain aspects of European culture (think of shoes, cocktails, and jazz!), and of the internationalization of still other aspects of all Western culture. This notwithstanding, the discerning traveller in foreign lands, or even his dumb brother, finds ample occasion to experience a shock of difference, of strangeness, at times to the extent of seeming absurdity, a shock induced by the numerous local customs, usages, attitudes, which cling to localities and the very existence of which may remain unknown or but dimly known to the outsider, unless he makes a point of finding out.

In the modern world the scene for culture contact is set on a grand scale. But diffusion continues to operate piecemeal, with variations in occasion, facility, and speed.

course, they borrow; but also, they abstain from borrowing; they take *some* things but not others. The borrowing then is selective. If this were not so, cultural differences would be promptly obliterated. As a matter of fact, they persist almost indefinitely.

Selection in borrowing cannot be altogether casual. There must be some reasons. A thing, custom, idea, is not taken because it is not needed, or because it is not liked; or it may be both liked and needed, but still is not taken because people prefer to leave good enough alone—even though 'good enough' may not be so good—rather than take the risk of substituting or adding something that might prove better but at the cost of certain dislocations in custom—the breaking of habits—which, as such, are resented and resisted as something evil, or at best, as a burden.

Finally, what people do take, they may cherish as foreign, or they might grow accustomed to it and accept it as a matter-of-fact, or they might make it 'their own' and forget the very fact that it was foreign once.

The psychology of borrowing, it would seem, deserves some words of comment.

Borrowing of Traits in a Uniform Cultural Medium. When the cultural highway runs on one level, borrowing proceeds smoothly. Under such conditions, it might not result in anything exciting, but unencumbered, it will go on almost indefinitely. Thus in primitive Australia, the old authors tell us, there existed certain more or less periodic bartering conclaves in which many tribes participated. On these occasions, while local products were being exchanged, the old men would pick up new rituals, songs, ceremonial designs, and introduce them to their own tribes. Backed by the authority of their sponsors, these innovations would easily find their place in the local cultural equipment. Similarly in Africa, where markets constitute one of the ancient forms of tribal and inter-tribal contact. Aided by the temporary intimacy of economic exchanges, customs and objects would meet and become disseminated over considerable areas. This also happened at the frequent town fairs which rose into prominence in Mediaeval Europe of the ninth and tenth centuries. It is here—so students of the period tell us—that we must look for the impetus to reintroduce a uniform coinage. This is interesting, for what we here observe is the emergence of a new feature, the stage for which was set by inter-group contacts. The credit for stressing this principle in its application to primitive conditions belongs to Rivers, and a striking illustration is provided by Australia, where the tribal old men found it necessary to readjust, with what seems obvious deliberation, the marriageable classes of certain tribes to meet the emergency of inter-tribal marriages.

As we saw before, it would be difficult to explain the relative uniformity of culture over wide geographical areas except by the assumption of waves of diffusion of particular customs and objects. And to this
we may now confidently add the further assumption that the progress
of such a wave became the smoother the greater the pre-existing uniformity of the local cultures achieved by the deposits from previous
waves of diffusion. It is thus that the Indian cultures of the North American Plains were welded, in a few centuries, into a Plains area of remarkable cultural uniformity. Similarly, in modern times: When Bismarck,
at the close of the Franco-Prussian War, proclaimed the German Empire,
a series of waves of diffusion was initiated as a result of which a thick
layer of cultural uniformity was promptly superimposed upon the local
individualities of the pre-existing states. What I have in mind here is
not particularly those changes in the direction of unification brought
about by the official acts of imperial legislation and administration, but
rather those less overt or conspicuous processes of percolation of objects
and customs made possible by the partial lifting of the political, economic, and legal boundaries of the separate states.

Rapid Diffusion When a Trait Fills a Need or Fits a Mood. Local
receptivity in the face of a new culture trait varies greatly. Also, it may
depend on a variety of conditions, not necessarily local in character.
Here the Plains Indians furnish another striking illustration. In pre-
Columbian days, these Indians were already buffalo-hunters. Though
successful in this pursuit, they were handicapped by the helplessness, in
attack or escape, of the pedestrian when confronted with a powerful and
speedy animal. Then the horse came, introduced, as we know, by the
Spaniards, in the sixteenth century. When the horse made its appearance
among Indian tribes, it aroused great wonderment and even awe. They
did not quite know what to make of it. According to a Pawnee tradition,
their tribal ancestors mistook a mule ridden by a man for a single animal
and shot at it. When the man fell, they captured the mule. When the
Aztecs of Mexico first saw the mounted men of Cortes, they were greatly
perturbed, and did not fail to fall into a similar error. The Dakota of the
Plains called the horse *sunka wakan,* 'mysterious dog.' The identification
with the dog was no doubt due to the use of the horse in transportation,
which linked it to the dog pulling the travois. Before long the horse,
having spread through the Plains in the sixteenth and seventeenth centuries, actually took the place of the dog in this latter capacity, while two
tipi poles were substituted for the lighter poles of the dog travois. Thus
transformed, the travois, of course, proved a far superior method of transport. The greatest addition to Plains culture, however, was contributed

by the horse as a mount. This was little short of a revolution. Armed, as before, with bow and arrow, and mounted, the new buffalo-hunter proved incomparably superior to his pedestrian ancestor, as he could now fearlessly approach the buffalo. At close quarters his weapon was not inferior to a fire-arm, at least not until the advent of the repeating rifle. The enhanced success of the chase may have had something to do with the abandonment of agriculture by some of the eastern Plains tribes which seems to have occurred about this time (although we are not quite certain about this). Horses became the prized possession of the Plains Indians, the stealing of horses a favourite pursuit, propped up by a moral standard suited to the occasion. Military tactics underwent a radical transformation. It now became possible to count *coup* on an enemy (acme of valour!) with all the old bravery but with a far better chance of getting away. By increasing the speed and frequency of inter-tribal communication, finally, the horse contributed to the dissemination of Plains culture traits, thus functioning as an important dynamic factor in the forging of the cultural unity of an area.

The rapid spread of an entire complex of associated traits is illustrated by the so-called Ghost-Dance religions of the American Indians, which we had occasion to review before, if from another angle. Messianic ideas had not been unknown among the Indians of South and North America in the sixteenth, seventeenth, and eighteenth centuries; but the Ghost Dance of the western tribes of the northern continent belongs to the nineteenth century. This Dance, as we saw, was very uniform in its content without excluding tribal variations. Whether we examine the messages of Smohalla, Taviho, or Wovoka, or the customs introduced by them, the mood is the same: on the mixed background of despondency and hope arises the millennial prophecy of the return of the buffalo, the going of the White man, accompanied by certain ethical doctrines of marked puritanical flavour; there are miracles, cures, dances, peyote-drinking, visions. The spread of these doctrines and practices from tribe to tribe proceeded with the impetuosity of a conflagration. Nor did the process subside with the century. By 1910 many of the Plains tribes had adopted the Dance. In 1912 the Crow took it up; in 1914, the Utes of the Plateau and the Woodland Menomine. In 1916, the various tribes of Oklahoma whom the Dance had formerly passed by, began to use peyote; and by 1919, the western Shoshone took it up.

We have here a striking example of how a common psychic disposition, or mood, coupled with similar sociological conditions, will favour the rapid spread of a trait or trait complex.

The tendency to absorb an entire trait complex—not the entire culture, be it noted, but a tight clump of functionally knit traits—is illustrated by the history of what Wissler called the 'maize culture complex.' Among the agricultural tribes of North America this complex is essentially similar: 'The fundamental concept is the propagation of maize which embraces the related processes of preparing the soil, planting the grain, protecting the crop, gathering the ears, and preserving the seed. Each of these is a fixed procedure and must be followed in a definite order. The food-production processes are numerous: maize was eaten green, hulled, and ground, with various forms of each. Mixed dishes of maize with beans, squash, or meat were prepared according to definite recipes. Numerous religious ceremonies and social observances [were] definitely associated with maize.' [7] The presence of such a complex in a series of contiguous tribes presents an unmistakable picture of diffusion, even though we may be ignorant, as in this case, of the chronology and other particulars of the process of spread. It should also be noted that, religious features apart, there was no question here of meanings or interpretations. What we have is a large series of objects and procedures associated in a technological whole. When discovering such a complex among its neighbours, an agricultural tribe, or one merely ready for agriculture, seizes upon it—and it takes it as it finds it. The case becomes even more suggestive when we remember (with Wissler) that the White American farmer, finding himself in the same situation, took over, object by object and process by process, the entire maize complex, as he discovered it among the Indians. The social and religious elements of the Indian setting, on the other hand, could not be fitted into the cultural background of the Whites; although even here there was one feature, the husking-bee of the old farmers, which had an Indian parallel.

What happened when maize was brought to Europe is something quite different. Rapidly it spread on the continent and beyond, as far as China. Together with manioc (from South America) and the common bean, maize was also introduced in Negro Africa, where it soon became quasi-indigenous and economically important. But in all these instances what reached Europe, Asia, and Africa was the maize plant isolated from its functional complex. It was taken as such, and its cultivation was fitted into the prevailing local patterns.

Migration and Culture. When culture travels together with its carriers —in the case of migration, that is, whether in the form of military invasion or otherwise—the range of cultural diffusion may become enormous. The direction of spread may vary: it may proceed from the resi-

[7] Clark Wissler, 'Aboriginal Maize Culture as a Typical Culture-Complex,' *American Journal of Sociology*, vol. XXI, No. 5, 1916.

dents to the migrants, or from the latter to the former, or it may take both directions.

In the case of the White American farmers cited above, the invaders, with their higher culture, military power, and superior numbers, swept everything before them. The Indians were annihilated, absorbed, or reduced to a precarious existence in a cultural No Man's Land. In the case of maize-cultivation, however, the White farmers were confronted with an unfamiliar task. Among the Indians they found a cultivation complex, adjusted to the physical environment, technically rather simple, and thoroughly elaborated in all essential particulars. As we saw, the farmers took over the complex practically entire.

Two other instances, within the range of Indian cultures, have been noted before. The Salish immigrants in the Northwest (Bella Coola) and the Athapascan ones in the Southwest (Navajo and Apache), kept the languages of their home-lands, but succumbed culturally to the influence of their hosts and neighbours. This process was so thoroughgoing that their original cultures were almost totally obliterated.

Under other conditions migrants have been known to preserve their original culture indefinitely. This is exemplified by Madagascar. The population here contains some Negroid elements, as among the Vazimba and Sakalava. Students of the region, however, hesitate to ally these with the African Negroes, while some incline to the theory of a Melanesian derivation. Certain it is that the main contingent of the population as well as the entire cast of the culture, including language, are Malay, traceable to the migration of the Hova tribes, mainly from Java, which occurred some time during the early centuries of the Christian era. Later, perhaps since the sixth century, small groups of Arabic and Indian 'invaders' repeatedly reached the island. These came to constitute the ruling class, but the culture of the common people remained Malay.

The striking cultural gulf between Madagascar and the African mainland must be primarily ascribed to the Malay invasion but, perhaps, also to the forbidding character of the Mozambique Straits which rendered communication with Africa exceedingly hazardous. Not only is Madagascar un-African in culture, but its Malay culture has not, to any extent, penetrated the African continent. The instance also shows how far primitive peoples will navigate and carry their culture—on occasion.

The outstanding example of a complete vanishing of an immigrant culture is, of course, that of the American Negro. The importation of Negro slaves from Portuguese West Africa to the West Indies became a going concern in the sixteenth century, as soon as the supply of native Indian labour (mostly also slaves) began to give out. To the North

American continent Negro slaves were imported during the seventeenth and eighteenth centuries in ever-increasing numbers. They multiplied, interbred—in and out of law—with Whites and Indians, until today they constitute somewhat less than 10 percent of the population of the United States (this includes, of course, all those counted as Negroes, that is, all ascertainable mulattoes). What became of the African culture of the Negro? It vanished, language and all. There may conceivably remain some splinters of that ancient culture in the customs and beliefs of the southern Negroes, but these hardly analyzable survivals are, at best, in-finitesimal. The culture of the Negro is that of the White American. In this case the diffusion of White culture to the Negro was more in the nature of a substitution or transfusion. The reasons for this are apparent. The Negroes did not come in a body, as a people, not even as families. They came, they were brought, as individuals, torn away from their homes, their past, all their social bonds. In order to persist, culture must be carried by a functioning social organism. Lacking this, it finds itself in a social vacuum—and withers. One by one, the Negroes were sucked in by White American culture.

During great movements of peoples, when culture is confronted with culture, much depends on the vitality of the two cultures at the moment of impact and on their relative prestige.

While engaged in an argument in defence of his thesis of the possible influence of a small body of immigrants on their hosts, Rivers somewhere remarks that this influence may become vast if the culture of the immi-grants 'seems great and wonderful to those among whom they settle.' This principle may work in either direction. In the fifth and sixth centu-ries, when the hordes of northern Europe were hammering at the Roman Empire, the prestige of Rome was still enormous. True, Rome, as a political power, was dying, whereas the northern 'barbarians' were awakening to a new life of conquest and progress; but the glamour of cultural superiority was on the side of Rome. With its failing breath it impregnated its conquerors with seeds of culture which lived on for centuries. The reverse had occurred in the fourth century B.C., when the Graeco-Macedonian legions of Alexander the Great descended upon the peoples of western Asia. Wealth and numbers were on the side of Asia, with the Persians and Indians. The genius of Alexander, of course, won the battles of soldiers. This was important, but merely as a wedge. The greater battle was won by Greek civilization, of which Alexander, disciple of Aristotle, was the herald. In their time Persia and India had also drunk deep at the source of culture, but in that age they had fallen into a rut. Their culture, if not moribund, was at least dormant. The luminous thought and policy of Greece, carried by a man-god, struck them like a fructifying ray, and it held them enthralled for a long time to come. In legend and folk-lore, the memory of this historic episode lingers on among these peoples to the present day.

It will be seen from these examples that a mere objective enumeration of cultural traits can never furnish a rationale of such occurrences: the psychological situation determines everything.

Varieties of Adoption and Assimilation. Diffusion then must not be viewed in too mechanical a way, as if exposing one culture to another were all that was necessary. Not at all! Some traits that might be borrowed are left alone; some travel fast, others slowly; some fit almost immediately into their new surroundings, others undergo various transformations before being moulded into the new patterns. This last point requires some further comment.

The relations of the Chinese to the Mongols, on the one hand, and to the Manjus, on the other, are illuminating in this connexion. Manchuria, home-land of Manju and Mongol, has been called the Chinese reservoir, from which wave upon wave of alien and semi-alien peoples swept into China, and into which Chinese immigration has flown until modern days. Now, the Mongols are pastoral and migratory. They love freedom of movement. In the past they have again and again turned conquerors on an enormous scale. When they did so, conquest to them became an art and an end, not a means; they never, it seems, took the time or the trouble to do anything with their conquests. Between them and the settled Chinese, partly agricultural, partly urbanized, there always existed a state of hostility, smouldering at times, and at times overt. This incompatibility is reflected in cultural diffusion. 'Mongol borrowings of Chinese cultural elements,' it has been said, 'are strongly reminiscent of plunder.' [8] They take only what they like and use it in their own way. For centuries China has been making Mongol clothes, hats, boots, saddles; but these were always made to Mongol specifications; and to this day Mongol attire, though shot through with Chinese features, remains recognizably Mongol. And again, Chinese engaged in frontier activities in Inner Mongolia or western Fengtien, as traders, merchants, interpreters, artisans, had to pay for their success by the surrender of some Chinese characteristics: in one way or another they had to 'go native,' if only to the extent of taking a Mongol wife. Even among Mongols who had turned to agriculture, the immigrant Chinese farmer never felt safe about the future. So he accumulated sheep, cattle, and horses as security. Then, in

[8] Owen Lattimore, *Manchuria, Cradle of Conflict.* (By permission of The Macmillan Company, publishers.)

case of hostilities, if the Mongols pressed by the Chinese were forced to move, the semi-Mongolized Chinese farmer moved with them, for his equipment no longer fitted him for residence in closely settled regions.

The Manju-Chinese relations took a very different turn. Here there was no hostility, and the balance of cultural prestige was in favour of China. The Chinese frontiersman, moving into Manju territory, was prepared to occupy a place among the privileged. Even though he was moving away from China, moreover, his face remained turned towards China, for it was there that he proposed to capitalize whatever success or power might come his way. The Manjus themselves are becoming Chinese, and the Manju language, moribund since the middle of the seventeenth century, when the Manchus were entering China as conquerors, is now rapidly disappearing before the Chinese. Mongols, on the contrary, even when surrounded by Chinese for several generations and settled in the Chinese manner, tend to preserve their own language.

Selective borrowing, in the following instances not unaccompanied by deliberation, is illustrated by the way Western industrial capitalism was or is being taken up by Japan, Soviet Russia, and China. Japan, having resolved upon modernization, has mastered the science and technology of the West with what seemed remarkable facility and success, while preserving much of her ancient religion and social customs, which she is showing no inclination to abandon. Soviet Russia, while following in the footsteps of old Russia by borrowing from the West, is making a very different selection. It is exerting stupendous efforts to acquire the scientific and technical equipment of Western industrialism, while rejecting the entire social, economic, and legal system rooted in that industrialism. The case of China differs from both of the preceding, but is perhaps even more interesting. To put it bluntly, China harbours no admiration for the standards and ideals of our civilization. Frankly, she prefers her own spiritual past. And 'the past to which China turns for its ideal of civilization,'—as a modern writer puts it,—'is neither one of mediaevalism nor one of oversimplified "natural simplicity," but one of great spiritual richness, creative achievement and elaborate structure, so indubitably noble that it is not unreasonable to argue a case attributing the misfortunes of China to a decline from its ancient standard, instead of to failure to assume an alien standard.' However this may be, China seems committed to make room for Western technique, after a fashion. It wants to use it but it cares little about mastering it. The results are curious. The man of technical training is classed as a mechanic. As such, he is regarded as something of a magician: the machine is his professional secret; if it is to function right, the mechanic, master of the machine, must be treated with circumspection. Mechanics apart, the Chinese are noted for their knack of making a half-dilapidated machine turn the trick and get away with it, but they will not take care of the machine. This applies to automobiles, as well as to factories and railroads. Machines are permitted to run down, and then new ones take their place. Thus China is using the mechanical tools of the West without really adopting them or caring for them or the technological complex they represent. Even the technical terms, though translated into Chinese or taken over through the Japanese, fail to articulate with the rest of Chinese thought. 'It is difficult for foreigners to appreciate'—we are told—'that such forms have a sort of unreality which keeps them alien from the body of the language, and that the processes of thought behind these terms are so alien to the language itself that many of them cannot be expressed in terms naturally evolved from the language, but must be dealt with in a language within the language.' [9]

A sad commentary on the psychological limits of diffusion is presented by the disheartening failure of White civilization to either leave primitives alone or pull them up to its own level. The story is told in a hundred versions wherever moderns and primitives have met: the English with the natives of Australia, Americans in Canada and the United States with the Indians, Russians in Siberia with the Koryak, Chukchee, Gilyak, and others, Europeans and Americans with the Melanesians and Polynesians. Apart from the prevailing spirit of selfish exploitation, the impact of White civilization has meant degeneration and dissolution to the primitives. Their standards collapsed, their arts deteriorated, then vanished altogether; they borrowed our vices, succumbed to our diseases; prevented by racial barriers, propped up by prejudice, from being absorbed in our civilization, their remnants are now leading the spiritless existence of social pariahs lost in a cultural void.

Whether, under a more understanding and kindly régime, this human tragedy might have been averted, it is difficult to say. In the dispassionate view of science, at any rate, these facts can only be read one way. Though history abounds in examples of the quickening effect of culture contact which has at times achieved veritable miracles of cultural rejuvenation, such contact under unfavourable conditions may bring about cultural decay or death.[10]

[9] The Chinese data and relevant comments here referred to are based on Owen Lattimore's *Manchuria, Cradle of Conflict*, a book I highly recommend to the student as an illuminating analysis of a little known or understood situation.

[10] As between moderns and primitives, the facts of lopsided diffusion have also a humorous side. It has often been reported that natives, after having adopted modern

Intra-Tribal and Inter-Tribal Diffusion. It should, in conclusion, be understood that the processes of diffusion may not be identified with the historical contacts of tribes. His mind intent on inter-tribal diffusion, the student is apt to forget that similar processes are taking place constantly and inevitably, within the boundaries of culture-areas or individual tribes, however territorially restricted. When studying diffusion between tribes, we usually take the particular traits, whether things or ideas, for granted: we are interested in their transfer, not in their origination or transformation *in loco*. When our concern is with a particular local culture, on the other hand, the local changes of traits, through innovations or inventions, claim at least a share of attention. Thus arose the notion, absurd at bottom, that origination, invention, occurs within tribes, whereas diffusion, transfer, takes place between tribes. The idea, to repeat, is absurd. Inter-tribal diffusion is inseparable from cultural mutation, as seen in the varieties and caprices of adoption and assimilation, while intra-tribal invention and creativeness are associated with the diffusion of the resulting innovations within the tribe. However important social factors may be in codetermining cultural changes, inventions—using the term broadly to cover all innovations, whether in things, processes, or ideas—come from the minds of individuals, whether deliberately or otherwise. A phonetic peculiarity, a new word, a new shade of meaning in an old word, a name, a new dance or song or modifications of old ones, a mechanical device, a twist in the form or content of a myth, a mannerism of technique, an artistic pattern or a new combination of old patterns, a new idea or interpretation, whether derived from insight or error—in short, anything new in a culture must start somewhere, and this 'somewhere' can only be an individual act or mind or, where cooperation of several is inherent—as in language or joint work—the acts or minds of a few individuals. What happens next? Well, the new feature spreads, or it does not. A phonetic peculiarity may remain an individual affair, to disappear as it appeared and be forgotten; or it may become characteristic of a group within a culture, perhaps to be perpetuated; or again, it may spread to the limits of the tribe or beyond. Similarly, with a new word or meaning. It may or may not be taken up by others.

clothes, insisted on taking them off when it rained. Similarly, in my days among the Iroquois of southeastern Canada, I often observed how indifferently they used the newly adopted 'White' clothes. At a public ceremonial, a chief—who in the old days would have appeared in full ritualistic regalia—thought nothing of officiating in the ragged and muddy, though modern, outfit of a farmer. In the ancient culture, the Indian's attire carried the full weight of graded distinctions. White man's clothes were taken over without the associated shadings; they were just clothes, 'fit' for work in the field as well as for ceremonial occasions.

If it is, it may become a momentary slang expression, presently to pass out again; or it may remain as a more permanent feature in the vocabulary of a professional, social, esoteric group; or again, it may prove a 'winged word,' soar far and wide, and persist indefinitely. A new mechanical device may prove too inconvenient, or require special skill, and as such be nipped in the bud; or having become known to others, it may be added to the technical equipment of the group; or if the device has special merits, it may take the place of pre-existing devices in the same field; finally, it may prove a revolutionary innovation, fated to transform a technique, an industry, or even the entire technological and economic existence of a tribe or of many tribes. And so throughout. In every case, the new may be accepted or rejected; if accepted, it may spread within narrow or wide limits; it may prove a passing ripple, a lasting phase, or a permanent achievement. The spread which transforms a new trait from a feature *in* a culture into a feature *of* the culture, is a process of diffusion, from individual to individual, from individual to a group, or from group to group. The new trait then does not become a feature of the culture until it has spread, more or less, by diffusion, and has been incorporated in an old cultural pattern. In both kinds of diffusion, moreover—intra-tribal or inter-tribal—the same limiting conditions prevail: the new things or ideas may be rejected or accepted, and if the latter, they may be absorbed in the culture, more or less readily and more or less completely.

Having made certain of this much, we are now prepared to find some differences. Patently enough, intra-tribal diffusion is a much more persistent and inevitable process than inter-tribal diffusion; also, it proceeds, by and large, more easily and smoothly. One is apt to overlook it because it is taken for granted. Inter-tribal diffusion, on the contrary, is spasmodic and halting; in numerous particular instances, moreover, the actuality of its occurrence, as was shown, can only be judged probable or inferred, rather than proved. Thus it presents problems and thereby commands attention.

But why, we must now ask, does intra-tribal diffusion proceed, on the whole, so easily and smoothly? The answer lies in the relation of the new features to the pre-existing culture. In a tribe, a local group, that is, with its traditional culture and culture-patterns, the new is held by the old: the 'inventor,' having absorbed tribal culture in his education, invents, but he does so with moderation: he may not and will not go off into something *entirely* new, for his innovation is rooted in that which is being innovated, the old and established. In modern culture the range of acceptable innovation is relatively wide, and the inventor's education is such that he may, on occasion, depart considerably from the old. In primitive culture the range of acceptable novelty is relatively slight, but then the primitive inventor is himself moulded to pattern to such an extent that he is not likely to originate anything outside the narrow range of novelty acceptable to his group. This being so, an enormous proportion of the new (most of which, it must be remembered, will only be *slightly* new, whatever the culture) finds little opposition to its spread within the culture when on its way to becoming one of its accepted and established features. Not so in inter-tribal diffusion. Here the whole of culture A may be regarded as new to culture B with which A is in contact, new because different. The newness of A in the eyes of B may, moreover, be of *any* degree, for the individual moulders of A (in the present or past), its 'inventors,' have not been moulded by the education in B. A then may be agricultural, while B is pastoral; or A's art may be entirely beyond the technical skill in B; or A's religion may be absurd, its morality revolting, in the eyes of B; A, finally, may be a modern group, B a primitive one. Most or all of the content of A may thus prove unacceptable to B and will not spread: there will be no diffusion. Or if there is, it may prove protracted, difficult, and perhaps imperfect.

The difference then between intra-tribal and inter-tribal diffusion, from this angle, lies in the following: In intra-tribal diffusion the selection exercised with reference to the new is administered by the same agency which has codetermined the new or limited its range, namely the tribal culture. Therefore, the new here is not likely to prove very new, or unacceptably so. As a consequence, spread or diffusion within the tribe will usually proceed without difficulty. In inter-tribal contact, these conditions favourable to unencumbered diffusion do not obtain. Hence diffusion here is subject more fully to the accidents of time, place, and occasion.

All this is relative, of course. Two tribes in contact may but need not be different or wholly different in culture. They might, for example, both be primitive, or belong to one culture-area. Now, the less the cultural difference of two tribes, the more common their historical background, the less will be the difference between the conditions of diffusion between two such tribes and those that obtain within one tribe. Diffusion within a culture-area, as we know, proceeds almost as readily as it does within the component tribes of the area. Or, in modern cultures: diffusion between the nations of the Western world is so constant and smooth because they already have so much in common. From this standpoint, the difference between intra-tribal and inter-tribal diffusion resolves itself into one of degree rather than of kind.

Chapter XXX

EVOLUTION AND PROGRESS

Pre-scientific Ideas on Evolution

Interest in the diffusion of cultural features is very keen today. In the extreme form of a diffusionistic dogma it is, as we saw, represented by such writers as Graebner, Rivers, Elliot Smith, Father W. Schmidt. In a more moderate form it characterizes the recent work of some American students, for example, Clark Wissler and A. L. Kroeber. In the intellectual climate of the Western world, where the concepts and methods of the natural and exact sciences have made their home, this appeal of diffusion as an approach to culture is easy to understand. People like concreteness, enumeration, proof. All this is possible, within limits, in the study of diffusion.

During the second half of the nineteenth century the orientation of the social sciences was a very different one. Under the powerful influence of Darwin's biological theories and the evolutionary philosophy of Herbert Spencer, anthropologists, sociologists, and less markedly other social scientists, were exerting their efforts in an attempt to subsume cultures under the concept of change or transformation.

The idea of linking the past to the present by a series of changes is not a new one. To ascribe the concept of social evolution too exclusively to the influence of Darwin's biological theories, is a mistake for which anthropologists are in part responsible. The influence of the science of life did, to be sure, give to evolutionary thought its modern flavour, but the thought itself antedates the dynamic standpoint in biology which, arising towards the end of the eighteenth century, established itself as the dominant ideological pattern in the nineteenth. Even the primitives did some thinking about such matters. It is, in fact, apparent that anyone who thinks of the past at all, in its relation to the present, finds himself limited to a few possible alternatives: either the past was like the present, or the present became what it is through some act of creation, or, finally, there was a process of change or development, gradual or otherwise, which linked the past to the present. All of these approaches are to be found in the thinking of the primitives. The Eskimo, for example, conceive of the past as little more than a reflection of the present: things

always were what they are now. This point of view may be described
as one of permanence or immutability. Many primitives find the standpoint of creation congenial to their thought. Creation, in this context, may
be described as a transformation of an idea into a fact: the thought of
the Creator becomes objective reality in the world of fact. The culture-
heroes of the American Indians, who established the arts and crafts and
taught man the ways of life, are embodiments of this conception. A
more impressive instance may be seen in the Polynesian god, Tane, the
Fertilizer.

According to a New Zealand version, Tane created man in the following way: When 'it was resolved' to create woman, Tane, the Fertilizer, as
representing the male element, was appointed to carry out the task. On
the body of the Earth Mother he fashioned an image in human form—
fashioned it of earth, a portion of the body of Papa. Into this body, this
lifeless form of earth, it was necessary to instil life. The spirit (the breath
of life) and the mind (the power of thought) were obtained from Io,
the Supreme God. When Tane introduced these, when the breath of life
entered the nostrils of the earthen image, the life-principle of man took
possession of it: breathing commenced, the eyes opened, a sneeze broke
from the nostrils; the forebear of the *ira tangata* was endowed with life;
a person, a female, lived. Woman had entered the world. The woman
thus fashioned, continues E. S. Craighill Handy,[1] was then impregnated
by the god and thus was the race of man originated. Nor is the idea of
creation foreign to some of the crudest tribes. The mythological brothers
of the Australians who operated upon the *inapertwa*, half-finished bodies
of men and women, by separating their arms and legs and making them
live as humans, were Creators.

The idea of change or transformation, finally, is also represented. The
genealogically minded Polynesians project the enormous family trees
of their chiefs into the remote traditional and mythological past, but
they also invent elaborate accounts of mythical transformations by
means of which the world came to be as it is. Thus in New Zealand we
find the following version of the formation of the world, the series here
given representing successive stages:

> The Void
> The First Void
> The Second Void
> The Vast Void
> The Far-Extending Void
> The Sure Void

. [1] *Polynesian Religion*, p. 99.

The Unpossessing Void
The Delightful Void
The Void Fast Bound
The Night
The Hanging Night
The Drifting Night
The Moaning Night
The Daughter of Troubled Sleep
The Night
The Dawn
The Abiding Day
The Bright Day
Space

In 'Space' two existences without shape were formed: a male, Maku
(Moisture), and a female, Mahora-nui-a-rangi(Great Expanse of Heaven).
From these sprang Rangi-potiki (The Heavens) who took to wife Papa
(Earth) and begat the gods.[2] In this series the idea of progressive development seems to be combined with that of individualized stages in the
form of a genealogical succession. 'According to the Hawaiian account,'
continues Dixon, 'the drama of creation is divided into a series of stages,
and in the first of these life springs from the shadowy abyss and dark
night. There is here, however, no long series of antecedent, vaguely
personified entities ranged in genealogical sequence, but the immediate
appearance of living things. At first the lowly zoophytes come into being,
and these are followed by worms and shellfish, each type being declared
to conquer and destroy its predecessor, a struggle for existence in which
the strongest survive. Parallel with this evolution of animal forms, plant
life begins on land and in the sea—at first with the algae, followed by
seaweeds and rushes. As type follows type, the accumulating slime of
their decay raises the land above the waters, in which, as spectator of
all, swims the octopus, the lone survivor from an earlier world. In the
next period Black Night and Wide-Spread Night give birth to leafy plants
and to insects and birds, while in the darkness the first faint glimmering
of day appears. The sea brings forth its higher forms, such as the medusae,
fishes, and whales; and in the dim twilight monstrous forms creep in the
mud. Food plants come into existence while all nature is thrown into an
uproar under the stress of its birth-pains. The fifth period sees the
emergence of swine (the highest mammal known to the Hawaiian), and
night becomes separated from day. In the sixth, mice appear on land,
and porpoises in the sea; the seventh period witnesses the development

2 Roland B. Dixon, *Oceanic Mythology*, p. 7.

of various abstract psychic qualities, later to be embodied in man, while in the eighth, the turmoil and uproar having subsided, from peace and quiet, fructified by the light, which is now brilliant, woman is born, and also man, together with some of the higher gods.' [3] While granting considerable dramatic force to this tale, we need not consider it a scientific hypothesis (compare here with our own surviving theological cosmogony!). What counts in this context is the presence of the idea of progressive development which is here exhibited with utmost clarity.

The ancient Greeks loved to play with the notion of evolution, as, for example, Heraclitus, the 'dark' philosopher, with his idea of universal change or transmutation. Among the Greeks also another idea took root, namely, that of human progress, the movement of society in the direction of improvement. In one form or another this notion pervades the political and ethical thinking of both Aristotle and Plato. Also they distinguished automatic changes from deliberate efforts at change. Aristotle's *Politics* and Plato's *Republic* are great depositories of such ideas. The Roman poet, Lucretius, writing in the first century A.D., returned to both themes in his *De Rerum Natura*, representing the history of nature as an unfoldment and that of human society as a progressive series. In the Middle Ages the prevailing theological dogmatism was inimical to the concept of change or progress in things physical or social. The revival of freer and more constructive thought during the Renaissance led to a recrudescence of these older notions. On the one hand, the path-breaking researches of such men as Copernicus, Kepler, da Vinci, Galileo, and Descartes resulted in the establishment of what came to be known as the modern mathematico-mechanical view of the world, presently to be perfected by the speculative genius of Newton and the great synthesizing ability of Laplace. On the other hand, such French thinkers as Bossuet, Turgot, and Condorcet revived the notion of progress in the development of mankind.

In the comprehensive ideological structure of Auguste Comte (1798–1857) both ideas are utilized. He bases his picture of the physical world on the mathematico-mechanical ideas of the science of his day and at the same time re-establishes the concept of human progress by applying a law of development to the social domain. In the days of later evolutionists it became fashionable to snub Comte's ideas in this matter. Herbert Spencer, for example, made quite a case of his alleged independence of Comte. When viewed without prejudice, however, Comte's work can be shown to contain all the germinating notions of the so-called classical

[3] Roland B. Dixon, *Oceanic Mythology*, pp. 15–16. (Reprinted by permission of The Archaeological Institute of America.)

evolutionists. He spoke of the universality of change in culture, of stages
of development, of the inevitability of progress. He was also the first
among social thinkers to use the comparative method on a comprehensive
scale. Comte claimed that all the stages through which mankind had
passed in its development can still be found exhibited among the living
tribes of the earth. This, he thought, was due to the fact that, whereas the
stages of historical change were fixed, the rate of progress was not everywhere the same. Numerous factors served both to precipitate and to re-
tard the cultural advance, and as a result the modern student, if he
searches patiently enough, can reconstruct from the horizontal plane of
present cultural conditions among tribes now living the whole vertical
picture of stages passed through in history by the ancestors of the present Western culture.

From Lamarck to Spencer

Towards the end of the eighteenth century and the beginning of the
nineteenth, while these ideas were already in the air, biological thought
continued with remarkable tenacity to hold on to the dogma of permanence, the so-called fixity or immutability of species. When Lamarck
(1744–1829) appeared on the scene with his radically different notions,
he could not in his lifetime make much headway against the greater authority of the famous French anatomist, Cuvier, who held on to the older
notion of stability. Lamarck's ideas, as developed in his *Zoological Philosophy* (1809) were, however, not forgotten. The two pillars on which
he erected his new idea-system were these: the function moulds the organ,
and acquired characteristics are inherited. Translating these propositions
into the concrete, this means that the organism becomes adjusted to its
natural environment by developing certain organs or strengthening others
in the course of exercise—such as, say, the claws of the cat family or
their powerful tusks, the elongated neck of the giraffe or the less marked
lengthening of the neck of the polar bear—and that these traits, once
having started on their way, are inherited in the offspring, who begin to
build where their progenitors left off. A mechanism was thus provided
which made it possible to link up the different species of plants or animals with each other and to transform the picture of permanence and
disparateness, as between species, into one of change and transmutation
from one species to the next. Lamarck, we think, was in error. The principle of the inheritance of acquired characteristics finds little favour
with modern biologists. The fact remains that at a time when the dynamic view of the history of life on earth was just beginning to forge

ahead, against authoritative and impassioned opposition, Lamarck was among the first to pave the way.[4]

After this the budding evolutionary approach was never wholly abandoned. The work of Robert Malthus proved a further stepping-stone in this direction. In his famous *Essay on Population* (first edition, 1798, second greatly enlarged edition, 1803), he established the so-called law of population based on the observation that, while both population and food-supply in a given community increase with time, the rate of increase is not the same. Whereas the population, taught Malthus, increases in a geometrical ratio, the food supply increases in an arithmetical one. The inevitable consequence is a shortage of food. This pressure on the population results in a struggle for existence in a world in which a scramble for food becomes a necessity. In the formative stages of their

---

[4] It is not uncommon among students of the subject to regard the Königsberg sage, Immanuel Kant, as an early evolutionist. In his critical study, 'Kant and Evolution' (*Popular Science Monthly*, vol. XXVIII, 1911), Professor Arthur O. Lovejoy has shown that this is wholly unfounded. Kant, it is true, was keenly sensitive to the intellectual currents of his time. Evolutionary gropings did not pass him by, but his mind remained set to the end against the idea of community of descent of the animal kingdom. He was even inclined to wax emotional when confronted with the notion. In his review (1785) of Herder's *Ideen* (full title: *Ideas for a Philosophy of Human History*), for example, occurs the following passage: 'The slightness of the degree of difference between species is, since the number of species is so great, a necessary consequence of their number. But a *relationship* between them—such that one species should originate from another and all from one original species, or that all should spring from the teeming womb of a universal Mother—this would lead to ideas so monstrous that the reason shrinks from them with a shudder.' (*Ibid.*, p. 46.)

Goethe, on the other hand, who was 36 when Kant was 61 (at the time he wrote the review just mentioned), is rightly placed in the very centre of that intellectual current which, revived in the eighteenth century, was headed straight for evolution. His contributions to the subject were, in fact, outstanding and speak eloquently both for his remarkable powers of observation and his imaginative daring. Goethe's views can be found in his observations on the intermaxillary bone and osteology generally and especially in his essay on the metamorphosis of plants, in which he reduces all parts of the plant, excepting the stem and root, to the leaf. This is what Thomas H. Huxley has to say of Goethe in his *Life of Owen* (vol. II, p. 290) : 'There was considerable reason, a hundred years ago, for thinking that an infusion of the artistic way of looking at things might tend to vivify the somewhat mummified body of technical zoology and botany. Great ideas were floating about; the artistic apprehension was needed to give these airy nothings a local habitation and a name; to convert vague suppositions into definite hypotheses.' Eckermann in his famous *Conversations with Goethe* relates how, on one occasion, he found Goethe exclaiming: 'Well, what do you think of the great event, etc.?' Naturally enough, he thought that Goethe was referring to the French Revolution of 1830 which had just taken place. To his amazement, however, he presently discovered that the reference was to the debate at the French Academy between Cuvier and Geoffroy Saint-Hilaire, the latter having taken up the cudgels in defence of evolution. (*Cf.* Merz, *History of European Thought in the XIXth Century*, vol. II, p. 246, note 2, and p. 253, note 3.)

thought, both Charles Darwin and Herbert Spencer became acquainted with Malthus's essay, and they left personal statements referring to the quickening effect exercised by this reading on their own evolutionary ideas.

A further item in the same direction was added by the cellular theory of organic matter. The seed of this notion, which had been germinating for some time, was kept from fruition in more concrete and experimental form by the inadequacies of technique. With the advent of the microscope it became possible to clinch the argument, which was done by Schleiden for botany and Schwann for zoology towards the end of the first quarter of the nineteenth century. If the ultimate base of all organic substance was the same, it could now be argued, the simplest explanation of this fact had to be seen in genetic continuity. Thus a further road was opened up along which species could be connected with each other in development.

The next significant contribution was that of Carl Ernst von Baer, a Russian-German biologist who specialized in embryology. Von Baer, a man of enormous erudition and a talented experimentalist, is best known in the history of biology for his epochal discovery of the human ovum. His contribution to the theory of organic evolution, however, rests in the formulation of a principle usually covered by the phrase, 'ontogeny recapitulates phylogeny,' which means that the individual organism in the course of its development retraces the stages through which the species of animals passed in their evolution from the unicellular organism to the particular organism in question. Von Baer himself, an exceedingly cautious and self-critical experimentalist, was very guarded in formulating this principle. In fact he was inclined to apply it to the different changes within the range of one species rather than to the transformation of one species into another. Some 30 years had to elapse after the publication of his great *History of the Development of Animals* (1828–1837) before the principle was presented in a more extreme form by Ernst Haeckel, the leading German protagonist of Darwinian ideas. In his *Anthropogenie* (1863) he restated the principle as the 'fundamental ontogenetic law.' Among other arguments and devices, he used photographs of embryos of different animals to prove his contention. It appeared before long that Haeckel had gone greatly beyond the facts. Under the constant pounding of biological criticism the principle was in time subjected to the following two important restrictions: First, while it was admitted that a recapitulation of phylogeny in ontogeny did take place and that this fact constituted one of the most impressive evidences for the genetic relationship of species, the recapitulation involved was now shown to be foreshortened in character, as if phylogenetic stages had been telescoped and condensed into the ontogenetic series. Not all the phases of development represented by the different species were in fact traceable in the embryonic stages of the later organism, but only certain peaks, as it were, the intermediate phases being slurred over. And second, what was recapitulated were not the adult nor even the precise embryonic forms of the preceding species, but rather the more generalized forms belonging to the main trunk of the tree of descent, of which forms the finished species were to be regarded as specialized developments. In this modified form the principle still holds and may be regarded as one of the pillars of modern biological thought in its genetic aspect.

Another important contribution to the dynamic point of view came from the side of geology. Building upon the researches of his predecessor, Hutton, Charles Lyell pointed out in his *Principles of Geology* (1830) that the different geological strata, when chronologized, could be utilized for transforming a spatial superposition into a temporal succession, the deepest-lying strata being, of course, those that were deposited earliest and so on with the rest. Thus the time-perspective, and with it, the principle of development, were introduced also into the realm of the history of the earth.

Upon these foundations Charles Darwin, the biologist, and Herbert Spencer, the philosopher, built up their comprehensive systems. Darwin, whose extraordinary gifts of observation were sharpened when he was still a youth by his five-year journey on H.M.S. *Beagle*, was greatly impressed by the evidences of variability in plants and animals which could be readily identified as belonging to the same general kind. He was particularly struck by this phenomenon in regions like South America and the Galapagos Islands where, as one travelled from island to island, the patent similarity of animals and birds was seen to be accompanied by more or less conspicuous variations characteristic of special localities. If animal forms varied in this fashion, argued the young Darwin, there must have been some sufficient reason to induce this process; as the variations, morever, corresponded to differences in environments, the advantage of these variations to the plant or animal organism must have been related, in some way, to the varying characteristics of the environments. Such were the thoughts that occupied Darwin's mind when he returned to England. Presently he set out on an experimental career covering many years, in the course of which he tried his hand, after the manner of animal fanciers, at the production of new varieties or subvarieties of organic creatures. Proceeding by the method of selective breeding, he was entirely successful in producing such new varieties.

His thought, in substance, ran as follows: Here I have achieved in my laboratory, argued Darwin, what nature, according to my previous observations, had achieved in her own. Now these results were obtained in pursuance of my conscious aim of determining upon certain traits and then perpetuating or enhancing them through selective breeding. Nature, without planning or selecting deliberately, has produced strictly comparable results. How could this be accounted for? It is here that Darwin made use of Malthus's concept of a struggle for existence.[5] He pointed out that certain traits were useful, others dangerous to animals in their particular environment. It was, for example, advantageous to possess the colour of one's normal *milieu*. Such a colour would act as an effective camouflage, thus decreasing the danger of being observed and destroyed by one's enemies, or successfully evaded by one's potential victims.[6] It is, for example, well known that the Arctic bear did not originally belong to the Arctic but represented one variant of the bear family which, in other regions, is brown or black, but not white. Why, then, would the bear, upon settling down in the Arctic, turn white? Sooner or later, continued Darwin, a white spot—discoloured region—might, for one reason or another, appear on the fur of the bear. This would provide a partial though far from perfect camouflage. Such a bear then would possess a slightly greater chance for survival and multiplicity of offspring. Among the latter some were likely to possess this trait even to a greater extent. They would be partly brown and partly white; a still greater advantage, therefore. Thus, ultimately, a white bear was the result. The long neck of the polar bear, a condition for successful navigation as well as for catching fish while planted on an ice block, could be accounted for in a similar way. It was clear to Darwin that the introduction of Lamarck's principle of the inheritance of acquired characteristics would greatly further the feasibility of his own principle, which he called 'natural selection.' But he also knew that the evidence did not favour Lamarck's idea. Reluctantly, therefore, he resolved to forego its application. Instead

[5] 'In October 1838,' writes Darwin in his brief autobiography, 'that is, fifteen months after I had begun my systematic enquiry, I happened to read for amusement "Malthus on Population," and being well prepared to appreciate the struggle for existence which everywhere goes on from long-continued observation of the habits of animals and plants, it at once struck me that under these circumstances favourable variations would tend to be preserved, and unfavourable ones to be destroyed. The result of this would be the formation of new species.' (*The Life and Letters of Charles Darwin*, edited by his son, Francis Darwin, vol. I, p. 83.) This was, as stated, in October, 1838. *The Origin of Species* appeared in November, 1859. Such is the cost of scientific method, in terms of time!

[6] How the initial variations occurred Darwin was unable to explain; instead he called them 'spontaneous variations' and simply took them for granted.

he built his own theory on the fact of variability, the general principle of heredity, and the gradual multiplication of the fit (those better adjusted to the environment) and reduction and ultimate elimination of the unfit (those less well adjusted to the environment).[7]

Though Darwin's thought proved a regular bomb-shell in the realm of biological theory and created an epoch, it cannot be said that Spencer's evolutionary philosophy was traceable to the influence of Darwin's work. Spencer thought of evolution and had formulated the main lines of evolutionary development in all aspects of natural phenomena before he knew of Darwin's conclusions. The first edition of his *Principles of Biology* (1855) appeared before the publication of Darwin's famous book. Instead, Spencer used the Lamarckian principle of the inheritance of acquired characteristics to explain the transmutation of species. He had, to be sure, no experimental evidence to sustain this principle but he accepted and defended it as a matter of logical necessity. 'Either there was inheritance of acquired characteristics,' exclaimed Herbert Spencer, 'or there was no evolution.'[8]

In his *Synthetic Philosophy* (started in 1862, completed in 1896), Herbert Spencer subsumed the whole of the known universe under the concept of evolution. Starting with the cosmic phenomena, then proceeding to the history of the earth,[9] he passed to the phenomena of organic life (*Principles of Biology*, 2 vols.), to those of the mind (*Principles of*

---

[7] Darwin's theory was presented to the world in his book, *The Origin of Species* (1859), the full title of which ran as follows: *The Origin of Species by Means of Natural Selection, or the Preservation of Favoured Races in the Struggle for Life.* In this title, 'origin of species' is, strictly speaking, a misnomer, because the 'origin' lies, of course, in those 'spontaneous variations' Darwin was unable to explain. 'Preservation of favoured races,' or the more common term, 'survival of the fittest,' designated a concept contributed by Herbert Spencer. 'Struggle for life' or, more frequently, 'struggle for existence,' is Malthus's term. 'Natural selection,' finally, is Darwin's particular contribution.

[8] An interesting historical episode referring to this period was Spencer's protracted controversy with August Weismann, the German biologist who spent half a lifetime experimenting with animals with the intention of either finding evidence of the inheritance of acquired characteristics or putting the principle definitely out of commission. Ultimately he came to a negative conclusion. But Spencer, to whom in the words of Huxley a tragedy was a hypothesis disproved by a fact, remained unshaken. Biologists are still busily at work in their efforts to reach light in this direction, the majority, at this stage of proceedings, refusing to concede the principle.

[9] Spencer's ideas on these two topics can be gleaned from his *First Principles*, the first volume of the *Synthetic Philosophy*. When he came to develop his system in detail he sidetracked these two originally planned volumes, as his interest was heavily weighted in the direction of living phenomena, especially those of human society and of ethics, with particular reference to the relations between the individual and the state. His ideas on this last topic are more concisely formulated in his two essays, *Social Statics* and *Man Versus the State*.

Psychology, 2 vols.), and finally to those of society (*Principles of Sociology,* 3 vols.) and of morality (*Principles of Ethics,* 2 vols.).

The three tenets of social evolution as formulated by Herbert Spencer were, in substance, these: Social evolution, representing the human or cultural aspect of universal evolution, is subsumable under the general law of change. Consequently, it is *uniform,* meaning that it everywhere proceeds in a similar way, passing through certain necessary and inevitable stages; it is *gradual,* meaning that sudden and violent changes, cataclysms, do not occur—instead, the changes are relatively slight in extent and slow in their incidence, conspicuous differences thus being the result of the accumulation of relatively inconspicuous increments of change,[10] and, it is *progressive,* meaning that the changes are in the direction of improvement.[11]

[10] The idea of gradual change, by small increments, must be traceable to Darwin's influence, although I have not been able to find definite evidence of this. In Darwin's scheme of organic evolution the 'imperceptible gradations' were the weakest link. He was attacked on this score even before the publication of the *Origin of Species,* and finally, in 1900, the botanical investigations of De Vries brought proof of the occurrence of variations both sudden, rather than gradual, and considerable, rather than imperceptible. De Vries's *The Mutation Theory* did, however, not weaken Darwin's major position, the theory of natural selection, as is sometimes assumed—it strengthened it. Before De Vries it was difficult to see how variations so small as to be imperceptible could be of advantage in the struggle for existence. De Vries's rectification improved the setting for natural selection: now it had something to start from!

[11] In fairness to Spencer I shall reproduce here a foot-note from my *Early Civilization:* 'Evolution,' says Spencer, 'is commonly conceived to imply in everything an intrinsic tendency to become something higher. This is an erroneous conception of it.' Spencer proceeds to note that evolution in organisms continues until equilibration with environmental conditions is reached. After this 'evolution practically ceases.' Then, as new conditions arise, there is further change, 'but it by no means follows that this change constitutes a step in evolution.' What is true of biological organisms is true of society: 'The social organism, like the individual organism, undergoes modifications until it comes into equilibrium with environing conditions and thereupon continues without any further change of structure. When the conditions are changed meteorologically, or biologically, or by alterations in the Flora and Fauna or by migration consequent on pressure of population, or by flight before usurping races, some change of social structure results. But this change does not necessarily imply advance.' (*Principles of Sociology,* vol. 1, pp. 95–96.) The insights thus reached by Herbert Spencer were, however, wasted on himself as far as his systematic philosophy was concerned.

Chapter XXXI

EVOLUTION AND PROGRESS (Continued)

Stages and Rate in Social Evolution: Construction and Critique

Of the three tenets of evolution the one of greatest interest here is the first, namely, the uniformity of cultural changes. No other writer has discussed this aspect of the subject with greater ingenuity or wealth of illustrative material than Spencer himself. Alone among social evolutionists, he undertook and carried out the task of tracing the different aspects of culture, such as ceremonial institutions, professional institutions, industrial institutions, and so on, through the different phases which presumably are re-enacted in identical or at least similar form whenever the particular institution develops in history. The details of Spencer's performance are too elaborate for reproduction; our concern here is with his method as well as the influence he exerted on the thought of other social scientists. The method used by Spencer in his *Sociology* and *Ethics* is the so-called comparative method introduced by the classical evolutionists. What, exactly, does this term imply? The procedure is, in brief, as follows: A more or less vast collection of material is made from numerous tribes in different parts of the world illustrating some aspect of culture, such as religion. Then the instances cited are arranged into a series of presumed stages. What makes it possible to arrange the concrete data thus collected into an allegedly successive series of stages is, of course, some preconceived idea of the nature of these stages and of their serial order, for no indication of that order can be gleaned from the facts themselves owing to the paucity and thinness of the historical perspective in most of our primitive data. We hear the evolutionist say, 'Now, here we are! Here is our historical development illustrated by concrete instances from zero to whatever the point in history may be. Evolution stands vindicated.' In the years following the publication of Spencer's treatises, and in fact, while he was still busy penning them, it has frequently been pointed out that many of the instances thus collected were inaccurate or misleading, in that they were torn out of their concrete setting in the culture or history of the tribe to which they referred. But let us waive this point, and suppose the instances all accurate and their connotation correct. Still the question remains: what right has the evolutionist to arrange instances of cultural facts or processes gathered from different tribes into a successive series, and then claim it as historical, claim, that is, that it has actually occurred in this form, that the different instances were comprised in a concrete historic series of stages at some particular place and time, or in all places and times, whenever the particular institution has developed in history? This is the crucial point. What is the theoretical justification of designating as historical, i.e., actual, a series of instances never observed in this successive form in history? The only answer the evolutionist could give here would be that according to the general principles of evolution such were the stages, and that now they were concretely illustrated; therefore the evolutionary hypothesis was correct. This reply cannot be accepted as valid. The instances may be factual and accurate enough as instances, but the ordering of them into a series of temporal succession, never as such observed nor deducible from the facts, could only be validated by the assumption of uniformity in development which is one of the tenets of evolution, the very hypothesis, that is, the procedure was intended to prove. The argument therefore is circular: something that is to be proved, or an inherent part of that something, is assumed in order to make the proof valid.

This aspect of the comparative method is illustrated even more impressively by the following circumstance: The evolutionist, unable to discover his stages in the historical perspective of one tribal culture, for the simple reason that such a perspective is never available except fragmentarily, proceeds to substitute an instance found in one tribe as a stage succeeding upon an instance drawn from another, and so on until the entire series is completed. The resulting collection of instances is therefore historically a hodge-podge. What makes the collection an historical or presumed historical series is once more the assumption of uniformity of development which makes the evolutionist feel at liberty to fill in the gaps in the series by instances wherever found. If the particular stage is not discoverable in the history of tribe A, the corresponding stage in the history of tribe B will do just as well, the assumption being that it must also have occurred in the history of tribe A but cannot be found for lack of evidence or, if it has not occurred, then it will occur in the future, if the tribe is permitted to develop normally, that is in line with the principles of evolution. Throughout, then, we find that what is to be demonstrated is already assumed to validate the demonstration.

Graphically this situation may be illustrated as follows:

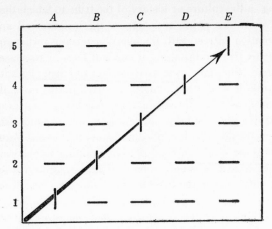

Fig. 80. Diagram in Refutation of the Comparative
Method as Used by the Evolutionists.

A, B, C, D, E are tribes; 1, 2, 3, 4, 5 are stages in the development of
a cultural feature; horizontal lines indicate that the stage has not actually been observed in the tribe, vertical lines, that it has. In connexion
with the cultural feature in question, stage 1 has been found in tribe A,
stage 2 in B, stage 3 in C, etc. So far, all is well: what we have is five
concrete descriptive data which merely show, at best, that such things
do actually occur. What the evolutionist proceeds to do is to link 1-A,
2-B, 3-C, 4-D and 5-E into a chronologically quasi-successive series, as
indicated by the arrow, and then declare evolution demonstrated as a
historic fact. But the arrow, as a unit, will not stand up under criticism;
it will disintegrate into five cultural features, geographically and historically distinct. To justify his flagrant disregard of space and time the
evolutionist would have to show that his 'substitutions' were legitimate.
Now, the only way he could do this would be by equating the developments through stages 1 to 5 in all five tribes; then whatever is missing in
A could be borrowed from B, C, etc. Ultimately, the arrow connecting into
a series 1-A, 2-B, 3-C, etc., could be equated with and used as a substitute for 1-A to 5-A, or 1-B to 5-B, etc. What prompts the evolutionist to
identify the series 1 to 5 in the five tribes is, however, nothing he has
discovered in the facts, but the evolutionary assumption of uniformity
in cultural development. In setting out to *prove* evolution, he cannot be
permitted to assume as true one of the tenets of evolution. The argument
is circular; there is no proof.

These and other criticisms on the procedure of the evolutionists were,
however, not passed until much later. In the last quarter of the nineteenth

century, on the other hand, the theory of social evolution, after an initial struggle against prevailing conceptions, won the field and occupied it practically without rivals for more than a generation. It is interesting in this connexion that the anthropologists were the ones to be most directly and powerfully affected, nor was this wholly accidental. In the anthropological field the concrete historic retrospect was then and remains today quite fragmentary; it is but seldom that a concrete series of historically successive stages of culture can be constructed on the basis of actually explored material. Under such conditions, if the past is to be reconstructed at all, the method must be speculative, and it is the speculative aspect of anthropological thought that was stimulated by the evolutionary theory. All the fields of cultural anthropology were affected. In the domain of economics, the famous three stages were established—hunting, pastoral life, and agriculture—which in this form and order were supposed to summarize the development of economy in all human societies. In the domain of technology another three stages or ages were formulated: the Stone Age, the Bronze Age, and the Iron Age. In the field of art, a number of evolutionary theories were propounded of which that of A. C. Haddon acquired the greatest vogue. In his book, *Evolution in Art,* Haddon taught that the earliest phase of decorative art was a realistic one in which the different things in nature, such as animals, birds, and plants, were represented realistically, that subsequently these realistic carvings or drawings underwent a gradual process of conventionalization in the direction of more purely geometrical patterns. This process went on until the patterns became wholly geometrical, the original realistic intent being now represented, if at all, by the imputed symbolic significance of the design or even merely by a name. In the domain of religion no one seemed to dare to construct as complete or detailed a series of stages as Spencer himself had attempted. In conjunction with E. B. Tylor he derived all the creatures of the supernatural realm from the original belief in spirits, which itself was traced to the double (shadow, echo, reflection) and the dream image. Further, he derived all religious ritual from a primal ancestor-worship, and finally reduced the emotional aspect of religion to the primitive attitude of fear which led him to formulate his famous dictum that all religion had come from the fear of the dead and all society from the fear of the living. Less complete or ambitious pictures of religious evolution were to be found in the works of other authors, for example in Jevons's book, *Introduction to the History of Religions,* in which totemism was featured as the earliest stage from which all nature-worship ultimately developed. Even Durkheim's more recent and in other respects much more critical study, *The Elementary*

Forms of the Religious Life, belongs here. Durkheim rejected the comparative method and based his study, in the main, on a very detailed and careful examination of the religious practices and beliefs of one cultural district, namely Australia, but then proceeded to declare the stages he had there discovered, or thought he had, as of general validity.

Another evolutionary scheme, which enjoyed a great vogue and exercised a profound influence on social thinking, referred to the development of society in the narrower sense. This theory was originally sponsored by three students who had reached their results independently of each other: J. J. Bachofen, a Swiss classicist, John Ferguson McLennan, a Scotch jurist, and Lewis H. Morgan, one of the first American anthropologists. The theory was enunciated in Bachofen's *Das Mutterrecht,* in McLennan's *Studies in Ancient History,* and in Morgan's *Ancient Society.* In main upshot the theory was as follows: In the domain of social organization proper, the earliest definite phase was assumed to have been the clan, subsequently followed by the gens, and much later by the family in the historic sense. Parallel with this went on an evolution of the forms of marriage which, starting from a stage of primitive promiscuity in which no regulations of any sort were observed between the sexes, then passed through two phases of group marriage (Morgan's contribution), to reach finally the stage of individual marriage as known to history. To this general conception Bachofen added the theory of the matriarchate, which to him appeared as a universal phase in the development of human society, coeval with the clan period, and characterized by the rule of women. While the vogue of evolution lasted, similar theories, dealing with the different aspects of culture, were springing up everywhere. People thus came to think that the past must be understood in evolutionary terms, and if it could not be thus expressed, then, it was thought, it remained ununderstood.

It is easy to see that the labours of the evolutionists introduced order and meaning, or a semblance of it, into the chaos of opinion with reference to the early human past. Thus simplicity took the place of complexity, and an apparently firm foundation was established for later historic periods. Again, there is no denying that the momentum of evolutionary thought proved a mighty stimulus to research, especially in the form of world-wide comparative studies of primitive institutions and beliefs. Before embarking on a critical discussion of these formulations, it will be well to remember that evolutionary writers universally employed the comparative method already referred to, a procedure which lent their works an air of great erudition and comprehensiveness. To this it may be added that most evolutionists, including Spencer, were strangely indifferent to their own methodology, in the sense that they were scarcely aware of what it was exactly that they were doing, and found it unnecessary to present a theoretical justification of the method they employed. But much time was to pass before the criticism against the comparative method as such was clinched, a criticism which, when finally made, came to constitute a major theoretical objection to evolutionary procedure. Instead the ambitious thought-structure of the evolutionists was attacked and destroyed bit by bit by arguments directed against the particular sets of stages posited by them as characteristic of the advance in the different aspects of culture.

In connexion with the three economic stages—hunting, pastoral life, and agriculture—the following strictures were made. It is, of course, true that hunting presupposes less technological equipment, hence less history, than either herding or agriculture. The latter two stages, one involving the domestication of animals, the other the cultivation of plants, obviously cannot belong to the earliest phases of man's career on earth. But it is also true that hunting, though fundamentally primitive and historically early, persists as an aspect of economy through all the stages of economic development and up into the present. Also, hunting never stood alone. The hunter everywhere was the man; while men hunted, women gathered the wild products of plant nature, a process requiring less energy and a narrower territory, and hence more nearly compatible with the various duties, maternal and domestic, which tied woman to the home. This feminine aspect of economy is everywhere associated with hunting, constituting together with it the true picture of primitive economic life.

The other two phases, herding and agriculture, as already said, are rooted in two fundamental, in fact, epochal, inventions or series of inventions, namely domestication and cultivation. Of these, domestication may with a high degree of probability be credited to man, who, in his capacity as hunter, had become familiar with the ways and habits of animals, and was thus placed in a position to make those discoveries and inventions which provided the link between hunting wild animals for food and clothing, and breeding and herding domesticated animals for the satisfaction of these and other wants. The cultivation of plants, on the other hand, can with equal probability be credited to woman, who was no less familiar with the plant kingdom than man was with that of animals. As to the assumed succession of these stages, their evolutionary position could be shown to have been hastily and uncritically formulated.

In surveying the primitive world, as we know it today, we find vast areas, such as those of the two Americas, in which agriculture is practised by many tribes, whereas domestication is unknown, with the sole exception of the dog, and, in one restricted area (Peru), the llama. The dog's omnipresence, in association with man, both among the present primitives and in prehistory, except in the earliest phase, justifies the assumption that the domestication of this particular animal had taken place a long time before that of any other animal, and thus constitutes a separate problem. In America, then, agriculture must be conceived as a condition developing directly out of the more primitive stage of the gathering of the wild plants of nature, without any intervening stage of domestication. In Africa, again, throughout wide areas, domestication, as we know, takes the form of herding and stock-breeding on an enormous scale and coexists with agriculture, the two occupations usually constituting the pursuits of separate social classes and probably being traceable, if not in all individual instances, to separate historic sources, not only as techniques but in the form of the coalescence of agricultural and herding tribes. Agriculture itself again cannot, as an historic phenomenon, be treated as a unit for the reason that a vast gulf separates what might be called primitive agriculture from historic agriculture. Primitive agriculture, which is the only kind present among modern primitives, precedes the invention of the plough, the digging-stick and hoe being used instead. It is generally, although not without exceptions, in the hands of women, and is not associated with the utilization of domesticated animals in the agricultural pursuits, not even in Africa where the animals needed for this were at hand.[1] Historic agriculture, on the other hand, is associated with the plough, the domesticated animal—whether cattle, horse, or mule—as man's helpmate in the pursuit, and the almost complete monopolization of agriculture by men. The subsequent reintroduction of women into agriculture as associates of men belongs to late historic times and represents a distinct problem. The resulting picture of the succession of the basic economic pursuits obviously lacks the simplicity of the evolutionary scheme, allowing as it does for a number of variants not foreseen in the evolutionary conception, but it has the merit of coming closer to the truth as revealed by unprejudiced research.

Similarly with the other three-stage theory, that of the Stone, Bronze, and Iron Ages. This generalization, originally derived from the study of

[1] It is, of course, obvious that the use of the hoe or digging stick does not create a situation in which a domesticated animal could be profitably used, such an occasion arising only with the introduction of the plough.

European prehistory, applies well enough in this particular field, but it falls down when extended to the vast region farther south, namely Africa, where a Stone Age was followed directly by an Age of Iron, the Bronze Age having failed to materialize.

The theories of Haddon and others, referring to the development of art from a realistic to a geometrical stage, also collapsed under critical scrutiny. The process of conventionalization or geometrization, in and by itself, is, of course, not a figment; it can be substantiated on primitive specimens—baskets, pots, or woodwork—as well as by a study of, say, the hats of modern ladies.[2] While this is true enough, it only establishes the above process as real but not as universal or exclusive or pristine. The burden of proof here lies on those who would claim that geometrical art never did or could arise as such, without any preceding naturalistic stages. This proof has never been produced; it has, moreover, been observed in more than one place where decorative pottery is common, for example among the Chiriqui Indians, that purely formal shapes tend in a later stage of development to become embellished by more or less realistic excrescences, which almost seem to be sprouting forth from under the surface of the pot. Here, then, the realistic is an emanation from the geometrical, the artist's imagination having been stimulated in the direction of naturalism either by vague resemblances to animal forms in the structure of the pot itself or by some external source. A region like that of the American Plains provides a convenient occasion for the study of the symbolic aspect of art in relation to its formal aspect. What we find here, as we saw, is a very uniform art in the form of coloured bead-work based on geometrical patterns reducible to a limited number of simple units. This art, with minor variations, is characteristic of the area as a whole. The art, we know, is also symbolic, but in this case the symbols are found to vary considerably as between tribe and tribe, or one group of tribes and another. In the absence of relevant historic data we cannot concretely demonstrate the priority of the geometrical art, but the likelihood of such priority must at least be regarded as very high. Otherwise the student would find himself in the difficult position of having to explain how and why similar or identical figures have among different tribes developed out of varying realistic patterns which, according to Haddon's theory, survived in the varying symbolic meanings in the different tribes. In this

[2] It will be found here that a period, some 35 years ago, when a lady's hat resembled a private horticultural establishment with an occasional bird or so, was followed by another in which the floral and faunal forms lost, more or less rapidly, their naturalistic suggestiveness, to be presently submerged altogether under curvilinear or angular patterns.

case, at any rate, the naturalistic theory would seem to be putting things on their heads.[3]

The same kind of stricture applies also to the scheme of social development. It is now conceded, by all but a few, that the family, frequently but not necessarily in the form of monogamy, is an omnipresent as well as the most primitive form of social unit, in conjunction, of course, with the local group. It stands to reason that sibs could not claim similar antiquity because in their very nature they carry evidence of a historic process: unilateral descent, sib names, not to speak of other features, could not have fallen from heaven ready-made. History must have been the moulder of these features. The family, on the other hand, is in comparison a primal and, as it were, an organic grouping, presupposing nothing but the sex urge and a tendency for sex-mates to remain together at least for some time while a child or children are conceived, carried, born, and nursed. It is for this reason that we can and do find one or another sort of family life among many of the higher animals, whereas such things as sibs or phratries are, of course, neither present nor conceivable below the stage of humanity. The major item in the evolutionary theory of social development, and the one most hotly debated, was the clan-gens succession, the notion, namely, that a universal clan stage was followed by a universal gentile stage. Now, this process of transition from maternal to paternal reckoning of group descent has, we know, never been observed historically. All we find is that many tribes are organized into clans, many others into gentes, and that both clans and gentes are defi-

---

[3] In view of the scantiness of our historic perspective in anthropology—a fact often stressed in these pages—it is well to remember, when thinking about such matters, that apart from specific cultural baggage, human imagination is the same today that it was thousands of years ago. Recall then what imagery Hamlet contrived to read into the curvy shapes of the clouds! And others did the same before him and do so now. Under proper atmospheric conditions and a suitable mood the silent branches of the forest still carry suggestions of cougars and owls and bats, if not gnomes and hobgoblins. Many an unknown hero lies buried or stands menacingly amidst the seductive outlines of a mountain chain. And conversely, human faces and figures suggest, on occasion, not merely other animals or birds—pig, bull, lion, monkey, wolf, fox, lynx, donkey, eagle, rooster—but also geometrical shapes: faces appear as triangles, apex down or up; noses as segments of circles or as straight lines; heads as triangles, squares, rhomboids; bellies as spheres or barrels; arms as sticks, derricks, or sides of ham. The art of the caricaturist finds an inexhaustible source of inspiration in these harmless suggestions. And so it was always. Man's experience has stocked his mind with patterns, naturalistic as well as geometrical; his imagination feeds on both, and at times goes riot with combinations, absurd or appropriate, aesthetic and grotesque, and it does so clumsily, gracefully, wittily, innocently, or offensively. In the light of all this it seems strangely penurious to want to limit the origin of man-made forms to naturalism or any other single factor.

nitely to be allocated to primitiveness, if not wholly pristine, as no evidence of sibs can be discovered among historic tribes. What the evolutionists had to do, therefore, in order to substantiate their position, was to look for evidences of pre-existing maternal organization among tribes with paternal descent. As such evidence, for example, was regarded a relatively high status of woman or the prominence of the maternal uncle, features which were assumed to be organically related to a maternal society and out of keeping with a paternal one. In other words, a high status of woman or the importance of the mother's brother were looked upon as survivals from a social condition to which, it was thought, they more fittingly belonged. In this utilization of the concept of survival in substantiation of an evolutionary hypothesis, we encounter once more that circular reasoning already dealt with in connexion with the comparative method. Seeing that the position of women in paternal or any other societies varies, and that maternal uncles, as well as fathers, may be more or less important, whatever the form of group descent, it is evident that the ascription of a survival character to these two features, high status of woman and importance of maternal uncle, derives its inspiration solely from the assumption of a pre-existing maternal condition, which is, of course, the very point to be proved. It can therefore not be used as an element in the proof.

Similarly, Bachofen's conception of a matriarchal era as well as that of a primitive stage of sexual promiscuity came to be recognized as pure fiction, the latter in particular representing nothing but a projection into presumed historical reality of a typical evolutionary starting-point: before order, chaos; before regulation, no regulation. The matriarchate, or the socio-political pre-eminence of woman, is not as wholly devoid of a factual foundation, considering that among some tribes, but only a very few—the Iroquois, the Pueblos, the Khasi of Assam (which other?) —women are important and might, by stretching the point, be described as predominant. But to admit this is one thing; to construct out of thin air a universal primitive matriarchate, an era of feminine dominance, is quite another.

A further argument against the stage theory in social evolution can be derived from the theory of diffusion discussed a while ago. It has been shown that every tribe develops its culture not merely out of its inner resources, but at least in part under the stimulation of extraneous cultural items coming from neighbouring tribes. As such items in their origins are obviously independent of the recipient culture, it follows that to admit them is to throw a monkey-wrench into the evolutionary scheme of necessary stages, in so far as this scheme, based solely on 'inner growth,' makes no provision for such extraneous factors. When confronted with this argument, the evolutionists attempted to defend their position on the ground that of the cultural features entering a group from the outside only those would prove acceptable and, therefore, assimilable, which fitted into the pre-existing culture of the recipient group. If they did not so fit they would be rejected or at best remain unassimilated, loosely afloat, as it were, in a hostile or uncongenial cultural medium. If, on the other hand, the extraneous features did fit and as a consequence were accepted and assimilated, then this very fact would bear evidence to the preparedness of the recipient group to accept such features and, if so, it should also be credited with the capacity or readiness to evolve them independently, had it not chanced to receive them from without. At first blush this argument sounds convincing enough; on analysis, however, it will be found that cultural preparedness is here taken in a much more precise sense than could be justified by a survey of what actually happens in such cases. Rather is it true that within certain broad limits all kinds of things or ideas can be accepted and assimilated by a group with a given culture. Barring a few obvious exceptions, have we really any proof of the inability of a culture to assimilate a given extraneous feature except the fact itself that, in a particular instance, it has not so assimilated it? Then we say that it was not prepared to do so. In other words, we can with a certain plausibility apply the concept of cultural preparedness *after the fact*, but we should be more than cautious in using it *before the fact*. For all we know to the contrary, when such an event does occur, it will not chime with our expectations. The rebuttal of the evolutionists being thus found wanting, the position is vindicated that the facts of diffusion or cultural borrowing are incompatible with dogmatic evolutionism of the quasi-organic sort.

The conception of uniform cultural development with its fixed stages must be regarded as the major one of the three tenets of evolutionism. Once it was overthrown, social evolutionism was shaken at its very base. But there were also the other tenets, the gradual character of evolutionary change and its progressive direction. These two tenets also suffered at the hands of numerous critics. Here the anthropologist ceded his monopoly in criticism to other social scientists, including the historian. As already stated and restated, we know very little about the particulars of cultural change among primitives for the simple reason that the relevant data on the history of primitive cultures, especially as to chronology, are so fragmentary. If we supplement what little we know in this regard by the evidence of later history, it becomes clear that gradual change does in fact occur. The question is whether the process implied and the accre-

tions to culture thus achieved correspond to what is meant by development or evolution. Being historical and propagated by the contact of
generations, human culture comprises a process of cultural accumulation. New items of knowledge, new ideas, new objects (or, shall I say,
more objects?), constantly make their appearance in addition to the pre-
existing ones. Most of these, however, whether material or mental, are
moulded after the pattern of the old. There is thus a gain in quantity
or mass, but is there also what might be called development or evolution?
Apparently not, unless we should care to identify accumulation with
evolution, which few evolutionists would allow. Now this process of
accumulation or amassing of things and ideas, the reality of which is undeniable, is in the nature of the case a slow and gradual affair. When
we speak of evolution, however, what is meant is not merely a change in
quantity or mass, but in quality or form, which implies creativeness or,
in a broad sense, invention. As we study invention or creativeness during
the only period available for such a study, namely that of written history,
periods fertile in ideas seem to come in spurts. These are followed, as a
rule, by a more or less protracted period during which spread, assimilation, acculturation of such things and ideas continues to go on, more or
less actively, but little origination takes place. Then, another spurt.
Whether the field explored is that of technique, mechanical inventions,
art, literature, science, or philosophy, everywhere the evidence of fact is
the same: a spurt followed by a relative quiescence or, to abandon the
metaphor, precipitation in development followed by mere passive reproduction of established patterns, or even relative retardation. Cultural
growth being in one of its aspects a form of learning, it is not surprising
to find that it should, in the main, bear the same character as does learning: peaks and plateaus, not a gradually ascending curve, will stand for
either process.

Whatever little we know about primitive cultures, in this respect, does
not militate against this conception. In religion, for example, when change
takes place, it takes, as we saw, the form of a rather sudden and violent
eruption; or at least, it does so at times. In the domain of technology,
where invention in the narrower sense reigns, little is available in the
form of concrete observation. But it is more than probable that here as
elsewhere radical inventions, such as the wheel, the making of fire, or
the bow and arrow, were followed by a more or less rapid succession of
other inventions thus engendered, and indeed made possible. After this
things would again come to a relative rest, for an indefinite period.
It must be remembered that there can be no transition between a wheel
and a no-wheel. Either a thing is a wheel or not a wheel, and when it is a

wheel it opens up innumerable opportunities, some of which must presently become apparent. Similarly with any device for making fire. Until the device works you simply cannot make fire; and when it does finally work, there is fire, and a method of producing it deliberately and *ad hoc* constitutes an epochal change. Leaning upon facts made known by later history, if not by that of primitives, unfortunately so dark, it seems safe to assume that primitives also knew the thrills of invention and discovery, accompanied by precipitation in development, and followed by periods of relative stability.[4]

Having arrived thus far, we find the task of dealing with these aspects of the theory of social evolution only partially carried out. When engaged on a critical venture, the temptation lies near to carry one's criticism too far and thus vitiate the result by absorbing into one's critique the same type of prejudice or dogma disclosed in the subject criticized. With all its faults and exaggerations, the theory of social evolution was not built on quicksand, nor has it wholly failed of contributing constructively to human thinking. As already noted, the sweeping character of evolutionary thought and the boldness of its generalizations have stimulated speculative as well as concrete investigations, a valuable result in itself which, though indirect, should not be underestimated. Then again, the evolutionists also brought into bold relief the desirability of looking upon history as an interconnected affair. After all, nothing is gained by adopting a view of history which conceives of it as a series of miracles, as it were, without any rhyme or reason. Nor would such a view correspond to the facts. It must further be admitted that there is an element of truth in the conception that the development of culture has been an unfoldment, that the different aspects of culture are interconnected, that certain phases of culture cannot materialize unless

[4] A mere note must suffice here with reference to another variety of evolutionary thought in which definite emphasis was placed on the cataclysmic nature of certain important periodic changes in the process of social development. The reference is, of course, to the historical philosophy of Karl Marx, who leaned but little on the classical evolutionists, his leading ideas having been formulated somewhat in advance of those of Herbert Spencer and his followers. As everyone knows, he derived his inspiration from the German philosopher, Friedrich Hegel, who had formulated an evolutionary or quasi-evolutionary scheme of history of his own. It is, however, interesting to note that the Marxian theory of revolutions in culture—the term 'revolution' here being used not in a narrow economic or political, but in a broad cultural sense—was widely accepted even by those who were most opposed to him in their social views. It is also important to realize that Marx by no means discarded the idea of gradual change in history; insisting, on the contrary, on its presence, he worked this concept into his very rigid scheme of historic determinism. Cataclysm to Marx was not *the* method of history but one of its two methods, the other being gradual change. 'Evolution through revolution,' said Kropotkin, the anarchist; but 'revolution through evolution' would describe the Marxian philosophy equally well.

certain other phases have preceded them. Let me try to illustrate these propositions as briefly as may be.

Take first the problem of the interrelations of the different aspects of culture. Granting that these aspects do not interlock in such a way that a change in one is inevitably accompanied or followed by a change or a corresponding change in another, it will yet be admitted that these aspects do not change or develop in utter independence of each other. We saw a while ago how the development of decorative art among primitives goes hand in hand with the rise of technique. By and large, a higher technique is accompanied by a more advanced art. Similarly we should not expect a high degree of political centralization in communities in which the means of communication have remained wholly primitive. The African state, for example, could scarcely exist without the extensive road-building itself furthered by the state but also constituting its most effective tool. In the absence of these arteries of power and wealth, effective military organization or any systematic fiscal policy would be impracticable. In modern days the enormous expansion of technology is by general recognition to be traced to a similarly amazing growth of scientific knowledge, while the demands of technology spur on still further advances in science. It is a commonplace of social theory that ever since the days of Rome, the economic, political, and legal aspects of European society have been strictly interrelated, both formally and functionally.

There is, then, a tendency for the different aspects of culture to stimulate and fructify each other. There is no fixed interrelation here nor any precise parallelism in change, but neither is there complete independence. Culture is neither an aggregate of disparate aspects nor is it a thoroughly integrated or organic whole. Rather is it a complex the different aspects of which, while preserving their autonomy, ever tend to enter into interrelations with each other, but at different rates and with varying degrees of completeness.

So also with the problem of stages. In the dogmatic evolutionary formulation we found it necessary to reject them, but in this also we should not go too far. Take, for example, chieftainship. It is probable that one or another kind of leadership has existed in human society from the beginning, but certainly not hereditary leadership. Before succession in office was established or could have been thought of, there must have been leaders or officials whose office was not hereditary. Similarly, leadership must have developed in relatively small groups; the presence of a chieftain wielding power over a populous tribe or group of tribes, could not possibly be regarded as a primary or truly primitive state of affairs. When speaking about sib organizations, I already had occasion to note that these forms of social structure could not be regarded as primary for the simple reason that such elements as unilateral inheritance of group membership, or sib names, could only have developed historically, a process which requires time. Even more obviously, tool making and using is a matter of achievement. Skill, within limits, may come in one lifetime, but knowledge and invention, props of technique, are functions of time. Everything else being equal, no one would place the woodwork of Australia on one level with that of Melanesia or Polynesia. Such things will be achieved and must be learned. Once more, time, as well as need, opportunity, chance. The same applies, if less clearly, in the domain of religion and magic. All the data indicate that the more primitive forms of supernatural creatures and magical devices are associated with single or at any rate simple purposes and functions. A primal magical rite is for fertility, protection, success in hunting or in love; a primitive spirit is of sickness or famine, of craftsmanship or of valour. The more comprehensive forms of magical power, the more versatile deities encountered among the more advanced primitives as well as in historic times, came into being through a process of syncretism—powers and functions originally connected with separate things, acts, or supernatural beings, now became concentrated in a single carrier. We cannot very well conceive of this process as reversed, except under very special conditions, without going both in the face of known facts and of theoretical probability.

Or take the field of economics. Once more, some sort of vague proprietary sense may, perhaps, be regarded as having belonged to man from the beginning. Do we not see incipient elements of it already among animals? But here also the idea of inheritance of property must have appeared later. This theoretically feasible conception is fully vindicated by a survey of primitive tribes; the cruder ones either manage without the notion of property inheritance or have no very definite regulations in this connexion. The exchange of goods or commodities, again, may be very old indeed, but before a medium of exchange developed there was exchange in kind, and it is out of the perplexities and inconveniences of the latter that the stimulus arose first to regard certain goods as a medium of exchange, then to devise a separate medium which no longer had much or any value except as a medium.

These examples could be multiplied indefinitely. Perhaps too eagerly absorbed in the process of tearing down evolution, we have been tempted to neglect the positive leads left behind by this school of thought. There is much room here for constructive work yet to be done.

Theory of Progress

Like the tenet of gradual change, the last and final tenet of the evolutionary scheme, that of progressive change, proved of special interest to social scientists other than anthropologists. Even among the classical evolutionists themselves the idea of progress played a very uneven part. Herbert Spencer, however, did emphasize it, presently to be dubbed the 'optimistic philosopher' by one of his continental expounders. The theory of progress, let us remember, has a long history of its own, reaching far back of the biological conception of evolution formulated in the nineteenth century. Now let me ask, to what extent does the notion of social progress reflect what we actually know of human affairs in their unfoldment in history? It is probably sufficient to have asked this question to realize that the idea of social progress corresponds far less to anything actual, in past or present, than to a widely shared desire that such might be the case. In other words, as Wundt, the psychologist, and Eduard Meyer expressed it, the idea of progress is far less a rational deduction than it is a moral postulate. It is a sort of prop to living which renders the past less disappointing, the present more endurable, and the future more rosy. If, however, the question is asked whether the notion of progress is true rather than merely agreeable, the answer can scarcely be in doubt. Should one attempt to envisage a historic period of any length from the standpoint of progress, it would at once be realized that the task bristles with difficulties. In the first place, what is progress but change in a desirable direction? And what is desirable? Well, something here, something else there; this to me, that to you. Or, to phrase it differently, progress is change in the direction of improvement. But what is improvement unless you have a standard? And standards notoriously differ. In other words, there is a core of subjectivity underlying the very idea of progressive change, unless one should be willing to assert that there are certain eternal values realized by progressive change in history. But who is there to determine these eternal values? As one listens to men, wise or otherwise, in present or past, expressing themselves on what is improvement or desirable, he is reminded of the confusion of tongues.

However, let us distinguish. Culture, as we saw, comprises various aspects which, though integrated in part, also preserve a degree of autonomy. So the question may well be asked, referring to primitives as well as to historic peoples, whether change or progressive change in one cultural aspect is invariably or usually accompanied by similar changes in another or others? The reverse seems only too patently true. Take for example the Australians, and it will appear that, whatever one's standards, the social system of these people will have to be recognized as more complex and at least in this sense more highly evolved than their material or technological equipment; this latter, adequate though it may be for the time and place, remains relatively crude, with distinct earmarks of, shall we say, 'primitiveness.' On the other hand, take the Eskimo, by way of contrast; their socio-political organization is of the crudest and simplest possible sort, whereas their technology is so elaborate and so obviously adequate to the solution of their many environmental problems as to be constantly cited as such by all investigators. Or compare from this standpoint the tribes of the Iroquois League with those of the Northwest. In political structure and consciousness the Iroquois are indubitably more advanced, but in the domain of art the Pacific Coast tribes are as clearly superior to the Iroquois. Similarly in other periods in the history of civilization. The Greeks of the Periclean Age or thereabouts did achieve a remarkably harmonious and integrated development in a number of cultural aspects, such as political and ethical ideas and practices, art, literature, and philosophy, but they lagged behind in the development of the economic aspect of life, both in practice and in idea. And again, in the more restricted field of politics: whereas their wisdom was of the highest within the boundaries of the City-state, they failed to develop corresponding insight or vision in inter-state relations, a fact also frequently commented upon by historians. The Romans of the imperial period contributed much to political and legal development and thought, but they failed to enhance creatively the fields of science, art, or philosophy. Or in modern days: however warmly we might feel towards the superiorities of our Western civilization, the fact is only too patent that our scientific and technological development, flowing directly or indirectly from the advancement of the exact and natural sciences in the nineteenth century, is far ahead of our habits and notions in matters social, political, economic, and moral, and is characterized by a far more rapid rhythm of change. This discrepancy is in fact so conspicuous as to be generally and rightly recognized as one of the most serious evils and puzzling problems of the present moment in history.[5]

Evidently then, if there is anything in the idea of progress at all, it cannot be used in the broad sense of a general, universal, and inevitable

---

[5] In connexion with this general subject of the relative development of the different aspects of culture I want to refer the student to W. F. Ogburn's stimulating book, *Social Change,* in which he expounds the pregnant concept of a 'cultural lag,' which is one way of formulating the facts reviewed in these pages.

tendency of the social process in history. If the concept of progress is to be retained, its form must be radically changed so as to bring it into harmony with the known facts. To this aspect of the subject we shall presently return.

Another interesting phase of the idea of progress is this: it is patently more readily applicable to certain aspects of culture than to others. In science, for example, or knowledge in general, as well as in technology, or knowledge in operation, the idea of progress can be and has been readily applied, in this case with a very precise connotation. Both knowledge and tools (symbols of technique) are goods, that is, positive social values. Now, both in science and in technology there has been a definite though not always steady advance from primitiveness to modern times, or more emphatically, from the Renaissance to the present. Now, if knowledge and technique are good, more knowledge and technique are better. Here, then, there has been progress. The idea of progress, in this connotation, though definite, is removed from the more basic concept of qualitative improvement. So that precisely where the idea of progress is most definitely applicable, it loses that aspect of its meaning which by general recognition constitutes its very core, namely the aspect of quality or value. In those aspects of culture, on the other hand, where the qualitative and valuational sides are pronounced, such as social organization, economic life, morality, religion, art, the application of the idea becomes difficult on account of the intrusion of a subjective element. A mere accumulation or amassing of content in these fields is, as such, devoid of meaning. More knowledge may be better than little knowledge, but what does more religion mean, or more art, or more morality? Perceptibly less than nothing, as Veblen might have said. Here values and standards must be appealed to, inevitably so; whence the subjective bias. Is Christianity, let us say, superior to Mohammedanism, Judaism, or Confucianism? Yes or no, according to who you are or what you believe in. Or, is modern art superior to that of the Greeks or that of the Chinese? Again we are in the same quandary. Or, is modern socio-political organization superior to that of the primitives, the Greeks, the Romans? How standards here can differ and how irreconcilable such differences may become, on occasion, is strikingly brought home by the basic cleft in modern opinion between those who advocate dictatorship, whether communist or fascist, and those others who cling to democracy with its recognized failings and compensating virtues.

Is it not clear, then, that we have to choose between abandoning the idea of progress altogether and preserving it, but with a radically changed connotation? I, for one, choose the second alternative, regarding the idea of progress as applicable but in a more modest and restricted sense. Once your subject-matter or problem has been defined and your standard or value made clear, the road is paved for the application of the concept of progress *within these limits*. There is, for example, no point in comparing Greek art with the Gothic with the aim of evaluating them as to superiority or inferiority; or the Gothic with the modern. But it is perfectly feasible to envisage the development of Greek art, say Greek architecture, from the sixth century B.C. to the fourth century B.C. It will then be seen that within that temporal range and accepting the ideals gradually emerging in the development of Greek art, there was progress, a steady movement towards the realization of those ideals. Similarly in the Gothic, if we study it beginning with its emergence from the Romanesque and through the several centuries of its unfoldment, up to say the fifteenth or sixteenth century, there is within this period, granting once more the ideals and problems of the Gothic, a steady advance in the solution of these problems in the light of these ideals. Similarly, if we study the development of the modern national state from its emergence or re-emergence in the late Renaissance and through the eighteenth and nineteenth centuries. There was here, granting again the ideals and associated problems, an advance which perhaps may be regarded as having reached its culmination in the Germany of the pre-War period. Or, as regards primitives—when the archaeologist is lucky enough to chance upon a series of superimposed cultural strata, and to study the pottery in these strata, as has occurred in the Pueblo region, he may, as in this case, discover a complete series of levels of pottery-making, beginning with technically imperfect and relatively crude shapes of unglazed pottery, followed by glazed pottery, and by a long range of progressively more complicated, technically more elaborate, and imaginatively richer designs, culminating in the extraordinary artistry of Zuñi, Hopi, or San Ildefonso pottery. It is both possible and, I think, helpful to use the concept of progress here.

When we say, finally, that in comparison to the primitives or to the Middle Ages we live in a progressive society, we cannot mean by this that progress, improvement, is somehow inherent in the very make-up of our society but not of theirs. What we do mean is that one of the ideals of modern more mobile society is to prepare courageously for impending changes, in part to foresee them, and in part to realize them by conscious planned effort. A very different point of view, it will be seen, and one scarcely applicable or possible in other ages. Even today, let us admit, this view remains more of a desideratum than of an accomplishment, but perhaps we are prepared to accept it as an ideal. In this more limited and highly transfigured sense, the concept of progress should, I think, be preserved in the social field. By way of clearing the ground for this new orientation, it will be well to forget, once and for all, the notion of a universal, automatic and inevitable progress in society or history. Progress to us is no longer a spectacle to be contemplated but a problem to be solved, a task to be accomplished.

BIBLIOGRAPHY

BIBLIOGRAPHY

With some exceptions, the books and articles referred to in the text are not included in this bibliography. Excepting one or two instances, only English works are cited. Obviously, a slight list like the following cannot aspire to completeness or even comprehensiveness. All that is intended by this necessarily subjective selection of titles is to guide the student on to a study of ethnographic and ethnological literature. A list different in all particulars might do as well, or better.

By way of introduction a word about encyclopaedias and journals. Though the 9th Edition of the *Encyclopaedia Britannica* (the greatest of the several editions) is now definitely dated, it is still useful to compare the articles on anthropology and ethnology in the several editions, especially Elliot Smith's 'Ethnology' (11th Ed.) with Malinowski's 'Anthropology' (the next edition). The articles on anthropological topics in Hastings' *Encyclopaedia of Religion and Ethics* are often excellent. See also the same topics in the *New International Encyclopaedia* (2nd Ed.). The *Encyclopedia of the Social Sciences* contains several first-rate articles, such as Boas's 'Anthropology' and 'Race,' Sapir's 'Cult,' Malinowski's 'Culture,' Lowie's 'Marriage,' Benedict's 'Religion' (Primitive), Kroeber's 'Art' (Primitive). See also my 'Evolution' (Social) and 'Totemism.'

Of the journals in English the following may be mentioned: *American Anthropologist, Journal of American Folk-Lore, American Journal of Physical Anthropology, Journal of the Anthropological Institute of Great Britain and Ireland, Man, Folk-Lore, Africa, International Journal of American Linguistics*.

Indispensable for students of the American Indians are the *Handbook of American Indians* (2 vols.) and the *Handbook of American Indian Languages* (2 vols.). See in the latter Boas's Introduction (vol. I, pp. 1–80).

Of the irregular serial publications the following should be noted: Columbia University Contributions to Anthropology, Harvard African Studies, Anthropological Publications of the University Museum (Pennsylvania), Memoirs of the American Anthropological Association, Anthropological Papers of the American Museum of Natural History (an enormous amount of material on the Plains Indians will be found here), Memoirs of the Geological Survey, Canada (Anthropological Series), Reports and Bulletins of the Bureau of American Ethnology (many comprehensive monographs on all phases of Indian life and thought), Publications of the Field Museum of Natural History (Anthropological Series), University of California Publications in American Archaeology and Ethnology (tribes of California and the Southwest), and Publications of the Jesup North Pacific Expedition (tribes of the Northwest Coast and Northeast Siberia).

ABBREVIATIONS

A	Africa
AA	American Anthropologist
AAA	American Anthropological Association

AJPhA .... *American Journal of Physical Anthropology*
AJS .... *American Journal of Sociology*
AMNH .... American Museum of Natural History
AP .... Anthropological Papers
AS .... Anthropological Series
BAE .... Bureau of American Ethnology
BM .... Brisbane Museum
BPBM .... Bernice Pauahi Bishop Museum
CAAS .... Connecticut Academy of Arts and Sciences
CES .... Comparative Ethnological Studies
F .... *Forum*
FMNH .... Field Museum of Natural History
HB .... *Human Biology*
INM .... Indian Notes and Monographs
JAF .... *Journal of American Folk-Lore*
JAI .... *Journal of the Anthropological Institute of Great Britain and Ireland*
JNPE .... Jesup North Pacific Expedition
JSPs .... *Journal of Social Psychology*
MAI .... Museum of the American Indian (Heye Foundation)
NYSM .... New York State Museum
O .... *Oceania*
PsB .... *Psychological Bulletin*
RSSA .... Royal Society of South Australia
Sc .... *Science*
UCPAAE .... University of California Publications in American Archaeology
and Ethnology
UMSSSc .... University of Minnesota Studies in the Social Sciences
USNM .... United States National Museum

ANIMAL, MAN, AND RACE

Alverdes, Fr., *Social Life in the Animal World* (1927).
Baer, Karl Ernst von, *History of the Development of Animals* (1828–1837).
Bauer, E., Fischer, E., and Lenz, F., *Human Heredity* (1931).
Boas, F., Abstract of the Report on Changes in Bodily Form of the Descendants of European Immigrants (1911).
Boas, F., 'Studies in Growth,' *HB*, vol. IV, 1932, pp. 307–350; vol. V, pp. 429–444.
Boas, F., 'This Nordic Nonsense,' *F*, vol. LXXIV, 1925, pp. 502–511.
Brigham, C. C., *A Study of American Intelligence* (1923). A fine example of bad reasoning.
Crookshank, F. G., *The Mongol in Our Midst* (1924). Interesting but fantastic.
Darwin, Ch., *The Descent of Man* (1871). More readable than his *Origin of Species* (1859). Worthy of study as a fine specimen of unrelenting self-criticism.
Davis, R. C., *Ability in Social and Racial Classes* (1932).
Dixon, R. B., *The Racial History of Man* (1923). Rich in valuable material, but conclusions vitiated by faulty method.
Fishberg, M., *The Jews* (1911). Dated but useful.
Garth, T. R., 'A Review of Racial Psychology,' *PsB*, 1925.

Grant, M., *The Passing of the Great Race* (1916). This and his *The Conquest of a Continent* (1933) are admirable as instances of prejudice in scientific disguise.

Haddon, A. C., and Huxley, J. S., *We Europeans, A Survey of 'Racial' Problems* (1936). Excellent and readable.

Hankins, F. H., *The Racial Basis of Civilization, A Critique of the Nordic Doctrine* (1926). The best historical survey in English.

Holmes, S. J., *The Trend of the Race* (1921).

Howard, H. E., *An Introduction to the Study of Bird Behavior* (1929).

Huntington, E., *The Character of the Races* (1924). This and his earlier *Climate and Civilization* are almost unique as bad reasoning and faulty method (very useful reading).

Jennings, H. S., *The Biological Basis of Human Nature* (1930).

Kantor, J. R., 'Anthropology, Race, Psychology, and Culture,' *AA*, vol. XXVII, 1925, pp. 267–283.

Keegan, J. J., 'The Indian Brain,' *AJPhA*, vol. III, 1920, pp. 26–62.
The student interested in human biology will find the *American Journal of Physical Anthropology* indispensable. With special reference to race, he will read there a number of important articles dealing with the so-called 'blood-groups,' a subject not discussed in this book.

Klineberg, O., *Race Differences* (1935). A first-rate study!

Pavlov, I. P., *Conditioned Reflexes* (1927).

Radin, P., *The Racial Myth*.

Reuter, E. B., *Race Mixture: Studies in Intermarriage and Miscegenation* (1931).

Ripley, W. Z., *The Races of Europe* (1899). Still useful.

Smith, G. Elliot, *Essays on the Evolution of Man* (1927).

Stoddard, L., *The Rising Tide of Color, Against White Supremacy* (also his *Racial Realities in Europe*). See remark on Grant.

Witty, P. A., and Lehman, H. C., 'Racial Differences: The Dogma of Superiority,' *JSPs*, vol. I, 1930, pp. 394–418.

Wood-Jones, F., *Man's Place Among the Mammals* (1929). Important, though very speculative, in part.

Woodworth, R. S., 'Racial Differences in Mental Traits,' *Sc*, N.S., vol. XXXI, 1910.

Yerkes, R. M. and A. W., *The Great Apes: A Study of Anthropoid Life* (1929). Most comprehensive study, though uneven in quality.

Zuckerman, S., *Functional Affinities of Man, Monkeys, and Apes* (1933). Purely behavioristic, but very good.

Zuckerman, S., *The Social Life of Monkeys and Apes*. Ditto.

BASIC WORKS, OLD AND NEW, ON PRIMITIVE CULTURE

Boas, F., *Anthropology and Modern Life*.

Boas, F., *Mind of Primitive Man*.

Durkheim, É., *Elementary Forms of the Religious Life*. Though written as a contribution to religious origins, it is an excellent study of primitive Australia.

Frazer, J. G. (Sir James), *The Golden Bough*. Negligible as theory, indispensable as a collection of material on primitive religion.

Frazer, J. G. (Sir James), *Totemism and Exogamy* (1909). Ditto.

Kroeber, A. L., *Anthropology*.

Lang, Andrew, *Magic and Religion*.

532 BIBLIOGRAPHY

Linton, Ralph, *The Study of Man, An Introduction* (1936). Original and readable.
Lowie, R. H., *Primitive Religion*.
Lowie, R. H., *Primitive Society*. Especially valuable as a criticism of L. H. Morgan.
Maine, Henry S., *Ancient Law*.
Maine, Henry S., *Lectures on the Early History of Institutions*.
Myres, J. L., *Position of Women in Primitive Society* (1926).
Radin, P., *Method and Theory of Ethnology*.
Radin, P., *Primitive Man as a Philosopher*. An important contribution on the role of the individual in primitive society.
Sapir, E., *Language, An Introduction to the Study of Speech* (1921). No other such book in English.
Schmidt, P. W., *The Origin and Growth of Religion* (1930).
Sollas, W. J., *Ancient Hunters and Their Modern Representatives*, 3d Ed. (1924).
Tylor, E. B., *Primitive Culture*, 2 vols. This and his *Anthropology and Researches into the Ancient History of Mankind* belong to the order of books that do not grow old.
Westermarck, E., *The History of Human Marriage*, 3 vols., 5th Ed. Now supplemented, but not superseded, by Robert Briffault's *The Mothers* (3 vols.).
Wissler, C., *Man and Culture*. Thought-provoking, though not always convincing.
Wissler, C., *The American Indian*. Still the only book dealing with primitive America as a whole.

PREHISTORY

Altogether irreplaceable here is the *Reallexikon der Vorgeschichte* in 15 vols. edited by Max Ebert (unfortunately in German).
Boule, M., *Fossil Men, Elements of Human Palaeontology* (1923).
MacCurdy, G. G., *Human Origins*, 2 vols. (1924).
Obermaier, H., *Fossil Man in Spain* (1924).
Osborn, H. F., *Men of the Old Stone Age* (1918).

AMERICA

Benedict, R. F., 'The Concept of the Guardian Spirit in North America,' *Memoirs, AAA*, vol. XXIX.
Bennett, W. C., and Zingg, R. M., *The Tarahumara, an Indian Tribe of New Mexico* (1935).
Boas, F., 'Comparative Study of Tsimshian Mythology,' *Reports, BAE*, vol. XXXI.
Boas, F., 'Mythology of the Bella Coola Indians,' *JNPE*, vol. I, Part 2, pp. 25–127.
Boas, F., 'Social Organization and Secret Societies of the Kwakiutl Indians,' *Reports, USNM*, 1895, pp. 311–737.
Crawford, M. D. C., 'Peruvian Fabrics,' *AP,AMNH*, vol. XII, 1916.
Crawford, M. D. C., 'Peruvian Textiles,' *AP,AMNH*, vol. XII.
Dixon, R. B., 'The Independence of the Cultures of the North American Indians,' *Sc*, vol. XXXV, 1912, pp. 46–55.
Goddard, P. E., *Indians of the Southwest* (1913).
Hewett, E. L., *Ancient Life of the American Southwest* (1930).
Karsten, R., *Civilization of the South American Indians* (1926).
Kroeber, A. L., 'Handbook of the Indians of California,' *Bulletins, BAE*, vol. LXXVIII.

Kroeber, A. L., 'Zuñi Kin and Clan,' *AP,AMNH*, vol. XVIII, Part 2.

Linné, S., *The Technique of South American Ceramics* (1925).

Lothrop, S. K., 'The Indians of Tierra del Fuego,' *MAI*, 1928.

Lowie, R. H., 'Plains Indians Age Societies,' *AP,AMNH*, vol. XI, 1916, pp. 877–1031.

Mead, C. W., *Old Civilizations of Inca Land* (1924).

Mead, M., *The Changing Culture of an Indian Tribe* (1932).

Nordenskiöld, E., 'An Ethno-Geographical Analysis of the Material Culture of Two Indian Tribes in the Gran Chaco,' *CES*, vol. I (1909).

Nordenskiöld, E., *The Copper and Bronze Ages in South America* (1921).

Parker, A. C., 'The Code of Handsome Lake, the Seneca Prophet,' *Bulletins, NYSM*, vol. CLXIII, 1913.

Redfield, R., *Tepoztlan, a Mexican Village* (1930).

Spinden, H. J., *Ancient Civilizations of Mexico and Central America*, 2nd Ed., 1922.

Thompson, J. E., *The Civilization of the Mayas* (1927).

Wilson, G. L., 'Agriculture of the Hidatsa Indians,' *UMSSSc*, No. 9, 1917.

Wilson, G. L., 'The Horse and the Dog in Hidatsa Culture,' *AP,AMNH*, vol. XV, 1924, pp. 125–311.

Wissler, C., 'Aboriginal Maize Culture as a Typical Culture Complex,' *AJS*, vol. XXI, 1916.

Wissler, C., 'The Influence of the Horse on the Development of Plains Culture,' *AA*, vol. XVI, 1914.

POPULAR WORKS OF SERIOUS IMPORT ON THE AMERICAN INDIANS

Linderman, F. B., *Red Mother* (1932).

Mathews, J. J., *Wah'kon-tah, The Osage and the White Man's Road* (1932).

Neihardt, J. G., *Black Elk Speaks, Being the Life Story of a Holy Man of the Ogalala Sioux* (1932).

Vestal, Stanley, *Sitting Bull, Champion of the Sioux* (1932).

AFRICA

Beech, M. W. H., *The Suk* (1911).

Burton, R. F., *A Mission to Gelele, King of Dahome*, 2 vols. (1864). Not strictly scientific but important as a picture of a now vanished scene.

Calloway, H. (Bishop), *The Religious System of the Amazulu* (1870). Ditto.

Delafosse, M., *The Negroes of Africa, History and Culture* (tr. from the French, 1931).

Dornan, S. S., *Pygmies and the Bushmen of the Kalahari* (1925).

Driberg, G. H., *The Lango* (1923).

Driberg, G. H., 'The Status of Women among the Nilotics and Nilo-Hamitics,' *A*, vol. V, 1932, pp. 404–421.

Ellis, A. B., *The Ewe-speaking Tribes of the Slave Coast of West Africa* (1899). See also the same author's studies of the Tshi and the Yoruba.

Hobley, C. W., *Bantu Beliefs and Magic* (1922).

Hollis, A. C., *The Masai* (1905).

Hollis, A. C., *The Nandi* (1909).

Junod, H. A., *The Life of a South African Tribe*, 2 vols. (1912). A capital work.

Lindblom, G., *The Akamba* (1920).

534 BIBLIOGRAPHY

Linton, R., 'The Tanala; a Hill Tribe of Madagascar,' *AS,FMNH*, vol. XXII, 1933.
Rattray, R. S., *The Ashanti* (1925). See also this author's books on Ashanti proverbs, art, law, and folk-tales.
Rattray, R. S., *The Tribes of the Ashanti Hinterland*, 2 vols. (1932).
Roscoe, J., *The Banyankole* (1923).
Roscoe, J., *Twenty-Five Years in East Africa* (1921).
Routledge, W. S. and K., *With a Prehistoric People, the Akikuyu of British East Africa* (1910).
Seligman, C. G. and B. Z., *Pagan Tribes of the Nilotic Sudan* (1932).
Smith, E. W., and Dale, A. M., *The Ha-speaking Peoples of Northern Rhodesia* (1920).
Stow, G. W., *The Native Races of South Africa* (1905). Valuable as an old survey, though preliminary.
Talbot, P. A., *The Peoples of Southern Nigeria*, 4 vols. (1921).
Torday, E., *On the Trail of the Bushongo* (1925).
Von Hornbostel, E. M., 'The Ethnology of African Sound Instruments,' *A*, vol. VI, 1933, pp. 129–157, 277–311.
Werner, A., *Language Families of Africa* (1925).

ASIA AND ITS ARCHIPELAGOES

On the Northeast Siberians see the works by Bogoras, Jochelson, and Sternberg on the Chukchee, Koryak and Yukaghir, and Gilyak respectively in the *JNPE*.
Cole, F. C., 'The Tinguian,' *AS, FMNH*, vol. XIV.
Radcliffe-Brown, A. R., *The Andaman Islanders* (1933 Ed.).
Rivers, W. H. R., *The Todas* (1906).
Seligman, C. G. and B. Z., *The Veddahs* (1911).
Skeat, W. W., and Blagden, Ch. O., *Pagan Races of the Malay Peninsula*, 2 vols. (1906).

THE SOUTH SEAS

On Polynesia see the *Memoirs* of the *BPBM*.
Christian, F. W., *The Caroline Islands*.
Codrington, R. H., *The Melanesians: Studies in Their Anthropology and Folk-lore* (1891). Original source of the *mana* concept.
Ellis, W., *Polynesian Researches*, 4 vols., 2nd Ed. (1836). Invaluable as an old source.
Gifford, E. W., 'Tougan Society,' *Bulletins, BPBM*, vol. LXI.
Handy, E. S. C. and W. C., 'Samoan House Building, Cooking, and Tattooing,' *Bulletins, BPBM*, vol. XV, 1924.
Handy, E. S. C., 'The Native Culture of the Marquesas,' *Bulletins, BPBM*, vol. IX, 1923, pp. 81 seq., 98 seq.
Ivens, W. G., *Melanesians of the Southeast Solomon Islands* (1927).
Ivens, W. G., *The Island Builders of the Pacific*.
Lewis, A. B., 'Ethnology of Melanesia,' *FMNH* Guides, vol. V, 1932.
Malinowski, B., *Argonauts of the Western Pacific* (1922).
Malinowski, B., 'The Natives of Mailu,' *Transactions, RSSA*, 1915, pp. 494–706.
Malinowski, B., *The Sexual Life of Savages*, 2 vols. Extraordinary.
Mead, M., *Growing Up in New Guinea* (1930). This and the author's *Coming of Age in Samoa* (1928) are highly suggestive and readable. Especially important in connection with primitive education.

Powdermaker, H., *Life in Lesu* (1933).

Rivers, W. H. R., Ed., *Essays on the Depopulation of Melanesia* (1922).

Rivers, W. H. R., *The History of Melanesian Society*, 2 vols., 1914. Vol. II of this work stands alone as an attempt at speculative historical reconstruction. Though far from convincing, it remains important as an effort.

Seligman, C. G., *The Melanesians of British New Guinea* (1910).

Thompson, B., *The Fijians: A Study of the Decay of Custom* (1908).

Tregear, E., *The Maori* (1904). For an extensive bibliography on the Maori see Firth, *Primitive Economics of the New Zealand Maori*.

Turner, Geo., *Nineteen Years in Polynesia* (1861).

Turner, Geo., *Samoa, a Hundred Years Ago and Long Before* (1884). See remark on Ellis.

Williams, Th., and Calvert, J., *Fiji and the Fijians* (1858). Old but good.

Williamson, R. W., *The Social and Political Systems of Central Polynesia*, 3 vols. (1924). Often faulty in particulars but valuable as a survey.

Wollaston, A. F. R., *Pygmies and Papuans: The Stone Age To-day in Dutch New Guinea* (1912).

AUSTRALIA

Howitt, A. W., *Native Tribes of Southeast Australia.*

Parker, K. L., *The Euahlayi Tribe* (1905).

Radcliffe-Brown, A. R., 'The Social Organization of Australian Tribes,' *O*, vol. I. Very important!

Roheim, G., *Australian Totemism* (1925). A wild Freudian excursion into ethnological interpretation.

Roth, W. E., 'North Queensland Ethnography,' *Bulletins*, *BM*, Nos. 3, 4, 5, 7, 8, 1901-06.

Spencer, B., and Gillen, F. J., *Native Tribes of Central Australia.* This and the authors' *Northern Tribes of Central Australia* and *Native Tribes of the Northern Territory of Australia*, while in a sense indispensable, do not by any means deserve their high reputation. The books, though rich in material, are open to much criticism both as to method and as to manner of presentation.

Various Authors, *Cambridge Anthropological Expedition to Torres Straits*, 6 vols.

Wheeler, G. C., *The Tribe and Inter-Tribal Relations in Australia* (1910). Though slight, this study is very good and should be used more than it is.

ART

Balfour, Henry, *The Evolution of Decorative Art* (1893).

Barrett, S. A., 'Pomo Indian Basketry,' *UCPAAE*, vol. VII, No. 3.

Boas, F., 'Decorative Designs of Alaskan Needle-cases,' *Reports*, *USNM*, vol. XXXIV, 1908, pp. 321-344.

Emmons, Geo. T., 'The Chilkat Blanket,' *Memoirs*, *AMNH*, vol. III, Part 4.

Haddon, A. C., *Decorative Art of British New Guinea* (1894).

Hirn, Yrjö, *The Origins of Art* (1900).

Kroeber, A. L., 'The Arapaho,' *Bulletins*, *AMNH*, vol. XVIII.

Lehman, W., and Doering, H., *The Art of Old Peru* (1924).

Lumholtz, C., 'Decorative Art of the Huichol Indians,' *Memoirs*, *AMNH*, vol. III.

MacCurdy, G. G., 'A Study of Chiriquian Antiquities,' *Memoirs*, *CAAS*, vol. III.

536   BIBLIOGRAPHY

Montell, G., *Dress and Ornaments in Ancient Peru* (1929).
Saville, M. H., 'The Goldsmith's Art in Ancient Mexico,' *INM*, No. 4, 1920.

LAW

Barton, R. F., 'Ifugao Law,' *UCPAAE*, vol. XV, 1919, pp. 1–127.
Hogbin, Ian, *Law and Order in Polynesia.*
Malinowski, B., *Crime and Custom in Savage Society* (1926).

PRIMITIVE PSYCHOLOGY

Benedict, R. F., *Patterns of Culture* (1934).
Lévy-Bruhl, L., *How Natives Think.* See also the same author's *Primitive Mentality, The Soul of the Primitives,* and *Primitives and the Supernatural* (1935).
Mead, M., 'An Investigation of the Thought of Primitive Children with Special Reference to Animism,' *JAI*, vol. LXII, 1932, pp. 173–190.
Mead, M., *Sex and Temperament in Three Primitive Societies* (1935).

CULTURE AND ENVIRONMENT

Lowie, R. H., *Culture and Ethnology.*
Myres, C. L., *The Dawn of History.*
Semple, E. C., *American History and Its Geographic Conditions.*
Semple, E. C., *Influences of Geographical Environment* (after Ratzel).
Thomas, F., *The Environmental Basis of Society* (1925). Contains a full bibliography up to the date of publication.

DIFFUSION (CRITICAL AND UNCRITICAL)

Boas, F., 'Dissemination of Tales Among the Natives of North America,' *JAF*, 1891, pp. 13–20.
Dixon, R. B., *The Building of Cultures* (1928). The only systematic examination to date of the writings of the diffusionists.
Laufer, B., 'The Reindeer and Its Domestication,' *Memoirs, AAA,* vol. IV, 1917, pp. 91–147.
Perry, W. J., *The Children of the Sun.*
Smith, G. Elliot, *Human History* (1929).
Smith, G. Elliot, *The Migrations of Early Culture* (1915).

SOCIAL EVOLUTION, PRO AND CON

See, by way of introduction, Spencer's *Principles of Sociology,* Bachofen's *Das Mutterrecht (Matriarchate),* MacLennan's *Studies in Ancient History.*
Boas, F., 'Review of Graebner's *Methode der Ethnologie*' (1909, *The Method of Ethnology*), *Sc,* 1911, pp. 804–810.
Briffault, R. L., *The Mothers,* 3 vols., 1927.
Hartland, E. S., 'Matrilineal Kinship and the Question of Its Priority,' *Memoirs, AAA,* vol. IV, pp. 1–90.
Hartland, E. S., *Primitive Paternity,* 2 vols.

Kroeber, A. L., Review of the above, *AA*, vol. XIX, pp. 578 seq. See also Hartland's reply and Kroeber's counter-reply, *AA*, vol. XX, pp. 224–227. (*Cf.* my review of Hartland's *Primitive Paternity*, *AA*, 1911.)

Lang, A., *Social Origins*.

Letourneau, Ch., *Evolution of Marriage and the Family*.

Lowie, R. H., *Are We Civilized?* (1929).

Lowie, R. H., 'The Matrilineal Complex,' *UCPAAE*, vol. XVI, pp. 29–45.

Lowie, R. H., *The Origin of the State* (1927). (*Cf.* F. Oppenheimer's *The State*.)

Tylor, E. B., 'On a Method of Investigating the Development of Institutions, Applied to Laws of Marriage and Descent,' *JAI*, vol. XVIII, 1889, pp. 245–272. Though abortive, Tylor's effort remains of considerable theoretical interest.

INDICES

INDEX OF PERSONAL NAMES

INDEX OF SUBJECTS

INDEX OF TRIBES [1]

[1] This list should be consulted in conjunction with the Tribal Map following. The black dots on the Map indicate the approximate locations. In cases where several dots occur in one square, the location of individual tribes will remain approximate for the student, until he learns to identify the tribes. The Map, as it stands, however, will serve the purpose of general orientation. For more detailed and precise information the student is referred to the special literature.

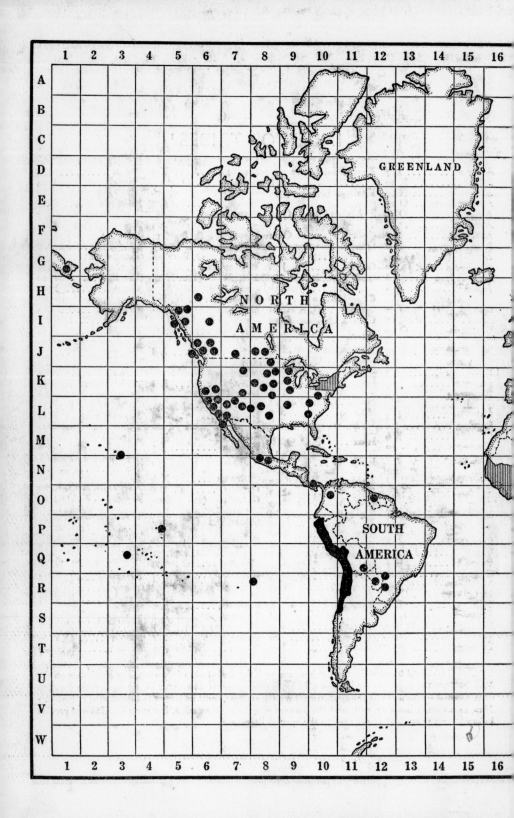